D0236798

DEDICATED TO

The Hunger Family
Jackson S. and Elizabeth C.
Betty
Kari, Suzi, Lori, Merry,
and Smokey!

The Wheelen Family
Thomas L. and Kathryn E.
Kathy, Tom, and Richard

PREFACE

This book has been class-tested in policy/strategic management courses and revised based on feedback from those classes and from reviews by authorities in the field. In response to students and professors, we have emphasized primarily those concepts that have proven to be most useful in understanding strategic decision making and in conducting case analysis. Our goal was to make the text as comprehensive as possible without getting bogged down in any one area. Extensive current references are provided at the end of each chapter for those who wish to learn more about any particular topic. The fact that previous editions of this book have been translated into Arabic and Italian and used in colleges around the world has caused us to emphasize international examples and considerations.

This text was originally part of a hardcover book titled *Strategic Management and Business Policy,* 4th edition, published by Addison-Wesley Publishing Company. The hardcover book includes the **fourteen chapters of this text plus forty-one comprehensive cases** in strategic management. Given the strong demand for the hardcover book, we decided to publish the text alone in a softcover version. This gives strategic management and business policy instructors the opportunity to continue using the same text material, but with different cases. The same Instructor's Manual originally prepared for the hardcover book can be used with this text.

TIME-TESTED FEATURES

This edition includes many of the same features and content that helped make previous editions successful. A **model of the strategic management process** is thoroughly presented in the first chapter and provides an organizing principle for the entire book. The **strategic audit**, based on the popularly used strategic decision-making process, is explained in Chapter 2 and serves to aid in case analysis. To enable the reader to understand the roles and responsibilities of people in corporations who have to make strategic decisions, a section in Chapter 2 is devoted to the **board of directors and top management.**

Special chapters dealing with strategic issues in **multinational corporations** (Chapter 11), **entrepreneurial ventures and small businesses** (Chapter 12), and **not-for-profit organizations** (Chapter 13) are included to give special emphasis to these types of organizations. International issues and examples, as well as stakeholder concerns, are integrated throughout the text. In contrast to other textbooks in this area, equal emphasis is placed on environmental scanning factors in the societal environment as well as factors in the task environment—an organization's particular industry.

FEATURES NEW TO THIS EDITION

In addition to updating and fine-tuning the time-tested features, other additions and changes to the chapters make the book more useful to students and professors, and more representative of the rapidly growing field of strategic management and business policy.

- **Increased coverage of strategy implementation (Chapters 8 and 9).** A *second chapter has been added on strategy implementation* to provide more information on organizational and job design as well as on managing organizational culture and action planning. Staffing issues after acquisitions and during retrenchment have been expanded. The concept of the organizational life cycle includes Danny Miller's work on declining organizations.
- **Increased coverage of business and functional strategies (Chapter 7).** A separate chapter *expands on Michael Porter's competitive strategies* at the business unit level and on the many possible strategies at the corporation's functional level. New information on competitive tactics is also included.
- **A separate chapter on social responsibility and ethics (Chapter 3).** To better deal with the increasing interest in environmental concerns and stakeholder issues, not only has content on *social responsibility been expanded,* but concepts and theories dealing with *ethics in strategic management* have been added.
- **Increased coverage of industry analysis (Chapter 4).** Information on *Porter's forces* determining competitive intensity has been *expanded* and combined with literature on *strategic groups, industry evolution, mobility barriers,* and *strategic types.*
- **Heightened emphasis on strategic factors (Chapters 4, 5, and 6).** Techniques are presented to better analyze and synthesize information gained from environmental scanning and to consolidate it into the useful categories of strengths, weaknesses, opportunities, and threats. Some of these are *EFAS—Synthesis of External Factors* (Chapter 4), *IFAS—Synthesis of Internal Factors* (Chapter 5), and *SWOT/TOWS Matrix* (Chapter 6).
- **Key concepts from Porter's *Competitive Advantage of Nations* (Chapter 11).** A new section on international trade using the concepts of *Smith, Ricardo, and Porter,* and an expanded section on *Hofstede's research on cultural values,* have been added to the international chapter dealing with strategic issues in multinational corporations.
- **Boxed examples of Maytag Corporation added to Chapters 1–12.** Instead of a long, integrative case at the end of each chapter, a short vignette of one company's (Maytag's) experience in strategic management serves to illustrate some of the issues in each chapter and to integrate the material.
- **A videotape on the Maytag Corporation made available to adopters of this book.** A short videotape describes the corporation, its products, and its strategic plan.
- **Information on strategic decision making and strategic managers combined into one chapter (Chapter 2) and case analysis moved to a separate chapter (Chapter 14).** This serves to "tighten up" the material and place it where it is most useful to the reader.

SUPPLEMENTS

INSTRUCTOR'S MANUAL

A comprehensive Instructor's Manual has been carefully constructed to accompany this book. It is composed of the following three parts:

- **Ideas for Instructors and Chapter Notes.** Suggested course outlines, case sequences, and teaching aids are included in this part. A standardized format is provided for each chapter: *chapter abstract, list of key concepts/terms,* and *suggested answers to discussion questions.* A reprinted article, "Facts and Impacts: A Comparative Analysis of the 1992 European Community Pact and the U.S.–Canadian Free Trade Agreement," is included with the notes for Chapter 11 as an added instructional resource.
- **Multiple-Choice Test Questions.** Approximately 60 multiple-choice questions are included for each chapter. Prepared by John E. Merchant, California State University at Sacramento, these questions are also available in a computerized test bank (see below).
- **Transparency Masters.** Selected figures and tables from the text chapters plus other masters highlighting key strategic management concepts and techniques are included in this part.

COMPUTERIZED TEST BANK

The same multiple-choice questions (approximately 60 per chapter) found in the Instructor's Manual are available free to adopters of this textbook in a computerized test bank on diskette. These questions cover all fourteen chapters of the book.

TRANSPARENCY ACETATES

Professionally drawn acetates of the transparency masters from the Instructor's Manual for use with overhead projectors are available free to adopters of the text.

VIDEOTAPE

A videotape of the Maytag Corporation is *available free to adopters of this book.* The tape is a presentation of the corporation's major divisions and product lines as shown at the 1990 annual shareholders meeting.

ACKNOWLEDGMENTS

We are grateful to the many people who reviewed drafts of the various editions of this book for their constructive comments and suggestions. Their thought and effort has resulted in a book far superior to our original manuscript.

Our special thanks go to Mac Mendelsohn, our editor at Addison-Wesley Publishing Company, for his support of this 4th Edition. Mac has been our in-house sponsor for many editions of our books, long before he became our editor. We thank him for his insights, concern, assistance, and especially for his friendship. Mac's emphasis on a quality book and quality supplementary materials helped make this book a success. He helped us keep our sanity when adversity threatened to swamp our revision. We are also grateful to Kazia Navas, Kim Kramer, and Nancy Benjamin for their help and supervision of the production process. The valuable contributions of the people at Addison-Wesley are reflected in the overall quality of the book and the fact that it was published on time—every time!

We especially thank Betty Hunger for her typing of the chapters and the Instructor's Manual accompanying this book. Typing camera-ready pages is no easy chore given the authors you had to work with! Thanks are due Hongwei Li for her energetic work on the complicated Name Index. We are also very grateful to Kathy Wheelen for her continued first-rate administrative support. Tom thanks Kathy for being his right arm for the past nine years: "Thank you. I love you. You're a great supporter, daughter, and friend."

In addition, we express our appreciation to Dr. David Shrock, Dean, and Dr. James McElroy, Management Department Chair, of Iowa State University's College of Business, for their support and provision of the resources so necessary to produce a textbook. Both of us acknowledge our debt to Dr. William Shenkir and Dr. Frank S. Kaulback, Dean and former Dean, respectively, of the McIntire School of Commerce of the University of Virginia for the provision of a work climate most supportive to the original development of this book. The dedication page reflects our debt to our families—those people who have cheerfully (usually) put up with us in our quest to write the very best text in strategic management and business policy. Tom Wheelen's father would have celebrated his centennial birthday on March 15, 1993.

Lastly, to the many strategy/policy instructors, teaching assistants, and students who have come to us with suggestions for the strategic management/business policy course: we have tried to respond to your concerns as best we could by providing a comprehensive yet usable text. To you, the people who work hard in the strategy/policy trenches, we acknowledge our debt. This book is yours.

Ames, Iowa   J. D. H.
Tampa, Florida   T. L. W.

23 may } TQM & Environmental Issues.
24
25 may → general revision

CONTENTS

INTRODUCTION TO STRATEGIC MANAGEMENT AND BUSINESS POLICY

CHAPTER ONE

Introduction

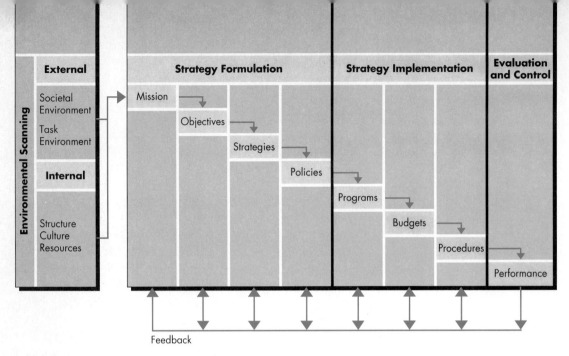

STRATEGIC MANAGEMENT MODEL

In management circles, there is no historic precedent for planning. The typical executive lives in a reactive environment. . . . Generally, most managers simply try to outdo what they did in previous years. The idea of determining in advance how to outdo oneself, then meeting the challenge, is a lot less fun than managing by the seat of one's pants.[1]

William W. Simmons,
Former Head of Corporate
Planning, IBM Corporation

During most of the 1980s, Quaker State was the market leader in motor oil, steadily increasing its sales and profits every year. In 1986, for example, management announced record earnings of $2.01 a share, or $50.3 million on sales of $926.8 million.

Everything fell apart, unfortunately, one year later. In 1987, the company recorded its first loss ever at $1.82 a share. Over the next two years, operating margins dropped from 12.8% to 6% as Pennzoil replaced Quaker State as Number One in market share. In attempting to reverse its misfortunes, the company changed its chief executive officer (CEO) three times in 15 months!

By mid-1988, the takeover sharks were gathering in anticipation of a quick killing. Given that the breakup value of the company was higher than the company's stock price and that the sale of profitable subsidiaries would be more than enough to finance the cost of the company's acquisition, Quaker State's days appeared to be numbered.

What went wrong? How could such a successful company fall on such hard times? "We made some bad calls," reported Jack Corn, Quaker State's latest CEO, who had been drawn out of retirement in July 1988 to salvage the company before it was too late. "We read the situation wrong, and didn't meet the competition head on," he stated.[2]

Jack Corn's comments suggest why the managers of today's business corporations must manage firms strategically. They cannot make decisions based on long-standing rules, historical policies, or simple extrapolations of current trends. Instead, they must look to the future as they plan organizationwide objectives, initiate strategy, and set policies. They must rise above their training and experience in such functional/operational areas as accounting, marketing, production, or finance, and grasp the overall picture. They must be willing to ask three *key strategic questions*:

1. Where is the organization now?
2. If no changes are made, where will the organization be in one year; two years; five years; ten years? Are the answers acceptable?
3. If the answers are not acceptable, what specific actions should management undertake? What are the risks and payoffs involved?

In 1986, Quaker State still sold a motor oil that was well suited only to the big, eight-cylinder engines that used to dominate U.S. and Canadian highways. Unfortunately, Quaker State's management failed to gauge the impact that the shift in the marketplace from large to small cars was having on oil sales. While Quaker State was spending approximately $280 million to expand Minit-Lube, its ten-minute oil-and-filter-change business, competitors Pennzoil and Valvoline were spending heavily on packaging and advertising for their higher-quality oil ideally suited for modern, smaller, hotter-running auto engines. Quaker State's management had failed to realize the environmental changes that had altered the rules for success. A poor job of environmental scanning had resulted in poor strategic planning.

Quaker State's management was not alone in its inability to anticipate environmental changes. Only a few years earlier, Levi Strauss and Company had been forced to close 22 of its plants when the demand for its clothing had fallen off precipitously. The number of potential customers had dropped as the baby boomer generation reached its thirties. A chagrined Chairman of Levi Strauss finally admitted: "The demographics have been against us."[3] He did not report, however, why Levi's management failed to include something as easy to predict as demographic trends in its planning!

These examples show how a leading company can quickly become an also-ran because of its failure to adapt to change or, even worse, its failure to create change. Current predictions are that the environment will become even more complex and turbulent as the world enters the twenty-first century. A recent report prepared by the American Assembly of Collegiate Schools of Business and the European Foundation for Management Development states, "Living with uncertainty is likely to be management's biggest challenge."[4]

Strategic management is a quickly developing field of study that has emerged in response to this environment of increasing turbulence. This field of study looks at the corporation as a whole and attempts to explain why some firms develop and thrive while others stagnate and go bankrupt. The distinguishing characteristic of strategic management is its emphasis on strategic decision making.[5] It therefore typically focuses on analyzing the problems and opportunities faced by people in top management. Unlike many decisions made at lower levels in a corporation, **strategic decisions** deal with the long-run future of the entire organization and have three characteristics:

1. *Rare:* strategic decisions are unusual and typically have no precedent to follow.
2. *Consequential:* strategic decisions commit substantial resources and demand a great deal of commitment.
3. *Precursive:* strategic decisions set precedents for lesser decisions and future actions throughout the organization.[6]

Because strategic decisions have these characteristics, the stakes can be very high. For instance, the strategic decision made after World War II by Sears, Roebuck and Company to expand from catalog sales into retail stores and insurance gave Sears many years of successful profits. A similar decision made independently during the 1960s by the top managements of General Motors, Ford, and Chrysler to emphasize the production of large, powerful automobiles over small, fuel-efficient ones resulted in their low profits and even the threat of bankruptcy in the early 1980s.

Thompson S.A. of France made another kind of high-stakes strategic decision in 1987, when management decided to give $800 million in cash plus the company's medical electronics unit to General Electric for GE's and RCA's television business. Although the acquisition made Thompson second in the world in television sales after the Dutch giant Philips, the company was facing a far-from-secure future. Japanese competitors were close on the company's heels and gaining. Thompson S.A. had been born in 1968 out of a merger between CSF, a defense electronics firm, and Thompson Brandt, a consumer electronics company. Saved from bankruptcy in 1982 by the arrival of Alain Gomez as its new chief executive, Thompson had been steadily improving its productivity, sales, and profits in both the consumer and defense electronics industries over the years.

Known as an aggressive CEO, Gomez wanted Thompson to become the world leader in televisions. Facing a more unified European market in 1993, Gomez felt that a stronger base, a measure of trade protection, and heavy investment in new technology would give companies like Thompson the ability to compete against strong Japanese competitors. Thompson was investing heavily in research and development to stay in the race with the Japanese to produce high-definition television.

Gomez broadcast his strategic decision to 17,000 Thompson employees in the U.S., Asia, and Europe via satellite from a Paris concert hall. He contended that huge profits would be reaped when consumers started replacing their current televisions with new high-definition models in the mid-1990s. He cautioned, however, that only a few companies will survive until then. "This is our opportunity," added Gomez. "We cannot miss it."[7]

1.1 STUDY OF STRATEGIC MANAGEMENT AND BUSINESS POLICY

Most business schools offer a strategic management or business policy course. Although this course typically serves as a capstone or final integrative class in a business administration program, it—also typically—takes on some of the characteristics of a separate discipline.

In the 1950s the Ford Foundation and the Carnegie Corporation sponsored investigations into the business school curriculum.[8] The resulting Gordon and Howell report, sponsored by the Ford Foundation, recommended a broad business education and a course in business policy to "give students an opportunity to pull together what they have learned in the separate business fields and utilize this knowledge in the analysis of complex business problems."[9] The report also suggested the content that should be part of such a course:

> The business policy course can offer the student something he [or she] will find nowhere else in the curriculum: consideration of business problems which are not prejudged as being marketing problems, finance problems, etc.; emphasis on the development of skills in identifying, analyzing, and solving problems in a situation which is as close as the classroom can ever be to the real business world; opportunity to consider problems which draw on a wide range of substantive areas in business; opportunity to consider the external, nonmarket implications of problems at the same time that internal decisions must be made; situations which enable the student to exercise qualities of judgment and of mind which were not explicitly called for in any prior course. Questions of social responsibility and of personal attitudes can be brought in as a regular aspect of this kind of problem-solving practice. Without the responsibility of having to transmit some specific body of knowledge, the business policy course can concentrate on integrating what already has been acquired and on developing further the student's skill in using that knowledge.[10]

By the late 1960s most business schools included such a business policy course in their curriculum. But since that time the typical policy course has evolved to one that emphasizes the total organization and strategic management, with an increased interest in business social responsibilities and ethics. This evolution is in line with a recent survey of business school deans that reported that a primary objective of undergraduate business education is to develop an understanding of the political, social, and economic environment of business.[11] This increasing concern with the effect of environmental issues on the management of the total organization has led leaders in the field to replace the term *business policy* with the more comprehensive *strategic management*.[12] **Strategic management** is that set of managerial decisions and actions that determines the long-run performance of a corporation. It includes environmental scanning, strategy formulation, strategy implementation, and evaluation and control. The study of strategic management therefore emphasizes the monitoring and evaluating of environmental opportunities and constraints in light of a corporation's strengths and weaknesses. In contrast, the study of **business policy,** with its integrative orientation, tends to look inward. By focusing on the efficient utilization of a corporation's assets, it thus emphasizes the formulation of general guidelines that will better accomplish a firm's mission and objectives. We see, then, that strategic management incorporates the concerns of business policy with a heavier environmental and strategic emphasis.

1.2 RESEARCH ON THE EFFECTIVENESS OF STRATEGIC MANAGEMENT

Many of the concepts and techniques dealing with long-range planning and strategic management have been developed and used successfully by business corporations such as General Electric and the Boston Consulting Group, among others. Nevertheless, not all organizations use these tools or even attempt to manage strategically. Many are able to succeed for a while with unstated objectives and intuitive strategies. American Hospital Supply Corporation (AHS) was one such organization until Karl Bays became chief executive and introduced strategic planning to a sales-dominated management. Previously, the company's idea of long-range planning was "Maybe in December we should look at next year's budget," recalled a former AHS executive.[13]

From his extensive work in the area, Bruce Henderson of the Boston Consulting Group concluded that intuitive strategies cannot be continued successfully if (1) the corporation becomes large, (2) the layers of management increase, or (3) the environment changes substantially.[14] Research suggests that the increasing risks of error, costly mistakes, and even economic ruin are causing today's professional managers to take strategic management seriously in order to keep their company competitive in an increasingly volatile environment.[15] Research by Gluck, Kaufman, and Walleck proposes that, as top managers attempt to better deal with their changing world, strategic planning evolves through *four sequential phases:*

Phase 1.   *Basic financial planning:* seeking better operational control through the meeting of budgets.

Phase 2.   *Forecast-based planning:* seeking more effective planning for growth by trying to predict the future beyond the next year.

Phase 3.   *Externally oriented planning (strategic planning):* seeking increased responsiveness to markets and competition by trying to think strategically.

Phase 4.   *Strategic management:* seeking to manage all resources to develop competitive advantage and to help create the future.[16]

The fourth phase, strategic management, includes a consideration of strategy implementation and evaluation and control, in addition to Phase 3's emphasis on strategic planning. By 1990, most large corporations around the world had begun the conversion from strategic planning to strategic management. In a recent speech, Lawrence A. Bossidy, the Vice-Chairman of the Board and Executive Officer of the General Electric Company, surprised his audience by stating that GE no longer conducted strategic planning. "But I want to make it clear," he continued, "that when we deserted strategic planning, we most emphatically did not abandon strategic *thinking* or strategic *management*. . . ."[17] This increasing concern with strategic management was echoed by F. A. Maljers, Chairman of the Board of Unilever. Emphasizing that strategy formulation and implementation are equally important and interdependent, Maljers stated: "The largest companies in the world all have to take strategic management seriously."[18]

William Rothschild, staff executive for business development and strategy at General Electric, notes the current trend to push strategic management duties down the organizational hierarchy to operating line managers. He observes that at GE, "over half of our managers are strategic thinkers. Another 20 percent to 25 percent lean that way. The rest don't understand it, and if they're fortunate enough to be in the right business where there is a stable environment, it doesn't matter too much."[19]

Many researchers have conducted studies of corporations to reveal whether organizations that engage in strategic planning outperform those that do not. One analysis of five companies with sales ranging from $1 billion to $17 billion reports that the impact of strategic planning has been to

- help the companies sort their businesses into "winners and losers,"
- focus attention on critical issues and choices, and
- develop a strategic frame of mind among top and upper-level managers.

The study concludes that management should expect strategic planning to improve a company's competitive position and long-term profits, plus yield growth in earnings per share.[20]

Research studies attempting to measure objectively this anticipated connection between a corporation's use of formal strategic planning and its performance have sometimes found mixed results.[21] Rhyne, however, explains these contradictory findings as resulting from the use of varying measures for planning and performance plus a typical failure to consider industry effects. When he controlled for industry variation, focused only on the total return to stockholders, and considered strategic planning as being different from less-evolved stages of planning (such as budgeting or annual planning), Rhyne found a positive relationship between strategic planning and performance. He concluded that "these results provide assurance that the prescriptions of strategic management theory are indeed valid."[22]

Additional research reveals that the attainment of an appropriate match or "fit" between an organization's environment and its strategy has positive effects on the organization's performance.[23] For example, a study of the impact of deregulation on U.S. railroads found that those railroads that changed their strategy as their environment changed outperformed those railroads that did not change their strategies.[24]

It is, nevertheless, not always necessary for strategic planning to be a formal process for it to be effective. Small corporations, for example, may plan informally and irregularly.[25] The president and a handful of top managers might get together casually to resolve strategic issues and plan their next steps. As will be discussed in Chapter 12, they need no formal, elaborate planning system because the number of key executives is small enough that they can meet relatively often to discuss the company's future.

In large, multidivisional corporations, however, the planning of strategy can become complex. A study of strategic decisions made in 30 large organizations in the U.K. revealed that the average amount of time elapsed from the beginning of situation assessment to final decision agreement was a little over 12 months.[26] Because of the relatively large number of people affected by a strategic decision in such a firm, a formalized, more sophisticated system is needed to ensure that strategic planning leads to successful performance. Otherwise, top management becomes isolated from developments in the divisions and lower-level managers lose sight of the corporate mission.

From this evidence we can conclude that a knowledge of strategic management is very important for business performance to be effective in a changing environment. The use of strategic planning and the selection of alternative courses of action based on an assessment of important external and internal factors are becoming key parts of a general manager's job.

1.3 INITIATION OF STRATEGIC CHANGE

After much research, Henry Mintzberg discovered that strategy formulation is typically not a regular, continuous process: "It is most often an irregular, discontinuous process, proceeding in fits and starts. There are periods of stability in strategy development, but also there are periods of flux, of groping, of piecemeal change, and of global change."[27] This view of strategy formulation as an irregular process can be explained by the very human tendency to continue on a particular course of action until something goes wrong or a person is forced to question his or her actions. Research does indicate that most organizations tend to follow a particular strategic orientation for about 15 to 20 years before they make a significant change in direction.[28] After this rather long period of fine-tuning an existing strategy, some sort of shock to the system is needed to motivate management to make a serious reassessment of the corporation's situation.

In a business corporation, the stimulus for a strategic change usually lies in one or more **triggering events**. Some of the possible triggering events are:

- New CEO.
- Intervention by an external institution, such as a bank.
- Threat of a change in ownership, that is, a takeover.
- Recognition by management of a performance gap.[29]

As shown in Illustrative Example 1.1, one act that is likely to serve as a triggering event is the emergence of a new chief executive officer. By asking a series of embarrassing questions, the new CEO cuts through the veil of complacency and forces people to question the very reason for the corporation's existence—a very frightening situation for most long-term employees.

A similar stimulus can result when a corporation's bank suddenly refuses to agree to a new loan or suddenly calls for payment in full on an old one. The bank may no longer be willing to underwrite what it perceives as a developing weakness in the company. The ensuing panic felt by the corporation's top management in finding financing may be the triggering event needed to initiate a complete strategic review.

ILLUSTRATIVE EXAMPLE 1.1

New CEO Transforms United Technologies

Just a few weeks after replacing Harry Gray as CEO at United Technologies Corporation (UTC), Robert F. Daniell summoned his top executives to a crucial meeting. The subject for discussion was UTC's questionable future. Customers of its Pratt and Whitney jet engines, outraged by UTC's poor service, had been switching to General Electric. The market shares of the corporation's once-dominant Otis elevator and Carrier air-conditioning units were rapidly falling. Profits were approaching a 13-year low. "Things had to change," said Daniell.

With the aid of a consultant, executives thrashed through the corporation's problems and began to devise some solutions. "Just the fact that we went through all of that yelling and screaming was unusual," commented one executive who attended. After two days, UTC's top management agreed to remake United Technologies into a leaner, more aggressive company providing significantly improved customer service.

Source: T. Vogel, "Where 1990s-Style Management Is Already Hard at Work," *Business Week* (October 23, 1989), pp. 92–100.

The threat of a takeover can, of course, create the same situation. For example, an attempt by the Belzberg family to acquire Armstrong World Industries led management in 1989 to sell its low-profit businesses, to reduce the number of upper managers, and to strengthen the company's marketing and service efforts. Referred to as Armstrong's "weight-loss program," the company's strategic change focused on making its lines of floor tiles, ceilings, and furniture more attractive to the customer. Commenting on the demand by a key buyer that all Armstrong products be supplied with bar codes for inventory control, CEO William Adams said, "I don't know how we're going to do it, but we are going to do it."[30]

Another triggering event is a *performance gap*—when corporate performance does not meet expectations. A typical performance gap occurs when sales and profits decline, or else sales and profits stagnate while those of competitors rise.[31] If top management chooses to confront the problem (and this is not always the case), the formulation process begins in earnest. People at all levels are urged by the board and top management to question present objectives, strategies, and policies. Even the mission may be questioned. Are we aiming too high? Do our strategies make sense? Environmental scanning of both internal and external variables begins. What went wrong? Why? Questions such as these prompt top management to review the corporation's current position and to initiate strategic change. Work begins in earnest to revitalize the corporation's process of strategic management.

1.4 DESCRIPTIVE MODEL OF STRATEGIC MANAGEMENT

The process of strategic management involves four basic elements: (1) **environmental scanning**, (2) **strategy formulation**, (3) **strategy implementation**, and (4) **evaluation and control**. Figure 1.1 shows how these four elements interact.

FIGURE 1.1   *Basic Elements of the Strategic Management Process*

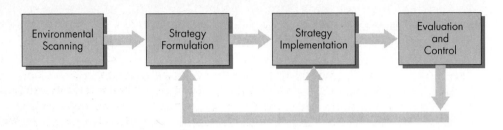

At the corporate level, the strategic management process includes activities that range from environmental scanning to the evaluation of performance. Top management scans both the external environment for opportunities and threats, and the internal environment for strengths and weaknesses. The factors that are most important to the corporation's future are referred to as strategic factors and are summarized with the acronym **S.W.O.T.**, standing for Strengths, Weaknesses, Opportunities, and Threats. Once these are identified, top management then evaluates the strategic factors and determines the corporate mission. The first step in the formulation of strategy, a statement of mission leads to a determination of corporate objectives, strategies, and policies. These strategies and policies are implemented through programs, budgets, and procedures. Finally performance is evaluated, and information is fed back into the system so that adequate control of organizational activities is ensured. Figure 1.2 depicts this process as a continuous one. It is an expansion of the basic model presented in Fig. 1.1.

ENVIRONMENTAL SCANNING: EXTERNAL

The *external environment* consists of variables (Opportunities and Threats) that are outside the organization and not typically within the short-run control of top management. These variables form the context within which the corporation exists. The external environment has two parts: task environment and societal environment. The **task environment** includes those elements or groups that directly affect and are affected by an organization's major operations. Some of these are stockholders, governments, suppliers, local communities, competitors, customers, creditors, labor unions, special interest groups, and trade associations. The task environment of a corporation is often referred to as its *industry*. The **societal environment** includes more general forces—ones that do not directly touch the short-run activities of the organization but that can, and often do, influence its long-run decisions. Such economic, sociocultural, technological, and political-legal forces are depicted in Fig. 1.3 in relation to a firm's total environment. (These external variables are discussed in more detail in Chapters 3 and 4.)

ENVIRONMENTAL SCANNING: INTERNAL

The *internal environment* of a corporation consists of variables (Strengths and Weaknesses) that are within the organization itself and are not usually within the short-run control of top management. These variables form the context in which work is done. They include the corporation's structure, culture, and resources. The **corporate structure** is the way a corporation is organized in terms of communication, authority, and workflow. It is often referred to as the "chain of command" and is graphically described in an organization chart. The **corporation's culture** is that pattern of beliefs, expectations, and values shared by the corporation's members. In a firm norms typically emerge that define the acceptable behavior of people from top management down to the operative employees. **Corporate resources** are those assets that form the raw material for the production of an organization's products or services. These assets include people and managerial talent as well as financial assets, plant facilities, and the skills and abilities within functional areas. (These internal variables in a firm's environment are discussed in more detail in Chapter 5.)

STRATEGY FORMULATION

Strategy formulation is the development of long-range plans for the effective management of environmental opportunities and threats, in light of corporate strengths and weaknesses. It includes defining the corporate mission, specifying achievable objectives, developing strategies, and setting policy guidelines.[32]

FIGURE 1.2 | **Strategic Management Model**

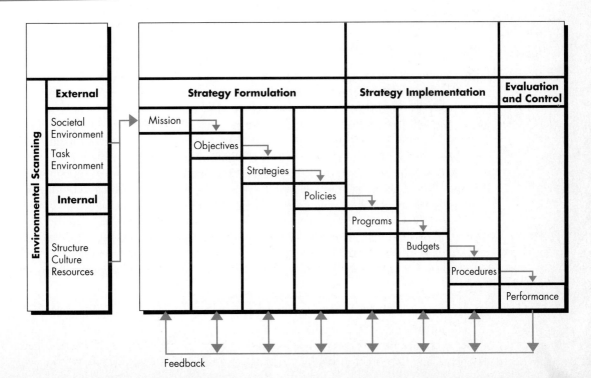

FIGURE 1.3	**Environmental Variables**

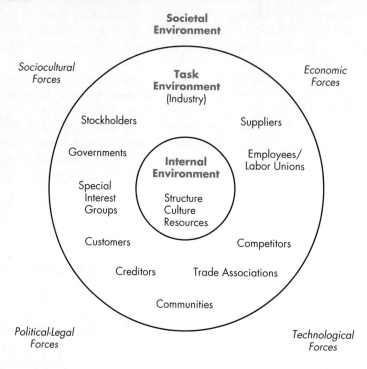

Mission

The corporate *mission* is the purpose or reason for the corporation's existence. For example, the mission of a savings and loan (S&L) association might be to provide mortgage money to people of the community. By fulfilling this mission, the S&L would hope to provide a reasonable rate of return to its depositors. A mission may be narrow or broad in scope. A **narrow mission** clearly limits the scope of the corporation's activities in terms of product or service offered, the technology used, and the market served. The above-mentioned S&L has the narrow mission of providing mortgage money to the people of the community. The problem with such a narrow statement of mission is that it might restrict the use of future opportunities for growth. A **broad mission** widens the scope of the corporation's activities to include many types of products or services, markets, and technologies. A broad mission of the same S&L might be to offer financial services to anyone, regardless of location. The problem with such a broad statement of mission is that it does not clearly identify which area the corporation wishes to emphasize and might confuse employees and customers. Other examples of narrow and broad missions follow:

Narrow Scope	Broad Scope
Railroads	Transportation
Insurance	Financial services
Typewriters	Office equipment
Television	Telecommunications

A well-conceived mission statement defines the fundamental, unique purpose that sets a business apart from other firms of its type and identifies the scope of the business's operations in terms of products offered and markets served. Surveys of large North American corporations reveal that approximately 60%–75% of them have formal, written statements of mission. A high percentage of the rest have an unwritten, informal mission.[33]

The concept of a corporate mission implies that throughout a corporation's many activities there should be a **common thread** or unifying theme and that those corporations with such a common thread are better able to direct and administer their many activities.[34] In acquiring new firms or in developing new products, such a corporation looks for "strategic fit," that is, the likelihood that new activities will mesh with present ones in such a way that the corporation's overall effectiveness and efficiency will be increased. A common thread may be common distribution channels or similar customers, warehousing economies or the mutual use of R&D, better use of managerial talent, or any of several possible synergistic effects. For example, Ralston Purina acquired Union Carbide's battery business, including the Eveready and Energizer brands. Ralston's CEO, William Stiritz, argued that Ralston Purina would earn better profit margins on batteries than did Union Carbide because of Ralston's expertise in developing and marketing branded consumer products.[35]

Objectives

The corporate mission, as depicted in Fig. 1.2, determines the parameters of the specific objectives to be defined by top management. These *objectives* are listed as the end results of planned activity. They state *what* is to be accomplished by *when* and should be quantified if possible. (The term *goal* is often confused with *objective*. In contrast to an objective, a *goal* is an *open-ended* statement of what one wishes to accomplish with *no* quantification of what is to be achieved and *no* time criteria for completion.[36] For example, a goal of an S&L might be to increase its rate of return—a rather vague statement.) The achievement of corporate objectives, however, should result in a corporation's fulfilling its mission. An S&L, for example, might set an objective for the year of earning a 10% rate of return on its investment portfolio.

Some of the areas in which a corporation might establish its goals and objectives are:

- Profitability (net profits).
- Efficiency (low costs, etc.).
- Growth (increase in total assets, sales, etc.).
- Shareholder wealth (dividends plus stock price appreciation).
- Utilization of resources (ROE or ROI).
- Reputation.
- Contributions to employees (employment security, wages).
- Contributions to society (taxes paid, participation in charities).
- Market leadership (market share).
- Technological leadership (innovations, creativity).
- Survival (avoiding bankruptcy).
- Personal needs of top management (using the firm for personal purposes, such as providing jobs for relatives).

The top management of most large, publicly traded U.S. corporations like to announce their long-term objectives for the company—partially because that sets measurable goals to work toward and partially because they hope to impress stockholders and financial analysts. Under the direction of Chairman John F. Welch, Jr., for example, General Electric identified in the early 1980s its primary objective of making GE worth more than any other U.S. company. By 1990, GE was on the verge of replacing IBM as the U.S. company with the highest stock market value![37] As CEO of The Limited, one of the fastest growing specialty-store companies in the U.S., Leslie Wexner announced high objectives for his corporation at the firm's 1990 annual meeting:

> It is our clear intention to become a $10 billion company with 10% after-tax profits by the mid-1990s. That is our dream, that is our common vision, and that is what we are working toward.[38]

It is likely, however, that some corporations have no formal objectives; rather, they have vague, verbal ones that are typically not ranked by priority. It is even more likely that such a corporation's specified, written objectives are not the "real" (personal and probably unpublishable) objectives of top management.[39]

Strategies

A *strategy* of a corporation forms a comprehensive master plan stating *how* the corporation will achieve its mission and objectives. It maximizes competitive advantage and minimizes competitive disadvantage. For example, to achieve its objective of a 10% rate of return, an S&L could increase demand for its mortgages by offering special terms to a particular market segment, such as young professional people who can't meet the normal down-payment requirements. In order to increase the amount of money deposited in savings accounts that fund the mortgages, the S&L might offer large depositors special privileges and interest rates not available from other financial institutions. A different strategy would be to offer financial services so that the S&L's income becomes less dependent on mortgages.

Just as many firms have no formal objectives, many CEOs have unstated, incremental, or intuitive strategies that have never been articulated or analyzed. If pressured, these executives might state that they are following a certain strategy. This stated or "explicit" strategy is one with which few could quarrel, such as the development and acquisition of new product lines. Further investigation, however, might reveal the existence of a very different "implicit" strategy. For example, the prestige of a banker in one community is strictly a function of the bank's asset size. Top management, therefore, tends to choose strategies that will increase total bank assets rather than profits. An extremely profitable small bank is in the eyes of the community still just another unimportant small bank. Often the only way to spot the implicit strategies of a corporation is to look not at what top management says, but at what it does. Implicit strategies can be derived from corporation policies, programs approved (and disapproved), and authorized budgets. Programs and divisions favored by budget increases and staffed by managers who are considered to be on the fast promotion track reveal where the corporation is putting its money and its energy.[40]

Policies

Flowing from the strategy, *policies* provide broad guidance for decision making throughout the organization. Policies are thus broad guidelines that serve to link the formulation of strategy with its implementation. In attempting to increase the amount of mortgage loans as well as the amount of deposits available for mortgages, an S&L might set policies of always evaluating a mortgage candidate on the basis of *potential* rather than on current or historical income and of developing *creative* incentives for savings depositors.

Corporate policies are broad guidelines for divisions to follow in compliance with corporate strategy. These policies are interpreted and implemented through each division's own objectives and strategies. Divisions may then develop their own policies that will be guidelines for their functional areas to follow. At General Electric, for example, Chairman Welch insists that GE be Number One or Number Two wherever it competes. This policy gives clear guidance to managers throughout the organization.[41] (Strategy formulation is discussed in greater detail in Chapters 6 and 7.)

STRATEGY IMPLEMENTATION

Strategy implementation is the process by which strategies and policies are put into action through the development of programs, budgets, and procedures. This process might involve changes within the overall culture, structure, and/or management sytem of the entire organization. Except when such drastic corporatewide changes are needed, however, the implementation of strategy is typically conducted by middle- and lower-level managers with review by top management. Sometimes referred to as operational planning, strategy implementation often involves day-to-day decisions in resource allocation.

Programs

A *program* is a statement of the activities or steps needed to accomplish a single-use plan. It makes the strategy action-oriented. It may involve restructuring the corporation or changing the company's internal culture concerning how people get things done. For example, one of the big stumbling blocks to any sort of strategic change at Walt Disney Productions during the early 1980s was the continued reliance by everyone in the company on the late founder's plans for guidance. Once the company had implemented the last of Walt's great visions (EPCOT Center at Disney World) no one was able to generate new concepts. It took a complete change in top management during 1984 plus the strong leadership of Michael Eisner as the new CEO to change the culture from keeping its sights on the past to one with a clear vision to the future.

Implementation might also include a series of advertising and promotional programs to boost customer interest in the company's products or services. For instance, to implement its strategy and policies, an S&L might initiate an advertising program in the local area, develop close ties with the local realtors' association, and offer free silverware with every $1,000 savings deposit.

Budgets

A *budget* is a statement of a corporation's programs in dollar terms. Used in planning and control, it lists the detailed cost of each program. Many corporations demand a certain percentage return on investment, often called a "hurdle rate," before top management will approve a new program. This is done to ensure that the new program will significantly add to the corporation's profit performance, and thus build shareholder value. The budget thus not only serves as a detailed plan of the new strategy in action, it also specifies through pro-forma financial statements the expected impact on the firm's future financial situation. For example, once the proposed budget for a series of programs is approved, the S&L mentioned earlier would probably draw up separate budgets for each of its three programs: the advertising budget, the public relations budget, and the premium budget.

Procedures

Sometimes termed Standard Operating Procedures (SOP), *procedures* are a system of sequential steps or techniques that describe in detail how a particular task or job is to be done. They typically detail the various activities that must be carried out for completion of the corporation's program. The S&L, for example, might develop procedures for the placement of ads in newspapers and on radio. They might list persons to contact, techniques for the writing of acceptable copy (with samples), and details about payment. They might establish detailed procedures concerning eligibility requirements for silverware premiums. (Strategy implementation is discussed in more detail in Chapters 8 and 9.)

EVALUATION AND CONTROL

Evaluation and control is the process in which corporate activities and performance results are monitored so that actual performance can be compared with desired performance. Managers at all levels use the resulting information to take corrective action and resolve problems. Although evaluation and control is the final major element of strategic management, it also can pinpoint weaknesses in previously implemented strategic plans and thus stimulate the entire process to begin again.

For evaluation and control to be effective, managers must obtain clear, prompt, and unbiased feedback from the people below them in the corporation's hierarchy. The model in Fig. 1.2 indicates how feedback in the forms of performance data and activity reports runs through the entire management process. Using this feedback, managers compare what is actually happening with what was originally planned in the formulation stage.

For example, the S&L management would probably ask its internal information systems people to keep track of both the number of mortgages being granted and the level of deposits at the end of each week for each S&L branch office. It might also wish to develop special rewards for loan officers who increase their mortgage lending.

To monitor and evaluate broad-scale results, top management of large corporations typically uses periodic reports dealing with key performance indicators, such as return on investment, net profits, earnings per share, and net sales. From what these

reports indicate, top management takes further action.
need to emphasize rewards for long-term performance
alter the corporation's current incentive system. To hel
areas with performance problems, corporations are some
centers, investment centers, expense centers, cost cen
(These are discussed in detail in Chapter 10.)

Activities are much harder to monitor and evalua
results. Because of the many difficulties in deciding whicl
because of the bias inherent in evaluating job performance, some firms now manage
by objectives. Management By Objectives (MBO) has been criticized, however, for
ignoring many of the intermediate activities that can lead to the desired results. To
counter this criticism, consulting firms have developed management "audits," which
assess key organizational activities and provide in-depth feedback to consultants and
managers. Management audits (to be discussed in more detail in Chapter 2) complement standard measures of performance and help to complete the picture of the
corporation's activities. (For an example of one company's strategic management
process, see the *boxed example* concerning Maytag Corporation on pp. 20–21.)

1.5 HIERARCHY OF STRATEGY

The typical large, multidivisional business firm has three levels of strategy: (1)
corporate, (2) business, and (3) functional.[42]

Corporate strategy describes a company's overall direction in terms of its
general attitude toward growth and the management of its various businesses and
product lines to achieve a balanced portfolio of products and services. It is the
pattern of decisions regarding the types of businesses in which a firm should be
involved, the flow of financial and other resources to and from its divisions, the
relationship of the corporation to key groups in its environment, and the ways in
which a corporation can increase its return on investment (ROI). Corporate strategy
may be one of *stability, growth,* or *retrenchment.*

Business strategy, in contrast, usually occurs at the divisional level, and emphasizes improvement of the competitive position of a corporation's products or services
in the specific industry or market segment served by the division. A division may be
organized as a **Strategic Business Unit** (SBU) around a group of similar products,
such as housewares or electric turbines. Top management usually treats an SBU as a
semi-autonomous unit with, generally, the authority to develop its own strategy
within corporate objectives and strategy. A division's business strategy probably
would stress the increasing of its profit margin in the production and sales of its
products and services. Business strategies also should integrate various functional
activities so that divisional objectives are achieved. Sometimes called **competitive
strategy**, business strategy may be one of *overall cost leadership* or *differentiation.*

The principal focus of **functional strategy** is the maximizing of resource productivity.[43] Within the constraints of the corporate and business strategies around them,
functional departments develop strategies in which their various activities and
competencies are pulled together for the improvement of performance. For example,

Maytag Corporation: Strategic Management Process

Maytag Corporation is a successful full-line manufacturer of major home appliances. Beginning with its very successful high-quality washers and dryers, it branched out through acquisitions into cooking appliances (Magic Chef, Hardwick, and Jenn-Air), refrigerators (Admiral), and vacuum cleaners (Hoover). Until 1978, however, the corporation (then known simply as Maytag Company) was strictly a laundry appliances manufacturer. Its only experience with any sort of strategic planning was in preparing the next year's budget!

In 1978, Daniel Krumm, Maytag's CEO, asked Leonard Hadley (at that time the company's Assistant Controller in charge of preparing the annual budget) and two others from manufacturing and marketing to serve as a strategic planning task force. Krumm posed these three people the question: *"If we keep doing what we're now doing, what will the Maytag Company look like in five years?"* The question was a challenge to answer, especially considering that the company had never done financial modeling and none of the three knew much about strategic planning. Hadley worked with a programmer in his MIS section to develop "what if" scenarios. The task force presented its conclusion to the board of directors: A large part of Maytag's profits (the company had the best profit margin in the industry) was coming from products and services with no future. These were repair parts, portable washers and dryers, and wringer washing machines.

This report triggered Maytag's interest in strategic change. After engaging in a series of acquisitions to broaden its product line, the corporation was poised in 1990 on the brink of becoming a global power in the major home appliance industry. Its 1988 purchase of Hoover gave Maytag not only a firm with worldwide strength in floor-care appliances, but also Hoover's strong laundry, cooking, and refrigeration appliance business in the U.K. and Australia. The trend toward the unification of Europe plus the rapid economic development of the Far East meant that Maytag could no longer survive simply as a specialty appliance manufacturer serving only North America.

The corporation's current strategic plan is updated every year and usually has a three-year time horizon. Although the latest plan does not list explicitly the corporation's mission, objectives, strategies, policies, and the like in a step-by-step fashion, the following can be inferred from the statements of top management and from corporate activities in mid-1990:

STRATEGY FORMULATION

Mission

Broad: Serve the best interests of shareowners, customers, and employees.
Narrow: Become a full-line globally oriented major home appliance manufacturer and marketer.

Objectives

1. Become the profitability leader in the industry for each product line manufactured.
2. Outperform the competition in the next five years striving for a 6.5% return on sales, a 10% return on assets, and a 20% return on equity.

Strategies

1. Grow horizontally in those major home appliance product lines and geographic areas,
   (continued)

Continued

such as Europe and Asia, where the corporation is not yet well represented, through external acquisitions or joint ventures.
2. Grow horizontally internally by improving efficiency and quality of acquired companies and by using one business unit's expertise in one area to introduce quality products to a business unit in another area.

Policies

1. No cost reduction proposal will be approved if it reduces product quality in any way.
2. Every product, from the least expensive to the highest priced, should be superior to the competition in overall quality and performance.
3. The corporation must not emphasize market share at the expense of profitability.
4. Business units must be managed for synergies, while simultaneously allowing the specialized expertise among those units to flourish.

STRATEGY IMPLEMENTATION

Programs

1. Initiate a program to identify other companies in Europe for the possibility of joint ventures, acquisitions, or supplier agreements.
2. Initiate a program to analyze and develop the Asian market—growing probably through current distributors and licensees and possibly through a joint venture partner.
3. Modernize Hoover's laundry and dishwasher plant in South Wales and the floor care plant in Scotland.
4. Develop plans to build a new dishwasher plant in Tennessee to consolidate all the dishwasher production currently being done separately by each of the U.S. business units.

Budgets

Prepare budgets showing a cost-benefit analysis of each planned program and a statement of how much the corporation can afford to spend for each program.

Procedures

1. Develop procedures for the sales of bonds or stock in quantities sufficient to finance any proposed acquisition.
2. Coordinate the marketing, manufacturing, and purchasing activities of the business units through corporate-wide planning committees chaired by representatives from the corporate planning staff.
3. Research and development activities for each major product line take place in the business unit where they are housed, but in coordination with experts specialized in that area from other parts of the corporation. For example, since Hoover is the corporation expert in front-loading washers, other units wishing to produce a front-loader should call on Hoover for assistance in development.

EVALUATION AND CONTROL

1. Require all business units to provide *monthly* status reports on sales and costs by product line plus any trends in expenses.
2. Require all business units to provide *annual* reports giving operating revenues, costs, and expenses as well as identifiable assets in dollars, plus property additions and deletions.
3. Require all business units to provide *quarterly* assessments of competitive activity and overall trends affecting each of their product lines.

a typical strategy of a marketing department might center on developing the means to increase the current year's sales over those of the previous year. With a *market development* functional strategy, the department would attempt to sell current products to different customers in the current market or to new customers in a new geographical area. Examples of R&D functional strategies are *technological followership* (imitate the products of other companies) and *technological leadership* (pioneer an innovation).

The three levels of strategy—corporate, business, and functional—form a **hierarchy of strategy** within a large corporation. They interact closely with each other and must be well integrated if the total corporation is to be successful. The model presented earlier in Fig. 1.2 reflects the strategic management process at all levels within the organization. As depicted in Fig. 1.4, each level of strategy forms the strategic environment of the next level in the corporation. A division's external environment, for example, includes not only those task and societal variables of special importance to the division, but also the mission, objectives, strategies, and policies of corporate headquarters. Similarly, both corporate and divisional constraints form a large part of the external environment of a functional department. Therefore, the strategic plan for each lower level is constrained by the strategic plan(s) of the next higher level(s). For example, the functional level is constrained by both the divisional and corporate levels.

Most major corporations are structured on both a divisional and a functional basis. As depicted in Fig. 1.5, the corporate level goes through all three elements of the strategic management process. Top management *with input from the divisions* formulates strategies and makes plans for implementation. These implementation plans stimulate the strategy formulation process at the divisional level. To accom-

---

FIGURE 1.4 | **Hierarchy of Strategy**

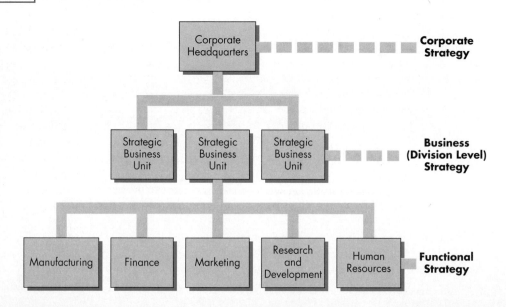

| **FIGURE 1.5** | **Strategic Management Process at Three Corporate Levels** |

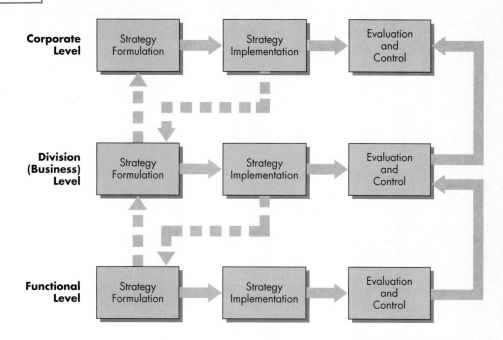

plish the corporate programs, each division formulates its own objectives, strategies, and policies. For example, a corporate-level program of CSX Corporation (a multidivisional major transportation company) was to dispose of unproductive and marginal assets. To implement this program, the railroad business segment (or division) formulates an objective specifying how many miles of track would be abandoned or/and sold during the coming year and develops a strategy for accomplishing that objective. Then, as the division acts on its strategy, it feeds its evaluation and control information upward to the corporate level for its use in evaluation and control.

Responding to each division's programs for implementation, separate functional departments within each division begin to formulate their own objectives and strategies. For example, American Commercial Lines (ACL), CSX's barge subsidiary, might set an objective of increasing its barge tonnage by 10% over the previous year and propose this business strategy: to differentiate its service from that of the competition, it will guarantee fewer losses in transit. In response to this strategy, each functional department—such as operations and marketing—develops its own objectives and strategies. ACL's operations department would set an objective for loss reduction and begin formulating a strategy for the reduction of damage to goods being transported. ACL's marketing department would also set objectives specifying how many new customers will have to be attracted and how much tonnage from its current customers will have to be increased, to fulfill ACL's overall objective. Marketing would then formulate the appropriate advertising and promotion strategies. In this way each level of the corporation develops its own objectives, strategies, policies, programs, budgets, and procedures to complement those of the level above.

The specific operation of the hierarchy of strategy may vary from one corporation to another. The one described here of CSX Corporation (and of Maytag Corporation as well) is an example of **top-down strategic planning**, in which corporate-level top management initiates the strategy formulation process and calls upon divisions and functional units to formulate their own strategies as ways of implementing corporate-level strategies. Another approach is **bottom-up strategic planning**, in which the strategy formulation process is initiated by strategic proposals from divisional or functional units. This approach is shown by the arrows pointing upward in Fig. 1.5; strategy formulation leads from the functional level to the divisional level and from the divisional to the corporate level. Bechtel Group, the largest construction and engineering company in the U.S., uses bottom-up strategic planning because it uses autonomous divisions as independent profit centers.[44] Although an **interactive approach** is sometimes proposed as a third means to strategic planning,[45] it is clear that in most companies the origin of the formulation process is not as important as the resultant interaction between levels. The process involves a lot of negotiation between levels in the hierarchy so that the various objectives, strategies, policies, programs, budgets, and procedures fit together and reinforce each other. It is a continuous process of adjustment between the formulation and implementation of each level of strategy.

F. A. Maljers, Chairman of the Board of Unilever, points out how this hierarchy of strategy must be integrated if the corporation is to be managed successfully:

> If a global company is to function successfully, strategies at different levels need to interrelate. The strategy at corporate level must build upon the strategies at lower levels in the hierarchy (the bottom-up element of strategy). However, at the same time, all parts of the business have to work to accommodate the overriding corporate goals (the top-down approach.)[46]

SUMMARY AND CONCLUSION

This chapter sets the stage for the study of strategic management and business policy. It explains the rationale for including the subject in a business school curriculum. In addition to serving as a capstone to integrate the various functional areas, the course provides a framework for the analysis of top management's decision process and the effects of environmental issues on the corporation. Research generally supports the conclusion that corporations that manage strategically perform at higher levels than do those firms that do not. Strategic management is thus an important area of study for anyone interested in organizational productivity.

Our model of strategic management includes environmental scanning, strategy formulation and implementation, plus evaluation and control. The mission of a corporation derives from the interaction of internal and external environmental factors, as modified by the needs and values of top management. A precise statement of mission guides the setting of objectives and the formulation of strategies and policies. Strategies are implemented through specific programs, budgets, and procedures. Management continuously monitors and evaluates performance and activities on the basis of measurable results and audits of key areas. These data feed back into the corporation at all phases of the strategic management process. If results and activities fail to measure up to the plans, managers may then take the appropriate actions.

Although top management and the board of directors have primary responsibility for the strategic management process, many levels of the corporation conduct strategy formulation, implementation, and evaluation and control. Large multidivisional corporations utilize divisional and functional levels that integrate the entire corporation by focusing their activities on the accomplishment of the corporate mission.

DISCUSSION QUESTIONS

1. What differentiates strategic decisions from other types of decisions?

2. How does strategic management typically evolve in a corporation? Why?

3. What is meant by the hierarchy of strategy?

4. Does every business firm have business strategies? Explain.

5. What information is needed for the proper formulation of strategy? Why?

6. What are the pros and cons of *bottom-up* as contrasted with *top-down* strategic planning?

NOTES

1. W. W. Simmons with R. B. Elsberry, "Vision Quest: Long-Range Planning at IBM," *The Futurist* (September-October 1988), p. 17.

2. K. Hannon, "Run Over By the Competition," *Forbes* (September 5, 1988), p. 80.

3. J. Mendes, "Profiting from a Changing America," *Fortune* (Investor's Guide—October 1988), p. 45.

4. J. Robertson, "The Changing Expectations of Society in the Next Thirty Years," in *Management for the XXI Century,* edited by the AACSB and EFMD (Boston/The Hague/London: Kluwer-Nijhoff Publishing, 1982), p. 5.

5. H. Mintzberg, "Strategy Formulation: Schools of Thought," in *Perspectives on Strategic Management,* edited by J. W. Fredrickson (New York: Harper Collins, 1990), p. 179.

6. D. J. Hickson, R. J. Butler, D. Cray, G. R. Mallory, and D. C. Wilson, *Top Decisions: Strategic Decision-Making in Organizations* (San Francisco: Jossey-Bass, 1986), pp. 26–42.

7. T. Peterson and L. Therrien, "Alain Gomez, France's High-Tech Warrior," *Business Week* (May 15, 1989), pp. 100–106.

8. R. A. Gordon and J. E. Howell, *Higher Education for Business* (New York: Columbia University Press, 1959).

   F. C. Pierson et al., *The Education of American Businessmen* (New York: McGraw-Hill, 1959).

9. Gordon and Howell, *Higher Education,* p. 206.

10. *Ibid.,* pp. 206–207.

11. J. D. Hunger and T. L. Wheelen, *An Assessment of Undergraduate Business Education in the United States* (Charlottesville, Va.: McIntire School of Commerce Foundation, 1980). Also summarized in "A Performance Appraisal of Undergraduate Business Education," *Human Resource Management* (Spring 1980), pp. 24–31.

12. D. Schendel and K. Cool, "Development of the Strategic Management Field," in *Strategic Management Frontiers,* edited by J. H. Grant (Greenwich, Conn.: JAI Press, 1988), pp. 17–31.

13. B. Lancaster, "American Hospital's Marketing Program Places Company Atop a Troubled Industry," *Wall Street Journal* (August 24, 1984), p. 19.

14. B. D. Henderson, *Henderson on Corporate Strategy* (Cambridge, Mass.: Abt Books, 1979), p. 33.

15. R. Lamb, *Advances in Strategic Management,* Vol. 2 (Greenwich, Conn.: JAI Press, 1983), p. x.

16. F. W. Gluck, S. P. Kaufman, and A. S. Walleck, "The Four Phases of Strategic Management," *The Journal of Business Strategy* (Winter 1982), pp. 9–21.

17. S. M. Millett, "How Scenarios Trigger Strategic Thinking," *Long Range Planning* (October 1988), p. 61.

18. F. A. Maljers, "Strategic Planning and Intuition at Unilever," *Long Range Planning* (April 1990), p. 63.

19. P. Pascarella, "Strategy Comes Down to Earth," *Industry Week* (January 9, 1984), p. 51.

20. W. B. Schaffir and T. J. Lobe, "Strategic Planning: The Impact at Five Companies," *Planning Review* (March 1984), pp. 40–41.

21. C. B. Shrader, L. Taylor, and D. R. Dalton, "Strategic Planning and Organizational Performance: A Critical Appraisal," *Journal of Management* (Summer 1984), pp. 149–179.

    P. R. Varadarajan and V. Ramanujam, "Strategic and Organizational Sources of Superior Corporate Performance," in *Handbook of Business Strategy, 1989/90 Yearbook,* edited by H. E. Glass (Boston: Warren, Gorham, & Lamont, 1989), pp. 17.1–17.16.

    J. A. Pearce II, E. A. Freeman, and R. B. Robinson, Jr., "The Tenuous Link Between Formal Strategic Planning and Financial Performance," *Academy of Management Review* (October 1987), pp. 658–675.

22. L. C. Rhyne, "The Relationship of Strategic Planning to Financial Performance," *Strategic Management Journal* (September-October 1986), p. 435.

23. N. Venkatraman and J. E. Prescott, "Environment-Strategy Coalignment: An Empirical Test of Its Performance Implications," *Strategic Management Journal* (January 1990), pp. 1–23.

    S. A. Zahra and W. R. Boxx, "A Multivariate Examination of Perceived Environmental Attributes, Competitive Strategy and Performance Links," *International Journal of Management* (June 1990), pp. 166–177.

24. K. G. Smith and C. M. Grimm, "Environmental Variation, Strategic Change and Firm Performance: A Study of Railroad Deregulation," *Strategic Management Journal* (July-August 1987), pp. 363–376.

25. R. B. Robinson, Jr., and J. A. Pearce, III, "Research Thrusts in Small Firm Strategic Planning," *Academy of Management Review* (January 1984), pp. 128–137.

26. Hickson et al., *Top Decisions*, pp. 100–101.

27. H. Mintzberg, "Planning on the Left Side and Managing on the Right," *Harvard Business Review* (July-August 1976), p. 56.

28. D. Miller and P. H. Friesen, "Momentum and Revolution in Organizational Adaptation," *Academy of Management Journal* (December 1980), pp. 600–601.

    H. Mintzberg and A. McHugh, "Strategy Formulation in an Adhocracy," *Administrative Science Quarterly* (June 1985), p. 190.

29. P. Grinzer and P. McKiernan, "Generating Major Change in Stagnating Companies," *Strategic Management Journal* (Summer 1990), pp. 131–146.

30. V. P. Goel, "Armstrong Sharpens Its Focus in Shadow of Belzbergs," *Wall Street Journal* (November 27, 1989), p. A5.

31. C. J. Fombrun and A. Ginsberg, "Shifting Gears: Enabling Change in Corporate Aggressiveness," *Strategic Management Journal* (May-June 1990), pp. 297–308.

32. Although some theorists propose that *both* objective setting and the consideration of competitive methods are a part of strategy, we agree with those who contend that objectives and strategy are separate means and ends considerations. See G. G. Dess, "Consensus on Strategy Formulation and Organizational Performance: Competitors in a Fragmented Industry," *Strategic Management Journal* (May-June 1987), pp. 259–260.

33. J. A. Pearce and F. David, "Corporate Mission Statements: The Bottom Line," *Academy of Management Executive* (May 1987), pp. 109–115.

    L. L. Byars and T. C. Neil, "Organizational Philosophy and Mission Statements," *Planning Review* (July-August 1987), pp. 32–35.

34. H. I. Ansoff, *The New Corporate Strategy* (New York: John Wiley & Sons, 1988), pp. 75–77.

35. K. Dreyfack, "What Purina Really Wanted From Carbide," *Business Week* (April 21, 1986), p. 33.

36. M. D. Richards, *Setting Strategic Goals and Objectives,* 2nd ed. (St. Paul, Minn.: West Publishing Co., 1987), p. 12.

37. D. B. Hilder and R. Smith, "Will GE Topple IBM's Crown As the Stock Market's Value King?" *Wall Street Journal* (July 23, 1990), pp. C1–C2.

38. J. A. Trachtenberg, "Leslie Wexner Pushes Limited's Fast Growth Despite Retailing's Ills," *Wall Street Journal* (August 15, 1990), p. A1.

39. M. D. Richards, *Setting Strategic Goals and Objectives,* 2nd ed. (St. Paul, Minn.: West Publishing Co., 1986), pp. 30–32.

40. K. R. Andrews, *The Concept of Corporate Strategy,* 2nd ed. (Homewood, Ill.: Irwin, 1987), p. 18.

41. E. Koerner, "GE's High-tech Strategy," *Long Range Planning* (August 1989), pp. 11–19.

42. Some theorists propose a fourth level of strategy called "enterprise," which seeks to position an organization within its broader environment. See R. E. Freeman and P. Lorange, "Theory Building in Strategic Management," in *Advances in Strategic Management, Volume 3,* edited by R. Lamb and P. Shrivastava (Greenwich, Conn.: JAI Press, 1985), p. 20. We chose, however, to include these broad environmental concerns with other factors considered in the development of corporate-level strategy. See Andrews, *Corporate Strategy,* p. 13.

43. C. W. Hofer and D. Schendel, *Strategy Formulation: Analytical Concepts* (St. Paul, Minn.: West, 1978), p. 29.

44. D. M. Slavick, "Planning at Bechtel: End of the Mega-project Era," *Planning Review* (September 1986), p. 20.

45. I. A. Marquardt, "Strategists Confront Planning Challenges," *Journal of Business Strategy* (May/June 1990), p. 6.

46. Maljers, "Strategic Planning at Unilever," p. 63.

CHAPTER TWO

Strategic Decision Makers: Strategic Managers and the Strategic Audit

CHAPTER OUTLINE

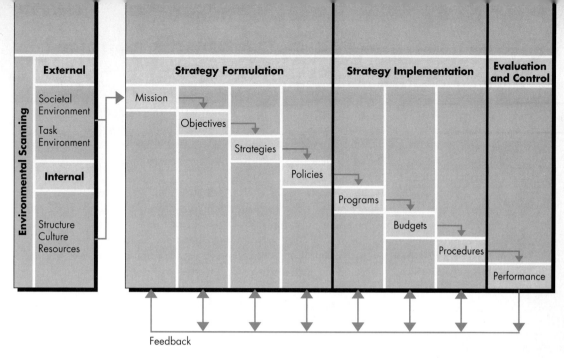

STRATEGIC MANAGEMENT MODEL

Long-range planning is not a process that occurs for three days once a year at a New England resort. You need to have your long-range plan and your strategies in mind all the time, particularly before you prepare the next year's budget.[1]

Worth Loomis, President,
Dexter Corporation

Strategic decision makers are the people in a corporation who are directly involved in the strategic management process. They are the strategic managers who (with some assistance from staff) scan the internal and external environments, formulate and implement objectives, strategies, and policies, and evaluate and control the results. The people with direct responsibility for this process are the board of directors and top management. The chief executive officer (CEO), the chief operations officer (COO) or president, the executive vice-president, and the vice-presidents in charge of operating divisions and functional areas typically form the top management group. Traditionally, boards of directors have engaged in strategic management only to the extent that they passively approved proposals from top management and hired and fired their CEOs. Their role, however, is changing dramatically. The strategic management process, therefore, is also changing.

2.1 CORPORATE BOARD OF DIRECTORS

Directors conduct a far different meeting from those in the past. Pressures—from regulatory agencies, shareholders, lenders, and the public—have practically forced greater awareness of directors' responsibilities. The board as a rubber stamp or a bastion of the "old-boy" selection system has largely been replaced by more active, more professional boards.[2]

Even in the recent past, boards of directors functioned rather passively. Members were selected because of their prestige in the community, regardless of their knowledge of the specific functioning of the corporation they were to oversee. Traditionally, members of the board were requested simply to approve proposals by top management or the firm's legal counsel, and the more important board activities generally were conducted by an executive committee composed of insiders. Even now, the boards in some family-owned corporations are more figureheads than overseers; they exist on paper because the laws of incorporation require their presence, but rarely, if ever, do they question management's plans.

Lee Iacocca describes how such a situation existed at the Ford Motor Company under Henry Ford II.

> The Ford Motor Company had gone public in 1956, but Henry never really accepted the change. As he saw it, he was like his grandfather, the rightful owner—Henry Ford, Prop. (Proprietor)—and the company was his to do [with] as he pleased. When it came to the board, he, more than most CEOs, believed in the mushroom treatment—throw manure on them and keep them in the dark. That attitude, of course, was fostered by the fact that Henry and his family, with only 12% of the stock, held on to 40% of the voting rights.[3]

Over the past decade, stockholders and various interest groups have seriously questioned the role of the board of directors. A recent survey by the National Association of Corporate Directors, for example, revealed that almost half of stockholders polled believe that directors ignore stockholder interests when considering a merger.[4] As a result of these and other doubts, the general public has become more aware and more critical of many boards' apparent lack of responsibility for corporate activities. For example, the Federal Home Loan Bank Board, concerned that the savings and loan (S&L) industry had become riddled with unscrupulous practices and unwise lending policies during the 1980s, sued the directors of 135 failed S&Ls for not properly supervising top management.[5] It was felt that board members were expected to closely monitor the actions of management and to actively intervene when necessary.

RESPONSIBILITIES OF THE BOARD

At this time, there are no national standards defining the accountability or responsibility of a board of directors. The law offers little guidance on this question. Specific requirements of directors vary, depending on the state in which the corporate charter is issued. According to Conference Board reports authored by Bacon and Brown, "State corporation laws give boards of directors rather sweeping powers couched in general language that does not specify to whom they are accountable nor clarify what it is they are accountable for."[6] There is, nevertheless, a developing consensus concerning the major responsibilities of a board.

The board of directors of a corporation is appointed or elected by the stockholders for the following purposes:

- To oversee the management of the corporation's assets.
- To establish or approve the corporation's mission, objectives, strategy, and policies.
- To review management's actions in light of the financial performance of the corporation.
- To hire and fire the principal operating officers of the corporation.

In a legal sense, the board is required to direct the affairs of the corporation but not to manage them. It is charged by law to act with "due care." As Bacon and Brown put it, "Directors must act with that degree of diligence, care and skill which ordinarily prudent [people] would exercise under similar circumstances in like positions."[7] If a director or the board as a whole fails to act with due care and, as a result, the corporation is in some way harmed, the careless director or directors can be held personally liable for the harm done. For example, the Delaware Supreme Court in 1985 fined directors of Trans Union Corporation, a railcar-leasing company, for negligence in connection with the sale of the company. It held the members of the board personally liable for the difference between the offer they accepted and the supposed value of the company.[8] Various studies indicate that personal liability lawsuits against corporate directors and officers are rising at a rate of up to 25% annually. In 1988, for example, lawsuits were filed against the officers and directors of 88% of U.S. corporations with assets over $1 billion![9] Although few of these suits ended unfavorably for individual directors, most members of today's boards of directors are now concerned that they might be held personally liable not only for their own actions, but also for the actions of the corporation as a whole. This concern is reinforced by the requirement of the Securities and Exchange Commission (SEC) that a majority of directors must sign the Annual Report Form 10-K.

Directors must make certain, in addition to the duties listed above, that the corporation is managed in accordance with the laws of the state in which it is incorporated. They must also ensure management's adherence to laws and regulations, such as those dealing with the issuance of securities, insider trading, and other conflict-of-interest situations. They must also be aware of the needs and demands of constituent groups, so that they can achieve a judicious balance among the interests of these diverse groups while ensuring the continued functioning of the corporation. For example, the Delaware Supreme Court in 1986 concluded that when Revlon's directors authorized management to negotiate the sale of the company, the legal duties of the directors changed. In the court's words, the directors' role became that of "*auctioneers* charged with getting the best price for the stockholders in the sale of the company!"[10]

ROLE OF THE BOARD IN STRATEGIC MANAGEMENT

In terms of strategic management, a board of directors has three basic tasks.[11]

- **To monitor.** By acting through its committees, a board can keep abreast of developments both inside and outside the corporation. It can thus bring to management's attention developments it might have overlooked.

- **To evaluate and influence.** A board can examine management's proposals, decisions, and actions; agree or disagree with them; give advice and offer suggestions; outline alternatives.
- **To initiate and determine.** A board can delineate a corporation's mission and specify strategic options to its management. Most boards still leave this task to top management.

Even though every board will be composed of people with varying degrees of commitment to the corporation, we can make some generalizations about a board of directors as a whole, in its attempt to fulfill these three basic tasks. We can characterize a board as being at a specific point on a continuum, on the basis of its degree of involvement in corporate strategic affairs. As types, boards can range from phantom boards with no real involvement to catalyst boards with a very high degree of involvement. Highly involved boards tend to be very active. They take their tasks of monitoring, evaluating and influencing, and initiating very seriously; they provide advice when necessary and keep management alert. As depicted in Fig. 2.1, they can be deeply involved in the strategic management process. At Control Data Corporation, for example, the board of directors spends the day before the official board meeting studying a business sector, such as computer peripherals, or an issue, such as efforts to improve quality.[12] (Other corporations with actively participating boards are Mead Corporation, Rolm and Haas, Whirlpool Corporation, Westinghouse, and Dayton-Hudson.[13])

As a board becomes less involved in the affairs of the corporation, it moves farther to the left on the continuum (see Fig. 2.1). On the far left are passive boards that typically *never* initiate or determine strategy unless a crisis occurs. For example, when Douglas Danforth, former Westinghouse Electric Corporation Chairman, joined the board of National Intergroup, Incorporated (NII) in 1986, he found the board unwilling even to criticize, let alone replace, CEO Howard "Pete" Love for his

---

FIGURE 2.1 | **Board of Directors Continuum**

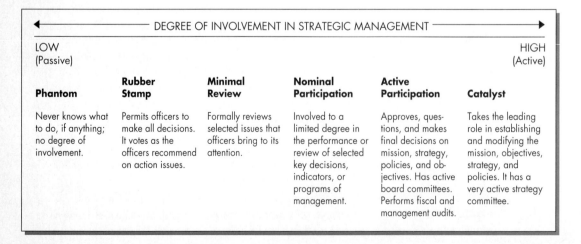

◀──────── DEGREE OF INVOLVEMENT IN STRATEGIC MANAGEMENT ────────▶

LOW   HIGH
(Passive)   (Active)

Phantom	Rubber Stamp	Minimal Review	Nominal Participation	Active Participation	Catalyst
Never knows what to do, if anything; no degree of involvement.	Permits officers to make all decisions. It votes as the officers recommend on action issues.	Formally reviews selected issues that officers bring to its attention.	Involved to a limited degree in the performance or review of selected key decisions, indicators, or programs of management.	Approves, questions, and makes final decisions on mission, strategy, policies, and objectives. Has active board committees. Performs fiscal and management audits.	Takes the leading role in establishing and modifying the mission, objectives, strategy, and policies. It has a very active strategy committee.

poor management. Eight of the eleven outside directors on NII's fifteen-person board had longtime social or business links to the CEO and his family. "They really like Pete," said a former director. "It got in the way of objectivity."[14] Until Danforth began asking probing questions of CEO Love, the board had passively agreed to every program of Love's, rarely challenging its faulty implementation.

Generally, the smaller the corporation, the less active is its board of directors. The board tends to be dominated by directors who are also owner-managers of the company. Other directors are usually friends or family members. As the corporation grows and goes public, however, the boards become more active in terms of roles and responsibilities.[15]

Most large, publicly owned corporations probably have boards that operate at some point between nominal and active participation. Few have catalyst boards, except for those with major problems (that is, pending bankruptcies, mergers, or acquisitions). Nevertheless, a recent survey of almost 600 publicly held and 250 privately held companies revealed that boards are now devoting more time to long-range strategic planning. When asked what they felt were the most critical issues that boards must contend with in the 1990s, directors listed strategic planning and long-term positioning (following unsolicited hostile takeover attempts) as most important.[16]

BOARD MEMBERSHIP

The boards of most publicly owned corporations are composed of both inside and outside directors. Inside directors (sometimes called management directors) are typically officers or executives employed by the corporation. The outside director may be an executive of another firm but is not an employee of the board's corporation. Recent surveys of large U.S. corporations found outsiders to form an increasing percentage of board membership. They now account for 74% of board members.[17] A survey of small companies found that although the number of outsiders on these boards may also be increasing, they constitute only 40% of the average board.[18]

This trend toward including a larger proportion of outsiders on a board is in line with guidelines proposed by the Securities and Exchange Commission, New York Stock Exchange, American Stock Exchange, National Association of Securities Dealers, and American Law Institute. For example, the New York Stock Exchange requires that all companies listed on the exchange have an audit committee composed entirely of independent, outside members.[19] These groups apparently take the view that outside directors are less biased and more likely to evaluate objectively management's performance than are inside directors. This view is in agreement with *agency theory*—a theory that states that problems arise in corporations because the agents (top management) are no longer willing to bear responsibility for their decisions unless they own a substantial amount of stock in the corporation. The theory suggests that a majority of a board needs to be from outside the firm, so that top management is prevented from acting selfishly to the detriment of the stockholders.[20] Vance, an authority on boards of directors, contends, however, that outside directors are less effective than are insiders because the outsiders have "questionable interest, availability, or competency."[21] At this time, the evidence is mixed regarding the relationship between the relative proportion of outside directors and a corporation's financial performance.[22]

The majority of outside directors are active or retired CEOs and COOs of other corporations. Others may be academicians, attorneys, former government officials, major shareholders, and bankers. A 1988 survey of 488 U.S. corporations found that 58% of the boards had at least one woman director—up from 45% only four years earlier.[23] Another survey revealed minority representation to have increased from 5.6% in 1983 to 7.8% of board membership in 1988.[24] Outside directors serving on the boards of large U.S. corporations earned on the average $28,219 in 1988 according to Korn/Ferry International.[25] Directors serving on the boards of small companies received less than $10,000 annually.

The vast majority of inside directors includes the chief executive officer, chief operating officer, and presidents or vice presidents of key operating divisions or functional units. Few if any inside directors receive any extra compensation for assuming this extra duty. Very rarely does a U.S. board include any lower-level operating employees.

Codetermination

The dearth of nonmanagement-employee directors on the boards of U.S. corporations may be changing. Codetermination, the inclusion of a corporation's workers on its board, began only recently in the U.S. Corporations such as Chrysler, Pan American Airlines, and Wheeling-Pittsburgh Steel have added representatives from employee associations to their boards as part of union agreements. Critics raise the issue of conflict of interest. Can a member of the board, who is privy to confidential managerial information, function, for example, as a union leader whose primary duty is to fight for the best benefits for his members? Research in 14 U.S. firms with workers on the board found that "worker board representation is no guarantee that workers will have an effective role in the governance of the organization."[26] The need to work for the corporation as a whole as well as to represent the workers creates role conflict and stress among the worker directors—thus cutting into their effectiveness.

Although the movement to place employees on the boards of directors of U.S. companies is only just beginning, the European experience reveals an increasing acceptance of worker participation on corporate boards. The Federal Republic of Germany pioneered the practice. Most other western European countries have either passed similar codetermination legislation or use worker councils to work closely with management.

Interlocking Directorates

Boards that are primarily composed of outside directors will not necessarily be more objective than those primarily composed of insiders. CEOs may nominate for board membership chief executives from other firms, for the exchange of important information and a guarantee of the stability of key marketplace relationships. These executives are very likely to be serving on both their own and other boards of directors. When two firms share a director or when an executive of one firm sits on the board of a second firm, this is called a direct *interlocking directorate*. An indirect interlock occurs when two corporations have directors who also serve on the board of a third firm.[27]

Although the Clayton Act and the Banking Act of 1933 prohibit interlocking directorates by U.S. companies competing in the same industry, interlocking continues to occur in almost all corporations, especially large ones.[28] Research has shown that the larger the firm, the greater the number of different corporations represented on its board of directors. Interlocking occurs because large firms have a large impact on other corporations; and these other corporations, in turn, have some control over the firm's inputs and marketplace. Interlocking directorates are also a useful method for gaining both inside information about an uncertain environment and objective expertise about a firm's strategy.[29] Family-owned corporations, however, are less likely to have interlocking directorates than are corporations with highly dispersed stock ownership, probably because family-owned corporations do not like to dilute their corporate control by adding outsiders to boardroom discussions.[30]

NOMINATION AND ELECTION OF BOARD MEMBERS

Traditionally, the CEO of the corporation decided whom to invite to board membership and merely asked the stockholders for approval. The chief criteria used by most CEOs in nominating board members were that the persons be compatible with the CEO and that they bring some prestige to the board.

There are some dangers, however, in allowing the CEO free reign in nominating directors. The CEO might select only board members who, in the CEO's opinion, will not disturb the company's policies and functioning. More importantly, directors selected by the CEO often feel that they should go along with any proposals made by the CEO. Thus, board members find themselves accountable to the very management they are charged to oversee. In the case of National Intergroup, most of the outside directors had personal, social, and business links to the CEO, Howard "Pete" Love, and would often go hunting or golfing with the CEO. Partially because of these close ties, the board tended to allow the CEO a large degree of discretion when it came to strategic decisions.[31] Because of the likelihood of these kinds of occurrences, there is an increasing tendency for a special board committee to nominate new outside board members for election by the stockholders. Surveys reveal that approximately 90% of large U.S. corporations now use nominating committees to identify potential directors (as contrasted with only 9% in 1976).[32]

A recent study of corporate boards by Spencer-Stuart, an executive search firm, found that in 1989 half of the boards surveyed elected outside directors for three-year terms, compared with only 17% in 1984.[33] Virtually every corporation whose directors serve terms of more than one year divides the board into classes and staggers elections so that only a portion of the board stands for election each year. Arguments in favor of this practice are that it provides continuity by reducing the chance of an abrupt turnover in its membership and that it reduces the likelihood of people unfriendly to management (who might be interested in a hostile takeover) being elected through cumulative voting.

The practice of **cumulative voting** allows a stockholder to concentrate his or her votes in an election of directors. Cumulative voting is required by law in 18 states and is mandatory on request or permitted as a corporate option in 32 other states or territories. Under cumulative voting, the number of votes allowed is determined by multiplying the number of voting shares held by the number of directors to be elected. Thus, a person owning 1,000 shares in an election of 12 directors would have 12,000 votes. These votes may then be distributed in any manner—for instance, divided evenly (or unevenly) between twelve directors or concentrated on one. This method is contrasted with straight voting in which the stockholder votes simply yes or no for each director to be elected. Although few stockholders use the privilege of cumulative voting, it is a powerful way for them to influence a board of directors. For example, a minority of stockholders could concentrate their voting power and elect one or more directors of their choice. In contrast, straight voting allows the holders of the majority of outstanding shares to prevent the election of any director not to their liking.

Those in favor of cumulative voting argue that it is the only system under which a candidate not on the management slate can hope to be elected to the board. Otherwise, under straight voting, an entrenched management could insulate itself from criticism and use the board as a rubber stamp. Critics of cumulative voting argue that it allows the board to deteriorate into interest groups more concerned with protecting their own special concerns than in working for the good of the corporation. This could become a serious problem if the corporation is in danger of being bought or controlled by another firm. For instance, by purchasing some shares, another firm (such as a potential acquirer) could, through cumulative voting, elect enough board members that it could directly influence or even incapacitate the board. It is for this reason that many U.S. corporations have recently re-incorporated in the state of Delaware, where cumulative voting is not mandatory.[34] Nevertheless, the practice of cumulative voting has been recommended as a way to achieve minority representation on the boards of directors of major corporations.

ORGANIZATION OF THE BOARD

The size of the board is determined by the corporation's charter and its bylaws in compliance with state laws. Although some states require a minimum number of board members, most corporations have quite a bit of discretion in determination of board size. A study of the boards of 100 large, publicly held U.S. corporations in 1989 found the median board size to be 14, down from 16 in the early 1980s.[35] The average size of the boards of privately held companies is probably closer to seven or eight members.

A fairly common practice in U.S. corporations is to have the chairman of the board also serve as the chief executive officer. The CEO concentrates on strategy, planning, external relations, and responsibility to the board. The chairman's responsibility is to ensure that the board and its committees perform their functions as stated in their charter. Further, the chairman schedules board meetings and presides over the annual stockholders' meeting. Approximately 75% of the top executives of U.S. Fortune 1000 corporations hold the dual designation of chairman and CEO. Although several people have argued that a CEO should not also serve as chairman because of conflict of interest, research reveals *no* significant performance differences between those corporations having combined CEO/Chairmen and those having the roles separated.[36]

The most effective boards of large corporations accomplish much of their work through committees.[37] Although the committees do not have legal duties, unless detailed in the bylaws, most committees are granted full power to act with the authority of the board between board meetings. Typical standing committees are the executive committee, audit committee, compensation committee, finance committee, and nominating committee. The executive committee is formed from local directors who can meet between board meetings to attend to matters that must be settled quickly. This committee acts as an extension of the board and, consequently, may have almost unrestricted authority in certain areas.[38]

TRENDS FOR THE FUTURE

The role of the board of directors in the strategic management of the corporation is likely to be a more active one in the future. Change is more likely to be evolutionary than radical or revolutionary. Different boards are at different levels of maturity and will not be changing in the same direction or at the same speed.[39]

The importance of the board of directors and its likely future is aptly summarized by James Worthy and Robert Neuschel in their study on corporate governance:

> Boards of directors will be importantly concerned with helping to achieve the balance (between the degree of freedom necessary for business to function profitably and the need for society to preserve other freedoms and institutions) in the years ahead. More and more, society will expect the board to provide the fine line between achieving the economic objectives of the corporation and meeting the broader needs of society.[40]

2.2 TOP MANAGEMENT

The top management function is usually conducted by the CEO of the corporation in coordination with the COO or president, executive vice-president, and vice-presidents of divisions and functional areas. An understanding of top management is especially important to the study of strategic management. Research consistently reports that chief executive officers not only have a strong impact on the strategic direction of their firms, but also directly affect corporate performance through their actions and statements.[41] In a survey of top investment analysts and money managers, almost half responded that their personal evaluation of top management is worth 60% of their total evaluation of the company.[42]

RESPONSIBILITIES OF TOP MANAGEMENT

Top management, and especially the CEO, is responsible to the board of directors for the overall management of the corporation. It is tasked with getting things accomplished through and with others, in order to meet the corporate objectives.

Top management's job is thus multidimensional and is oriented toward the welfare of the total organization. Specific top management tasks vary from firm to firm and are developed from an analysis of the mission, objectives, strategies, and key activities of the corporation. But all top managers are people who see the business as a whole, who can balance the present needs of the business against the needs of the future, and who can make final and effective decisions.[43] The chief executive officer, in particular, must successfully handle three responsibilities crucial to the effective strategic management of the corporation: (1) fulfill key roles, (2) provide executive leadership, and (3) manage the strategic planning process.

Fulfill Key Roles

From five weeks of in-depth observation of five chief executives, Henry Mintzberg concluded that the job of a top manager contains ten interrelated *roles*. The importance of each role and the amount of time demanded by each probably vary from one job to another. These roles are as follows:

- **Figurehead:** Acts as legal and symbolic head and performs obligatory social, ceremonial, or legal duties.
- **Leader:** Motivates, develops, and guides subordinates.
- **Liaison:** Maintains a network of contacts and information sources with key people in the task environment.
- **Monitor:** Seeks and obtains information needed for understanding the corporation and its environment.
- **Disseminator:** Transmits information to the rest of the top management team and other key people in the corporation.
- **Spokesperson:** Transmits information to key groups and people in the task environment.
- **Entrepreneur:** Searches the corporation and its environment for projects to improve products, processes, procedures, and structures.
- **Disturbance Handler:** Takes corrective action in times of trouble or crisis.
- **Resource Allocator:** Allocates corporate resources by making and/or approving decisions.
- **Negotiator:** Represents the corporation in negotiating important agreements.[44]

Provide Executive Leadership

People who work in corporations look to top management for leadership. Their doing so, says Drucker, reflects a need for standard setting and example setting.[45] According to Mintzberg, this is a key role of any manager. Executive leadership is important because it sets the tone for the entire corporation. Researchers in this area describe the importance of developing a **strategic vision** that sets forth the corporation's mission and objectives for all to follow. Many actually go beyond this by proposing that the primary job of the CEO is to be a "manager of meaning," that is, to make sense for others in the organization of the many things that are going on both inside and outside of the firm.[46]

Most middle managers look to their boss for guidance and direction and so tend to emulate the characteristics and style of successful top managers. People in an organization want to have a vision of what they are working toward—a sense of mission. Only top management is in the position to specify and communicate this sense of mission to the general work force. Top management's enthusiasm (or lack of it) about the corporation tends to be contagious.

For instance, a positive attitude characterizing many well-known industrial leaders—such as Alfred Sloan at General Motors, Ed Watson at IBM, Robert Wood at Sears, Ray Kroc at McDonald's, and Lee Iacocca at Chrysler—has energized their respective corporations. In their book *In Search of Excellence,* Peters and Waterman report that "associated with almost every excellent company was a strong leader (or two) who seemed to have a lot to do with making [the] company excellent in the first place."[47] A two-year study by McKinsey & Co. found the CEOs of midsized, high-growth companies to be "almost inevitably consummate salesmen who radiate enormous contagious self-confidence" and "take pains to communicate their strong sense of mission to all who come in contact with them."[48]

Chief executive officers with a clear sense of mission are often perceived as dynamic and charismatic leaders. They are able to command respect and to influence strategy formulation and implementation because they tend to have three key characteristics.

1. The CEO *articulates a transcendent goal* for the corporation. The CEO's vision of the corporation goes beyond the petty complaints and grievances of the average work day. Because this vision puts activities and conflicts in a new perspective, it gives renewed meaning to everyone's work activities and enables them to see beyond the details of their own jobs to the functioning of the total corporation. As John W. Teets, CEO and Chairman of The Greyhound Corporation, states, "Management's job is to see the company not as it is . . . but as it can become."[49]

2. The CEO *presents a role* for others to identify with and to follow. The leader sets an example in terms of behavior and dress. The CEO's attitudes and values concerning the corporation's purpose and activities are clear-cut and constantly communicated in words and deeds.

3. The CEO *communicates high performance standards* but also *shows confidence* in the followers' abilities to meet these standards. No leader ever improved performance by setting easily attainable goals that provide no challenge. The CEO must be willing to follow through by coaching people.[50]

As an example of a top manager providing executive leadership, John Welch, Jr., Chairman and CEO of General Electric Company (GE), transformed GE after he took office in 1981. Welch dismantled GE's sectors and groups and now has 14 separate businesses reporting directly to him and his two vice-chairmen. According to Welch: "Good business leaders create a vision, articulate the vision, passionately own the vision, and relentlessly drive it to completion."[51]

Manage Strategic Planning Process

Top management must initiate and manage the strategic planning process. To specify the corporate mission, delineate corporate objectives, and formulate appropriate strategies and policies, it must take a very long-range view. As depicted in Fig. 2.2, the ideal time horizon for management's planning varies according to level in

| FIGURE 2.2 | "Ideal" Allocations of Time for Planning in the "Average" Company |

	Today	1 Week Ahead	1 Month Ahead	3-6 Months Ahead	1 Year Ahead	2 Years Ahead	3-4 Years Ahead	5-10 Years Ahead
President	1%	2%	5%	10%	15%	27%	30%	10%
Executive Vice-President	2%	4%	10%	29%	20%	18%	13%	4%
Vice-President of Functional Area	4%	8%	15%	35%	20%	10%	5%	3%
General Manager of a Major Division	2%	5%	15%	30%	20%	12%	12%	4%
Department Manager	10%	10%	24%	39%	10%	5%	1%	1%
Section Supervisor	15%	20%	25%	37%	3%			
Group Supervisor	38%	40%	15%	5%	2%			

Source: Reprinted with permission of The Free Press, a division of Macmillan, Inc. from *Top Management Planning* by G. A. Steiner. Copyright © 1969 by the Trustees of Columbia University in the City of New York.

the corporate hierarchy. The president of a corporation, for example, should allocate the largest proportion of planning time to looking two to four years ahead. One reason given for the worldwide economic success of many Japanese corporations is the reputed ability of their top managers to conceptualize corporate mission and strategy far into the future. Mr. Ishihara, President of Nissan, has been quoted as saying "In what I do now, I am thinking twenty or thirty years ahead."[52] A department manager, however, should put the heaviest proportion of planning time on looking only three to six *months* ahead.

To accomplish its tasks, top management must use information provided by three key corporate groups: a long-range planning staff, divisional or SBU managers, and managers of functional departments.

A **long-range planning staff** typically consists of six people, headed by a senior vice-president or director of corporate planning.[53] To generate data for strategic decisions by top management, it continuously monitors both internal and external environments. It also suggests to top management possible changes in the corporate mission, objectives, strategies, and policies. Although only one in five companies with sales under $100 million has a separate, formal planning department, nearly all corporations with sales of at least $2 billion have such departments.[54] The size of corporate planning staffs in large corporations is currently decreasing, however, as strategic planning responsibilities are being shifted to line managers.

Divisional or SBU managers, with the assistance of the long-range planning staff and with input from their product managers, perform the strategic planning function for each division. These SBU managers typically initiate proposals for top management's consideration and/or respond to requests for such proposals by corporate headquarters. They may also be tasked to carry out strategies and policies decided upon at the corporate level for organizationwide implementation. These division managers typically work with the heads of various functional units within the division to develop the appropriate functional strategies for the implementation of planned business-level strategies.

Managers of functional departments (marketing, engineering, R&D managers, etc.) report directly either to divisional managers in a multidivision corporation or to top management if the corporation has no divisions. Although they may develop specific functional strategies, they generally do so within the framework of divisional or corporate strategies. They also respond to initiatives from above that ask for input or require them to develop strategies for the implementation of divisional plans.

CHARACTERISTICS OF TOP MANAGEMENT TASKS

Top management tasks have two characteristics that differentiate them from other managerial tasks.[55] First, *very few of them are continuous*. Rarely does a manager work on these tasks all day. The responsibilities, however, are always present, even though the tasks themselves are sporadic. And when the tasks do arise, they are of crucial significance, such as the selection of a person to head a new division.

Mintzberg reports that the activities of most executives are characterized by brevity, variety, and fragmentation: "Half of the observed activities were completed in less than nine minutes and only one-tenth took more than an hour. In effect, the managers were seldom able or willing to spend much time on any one issue in any one session."[56]

The second characteristic of top management tasks is that *they require a wide range of capabilities and temperaments*. Some tasks require the capacity to analyze and carefully weigh alternative courses of action. Some require an awareness of and an interest in people, whereas others call for the ability to pursue abstract ideas, concepts, and calculations.

One effect of tasks having these two characteristics is that top managers are often drawn back into the functional work of the corporation. Because their activities are not continuous, people in top management often have unplanned free time. They tend therefore to get caught up in the day-to-day work in manufacturing, marketing, accounting, engineering, or in other operations of the corporation. They may find themselves constantly solving crises that could probably have been better handled by lower-level managers. These managers are also usually fond of protesting, "*How can I be expected to drain the swamp when I'm up to my eyeballs in alligators!?*"

A second effect of the tasks' characteristics is that top managers tend to perceive only those aspects and responsibilities of the top management function that are compatible with their abilities, experience, and temperaments. And, if the board of directors fails to state explicitly what it considers to be the key responsibilities and activities of top management, the top managers are free to define the job themselves. Therefore, important tasks can be overlooked until a crisis occurs.

MODES OF STRATEGY FORMULATION

From his studies of chief executives, Henry Mintzberg proposes that a corporation's mission, objectives, and strategies are strongly affected by top management's perception of the world.[57] This perception determines the approach or "mode" used by the CEO and his or her staff in strategy formulation. He names three basic modes: entrepreneurial, adaptive, and planning.

- **Entrepreneurial mode.** Strategy is made by one powerful individual. The focus is on opportunities. Problems are secondary. Strategy is guided by the founder's own vision of direction and is exemplified by large, bold decisions. The dominant goal is growth of the corporation.

  Bill Gates, founder and Chairman of Microsoft Corporation, is an example of this mode of strategic planning. The company reflects his vision of the personal computer industry. Although Microsoft's clear mission—competitiveness, tenacity, and technological self-confidence, which emanate from Gates—are certainly advantages of the entrepreneurial mode, its tendency to introduce products before they are ready is a significant disadvantage. "Microsoft is a very seat-of-the-pants operation, . . ." comments Michael Swavely, President of Compaq Computer's North American operations.[58]

- **Adaptive mode.** Sometimes referred to as "muddling through," this strategy-formulation mode is characterized by reactive solutions to existing problems, rather than a proactive search for new opportunities. Much bargaining goes on concerning priorities of objectives. Strategy is fragmented and is developed to move the corporation forward in incremental steps.

  This mode is typical of most universities, many large hospitals, a large number of governmental agencies, and a surprising number of large corporations. Western Union, for example, has for years successfully plodded along earning a small but predictable annual profit from businesses that largely were outgrowths of the telegraph. Only recently, when it tried to change modes and become more aggressive, did it fall on hard times.[59]

- **Planning mode.** Analysts assume major responsibilities for strategy formulation. Strategic planning includes both the proactive search for new opportunities and the reactive solution of existing problems. Systematic comprehensive analysis is used for the development of strategies that integrate the corporation's decision-making processes.

  As shown in the following *boxed example* of Maytag, the current Maytag Corporation is an example of the planning mode in strategy formulation. After realizing how the major home appliance industry was changing in the U.S. and throughout the world, Maytag's top management deliberately chose to transform the company from a domestic high-quality niche producer of laundry appliances to a full-line global competitor.

In the *entrepreneurial* mode, top management believes that the environment is a force to be used and controlled. In the *adaptive* mode, it assumes the environment is too complex to be completely comprehended. In the *planning* mode, it works on the assumption that systematic scanning and analysis of the environment can provide

MAYTAG CORPORATION:
EVOLUTION OF PLANNING MODE

During the lifetime of F. L. Maytag, the firm's approach to strategic planning could be called entrepreneurial. As both founder and owner of the company, F. L. based his key decisions on his evolving vision of the company's future. He slowly phased out the company's original line of farm equipment as his new line of washing machines increased in sales. Between 1909 and 1911, F. L. worked with the famed Duesenberg brothers to build a Maytag-Mason automobile in Waterloo, Iowa. He experimented with several marginal ventures until he decided to devote all of the company's energies to the manufacture and sale of washing machines.

After F. L.'s departure from the company's management in the 1920s, the firm's approach to strategic planning changed from an entrepreneurial to an adaptive mode. Maytag family descendants and professional managers continued to follow F. L.'s ideas concerning washing machines and generally made strategic changes as a way of adapting to a changing environment. The innovative genius and entrepreneurial drive of the company's early years were no longer present. The firm's slowness in converting from wringer to automatic washing machines in the 1940s cost the company its leadership of the industry. Its share of the U.S. washing machine market dropped from 40%–45% during the 1920s and 1930s to 8% in 1954. Although management continued to add to and improve Maytag's product line throughout the 1950s and 1960s, the company remained primarily a high-quality niche producer of laundry appliances.

As mentioned in the boxed example of Maytag in Chapter 1, Maytag Company's strategic planning process changed radically in 1978. CEO Daniel Krumm took a hard look at Maytag's position in the industry, established a strategic planning task force, and asked its members to answer the question: "If we keep doing what we're doing now, what will the Maytag Company look like in five years?" The resulting report shook the company from top to bottom and initiated the corporation's current planning mode of strategy formulation.

The corporation's current strategic plan is updated every year and usually has a three-year time horizon. Maytag's top management usually begins the process by scanning the firm's external and internal environments. After much brainstorming, the strategic issues committee, which is composed of top management, generates a strategic proposal for the corporation. The committee then invites the rest of the top-level staff and the business-unit heads to an annual meeting for an open discussion to flesh out the proposal. The resulting strategic plan deals with implementation as well as formulating a general direction for the firm as a whole.

the knowledge it needs to influence the environment to the corporation's advantage. The use of a specific planning mode reflects top management's perception of the corporation's environment. If we categorize a corporation's top management according to these three planning modes, we can better understand how and why key decisions are made. Then if we look at these decisions in light of the corporation's mission, objectives, strategies, and policies, we can then determine whether the dominant planning mode is appropriate.

In some instances, a corporation might follow an approach called **logical incrementalism,** which is a synthesis of the planning, adaptive, and to a lesser extent, the entrepreneurial modes of strategy formulation. As described by Quinn, top management might have a reasonably clear idea of the corporation's mission and objectives, but, in its development of strategies, chooses to use "an interactive process in which the organization probes the future, experiments and learns from a series of partial (incremental) commitments rather than through global formulations of total strategies."[60] This approach appears to be useful when the environment is changing rapidly and when it is important to build consensus and develop needed resources before the entire corporation is committed to a specific strategy.

IMPORTANCE OF CONCEPTUAL SKILLS

Conceptual skills are very important for the successful management of organizations. Top managers face a **strategic management paradox.** On the one hand, top managers are charged with maintaining organizational efficiency and internal stability in order to earn a predictable stream of profits. On the other hand, however, they must be able to change the organization quickly when external pressures pose new threats or opportunities. Unfortunately, those executives who succeed in making their companies very efficient in the use of resources might also be making the firms more passive and less prepared for radical environmental shifts. Top managers who are successful in making their corporations flexible and responsive to new environmental challenges, in contrast, will not ensure the firm's survival if they ignore their responsibility to maintain efficient performance in the face of competitive pressures.[61] How does one balance these seemingly conflicting priorities?

Research by Lamb of 89 current and former CEOs, from David Rockefeller and Lee Iacocca to Harold Geneen, revealed that 90% of the chief executives said they were unprepared to deal with the external environment—community groups, the media, Wall Street analysts, leaders, and government agencies—and yet such activities consumed as much as 50% of their time.[62] Until recently, the route to the top in most large corporations had been through specialized training and functional job responsibilities. Now and in the future, however, specific functional backgrounds such as marketing or finance are becoming less important for chief executives. "It will be very difficult for a single-discipline individual to reach the top," comments Douglas Danforth, former Chairman of Westinghouse Electric Company and influential director on the boards of many corporations.[63] A survey of CEOs conducted jointly in 1988 by the executive-search firm Korn/Ferry International and Columbia University Graduate School of Business concluded that specific industry experience will also become less relevant to top management success because there are likely to be fewer one-industry companies in the future.[64] These CEOs agreed that the most important talents required for top managers in the next century will be strategy formulation and human resource management.[65]

One reason top executives often run into difficulty in managing an organization—especially a large organization in a changing environment—is because they have not adequately developed their conceptual skills. The very skills and abilities that were so helpful in succeeding in a narrowly defined entry-level job are usually of little value in a more broadly defined top management position.

Robert L. Katz suggests that effective administration depends on a proper mix of three basic skills: technical, human, and conceptual.[66]

- **Technical skills** pertain to *what* is done and to working with *things*. They comprise one's ability to use technology to perform an organizational task.
- **Human skills** pertain to *how* something is done and to working with *people*. They comprise one's ability to work with people in the achievement of goals.
- **Conceptual skills** pertain to *why* something is done and to one's view of the corporation as a *whole*. They comprise one's ability to understand the complexities of the corporation as it affects and is affected by its environment.

Katz further suggests that the optimal mix of these three skills varies at the different corporate levels:

> At lower levels, the major need is for technical and human skills. At higher levels, the administrator's effectiveness depends largely on human and conceptual skills. At the top, conceptual skill becomes the most important of all for successful administration.[67]

Results of a survey of 300 presidents of *Fortune*'s list of the top 50 banking, insurance, public utility, retailing, and 100 top industrial firms support Katz's conclusion regarding the different skill mixes needed at the different organizational levels.[68] As shown in Fig. 2.3, the need for technical skills decreases and the need for conceptual skills increases as a person moves from first-line supervision to top management. Further research also notes that middle managers recognized as having top management potential tend to be able to conceptualize problems and use information across five functional areas within their organizations.[69] This transition from primarily technical to an emphasis on conceptual skills is important given that most theorists agree that conceptual work carried out by an organization's executives is the heart of strategy making.[70]

| **FIGURE 2.3** | **Optimal Skill Mix of a Manager by Hierarchical Level** |

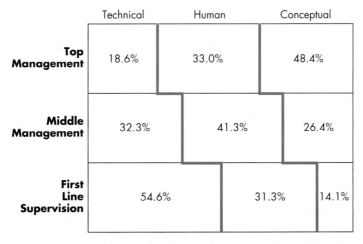

Source: T. L. Wheelen, C. E. Michaels, Jr., and J. D. Hunger, "A Longitudinal Study of the Skills of an Effective Executive," Working Paper. Copyright © 1991 by T. L. Wheelen. Reprinted by permission.

2.3 STRATEGIC AUDIT: AN AID TO STRATEGIC DECISION MAKING

As business corporations become larger and more complex, strategic decision making becomes more complicated. Executives often need some sort of checklist or guideline to aid them in collecting the necessary data and organizing it for strategic analysis and the development of alternative strategies and programs. Consulting firms, management scholars, boards of directors, and practicing managers suggest the use of management audits of corporate activities.[71]

A **management audit** provides a checklist of questions that forms the basis for an in-depth analysis of a particular area of importance to the corporation. It is extremely useful as a diagnostic tool to pinpoint problem areas and to highlight strengths and weaknesses. Rarely, however, does it include consideration of more than one issue or functional area such as a corporation's sales force, social responsibility, or its human resource management. The **strategic audit** is, in contrast, a *type of management audit* that takes a corporatewide perspective and provides a comprehensive assessment of a corporation's strategic situation.

As contrasted with the typically more specialized management audit, the strategic audit considers external as well as internal factors and includes alternative selection, implementation, and evaluation and control. It therefore covers the key aspects of the strategic management process and places them within a decision-making framework. This framework is composed of the following eight interrelated steps:

1. **Evaluation of a corporation's current performance results** in terms of (a) return on investment, profitability, and so forth, and (b) the current mission, objectives, strategies, and policies.
2. **Examination and evaluation of a corporation's strategic managers**—its board of directors and top management.
3. **A scan of the external environment** to locate strategic factors that pose opportunities and threats.
4. **A scan of the internal corporate environment** to determine strategic factors that are strengths and weaknesses.
5. **Analysis of the strategic factors** to (a) pinpoint problem areas, and (b) review and revise the corporate mission and objectives as necessary.
6. **Generation, evaluation, and selection of the best alternative strategy** in light of the analysis conducted in Step 5.
7. **Implementation** of selected strategies via programs, budgets, and procedures.
8. **Evaluation** of the implemented strategies via feedback systems, and the **control** of activities to ensure their minimum deviation from plans.

This strategic decision-making process, depicted in Fig. 2.4, basically reflects the approach to strategic management being used successfully by corporations such as Warner-Lambert, Dayton Hudson, Avon Products, Bechtel Group, Inc., and Taisei Corporation.[72] Although some research suggests that this "rational" approach to strategic decision making might not work so well for firms in very unstable environ-

FIGURE 2.4 | **Strategic Decision-Making Process**

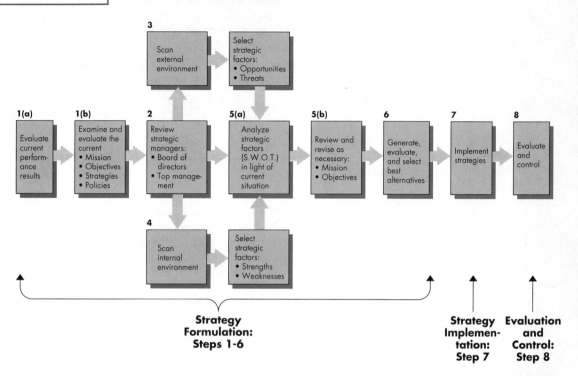

ments,[73] other research concludes that increasing environmental complexity seems to increase planning extensiveness.[74] Generally, there appears to be a relationship between organizational performance and comprehensive, sophisticated strategic analysis.[75] The strategic decision-making process recommended in this chapter is one way to achieve more comprehensive and better-integrated strategic management. The key is to monitor environmental conditions and to keep the process flexible in light of changing circumstances.

The strategic decision-making process is made operational through the strategic audit. The audit presents an integrated view of strategic management in action. It describes not only how objectives, strategies, and policies are formulated as long-range decisions, but also how they are implemented, evaluated, and controlled by programs, budgets, and procedures. The strategic audit, therefore, enables a person to better understand the ways in which various functional areas are interrelated and interdependent, as well as the manner in which they contribute to the achievement of the corporate mission. Consequently, the strategic audit is very useful to those people, such as boards of directors and top management, whose jobs are to evaluate the overall performance of a corporation.

The appendix at the end of this chapter is an example of a strategic audit proposed for use in the analysis of complex business policy cases and for strategic decision making. The questions in the audit parallel the eight steps depicted in Fig.

2.4, the strategic decision-making process. It is *not* an all-inclusive list, but it does present many of the critical questions needed for the strategic analysis of any business corporation. A person should consider the audit as a guide for analysis. Some questions or even some areas might be inappropriate for a particular situation; in other cases, the questions may be insufficient for a complete analysis. However, each question in a particular area of the strategic audit can be broken down into an additional series of subquestions. It is up to the individual to develop these subquestions when they are needed.

SUMMARY AND CONCLUSION

The strategy-makers of a modern corporation are the board of directors and top management. Both must be actively involved in the strategic management process if the corporation is to have long-term success in accomplishing its mission.

An effective board is the keystone of the modern corporation. Without it, management would tend to focus on short-run problems and solutions or go off on tangents at odds with the basic mission. The personal needs and goals of executives would tend to overrule the interests of the corporation. Even the strongest critics of boards of directors are more interested in improving and upgrading boards than in eliminating them. An active board is critical in determining an organization's mission, objectives, strategy, and policies.

Top management, in contrast, is responsible for the overall functioning of the corporation. People in top management must view the corporation as a whole rather than as a series of functional departments or decentralized divisions. They must constantly visualize and plan for the future, and set objectives, strategies, and policies that will allow the corporation to successfully realize that future. They must set standards and provide a vision not only of what the corporation is but also of what it is trying to become. They must develop working relationships with the board of directors, key staff personnel, and managers from divisions and functional areas.

The strategic audit is proposed as an aid to top managers and boards of directors for a more comprehensive analysis of a corporation's situation. It is a way of operationalizing the strategic decision-making process commonly used in large business corporations.

DISCUSSION QUESTIONS

1. Does a corporation really need a board of directors? Why or why not?

2. What aspects of a corporation's environment should be represented on a board of directors?

3. Should cumulative voting for the election of board members be *required* by law in all political jurisdictions?

4. Do you agree that a chief executive office (CEO), in order to be effective, should fulfill Mintzberg's ten roles?

5. Should people be selected for top management positions primarily on the basis of their having a particular combination of skills? Explain.

6. Reconcile the strategic decision-making process depicted in Fig. 2.4 with the strategic management model depicted in Fig. 1.2.

7. What are the strengths and weaknesses of the strategic audit as a technique for assessing corporate performance?

NOTES

1. W. Loomis, "The Real Drivers of Strategy," *Planning Review* (May–June 1988), p. 5.

2. J. W. Lorsch with E. MacIver, *Pawns or Potentates: The Reality of America's Corporate Boards* (Boston: Harvard Business School Press, 1989), pp. 4–6.

3. L. Iacocca, *Iacocca: An Autobiography* (Toronto: Bantam Books, 1984), p. 104.

4. M. L. Weidenbaum, "The Best Defense Against the Raiders," *Business Week* (September 23, 1985), p. 21. This belief is supported by research reporting that the stockholders of an acquiring firm tend to lose in the transaction. See M. Weidenbaum and S. Vogt, "Takeovers and Stockholders: Winners and Losers," *California Management Review* (Summer 1987), pp. 157–168.

5. J. H. Dobrzynski, M. Schroeder, G. L. Miles, and J. Weber, "Taking Charge," *Business Week* (July 3, 1989), p. 69.

6. J. Bacon and J. K. Brown, *Corporate Directorship Practices: Role, Selection and Legal Status of the Board* (New York: The Conference Board, Report no. 646, 1975), p. 7.

7. Bacon and Brown, *Corporate Directorship Practices*, p. 75.

8. M. Galen, "A Seat on the Board Is Getting Hotter," *Business Week* (July 3, 1989), p. 72.

9. J. Irish, "Director Exposure Goes Global," *Directors & Boards* (Fall, 1989), pp. 18–19.

   W. E. Green, "Directors' Insurance: How Good a Shield," *Wall Street Journal* (August 14, 1989), p. B1.

   I. F. Kesner and R. B. Johnson, "Crisis in the Boardroom: Fact and Fiction," *Academy of Management Executive* (February 1990), pp. 23–35.

10. L. A. Hamermesh, "The Director As Auctioneer," *Directors and Boards* (Winter 1987), p. 26.

11. Bacon and Brown, *Corporate Directorship Practices*, p. 15.

12. Dobrzynski et al., "Taking Charge," p. 71.

13. J. Rosenstein, "Why Don't U.S. Boards Get More Involved in Strategy?" *Long Range Planning* (June 1987), pp. 32–33.

14. G. L. Miles, "National Intergroup: How Pete Love Went Wrong," *Business Week* (March 6, 1989), p. 64.

15. C. N. Waldo, *Boards of Directors* (Westport, Conn.: Quorum Books, 1985), p. 2.

   A. V. Bruno and J. K. Leidecker, "When to Convert from a Perfunctory Board or 'Staff Meeting' to an Operating Board of Directors," in *Handbook of Business Strategy, 1985/1986 Yearbook*, edited by W. D.

16. T. Tilghman and D. Hickey, "Critical Emerging Issues in Board Renewal and Rewards," *Directors and Boards* (Spring 1989), p. 32.

17. Lorsch with MacIver, "Pawns or Potentates," p. 17.

   J. W. Hoft, J. D. Hunger, and C. B. Shrader, "Characteristics of Boards of Directors and Corporate Social Responsibility," *Proceedings, Midwest Management Society*, 1990, p. 22.

   Tilghman and Hickey, "Critical Emerging Issues," p. 33.

18. R. J. Bronstein, "Good Pay on Small Boards," *Directors and Boards* (Spring 1987), pp. 36–37.

19. I. F. Kesner, "Directors' Characteristics and Committee Membership: An Investigation of Type, Occupation, Tenure, and Gender," *Academy of Management Journal* (March 1988), p. 67.

20. For a good summary of agency theory as applied to corporate governance, see: J. P. Walsh and J. K. Seward, "On the Efficiency of Internal and External Corporate Control Mechanisms," *Academy of Management Review* (July 1990), pp. 421–458; K. M. Eisenhardt, "Agency Theory: An Assessment and Review," *Academy of Management Review* (January 1989), pp. 57–74.

21. S. C. Vance, *Corporate Leadership: Boards, Directors and Strategy* (New York: McGraw-Hill, 1983), p. 274.

22. M. H. Schellenger, D. D. Wood, and A. Tashakori, "Board of Director Composition, Shareholder Wealth, and Dividend Policy," *Journal of Management* (September 1989), pp. 457–467.

   I. F. Kesner, "Directors Stock Ownership and Organizational Performance: An Investigation of Fortune 500 Companies," *Journal of Management* (Fall 1987), pp. 499–507.

23. "Companies Court Women for Boards," *Nation's Business* (January 1990), p. 52.

24. "All-White Male Boards Fell," *Wall Street Journal* (March 23, 1989), p. 1.

25. "Companies Court Women for Boards," p. 52.

26. T. H. Hammer and R. N. Stern, "Worker Representation on Company Boards of Directors," *Proceedings, Academy of Management* (1983), p. 368.

27. J. R. Lang and D. E. Lockhart, "Increased Environmental Uncertainty and Changes in Board Linkage Patterns," *Academy of Management Journal* (March 1990), p. 106.

28. M. H. Bazerman and F. D. Schoorman, "A Limited

Guth (Boston: Warren, Gorham, and Lamont, 1985), pp. 29.1–29.9.

Rationality Model of Interlocking Directorates," *Academy of Management Review* (April 1983), pp. 206–217.

29. M. S. Mizruchi and L. B. Stearns, "A Longitudinal Study of the Formation of Interlocking Directorates," *Administrative Science Quarterly* (June 1988), pp. 194–210.

30. For a more in-depth discussion of this topic, refer to J. M. Pennings, *Interlocking Directorates* (San Francisco: Jossey-Bass, 1980), and M. S. Mizruchi, *The American Corporate Network 1904–1974* (Beverly Hills, Calif.: Sage Publications, 1982).

31. Miles, "National Intergroup," pp. 56–64.

32. Kesner, "Directors' Characteristics," p. 67.

G. R. Roche, "Committees Come to the Fore," *Directors and Boards* (Fall 1986), pp. 22–23.

33. "Downsized Boards and Upped Outsiders," *Directors and Boards* (Winter 1990), p. 40.

34. A. C. Regan and A. Reichel, " 'Shark Repellents': How to Avoid Hostile Takeovers," *Long Range Planning* (December 1985), p. 62.

35. "Downsized Boards and Upped Outsiders," p. 40.

36. R. Mims and E. Lewis, "Portrait of the Boss," *Business Week: The Corporate Elite* (October 19, 1990), p. 13.

P. L. Reckner and D. R. Dalton, "The Impact of CEO As Board Chairman on Corporate Performance: Evidence vs. Rhetoric," *Academy of Management Executives* (May 1989), pp. 141–143.

37. J. C. Worthy and R. P. Neuschel, *Emerging Issues in Corporate Governance* (Evanston, Ill.: Northwestern University Press, 1983), pp. 15–18.

38. For further information on board committees, refer to Kesner, "Directors' Characteristics," pp. 66–84.

39. Waldo, Boards of Directors, p. 172.

40. Worthy and Neuschel, Corporate Governance, p. 100.

41. E. J. Zajac, "CEO Selection, Succession, Compensation and Firm Performance: A Theoretical Integration and Empirical Analysis," *Strategic Management Journal* (March-April 1990), pp. 217–230.

K. M. Eisenhardt and C. B. Shoonhoven, "Organizational Growth: Linking Founding Team, Strategy, Environment and Growth Among U.S. Semiconductor Ventures, 1978–1988," *Administrative Science Quarterly* (September 1990), pp. 504–529.

S. Finkelstein and D. C. Hambrick, "Top-Management-Team Tenure and Organizational Outcomes: The Moderating Role of Managerial Discretion," *Administrative Science Quarterly* (September 1990), pp. 484–503.

42. T. H. Pincus, "A Crisis Parachute: Helping Stock Prices Have a Soft Landing," *Journal of Business Strategy* (Spring 1986), pp. 35–36.

43. P. F. Drucker, *Management: Tasks, Responsibilities, Practices* (New York: HarperCollins, 1974), p. 613.

44. H. Mintzberg, *The Nature of Managerial Work* (New York: HarperCollins, 1973), pp. 54–94.

45. Drucker, *Management,* pp. 611–612.

46. D. C. Limerick, "Managers of Meaning: From Bob Geldof's Band Aid to Australian CEOs," *Organizational Dynamics* (Spring 1990), pp. 22–33.

H. S. Jonas III, R. Fry, and S. Srivastva, "The Office of the CEO, Understanding the Executive Experience," *Academy of Management Executive* (August 1990), pp. 36–48.

J. P. Kotler, *The Leadership Factor* (New York: Free Press, 1988).

47. T. J. Peters and R. H. Waterman, *In Search of Excellence* (New York: HarperCollins, 1982), p. 26.

48. A. Levitt, Jr., and J. Albertine, "The Successful Entrepreneur: A Personality Profile," *Wall Street Journal* (August 29, 1983), p. 12.

49. Advertisement in *Business Week* (October 23, 1987), p. 118–119.

50. Adapted from R. J. House, "A 1976 Theory of Charismatic Leadership," *Leadership: The Cutting Edge,* edited by J. G. Hunt and L. L. Larson (Carbondale, Ill.: SIU Press, 1977), pp. 189–207.

This view of executive leadership is also referred to as *transformational leadership.* See B. M. Bass, "From Transactional to Transformational Leadership: Learning to Share the Vision," *Organizational Dynamics* (Winter 1990), pp. 19–31.

51. N. Tichy and R. Charan, "Speed, Simplicity, Self-Confidence: An Interview with Jack Welch," *Harvard Business Review* (September-October 1989), p. 113

52. M. Trevor, "Japanese Decision-making and Global Strategy," in *Strategic Management Research: A European Perspective,* edited by J. McGee and H. Thomas (Chichester, U.K.: John Wiley and Sons, 1986), p. 301.

53. S. Matlins and G. Knisely, "Update: Profile of the Corporate Planners," *Journal of Business Strategy* (Spring 1981), pp. 75, 77.

54. C. D. Burnett, D. P. Yeskey, and D. Richardson, "New Roles for Corporate Planners in the 1980's," *Journal of Business Strategy* (Spring 1984), p. 67.

55. Drucker, *Management,* pp. 615–617.

56. Mintzberg, *Managerial Work,* p. 33.

57. H. Mintzberg, "Strategy-Making in Three Modes," *California Management Review* (Winter 1973), pp. 44–53.

58. B. Schlender, "How Bill Gates Keeps the Magic Going," *Fortune* (June 18, 1990), pp. 82–89.

59. J. Guyon, "Western Union, Saved by a Junk-Bond Deal, Needs Rescuing Again," *Wall Street Journal* (October 13, 1989), p. 1.

60. J. B. Quinn, *Strategies for Change: Logical Incrementalism* (Homewood, Ill.: Irwin, 1980), p. 58.

61. A. Ginsberg and A. Buchholtz, "Converting to For-Profit Status: Corporate Responsiveness to Radical Change," *Academy of Management Journal* (September 1990), p. 470.

62. R. B. Lamb, *Running American Business* (New York: Basic Books, 1987).

63. A. Bennett, "The Chief Executives in Year 2000 Will Be Experienced Abroad," *Wall Street Journal* (February 27, 1989), p. A1.

64. L. B. Korn, "How the Next CEO Will Be Different," *Fortune* (May 22, 1989), p. 157.

65. *Ibid.*

66. R. L. Katz, "Skills of an Effective Administrator," *Harvard Business Review* (January-February 1955), pp. 33–42.

67. *Ibid.*, p. 42.

68. T. L. Wheelen, C. E. Michaels, Jr., and J. D. Hunger, "A Longitudinal Study of the Skills of an Effective Executive," Working Paper, 1991.

69. J. P. Walsh, "Selectivity and Selective Perception: An Investigation of Managers' Belief Structures and Information Processing," *Academy of Management Journal* (December 1988), pp. 873–896.

70. E. E. Chaffee, "Three Models of Strategy," *Academy of Management Review* (January 1985), pp. 89–90.

D. Norburn, "GOGOs, YOYOs and DODOs: Company Directors and Industry Performance," *Strategic Management Journal* (March-April 1986), p. 112.

B. C. Reimann, "Doers as Planners," *Planning Review* (September 1986), p. 45.

71. T. L. Wheelen and J. D. Hunger, "Using the Strategic Audit," *SAM Advanced Management Journal* (Winter 1987), pp. 4–12.

R. B. Buchele, "How to Evaluate a Firm," *California Management Review* (Fall 1962), pp. 5–16.

M. Lauenstein, "The Strategy Audit," *Journal of Business Strategy* (Winter 1984), pp. 87–91.

T. Barry, "What a Management Audit Can Do for You," *Management Review* (June 1977), p. 43.

72. H. Okuzumi, "Taisei Corporation Plans for the Year 2000," *Long Range Planning* (February 1990), pp. 53–65.

E. E. Tallett, "Repositioning Warner-Lambert as a High-Tech Health Care Company," *Planning Review* (May 1984), pp. 12–16, 41.

K. A. Macke, "Managing Change: How Dayton Hudson Meets the Challenge," *Journal of Business Strategy* (Summer 1983), pp. 78–81.

D. M. Slavick, "Planning at Bechtel: End of the Megaproject Era," *Planning Review* (September 1986), pp. 16–22.

H. Waldron, "Putting a New Face On Avon," *Planning Review* (July 1985), pp. 18–23.

73. J. W. Fredrickson and A. L. Iaquinto, "Inertia and Creeping Rationality in Strategic Decision Processes," *Academy of Management Journal* (September 1989), pp. 516–542.

74. S. Kukalis, "The Relationship Among Firm Characteristics and Design of Strategic Planning Systems in Large Organizations," *Journal of Management* (December 1989), pp. 565–579.

75. R. B. Robinson and J. A. Pearce II, "Planned Patterns of Strategic Behavior and Their Relationship to Business-Unit Performance," *Strategic Management Journal* (January-February 1988), pp. 43–60.

R. E. Jones, L. W. Jacobs, and R. D. Von Riesen, "Comprehensive Strategic Decision Processes in High Technology Firms," Working Paper, University of Wyoming, February 1990.

APPENDIX

Strategic Audit of a Corporation

I. CURRENT SITUATION

A. Performance
How is the corporation performing in terms of return on investment, overall market share, profitability trends, earnings per share, etc.?

B. Strategic Posture
What are the corporation's current mission, objectives, strategies, and policies?

1. Are they clearly stated or are they merely implied from performance?
2. *Mission:* What business(es) is the corporation in? Why?
3. *Objectives:* What are the corporate, business, and functional objectives? Are they consistent with each other, with the mission, and with the internal and external environments?
4. *Strategies:* What strategy or mix of strategies is the corporation following? Are they consistent with each other, with the mission and objectives, and with the internal and external environments?
5. *Policies:* What are they? Are they consistent with each other, with the mission, objectives, and strategies, and with the internal and external environments?

Source: T. L. Wheelen and J. D. Hunger, "Strategic Audit of a Corporation." Copyright © 1982 by Wheelen and Hunger Associates. Reprinted by permission. Revised 1988 and 1991.

II. STRATEGIC MANAGERS

A. Board of Directors
1. Who are they? Are they internal or external?
2. Do they own significant shares of stock?
3. Is the stock privately held or publicly traded?
4. What do they contribute to the corporation in terms of knowledge, skills, background, and connections?
5. How long have they served on the board?
6. What is their level of involvement in strategic management? Do they merely rubber-stamp top management's proposals or do they actively participate and suggest future directions?

B. Top Management
1. What person or group constitutes top management?
2. What are top management's chief characteristics in terms of knowledge, skills, background, and style?
3. Has top management been responsible for the corporation's performance over the past few years?
4. Has it established a systematic approach to the formulation, implementation, and evaluation and control of strategic management?
5. What is its level of involvement in the strategic management process?
6. How well does top management interact with lower-level management?
7. How well does top management interact with the board of directors?

8. Is top management sufficiently skilled to cope with likely future challenges?

III. EXTERNAL ENVIRONMENT: OPPORTUNITIES AND THREATS (S.W.<u>O</u>.T.)

A. **Societal Environment**
   1. What general environmental factors among the sociocultural, economic, political-legal, and technological forces are currently affecting both the corporation and the industries in which it competes? Which present current or future threats? Opportunities?
   2. Which of these are currently the most important (that is, are **strategic factors**) to the corporation and to the industries in which it competes? Which will be important in the future?

B. **Task Environment**
   1. What forces in the immediate environment (that is, threat of new entrants, bargaining power of buyers, threat of substitute products or services, bargaining power of suppliers, rivalry among competing firms, and the relative power of unions, governments, etc.) are currently affecting the level of competitive intensity within the industries in which the corporation offers products or services?
   2. What key factors in the immediate environment (that is, customers, competitors, suppliers, creditors, labor unions, governments, trade associations, interest groups, local communities, and stockholders) are currently affecting the corporation? Which present current or future threats? Opportunities?
   3. Which of these forces and factors are the most important (that is, are **strategic factors**) at the present time? Which will be important in the future?

IV. INTERNAL ENVIRONMENT: STRENGTHS AND WEAKNESSES (<u>S.W</u>.O.T.)

A. **Corporate Structure**
   1. How is the corporation structured at present?
      a) Is decision-making authority centralized around one group or decentralized to many groups or units?
      b) Is it organized on the basis of functions, projects, geography, or some combination of these?
   2. Is the structure clearly understood by everyone in the corporation?
   3. Is the present structure consistent with current corporate objectives, strategies, policies, and programs?
   4. In what ways does this structure compare with those of similar corporations?

B. **Corporate Culture**
   1. Is there a well-defined or emerging culture composed of shared beliefs, expectations, and values?
   2. Is the culture consistent with the current objectives, strategies, policies, and programs?
   3. What is the culture's position on important issues facing the corporation (that is, on productivity, quality of performance, adaptability to changing conditions)?

C. **Corporate Resources**
   1. **Marketing**
      a) What are the corporation's current marketing objectives, strategies, policies, and programs?
         i) Are they clearly stated, or merely implied from performance and/or budgets?
         ii) Are they consistent with the corporation's mission, objectives, strategies, policies, and with internal and external environments?
      b) How well is the corporation performing in terms of analysis of market position and marketing mix (that is, product, price, place, and promotion)?
         i) What trends emerge from this analysis?
         ii) What impact have these trends had on past performance and how will they probably affect future performance?
         iii) Does this analysis support the corporation's past and pending strategic decisions?
      c) How well does this corporation's marketing performance compare with those of similar corporations?
      d) Are marketing managers using accepted marketing concepts and techniques to eval-

uate and improve product performance? (Consider product life cycle, market segmentation, market research, and product portfolios.)

e) What is the role of the marketing manager in the strategic management process?

2. **Finance**

a) What are the corporation's current financial objectives, strategies, policies, and programs?

  i) Are they clearly stated or merely implied from performance and/or budgets?

  ii) Are they consistent with the corporation's mission, objectives, strategies, policies, and with internal and external environments?

b) How well is the corporation performing in terms of financial analysis? (Consider liquidity ratios, profitability ratios, activity ratios, leverage ratios, capitalization structure, and constant dollars.)

  i) What trends emerge from this analysis?

  ii) Are there any significant differences when statements are calculated in constant versus reported dollars?

  iii) What impact have these trends had on past performance and how will they probably affect future performance?

  iv) Does this analysis support the corporation's past and pending strategic decisions?

c) How well does this corporation's financial performance compare with that of similar corporations?

d) Are financial managers using accepted financial concepts and techniques to evaluate and improve current corporate and divisional performance? (Consider financial leverage, capital budgeting, and ratio analysis.)

e) What is the role of the financial manager in the strategic management process?

3. **Research and Development (R&D)**

a) What are the corporation's current R&D objectives, strategies, policies, and programs?

  i) Are they clearly stated, or implied from performance and/or budgets?

ii) Are they consistent with the corporation's mission, objectives, strategies, policies, and with internal and external environments?

  iii) What is the role of technology in corporate performance?

  iv) Is the mix of basic, applied, and engineering research appropriate given the corporate mission and strategies?

b) What return is the corporation receiving from its investment in R&D?

c) Is the corporation technologically competent?

d) How well does the corporation's investment in R&D compare with the investments of similar corporations?

e) What is the role of the R&D manager in the strategic management process?

4. **Operations (Manufacturing/Service)***

a) What are the corporation's current manufacturing/service objectives, strategies, policies, and programs?

  i) Are they clearly stated, or merely implied from performance and/or budgets?

  ii) Are they consistent with the corporation's mission, objectives, strategies, policies, and with internal and external environments?

b) What is the type and extent of operations capabilities of the corporation?

  i) If product-oriented, consider plant facilities, type of manufacturing system (continuous mass production or intermittent job shop), age and type of equipment, degree and role of automation and/or robots, plant capacities and utilization, productivity ratings, availability and type of transportation.

  ii) If service-oriented, consider service facilities (e.g., hospital, theater, or school buildings), type of operations systems

---

* Research suggests that the stretegic approach developed for manufacturing companies is very useful for service firms. See H. M. O'Neill, "Do Strategic Paradigms Work in Service Industries?" in *Handbook of Business Strategy, 1986/87 Yearbook*, edited by W. D. Guth (Boston: Warren, Gorham, and Lamont, 1986), pp. 19.1–19.14.

(continuous service over time to same clientele or intermittent service over time to varied clientele), age and type of supporting equipment, degree and role of automation and/or use of mass communication devices (e.g., diagnostic machinery, videotape machines), facility capacities and utilization rates, efficiency ratings of professional/service personnel, availability and type of transportation to bring service staff and clientele together.

c) Are manufacturing or service facilities vulnerable to natural disasters, local or national strikes, reduction or limitation of resources from suppliers, substantial cost increases of materials, or nationalization by governments?

d) Is operating leverage being used successfully with an appropriate mix of people and machines, in manufacturing firms, or of support staff to professionals, in service firms?

e) How well does the corporation perform relative to the competition? Consider costs per unit of labor, material, and overhead; downtime; inventory control management and/or scheduling of service staff; production ratings; facility utilization percentages; and number of clients successfully treated by category (if service firm), or percentage of orders shipped on time (if product firm).

   i) What trends emerge from this analysis?
   ii) What impact have these trends had on past performance and how will they probably affect future performance?
   iii) Does this analysis support the corporation's past and pending strategic decisions?

f) Are operations managers using appropriate concepts and techniques to evaluate and improve current performance? Consider cost systems, quality control and reliability systems, inventory control management, personnel scheduling, learning curves, safety programs, engineering programs that can improve efficiency of manufacturing or of service.

g) What is the role of the operations manager in the strategic management process?

5. **Human Resources Management (HRM)**

a) What are the corporation's current HRM objectives, strategies, policies, and programs?

   i) Are they clearly stated, or merely implied from performance and/or budgets?
   ii) Are they consistent with the corporation's mission, objectives, strategies, policies, and with internal and external environments?

b) How well is the corporation's HRM performing in terms of improving the fit between the individual employee and the job? Consider turnover, grievances, strikes, layoffs, employee training, quality of work life.

   i) What trends emerge from this analysis?
   ii) What impact have these trends had on past performance and how will they probably affect future performance?
   iii) Does this analysis support the corporation's past and pending strategic decisions?

c) How does this corporation's HRM performance compare with that of similar corporations?

d) Are HRM managers using appropriate concepts and techniques to evaluate and improve corporate performance? Consider the job analysis program, performance appraisal system, up-to-date job descriptions, training and development programs, attitude surveys, job design programs, quality of relationship with unions.

e) What is the role of the HRM manager in the strategic management process?

6. **Information Systems (IS)**

a) What are the corporation's current IS objectives, strategies, policies, and programs?

   i) Are they clearly stated, or merely implied from performance and/or budgets?
   ii) Are they consistent with the corporation's mission, objectives, strategies, policies, and with internal and external environments?

b) How well is the corporation's IS performing in terms of providing a useful database, automating routine clerical operations, assisting managers in making routine decisions, and providing information necessary for strategic decisions?
   i) What trends emerge from this analysis?
   ii) What impact have these trends had on past performance and how will they probably affect future performance?
   iii) Does this analysis support the corporation's past and pending strategic decisions?

c) How does this corporation's IS performance and stage of development compare with that of similar corporations?

d) Are IS managers using appropriate concepts and techniques to evaluate and improve corporate performance? Do they know how to build and manage a complex data-base, conduct system analyses, and implement interactive decision-support systems?

c) What is the role of the IS manager in the strategic management process?

V. ANALYSIS OF STRATEGIC FACTORS

A. What are the key internal and external factors (S.W.O.T.) that strongly affect the corporation's present and future performance?
   1. What have been the key historical strategic factors for this corporation?
   2. What are the key short-term (0–1 year) strategic factors for this corporation?
   3. What are the key intermediate-term (1–3 year) strategic factors for this corporation?
   4. What are the key long-term (3–10 year) strategic factors for this corporation?

B. Are the current mission and objectives appropriate in light of the key strategic factors and problems?
   1. Should the mission and objectives be changed? If so, how?
   2. If changed, what will the effects on the firm be?

VI. STRATEGIC ALTERNATIVES

A. Can the current or revised objectives be met by the simple, more careful implementing of those strategies presently in use (for example, fine tuning the strategies)?

B. What are the major feasible alternative strategies available to this corporation? What are the pros and cons of each? Can *scenarios* be developed and agreed upon?
   1. Consider stability, growth, and retrenchment as corporate strategies.
   2. Consider cost leadership and differentiation as business strategies.
   3. Consider any functional strategic alternatives that might be needed for reinforcement of an important corporate or business strategic alternative.

VII. RECOMMENDATION

A. Specify which of the strategic alternatives you are recommending for the corporate, business, and functional levels of the corporation. Do you recommend different business or functional strategies for different units of the corporation?

B. Justify your recommendation in terms of its ability to resolve both long- and short-term problems and effectively deal with the key strategic factors.

C. What policies should be developed or revised to guide effective implementation?

VIII. IMPLEMENTATION

A. What kinds of programs (for example, restructuring the corporation) should be developed to implement the recommended strategy?
   1. Who should develop these programs?
   2. Who should be in charge of these programs?

B. Are the programs financially feasible? Can *pro forma* budgets be developed and agreed upon? Are priorities and timetables appropriate to individual programs?

C. Will new standard operating procedures need to be developed?

IX. Evaluation and Control

A. Is the current information system capable of providing sufficient feedback on implementation activities and performance?
  1. Can performance results be pinpointed by area, unit, project, or function?
  2. Is the information timely?

B. Are adequate control measures, to ensure conformance with the recommended strategic plan, in place?
  1. Are appropriate standards and measures being used?
  2. Are reward systems capable of recognizing and rewarding good performance?

SCANNING THE ENVIRONMENT

PART TWO

CHAPTER THREE

Social Responsibility and Ethics in Strategic Management

CHAPTER OUTLINE

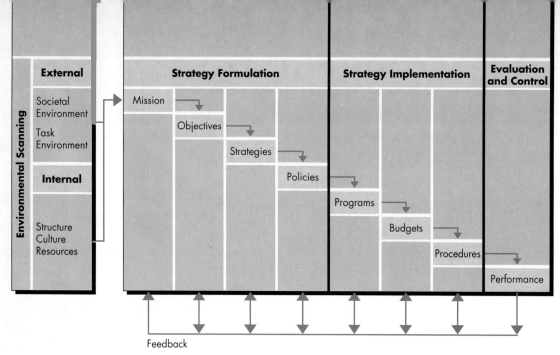

STRATEGIC MANAGEMENT MODEL

The officer of every corporation should feel in his heart—in his very soul—that he is responsible, not merely to make dividends for the stockholders of his company, but to enhance the general prosperity and the moral sentiment of the United States.[1]

Adolphus Green,
Founder of Nabisco

During much of its history, Beech-Nut Nutrition Corporation successfully manufactured and sold popular consumer products such as chewing gum and baby foods. Founded in 1891, the company traditionally emphasized product purity, high quality, and natural ingredients in its marketing programs and corporate culture. Eventually, reduced to a single product line of baby food, Beech-Nut was purchased from Squibb Corporation in 1973 by a group headed by Frank Nicholas. Known as "Mr. Natural," Nicholas promoted Beech-Nut's promise to use only natural ingredients—no artificial flavorings, no preservatives, no colorings—in its advertising. The label on its apple juice, for example, read "100% fruit juice, no sugar added."

Operating with very tight finances and a 15% market share (compared to the leader, Gerber Products Company's, 70% share), Beech-Nut couldn't begin to match the marketing expenditures of Gerber. After many attempts to cut costs, Nicholas sold the company to Nestlé S. A. in 1979 for $35 million. Nestlé invested an additional $60 million in Beech-Nut, but the losses continued. Neils Hoyvald joined Beech-Nut in 1980, and replaced Nicholas as President in 1981. Hoyvald promised Nestlé's management that Beech-Nut would be profitable in 1982. "The pressure was on," stated Hoyvald.

Given the continuous pressures on Beech-Nut's top management to reduce costs, it's no surprise that in 1977 the company quickly accepted an offer from Interjuice & Universal Juice Company to sell its apple-juice concentrate to them at 20% below market price. This amounted to a cost savings of approximately $250,000 annually. No questions were asked concerning the deal's amazing figures until a few years later. Even a 1978 visit by two Beech-Nut employees to inspect Interjuice's concentrate source plant in Queens, New York, during which they were denied access to the concentrate processing facility, failed to stir misgivings. What Beech-Nut may not have realized at first was that chemists at the Queens plant had secretly learned how to replicate precisely and more cheaply the numerous components of apple juice.

Concerned that the purchased apple juice appeared to be diluted with corn syrup and cane sugar, Jerome Li Cari, Beech-Nut's Director of R&D, urged management to switch to another supplier. Arguing that the tests were inconclusive, management refused to cancel the contract and instead asked the supplier to sign a "hold-harmless agreement." This agreement indemnified Beech-Nut against damages if the juice later proved to be adulterated. An important fact: Products containing apple juice accounted for 30% of Beech-Nut's sales; savings from the cheap concentrate were helping to keep the company alive.

Li Cari continued to look for more accurate test methods, and in 1981 found the apple juice to be adulterated with artificial malic acid—an ingredient not found in earlier tests. In an August 1981 memo sent to senior executives, Li Cari concluded that "a tremendous amount of circumstantial evidence" presented "a grave case against the current supplier." He again urged the company to switch to another supplier. In response, John Lavery, Beech-Nut's Head of Operations, told Li Cari that he wasn't a "team player" and threatened to fire him. Convinced that Beech-Nut was knowingly breaking the law, Li Cari resigned. "I felt there was nothing I could ever do to stop them from using that juice," admitted Li Cari.

At a Fall 1981 budget meeting, Lavery (who had sometimes referred to Li Cari as "Chicken Little") suggested changing apple concentrate suppliers even though it would add costs. Warned by Lavery that Universal's concentrate was bogus, President Hoyvald refused to switch. He told Lavery the new budget was already too high. Costs had to be kept as low as possible.

Evidence compiled by *Business Week* suggests that Beech-Nut employees used two main arguments to justify their conduct. First, they believed that many other companies were selling fake juice. (In reality, only 5% of apple juice then being sold was adulterated, according to industry sources.) Second, they were convinced that even if the apple juice was adulterated, it was perfectly safe. In looking back on the incident, one Beech-Nut executive asked: "So suppose the stuff was all water and flavor and sugar. Why get upset about it? Who were we hurting?" Outside of the R&D department, there was an almost total absence of inquiry. A longtime Beech-Nut employee admitted, "It was something you just hoped would go away."

In June 1982, a private investigator, hired by the Processed Apples Institute, told

Beech-Nut officials that a new adulteration test plus documents retrieved from a dumpster near the Queens plant proved that Universal's apple concentrate was fake. Refusing to join other juicemakers in a lawsuit against the supplier, top management canceled its supplier contract, but continued to sell products made from the synthetic concentrate. When investigators from the U.S. Food and Drug Administration (FDA) confronted Beech-Nut executives with evidence that Beech-Nut apple juice contained little or no apple juice, the executives responded that they had no knowledge of any reliable method to test the authenticity of apple juice. The company refused to allow the FDA to review Beech-Nut's juice-testing records or its shipping records. According to *Consumer Reports,* Beech-Nut management could have avoided a scandal at this point by conceding that its juice was sugared water and by agreeing to relabel it as apple-flavored drink rather than juice. Instead, Beech-Nut management told government investigators that all the adulterated juice had been shipped and wouldn't be recalled since it posed no health hazard. "We were trying to delay the FDA from finding the product," admitted Beech-Nut's Director of Distribution.

Worried that the State of New York might seize their entire inventory of fake apple juice products valued at $3.5 million, Hoyvald in August 1982 ordered it distributed "fast, fast, fast" at deep discounts. Much was exported to the Caribbean, and to Puerto Rico—a major Beech-Nut market. During the months when Beech-Nut executives were meeting with FDA officials to discuss a nationwide recall of the apple "juice" manufactured with imitation concentrate, the company initiated a special promotion: Buy 12 jars of baby food and get six jars of fruit juice free. A recall was finally instituted in October 1982. One month after the recall, Hoyvald wrote in a report to his superiors at Nestlé S.A.:

> It is our feeling that we can report safely now that the apple juice recall has been completed. If the recall had been effectuated in early June, over 700,000 cases in inventory could have been affected. . . . Due to our many delays, we were only faced with having to destroy approximately 20,000 cases.[2]

The company continued to sell mixed juices made from the synthetic concentrate until March 1983.

Several months after the recall, Jerome Li Cari attended a cocktail party at a meeting of the National Food Processors Association, where he overheard Beech-Nut executives laughing that they "got away with it, that the matter was dead." Li Cari then sent a letter to the FDA providing details of Beech-Nut's actions, signing it "Johnny Appleseed." Although the FDA knew that Beech-Nut had violated federal food and drug laws, Li Cari's letter suggested that Beech-Nut's managers had knowingly and intentionally broken the law.

In June 1985, the U.S. Justice Department began a criminal investigation into the Beech-Nut case. On November 13, 1987, Beech-Nut pleaded guilty to charges that it intentionally sold adulterated and misbranded juice in 20 states, Puerto Rico, the Virgin Islands, and five foreign countries. The company was fined $2.2 million—the largest fine in FDA history. On February 17, 1988, a jury convicted Hoyvald on 359 counts of violating federal food and drug laws. It also convicted Lavery on 448 counts, including conspiracy and mail-fraud charges. In addition to Li Cari, witnesses in the trials included two Universal Juice executives who had earlier pleaded guilty to charges against them. Hoyvald and Lavery were each sentenced to a year and a day in prison and fined $100,000. Early in 1989, a federal appeals court overturned the convictions of Hoyvald and Lavery on technicalities, but left intact Lavery's conviction on certain other charges. Beech-Nut's market share went from 19% in 1986 to 15.3% in 1988. Thanks to a $15 million advertising campaign featuring the co-host of "Good Morning America," Joan Lunden, Beech-Nut's share returned to 18% by May 1989. In September 1989, the *Wall Street Journal* announced that Nestlé had quietly found a buyer for its Beech-Nut subsidiary. The buyer, Ralston Purina Company, paid $85 million—little more than half the value of Beech-Nut's current sales.

In reviewing the 1981 performance report of Jerome Li Cari written by John Lavery, a Justice Department Lawyer noted that the report praised Li Cari's loyalty and technical ability, but said his judgment was "colored by naivete and impractical ideas." The lawyer asked Li Cari if he had been naive. Li Cari responded: "I guess I was. I thought apple juice should be made from apples."[3]

3.1 BUSINESS AND SOCIETY: AN INTERACTIVE RELATIONSHIP

Organizations such as Beech-Nut Nutrition Corporation do not exist in a social and ethical vacuum. They exist because society or a segment of it needs a particular product or service, and they can continue to exist relatively unchecked only so long as they take responsibility for their actions and acknowledge their role in the larger society. As a result, organizations must be constantly aware of the key variables in their environment. These variables may exist within a firm's task environment or in its larger societal environment (see Fig. 1.3). As mentioned in Chapter 1, the **task environment** includes those elements or groups that directly affect the organization and, in turn, are affected by it. These are governments, local communities, suppliers, competitors, customers, creditors, employees/labor unions, special-interest groups, and trade associations. The **societal environment** includes the more general economic, sociocultural, technological, and political-legal forces that do not directly touch on the short-run activities of the organization but that can, and often do, influence its long-run decisions.

All of these variables and forces constantly interact with each other. In the short run, societal forces affect the decisions and actions of an organization through the groups in its task environment. In the long run, however, the organization also affects these groups through its activities. For example, the decision by several U.S. business corporations to relocate their manufacturing facilities to Asia and Latin America in order to reduce labor costs has increased the unemployment of U.S. blue-collar workers—thus reducing union membership, adversely affecting the country's balance of trade with other nations, and creating economic depressions in those communities dependent for employment and tax revenue on the now-closed plants.

The relationship between business organizations and society, as depicted in

TABLE 3.1	Brief History of Society's Attitude Toward Business Organizations

Time Period	Society's Attitude
Greek/Roman Period (**100** B.C)	Tolerate Them
Middle Ages (**1000** A.D)	Restrict Them
Renaissance–W. Europe "Protestant Ethic" "Mercantilism" (**1500s**)	Use Them
Industrial Expansion "Laissez Faire" (**1800s**)	Glorify Them
Industrial Domination Monopolies, Cartels, Sweatshops, Depressions (**late 1800s**)	Dillusionment and Betrayal
Nationalism Battle of Ideologies (**early 1900s**)	*Capitalism:* Restrict Them Via Laws *Socialism:* Nationalize Them Via Government Ownership *Marxist Communism:* Outlaw Them
Developing Global Village World Trade Modern Mercantilism (**late 1900s**)	Encourage/Support Them (Capitalism, Socialism, and Communism)

Table 3.1, has varied through the ages. In ancient times, commercial activities, such as trading and money-lending, were regarded as necessary but distasteful. They were tolerated. During Europe's Middle Ages, the Roman Catholic Church held business and commercial activity in disdain and restricted it through strict rules and limitations. Trade itself was of dubious purity, and the gathering of wealth was considered contrary to the charitable teachings of Jesus Christ. With the coming of the Renaissance and the Protestant Reformation, however, values began to change and business activities were viewed more positively. A new spirit of individualism was encouraged. Following the economic concept of **mercantilism** (in which all business activity was considered an instrument of the state), governments in the West encouraged the formation of business ventures as a way to support the economic development of society.

In 1776, economist Adam Smith advanced a theory justifying capitalism in his book *An Inquiry into the Nature and Causes of the Wealth of Nations.* Smith argued that economic freedom would enable individuals, through self-interest, to fulfill themselves and thereby benefit the total society. Arguing against the centralized planning aspects of mercantilism, Smith used the term **laissez-faire** to suggest that government should leave business alone. The "invisible hand" of the marketplace would, through pure competition, ensure maximum benefit to society. With changes in sociocultural values fed by the benefits of new technology and laissez-faire economics, governments in the West began to not only give developing business organizations increasing autonomy, they also began to support and even glorify business as key to increasing the material well-being of society.

The resulting industrial revolution also had its negative side, which increasingly caused people to question the autonomy given business firms. Karl Marx, who wrote *The Communist Manifesto* with Friedrich Engels in 1848 and *Das Kapital* in 1867, rejected capitalism because of its many unsavory side effects, such as child labor, unsafe working conditions, and subsistence wages. Society's response to the development of self-centered monopolistic corporations and cartels varied from a government's passing legislation restricting business autonomy, to taking over ownership of a firm, to completely outlawing business activities and absorbing them within the state. Consequently, business people were increasingly constrained during much of the twentieth century by laws regarding air and water pollution, product safety, and employment practices, among others.

Faced with serious problems of unemployment and balance of trade problems during the 1980s, governments around the world acted to reduce some of the constraints they had previously placed on business activity. The general feeling appeared to be that state-controlled or heavily regulated business organizations could not operate as efficiently or as effectively as those given more autonomy. This became increasingly important as more countries found that their people and institutions were being forced to compete on a global scale. As a result, countries acted to support and encourage business activity. This developing view that it was government's job to encourage business activity as a way of improving or protecting its people's standard of living was more in line with the philosophy of mercantilism than it was with Adam Smith's laissez-faire capitalism.

Unfortunately, this strong support of business by governments around the world was tempered by business's ever-present tendency to take advantage of and exploit the very society that was supporting it. Allegations of insider trading and revelations of negligence, bribery, and fraud revealed some business people to have very low standards of ethics. As the twentieth century was coming to a close, strategic managers in business firms were coming to realize that they might lose their new-found support and autonomy if they failed to show some social responsibilty.

3.2 ISSUES IN SOCIAL RESPONSIBILITY AND ETHICS

The concept that business must be socially responsible sounds appealing until one asks, "Responsible to whom?" As was shown in Fig. 1.3, the task environment includes a large number of groups with interest in a business organization's activities. These groups are referred to as **stakeholders** because they affect or are affected by the achievement of the firm's objectives.[4] Should a corporation be responsible only to some of these groups, or does business have an equal responsibility to all of them?

As pointed out in Illustrative Example 3.1, the tendency of several business corporations in the U.S. and Canada to give their top executives large raises at the

ILLUSTRATIVE EXAMPLE 3.1

Why Are Workers Asked to Take Pay Cuts When Top Executives Receive Boosts in Salaries?

In response to continued requests by the top managements of both Armstrong Tire Company and the Firestone Tire and Rubber Company for employees at their plants in Des Moines, Iowa, to accept pay cuts in order to reduce costs, the *Des Moines Register* published the following editorial in 1987:

> The caller was distraught. The Register had published an editorial critical of the way the Armstrong Tire Co. was dealing with its workers, and she was worried—frightened, really—about the effect it might have.
>
> Years of work, years of a family's investment in a career were hanging by a thread. It wouldn't take much and it would be all gone. The plant would shut down. A newspaper editorial. A wrong word. That's all it might take.
>
> In the muted agony of an industrial plant on the brink, lives might be shattered, and a community must walk on eggs.
>
> There are bitterness and anger and fear, and there is the frustration of knowing that there are no good guys or bad guys. There are just people—em-

ployees, executives, the community—trapped in roles they must play.

> In the abstract, it is easy to understand what's happening. Basic industry is in the throes of change. There is the need to adopt new technology, and there are tough foreign competitors whose labor costs are lower. Some adjustments are unavoidable.
>
> That abstract understanding doesn't help much in the real world of people where those adjustments are being felt. What makes it so agonizing isn't so much the adjustments themselves—although they're bad enough—but the way they're being made.
>
> Des Moines is witnessing the events at the Firestone and Armstrong plants here, but much the same is happening in other industries in other communities.
>
> The ultimatum to workers is: Give back wages or the plant will close. It is non-debatable.
>
> Fellow employees of the same company in different communities must bid against each other. Who will give up the most? Communities are told to give money or tax breaks, or lose the plant.
>
> Meanwhile, the board rooms seem

(continued)

very time they are asking their employees to accept large pay cuts has created some real resentment, not only among employees/union members but among other concerned stakeholders as well. In its haste to satisfy one group of people, management may create future problems with other concerned parties.

The emphasis being placed on increasing shareholder wealth as the primary objective of business activity is being increasingly criticized. In his book *Tyranny of the Bottom Line: Holding Corporations Accountable,* Ralph Estes points out that many others besides stockholders invest heavily in a business corporation. These are the workers, the customers, and the taxpayers of the communities that support the corporation. Estes says: "These forgotten investors are often called stakeholders,

CONTINUED

to be doing just fine. About the same time Firestone workers were accepting pay cuts, Chairman John Nevin was on the cover of *Business Week* as America's fourth-highest-paid executive, at more than $6.3 million a year.

The gap widens. An economist could justify the gap as the way the free marketplace works, but it is hard to justify to a family that just made a sacrifice.

The companies say they are doing what they must do, but it is brutal and ugly.

And in the long run it is self-destructive. Sullen, embittered workers are not the most productive workers, nor are the plants they work in likely to produce the highest-quality products.

Then, as surely as business cycles turn, the workers will regain the upper hand someday, and when they do, their revenge will be no less self-destructive than the companies' hardball tactics now.

This country loses more production hours to labor-management disputes than any other major industrial nation. There is no way to measure losses in quality, innovation and productivity where walls of resentment and secrecy divide workers and managers.

If the United States has learned one lesson from the new international marketplace, it is that nations where there is harmony between workers and managers have an edge. Yet too much of American industry remains trapped in a 19th-century adversarial mentality in which workers and managers regard one another as the enemy, with relations between the two framed in terms of who "wins" and who "loses."

Actually, everyone loses. Workers lose, companies lose, communities lose. America loses.

Still, the mentality is so entrenched that anyone who suggests there ought to be a better way is accused by one side of being a union-buster and by the other of being anti-business. This subject is hard even to discuss rationally.

How can the pattern ever be broken?

Source: "Tradition of Bad Relations," *Des Moines Register* (July 21, 1987), p. 6A. Reprinted with permission.

and they are owed an accounting because they, too, invest by committing valuable resources, including not only money but their work, their careers, sometimes their lives to the corporation."[5]

JUGGLING STAKEHOLDER PRIORITIES

In any one decision the interests of one stakeholder can conflict with another. For example, a business firm's decision to build a plant in an inner-city location may have a positive effect on community relations but a negative effect on stockholder dividends. Which group's interests have priority?

TABLE 3.2	Importance to Executives of Various Stakeholders

Stakeholders	Rank[1]
Customers	6.40
Employees	6.01
Owners	5.30
General public	4.52
Stockholders	4.51
Elected public officials	3.79
Government bureaucrats	2.90

[1] The ranking is calculated on a scale of 7 (most important) to 1 (least important).

Source: Adapted from B. Z. Posner and W. H. Schmidt, "Values and the American Manager: An Update." Copyright © 1984 by The Regents of the University of California. Reprinted from the *California Management Review*, Vol. 26, No. 3, p. 206. By permission of The Regents.

In a survey sponsored by the American Management Association, 6,000 managers and executives were asked to rate on a seven-point scale the importance of several organizational stakeholders.[6] As shown in Table 3.2, executives felt customers to be the most important concern. Employees were also rated highly. Interestingly, the general public was felt to be of similar importance to stockholders. Owners (presumably those who own large blocks of stock), however, were rated as more important than either the public or more typical stockholders. Government representatives were rated as least important of all the groups considered.

In another survey, chief executive officers were asked to rate the importance of various objectives: net profits, rate of growth, market share, employee rewards and benefits, international market penetration, innovation, assets and reserves, dividend payout, price leadership, community service, plant and equipment modernness, and productivity. The most popular objectives were profit, rate of growth, market share, international market penetration, productivity, and innovation. Community service and dividend payout were the lowest-rated objectives. The authors of the research concluded: "Perhaps social responsibility and maximizing shareholder wealth are not as important as the popular press often suggests."[7]

Given the wide range of interests and concerns present in any organization's task environment, one or more groups, at any one time, probably will be dissatisfied with an organization's activities. For example, consider Maytag Corporation's decision in 1990 to build a new plant in Jackson, Tennessee. The new plant was to manufacture automatic dishwashers in one location for all the brands marketed by the corporation. As detailed in the *boxed example* on Maytag (pp. 72–73), the decision made stockholders happy because it meant that the firm would no longer have to purchase dishwashers from a competitor to sell under the corporation's lower-priced brand names. A new plant would also improve Maytag's efficiency in a very competitive industry. The local union and state politicians were, however, very upset with this decision. They wanted the new plant to be built in Newton, Iowa, where the company was currently manufacturing its Maytag-brand dishwashers.

Lonnie White, President of United Auto Workers Local 997 in Newton, argued that his people were against "community cannibalism" in which one location took work away from another location. Maytag's top management was being criticized by its stockholders if it kept dishwasher production in Newton and criticized by labor and the local community if it moved dishwasher production out.

Another recent controversial issue in juggling stakeholder concerns was charitable contributions. Even though corporations, like individuals, have the right to donate money to any charitable cause of their choice, some companies found themselves inundated by letters and phone calls in 1989 and 1990 from groups protesting donations to one charity in particular—Planned Parenthood. Even though well-known companies such as BP America, Dayton Hudson, and Pillsbury supported Planned Parenthood because of its prenatal care for low-income families, contraceptive research, and counseling programs to reduce unwanted pregnancies among teens, they were strongly criticized by "pro-life" groups against Planned Parenthood's advocacy of abortion. Doug Scott, Director of Public Policy at the Christian Action Council, urged consumers to boycott the products of those companies supporting Planned Parenthood. He contended that opponents of abortion had a moral duty to oppose organizations that were, in his words, "antichild and antifamily." Primarily as a result of this pressure, J. C. Penney, AT&T, and Union Pacific stopped their annual donations to Planned Parenthood. Dayton Hudson, in contrast, first canceled its contribution to Planned Parenthood and then reversed its decision after "pro-choice" groups favoring abortion as a woman's right mobilized their members to cancel their Dayton Hudson charge accounts. The Minneapolis-based department store chain entered the 1990 Christmas buying season facing a threatened boycott from either pro-life or pro-choice interest groups depending upon their final funding decision.[8]

UNETHICAL AND ILLEGAL BEHAVIOR

The examples just mentioned indicate how easily a business corporation can run into problems—even when top management is trying to achieve the best outcome for all involved. There are other examples, however, of business firms engaging in very questionable, unethical, or even illegal actions. These examples reveal the dark side of corporate decision making and support those who favor more governmental regulation and less business autonomy. There is no doubt that the top management of some business firms (including Beech-Nut) has sometimes made decisions emphasizing short-term profitability or personal gain over long-term relations with governments, local communities, suppliers, and even customers and employees. During the 1980s, 11% of the largest U.S. firms were convicted of bribery, criminal fraud, illegal campaign contributions, tax evasion, or some sort of price fixing.[9] The following is a list of some of the questionable practices that have been exposed in recent years:

- Possible negligent construction and management practices at nuclear power, weapons, and chemical plants (for example, nuclear plants at Three Mile Island and Rocky Flats, Colorado, and Union Carbide's chemical plant in Bhopal, India).[10]

MAYTAG CORPORATION: LOCATION DECISION

Throughout its history, Maytag Corporation has tried to act responsibly in light of the various concerns of its many stakeholder groups. Even though the corporation has kept its headquarters in Newton, Iowa, the recent acquisitions of Magic Chef and Hoover has meant that Maytag *Corporation* had to view things differently from Maytag *Company*. The *company* made Maytag-brand major appliances in Newton, Iowa, only. The *corporation* now makes Maytag, Admiral, Magic Chef, Jenn-Air, Hardwick, Norge, and Hoover brand appliances, as well as Dixie-Narco vending machines, throughout North America and the world. Maytag Corporation's top management (most of whom came from Maytag Company) now has had to consider not only their responsibilities to the stakeholders of Maytag Company, but also responsibilities to the various stakeholders of Magic Chef, Jenn-Air, Hoover, Admiral, and Dixie-Narco, as well as those stakeholders of the corporation as a whole. This has not been an easy matter.

Maytag's reputation as a good corporate citizen was tarnished in some people's eyes when the decision was announced at the April 24, 1990, stockholder meeting to move dishwasher manufacturing from Newton to Jackson, Tennessee.

Chairman and CEO Daniel Krumm announced that the plant would consolidate the manufacturing of all the brands marketed by the corporation into one large, highly efficient plant. Krumm said:

> Currently, the only dishwasher manufacturing operation we have is here in Newton, where we only have the ability to manufacture dishwashers for Maytag Company and some Jenn-Air models. We must purchase all the dishwashers for our medium-priced brands from a competitor [General Electric]. . . . Consequently, we are completely redesigning all corporate dishwasher models to facilitate single-plant production of distinctly different units for our Magic Chef, Maytag, Jenn-Air, Admiral, and Norge brands. . . . We expect to invest about $42 million in the Jackson plant, which will incorporate all new equipment, state-of-the-art technology and advanced automation, coupled with the ability and capacity to manufacture highly differentiated products. . . .

(continued)

- Improper disposal of toxic wastes (for instance, Hooker Chemical at Love Canal, New York, and Shell Oil Company at a pesticide plant near Denver, Colorado).[11]
- Production and sale of defective products (for example, A. H. Robbins's Dalkon Shield birth control device and Dow Chemical's corrosive cement additive, Sarabond).[12]
- Declaring bankruptcy to cancel a labor contract and cut wages (for instance, Wilson Foods).[13]
- Insufficient safeguarding of employees from exposure to dangerous chemicals and materials in the workplace (for instance, the asbestos problem at Johns-Manville and the overexposure of workers to lead and arsenic at Chrysler Corp.).[14]

CONTINUED

We are nearing the upper limits of our production capacity for Maytag brand dishwashers and there is no efficient way that our manufacturing facilities in Newton could accommodate the new dishwasher design, let alone provide the capacity we require to supply all corporate brands. Beyond that, phasing out dishwasher production at Maytag Company's Newton plant will provide the necessary space for extensive manufacturing revisions needed to meet anticipated demand for Maytag washers and dryers later in the 1990s.

Lonnie White, President of United Auto Workers Local 997—the bargaining unit representing Maytag Company unionized employees in Newton, Iowa—responded with dismay to top management's decision. "Where is their commitment to the community and the state of Iowa?" asked White. "They can add a facility here in Newton to do the same thing that they're doing in Jackson, Tennessee."

Pointing out that Maytag owned plenty of unused land in Newton, White contended that there could be only three reasons management would move dishwasher production to Tennessee: (1) to escape union shop, (2) to reduce wage costs, and (3) to cut benefits. "The Newton dishwasher line is only running one shift. Other lines run two shifts," said White in response to the statement that the line was near capacity. He indicated that the union was not so much concerned with itself as it was with the impact on local communities and the need to avoid "community cannibalism." White argued that there was a sufficient supply of workers in the area to expand production. "When Maytag Company last had a production increase in the mid-'80s and wanted to hire around 300 new workers, they [the company] received around 4,000 applications from all over the area."

One of White's concerns was the perceived change in the relationship between labor and management after Maytag became a large corporation in 1989. Management now seemed more formal and less flexible. Somewhat ruefully, White summed up the situation: "We're no longer dealing with Mother Maytag. Now we're dealing with a corporation."

- Continual instances of fraud, bribery, and price fixing at corporations of all sizes and locations (for example, Sundstrand's billing the U.S. Defense Department "millions of dollars" for such "unallowable" expenses as babysitting, saunas, golf, movies, dog kennels, and servants for Sundstrand executives and snowplowing at the executives' homes; also Drexel Burnham Lambert's involvement in mail, wire, and securities fraud).[15]

3.3 ETHICS: A QUESTION OF VALUES

Such questionable practices by business corporations run counter to the values of society as a whole and are justly criticized and prosecuted. Why are actions taken that so obviously harm important stakeholders in the organization's task environment? Are business corporations and the people who run them amoral, or are they simply ignorant of the many consequences of their actions?

CULTURAL DIFFERENCES

One reason for such behavior is that there is no worldwide standard of conduct for businesspeople. Cultural norms and values vary between countries and even between different geographic regions and ethnic groups within a country. One example is the use of payoffs and bribes to influence a potential customer to buy from a particular supplier. Although this practice is considered illegal in the U.S., it is deeply entrenched in many other countries. "Dash," or bribery, for instance, permeates Nigerian society and though technically illegal is widely accepted as a normal part of life. Dashing in Nigeria is considered by many to be a lubricant for an economy of scarcities and rigid government control. The dilemma facing a manager of a multinational corporation in Nigeria is either to dash a customs officer to expedite shipping or to abstain from bribery and run the risk that the goods will be permanently "lost." Although the U.S. Foreign Corrupt Practices Act of 1977 forbids U.S. citizens from engaging in such bribery, it does not affect non–U.S. citizens.[16]

PERSONAL DIFFERENCES

Another possible reason for an organization's questionable practices lies in differences in values between top management and key stakeholders in the task environment. Some businesspeople may believe profit maximization is the key goal of their firm, whereas concerned interest groups may have other goals as a priority, such as the hiring of minorities and women or the safety of their neighborhoods.

Economist Milton Friedman, in urging a return to a laissez-faire worldwide economy with a minimum of government regulation, argues against the concept of social responsibility. If a businessperson acts "responsibly" by cutting the price of the firm's product to prevent inflation, or by making expenditures to reduce pollution, or by hiring the hard-core unemployed, that person, according to Friedman, is spending the stockholder's money for a general social interest. Even if the businessperson has stockholder permission or encouragement to do so, he or she is still acting from motives other than economic and may, in the long run, cause harm to the very society the firm is trying to help. By taking on the burden of these social costs, the business becomes less efficient; and either prices go up to pay for the increased costs, or investment in new activities and research is postponed. These results negatively affect—perhaps fatally—the long-term efficiency of a business. Friedman thus referred to the social responsibility of business as a "fundamentally subversive doctrine" and stated that "there is one and only one social responsibility of business—to use its resources and engage in activities designed to increase its profits so long as it stays within the rules of the game, which is to say, engages in open and free competition without deception or fraud."[17]

Friedman's stand on free enterprise has been both criticized and praised. Businesspeople tend to agree with Friedman because his views are compatible not only with their own self-interests but also with their hierarchy of values. Of the six values measured by the Allport-Vernon-Lindzey Study of Values test (aesthetic, economic, political, religious, and social, and theoretical), both U.S. and British executives score high on economic and political values and low on social and religious ones. This is similar to the value profile of managers from Japan, Korea, India, and Australia. U.S. Protestant ministers, in contrast, score high on religious and social values and very low on economic values.[18]

Imagine the controversy that would result if a group composed of ministers and executives had to decide the following issues: *Should business firms close on Sunday? Should the corporation hire handicapped workers and accept the increased training costs associated with their employment?* In discussing these issues, the executive would probably be very concerned with the effects on the bottom line of profits, whereas the minister would probably be concerned with the effects on society and salvation (a very different bottom line).

This conclusion is supported by studies of executives that reveal a desire by businesspeople to limit their social responsibilities to those areas in which they can clearly see benefits to the corporation, in terms of increased sales, reduced costs, or less governmental regulation.[19] This very narrow view of businesses' responsibilities to society will typically cause conflicts between the business corporation and certain members of its task environment.

RELATIVISM

A serious challenge to the study of ethics and ethical behavior is the doctrine of moral relativism. Simply put, **moral relativism** claims that morality is relative to some personal, social, or cultural standard and that there is no method for deciding whether one decision is better than another. There are four types of relativism.[20] Each of them may be used at one time or another to justify questionable behavior.

- **Naive Relativism:** based on the beliefs that all moral decisions are deeply personal and that individuals have the right to run their own lives; each person should be allowed to interpret situations and act on his or her own moral values. Critics of naive relativism argue that tolerance is good up to a point, but that it can be taken too far. It is the lazy way out of ethical problems. It is not a belief, but an excuse for not having a belief or is an excuse for inaction.
- **Role Relativism:** proposes that social roles carry with them certain obligations to the role only. A manager in charge of a department, for example, must put aside his/her personal beliefs and do instead what the role requires, that is, acting in the best interests of the department. The Beech-Nut executives described earlier in this chapter might have said: "I was only doing my job," if personally challenged regarding their integrity.
- **Social Group Relativism:** based on the belief that morality is simply a matter of following the norms of one's peer group, decisions are made based on accepted practices. If an action is considered accepted practice, then it appears to have some legitimacy. Echoing the often-heard teenage refrain that "everyone is doing it" so it must be all right, Beech-Nut managers used synthetic

apple juice concentrate. Social Group Relativism is a pervasive phenomenon in the day-to-day business world.[21] A real danger in following this concept is that, like the Beech-Nut managers, a person may incorrectly believe a certain action is commonly accepted practice in the trade when it is not the case.

- **Cultural Relativism:** proposes that morality is relative to a particular culture, society, or community. People should therefore "understand" the practices of other countries, but not judge them. If the norms and customs are shared by members of another country, what right does an outsider have to criticize them? The concept may be summed up: "When in Rome, do as the Romans do." This type of relativism suggests that a business corporation must be "all things to all people" and warns against *moral imperialism*—imposing one's morality on others and judging them by standards they do not accept. Again, critics of this view state that it is the lazy way out of ethical problems.

BASIC APPROACHES TO ETHICAL BEHAVIOR

According to Von der Embse and Wagley, **ethics** is defined as the consensually accepted standards of behavior for an occupation, trade, or profession. **Morality,** in contrast, is the precepts of personal behavior, based on religious or philosophical grounds. **Law** refers to formal codes that permit or forbid certain behaviors and may or may not enforce ethics or morality.[22] Given these definitions, how does one arrive at a comprehensive statement of ethics to use in making decisions in a specific occupation, trade, or profession? A starting point for such a code of ethics is to consider the three basic approaches to ethical behavior: utilitarian, individual rights, and justice.[23]

- **Utilitarian Approach:** proposes that actions and plans should be judged by their consequences. One should therefore behave in such a way that will produce the greatest benefit to society and produce the least harm or the lowest cost. A problem with this approach is the difficulty in recognizing all the benefits and the costs of any particular decision. It is likely that only the most obvious stakeholders may be considered, whereas others may be "conveniently" forgotten.[24]
- **Individual Rights Approach:** proposes that human beings have certain fundamental rights that should be respected in all decisions. One need, therefore, avoid interfering with the rights of others who might be affected by a particular decision or behavior. A problem with this approach is one's definition of "fundamental rights." The U.S. Constitution includes a Bill of Rights that may or may not be accepted throughout the world. The approach can also encourage selfish behavior.
- **Justice Approach:** proposes that decision makers be equitable, fair, and impartial in the distribution of costs and benefits to individuals and groups. It follows the principles of *distributive justice* (people who are similar on relevant dimensions such as job seniority should be treated in the same way) and *fairness* (liberty should be equal for all persons). The justice approach can also include the concepts of retributive justice and compensatory justice. *Retributive justice* proposes that punishment should be determined on a proportional basis to the "crime." *Compensatory justice* argues that wrongs

FIGURE 3.1 | **Decision Tree for Incorporating Ethics into Decision Making**

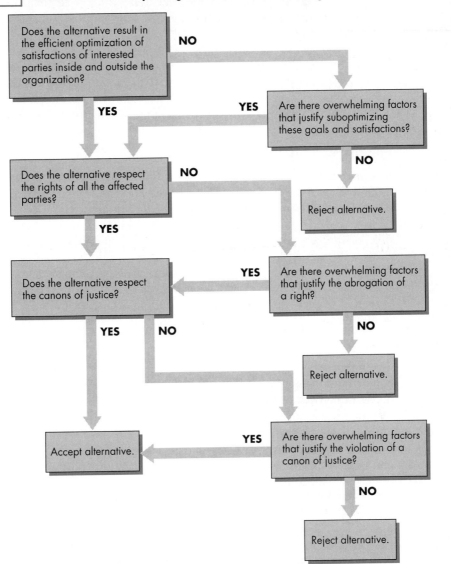

Source: Adapted from G. F. Cavanagh, D. J. Moberg, and M. Velasquez, "The Ethics of Organizational Politics," *Academy of Management Review* (July 1981), p. 368. Reprinted by permission.

should be compensated in proportion to the offense suffered. Issues in affirmative action such as reverse discrimination are examples of conflicts between distributive and compensatory justice.

Each of these three basic approaches to ethical behavior has strengths and weaknesses. Cavanagh, Moberg, and Velasquez, therefore, propose a decision tree (see Fig. 3.1) incorporating all three approaches to use whenever a decision with ethical issues needs to be made. They include the concept of the *overwhelming factor*—a situational factor that may, in a given case, justify overriding one of the three ethical criteria of utilitarian outcomes, individual rights, and equal justice.[25] This is where individual judgment comes into play. There are no hard-and-fast rules in ethics, only principles and approaches. When overwhelming factors are present in a situation, one good rule of thumb is to choose that alternative that a person can clearly explain to a jury in a court of law. If the intent is to achieve the maximum of good with the minimum of bad effects, one is following the *principle of double effect* and is likely to receive a sympathetic response if questioned later.[26]

PROMOTING ETHICAL BEHAVIOR

It is one thing to have a set of business ethics and yet another thing to protect and uphold them in the everyday rough-and-tumble world of business competition. For example, a survey by the *Wall Street Journal* of its subscribers found that although 93% agreed that lying is wrong, 43% believed that lying is sometimes justified to protect company secrets. In addition, several felt that lying was sometimes justified to avoid upsetting bosses and colleagues (13%) and to avoid negative publicity (12%).[27] Another survey of 1,000 corporate executives revealed that nearly one in four believe that ethical standards can impede successful careers. Sixty-eight percent agree that younger managers are driven to compromise their ethics "by the desire for wealth and material things."[28] This agrees with a survey conducted by *Personnel Journal*. Human resource managers surveyed state that the people most likely to be unethical are the middle managers in the 40-to-45-year-old age group who are driven by the desire to "make it before it's too late." The next group most likely to be unethical are top managers who tell subordinates to "do whatever you have to do, just don't tell me about it."[29]

Stages of Moral Development and Ethics Codes

A person's ethical behavior will be affected by his or her stage of moral development and other personality variables in addition to situational factors such as the job itself, one's supervisor, and the organizational culture.[30] Kohlberg proposes that a person's individual moral development progresses through three levels.[31] Similar in some ways to Maslow's hierarchy of needs, the individual moves from total self-centeredness to a concern for universal values.[32] The first level, **preconventional,** is characterized by a concern for self. Small children and others who have not progressed beyond this stage evaluate behaviors on the basis of personal interest—avoiding punishment or quid pro quo. The second level, **conventional,** is characterized by considerations of society's laws and norms. Actions are justified by an external code of conduct. The third level, **principled,** is characterized by a person's adherence to an internal moral code. The individual at this level looks beyond norms or laws to find universal values or principles. Kohlberg places most people in the conventional level, with less than 20% of U.S. adults in the principled level of development.[33]

Given the likelihood that most people working in a business organization will be in Kohlberg's conventional level of moral development, the use of codes of ethics can be a useful way to promote ethical behavior. Such codes are currently being used by 93% of the largest U.S. corporations.[34] According to a report by The Business Roundtable, an association of CEOs from 200 major U.S. corporations, the importance of a code is that it (1) clarifies company expectations of employee conduct in various situations and (2) makes clear that the company expects its people to recognize the ethical dimensions in decisions and actions.[35] The topics generally covered in these codes range from basic honesty and adherence to laws to product safety, health and safety, employment practices, conflicts of interest, supplier relationships, acquiring and using information, the protection of the environment, and payments to obtain business. Unfortunately, not all companies address all of these issues. A survey of U.S. Fortune 500 corporations reveals that although 75% of the codes in existence deal with conflicts of interest, only 25% deal with the company's role in civic and community affairs, consumer relations, or environmental and product safety.[36] The top management of a company wishing to improve the ethical behavior of its employees should not only develop a comprehensive code of ethics, but also communicate the code in its training programs, performance appraisal system, and in policies and procedures.

Promote Ethical Criticism

Even if a company has a code of ethics, employees may not believe that top management is serious about ethics until they see the code in action. A study of Champion International Corporation, for example, revealed that the lower the level of employees, the greater was their cynicism and hostility toward ethics codes. One manager reported that it is what the company *does,* not what it *says,* that counts.[37]

Nielsen proposes several alternative actions a person can take when he or she feels caught in a serious ethical dilemma.[38] Table 3.3 lists seven possible responses and the pros and cons for each. Nielsen recommends building consensus for change internally (#7) as the best approach if there is enough time and the key people in authority are reasonable. Avoiding thinking about the problem, obeying, or leaving doesn't improve the situation. Conscientiously objecting typically doesn't work. Telling the press or government can resolve the problem, but can result in many negative consequences. Nielsen recommends the following:

> In all but the most extreme and unusual circumstances one should first try negotiating a consensus. If that doesn't succeed, then a good move is to simultaneously conscientiously object and go public. . . . If you cooperate instead of conscientiously objecting, then you're acting just as unethically as everybody else. And if you go outside the organization secretly instead of publicly, you're not standing up for what you profess to believe in.[39]

Following Nielsen's view, it makes sense for management to promote ethical criticism. If people are encouraged to consider ethical issues and to discuss them openly without fear of retaliation or disapproval, more people would follow the consensus-building approach. Certainly Beech-Nut Nutrition Corporation and its parent, Nestlé S.A., would have done better in the long run if Beech-Nut's top management had welcomed instead of punished ethical criticism.

TABLE 3.3	Possible Responses to Ethical Dilemmas

Action	Pros	Cons
1. Avoid thinking about it.	Avoids conflict; good team player.	Prevents finding a solution.
2. Obey orders.	Avoids conflict; good performance evaluation.	Become part of the problem. Where draw the line?
3. Leave.	Revenge on company; good feelings in short run.	Lack courage to stay and fight; quickly replaced.
4. Conscientiously object.	Courageous feelings; encourages other people; may resolve the problem.	Likely to be threatened or fired; seen as a troublemaker.
5. Secretly tell the press or government.	Likely to resolve the problem; safe from retaliation.	Feel like a coward; must lie to keep safe.
6. Publicly tell the press or government.	Likely to resolve the problem; treated as a hero by public.	Likely to be fired or harassed; no longer able to resolve problem internally.
7. Build consensus for change internally.	Resolves problem from within; encourages others to help; may become an internal hero.	May take a long time; may be manipulated by others.

Source: R. P. Nielsen, "Alternative Managerial Responses to Ethical Dilemmas," *Planning Review* (November 1985), pp. 24–29, 43.

3.4 RESPONSIBILITIES OF BUSINESS

From a strategic point of view, a business corporation needs to consider its responsibilities to the society of which it is a part. The history of business and society clearly suggests that when business ignores its responsibilities to its stakeholders, society tends to respond through government to restrict business' autonomy. Business corporations must therefore be cognizant of their responsibilities if they wish to have the autonomy needed to be effective and efficient. But what are the responsibilities of a business firm?

FOUR RESPONSIBILITIES OF BUSINESS

Carroll proposes that the managers of business organizations have four responsibilities: economic, legal, ethical, and discretionary.[40] The **economic** responsibilities of a business organization's management are to produce goods and services of value to society so that the firm may repay its creditors and stockholders. **Legal** responsibilities are defined by governments in laws that management is expected to obey. The **ethical** responsibilities of an organization's management are to follow the generally held beliefs about how one should act in a society. For example, although there may be no law requiring an organization to find other work for employees laid off during a plant closing, society generally expects the firm to work with the employees and the community in planning for such a plant closing. The affected people can get very upset if an organization's management fails to act according to generally prevailing ethical values. **Discretionary** responsibilities, in contrast, are the purely voluntary obligations a corporation assumes. Examples are philanthropic contributions, training the hard-core unemployed, and providing day-care centers. The difference between ethical and discretionary responsibilities is that no one expects an organization to fulfill discretionary responsibilities, whereas many expect an organization to fulfill ethical ones.

The term **social responsibility** can thus be viewed as the *combination of an organization's ethical and discretionary responsibilities*. The discretionary responsibilities of today may become the ethical responsibilities of tomorrow. The provision of day-care facilities is, for example, moving rapidly from a discretionary to an ethical responsibility. Carroll suggests that to the extent that business corporations fail to acknowledge discretionary or ethical responsibilities, society, through government, will act, making them legal responsibilities. This may be done by government, moreover, without regard to an organization's economic responsibilities. As a result, the organization may have greater difficulty in earning a profit than it would have had in assuming voluntarily some ethical and discretionary responsibilities. For example, it has been suggested by some people in the U.S. automobile industry that the many safety and pollution regulations passed in the 1960s and 1970s were partially responsible for the poor health of the industry in the early 1980s.[41]

REASONS OFTEN GIVEN FOR SOCIAL RESPONSIBILITY

The many arguments proposed in favor of a business corporation's management acting in a socially responsible manner boil down to four:

1. **Morality.** A firm should be responsible to its many stakeholders because it is the "right thing to do." Based primarily on religious values or on some personally held moral code, actions are justified on the basis of the good of society in general. This rationale is altruistic; there is no expectation of receiving anything in return. For example, Tom Monaghan, Chairman and CEO of Domino's Pizza, donates profits from the six Domino's Pizza outlets in Central America to Father Enrique Silvestre, a Catholic priest working in the mountains of Honduras. Interested in missionary work, Monaghan likes to aid Father Silvestre in building homes for his people and setting up an experimental farm.[42]

2. **Enlightened Self-Interest.** A firm should be responsible to its stakeholders because of "quid pro quo" considerations. Sometimes expressed in terms of "what goes around, comes around," this reason proposes that the corporation is likely to be rewarded for its responsible actions either in the short or long term. For example, Procter & Gamble has found that because of its reputation for treating its employees well, the company has little difficulty hiring and keeping well-qualified people whenever it needs them. Although there may be no direct connection with profits, this rationale implies the existence of some eventual return for responsible actions. For example, Minneapolis-based Dayton Hudson was able to use its positive relationship

with its stakeholder groups throughout Minnesota to influence the state to enact a tough antitakeover law in 1987 when the company was in danger of being bought out by Dart Group Corporation of Landover, Maryland.[43]

3. **Sound Investment Theory.** A firm should be responsible to its stakeholders because such actions will be reflected in higher profits and in the price of its stock. This rationale proposes a direct connection between socially responsible actions and the corporation's financial performance. Unfortunately, studies in the area have found mixed results.[44] Examples can be cited of both highly profitable and marginally profitable companies with both poor and excellent social records. One interesting example is Control Data Corporation. Under the leadership of socially concerned William C. Norris as founder, Chairman, and CEO, Control Data had organized assembly plants in ghettos and prisons and spent millions of dollars on computer systems for education and training in schools and industry. Unfortunately, corporate earnings fell and Norris was criticized for allowing his "pet businesses" to drain investment away from the company's profitable ventures. He was forced to resign from the company.[45]

4. **Retain Autonomy.** A firm should be responsible to its stakeholders in order to avoid interference in managerial decision making by groups in its task environment. This reason is similar to Carroll's argument that the failure to fulfill ethical and discretionary responsibilities will eventually result in an enlargement of a corporation's legal responsibilities to the detriment of its economic responsibilities. Even with the finding that social responsibility has no clear direct connection to profits or stock price, one conclusion seems clear. The **iron law of responsibility** does apply. As Keith Davis points out, "In the long run those who do *not* use power in a manner that society considers responsible will tend to lose it."[46] If business organizations are unable or unwilling to police themselves by considering their responsibilities to all stakeholders in their task environment, then society— usually in the form of government—will police their doing so, and once again governments will reduce business's autonomy via increased rules and regulations.

SOCIAL AUDIT

Even though many examples of socially irresponsible behavior by business executives can be cited, many responsible actions can also be cited. The Reebok Foundation, for example, is a part of Reebok International and is well known for its work supporting Amnesty International—the Nobel prize-winning human rights organization. As another example, the chief executives of the top 50 companies of Cleveland, Ohio formed an organization in 1982 called "Cleveland Tomorrow" to rescue the city from serious decline. Member companies provided $2.5 million, in one instance, to help another organization buy and refurbish houses to sell to low-income people on a lease-purchase plan. To provide incentives for children to stay in school, companies give hiring preference to graduates of Cleveland high schools. McDonald's, the fast-food restaurant chain, established its McJobs Training Program to hire, train, and employ people with physical or mental disabilities who might not otherwise get jobs in the competitive marketplace.[47]

To keep track of their socially related activities, many large companies in North America and Western Europe conduct social audits. The **social audit** is a process used to identify, monitor, measure, evaluate, and report the effects a business organization is having on society or on certain segments of society that are not covered in the traditional financial reports.[48] It is a way to measure a company's progress toward achieving social goals such as minority employment, pollution cleanup, improvement of working conditions, community development, philanthropic contributions, and various consumer issues.[49] Although there are several different social audit approaches,[50] the following five-part approach is suggested by the U.S. Committee for Economic Development:

- A summary of program areas, such as consumer affairs, and the reasoning for undertaking certain activities and not others.
- A report of specific programs and the priorities for each set of activities.
- A listing of objectives for each priority activity and a description of how the organization is striving to reach the objectives.
- A summary report of the costs of each program area and activity to the company.
- A summary using quantitative measures whenever possible of the extent of achievement of each social objective.[51]

Conducting a social audit of a firm is not an easy task. The list of social areas of concern is almost endless. Nevertheless, a line must be drawn somewhere to make social responsibility a doable task. Measurement is even more difficult. Should measures be input-oriented (pollution control expenditures) or output-oriented (reduction of pollution)? If a company is only one of many companies dumping waste into a river, how can it pinpoint the effect of its efforts alone on the purity of the river's water? Evaluation of standards is equally difficult. Should government minimum standards for pollution, for example, be accepted as the company's standard? Given that pesticides and herbicides are necessary to grow sufficient food to feed a society, how much of these poisons is acceptable in local drinking water? The lack of common measures or of a common reporting format makes it difficult to compare the social performance of different companies.[52]

Although the problems inherent in conducting a social audit are many, a company needs to take this step. Given the recent swing in public attitudes against business (see Table 3.4), outside organizations are beginning to conduct their own social audits of business firms and to lobby government for more legislation. According to Stephen Brobeck, Executive Director of the Consumer Federation of America, "Overall national consumer organizations are much stronger than they were a decade ago, and they've never been better funded."[53] The Council on Economic Priorities, for example, publishes *Rating America's Corporate Conscience* and *Shopping for a Better World.* In *Shopping for a Better World,* the Council evaluates companies on the basis of (1) charitable contributions, (2) women's advancement, (3) minority advancement, (4) military contracts, (5) animal testing, (6) disclosure of information, (7) community outreach, (8) nuclear power involve-

---

| **TABLE 3.4** | **Recent U.S. Attitudes Toward Business** |

1. How would you describe your own attitude toward business in this country?

Very favorable	Somewhat favorable	Somewhat unfavorable	Very unfavorable	Not sure
18%	54%	18%	6%	4%

2. Federal regulation of business had once been too tough, but now has gone too much the other way and is too lax.

Agree	Disagree	Not sure
50%	45%	5%

3. How would you rate the ethical standards of business executives?

Excellent	Pretty good	Only fair	Poor	Not sure
2%	38%	46%	12%	2%

4. Business has gained too much power over too many aspects of American life.

Agree	Disagree	Not sure
69%	29%	2%

5. Which of the following do you think business would do to obtain greater profits? (% agreeing)

Deliberately charge inflated prices	62%
Harm the environment	47%
Knowingly sell inferior products	44%
Put its workers' health and safety at risk	42%
Endanger public health	38%
Sell unsafe products	37%

Source: Items 1–3 taken from a nationwide survey of 1,250 adults in the U.S. conducted May 8–12, 1987, by Louis Harris & Associates and reported in *Business Week* (July 20, 1987), p. 71. Items 4–5 taken from a similar survey conducted May 12–16, 1989, by Louis Harris & Associates and reported in *Business Week* (May 29, 1989), p. 29.

ment, (9) activities in South Africa, (10) environmental pollution, and (11) family benefits. Evaluations are listed for products commonly marketed to the consumer, such as Crest Toothpaste (P&G) or Jimmy Dean Sausage (Sara Lee). The publication states:

> Using the information gathered here, you'll have a greater chance to influence corporate policy than ever before. You truly can go "shopping for a better world."[54]

SUMMARY AND CONCLUSION

Anyone concerned with how strategic decisions are made in large corporations should be aware of the impact of the external environment on strategic decision makers. Long-run developments in the economic, technological, political-legal, and sociocultural aspects of the societal environment strongly affect the corporation's activities through the more immediate pressures in its task environment. These pressures are typically exerted by *stakeholder* groups, ranging from shareholders to environmental groups, who have an interest in a business organization's activities.

In any one corporate decision, the interests of one stakeholder can conflict with another. It is the job of the strategic manager to consider the many stakeholder interests and to balance their needs and desires against the interests of the corporation using priorities in goal setting.

Problems can arise between a business corporation and some of its stakeholders because of differences in basic values. Following Milton Friedman, some businesspeople may believe profit maximization to be not just the key goal, but the *only* goal of their firms, whereas concerned interest groups may have other goals as a priority, such as cleaning the environment or hiring minorities. Even though moral relativism may challenge the value of the imposition of any particular ethical standard on a corporation's managers, most companies are beginning to promote the value of ethical criticism as a way to improve the decision making of their executives.

From a strategic point of view, a business corporation needs to consider its responsibilities to the society of which it is a part. The history of business and society clearly suggests that when business ignores its responsibilities to its stakeholders, society tends to respond through government intervention to restrict business's autonomy. This is usually very costly to business firms. According to Carroll, managers of a business organization have ethical and discretionary responsibilities in addition to the normally accepted economic and legal ones. This concept of ethical and discretionary responsibilities as forming a company's social responsibility suggests that unless a company is voluntarily socially responsible to society, that company will be forced to be more responsible by government's expanding the firm's legal responsibilities. Undertaking social audits is one suggested approach to help corporations evaluate and improve their socially responsible behavior.

DISCUSSION QUESTIONS

1. What was Nestlé's role in the problems at Beech-Nut? Should Nestlé's top management be held partially responsible for the unethical and illegal practices engaged in by the managers of its Beech-Nut subsidary? What should Nestlé have done?

2. Should ethics and social responsibility be important topics in the study of strategic management and business policy? Why or why not?

3. How appropriate is the theory of *laissez-faire* in today's world?

4. Should Maytag Corporation move its dishwasher production from Newton, Iowa, to Jackson, Tennessee? What are the pros and cons of this decision?

5. Select a local business corporation and develop a list of its likely stakeholders. Put them in order of most important to least important and justify your priorities.

6. According to a recent article in the *Wall Street Journal,* tobacco companies are increasing their marketing efforts in Third World countries. Faced with a decline in tobacco usage in the developed countries (down 9% in the U.S. and 25% in the U.K. between 1970 and 1985), these corporations are using their advertising expertise and political connections to open new markets in Japan, Taiwan, Thailand, and South Korea, as well as in the Soviet Union.[55] Given the accumulating evidence regarding the link between tobacco usage and cancer, should the strategic managers in these tobacco companies be criticized for taking socially irresponsible actions? Should the making and selling of tobacco products be declared illegal by the government?

7. Do you agree with the economist Milton Friedman that social responsibility is a "fundamentally subversive doctrine" that will only hurt a business corporation's long-term efficiency?

8. Why is moral relativism a challenge to improving a strategic manager's ethical behavior?

9. Using Carroll's list of four responsibilities, should a company be concerned about *discretionary* responsibilities?

10. Is there a correlation between a corporation's level of social responsibility and its financial performance? Explain.

Notes

1. B. Burrough and J. Helyar, *Barbarians at the Gate* (New York: HarperCollins, 1990), p. vii.
2. "Bad Apples in the Executive Suite," *Consumer Reports* (May 1989), p. 296.
3. Summarized from: "Nestlé's Beech-Nut Enters Guilty Plea in Apple Juice Case," *Wall Street Journal* (November 16, 1987), p. 19; C. Welles, "What Led Beech-Nut Down the Road to Disgrace," *Business Week* (February 22, 1988), pp. 124–128; "Bad Apples" pp. 294–296; A. M. Freedman, "Nestlé Quietly Seeks to Sell Beech-Nut, Dogged by Scandal of Bogus Apple Juice," *Wall Street Journal* (July 6, 1989), p. A12; R. Johnson, "Ralston to Buy Beech-Nut, Gambling It Can Overcome Apple Juice Scandal," *Wall Street Journal* (September 18, 1989), p. B11.
4. R. E. Freeman, *Strategic Management: A Stakeholder Approach* (Boston: Pitman Publishing Co., 1984), p. 25.
5. R. Estes, "How to Save Corporate America," *Des Moines Register* (October 7, 1990), p. C1.
6. B. Z. Posner and W. H. Schmidt, "Values and the American Manager: An Update," *California Management Review* (Spring 1984), pp. 202–216.
7. K. Roth and D. A. Ricks, "Objective Setting in International Business: An Empirical Analysis," *International Journal of Management* (March 1990), p. 16.
8. B. Tierney, "Planned Parenthood Didn't Plan on This," *Business Week* (July 3, 1989), p. 34.
   K. Kelly, "Dayton Hudson Finds There's No Graceful Way to Flip-Flop," *Business Week* (September 24, 1990), p. 50.
9. G. F. Cavanagh, *American Business Values*, 3rd ed. (Englewood Cliffs, N.J.: Prentice-Hall, 1990), p. 173.
10. "Three Mile Island's Lingering Ills," *Business Week* (October 22, 1979), p. 75.
    "Dangerous Mind-Set," *Time* (July 3, 1989), p. 18.
    J. H. Dobrzynski, W. B. Glaberson, R. W. King, W. J. Powell, Jr., and L. Helm, "Union Carbide Fights for Its Life," *Business Week* (December 24, 1984), pp. 52–56.
11. "Who Will Be Liable for Toxic Dumping?" *Business Week* (August 28, 1978), p. 32.
    "Pollution: Who Will Pay?" *Fortune* (March 13, 1989), p. 12.
12. M. W. Walsh, "A. H. Robbins Seeks a Consolidated Trial for All Dalkon Punitive-Damage Claims," *Wall Street Journal* (October 23, 1984), p. 4.
    G. Stricharchuk and R. Wartzman, "Dow Chemical Product Is Assailed as Causing Brickwork to Collapse," *Wall Street Journal* (March 21, 1989), p. 1.
13. L. Sorenson, "Chapter 11 Filing by Wilson Foods Roils Workers' Lives, Tests Law," *Wall Street Journal* (May 23, 1983), p. 25.
14. S. Soloman, "The Asbestos Fallout at Johns-Manville," *Fortune* (May 7, 1979), pp. 197–206.
    A. R. Karr, "Chrysler Agrees to Pay $1.6 Million Fine to Settle OSHA Health Safety Charges," *Wall Street Journal* (July 7, 1987), pp. 3, 8.
15. J. Valente, "Sundstrand to Plead Guilty to Fraud on Defense Work, Pay U.S. $115 Million," *Wall Street Journal* (October 13, 1988), p. A3.
    E. T. Pound, "Honored Employee Is Key in Huge Fraud in Defense Purchasing," *Wall Street Journal* (March 2, 1988), p. 1.
    "Mixed Feelings About Drexel's Decision," *Wall Street Journal* (December 23, 1988), p. B1.
16. T. Clark, "Ethical Dilemmas in International Business," *International Journal of Management* (December 1988), p. 440.
17. M. Friedman, "The Social Responsibility of Business Is to Increase Its Profits," *New York Times Magazine* (September 13, 1970), pp. 30, 126–127; and *Capitalism and Freedom* (Chicago: University of Chicago Press, 1963), p. 133.
18. M. Gable and P. Arlow, "A Comparative Examination of the Value Orientations of British and American Executives," *International Journal of Management* (September 1986), pp. 97–106.
    W. D. Guth and R. Tagiuri, "Personal Values and Corporate Strategy," *Harvard Business Review* (September-October 1965), pp. 126–127.
    G. W. England, "Managers and Their Value Systems: A Five Country Comparative Study," *Columbia Journal of World Business* (Summer 1978), p. 35.
19. Posner and Schmidt, "Values and the American Manager" pp. 203–205.
    S. N. Brenner and E. A. Molander, "Is the Ethics of Business Changing?" *Harvard Business Review* (January-February 1977), p. 70.
20. Summarized from R. E. Freeman and D. R. Gilbert, Jr., *Corporate Strategy and the Search for Ethics* (Englewood Cliffs, N.J.: Prentice-Hall, 1988), pp. 24–41.
21. *Ibid.* p. 34.
22. T. J. Von der Embse and R. A. Wagley, "Managerial Ethics: Hard Decisions on Soft Criteria," *SAM Advanced Management Journal* (Winter 1988), p. 6.
23. Summarized from G. F. Cavanagh, D. J. Moberg, and M. Velasquez, "The Ethics of Organizational Politics," *Academy of Management Review* (July 1981), pp. 363–374; and J. E. Smith, J. B. Forbes, and M. M. Extejt, "Ethics in the Organizational Behavior Course," *The Organizational Behavior Teaching Review*, Vol. XIII, Issue 1 (1988-89), pp. 85–95. See also Cavanagh, *American Business Values*, pp. 186–199.

24. Smith et al., "Ethics in the Organizational Behavior Course," p. 86.

25. Cavanagh et al., "Ethics of Organizational Politics," p. 370.

26. *Ibid.*

27. "From Beer to Buy-Outs, Readers Share Their Thoughts," *Wall Street Journal* (Centennial Edition, June 23, 1989), p. C5.

28. T. D. Schellhardt, "What Bosses Think About Corporate Ethics," *Wall Street Journal* (April 6, 1988), p. 21.

29. Summarized from *Personnel Journal* by P. Plawin and A. Blum, "The Young and the Ruthless," *Changing Times* (August 1988), p. 76.

30. L. K. Trevino, "Ethical Decision Making in Organizations: A Person-Situation Interactionist Model," *Academy of Management Review* (July 1986), pp. 601–617.

31. L. Kohlberg, "Moral Stage and Moralization: The Cognitive-Development Approach," in *Moral Development and Behavior*, edited by T. Lickona (New York: Holt, Rinehart & Winston, 1976).

32. A. H. Maslow, "A Theory of Human Motivation," *Psychological Review*, Vol. 50 (1943), pp. 370–396.

33. Trevino, "Ethical Decision Making," p. 606.

34. T. J. Murray, "Ethics Program: Just a Pretty Face," *Business Month* (September 1987), p. 30.

35. J. Keogh, ed., *Corporate Ethics: A Prime Business Asset* (New York: The Business Roundtable, 1988), p. 5.

36. A Bennett, "Ethics Codes Spread Despite Skepticism," *Wall Street Journal* (July 15, 1988), p. 13.

37. Keogh, *Corporate Ethics*, p. 24.

38. R. P. Nielsen, "Alternative Managerial Responses to Ethical Dilemmas," *Planning Review* (November 1985), pp. 24–29, 43.

   R. P. Nielsen, "Changing Unethical Organizational Behavior," *Academy of Management Executive* (May 1989), pp. 123–130.

39. Nielsen, "Alternative Managerial Responses," p. 43.

40. A. B. Carroll, "A Three-Dimensional Conceptual Model of Corporate Performance," *Academy of Management Review* (October 1979), pp. 497–505. Another way of conceptualizing responsibilities is proposed by S. P. Sethi in "Dimensions of Corporate Social Responsibility," *California Management Review* (Spring 1975), pp. 58–64. Economic and legal responsibilities may be considered as *social obligation;* ethical responsibilities may be considered as *social responsibility;* discretionary responsibilities may be considered as *social responsiveness.* We prefer to use Carroll's conceptualization since it views social responsibility as including ethical and discretionary responsibilities.

41. L. Iacocca, *Iacocca: An Autobiography* (Toronto: Bantam Books, 1984), pp. 196–197.

42. M. Alpert, "Holy Pepperoni!" *Fortune* (July 17, 1989), p. 116.

43. S. Kilman and F. Schwadel, "A 'Merchant's Merchant' Buys Some Time," *Wall Street Journal* (June 29, 1987), p. 28.

44. K. E. Aupperle, A. B. Carroll, and J. D. Hatfield, "An Empirical Examination of the Relationship Between Corporate Social Responsibility and Profitability," *Academy of Management Journal* (June 1985), p. 459. Since one recent study found that successful companies are more likely to be socially responsible than are less successful ones, one could conclude that high financial performance leads to increased social responsibility, rather than the reverse! See J. B. McGuire, A. Sundgren, and T. Schneeweis, "Corporate Social Responsibility and Firm Financial Performance," *Academy of Management Journal* (December 1988), pp. 854–872.

45. S. Koepp and M. Hequet, "Two in Pursuit of a Turnaround," *Time* (February 16, 1987), p. 48.

46. K. Davis, "The Meaning and Scope of Social Responsibility," in *Contemporary Management: Issues and Viewpoints,* edited by J. W. McGuire (Englewood Cliffs, N.J.: Prentice-Hall, 1974), p. 631.

47. B. Carton, "Reebok's Image of Conscience," *Boston Globe* (September 20, 1988), pp. 51, 58.

   C. Gustke, "How Business Bosses Saved a Sick City," *Fortune* (March 17, 1989), pp. 106–110.

   A. Dolan, "McJobs Opens New Doors for the Disabled," *The Daily Tribune* (Ames, Iowa), Business Times edition (April 9, 1990), p. C10.

48. R. A. Buchholz, *Business Environment and Public Policy,* 3rd ed. (Englewood Cliffs, N.J.: Prentice-Hall, 1989), p. 471.

49. A. B. Carroll and G. W. Beiler, "Landmarks in the Evolution of the Social Audit," *Academy of Management Journal* (September 1975), p. 598.

50. J. L. Hysom and W. J. Bolce, *Business and Its Environment* (St. Paul, Minn.: West, 1983), pp. 48–49.

51. J. J. Corson and G. A. Steiner, *Measuring Business's Performance: The Corporate Social Audit* (New York: Committee for Economic Development, 1974).

52. Buchholz, *Business Environment,* pp. 473–475.

53. J. Bodnar and M. Dovel, "Whatever Happened to the Consumer Movement?" *Changing Times* (August 1989), p. 45.

54. R. Will, A. T. Marlin, B. Carson, and J. Schorsch, *Shopping for a Better World* (New York: Council on Economic Priorities, 1989), p. 1.

55. A. Cockburn, "The Other Drug War, Where Tobacco Firms Are the Pushers," *Wall Street Journal* (September 27, 1990), p. A15. See also K. Deveny and K. H. Bacon, "Tobacco Is Facing New Attacks," *Wall Street Journal* (May 24, 1990), p. B1.

CHAPTER FOUR

Environmental Scanning and Industry Analysis

CHAPTER OUTLINE

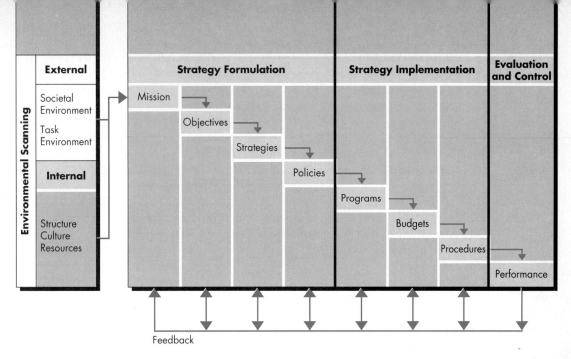

STRATEGIC MANAGEMENT MODEL

The central problem for complex organizations is one of coping with uncertainty.[1]

J. D. Thompson

Who remembers Beaunit Mills, Hercules Powder, or Liebmann Breweries? These companies, along with 250 others that appeared in the first Fortune 500 list of top business corporations in 1955, have vanished from the major ranks of U.S. industry. Why did so many fail to thrive? Although some of the changes are the result of mergers and acquisitions, most of the turnover can be attributed to a company's inability to adapt to changing conditions.[2]

With an 80% share of the market, National Cash Register (NCR) of Dayton, Ohio, dominated the U.S. mechanical cash register business in 1971. NCR's management had invested millions of dollars in a highly sophisticated manufacturing facility. Also in 1971, Data Terminal Systems introduced the first electronic cash register in the U.S. NCR, however, ignored what was quickly to be the dominant technology and continued to emphasize its mechanical products until, finally, its profits turned to losses. In a frantic effort to recover lost sales, the company fired 80% of its top managers and destroyed its expensive manufacturing facility to make room for a new plant. Despite the introduction of NCR's own electronic cash register, it was too late; NCR's market share dropped from 80% in 1971 to 25% in 1978. It never regained industry dominance.[3]

The above example shows how quickly a leading company can become an also-ran because of its failure to adapt to environmental change or, even worse, its failure to create change. To be successful over time, an organization needs to be in tune with its external environment. There must be a **strategic fit** between what the environment wants and what the corporation has to offer, as well as between what the corporation needs and what the environment can provide.[4] Current predictions are that the environment for all organizations will become even more uncertain as the world enters the twenty-first century. **Environmental uncertainty** refers to the combination of the degree of *complexity* and the degree of *change* existing in an organization's external environment.[5] Environmental uncertainty is a threat to strategic managers because it hampers their ability to develop long-range plans and to make strategic decisions to keep the corporation in equilibrium with its external environment.

Faced with increasing uncertainty, and based on their degree of willingness to change their corporation and/or to change their environment, strategic managers may take one of four basic orientations for dealing with uncertainty, depicted in Fig. 4.1

If managers do not wish to change their firm's way of doing things or to change how the environment affects their firm, they may choose simply to **avoid** change completely by either ignoring the situation or by hiding in a small, secure market niche. If they choose, in contrast, to change the environment in some way so that the firm can continue its activities unchanged, managers may attempt to **influence** key groups in the firm's environment by advertising the firm's virtues, lobbying the government for favors, or co-opting antagonistic groups by inviting one of the firm's critics to join the corporation's board of directors. (These actions are sometimes called *political strategies*.) If managers fear changing the firm's environment, they may respond to increasing environmental uncertainty by **reacting** to a new situation, either by simply imitating the actions of the industry leader ("If it's good enough for IBM it's good enough for us") or by reorganizing to cut costs. None of these three

---

| **FIGURE 4.1** | **Basic Orientations for Dealing with Environmental Uncertainty** |

The Environment

		Don't Change Environment	Change Environment
The Corporation	Don't Change Corporation	**Avoid** • Ignore • Hide	**Influence** • Advertise • Lobby • Cooptation
	Change Corporation	**React** • Follow leader • Reorganize	**Anticipate** • Strategic planning

orientations, however, can be thought of as true strategic planning. They are simply temporary approaches used to postpone the inevitable adjustments needed to gain and keep strategic fit.

Managers who are willing to actively embrace the increasing uncertainty facing their organization in order to **anticipate** future developments engage in strategic planning. To be successful, however, they must have the will not only to change the way their firm operates, but also to attempt to change or modify certain elements in their environment to help create a future more favorable to their corporation. If the company is in dire straits, however, management may have to take a few short-term measures to beat off a few alligators before they can get down to the strategic business of draining the swamp!

During the 1970s, for example, Chrysler Corporation dealt with uncertainty in the automobile industry by *reacting*. It tried to follow General Motors' example. When that failed, Chrysler emphasized cost cutting. Under the threat of bankruptcy, Chrysler's board of directors hired Lee Iacocca as Chief Executive Officer. Iacocca immediately reorganized the company by selling off units to get its production facilities more in line with its market demands. He also moved to an *influence* orientation by lobbying the federal government for a loan guarantee, advertising the "new" Chrysler Corporation to regain consumer confidence, and co-opting the union by placing the President of the United Auto Workers on the board of directors. Iacocca and his team of strategic managers then changed to an *anticipation* orientation. Based on in-depth environmental scanning (and a certain amount of intuition!), top management focused production on small, front-wheel-drive cars and on manufacturing a series of cars with strong market appeal that other auto companies had overlooked, such as minivans and convertibles. Chrysler's strategic managers correctly anticipated the trend toward front-wheel drive and toward flashier, more exciting automobiles. They not only transformed Chrysler into a more innovative, successful organization, they also helped change the environment by getting key stakeholder groups to accept Chrysler's view of the future, as well as to support it.

4.1 Environmental Scanning

The first step in strategic planning is environmental scanning. Before strategy makers can begin formulating specific strategies, they must scan the external environment to identify possible *opportunities* and *threats*. **Environmental scanning** is the monitoring, evaluating, and disseminating of information from the external environment to key people within the corporation.[6] It is a tool that a corporation uses to avoid strategic surprise and to ensure its long-term health. In 1973, for example, the Arab oil embargo caught many firms completely by surprise, with the result that goods dependent on oil as a raw material or energy source could not be produced, which, in turn, caused chaos throughout the world's economy. The top managements of many corporations then realized just how dependent they were on seemingly unpredictable external events. It was in the early 1970s that many corporations established for the first time formal strategic planning systems. By 1984, between 92% and 95% of the world's largest corporations were using planning departments to monitor the environment and to prepare forecasts.[7]

ENVIRONMENTAL VARIABLES

In undertaking environmental scanning, strategic managers must first be aware of the many variables within a corporation's task and societal environments. (See Fig. 4.2.) The **task environment** includes those elements or groups that directly affect the corporation and, in turn, are affected by it. These are governments, local communities, suppliers, competitors, customers, creditors, employees/labor unions, special-interest groups, and trade associations. A corporation's task environment is the specific **industry** within which that corporation operates. The **societal environment** includes the more general forces that do not directly touch on the short-run activities of the organization but that can, and often do, influence its long-run decisions. These, also shown in Fig. 4.2, are as follows:

- **Economic forces** that regulate the exchange of materials, money, energy, and information.
- **Technological forces** that generate problem-solving inventions.
- **Political-legal forces** that allocate power and provide constraining and protecting laws and regulations.
- **Sociocultural forces** that regulate the values, mores, and customs of society.

Both the societal and task environments must be monitored so that strategic factors that are likely to have a strong impact on corporate success or failure can be detected.

FIGURE 4.2   **Key Environmental Variables**

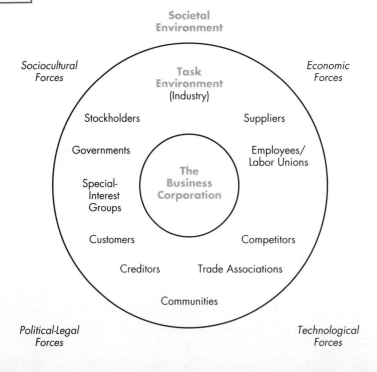

MONITORING STRATEGIC FACTORS

Strategic managers should engage in environmental scanning through use of a *Strategic Issues Management System.*[8] By monitoring for weak as well as strong environmental signals, such a system continuously scans for possible trends and future developments. As mentioned earlier, NCR paid little attention to the appearance of the first electronic cash register in 1971—an example of a weak signal. By 1978, however, NCR's market share had dropped from 80% to 25%—a rather strong signal!

One way to identify and analyze developments in the societal environment is to use the matrix provided in Fig. 4.3. *First,* identify approximately three or more trends emerging in each of the four forces in the societal environment. *Second,* attempt to ascertain the likely impact, if any, of each of these trends on each of the ten primary elements (stakeholder groups) in the corporation's task environment. For example, if a period of low economic growth appears to be developing, list that

FIGURE 4.3 | **Matrix For Environmental Trend Analysis**

Societal Forces

Task Elements	Economic	Technological	Political-Legal	Sociocultural
	1. 2. 3.	1. 2. 3.	1. 2. 3.	1. 2. 3.
Communities				
Competitors				
Creditors				
Customers				
Employees/ Labor unions				
Governments				
Special-interest groups				
Stockholders				
Suppliers				
Trade associations				

Source: Suggested by J. C. Camillus, *Strategic Planning and Management Control* (Lexington, Mass.: D. C. Heath & Co., 1986), pp. 59–67.

as one of the economic forces in the societal environment and attempt to identify its impact on those task elements likely to be affected. This enables the strategic manager to see how an economic development may affect the firm through its impact on elements in the company's task environment.

When analyzed, environmental data form a series of **strategic issues**—those trends and developments that are very likely to determine the future environment. Insofar as a corporation's strategic managers are concerned, however, these strategic environmental issues must be further analyzed so that those of most importance to the corporation's own future are identified. A corporation's **strategic factors** are those environmental strategic issues that are judged to have a high probability of occurrence and a high probability of impact on the corporation. As shown in Fig. 4.4, an **issues priority matrix** can be used to help managers decide which strategic issues should be merely scanned (low priority) and which should be monitored as strategic factors (high priority). Those environmental issues judged to be a corporation's strategic factors are then categorized as *opportunities* and *threats*, and are included in strategy formulation.

Few firms, unfortunately, successfully monitor strategic issues.[9] The personal values of a corporation's top managers are likely to bias both their perception of what is important to monitor in the external environment and their interpretations of what they perceive. Therefore, different companies often respond differently to the same environmental changes because of differences in the ability of their strategic managers to recognize and understand strategic issues and factors.[10] For example, a study of presidents of savings and loan associations revealed that a president's perception of the environment strongly affected strategic planning. Those presidents who believed the present uncertain environment to be only temporary used no long-term planning staff or planning committees. They simply chose to wait for the "good old days" to return. In contrast, those presidents who believed the days of the stable,

| FIGURE 4.4 | **Issues Priority Matrix** |

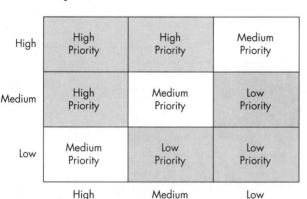

Source: Adapted from L. L. Lederman, "Foresight Activities in the U.S.A.: Time for a Re-Assessment?" *Long-Range Planning* (June 1984), p. 46. Copyright © 1984 by Pergamon Press, Ltd. Reprinted by permission.

regulated environment to be long gone spent 30%–50% of their time considering long-range strategic issues and used planning staffs extensively.[11]

Societal Environment

The number of possible strategic factors in the societal environment is very high. The number becomes enormous when one realizes that, generally speaking, each country in the world can be represented by its own unique set of societal forces—some of which are very similar to neighboring countries and some of which are very different. For example, as members of the European Community (Common Market), the U.K. and France share many of the same economic forces in their two societal environments. To the extent, however, that France's judicial system is based on the Napoleonic Code and the U.K.'s emphasis is on its tradition of common law, the political-legal forces in their societal environments are very different. (Additional examples of various societal forces in countries around the world are presented in Chapter 11.)

As noted in Table 4.1, large corporations categorize the societal environment into four areas and focus their scanning in each area on trends with corporatewide relevance. The economic area is usually the most significant, followed by the technological, political-legal, and sociocultural, in decreasing order of importance.[12] Obviously, trends in any one area may be very important to the firms in one industry but of lesser importance to firms in other industries. For example, the demographic bulge in the U.S. population caused by the "baby boom" in the 1950s strongly affected the brewing industry, among others. As this demographic group grew older during the 1980s, the percentage of the population that fell within the 18–25 years

TABLE 4.1	Some Important Variables in the Societal Environment

Economic	Technological	Political-Legal	Sociocultural
GNP trends	Total federal spending for R&D	Antitrust regulations	Life-style changes
Interest rates		Environmental protection laws	Career expectations
Money supply	Total industry spending for R&D		Consumer activism
Inflation rates		Tax laws	Rate of family formation
Unemployment levels	Focus of technological efforts	Special incentives	
Wage/price controls		Foreign trade regulations	Growth rate of population
Devaluation/revaluation	Patent protection		Age distribution of population
Energy availability and cost	New products	Attitudes toward foreign companies	
	New developments in technology transfer from lab to marketplace	Laws on hiring and promotion	Regional shifts in population
Disposable and discretionary income		Stability of government	Life expectancies
	Productivity improvements through automation		Birth rates

of age category—prime beer-drinking age—declined. Thus sales and profits of breweries decreased and corporations like Anheuser-Busch found that they had to diversify if they were to stay profitable. In contrast, as the number of dual-career married couples in the 25–34 years of age category became larger, demand increased for day-care facilities like Kinder-Care Learning Centers.

Corporations throughout the developed nations of the world face some demographic societal pressures regardless of industry. The falling birth rates plus changing economic factors, for example, are leading to an aging of the work force and to pressure for both men and women to have fulltime jobs. Because more than 60% of U.S. mothers with children under the age of 14 were actively employed by 1987 and there were predictions that the percentage would continue to rise, pressures were building on organizations to deal with the increasingly severe child-care dilemma facing their employees.[13] As the percentage of people in the workforce of the developed world over 45 years of age increases from 32% in 1990 to 41% by 2040, personnel practices and competitive strategies will be forced to change.[14] McDonald's fast-food chain has already begun to replace some of its teenage employees with retired adults. In attempts to change their offerings to match the changing life-styles of their aging clientele, ski resorts are deemphasizing steep downhill slopes in favor of family-oriented lodges and scenic views.

John Naisbitt, in his influential book *Megatrends,* states that the U.S.'s present societal environment is turbulent because we are moving from one era to another. Having performed a content analysis of newspapers, he proposes that U.S. society is being restructured by *ten broad influences* or "megatrends" that are defining the new society.

1. We are moving from an industrial to an information society.
2. We are moving from forced technology to a matching of each new technology with a compensatory human response ("Hi tech–hi touch").
3. We are moving from a national to a world economy.
4. We are moving from short-term to long-term considerations, with an emphasis on strategic planning.
5. We are moving from a period of centralization to decentralization of power.
6. We are shifting from reliance on institutional help to more self-reliance.
7. We are moving from representative democracy to more participative democracy, in politics as well as in the workplace.
8. We are giving up our dependence on traditional hierarchical structures in favor of informal networks of contacts.
9. We are moving geographically from the North to the South and West.
10. We are moving from a society with a limited number of personal choices to a multiple-option society.[15]

Comments by other analysts of societal trends, such as Alvin Toffler and Peter Drucker, suggest that many of Naisbitt's megatrends are already having an enormous impact not only on the U.S. but on world society in general.[16]

Most of the variables in each of the societal forces constantly interact with and influence each other. For example, the trend toward dual-career couples in the U.S. and Canada in the 1980s may have developed partially from the combination, prevalent in the late 1970s, of high interest rates (increasing the cost of home ownership) and inflation (reducing the purchasing power of the paycheck), coupled with changing sociocultural values regarding the role of women (leading to an increase in the number of women in nontraditional occupations). This trend, along with the trend toward single-parent households in the U.S. and Canada, interacts with political-legal forces to result in an increasing governmental awareness of a child-care "problem," which politicians attempt to help "solve."

Trends such as these develop out of the interaction of variables in the societal environment and tend to affect the decisions and actions of a corporation through their impact on groups in the firm's task environment. The trend toward dual-career couples, for example, affects companies today in terms of direct requests from employee/union groups and from pressure by special-interest groups on governments to provide or require child-care assistance for working parents. The trend may also affect how a company reaches its customers. For example, when Avon's sales began to drop because fewer and fewer women were at home to buy cosmetics from the visiting Avon representative, the Avon "lady" moved to the office to sell cosmetics during the lunch hour! To the extent that trends such as these in the societal environment are likely to have a strong impact on a particular corporation, they must be considered as strategic factors and be monitored closely by that firm's planners.

Task Environment

As was shown in Fig. 4.2, the task environment includes a large number of groups with an interest in a business corporation's activities. These groups are referred to as **stakeholders** because they directly affect or are affected by the organization's decisions. In effect, each of them has a "stake" in what the organization does or fails to do. Each stakeholder uses its own criteria to determine how well a corporation is performing, and each is constantly judging management's actions in terms of their effect on itself. To the extent that a stakeholder group feels that it is not being treated properly, it will put direct pressure on the organization to remedy the situation. Therefore, management must be aware not only of the key stakeholders in the corporation's task environment, but also of the criteria each group uses to judge the corporation's performance. The following is a list of some of these stakeholders and their probable criteria:

Stockholders	Price appreciation of securities. Dividends (how much and how often?).
Unions	Comparable wages. Stability of employment. Opportunity for advancement. Working conditions.
Governments	Support of government programs. Adherence to laws and regulations.
Suppliers	Rapidity of payment. Consistency of purchases.

Creditors	Adherence to contract terms.
	Dependability.
Customers/	Value given for the price paid.
distributors	Availability of product or service.
Trade associations	Participation in association programs (time).
	Participation in association programs (money).
Competitors	Rate of growth (encroachment on their markets).
	Product or service innovation (source of new ideas to use).
Communities	Contribution to community development through taxes, participation in charitable activities, etc.
	Employment of local people.
	Minimum of negative side-effects (e.g., pollution).
Special-interest groups	Employment of minority groups.
	Contributions to urban improvement programs.
	Provision of free services to the disadvantaged.

As shown in Fig. 4.5, a corporation's scanning of the environment will include analyses of all the relevant elements in the task environment—customers, competitors, suppliers, creditors, and governments, to name a few. These analyses take the form of individual reports written by various people in different parts of the firm. At Procter & Gamble (P&G), for example, each quarter people from each of the brand management teams work with key people from the sales and market research

---

FIGURE 4.5 | **Scanning the External Environment**

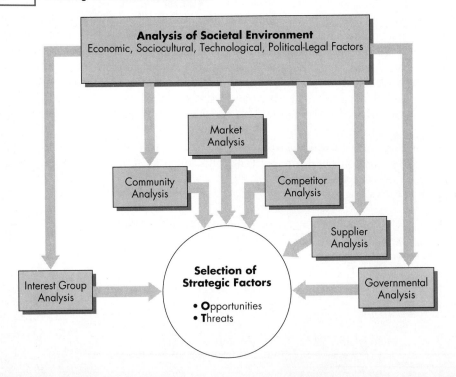

departments to research and write a "competitive activity report" on each of the product categories in which P&G competes. People in purchasing also write similar reports concerning new developments in the industries that supply P&G. These and other reports are then summarized and transmitted up the corporate hierarchy for top management to use in strategic decision making. If a new development is reported regarding a particular product category, top management may then send memos to people throughout the organization to watch for and report on developments in related product areas. The many reports resulting from these scanning efforts, when boiled down to their essentials, act as a detailed list of strategic factors—those opportunities and threats facing the corporation from its task environment.

4.2 INDUSTRY ANALYSIS

The task environment of a particular company may also be regarded as the company's industry. An *industry* is a group of firms producing a similar product or service, such as automobiles or soft drinks. An examination of the important stakeholder groups in a particular corporation's task environment may thus be called *industry analysis*.

COMPETITIVE INTENSITY

Porter, an authority on competitive strategy, contends that a corporation is most concerned with the intensity of competition within its industry. The level of this intensity is determined by basic competitive forces, which are depicted in Fig. 4.6. "The collective strength of these forces," he contends, "determines the ultimate profit potential in the industry, where profit potential is measured in terms of long-run return on invested capital."[17] The stronger each of these forces, the more companies are limited in their ability to raise prices and earn greater profits. Although Porter mentions only five forces, a sixth—other stakeholders—is added here to reflect the power that unions, governments, and other groups from the task environment wield over industry activities.

Using the model in Fig. 4.6, a strong force can be regarded as a threat, since it is likely to reduce profits. A weak force, in contrast, can be viewed as an opportunity, since it may allow the company to earn greater profits. In the short run, these forces act as constraints on a company's activities. In the long run, however, it may be possible for a company, through its choice of strategy, to change the strength of one or more of the forces to the company's advantage.

In carefully scanning its industry, the corporation must assess the importance to its success of each of the following six forces:[18]

1. **Threat of New Entrants:** New entrants to an industry typically bring to it new capacity, a desire to gain market share, and substantial resources. They are, therefore, threats to an established corporation. The threat of entry depends on the presence of entry barriers and the reaction that can be expected from existing competitors. For example, there have been very few

FIGURE 4.6 | **Forces Driving Industry Competition**

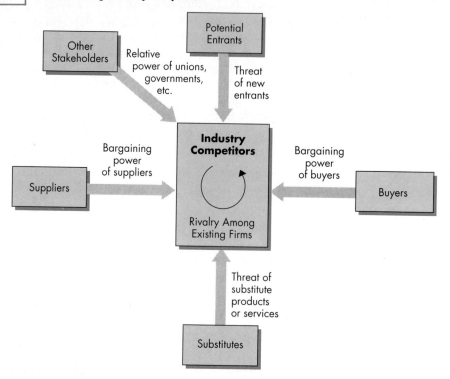

Source: Adapted/Reprinted with permission of The Free Press, a Division of Macmillan, Inc. from *Competitive Strategy: Techniques for Analyzing Industries and Competitors* by Michael E. Porter. Copyright © 1980 by The Free Press.

new automobile companies successfully established in the U.S. since the 1930s because of the high capital requirements to build production facilities and to develop a dealer distribution network. Some of the *barriers to entry* are:

Economies of Scale. Economies of scale refer to the cost advantages associated with large size. Scale economies deter new entrants by forcing the entrant to enter the industry at a large scale (usually with high costs) and so risk reaction from existing firms, or to enter the industry at a small scale and accept a cost disadvantage. Scale economies in the production and sale of mainframe computers, for example, give IBM a significant advantage over any new rival.

Product Differentiation. Brand identification creates a barrier to entry by forcing entrants to spend heavily to overcome existing customer loyalty. Advertising, customer service, and being first with a new product foster brand identification. Corporations like Procter & Gamble and General Mills, which manufacture consumer products, create high entry barriers through their high levels of advertising and promotion.

Capital Requirements. The need to invest huge financial resources in order to compete creates a significant barrier to entry—particularly if it is for unrecoverable up-front expenses such as R&D. Xerox's original decision to rent instead of sell copiers created an entry barrier for competitors. A new entrant had to have a lot of working capital to support a similar rental policy.

Switching Costs. Switching costs are the one-time costs facing a buyer when that buyer switches from one supplier's product to another's. If these switching costs are high, a new entrant must offer a major improvement in cost or performance to entice a potential customer to change from its current supplier. Computer software is one example of an industry with high switching costs. Once a software program like Lotus 1-2-3 or WordPerfect becomes established in an office, office managers are very reluctant to switch to a new program because of the high training costs.

Access to Distribution Channels. A barrier to entry can be the new entrant's need to secure distribution for its products. To the extent that appropriate distribution channels have already been served by the established firms, the new entrant must persuade the channels to accept its products through costly promotion allowances. For example, small entrepreneurs have a difficult time obtaining supermarket shelf space for their goods because large retailers charge for space on their shelves and give priority to the established firms who can pay not only the shelf fees, but also the advertising needed to generate high customer demand.

Cost Disadvantages Independent of Size. Established companies may have cost advantages not easily imitated by new entrants. These may be proprietary product knowledge protected by patents, favorable access to raw materials, favorable locations, or government subsidies. Sears, for example, expanded rapidly after World War II into newly built suburban shopping malls and thus kept Montgomery Ward and other potential competitiors out of the best locations. A cost advantage can also derive from the effects of an *experience* (or learning) *curve*. In some industries, like aerospace, there is a tendency for unit costs to decline as the firm gains cumulative experience in making and selling the product. In such an industry, a new entrant will find it very costly to compete against an established firm with a low cost position based on experience. (The experience curve and its implications for strategic management will be discussed in more detail in Chapter 5.)

Government Policy. The government can limit entry into an industry through licensing requirements and limits on access to needed raw materials. For example, the U.S. federal government limits access to off-shore drilling sites for petroleum companies to reduce the likelihood of contamination of the nation's coastline.

2. **Rivalry Among Existing Firms:** In most industries, corporations are mutually dependent. A competitive move by one firm can be expected to have a noticeable effect on its competitors and thus may cause retaliation or counter-

efforts. For example, the entry of Philip Morris into the beer industry through the acquisition of Miller Brewing increased the level of competitive activity to such an extent that any introduction of a new product or promotion is now quickly followed by similar moves from other brewers. According to Porter, *intense rivalry* is related to the presence of several factors, such as:

Competitors. Competitors are either numerous or roughly equal in size and power. When competitors are numerous, there is plenty of room for new strategies to be tried by one firm and copied by others. When competitors are roughly equal in size, they watch each other carefully to make sure that any move by another firm is matched by an equal countermove.

Industry Growth. Industry growth is slow, generating fights for market share by expansion-oriented companies. When an industry is growing rapidly, there is usually plenty of opportunity for many firms to grow within it. When industry growth slows, however, it becomes much more difficult for any one firm to continue sales growth unless it takes sales away from a competitor. For example, any slowing in passenger traffic tends to set off price wars in the airline industry.

The Product or Service. The product or service is undifferentiated or lacks switching costs. When a product or service is basically the same regardless of the company offering it, that product or service becomes like a commodity. Commodities, such as grain or petroleum, are usually graded into categories and compete within each category only on price and service. If switching costs are low, customers will jump from one supplier to another to reduce their costs—and the resulting rivalry among suppliers will be high. For example, many car owners commonly choose a gas station based on the station's location and its posted price of unleaded gasoline without regard for differences in gasoline quality.

Fixed Costs. Fixed costs are high or the product is perishable. To the extent that a company's fixed costs are high, it may be willing to cut prices below its total costs in order at least to cover its fixed costs. Airlines, for example must fly their planes on a schedule regardless of the number of paying passengers for any one flight. As a result, cheap standby or excursion fares are used whenever a plane has empty seats. Although these fares may not pay for the complete cost of the tickets, they at least contribute to the relatively fixed costs of fuel, crew salaries, and administration, which must be paid regardless of the number of tickets sold. To the extent that a product is perishable (like fresh fruits or vegetables), it must be sold at whatever price can be obtained before the product deteriorates.

Capacity. Capacity is normally added in large increments. If the only way a company can increase its manufacturing capacity is to add it in a large increment by building a new plant, it will run that new plant at full capacity to keep its unit costs as low as possible. This is especially likely if there are economies of scale present in the production of that product. Since the company will be producing more than market demand at the current price, the company will probably reduce its price and hope that it can recoup its costs in a greater number of sales.

Exit Barriers. Exit barriers are high. The reverse of entry barriers, exit barriers keep a company from leaving an industry. These barriers may be specialized assets or management's loyalty to an existing business. To the extent that a firm finds it very difficult to exit an industry, it will continue to compete as long as it can avoid losing significant amounts of money, while management hopes that better times are on the way. The brewing industry, for example, has a high degree of rivalry because there are few uses for breweries except for making beer. The same thing is true in the steel industry.

Rivals. Rivals are often diverse in their strategies used, origins, and corporate cultures. Since diverse rivals have very different ideas of how to compete, they are likely to cross paths often and unknowingly challenge each other's position.

3. **Threat of Substitute Products or Services:** In effect, all corporations within one industry are competing with firms in other industries that produce substitute products. *Substitute products* are those products that appear to be different, but can satisfy the same need as another product. According to Porter, "Substitutes limit the potential returns of an industry by placing a ceiling on the prices firms in the industry can profitably charge."[19] To the extent that switching costs are low, substitutes may have a strong effect on an industry. In the 1970s, for example, the high price of cane sugar caused soft drink manufacturers to turn to high-fructose corn syrup as a sugar substitute. Since switching costs to convert the soft drink manufacturing process were high, companies did not change to corn syrup until the price of sugar was sufficiently high to justify the switch. Similarly, the price of sugar has to drop substantially for a long period of time before the soft drink companies would consider a switch back to sugar. Sometimes a difficult task, the identification of possible substitute products or services means searching for products or services that can perform the same function, even though they may not appear to be easily substitutable. Videocassette recorders, for example, have become substitutes for home motion-picture projectors. The television screen thus substitutes for the portable projection screen.

4. **Bargaining Power of Buyers:** Buyers affect an industry through their ability to force down prices, bargain for higher quality or more services, and play competitors against each other. A buyer or a group of buyers is powerful if some of the following hold true:
   - It purchases a large proportion of the seller's product or service.
   - It has the potential to integrate backward by producing the product itself.
   - Alternative suppliers are plentiful because the product is standard or undifferentiated.
   - Changing suppliers costs very little.
   - The purchased product represents a high percentage of the buyer's costs, thus providing an incentive to shop around for a lower price.

- It earns low profits and is thus very sensitive to costs and service differences.
- The purchased product is unimportant to the final quality or price of the buyer's products or services and thus can be easily substituted without affecting the final product adversely.

For example, to the extent that General Motors purchases a large percentage of Goodyear's total tire production, GM's purchasing department can easily make all sorts of demands on Goodyear's marketing people. This would be the case especially if GM could easily get its tires from Bridgestone or Michelin at no extra trouble or cost. Increasing demands by large manufacturing companies for "just-in-time delivery" means that, to get the orders, a small supplier dependent on the large firm's business must take over the warehousing functions previously handled by the large firm.

5. **Bargaining Power of Suppliers:** Suppliers can affect an industry through their ability to raise prices or reduce the quality of purchased goods and services. A supplier group is powerful if some of the following apply:
   - The supplier industry is dominated by a few companies, but sells to many.
   - Its product or service is unique and/or it has built up switching costs.
   - Substitutes are not readily available.
   - Suppliers are able to integrate forward and compete directly with their present customers. An example is IBM's willingness in 1980 to open its own personal-computer stores instead of selling only through other established retailers.
   - A purchasing industry buys only a small portion of the supplier group's goods and services and is thus unimportant to the supplier. For example, major oil companies in the 1970s were able to raise prices and reduce services because so many companies that purchased oil products had heavy energy needs and, in the short run, were unable to switch to substitute fuels, such as coal or nuclear power. Wishing to be less dependent on suppliers for the raw material so necessary to produce its synthetic materials, Dupont, a heavy user of oil-based products, chose to buy Conoco, a major oil company.

6. **Relative Power of Other Stakeholders:** Freeman recommends adding this sixth force to Porter's list to include a variety of stakeholder groups from the task environment.[20] Some of these groups are governments, unions, local communities, creditors (if not included with suppliers), trade associations, special-interest groups, and stockholders. The importance of these stakeholders will vary by industry. For example, environmental groups in Maine, Michigan, Oregon, and Iowa successfully fought to pass bills outlawing disposable bottles and cans, and thus deposits for most drink containers are now required. This effectively raised costs across the board, with most impact on the marginal producers who could not internally absorb all of these costs. Although Porter contends that the government influences the level of competitive activity through the previously mentioned five forces, it is sug-

gested here that governments deserve a special mention because of their strong relative power in all industries.

INDUSTRY EVOLUTION

Over time most industries evolve through a series of stages from growth through maturity to eventual decline. The strength of each of the six forces mentioned above varies according to the stage of industry evolution. Based on the product life cycle (to be discussed in Chapter 5), this industry life cycle is useful for explaining and predicting trends among the six forces driving industry competition. For example, when an industry is new, people will often buy the product regardless of price because it fulfills a unique need. As new competitors enter the industry, prices drop as a result of competition. Companies use the experience curve and economies of scale to reduce costs faster than the competition. Companies integrate to reduce costs even further by acquiring their suppliers and distributors. Competitors try to differentiate their products from one another's in order to avoid the fierce price competition common to the "competitive turbulence" part of the growth stage (see Fig. 5.3).

By the time an industry enters maturity, products tend to become more like commodities. As buyers become more sophisticated over time, purchasing decisions are based on better information. Price becomes a dominant concern given a minimum level of quality and features. One example of this trend is the videocassette recorder industry. By 1990, VCRs had reached the point where there were few major differences among them. Consumers realized that since slight improvements cost significantly more money, it made little sense to pay more than the minimum for a VCR. Porter thus argues that "there is a natural force reducing product differentiation over time in an industry."[21] Supporting this tendency is the diffusion of technology from one company to another. For example, when Xerox was facing strong competition from Japanese firms able to sell copiers more cheaply than Xerox, management introduced "competitive benchmarking." In effect, the company purchased a competitor's product in order to take it apart and through "reverse engineering" discover how to get around patented technology to make a similar or better product.

As an industry moves through maturity into decline, its products' growth rate of sales slows and may even begin to decrease. To the extent that exit barriers are low, firms will begin converting their facilities to alternate uses or will sell them to another firm. The industry tends to consolidate around fewer but larger competitors. As in the case of the U.S. major home appliance industry described in the *boxed example* of Maytag (p. 106), the industry changed from being a "fragmented" industry composed of hundreds of appliance manufacturers in the industry's early years to an oligopoly composed of five companies (including Maytag) controlling over 90% of U.S. appliance sales. These firms then realized that they needed access to less mature European and Asian markets if they were to remain profitable in such a competitive industry.

MAYTAG CORPORATION:
EVOLUTION OF THE U.S. MAJOR HOME APPLIANCE INDUSTRY

In 1945, there were approximately 300 U.S. appliance manufacturers in the United States. By 1990, however, the "big four" of Whirlpool, General Electric, A.B. Electrolux (*no* relation to Electrolux Corporation, a U.S. company selling Electrolux-brand vacuum cleaners), and Maytag controlled over 90% of the U.S. market, with Raytheon having a significant part of the remainder. The consolidation of the industry over the period was a result of fierce domestic competition. Emphasis on quality and durability coupled with strong price competition drove the surviving firms to increased efficiencies and a strong concern for customer satisfaction.

Prior to World War II, most appliance manufacturers produced a limited line of appliances derived from one successful product. General Electric made refrigerators. Maytag focused on washing machines. Hotpoint produced electric ranges. Each offered variations of its basic product, but not until 1945 did firms begin to offer full lines of various appliances. By 1955, the major appliance industry began experiencing overcapacity, leading to mergers and acquisitions and a proliferation of national and private brands. Product reliability improved during the 1960s even though real prices (adjusted for inflation) declined around 10%.

During the 1970s, inflation put increasing pressure on operating costs for all manufacturers. Profit margins were squeezed even more and the industry continued to consolidate around fewer firms. Whereas antitrust considerations prevented GE and Whirlpool from acquiring other appliance units, White was able to buy the troubled appliance divisions of all the automobile manufacturers plus Westinghouse's as they were put up for sale.

By the 1980s, most appliance manufacturers offered a full range of products even if they did not make all the items themselves. A company would fill the gaps in its line by putting its own brand name on products it purchased from another manufacturer. Nevertheless, there were some indications that in 1990 this situation might be coming to an end. In his remarks to the annual meeting of stockholders in April 1990, Maytag's Daniel Krumm stated that one of the reasons the company was building a new dishwasher plant was to be able to produce all of its dishwashers itself. CEO Krumm stated that Maytag "must now purchase our medium-price brands from a competitor. There's no future in that!"

The U.S. major home appliance industry faced some significant threats as well as opportunities as it entered the last decade of the twentieth century. After 40 years of rising sales in units, as well as in dollars, the North American market had reached maturity. Future unit sales were expected to grow only 1%–2% annually on average for the foreseeable future. Operating margins had been dropping as appliance manufacturers were forced to hold prices low to be competitive, even though costs kept increasing. In Western Europe, however, a market already 25% larger than the mature North American appliance market, unit sales were expected to grow 5% annually. This figure was expected to increase significantly once Eastern European countries opened their economies to world trade. In addition, the expected economic integration in 1992 of the 12 member countries of the European Community (EC)—the Netherlands, Belgium, Luxembourg, Germany, France, Italy, Denmark, Great Britain, Irish Republic, Greece, Spain, and Portugal—had tremendous implications for the emerging global appliance industry.

STRATEGIC GROUPS AND STRATEGIC MAPPING

In the analysis of a particular industry, it can be useful to categorize the various competitors within that industry into strategic groups. According to Hatten and Hatten, a **strategic group** is a set of business units or firms that "pursue similar strategies with similar resources."[22] Because a corporation's structure and culture tend to reflect the kinds of strategies it follows (to be discussed further in Chapter 8), companies or business units belonging to a particular strategic group within the same industry tend to be strong rivals and tend to be more similar to each other than to competitors in other strategic groups within the same industry. For example, although Chevrolet and Rolls-Royce are a part of the same automobile industry, they have different missions, objectives, and strategies, and thus belong to different strategic groups. They generally have very little in common and pay little attention to each other when planning competitive actions. Ford and Plymouth, however, have a great deal in common with Chevrolet in terms of their similar strategy of producing a high volume of low-priced automobiles targeted for sale to the average person. Consequently, they are strong rivals and are organized and operated in a similar fashion.

Strategic groups in a particular industry can be "mapped" by plotting the market positions of industry competitors on a two-dimensional graph using two strategic variables as the vertical and horizontal axes. *First,* select two broad variables or characteristics that differentiate the companies in an industry from one another. *Second,* plot the firms using these two characteristics as the dimensions. *Third,* draw a circle around those companies that are closest to one another as one strategic group, varying the size of the circle in proportion to the group's share of total industry sales.

As shown in Fig. 4.7, the restaurant chain industry can be mapped by using the dimensions of price and product-line breadth. Other dimensions, such as quality and degree of vertical integration, can also be used in additional graphs of the industry to gain a better understanding of how the various firms in the industry compete. Keep in mind, however, that when choosing the two dimensions, they should *not* be highly correlated; otherwise, the circles on the map will simply lie along the diagonal, providing very little new information other than the obvious. Note that in Fig. 4.7, although product-line breadth generally seems to be correlated with price (that is, the wider the selection of offerings at a restaurant, the higher the price per offering), this is not always the case. Long John Silvers, for example, charges a higher price for its fish offerings than does the typical hamburger-oriented fast food restaurant, even though its offerings are no broader than are those of McDonald's.

MOBILITY BARRIERS

A corporation or business unit within a particular industry or strategic group makes strategic decisions that competitors outside the group cannot easily imitate without substantial costs and a significant amount of time. These obstacles to casual imitation of a firm's strategy form entry barriers. These barriers are of great importance to a strategic manager because their presence in an industry can either reduce or increase the likelihood of competitors in a particular market segment.

| **FIGURE 4.7** | **Mapping Strategic Groups in the U.S. Restaurant Chain Industry** |

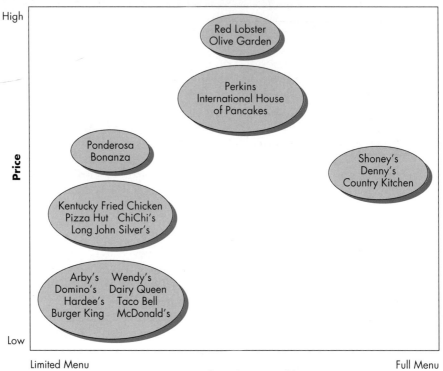

Barriers may not just protect companies in a strategic group from entry by firms outside the industry; they may also provide barriers to moving from one strategic group to another. Porter thus recommends the use of the term *mobility barriers* when doing strategic group analysis. These **mobility barriers** are, according to Porter, "factors that deter the movement of firms from one strategic position to another."[23]

The huge, vertically integrated manufacturing and distribution facilities of General Motors, Chrysler, and Ford acted as a mobility barrier for many years in the U.S. It prevented American Motors from successfully moving outside its niche in small cars and utility vehicles. The heavy costs involved in competing at even a small level in the U.S. acted as a mobility barrier to most foreign-based auto companies, until Volkswagen found a lucrative niche in the 1960s, one that the Japanese soon explored and expanded. Some of the possible entry/mobility barriers and ways in which they can be avoided or overcome are presented in Table 4.2.

STRATEGIC TYPES

In analyzing the level of competitive intensity within a particular industry or strategic group, it is useful to characterize the various competitors for predictive purposes.

TABLE 4.2	Examples of Entry/Mobility Barriers and Ways to Avoid or Overcome Them

Examples of Entry/Mobility Barriers in Some Industries
- High fixed asset requirement (steel industry)
- Heavy advertising expenses (beer industry)
- Scarce raw materials (petroleum industry)
- Difficult government requirements (electric utilities)
- Credit sales required (appliance industry)
- Ability to handle trade-ins (retail auto industry)
- Products protected by patents, trademarks, and trade secrets (drug industry)
- Control of key distribution channels (network television)
- Very low competitive prices (consumer electronics industry)

Ways in Which Entry/Mobility Barriers Can Be Avoided or Overcome
- Find an open niche (Neutrogena's mild soap)
- Find a substitute product (personal computers replace typewriters)
- Develop a technological improvement (P&G's low-fat cooking oil)
- Differentiate product through marketing mix (Zenith's sales of computers to colleges)
- Locate spot where competitors are weak (Toyota's emphasis on low-cost quality)
- Create process improvements (Deere's flexible manufacturing)

According to Miles and Snow, competing firms within a single industry can be categorized on the basis of their general strategic orientation into one of four basic types: the *Defender,* the *Prospector,* the *Analyzer,* and the *Reactor.*[24] Each of these types has its own favorite strategy for responding to the environment, and has its own combination of structure, culture, and processes consistent with that strategy. This distinction helps explain why companies facing similar situations behave differently and why they continue to do so over a long period of time. These general types have the following characteristics:

- **Defenders** are companies with a limited product line that focus on improving the efficiency of their existing operations. This cost orientation makes them unlikely to innovate in new areas. An example of such a corporation is the Adolph Coors Company, which for many years emphasized production efficiency in its one Colorado brewery and virtually ignored marketing.

- **Prospectors** are companies with fairly broad product lines that focus on product innovation and market opportunities. This sales orientation makes them somewhat inefficient. They tend to emphasize creativity over efficiency. An example is the Miller Brewing Company, which successfully promoted "light" beer and generated aggressive, innovative advertising campaigns, but had to close a brand-new brewery when management overestimated market demand.

- **Analyzers** are corporations that operate in at least two different product-market areas, one stable and one variable. In the stable areas, efficiency is emphasized. In the variable areas, innovation is emphasized. An example is Anheuser-Busch, which can take a defender orientation to protect its massive market share in beer and a prospector orientation to generate sales in its snack foods and amusement parks.
- **Reactors** are corporations that lack a consistent strategy-structure-culture relationship. Their (often ineffective) responses to environmental pressures tend to be piecemeal strategic changes. An example is the Pabst Brewing Company, which, because of numerous takeover attempts, has been unable to generate a consistent strategy to keep its sales from dropping.

Dividing the competition into these four categories enables the strategic manager not only to monitor the effectiveness of certain strategic orientations, but also to develop scenarios of future industry developments (discussed later in this chapter).

4.3 SOURCES OF INFORMATION

Studies have shown that much environmental scanning is done on an informal and individual basis. Information is obtained from a variety of sources, such as customers, suppliers, bankers, consultants, publications, personal observations, subordinates, superiors, and peers. For example, scientists and engineers working in a firm's R&D lab can learn about new products and competitors' ideas at professional meetings; someone from the purchasing department, speaking with supplier-representatives' personnel, may also uncover valuable bits of information about a competitor. A study of product innovation in the scientific instrument and machine tool industries found that 80% of all product innovations were initiated by the *customer* in the form of inquiries and complaints.[25] In these industries, the sales force and service departments must be especially vigilant.

Some of the main sources of information about an industry's environment are shown in Fig. 4.8. Because people throughout a corporation can obtain an extraordinary amount of data in any given month, top management must develop a system to get these data from those who obtained them to the people who can integrate them with other information to form a comprehensive environmental assessment.

As one would suspect, research suggests that corporations develop and implement more scanning procedures for following, anticipating, and responding to changes in the activities of *competitors* than of any other stakeholder in the environment.[26] At General Mills, for example, all members of the company have been trained to recognize and tap sources of competitive information. Janitors no longer simply place orders with suppliers of cleaning materials, they also ask about relevant practices at competing firms![27]

There is danger in focusing one's scanning efforts too closely on one's own industry, though. According to research by Snyder, "History teaches that most new developments which threaten existing business practices and technologies do not come from traditional industries."[28] For instance, **technology transfer**, the process of taking new technology from the laboratory to the marketplace, has become an

| FIGURE 4.8 | Sources of Data for Industry Analysis |

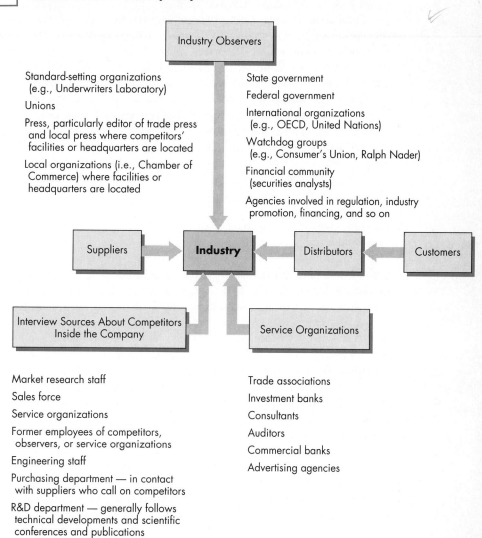

Industry Observers

Standard-setting organizations
(e.g., Underwriters Laboratory)

Unions

Press, particularly editor of trade press
and local press where competitors'
facilities or headquarters are located

Local organizations (i.e., Chamber of
Commerce) where facilities or
headquarters are located

State government

Federal government

International organizations
(e.g., OECD, United Nations)

Watchdog groups
(e.g., Consumer's Union, Ralph Nader)

Financial community
(securities analysts)

Agencies involved in regulation, industry
promotion, financing, and so on

Suppliers → **Industry** ← Distributors ← Customers

Interview Sources About Competitors
Inside the Company

Service Organizations

Market research staff

Sales force

Service organizations

Former employees of competitors,
observers, or service organizations

Engineering staff

Purchasing department — in contact
with suppliers who call on competitors

R&D department — generally follows
technical developments and scientific
conferences and publications

Trade associations

Investment banks

Consultants

Auditors

Commercial banks

Advertising agencies

Source: Adapted/Reprinted with permission of The Free Press, a Division of Macmillan, Inc. from *Competitive Strategy: Techniques for Analyzing Industries and Competitors* by Michael E. Porter. Copyright © 1980 by The Free Press.

important issue in recent decades. Consider just one example. With the development of the integrated circuit, electronics firms, such as Texas Instruments, were able to introduce high-volume, low-cost electronic digital watches. These firms' entry into the watch-making industry took well-established mechanical watchmakers by surprise. Timex, Seiko, and especially the Swiss firms found that their market had changed overnight. Their production facilities, however, had not; and they spent a lot of money buying the new technology.

Most corporations rely on outside organizations to provide them with environmental data. Firms such as A. C. Nielsen Co. provide subscribers with bimonthly data on brand share, retail prices, percentages of stores stocking an item, and percentages of stock-out stores. These data can be used by management to spot regional and national trends as well as to assess market share. Information on market conditions, government regulations, competitors, and new products can be bought from "information brokers." Such firms as FIND/SVP, a New York company, and Finsbury Data Services, owned by Reuters in London, get their data from periodicals, reference books, computer data banks, directors, and experts in the area. Other firms, like Chase Econometrics, offer various data bases plus a software package that enables corporate planners to gain computer access to a large number of key indicators. Typically, the largest corporations spend from $25,000 to $30,000 per year for information services.[29] Close to 6,000 firms in the U.S. and Canada have established their own in-house libraries to deal with the growing mass of available information.[30]

Some companies, however, choose to use industrial espionage or other intelligence-gathering techniques to get their information straight from their competitors. For example, Hitachi Ltd., the large Japanese electronics firm, pleaded guilty to conspiring to transport stolen IBM material to Japan.[31] In 1986, Kellogg Company closed its Battle Creek, Michigan, plant to public tours when it learned that industrial spies from two foreign competitors had gathered valuable information during visits. Experts report that modern "pirates" of information are inflicting billions of dollars worth of damage annually in missed sales and wasted R&D costs. Valuable information can slip out through managers, salespeople, and suppliers. Even cleaning workers have been caught selling trash to rival competitors.[32]

4.4 FORECASTING

Once a business corporation has collected data about its current environmental situation, it must analyze present trends to learn if they will continue into the future. The strategic planning horizon for many large corporations is from five to ten years in the future. A long-term planning horizon is especially necessary for large, capital-intensive corporations, such as automobile or heavy-machinery manufacturers. In these corporations, moving from an accepted proposal to a finished product requires many years. Therefore, most corporations must base their future plans on a forecast, a set of assumptions about what that future will look like. These assumptions can be derived from an entrepreneur's vision, from a head-in-the-sand hope that the future will be similar to the present, or from the opinions of experts. Figure 4.9 depicts the role of forecasting in the strategy formulation process.

THE DANGER OF ASSUMPTIONS

A forecast is nothing more than a leap of faith into the future. Environmental scanning provides reasonably hard data on the present situation, but intuition and

FIGURE 4.9 | The Role of Forecasting

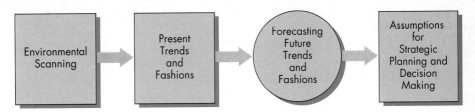

luck are needed to accurately predict the future. Faulty underlying assumptions appear to be the most frequent cause of forecasting errors.[33] Nevertheless, many managers who formulate and implement strategic plans have little or no realization that their success is based on a series of assumptions. Many long-range plans are simply based on projections of the current situation. One example of what can happen when a corporate strategy rests on the very questionable assumption that the future will simply be an extension of the present is that of the Miller Brewing Company, a subsidiary of Philip Morris.

In 1980, Miller Brewing decided to construct a $412 million brewery in Trenton, Ohio. The decision was made after a decade of growth that saw Miller's beer volume increase 640% while that of the industry as a whole grew by only 40%. Miller's strategic managers assumed that with Philip Morris's marketing genius supporting the company, the sky was the limit for Miller beer. Unfortunately, that trend was not to continue. Of the total U.S. population, that percentage aged 18–25 began to drop, and so did the overall demand for beer. The competition also increased its challenge: having been stung by Miller's marketing successes during the 1970s, Anheuser-Busch tripled its advertising budget and launched a $2 billion capital-expansion program. It became an aggressive competitor. Miller's Trenton brewery, completed in 1982, never opened. In 1986, the sales volume of Miller High Life (once the Number Two beer in the U.S.) had declined by 50% since the decade's beginning. Unable to reverse the trend, Miller took a $280 million write-off on the Trenton brewery.[34]

TECHNIQUES

As depicted in Table 4.3, various techniques are used to forecast future situations. Each has its proponents and critics. A study of nearly 500 of the world's largest corporations revealed **trend extrapolation** to be the most widely practiced form of forecasting—over 70% use this technique either occasionally or frequently.[35] Simply stated, extrapolation is the extension of present trends into the future. As shown in the Miller Brewing example, it rests on the assumption that the world is reasonably consistent and changes slowly in the short run. Time-series methods are approaches of this type; these attempt to carry a series of historical events forward into the future. The basic problem with extrapolation is that a historical trend is based on a series of patterns or relationships among so many different variables that a change in any one can drastically alter the future direction of the trend. As a rule of thumb, the further back into the past one can find relevant data supporting the trend, the more confidence one can have in the prediction. Nevertheless, even experts in forecasting admit: "Forecasts that cover a period of two years or more are typically very inaccurate.[36]

As shown in Table 4.3, brainstorming and statistical modeling are also very popular forecasting techniques. **Brainstorming** is a nonquantitative approach requiring simply the presence of people with some knowledge of the situation to be predicted. The basic ground rule is to propose ideas without first mentally screening them. No criticism is allowed. Ideas tend to build on previous ideas until a consensus is reached. This is a good technique to use with operating managers who have more faith in "gut feel" than in more quantitative "number-crunching" techniques.

Statistical modeling is a quantitative technique that attempts to discover causal or at least explanatory factors that link two or more time series together. Examples of statistical modeling are regression analysis and other econometric methods. Although very useful in the grasping of historic trends, statistical modeling, like trend extrapolation, is based on historical data. As the patterns of relationships change, the accuracy of the forecast deteriorates.[37]

Other forecasting techniques, such as *cross-impact analysis, trend-impact analysis,* and *relevance trees,* have not established themselves successfully as regularly employed tools. Research by Klein and Linneman reports that corporate planners

TABLE 4.3	**Degree of Usage of Forecasting Techniques[1]**			
Technique	Top 1,000 U.S. Industrials (n = 215)	Top 100 U.S. Industrials (n = 40)	Top 300 U.S. Non-Industrials (n = 85)	Top 500 Foreign Industrials (n = 105)
Trend extrapolation	73%	70%	74%	72%
Statistical modeling (e.g., regression analysis)	48	61	51	45
Scenarios	57	67	67	61
Relevance trees	5	3	7	4
Simulation	34	45	38	27
Brainstorming	65	61	69	52
Trend-impact analysis	34	33	31	29
Expert opinion/Delphi	33	42	24	35
Morphological analysis	2	0	0	5
Signal monitoring	15	19	14	18
Cross-impact analysis	12	22	11	5

[1] Figures reflect the percentage of respondents indicating either "frequent" or "occasional" use. Respondents had been asked to classify their frequency of technique use as "not used," "rarely used," "used occasionally," or "used frequently."

Source: H. E. Klein and R. E. Linneman, "Environmental Assessment: An International Study of Corporate Practices," *Journal of Business Strategy* (Summer 1984), p. 72. Copyright © 1984 by Warren, Gorham & Lamont, Inc. Reprinted by permission. All rights reserved.

found these techniques to be complicated, time-consuming, expensive, and academic. Usage was therefore concentrated among the very largest companies and there it was generally used to provide input for scenario-writing.[38]

Research further reports that **scenario-writing** appears to be the most widely used forecasting technique after trend extrapolation. Among corporations in the top Fortune 1000 Industrials, the usage of scenarios increased from 22% in 1977 to 57% in 1981. Klein and Linneman predict that usage of this popular forecasting technique will increase, but point out that "most companies follow a very informal scenario-writing approach with little reliance on rigorous methodologies."[39] The scenario thus may be merely a written description of some future state, in terms of key variables and issues, or it may be generated in combination with other forecasting techniques.

A more complex version used by General Electric (depicted in Fig. 4.10) is based on a Delphi panel of experts, a trend-impact analysis, and a cross-impact analysis. The **Delphi technique** involves an anonymous panel of experts who are asked individually to estimate the probability of certain events' occurrence in the future. After seeing the anonymous responses from the other experts on the panel, each member of the panel is given several opportunities to revise his/her estimate. **Cross-impact analysis** (CIA), which is typically done on a computer, produces a matrix showing the interaction of the various likely developments that had been generated earlier by the Delphi panel. For example, in the lower right corner of Fig. 4.10, the CIA matrix indicates a prediction that the development of usable nuclear energy by the fusion (instead of the current fission) process will probably result in oil price-cuts by the members of OPEC and an increase in safety and environmental laws regarding the mining and burning of coal. **Trend-impact analysis** (TIA), in contrast, begins with an outside expert's or a Delphi panel's forecast of a trend or phenomenon. For example, if someone were interested in the future of cigarette smoking, one might use extrapolation to forecast a continuing downward trend in the number of smokers. Various possible influencing factors are then added to the forecast, and predictions of three or more alternative future trends result. For example, the likelihood that campaigns against public smoking will increase might cause the trend in number of smokers to decline faster. The invention of smokeless tobacco might cause the trend to reverse its decline. The output from the Delphi panel, the cross-impact analysis, and the trend-impact analysis are then used in the development of a series of probable future scenarios.

In his book *Competitive Advantage*, Michael Porter strongly recommends the use of scenarios because they (1) allow a firm to move away from use of dangerous, single-point forecasts of the future in instances when the future cannot be predicted, and (2) encourage managers to make their assumptions explicit.[40] He recommends the use of **industry scenarios,** which utilize variables from the societal environment in terms of their effect on the key stakeholders in a corporation's task environment (industry). The process may operate as follows:[41]

1. **Examine possible shifts in the societal variables** (e.g., economic, sociocultural, technological, and political-legal). Begin with the obvious variables listed in Table 4.1 and included in Fig. 4.3 and decide which of them might be

| **FIGURE 4.10** | **Scenario Construction at General Electric** |

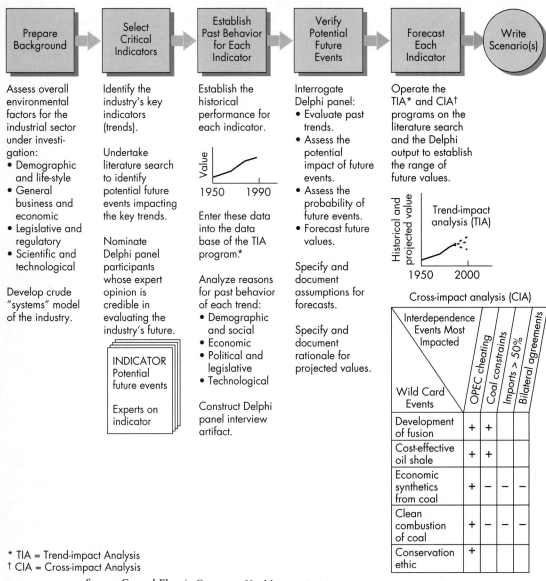

Prepare Background

Assess overall environmental factors for the industrial sector under investigation:
• Demographic and life-style
• General business and economic
• Legislative and regulatory
• Scientific and technological

Develop crude "systems" model of the industry.

Select Critical Indicators

Identify the industry's key indicators (trends).

Undertake literature search to identify potential future events impacting the key trends.

Nominate Delphi panel participants whose expert opinion is credible in evaluating the industry's future.

INDICATOR
Potential future events

Experts on indicator

Establish Past Behavior for Each Indicator

Establish the historical performance for each indicator.

Enter these data into the data base of the TIA program.*

Analyze reasons for past behavior of each trend:
• Demographic and social
• Economic
• Political and legislative
• Technological

Construct Delphi panel interview artifact.

Verify Potential Future Events

Interrogate Delphi panel:
• Evaluate past trends.
• Assess the potential impact of future events.
• Assess the probability of future events.
• Forecast future values.

Specify and document assumptions for forecasts.

Specify and document rationale for projected values.

Forecast Each Indicator

Operate the TIA* and CIA† programs on the literature search and the Delphi output to establish the range of future values.

Write Scenario(s)

Trend-impact analysis (TIA)

Cross-impact analysis (CIA)

Interdependence Events Most Impacted / Wild Card Events	OPEC cheating	Coal constraints	Imports > 50%	Bilateral agreements
Development of fusion	+	+		
Cost-effective oil shale	+	+		
Economic synthetics from coal	+	−	−	−
Clean combustion of coal	+	−	−	−
Conservation ethic	+			

* TIA = Trend-impact Analysis
† CIA = Cross-impact Analysis

Source: General Electric Company. Used by permission.

changing to create a strategic issue. In order to identify those issues of most importance to the corporation and/or the industry, plot these variables on the issues priority matrix depicted in Fig. 4.4.

2. **Identify uncertainties in each of the six forces from the task environment** (e.g., competitors, buyers, suppliers, likely substitutes, potential entrants, and

other key stakeholders) as depicted in Fig. 4.6. Make sure that all the high-priority strategic issues identified in the first step are specified in terms of the appropriate forces in the task environment.

3. **Identify the causal factors behind the uncertainties.** These sources of uncertainty can be inside the industry (e.g., competitor behavior) or outside the industry (e.g., new regulations). It is likely that many of these causal factors were identified earlier when the societal environment was analyzed. It is also likely that new ones surfaced when the task environment was analyzed.

4. **Make a range of plausible assumptions about each important causal factor.** For example, if the price of oil is a causal factor, make reasonable assumptions about its future level in terms of high, low, and most probable price. A trend-impact analysis may be of some value here.

5. **Combine assumptions about individual causal factors into internally consistent scenarios.** Put various combinations of the assumptions together into sets of scenarios. Because one assumption may affect another, ensure that the scenarios are internally consistent. A simplified cross-impact analysis may be of some value in one's determining the interaction of likely trends. For example, if a scenario includes the assumptions of high oil prices and a low level of economic inflation, that scenario is not internally consistent and should be rejected. (It is an unlikely event because high oil prices tend to drive inflation upward.)

6. **Analyze the industry situation that would prevail under each scenario.** For example, if one scenario assumes that generic drugs will be more in demand than brand name drugs, the situation in the drug industry under that assumption will be very different than under the assumption that the demand for generic drugs will be negligible. For example, an industry dominated by generic drugs would have low profit margins for all firms and a very heavy degree of competition. It is likely that in that industry situation a few firms would leave the drug industry.

7. **Determine the sources of competitive advantage under each scenario.** For example, in an industry dominated by generic drugs, the combination of low price backed up by low operating costs would provide competitive advantage to a firm. If brand name drugs dominated, the combination of strong advertising, high-quality production, and heavy promotion would provide competitive advantage to the firm using them.

8. **Predict competitors' behavior under each scenario.** As the industry moves toward a particular scenario, each competitor will make some adjustment. Some might leave the industry. New competitors might enter. Using each competitor's history and what is known about its management, estimate what each competitor is likely to do. Once this is done, management should be able to specify the *strategic factors* that are necessary for success (opportunities) as well as those that could cause failure (threats), in a variety of future scenarios. In order to choose the ones most likely to occur, one can also attach probabilities to each of the developed scenarios.[42]

4.5 SYNTHESIS OF EXTERNAL STRATEGIC FACTORS—EFAS

Once strategic managers have scanned the external societal and task environments and identified strategic factors for their particular corporation, they may wish to summarize their analysis of these strategic factors using a form such as that given in Table 4.4. This form (External Strategic Factors Analysis Summary—EFAS) is one way to organize the external strategic factors into the generally accepted categories of opportunities and threats as well as to analyze how well a particular company is responding to these specific factors in light of the perceived importance of these

TABLE 4.4 | **External Strategic Factor Analysis Summary (EFAS): Maytag as Example**

External Strategic Factors	Weight	Rating	Weighted Score	Comments
	1	2	3	4	5
Opportunities:				
■ Economic integration of European Community	.20	4	.80	Acquisition of Hoover
■ Demographics favor quality appliances	.10	5	.50	Maytag quality
■ Economic development of Asia	.05	1	.05	Low Maytag presence
■ Opening of Eastern Europe	.05	2	.10	Will take time
■ Trend to "Super Stores"	.10	2	.20	Maytag weak in this channel
Threats:				
■ Increasing government regulations	.10	4	.40	Well positioned
■ Strong U.S. competition	.10	4	.40	Well positioned
■ Whirlpool and Electrolux strong globally	.15	3	.45	Hoover weak globally
■ Fuzzy logic technology	.05	1	.05	Questionable
■ Predicted recession	.10	2	.20	High Maytag debt load
Total Weighted Score	**1.00**		**3.15**	

Notes: 1. List opportunities and threats (5–10 each) in column 1.

2. Weight each factor from 1.0 (Most Important) to 0.0 (Not Important) in Column 2 based on that factor's probable impact on the company's strategic position. **The total weights must sum to 1.00.**

3. Rate each factor from 5 (Outstanding) to 1 (Poor) in Column 3 based on the company's response to that factor.

4. Multiply each factor's weight times its rating to obtain each factor's weighted score in Column 4.

5. Use Column 5 (comments) for rationale used for each factor.

6. Add the weighted scores to obtain the **total weighted score** for the company in Column 4. This tells how well the company is responding to the strategic factors in its external environment.

factors to the company. To use the EFAS form given in Table 4.4, complete the following steps:

First, identify and list in Column 1 about 5 to 10 opportunities and about the same number of threats. *Second,* assign a **weight** in Column 2 to each factor from 1.0 (Most Important) to 0.0 (Not Important) based on that factor's probable impact on a particular company's strategic position. (All weights must sum to 1.0 regardless of the number of strategic factors.) *Third,* assign a **rating** in Column 3 to each factor from 5 (Outstanding) to 1 (Poor) based on that particular company's current response to that particular factor.

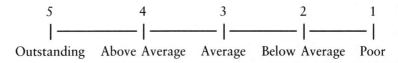

$$5 \qquad 4 \qquad 3 \qquad 2 \qquad 1$$

Outstanding   Above Average   Average   Below Average   Poor

Fourth, multiply the weight (Column 2) for each factor times its rating (Column 3) to obtain that factor's **weighted score** in Column 4. This results in a weighted score for each factor. *Fifth,* use Column 5 (comments) to note why a particular factor was selected and how its weight and rating were estimated. *Sixth,* add the weighted scores for all the external factors in Column 4 to determine the total weighted score for that particular company. The *total weighted score* ranges from 5.0 (Outstanding) to 1.0 (Poor) with 3.0 as Average and indicates how well a particular company is responding to current and expected strategic factors in its external environment. The score can be used to compare that firm to other firms in its industry.

As an example of this procedure, Table 4.4 includes a number of external strategic factors for Maytag Corporation with corresponding weights, ratings, and weighted scores provided.

Once strategic managers have completed their analysis of a firm's external strategic factors in terms of opportunities and threats, they must do the same for the corporation's internal strategic factors in terms of strengths and weaknesses. (A form similar to that shown in Table 4.4 may then be completed for an *Internal Strategic Factors Analysis Summary—IFAS;* see Table 5.3) This is the topic covered next in Chapter 5.

SUMMARY AND CONCLUSION

Anyone concerned with how strategic decisions are made in large corporations should be aware of the impact of the external environment on top management and the board of directors. Long-run developments in the economic, technological, political-legal, and sociocultural aspects of the societal environment strongly affect the corporation's activities through the more immediate pressures in its task environment.

Before strategy can be formulated, strategy makers must scan the external environment for possible opportunities and threats. They must identify strategic issues to be monitored, as well as assess which are likely to affect the corporation in the future. They must investigate the six forces driving industry competition to find which are becoming stronger and which are becoming weaker. Then they must analyze the resulting information and disseminate it to the people involved in strategic planning and decision making.

Just as environmental scanning provides an understanding of present trends in the environment, forecasting provides assumptions about the future that are crucial for strategic management. Most modern corporations use the techniques of trend extrapolation, scenario-writing, brainstorming, and statistical modeling to predict their future environment. Even if the predictions prove to be wrong, the very act of scanning and forecasting the environment helps managers take a broader perspective. These techniques also help prevent the development of reactive managers, who dare not take the time to plan for the future because they are caught up in the crises and problems of the present. Ward Hagan, Chief Executive Officer of Warner-Lambert, makes a strong argument in favor of environmental scanning and forecasting:

> Nobody can plan accurately, strategically, five years ahead. But the intellectual discipline that it imposes on operating people once a year is the best possible medicine I know for clear, sequential thinking.[43]

DISCUSSION QUESTIONS

1. Why is environmental uncertainty an important concept in strategic management?

2. Discuss how a development in a corporation's societal environment can affect the corporation through its task environment. Provide an example.

3. How can one identify strategic factors in a particular corporation's external environment?

4. What can a corporation do to ensure that information about strategic environmental factors gets to the attention of strategy makers?

5. What factors, according to Porter, determine the level of competitive intensity among companies? Briefly describe each factor.

6. Describe the importance of entry/mobility barriers in an industry. Provide an example.

7. According to Miles and Snow, competing firms within a single industry can be classified into four basic types based on their generic strategy orientation. Briefly describe each of these four types.

8. Why is industrial espionage becoming an important issue in strategic management?

9. If most long-term forecasts are usually incorrect, why bother doing them?

10. Compare and contrast trend extrapolation with the writing of scenarios, as forecasting techniques.

NOTES

1. J. D. Thompson, *Organizations in Action* (New York: McGraw-Hill, 1967). Copyright © 1967. Reproduced by permission of McGraw-Hill, Inc.

2. W. Shanklin, "Fortune 500 Dropouts," *Planning Review* (May 1986), pp. 12–17.

3. S. R. Craig, "Seeking Strategic Advantage with Technology? Focus on Customer Value!" *Long Range Planning* (April 1986), p. 53.

4. The concept that the business organization must be in proper "alignment" with its environment in order to be successful is a central feature of work in business policy and strategic management. See C. E. Summer et al. in "Doctoral Education in the Field of Business Policy and Strategy," *Journal of Management* (June 1990), pp. 364–365.

5. R. B. Duncan, "Characteristics of Organizational Environments and Perceived Environmental Uncertainty," *Administrative Science Quarterly* (September 1972), pp. 313–327.

6. N. H. Snyder, "Environmental Volatility, Scanning Intensity and Organization Performance," *Journal of Contemporary Business* (September 1981), p. 7.

7. H. E. Klein and R. E. Linneman, "Environmental Assessment: An International Study of Corporate Practices," *Journal of Business Strategy* (Summer 1984), p. 67.

8. J. E. Dutton and E. Ottensmeyer, "Strategic Issue Management Systems: Forms, Functions, and Contexts," *Academy of Management Review* (April 1987), pp. 355–365.

P. Lorange, M. F. S. Morton, and S. Ghoshal, *Strategic Control* (St. Paul, Minn.: West Publishing Co., 1986), pp. 101–104.

9. P. V. Jenster, "Using Critical Success Factors in Planning," *Long Range Planning* (August 1987), p. 108.

10. J. B. Thomas, "Interpreting Strategic Issues: Effects of Strategy and the Information-Processing Structure of Top Management Teams," *Academy of Management Journal* (June 1990), pp. 286–306.

11. M. Javidan, "The Impact of Environmental Uncertainty on Long-Range Planning and Practices of the U.S. Savings and Loan Industry," *Strategic Management Journal* (October-December 1984), pp. 381–392.

12. S. C. Jain, "Environmental Scanning in U.S. Corporations," *Long Range Planning* (April 1984), p. 119.

13. C. Wallis, "The Child-Care Dilemma," *Time* (June 22, 1987), pp. 54–60.

14. P. Johnson, "Our Aging Population—The Implications for Business and Government," *Long Range Planning* (April 1990), p. 57.

15. J. Naisbitt, *Megatrends* (New York: Warner Books, 1982).

16. A. Toffler, "Powershift," *Newsweek* (October 15, 1990), pp. 86–92.

   E. Reingold, "Facing the 'Totally New and Dynamic,'" *Time* (January 22, 1990), pp. 6–7.

17. M. E. Porter, *Competitive Strategy* (New York: The Free Press, 1980), p. 3.

18. This summary of the forces driving competitive strategy is taken from Porter, *Competitive Strategy*, pp. 7–29.

19. *Ibid., p. 23.*

20. R. E. Freeman, *Strategic Management: A Stakeholder Approach* (Boston: Pitman Publishing, 1984), pp. 140–142.

21. Porter, *Competitive Strategy*, p. 170.

22. K. J. Hatten and M. L. Hatten, "Strategic Groups, Asymmetrical Mobility Barriers, and Contestability," *Strategic Management Journal* (July-August 1987), p. 329.

23. Porter, *Competitive Strategy*, pp. 133–134.

24. R. E. Miles and C. C. Snow, *Organizational Strategy, Structure, and Process* (New York: McGraw-Hill, 1978).

25. R. T. Pascale, "Perspective on Strategy: The Real Story Behind Honda's Success," *California Management Review* (Spring 1981), p. 70.

26. B. Rosenbloom and R. V. Tripuraneni, "Strategic Planning Catches On in U.S. Retailers," *Long Range Planning* (August 1985), p. 59.

27. D. C. Smith and J. E. Prescott, "Demystifying Competitive Analysis," *Planning Review* (September/October 1987), p. 13. For more in-depth information on the gathering of competitor intelligence, refer to the entire September/October 1987 issue of *Planning Review*.

28. Snyder, "Environmental Volatility," p. 16.

29. C. Cox, "Planning in a Changing Environment: The Search for External Data," in *Handbook of Business Strategy, 1985/86 Yearbook*, edited by W. D. Guth (Boston: Warren, Gorham, and Lamont, 1985), p. 5.2.

30. J. L. Roberts, "As Information Swells, Firms Open Libraries," *Wall Street Journal* (September 25, 1983), p. 25.

31. J. Drinkhall, "Hitachi Ltd. Pleads Guilty in IBM Case," *Wall Street Journal* (February 9, 1983), p. 4.

32. G. L. Miles, "Information Thieves Are Now Corporate Enemy No. 1," *Business Week* (May 5, 1986), pp. 120–125.

33. S. P. Schnaars, "How to Develop and Use Scenarios," *Long Range Planning* (February 1987), p. 106.

34. J. Merwin, "A Billion in Blunders," *Forbes* (December 1, 1986), p. 104.

35. Klein and Linneman, "Environmental Assessment," p. 72.

36. S. Makridakis and S. C. Wheelwright, "Introduction to Management Forecasting," *The Handbook of Forecasting* (New York: John Wiley and Sons, 1982), p. 8.

37. *Ibid.*, p. 6.

38. Klein and Linneman, "Environmental Assessment," p. 72.

39. *Ibid.*, p. 73.

40. M. E. Porter, *Competitive Advantage* (New York: The Free Press, 1985), p. 447.

41. This process of scenario development is adapted from Porter, *Competitive Advantage*, pp. 448–470.

42. For further information on forecasting, see S. Makridakis and S. C. Wheelwright, *Forecasting Methods for Management*, 5th ed. (New York: John Wiley and Sons, 1989).

43. M. Magnet, "How Top Managers Make a Company's Toughest Decisions," *Fortune* (March 18, 1985), p. 55.

CHAPTER FIVE

Internal Scanning and Analysis

CHAPTER OUTLINE

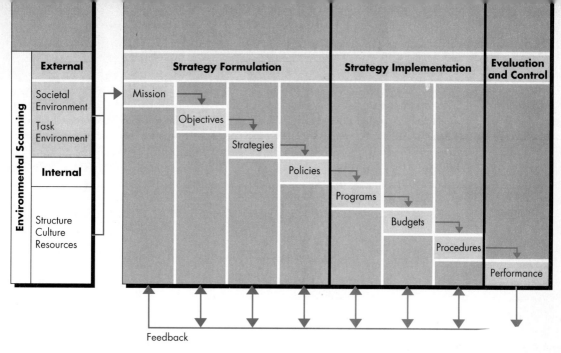

STRATEGIC MANAGEMENT MODEL

separate; discontinuous [handwritten annotation]

Competitive advantage . . . stems from the many discrete activities a firm performs in designing, producing, marketing, delivering, and supporting its product. . . . A firm gains competitive advantage by performing these strategically important activities more cheaply or better than its competitors.[1]

Michael Porter

When Barry Gibbons arrived at Burger King in 1989 as its new CEO, he knew the fast food chain had lots of problems—questionable marketing, dirty restaurants, an unimaginative menu, and poor service. The biggest problem was that no one seemed to know which was doing the most damage. During his first three months on the job, Gibbons established an intelligence network that included employee and supplier surveys and the installation of an 800-number hot line for customer complaints. He also hired "mystery customers" to visit every Burger King restaurant once a month and report on their dining experience. This approach to internal environmental scanning resulted in 80,000 reports and thousands of calls from customers every month. From this information, Gibbons was able to identify the internal strategic factors that were helping and hurting the company, and therefore turn the company around. As a result of significant changes, operating results rose 25% during the last quarter of fiscal year 1989 compared to the year before. In 1990's first quarter the

123

company posted its best same-store sales growth since 1986. According to Gibbons, the key to his success was in "telling people what's happening to the organization, where it's been, who you are, what you're going to do, and what you stand for."[2]

Barry Gibbons's experience at Burger King indicates the importance of internal scanning and analysis. Before deciding which possible strategies are appropriate for the corporation's future, top management should scan and analyze not only the external environment, but also the firm's own internal situation—the environment within the firm itself.

5.1 APPROACHES TO INTERNAL SCANNING AND ANALYSIS

Strategic managers should identify those variables within their company that may be important strengths or weaknesses. A variable is a strength if it provides a company a competitive advantage. It is something the firm does or has the potential to do particularly well relative to the abilities of existing or potential competitors. A variable is a weakness if it is something the corporation does poorly or doesn't have the capacity to do although its competitors have that capacity. Evaluate the importance of these variables to ascertain if they are **internal strategic factors**—those particular strengths and weaknesses that will help determine the future of the company. This can be done by comparing measures of these variables with measures of (1) the company's past performance, (2) the company's key competitors, and (3) the industry as a whole. To the extent that a variable (such as a firm's financial situation) is significantly different from the firm's own past, its key competitors, or the industry average, the variable is likely to be a strategic factor and should be considered in strategic decisions.

Strategic managers can scan and analyze internal variables by following one or a combination of four distinct approaches: 7-S Framework, PIMS analysis, value chain analysis, and functional analysis.

7-S FRAMEWORK

Popularized by Peters and Waterman in their book *In Search of Excellence*, the 7-S Framework approach to internal scanning and analysis involves gathering information on seven organizational variables, the seven S's: *structure, strategy, staff, management style, systems and procedures, skills,* and *shared values.*[3] These variables form a pattern that managers must somehow balance to be successful. This approach was developed by the management consulting firm McKinsey and Company and has been used by many business corporations to assess their internal situation. Unfortunately, this approach has not always been fruitful, so companies have looked to other methods for additional insight.[4]

PIMS ANALYSIS

A current research effort to help pinpoint relevant internal strategic factors for business corporations is being made by the Strategic Planning Institute. Its *PIMS*

Program (Profit Impact of Market Strategy) is composed of various anal[y] data bank containing about 100 items of information on the strategic experien[ce] nearly 3,000 strategic business units throughout North America and Europe, [f] periods ranging from 2 to 12 years. The research conducted with the data has been aimed at discovering the empirical "principles" that determine which strategy, under which conditions, produces what results in terms of return on investment and cash flows, regardless of the specific product or services. To date, PIMS research has identified nine major strategic factors that account for around 80% of the variation in profitability across the businesses in the data base.[5] In working with these factors, the Strategic Planning Institute has prepared profiles of high return on investment (ROI) companies as contrasted with low ROI companies. They found that the companies with high rates of return had the following characteristics:

- Low investment intensity (the amount of fixed capital and working capital required to produce a dollar of sales).
- High market share.
- High relative product quality.
- High capacity utilization.
- High operating effectiveness (the ratio of actual to expected employee productivity).
- Low direct costs per unit, relative to competition.[6]

These and other PIMS research findings are controversial. For example, PIMS research has consistently reported that a large market share should lead to greater profitability.[7] The reason appears to be that high market share results in low unit costs because of economies of scale. Unfortunately, several studies have found that high market share does not always lead to profitability. Firms selling products of high quality relative to the competition have been found to be very profitable even though they do not have large market share.[8] PIMS researchers respond, however, that the single most important factor affecting a business unit's performance relative to its competitors' is the quality of its products or services. They also state that market leaders tend to have products of higher quality relative to those of its competitors and market followers.[9]

From a practitioner's point of view, the most important criticism of PIMS research is that the "significant predictors of performance (investment intensity, market share, relative product quality, capacity utilization, etc.) generally have tended to be variables outside of management's control, at least in the short run."[10] As a result of these and other limitations, one can conclude that we are still quite a distance away from discovering universal strategic laws.

Nevertheless, the PIMS program is useful in helping strategic managers identify key internal variables, such as investment intensity, market share, product quality, capacity utilization, operating effectiveness, and direct costs per unit. In the assessment of a corporation's relative strengths and weaknesses, these factors can be measured and compared with those of other firms in the same industry. The resulting *PAR ROI Report* calculates for the company a "normal" or expected level of ROI given the company's scores on key variables. If the company is not achieving this level of return on investment, the PIMS data base can generate a "look-alikes"

examines how businesses starting with similar strategic profiles were able
higher profits. These reports then suggest which internal variables the
hould change to improve performance.[11]

AIN ANALYSIS

in analysis, as proposed by Porter, is a way of examining the nature and
extent of the synergies that do or do not exist between the internal activities of a
corporation. The systematic examination of individual value activities can lead to a
better understanding of a corporation's strengths and weaknesses. According to
Porter, "Every firm is a collection of activities that are performed to design, produce,
market, deliver, and support its product. All of these activities can be represented
using a value chain [shown in Figure (5.1)]. . . . Differences among competitor value
chains are a key source of competitive advantage."[12]

First, examine the value chain of a particular product or service in terms of the
various activities involved in the production of a product or service. As depicted in
Fig. 5.1, Porter identifies five **primary** activities that usually occur in any business
corporation: (1) inbound logistics of raw materials, (2) operations, (3) outbound
logistics of the finished goods, (4) marketing and sales, and (5) customer service—
and four **support** activities: (1) the procurement process, (2) technology development, (3) human resource management, and (4) the infrastructure of planning,
accounting, finance, legal, government affairs, and quality management.

Second, examine the "linkages" among the product's or service's value activities. Linkages are the connections between the way one value activity is per-

| FIGURE 5.1 | The Value Chain |

Source: Adapted from Michael E. Porter, *Competitive Advantage: Creating and Sustaining Superior
Performance* (New York: The Free Press, 1985), p. 37. Reprinted with permission of The Free Press,
a Division of Macmillan, Inc. Copyright © 1985 by The Free Press.

formed and the cost of performance of another activity. In seeking ways for a corporation to gain competitive advantage in the marketplace, the same function can be performed in different ways with different results. For example, quality inspection of 100% of output instead of the usual 10% would increase production costs, but that increase might be more than offset by the savings obtained from the reduction in the number of repair people needed to fix defective products and the increase in the amount of salespeople's time devoted to selling instead of exchanging already-sold, but defective, products.

Third, examine the potential synergies among the corporation's products or business units. Not only does each value element, such as advertising or manufacturing, include an inherent economy of scale in which activities are conducted at their lowest possible cost per unit of output, but economies of scope across elements as well. Such *economies of scope* result when the value chains of two separate products or services share activities, such as the same marketing channels or manufacturing facilities. For example, the cost of joint production of multiple products can be less than the cost of separate production. The same can be true of marketing. Ralston Purina, a successful marketer of consumer goods, bought Union Carbide's battery business because it could apply its existing expertise in the marketing of its current products to the value chains of the acquired Eveready and Energizer brands.

FUNCTIONAL ANALYSIS

One of the simplest ways to scan and analyze the internal environment of a corporation is through functional analysis. Ansoff, an authority in strategic management, proposes that a corporation's skills and resources can be organized into a "competence profile" according to the typical business functions of marketing, finance, research and development, and operations, among others.[13] The strategic management model depicted in the figure that begins each chapter agrees with Ansoff and proposes that strategic managers conduct internal scanning and analysis by examining the corporation's current *structure, culture,* and *resources.* Because of its simplicity and widespread usage, functional analysis is recommended both in this chapter and in the strategic audit presented earlier in Chapter 2.

5.2 STRUCTURE

The structure of a corporation is often defined in terms of communication, authority, and work flow. It is the corporation's pattern of relationships, its "anatomy." It is a formal arrangement of roles and relationships of people, so that the work is directed toward meeting the goals and accomplishing the mission of the corporation. Sometimes it is referred to as the chain of command, and it is often graphically described by an organization chart.[14]

An understanding of how a particular corporation is structured is very useful in the formulation of a strategy. If the structure is compatible with a proposed change in strategy, it is a corporate strength. If, however, the structure is not compatible with either the present or proposed strategy, it is a definite weakness, and will act to keep the strategy from being implemented properly. Intel Corporation, for example, has had some problems because its successful growth strategy became incompatible with its centralized decision-making structure. The company grew too big and its markets too turbulent for the CEO, Andy Grove, to control it closely. Opportunities were in danger of being missed because of managers' dependence on Grove for guidance.[15]

A corporation's particular structure can predispose its strategic managers toward the selection of one strategy over another.[16] For example, research has revealed that diversified corporations using a divisional structure are more likely to move into international activities than are centralized companies using a functional structure.[17]

Although there is an almost infinite variety of structural forms, certain basic types predominate in modern complex organizations. These are simple, functional, divisional, and conglomerate structures.[18] Figure 5.2 illustrates these basic struc-

| **FIGURE 5.2** | **Basic Structures of Corporations** |

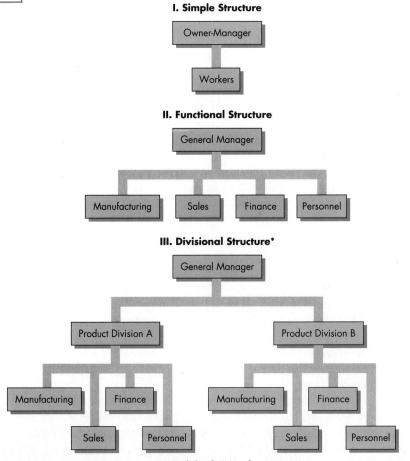

* Conglomerate structure is a variant of the divisional structure.

tures. Generally speaking, each structure tends to support some corporate strategies over others.[19]

- **Simple** structure has no functional or product categories and is appropriate for a small, entrepreneur-dominated company with one or two product lines that operates in a reasonably small, easily identifiable market niche. Employees tend to be generalists and jacks-of-all-trades.
- **Functional** structure is appropriate for a medium-sized firm with several product lines in one industry. Employees tend to be specialists in the business functions important to that industry, such as manufacturing, marketing, finance, and human resources.
- **Divisional** structure is appropriate for a large corporation with many product lines in several *related* industries. Employees tend to be functional specialists organized according to product/market distinctions. General Motors, for example, groups its various auto lines into the separate divisions of Chevrolet, Pontiac, Oldsmobile, Buick, and Cadillac. Management attempts to find some synergy among divisional activities through the use of committees and horizontal linkages.
- **Conglomerate** structure is appropriate for a large corporation with many product lines in several *unrelated* industries. A variant of the divisional structure, the conglomerate structure (sometimes called a holding company), is typically an assemblage of separate firms operating under one corporate umbrella. Employees are functional specialists as in the divisional structure, but the holding company nature of the corporation prevents any attempt at gaining synergy among the divisions.

If the current basic structure of a corporation does not easily support a strategy under consideration, top management must decide if the proposed strategy is feasible or if the structure should be changed to a more advanced structure such as the SBU, matrix, or network. Additional information regarding advanced structures is presented in Chapter 8 under strategy implementation.

5.3 CULTURE

A **corporation's culture** is the collection of beliefs, expectations, and values *learned* and *shared* by the corporation's members and *transmitted* from one generation of employees to another.[20] These create norms (rules of conduct) that define acceptable behavior from top management to the operative employee. Myths and rituals, often unrecorded, that emerge over time will emphasize certain norms or values and explain why a certain aspect of the culture is important. Like the retelling of the vision and perseverance of the founder(s) of the corporation, the myth is often tied closely to the corporate mission.

Corporate culture shapes the behavior of people in the corporation. Analysts Schwartz and Davis point out: "Apparently, the well-run corporations of the world have distinctive cultures that are somehow responsible for their ability to create, implement, and maintain their world leadership positions."[21] Because these cultures

Maytag Corporation: Culture as a Key Strength

In 1990, the Maytag Corporation still reflected the strong ideas of Maytag Company founder F. L. Maytag. The corporate headquarters were housed on the second floor of a relatively small and modest building. Built in 1961, the Newton, Iowa, building also housed Maytag Company administrative offices on the first floor. Responding to a comment from outside observers that the corporation had "spartan" offices, Leonard Hadley, Chief Operating Officer, looked around at his rather small, windowless office and said, "See for yourself. We want to keep corporate staff to a minimum." Hadley felt that the headquarters' location, coupled with the fact that most of the corporate officers had originally been with the Maytag Company, resulted in an overall top management concern for product quality and financial conservatism.

When asked to discuss specific resources that gave the corporation a competitive edge, Chairman and CEO Daniel Krumm pointed to the firm's roots and focused on *dedication to quality* above corporate perquisites.

That, of course, has been Maytag's hallmark for as long as any of us can remember. We believe quality and reliability are, ultimately, what the consumer wants. That has been a challenge to us as we have acquired companies that may have had a different emphasis, but we have made significant recent strides in improving the quality of all our products.

have a powerful influence on the behavior of managers, they can strongly affect a corporation's ability to shift its strategic direction. See the *boxed example* of Maytag for how its corporate culture affects the company's strategic managers.

Corporate culture generally reflects the mission of firms. It gives a corporation a sense of identity: "This is who we are. This is what we do. This is what we stand for." The culture includes the dominant orientation of the company.[22] Some companies are *market-oriented*. Like IBM and John Deere, they define themselves in terms of their customers and their customers' needs. For example, one of the secrets given for the success of Deere and Company during a period of agricultural recession was its rural roots. Unlike International Harvester, which had its headquarters in downtown Chicago, Deere has its headquarters in East Moline, Illinois, in the heart of an agricultural region responsible for two of the nation's major crops, corn and soybeans. Deere has "geographical awareness, because most of its executives live on a farm or near one. . . ."[23]

Other companies may be *material-* or *product-oriented*. They define themselves in terms of the material they work on, the product they make, or the service they provide. They are first and foremost oil companies, steel companies, railroads, banks, or hospitals. This means that the people working for the company tend to identify themselves in the same way. They don't just work for a company; they *are* truckers, railroaders, bankers. This heavy emphasis on material or product can partially explain why some industries, such as the automobile or steel industry, have their own distinct culture that reflects and is reflected in the individual cultures of the member companies.[24] This sharing of a common set of beliefs, values, and assumptions makes it easier for people to move among companies within the same industry than to move to companies in other industries with a different culture. For example, when he left Ford Motor Company, Lee Iacocca stated that he had no interest in pursuing possible offers from International Paper, Lockheed, or Tandy Corporation. Said Iacocca, ". . . cars were in my blood."[25]

Other companies are *technology-oriented*. These companies define themselves in terms of the technology they are organized to exploit. Eastman Kodak, for example, ignored the development of xerography and almost missed out on the change to electronic photography because of its strong commitment to the chemical film technology pioneered by George Eastman. Similarly, high-tech firms in Silicon Valley think of themselves primarily as technological entrepreneurs.

The managers' understanding of a corporation's (or division's) culture is thus imperative if the firm is to be managed strategically. As suggested in Chapter 4's discussion of environmental scanning, an organization's culture can produce a **strategic myopia,** in which strategic managers fail to perceive the significance of changing external conditions because they are partially blinded by strongly held common beliefs. In this instance, a strongly held corporate culture can become a major deterrent to success at a time when the corporation most needs to change its strategic direction.[26]

An additional problem with a strong culture is that a change in mission, objectives, strategies, or policies is not likely to be successful if it is in opposition to the accepted culture of the corporation.[27] Foot-dragging and even sabotage may result, as employees fight to resist a radical change in corporate philosophy. Like structure, if a corporation's culture is compatible with a new strategy, it is an internal strength. But if the corporate culture is not compatible with the proposed strategy, it is a serious weakness. This does not mean that a manager should never consider a strategy that runs counter to the established culture. However, if such a strategy is to be seriously considered, top management must be prepared to attempt to change the culture as well, a task that will take much time, effort, and persistence.

Additional information regarding corporate culture and techniques to change culture is presented in Chapter 8.

5.4 RESOURCES

William Newman, an authority on strategic management, points out that a practical way to develop a corporation's master strategy is to "pick particular roles or niches that are appropriate in view of competition and the company's resources" [propitious niche].[28] The company's resources are typically considered as financial, physical, and human; organizational systems and technological capabilities are also considered resources. Because these resources have functional significance, we can discuss them under the commonly accepted functional headings of marketing, finance, research and development, operations, human resources, and information systems. These resources, among others, should be audited so that internal strengths and weaknesses can be ascertained.

Strategic managers must be aware of the many contributions each functional area can make to divisional and corporate performance. Functional resources include not only the financial, physical, and human resources in each area but also the ability of the people in each area to formulate and implement under corporate guidance the necessary functional objectives, strategies, and policies. Thus the resources include both the *knowledge* of analytical concepts and procedural techniques common to each area and the *ability* of the people in each area to utilize them effectively. Some of the most valuable and well-known concepts and techniques are: market segmentation, product life cycle, capital budgeting, financial leverage, technological competence, operating leverage, experience-curve analysis, job analysis, job design, and decision-support systems. There are many others, of course, but these are the basic ones. If used properly, these resources serve as strengths to support strategic decisions.

MARKETING

The major task of the marketing manager from a corporation's point of view is to regulate the level, timing, and character of demand, in a way that will help the corporation achieve its objectives.[29] The marketing manager is the corporation's primary link to the customer and the competition. The manager must therefore be especially concerned with the market position and marketing mix of the firm.

Market position deals with the question, "Who are our customers?" It refers to the selection of specific areas for marketing concentration, and can be expressed in terms of market, product, and geographical locations. Through market research, corporations are able to practice **market segmentation** with various products or services so that management can discover what niches to seek, which new types of products to develop, and how to ensure that a company's many products do not directly compete with one another.[30] For example, brand managers at Procter & Gamble noticed that vacuum brick-packs of ground coffee were popular in the southern U.S. So they repackaged their Folgers® brand specifically for that market. As a result of such efforts at tailoring the brand to suit segments of the market plus a new advertising campaign, Folgers® coffee increased its share of the total U.S. market to 32% in 1988 from 24% six years earlier.[31]

The **marketing mix** refers to the particular combination of key variables under the corporation's control that can be used to affect demand and to gain competitive advantage. These variables are *product, place, promotion,* and *price.* Within each of these four variables are several subvariables, listed in Table 5.1, that should be analyzed in terms of their effects on divisional and corporate performance.

One of the most useful concepts in marketing, insofar as strategic management is concerned, is that of the **product life cycle.** As depicted in Fig. 5.3, the product life cycle is a graph showing time plotted against the dollar sales of a product as it moves from introduction through growth and maturity to decline. This concept enables a marketing manager to examine the marketing mix of a particular product or group

| FIGURE 5.4 | **Breakeven Chart** |

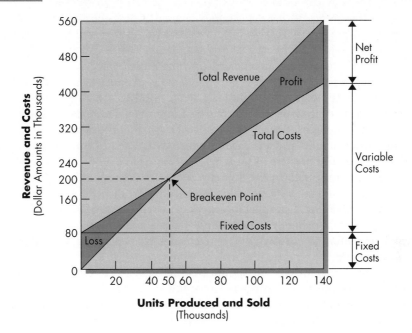

variable costs are $2.40 per unit. Total costs rise by $2.40, the amount of the variable costs, for each additional unit produced past $80,000, and the product is sold at $4.00 per unit. The total revenue line is a straight line increasing directly with production. As is usual, the slope of the total revenue line is steeper than that of the total cost line because, for every unit sold, the firm receives $4.00 of revenue for every $2.40 paid out for labor and material. Up to the breakeven point (the intersection of the total revenue and total cost lines), the firm suffers losses. After that point, the firm earns profits at an increasing amount as volume increases. In this instance, the breakeven point for the firm is at a sales and cost level of $200,000 and a production level of 50,000 units.

The financial manager must be knowledgeable of these and other more sophisticated analytical techniques if management is successfully to implement functional strategies, such as internal financing or leveraged buy outs (to be discussed in Chapter 7).

RESEARCH AND DEVELOPMENT

A corporation's technology helps define its market niche and the type of competition it faces.[36] The R&D manager is responsible for suggesting and implementing a corporation's technological strategy in light of its corporate objectives and policies. The manager's job therefore involves (1) choosing among alternative new technologies to use within the corporation, (2) developing methods of embodying the new technology in new products and processes, and (3) deploying resources so that the new technology can be successfully implemented.[37]

The term *research and development* is used to describe a wide range of activities. In some corporations R&D is conducted by scientists in well-equipped laboratories where the focus is on theoretical problem areas. This is called **basic R&D.** In other firms, R&D is concentrated on marketing and is concerned with product or product-packaging improvements. This is referred to as **product R&D.** In still other firms, R&D is concerned with engineering, concentrating on quality control, and the development of design specifications and improved production equipment. This is usually called **engineering** or **process R&D.** Most corporations will have a mix of basic, product, and process R&D, which will vary by industry, company, and product line. The balance of these types of research is known as the **R&D mix** and should be appropriate to the strategy being considered and to each product's life cycle. For example, it is generally accepted that product R&D normally dominates the early stages of a product's life cycle (when the product's optimal form and features are still being debated), whereas process R&D becomes especially important in the later stages (when the product's design is solidified and the emphasis is on reducing costs and improving quality).[38]

A company's R&D unit should be evaluated for **technological competence** in both the development and the use of innovative technology. Not only should the corporation make a consistent research effort (as measured by reasonably constant corporate expenditures that result in usable innovations), it should also be proficient

ILLUSTRATIVE EXAMPLE 5.1

A Problem in Technology Transfer at Xerox Corporation

In the mid-1970s, Xerox Corporation's Palo Alto Research Center (PARC) had developed a new type of computer with some innovative features, called Alto. Although Alto was supposed to serve as a research prototype, it became so popular among PARC personnel that some researchers began to develop Alto as a commercial product. Unfortunately, this put PARC into direct conflict with Xerox's product development group, which was at the same time developing a rival machine called the Star. Because the Star was in line with the company's expressed product development strategy, Alto was ignored by top management, who placed all its emphasis on the Star.

In 1979, Steve Jobs, cofounder of Apple Computer, Inc., made a now-legendary tour of the normally very secretive PARC. Researchers gave Jobs a demonstration of the Alto. Unlike the computers that Apple was then building, Alto had the power of a minicomputer. Its user-friendly software generated crisp text and bright graphics. Jobs fell in love with the machine. He promptly asked Apple's engineers to duplicate the look and feel of Alto. The result was the Macintosh—a personal computer that soon revolutionized the industry.

Sources: J. D. Hunger, T. L. Conquest, and W. Miller, "Xerox Corporation: Proposed Diversification," in *Cases in Strategic Management,* 3rd ed., edited by T. L. Wheelen and J. D. Hunger (Reading, Mass.: Addison-Wesley, 1990), pp. 142–143; J. W. Verity, "Rethinking the Computer," *Business Week* (November 26, 1990), p. 116.

in managing research personnel and integrating their innovations into its day-to-day operations. If a company is not proficient in **technology transfer,** the process of taking a new technology from the laboratory to the marketplace, it will not gain much advantage from new technological advances. Both American Telephone and Telegraph (AT&T) and Xerox Corporation have been criticized for their inability to take the research, ideas, and innovations developed in their sophisticated R&D facilities (AT&T's Bell Labs and Xerox's Palo Alto Research Center) and package them in improved products and services. See Illustrative Example 5.1 for a problem in the transfer of technology at Xerox Corporation.

Corporations operating in technology-based industries must be willing to make substantial investments in R&D. Research indicates that a company's R&D intensity (its spending on R&D as a percentage of sales revenue) is a principal means of gaining market share in global competition.[39] The amount spent on R&D will often vary by industry. For example, the computer and drug industries spent an average of 9.0% and 10.1%, respectively, of their sales dollar for R&D in 1990. As shown in Table 5.2, other industries, such as food and textiles, spent less than 1%. General Electric spends a large amount of money on R&D. Michael Carpenter, Vice-President of Corporate Business Development and Planning at GE, points out that much of the company's growth has developed internally from its R&D efforts. He states: "We spend half as much money each year on R&D as all the money going into the venture capital industry. . . . As a result GE has always been at the leading edge of technology."[40] A good rule of thumb for R&D spending is that a corporation should spend at a "normal" rate for that particular industry. According to PIMS data, those companies that spend 1% of sales more or less than the industry average have lower ROIs.[41]

Simply spending money on R&D or new projects does not mean, however, that the money will produce useful results. Between 1950 and 1979, the U.S. steel industry spent 20% more on plant maintenance and upgrading for each ton of production capacity added or replaced than did the Japanese steel industry. Nevertheless, the top managements of U.S. steel firms failed to recognize and adopt two breakthroughs in steelmaking—the basic oxygen furnace and continuous casting. Their hesitancy to adopt new technology caused them to lose the world steel market.[42]

In addition to money, another important consideration in the effective management of research and development is the time factor. It is generally accepted that the time needed for meaningful profits to result from the inception of a specific R&D program is typically 7 to 11 years.[43] According to Karlheinz Kaske, CEO of Siemans AG, however, the time needed to complete the cycle is getting shorter. In the past, he says, "ten to fifteen years went by before old products were replaced by new ones . . . now, it takes only four or five years."[44]

If a corporation is unwilling to invest the large amounts of money and time for its own program of research and development, it might be able to purchase or lease the equipment, techniques, or patents necessary to stay abreast of the competition. For example, Ford Motor Company paid $100 million in 1990 for 10.8% of the common stock of Cummins Engine Co., an expert in diesel engine technology. In return for its money, Ford got exclusive access to Cummins's truck-engine tech-

TABLE 5.2	R&D Expenditures by Industry in 1990 as a Percentage of Sales Revenues		

Aerospace	4.1	Manufacturing:	
Automotive:		General manufacturing	3.2
Cars and trucks	3.6	Machine and hand tools	2.0
Parts and equipment	2.1	Special machinery	2.6
Tire and rubber	2.4	Textiles	0.8
Chemicals	3.8	Metals and mining:	
Conglomerates	2.3	Aluminum	1.3
Consumer products:		Steel	1.0
Appliances/home furnishings	1.6	Other metals	0.8
Other consumer goods	0.7	Nonbank financial	0.7
Personal care	2.5	Office equipment and services:	
Containers and packaging	0.9	Business machines/services	2.2
Electrical and electronics:		Computer communications	9.8
Electrical products	2.3	Computers	9.0
Electronics	5.0	Data processing	5.4
Instruments	5.8	Disk and tape drives	6.4
Semiconductors	9.3	Peripherals and other	4.8
Food	0.7	Software and services	13.2
Fuel		System design	10.1
Oil, gas, and coal	0.7	Paper and forest products	1.0
Petroleum services	2.7	Publishing and broadcasting	1.0
Health care		Service industries	1.1
Drugs and research	10.1	Telecommunications	4.7
Medical products/services	6.2		
Housing	1.9	**All-industry composite**	**3.4**
Leisure-time products	4.9		

Source: Taken from "R&D Scoreboard," *Business Week* (June 15, 1990), pp. 197–223.

nology. This allowed Ford to forgo the $300 million expense of designing a new engine on its own to meet the 1994 U.S. emission standards.[45]

Those corporations that do purchase an innovative technology must, nevertheless, have the technological competence to make good use of it. Unfortunately, some managers who introduce the latest technology into their company's processes do not adequately assess the competence of their organization to handle it. For example, a survey conducted in the U.K. found that 44% of all companies that started to use robots met with initial failure, and that 22% of these firms abandoned the use of robots altogether, mainly because of inadequate technological knowledge and skills.[46] Similar problems with the introduction of robotization and computer-aided manufacturing have been noted at General Motors' new assembly plant in

| FIGURE 5.5 | **Technological Discontinuity** |

What the S-Curves Reveal

In the corporate planning process, it is generally assumed that incremental progress in technology will occur. But past developments in a given technology cannot be extrapolated into the future, because every technology has its limits. The key to competitiveness is to determine when to shift resources to a technology with more potential.

Source: P. Pascarella, "Are You Investing in the Wrong Technology?" *Industry Week* (July 25, 1983), p. 38. Copyright © 1983 by Penton/IPC. All rights reserved. Reprinted by permission.

Hamtramck, Michigan, and at Ford's recently remodeled St. Louis assembly plant. "They're now discovering that if you don't have good management, you'll end up with a rotten automated plant," concluded David Cole, Director of the University of Michigan's Office for the Study of Automotive Transportation.[47]

The R&D manager must determine when to abandon present technology and when to develop or adopt new technology. Richard Foster of McKinsey and Company states that the displacement of one technology by another (**technological discontinuity**) is a frequent and strategically important phenomenon. For each technology within a given field or industry, the plotting of product performance against research effort/expenditures on a graph results in an S-shaped curve. Foster describes the process depicted in Fig. 5.5:

> Early in the development of the technology a knowledge base is being built and progress requires a relatively large amount of effort. Later, progress comes more easily. And then, as the limits of that technology are approached, progress becomes slow and expensive. That is when R&D dollars should be allocated to technology with more potential. That is also—not so incidentally—when a competitor who has bet on a new technology can sweep away your business or topple an entire industry.[48]

The presence of such a technological discontinuity in the world's steel industry during the 1960s can explain why the large capital expenditures by U.S. steel companies failed to keep them competitive with the Japanese firms adopting the new technologies. As Foster points out: "History has shown that as one technology nears the end of its S-curve, competitive leadership in a market generally changes hands."[49] Interestingly, the phenomenon continues to occur in the semiconductor industry with each new wave of microchip technology. Each time, the more established firms, which have much invested in the old technology risk cannibalizing themselves in a bet on future technology and are subsequently left behind.[50]

Even though many companies in various industries have invested substantially in the energy and resources needed for their conversion to leading-edge technologies, there have been relatively few successes.[51] Ansoff recommends that strategic managers deal with technology substitution by (1) continuously searching for sources from which new technologies are likely, (2) as the technology surfaces, making a timely commitment either to acquire the new technology or to prepare to leave the market, and (3) reallocating resources from improvements in the older process-oriented technology to investments in the newer, typically product-oriented, technology as the new technology approaches commercial realization.[52]

OPERATIONS (MANUFACTURING/SERVICE)

If the corporation is in business to transform tangible raw materials, like iron ore or petroleum, into usable products, like automobiles, machine parts, or plastic raincoats, the transformation process is called *manufacturing*. If, however, the corporation is in the business of using people's skills and knowledge, such as those of doctors, lawyers, or loan officers, to provide services through hospitals, legal clinics, or banks, the work involved is called *service*. These functions can be found in any corporation producing and providing either a tangible product or an intangible service. Many of the key concepts and techniques popularly used in manufacturing can therefore be applied to service businesses.[53]

The primary task of the manufacturing or service manager is to develop and operate a system that will produce the required number of products or services, with a certain quality, at a given cost, within an allotted time. However, manufacturing plants vary significantly depending on the type of product made. In very general terms, manufacturing can be intermittent or continuous. In **intermittent systems** (job shops), the item is normally processed sequentially, but the work and sequence of the process vary. At each location, the tasks determine the details of processing and the time required for them. In contrast, **continuous systems** are those laid out as lines on which products can be continuously assembled or processed. An example is an automobile assembly line.

The type of manufacturing system used by a corporation determines divisional or corporate strategy. It makes no sense, for example, to plan to increase sales by saturating the market with low-priced products if the corporation's manufacturing process was designed as an intermittent "job shop" system that produces one-time-only products to a customer's specifications. Conversely, a plan to produce several specialty products might not be economically feasible if the manufacturing process was designed to be a mass-producing, continuous system using low-skilled labor or special-purpose robots.

Continuous systems are popular because they allow a corporation to take advantage of manufacturing **operating leverage.** According to Weston and Copeland, operating leverage is the impact of a given change in sales volume on net operating income.[54] For example, a highly labor-intensive firm has little automated machinery and thus a small amount of fixed costs. It has a fairly low breakeven point, but its variable cost line has a relatively steep slope. Because most of the costs associated with the product are variable (many employees earn piece-rate wages), its variable costs are higher than those of automated firms. Its advantage over other firms is that it can operate at low levels and still be profitable. Once its sales reach breakeven, however, the huge variable costs as a percentage of total costs keep the profit per unit at a relatively low level. Its low operating leverage thus prevents the firm from gathering the huge profits possible from a high volume of sales. In terms of strategy, this firm should look for a niche in the marketplace for which it can produce and sell a reasonably small quantity of goods.

In contrast, a capital-intensive firm has a lot of money in fixed investments, such as automated processes and highly sophisticated machinery. Its labor force, relatively small but highly skilled, earns salaries rather than piece-rate wages. Consequently, this firm has a high amount of fixed costs. It also has a relatively high breakeven point, but its variable cost line rises slowly. Its advantage is that once it reaches breakeven, its profits rise faster than do those of less automated firms. In terms of strategy, this firm needs to find a high-demand niche in the marketplace for which it can produce and sell a large quantity of goods. Its high operating leverage makes it an extremely profitable and competitive firm once it reaches its high breakeven point. Changes in the level of sales have a magnified (leveraged) impact on profits. In times of recession, however, this type of firm is likely to suffer huge losses. During an economic downturn, the firm with less automation and thus less leverage is more likely to survive comfortably, because a drop in sales primarily affects variable costs. It is often easier to lay off labor than to sell off specialized plants and machines.

The operations of a service business can also be continuous or intermittent. Continuous operations describe fairly similar services provided to the *same* clientele over a period of time (such as treatment of patients in a long-term-care hospital), whereas intermittent operations describe somewhat variable services provided to *different* clientele over a period of time (such as once-a-year auditing or income tax counseling by a CPA firm). To use operating leverage, service firms that use continuous operations might be able to substitute diagnostic machinery or videotape machines for highly paid professional personnel. Those using batch or intermittent operations might be able to substitute lower-paid support personnel for some of the more routine services performed by highly paid professionals.

A conceptual framework that many large corporations have used successfully is the **experience curve** (originally called the learning curve). The concept as it applies to manufacturing is that unit production costs decline by some fixed percentage (commonly 20%–30%) each time the total accumulated volume of production in units doubles. The actual percentage varies by industry and is based on many variables: the amount of time it takes a person to learn a new task, scale economies, product and process improvements, and lower raw materials costs, among others. For example, in an industry where an 85% experience curve can be expected, a corporation might expect a 15% reduction in costs for every doubling of volume. The total costs per unit (adjusted for inflation) can be expected to drop from $100 when the total production is 10 units, to $85 ($100 × 85%) when production increases to 20 units, and to $72.25 ($85 × 85%) when it reaches 40 units.[55] Achieving these results often means making investments in R&D and fixed assets; higher operating leverage and less flexibility thus result. Nevertheless, the manufacturing strategy is one of building capacity ahead of demand, in order to achieve the lower unit costs that develop from the experience curve. On the basis of some future point on the experience curve, price the product or service very low, to preempt competition and increase market demand. The resulting high number of units sold and high market share should result in high profits, based on the low unit costs.[56] This idea of management's using the anticipated experience curve to price low, in order to gain high market share and thus high profits, underlies the Boston Consulting Group's portfolio matrix (discussed in Chapter 6).

The experience curve is commonly used in management's estimating the production costs of (1) a product never before made with the present techniques and processes or (2) current products produced by newly introduced techniques or processes. The concept was first applied in the airframe industry and can be applied in the service industry as well. Although many firms have used experience curves extensively, an unquestioning acceptance of the industry norm (such as 80% for the airframe industry or 70% for integrated circuits) is very risky. The experience curve of the industry as a whole might not hold true for a particular company for a variety of reasons.

Recently, the use of large mass-production facilities to take advantage of experience-curve economies has been criticized. The use of Computer-Assisted Design and Computer-Assisted Manufacturing (CAD/CAM) and robot technology means that learning times are shorter and products can be economically manufactured in small, customized batches. Emphasizing *economies of scope* over *economies of scale,* several firms have introduced "flexible manufacturing." The new flexible factories permit a low-volume output of custom-tailored products to produce a profit.[57] It is thus possible to have the cost advantages of continuous systems with the customer-oriented advantages of intermittent systems. For example, Caterpillar, Inc. changed its production process at its steel tractor-tread plant in East Peoria, Illinois. Under the old "batch" system, steel beams were cut, drilled, and heat-treated on three distinct assembly lines. The new system, in contrast, feed steel beams on automated conveyor belts through a tractor-tread cell where all three operations are accomplished. Computers adjust machine tools within seconds to meet the new specifications on any new order. Previously, changing specifications meant idling the line for a full day.[58]

In conclusion, the operations manager in charge of either manufacturing or services must be knowledgeable about forecasting, scheduling, purchasing, quality assurance, process design, job design, work measurement, just-in-time production systems, and maintenance and reliability, among other things, in order to develop an appropriate operations functional strategy.

HUMAN RESOURCES

In many business firms, labor costs still account for more than 50% of the total costs of doing business.[59] Human resources are therefore likely to be an internal strategic factor in many corporations. The primary task of the manager of human resources is to improve the match between individuals and jobs. The quality of this match influences job performance, employee satisfaction, and employee turnover.[60] Consequently, human resource management (HRM) is concerned with the selection and training of new employees, appraisal of employee performance, the assessment of employees' promotion potential, and recruitment and personnel planning for the future. HRM is also concerned with wage and salary administration, labor negotiations, job design, and employee morale.

A good HRM department should know how to use attitude surveys and other feedback devices to assess employees' satisfaction with their jobs and with the corporation as a whole. HRM managers should also use job analysis. **Job analysis** is a means of obtaining job-description information about what needs to be accomplished by each job in terms of quality and quantity. Up-to-date job descriptions are essential not only for proper employee selection, appraisal, training, and development; wage and salary administration; and labor negotiations, but also for summarizing the corporatewide human resources in terms of employee-skill categories. Just as a corporation must know the number, type, and quality of its manufacturing facilities, it must also know the kinds of people it employs and the skills they possess. This knowledge is essential for the formulation and implementation of corporate strategy. The best strategies are meaningless if employees do not have the skills to carry them out or if jobs cannot be designed to accommodate the available workers. Honeywell, Inc., for example, uses *talent surveys* to ensure that it has the right mix of talents for implementation of its planned strategies.[61]

Strategic managers are beginning to realize that they must be more flexible in their utilization of employees in order for human resources to be a strength. Human resource managers therefore need to be knowledgeable about work options such as part-time work, job sharing, flextime, extended leaves, contract work, and the proper use of teams. For example, as a way to move a product more quickly through its development stage, companies like Motorola, NCR, and General Electric have begun using cross-functional work teams. Instead of developing products in a series of steps—beginning with a request from sales, which leads to design, then to engineering and on to purchasing, and finally to manufacturing (and often resulting in a costly product rejected by the customer)—companies are tearing down the traditional walls separating the departments so that people from each discipline can get involved in projects early on. In a process called "concurrent engineering," the once-isolated specialists now work side by side and compare notes constantly in an effort to design cost-effective products with features customers want.[62]

If the corporation is unionized, a good human resource manager should be able to work closely with the union. Although union membership in the U.S. has dropped to 12% of private-sector workers (16% if government workers are included) in 1989 from 25% in 1973, unions still represent 24% of workers in manufacturing in the U.S.[63] Interestingly, the average proportion of unionized workers among 17 major industrialized competitor nations of the U.S. actually increased from 48% in 1970 to 53% in 1987.[64] These developments have significant implications for the management of multinational corporations.

A recent development is the increasing desire by union leaders to work jointly with management in the formulation and implementation of strategic changes. For example, when General Electric announced its intention to close its Charleston, South Carolina, steam-turbine generator plant, the United Electrical Workers proposed to management 11 alternative products that the plant could produce. To save jobs, U.S. unions are increasingly willing to support *employee involvement* programs designed to increase worker participation in decision making.[65] Jerome M. Rosnow, President of the Work in America Institute, states that the involvement of union leaders in business decision making is a "major breakthrough which has great potential for improving the competitive edge of those companies.[66]

Human resource departments have found that to reduce employee dissatisfaction and unionization efforts (or, conversely, to improve employee satisfaction and existing union relations), they must consider the quality of work life (QWL) in the design of jobs. Partially a reaction to the traditionally heavy emphasis on technical and economic factors in job design, QWL emphasizes the human dimension of work. In general, **quality of work life** is "the degree to which members of a work organization are able to satisfy important personal needs through their experiences in the organization."[67] The knowledgeable human resource manager should therefore be able to improve the corporation's quality of work life by (1) introducing participative problem solving, (2) restructuring work, (3) introducing innovative reward systems, and (4) improving the work environment. It is hoped that these improvements will lead to a more participative corporate culture and thus higher productivity and quality products.

A corporation's human resources are especially important in today's world of global communication and transportation systems. Advances in technology are copied almost immediately by competitors around the world. People, however, are not as willing to move to other companies in other countries. Porter, among others, therefore proposes that the only long-term resource advantage remaining to corporations operating in the industrialized nations lies in the area of skilled human resources.[68] Paul Hagusa, President of the U.S. subsidiary of Sharp Corporation of Japan, makes this point very clearly.

> Once there was a time when the Americans had very efficient machines and equipment, and Japan did not. At that time—regardless of the workers—those with the most modern machines had the competitive advantage. But now, one country soon has the same machinery as another. So, what makes the difference today is the quality of the people.[69]

INFORMATION SYSTEMS

The primary task of the manager of information systems (IS) is to design and manage the flow of information in a corporation in ways that improve productivity and decision making. Information must be collected, stored, and synthesized in such a manner that it will answer important operating and strategic questions. This function is growing in importance.

A corporation's information system can be a strength or a weakness in all three elements of strategic management: formulation, implementation, and evaluation and control. It can not only aid in environmental scanning and in controlling a corporation's many activities, it can also be used as a strategic weapon in gaining competitive advantage. For example, American Hospital Supply (AHS), a leading manufacturer and distributor of a broad line of products for doctors, laboratories, and hospitals, has developed an order entry–distribution system that directly links the majority of its customers to AHS computers. The system has been successful because it simplifies ordering processes for customers, reduces costs for both AHS and the customer, and allows AHS to provide pricing incentives to the customer. As a result, customer loyalty is high and AHS's share of the market has become large.

Information systems can fulfill four major purposes:

- **Provide a basis for the analysis of early warning signals** that can originate both externally and internally. Any information system has a data base. Like a library, the system collects, categorizes, and files the data so that the system can be used by other departments in the corporation.
- **Automate routine clerical operations.** Payroll, inventory reports, and other records can be generated automatically from the data base and thus the need for file clerks is reduced.
- **Assist managers in making routine (programmed) decisions.** Scheduling orders, assigning orders to machines, and reordering supplies are routine tasks that can be automated through a detailed analysis of the company's work flow.
- **Provide the information necessary for management to make strategic (non-programmed) decisions.** Increasingly, personal computers coupled with sophisticated software are being used to analyze large amounts of information and to calculate likely payoffs from alternate strategies. In order to fulfill this purpose, decision-support systems are needed that allow easy interaction with the computer for the user.[70]

In assessing a corporation's strengths and weaknesses, one should note the level of development of the firm's information system. Based on research conducted by M.I.T.'s Sloan School of Management sponsored by Arthur Anderson and others, there are at least four distinct phases of information system development.

In **Phase One,** companies use information systems to improve the efficiency of existing businesses through customer billing, data entry, and report writing. In this phase the IS helps companies save money, but cannot yet be used for competitive advantage. For example, American Airlines first installed its Sabre computerized reservation system to keep better track of available seats on its flights.

In **Phase Two,** companies attempt to differentiate themselves from their competitors by using their installed IS to introduce new, electronically delivered products and services to *existing* customers. During this phase, for example, American Airlines connected its Sabre system to travel agents' offices. Because this made reservations easier for agents, American's ticket sales increased.

In **Phase Three,** companies attempt to sell new information-based products and services to *new* customers. American in this phase opened up its Sabre system to competing airlines. It not only gained revenues from processing other airlines' tickets, it further increased its own ticket sales.

In **Phase Four,** firms develop new, innovative information-based products and services on an ongoing basis. During this phase American Airlines began selling information gathered from travel agents on Sabre. American used its data base on fliers for its Advantage program by tracking their mileage and offering free flights for specific amounts of mileage on American flights. According to John Sifonis, an information technology strategist who directed Arthur Young's participation in the M.I.T. program, the fourth phase is the hardest to achieve. "Success in the fourth phase requires a continuing investment in information systems and a constant commitment to innovation in products and services."[71]

The information system is quickly becoming a corporation's strategic resource. Based on its phase of development and the abilities of the IS personnel, it can be used to monitor environmental changes, counter competitive threats, and assist in the implementation of strategy.[72]

5.5 SYNTHESIS OF INTERNAL STRATEGIC FACTORS—IFAS

Once strategic managers have scanned the internal organizational environment and identified strategic factors for their particular corporation, they may wish to summarize their analysis of these strategic factors using a form such as that given in Table 5.3. This form (Internal Strategic Factors Analysis Summary—IFAS) is one way to organize the internal strategic factors into the generally accepted categories of strengths and weaknesses as well as to analyze how well a particular company is responding to these specific factors in light of the perceived importance of these factors to the company. To use the IFAS form given in Table 5.3, complete the following steps:

First, identify and list in Column 1 about 5 to 10 strengths and about the same number of weaknesses. *Second,* assign a **weight** in Column 2 to each factor from 1.0 (Most Important) to 0.0 (Not Important) based on that factor's probable impact on a particular company's strategic position. (All weights must sum to 1.0 regardless of the number of strategic factors.) *Third,* assign a **rating** in Column 3 to each factor from 5 (Outstanding) to 1 (Poor) based on that particular company's current response to that particular factor.

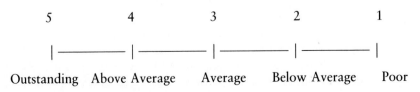

TABLE 5.3	Internal Strategic Factor Analysis Summary (IFAS): Maytag as Example

Internal Strategic Factors	Weight	Rating	Weighted Score	Comments
	1	2	3	4	5
Strengths:				
■ Quality Maytag culture	.15	5	.75	Quality key to success
■ Experienced top management	.05	4	.20	Know appliances
■ Vertical integration	.10	4	.40	Dedicated factories
■ Employee relations	.05	3	.15	Good, but deteriorating
■ Hoover's international orientation	.15	3	.45	Hoover name in cleaners
Weaknesses:				
■ Process-oriented R&D	.05	2	.10	Slow on new products
■ Distribution channels	.05	2	.10	Superstores replacing small dealers
■ Financial position	.15	2	.30	High debt load
■ Global positioning	.20	2	.40	Hoover weak outside U.K. and Australia
■ Manufacturing facilities	.05	4	.20	Investing now
Total Weighted Score	**1.00**		**3.05**	

Notes: 1. List strengths and weaknesses (5–10 each) in Column 1.

2. Weight each factor from 1.0 (Most Important) to 0.0 (Not Important) in Column 2 based on that factor's probable impact on the company's strategic position. **The total weights must sum to 1.00.**

3. Rate each factor from 5 (Outstanding) to 1 (Poor) in Column 3 based on the company's response to that factor.

4. Multiply each factor's weight times its rating to obtain each factor's weighted score in Column 4.

5. Use Column 5 (comments) for rationale used for each factor.

6. Add the weighted scores to obtain the **total weighted score** for the company in Column 4. This tells how well the company is responding to the strategic factors in its internal environment.

Source: T. L. Wheelen and J. D. Hunger, "Internal Strategic Factor Analysis Summary (IFAS)." Copyright © 1991 by Wheelen and Hunger Associates. Reprinted by permission.

Fourth, multiply the weight (Column 2) for each factor times its rating (Column 3) to obtain that factor's weighted score in Column 4. This results in a **weighted score** for each factor. *Fifth,* use Column 5 (comments) to note why a particular factor was selected and how its weight and rating were estimated. *Sixth,* add the weighted scores for all the internal factors in Column 4 to determine the total weighted score for that particular company. The *total weighted score* ranges from 5.0 (Outstanding) to 1.0 (Poor) with 3.0 as Average and indicates how well a particular company is responding to current and expected strategic factors in its internal environment. The score can be used to compare that firm to other firms in its industry.

As an example of this procedure, Table 5.3 includes a number of internal strategic factors for Maytag Corporation with corresponding weights, ratings, and weighted scores provided. It is thus very similar to Table 4.4 (EFAS) in which external strategic factors are summarized.

Once strategic managers have completed their analysis of a firm's internal strategic factors in terms of strengths and weaknesses, they must then analyze these factors in light of the corporation's previously considered external strategic factors. This overall situation analysis is the topic covered next in Chapter 6.

SUMMARY AND CONCLUSION

Before strategies can be developed, top management needs to scan and analyze its internal corporate environment for strengths and weaknesses that may be strategic factors. Strategic managers may choose among four distinct approaches in conducting their internal assessment: *7-S Framework, PIMS Analysis, Value Chain Analysis,* and *Functional Analysis.* The strategic management model underlying this book takes the functional approach by proposing that strategic managers scan and analyze their company's structure, culture, and resources.

A corporation's **structure** is its anatomy. It is often described graphically through an organization chart. Basic structures range from the simple structure of an owner-manager–operated business to the conglomerate. Each of these structural designs has its advantages and limitations. If compatible with present and potential strategies, a corporation's structure is a great internal strength. Otherwise, it can be a serious weakness that will either prevent a good strategy from being implemented properly or reduce the number of strategic alternatives available to the firm.

A corporation's **culture** is the collection of beliefs, expectations, and values learned and shared by its members and transmitted from one generation of employees to another. A culture produces norms that shape the behavior of employees. Top management must be aware of this culture and include it in its assessment of strategic factors. Those strategies that run counter to an established corporate culture are likely to be doomed by the poor motivation of the work force. If a culture is thus antagonistic to a strategy change, the implementation plan will also have to include plans to change the culture.

A corporation's **resources** include not only such generally recognized assets as people, money, and facilities, but also those analytical concepts and procedural techniques known and in use within the functional areas. Because most top managers view their corporations in terms of functional activities, it is simplest to assess resource strengths and weaknesses by functional area. Some of these areas are marketing, finance, research and development, operations, human resources, and information systems. Each area should be audited in terms of its financial, physical, and human resources, as well as its competencies and capabilities. Just as the knowledge of key functional concepts and techniques is a corporate strength, its absence is a weakness.

DISCUSSION QUESTIONS

1. Compare and contrast the four approaches to scanning and analyzing a corporation's internal environment.

2. Describe Porter's value chain analysis and how it relates to strategic management.

3. What is the role of breakeven analysis in the production of a new product or service?

4. In what ways can a corporation's structure and culture act as internal strengths or weaknesses?

5. What kind of internal factors help determine whether a firm should emphasize the production and sales of a large number of low-priced products or a small number of high-priced products?

6. What is the difference between operating and

financial leverage? What are their implications for strategic planning?

7. Why is technological competence important in strategy formulation?

8. How can management's knowledge of technological discontinuity help to improve a corporation's efficiency?

9. What are the pros and cons of management's using the experience curve to determine strategy?

10. Why should information systems be included in the analysis of a corporation's strengths and weaknesses?

NOTES

1. From COMPETITIVE ADVANTAGE: Creating and Sustaining Superior Performance by Michael E. Porter. Copyright © 1985 by Michael E. Porter. Used with permission of The Free Press, a Division of Macmillan, Inc.

2. B. Dumaine, "The New Turnaround Champs," *Fortune* (July 16, 1990), p. 39.

3. T. J. Peters and R. H. Waterman, Jr., *In Search of Excellence* (New York: HarperCollins, 1982), pp. 9–11.

4. G. Kellinghusen and K. Wubbenhorst, "Strategic Control for Improved Performance," *Long Range Planning* (June 1990), pp. 31–32. This article describes a company's negative experience with the 7-S approach before trying PIMS analysis.

5. S. Schoeffler, "Nine Basic Findings on Business Strategy," *The PIMSletter on Business Strategy,* No. 1 (Cambridge, Mass.: The Strategic Planning Institute, 1984), pp. 3–5.

6. G. Badler, "Strategizing for a Spectrum of Possibilities," *Planning Review* (July 1984), pp. 28–31.

7. R. D. Buzzell and B. T. Gale, *The PIMS Principles* (New York: The Free Press, 1987), pp. 8–10.

8. Many of these studies are summarized by M. S. Williams, "The Impact of Market Share on Return on Investment: Contemporary Theories and Implications for Management," in *Handbook of Business Strategy 1989/90 Yearbook*, edited by H. E. Glass (Boston: Warren, Gorham and Lamont, 1989), pp. 33.1–33.6.

9. Buzzell and Gale, *The PIMS Principles,* pp. 7, 183.

B. T. Gale, "Advertising, Profitability and Growth for Consumer Businesses," *The PIMSletter on Business Strategy,* No. 43 (Cambridge, Mass.: The Strategic Planning Institute, 1989), p. 9.

10. V. Ramanujan and N. Venkatraman, "An Inventory and Critique of Strategy Research Using the PIMS Database," *Academy of Management Review* (January 1984), p. 147.

11. For more details on PAR ROI and look-alikes PIMS reports, refer to B. T. Gale and D. J. Swire, "Business Strategies That Create Wealth," *Planning Review* (March/April 1988), pp. 6–13, 47. See also Kellinghusen and Wubbenhorst, "Strategic Control."

12. Porter, *Competitive Advantage,* p. 36.

13. H. I. Ansoff, *The New Corporate Strategy* (New York: John Wiley and Sons, 1988), pp. 66–71.

14. R. L. Daft, *Organization Theory and Design* (St. Paul, Minn.: West Publishing Co., 1986), pp. 211–212.

15. J. W. Wilson, "Can Andy Grove Practice What He Preaches?" *Business Week* (March 16, 1987), pp. 68–69.

16. J. W. Fredrickson, "The Strategic Decision Process and Organizational Structure," *Academy of Management Review* (April 1986), pp. 280–297.

D. Miller, "Configurations of Strategy and Structure: Towards a Synthesis," *Strategic Management Journal* (May-June 1986), pp. 233–249.

17. L. E. Fouraker and J. M. Stopford, "Organization Structure and the Multinational Strategy," *Administrative Science Quarterly* (June 1968), pp. 47–64.

18. R. H. Miles, *Macro Organizational Behavior* (Santa Monica, Calif.: Goodyear Publishing Co., 1980), pp. 28–34.

19. Based on J. R. Galbraith and R. K. Kazanjian, *Strategy Implementation: Structure, Systems, and Process,* 2nd ed. (St. Paul, Minn.: West Publishing Co., 1986), pp. 67–68.

20. W. J. Duncan, "Organizational Culture: 'Getting a Fix' on an Elusive Concept," *Academy of Management Executive* (August 1989), p. 229.

21. H. Schwartz and S. M. Davis, "Matching Corporate Culture and Business Strategy," *Organizational Dynamics* (Summer 1981), p. 30.

22. S. C. Wheelwright, "Manufacturing Strategy: Defining the Missing Link," *Strategic Management Journal* (January-March 1984), p. 79.

23. D. Muhm, "John Deere's Company: 145 Years of Farming History," *Des Moines Register* (November 11, 1984), p. 2F.

24. I. I. Mitroff and S. Mohrman, "Correcting Tunnel Vision," *Journal of Business Strategy* (Winter 1987), pp. 49–59.

25. L. Iacocca, *Iacocca: An Autobiography* (Toronto: Bantam Books, 1984), p. 141.

26. J. Lorsch, "Strategic Myopia: Culture as an Invisible Barrier to Change," in *Gaining Control of the Corporate Culture,* edited by R. H. Kilmann, M. J. Saxton, R. Serpa, and Associates (San Francisco: Jossey-Bass, 1985), pp. 84–102.

   H. I. Ansoff and T. E. Baker, "Is Corporate Culture the Ultimate Answer?" in *Advances in Strategic Management,* Vol. 4, edited by R. Lamb and P. Shrivastava (Greenwich, Conn.: JAI Press, 1986), p. 84.

27. Y. Wiener, "Forms of Value Systems: A Focus on Organizational Effectiveness and Cultural Change and Maintenance," *Academy of Management Review* (October 1988), p. 536.

28. W. H. Newman, "Shaping the Master Strategy of Your Firm," *California Management Review,* Vol. 9, No. 3 (1967), p. 77.

29. P. Kotler, *Marketing Management,* 4th ed. (Englewood Cliffs, N.J.: Prentice Hall, 1980), p. 22.

30. C. A. Swenson, "How to Sell to a Segmented Market," *Journal of Business Strategy* (January/February 1988), pp. 18–22.

31. Z. Schiller, "Stalking the New Consumer," *Business Week* (August 28, 1989), p. 55.

32. M. Schofeld and D. Arnold, "Strategies for Mature Businesses," *Long Range Planning* (October 1988), pp. 69–76.

33. C. M. Sandberg, W. G. Lewellen, and K. L. Stanley, "Financial Strategy: Planning and Managing the Corporate Leverage Position," *Strategic Management Journal* (January-February 1987), pp. 15–24.

34. For further information on capital budgeting, discounted cash flow, CAPM, and APM Techniques, see J. F. Weston and T. E. Copeland, *Managerial Finance,* 8th ed. (Chicago: Dryden Press, 1986), pp. 99–138 and 427–478.

35. T. E. Conine, Jr., "The Potential Overreliance on Break-Even Analysis," *Journal of Business Strategy* (Fall 1986), pp. 84–86.

36. W. P. Barnett, "The Organizational Ecology of a Technological System," *Administrative Science Quarterly* (March 1990), pp. 31–60.

37. M. A. Maidique and P. Patch, "Corporate Strategy and Technological Policy" (Boston: Intercollegiate Case Clearing House, No. 9-769-033, 1978, rev. March 1980), p. 3.

38. W. J. Abernathy and J. M. Utterback, "Innovation Over Time and in Historical Context," in *Readings in the Management of Innovation,* 2nd ed., edited by M. L. Tushman and W. L. Moore (Cambridge, Mass.: Ballinger, 1988), pp. 25–36.

   R. E. Gomory, "From the 'Ladder of Science' to the Product Development Cycle," *Harvard Business Review* (November-December 1989), pp. 99–103.

39. L. G. Franko, "Global Corporate Competition: Who's Winning, Who's Losing, and the R&D Factor as One Reason Why," *Strategic Management Journal* (September-October 1989), pp. 449–474.

40. R. J. Allio, "G.E. = Giant Entrepreneur?" *Planning Review* (January 1985), p. 21.

41. M. J. Chussil, "How Much to Spend on R&D?" *The PIMSletter of Business Strategy,* No. 13 (Cambridge, Mass.: The Strategic Planning Institute, 1978), p. 5.

42. T. F. O'Boyle, "Steel's Management Has Itself to Blame," *Wall Street Journal* (May 17, 1983), p. 32.

43. E. F. Finkin, "Developing and Managing New Products," *Journal of Business Strategy* (Spring 1983), p. 45.

44. M. Silva and B. Sjogren, *Europe 1992 and the New World Power Game* (New York: John Wiley and Sons, 1990), p. 231.

45. K. Kelly and M. Ivey, "Turning Cummins into the Engine Maker That Could," *Business Week* (July 30, 1990), pp. 20–21.

46. "The Impact of Industrial Robotics on the World of Work," *International Labour Review,* Vol. 125, No. 1 (1986). Summarized in "The Risks of Robotization," *The Futurist* (May-June 1987), p. 56.

47. R. Mitchell, "Detroit Stumbles on Its Way to the Future," *Business Week* (June 16, 1986), p. 103.

48. P. Pascarella, "Are You Investing in the Wrong Technology?" *Industry Week* (July 25, 1983), p. 37.

49. *Ibid.,* p. 38.

50. M. S. Malone, "America's New Wave Chip Firms," *Wall Street Journal* (May 27, 1987), p. 30.

51. W. P. Sommers, J. Nemec, Jr., and J. M. Harris, "Repositioning with Technology: Making It Work," *Journal of Business Strategy* (Winter 1987), p. 16.

52. H. I. Ansoff, "Strategic Management of Technology," *Journal of Business Strategy* (Winter 1987), p. 35.

53. L. J. Krajewski and L. P. Ritzman, *Operations Management* (Reading, Mass.: Addison-Wesley, 1987), p. 10.

54. Weston and Copeland, *Managerial Finance,* p. 220.

55. J. D. Camm, "A Note on Learning Curve Parameters," *Decision Sciences* (Summer 1985), pp. 325–327.

   A. C. Hax and N. S. Majuf, "Competitive Cost Dynamics: The Experience Curve," in *Readings on Strategic Management,* edited by A. C. Hax (Cambridge, Mass.: Ballinger, 1984), pp. 49–60.

56. B. D. Henderson, *Henderson on Corporate Strategy* (Cambridge, Mass.: Abt Books, 1979), p. 11.

57. J. Meredith, "The Strategic Advantages of New Man-

ufacturing Technologies for Small Firms," *Strategic Management Journal* (May-June 1987), pp. 249–258.

J. D. Goldhar and M. Jelinek, "Plan for Economies of Scope," *Harvard Business Review* (November-December 1983), pp. 141–148.

58. B. Bremner, "Can Caterpillar Inch Its Way Back To Heftier Profits?" *Business Week* (September 25, 1989), pp. 75–78.

59. C. A. Lengnick-Hall and M. L. Lengnick-Hall, "Strategic Human Resources Management: A Review of the Literature and a Proposed Typology," *Academy of Management Review* (July 1988), p. 456.

60. H. G. Heneman, D. P. Schwab, J. A. Fossum, and L. D. Dyer, *Personnel/Human Resource Management* (Homewood, Ill.: Irwin, 1986), p. 7.

61. N. Tichy, "Conversation with Edson W. Spencer and Foster A. Boyle," *Organization Dynamics* (Spring 1983), p. 30.

62. J. Carey and Z. Schiller, "A Smarter Way to Manufacture," *Business Week* (April 30, 1990), pp. 110–115.

L. Therrien, "The Rival Japan Respects," *Business Week* (November 13, 1989), pp. 108–118.

A. Kumar Naj, "GE's Latest Invention: A Way to Move Ideas from Lab to Market," *Wall Street Journal* (June 14, 1990), pp. A1, A9.

63. "Union Membership Could Drop to One in 20 Workers by Decade's End," *Wall Street Journal* (April 17, 1990), P. A1.

J. Hoerr, "The Payoff from Teamwork," *Business Week* (July 10, 1989), p. 58.

64. G. Koretz, "Why Unions Thrive Abroad—But Wither in the U.S." *Business Week* (September 10, 1990), p. 26.

65. Hoerr, "The Payoff from Teamwork," pp. 56–62.

66. J. Hoerr, "Now Unions Are Helping to Run the Business," *Business Week* (December 24, 1984), p. 69.

67. J. L. Suttle, "Improving Life at Work—Problems and Perspectives," in *Improving Life at Work: Behavioral Science Approaches to Organizational Change*, edited by J. R. Hackman and J. L. Suttle (Santa Monica, Calif.: Goodyear Publishing, 1976), p. 4.

68. M. E. Porter, *The Competitive Advantage of Nations* (New York: The Free Press, 1990), pp. 158, 582, 628.

69. L. E. Calonius, "In a Plant in Memphis, Japanese Firm Shows How to Attain Quality," *Wall Street Journal* (April 29, 1983), p. 14.

70. R. G. Murdick, *MIS: Concepts and Designs* (Englewood Cliffs, N.J.: Prentice Hall, 1980), p. 253.

71. J. G. Sifonis, "Mining for Gold in Your Information Systems," *Directors and Boards* (Summer 1989), p. 23.

72. J. M. Ward, "Integrating Information Systems into Business Strategies," *Long Range Planning* (June 1987), pp. 19–29.

PART THREE

STRATEGY FORMULATION

CHAPTER SIX

Situation Analysis and Corporate Strategy

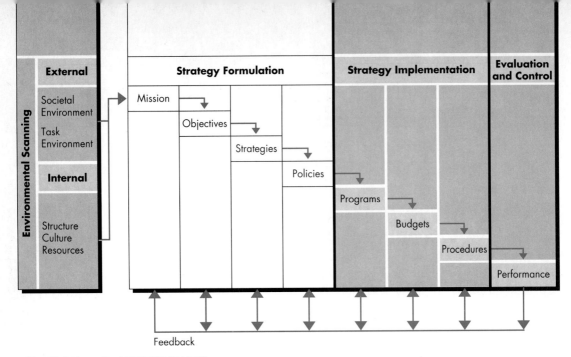

STRATEGIC MANAGEMENT MODEL

The job of a leader is to take the available resources—human and financial—and allocate them rigorously. Not to spread them out evenly like butter on bread. . . . We cut and ran from the ones that didn't stand a chance of becoming No. 1.[1]

Jack Welch, CEO
General Electric Company

Strategy formulation is often referred to as strategic planning or long-range planning. Regardless of the term used, the process is primarily analytical, not action-oriented. The basic strategic management model, discussed first in Chapter 1, reflects this distinction between strategy formulation and strategy implementation. As shown in the model, the formulation process is concerned with developing a corporation's mission, objectives, strategies, and policies. In order to do this, strategy makers must analyze the corporation's strategic factors (key strengths, weaknesses, opportunities, and threats) in light of the current situation. This is known as *situation analysis* and is shown in Fig. 6.1 (also Fig. 2.4) as Step 5(a) of the strategic decision-making process.

This chapter presents S.W.O.T. analysis and portfolio analysis as two popular methods of situation analysis. It further suggests that before generating feasible alternative strategies, strategic managers should review and revise as necessary the firm's current mission and objectives, as shown in Step 5(b) of Fig. 6.1. This leads to

| FIGURE 6.1 | **Strategic Decision-Making Process** |

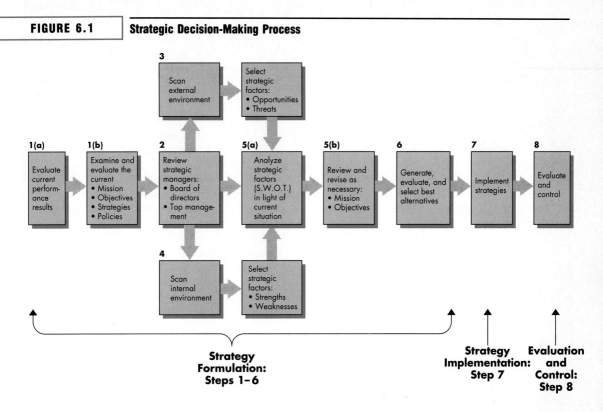

Step 6: the generation, evaluation, and selection of the best strategic alternatives. This chapter presents some of the many possible alternative corporate strategies and suggests when some of them might be most useful. Alternative business and functional strategies are presented and discussed in the next chapter.

6.1 SITUATION ANALYSIS

Situation analysis requires that top management attempt to find a strategic fit between external opportunities and internal strengths while working around external threats and internal weaknesses. This can result in the identification of a corporation's **distinctive competence**—the particular skills and resources a firm possesses and the superior way in which they are used.[2] For example, the emphasis by Urschel Laboratories on building high-quality, low-cost food processing machines has provided it a distinctive competence in manufacturing that enables it to dominate the industry. Management's willingness to pass cost-savings on to the customer in the form of lower prices, instead of maintaining prices and realizing more profits, has created an entry barrier to Urschel's prospective competitors. Prices are just too low to attract another company into the business!

Two useful and popular methods of analyzing a corporation's current situation are S.W.O.T. analysis and portfolio analysis.

ILLUSTRATIVE EXAMPLE 6.1

Internal Weakness Negatively Affects Implementation of Growth Strategy at U.S. Sprint

When United Telecommunications, Inc. and GTE Corporation formed U.S. Sprint Communications Company in 1985, they had great expectations that the new joint venture would succeed in the recently deregulated U.S. long-distance telephone industry. Competing against American Telephone and Telegraph Co. (AT&T) and MCI Communications Corp. did not, however, prove to be easy. Charles Skibo, Sprint's President, implemented an aggressive growth strategy to quickly gain market share while the giant AT&T was still recovering from the loss of its monopoly. Owing to an advertising campaign promising Sprint's fiber-optic network's transmission to be so clear that "you can hear a pin drop," Sprint added millions of residential and business customers. Unfortunately, Skibo failed first to upgrade the company's accounting systems and electronic call-routing switches necessary to handle the flood of new customers. These were serious internal weaknesses that led to $3 billion in losses over the next two years.

The company was unable to keep up with the flood of new customers. One U.S. Sprint customer-service representative was forced to keep 200 people on hold at one time! "It was a nightmare," commented an executive. "The attitude was, we'll just make it work." Even though President Skibo was replaced by Robert Snedaker in 1987, the problems continued. By 1988 Sprint was claiming that complaints had declined by a third, but customers still had problems with bills. When the bills arrived, customers were surprised by huge charges. Some said that they were charged for calls they didn't make and were never credited for their payments. Fifty-five corporate users listed Sprint near the bottom in customer service. According to Robert Morris, a financial analyst, "No one likes them."

President Snedaker continued to follow the previous president's growth strategy while he attempted to fix Sprint's weaknesses. Unfortunately, newly introduced Sprint services just aggravated matters. Offerings such as 800 numbers, WATS lines, and the highly promoted FON credit card taxed Sprint's network computers, leading to capacity shortages. One executive reported that "even though the card wasn't ready, [Sprint marketers] kept saying: 'Get it to market.'" As a result, many Sprint customers couldn't complete calls because switches in some cities didn't recognize their card codes. This was especially aggravating to customers because the company charged $0.55 every time the card was used.

Sprint's internal problems endangered the company's goal of increasing its 1988 market share of 7% compared with AT&T's share of 77% and MCI's share of 10%. With the train "already moving at 150 miles per hour," cautioned a former Sprint executive, "it's going to be tough to get off and fix the track."

Source: M. Ivey, F. Seghers, and T. Mason, "Will Sprint Ever Get Its Lines Untangled?" *Business Week* (April 25, 1988), pp. 64–65.

S.W.O.T. ANALYSIS

Research indicates that corporate performance is determined by a combination of internal and external factors.[3] Both sets of factors must therefore be considered when performing situation analysis. S.W.O.T. is an acronym for a corporation's key internal **S**trengths and **W**eaknesses and its external **O**pportunities and **T**hreats. These are the strategic factors to be analyzed in Step 5(a) of Fig. 6.1. They should include not only those external factors that are most likely to occur and to have a serious impact on the company, but also those internal factors that are most likely to affect the implementation of present and future strategic decisions.

In the case of Illustrative Example 6.1, which discusses U.S. Sprint's entry into the long-distance telephone business in the U.S., a S.W.O.T. analysis should have reflected the great opportunities for profits in the 1980s as a result of deregulation. It should also have shown the potentially serious threat not only from a then-lethargic AT&T, but also from market-oriented, aggressive companies like MCI. The S.W.O.T. analysis should also have listed the strong R&D and financial support that Sprint got from its relationship with United Telecommunications and GTE. An objective assessment of weaknesses should have highlighted Sprint's weaknesses in its operations and accounting system and raised a "red flag" for management to consider seriously before it chose a corporate growth strategy based on aggressive marketing. Because Sprint's top management failed to note the seriousness of the company's internal weaknesses before proceeding, the firm lost over $3 billion in two years and alienated many of its customers.

Generating a S.W.O.T. (TOWS) Matrix

A means of summarizing a firm's strategic factors is the S.W.O.T. (also called TOWS) Matrix provided in Figure 6.2. It illustrates how the external opportunities and threats facing a particular corporation can be matched with that corporation's internal strengths and weaknesses to result in four sets of possible strategic alternatives. To generate a S.W.O.T. (TOWS) Matrix like that shown in Fig. 6.2, take the following steps:

FIGURE 6.2 | **Generating a S.W.O.T. (TOWS) Matrix**

INTERNAL FACTORS (IFAS) EXTERNAL FACTORS (EFAS)	**Strengths (S)** List 5–10 *internal* strengths here	**Weaknesses (W)** List 5–10 *internal* weaknesses here
Opportunities (O) List 5–10 *external* opportunities here	**SO Strategies** Generate strategies here that use *strengths* to take *advantage* of *opportunities*	**WO Strategies** Generate strategies here that take *advantage* of *opportunities* by *overcoming weaknesses*
Threats (T) List 5–10 *external* threats here	**ST Strategies** Generate strategies here that use *strengths* to *avoid threats*	**WT Strategies** Generate strategies here that *minimize weaknesses* and *avoid threats*

Source: Adapted from H. Weihrich, "The TOWS Matrix—A Tool for Situational Analysis," *Long Range Planning* (April 1982), p. 60. Copyright © 1982 by Pergamon Press. Reprinted by permission.

1. In the block labeled *Opportunities*, list 5–10 external opportunities available in the corporation's current and future environment. Using the example of U.S. Sprint mentioned in Illustrative Example 6.1, this block should include deregulation of the industry as one strategic factor (EFAS from Table 4.4)

2. In the block labeled *Threats*, list 5–10 external threats facing the corporation now and in the future. Two of Sprint's strategic factors in this block should be the danger of AT&T becoming actively competitive and the current aggressiveness of MCI as a rival for market share (EFAS from Table 4.4).

3. In the block labeled *Strengths*, list 5–10 specific areas of current and future strength for the corporation under consideration. Two of Sprint's strengths were the strong R&D and financial support it could draw upon from its relationships with United Telecommunications and GTE (IFAS from Table 5.3).

4. In the block labeled *Weaknesses*, list 5–10 specific areas of current and future weakness for the corporation under consideration. Two of Sprint's strategic factors in this block were its weakness in operations technology and the fact that its accounting systems could not quickly handle a large number of new customers (IFAS from Table 5.3).

5. Generate a series of possible strategies for the corporation under consideration based on particular combinations of the four sets of strategic factors. **SO Strategies**, for instance, are generated by thinking of ways a corporation could choose to use its *strengths* to take advantage of *opportunities*. In U.S. Sprint's case, it could take advantage of deregulation by growing through emphasizing innovations developed by R&D and using its financial resources to compete directly against AT&T and MCI. **ST Strategies**, in comparison, consider a corporation's *strengths* as a way to avoid *threats*. For example, Sprint could use its R&D potential to generate products/services that were not currently offered by AT&T or MCI and thus avoid direct competition. **WO Strategies**, in contrast, attempt to take advantage of *opportunities* by overcoming *weaknesses*. In Sprint's case, it would cautiously delay major marketing efforts until it first upgraded its operations and accounting systems to ensure quality service. The fourth set of strategies, **WT Strategies**, are basically defensive and primarily act to minimize *weaknesses* and avoid *threats*. For example, Sprint could have accepted its weaknesses in operations and accounting as well as the dangers inherent in a large-scale battle for market share by focusing on a small niche of customers who were not being effectively served by the mass-marketing efforts of AT&T and MCI.

One way to generate a S.W.O.T. Matrix is to use the External and Internal Strategic Factor Analysis Summaries (EFAS and IFAS) presented earlier in Chapters 4 and 5. Follow steps 1 through 4 as mentioned above. Transfer the key opportunities and threats (steps 1 and 2) from Table 4.4 plus the key strengths and weaknesses (steps 3 and 4) from Table 5.3 into the appropriate blocks in Figure 6.2. Taking this approach, a strategic manager could generate a set of possible SO, ST, WO, and WT alternative strategies (step 5) for Maytag Corporation as shown in Figure 6.3.

FIGURE 6.3	A S.W.O.T. (TOWS) Matrix for Maytag Corporation

Internal Factors (*IFAS from Table 5.3*) / External Factors (*EFAS from Table 4.4*)	STRENGTHS (S) ■ Quality Maytag culture ■ Experienced top management ■ Vertical integration ■ Employee relations ■ Hoover's international orientation	WEAKNESSES (W) ■ Process-oriented R&D ■ Distribution channels ■ Financial position ■ Global positioning ■ Manufacturing facilities
OPPORTUNITIES (O) ■ Economic integration of European Community ■ Demographics favor quality appliances ■ Economic development of Asia ■ Opening of Eastern Europe ■ Trend toward super stores	SO STRATEGIES ■ *Use worldwide Hoover distribution channels to sell both Hoover and Maytag major appliances.* ■ *Find joint venture partners in Eastern Europe and Asia.*	WO STRATEGIES ■ *Expand Hoover's presence in continental Europe by improving Hoover quality and reducing manufacturing and distribution costs.* ■ *Emphasize superstore channel for all non-Maytag brands.*
THREATS (T) ■ Increasing government regulation ■ Strong U.S. competition ■ Whirlpool and Electrolux positioned for global economy ■ Fuzzy logic technology by Japanese ■ Predicted recession	ST STRATEGIES ■ *Acquire Raytheon's appliance business to increase U.S. market share.* ■ *Merge with a Japanese major home appliance company.* ■ *Sell off all non-Maytag brands and strongly defend Maytag's U.S. niche.*	WT STRATEGIES ■ *Sell off Dixie-Narco Division to reduce debt.* ■ *Emphasize cost reduction to reduce break-even point.* ■ *Sell out to Raytheon or a Japanese firm.*

Finding a Propitious Niche

William Newman suggests that a corporation should seek a **propitious niche** in its strategy formulation process.[4] This niche is a corporation's specific competitive role. It should be so well suited to the firm's internal and external environment that other corporations are not likely to challenge or dislodge it. The corporation thus has a distinctive competence that enables it to take advantage of specific environmental opportunities.

Finding such a niche is not always easy. A firm's management must be always looking for **strategic windows,** that is, market opportunities.[5] As shown in the case

ILLUSTRATIVE EXAMPLE 6.2

Fadal Engineering Company Finds a Propitious Niche

The machine tool industry in 1990 was not a very attractive enterprise for most U.S. companies. Led by Japanese corporations, importers were responsible for 43% of the $4.9 billion industry. U.S. companies such as Cincinnati Milicron and Giddings & Lewis had been successful by catering to multibillion-dollar customers like Caterpillar and Boeing, but were also threatened by foreign competition. All in all, this did not appear to be a good industry for a small, family-run business.

When Francis de Caussin, a Detroit machinist, moved his family to North Hollywood, California, in 1953, he formed a company whose name was the acronym of the first initials of the founder and his sons Adrian, David, and Larry: Fadal Engineering Company (pronounced *fuh-dal*). From their garage, the family built a business by making high-precision machine parts. Early in the 1980s, the family branched into the machine tool business. After considerable work, they made a no-frills vertical machining center to drill, bore, and mill metal pieces. Compared with the machine tools made for big manufacturers, Fadal's machine had fewer parts and simpler electronic controls.

The company soon expanded into other machine tools that were designed to appeal to smaller manufacturers that could not afford the more sophisticated, complex machines made by larger outfits. The machines made by Fadal were functional and durable, but far cheaper than the typical lowest-priced competing machine. Since Fadal generally used U.S.–made standard parts, repairs were usually a simple matter. By 1990, Fadal's sales reached the $80 million range, ten times what they were in 1985. The company controlled nearly 20% of the $400 million metalworking machine market tailored to the needs of small manufacturers.

Why was a small, family-run machine toolmaker successful in a relatively unattractive industry? Given its small size and the fact that existing competition was ignoring the small manufacturer's needs, Fadal took advantage of the market opportunity. The company designed products with a minimum of parts and frills, making its machines inexpensive and reliable. It kept overhead low. R&D was minimal. Only 20 of its 200 employees were salaried. The company has prospered. According to Adrian de Caussin, the eldest brother and Fadal's electronics chief, "We have vigor. Big, old-time toolmakers have lost that and if we lose ours, we'll go the same way."

Source: Z. Schiller, "Fadal's Attractions," *Business Week* (October 22, 1990), pp. 62–66.

---

of Fadal Engineering, presented in Illustrative Example 6.2, the first one through the strategic window can occupy a propitious niche and discourage competition (if the firm has the required internal strengths).

A recent study of high-performing, midsized growth companies found these successful corporations to have four characteristics in common.

- They innovate as a way of life.
- They compete on value, not price.
- They achieve leadership in *niche* markets.
- They build on their strengths by competing in *related niches*.[6]

In summary, research reveals that corporate performance is strongly influenced by how well a company positions itself within an industry.[7] A specific niche in which a corporation's strengths fit well with environmental opportunities is thus a desired

company is to maintain a balanced portfolio so that the firm can be self-sufficient in cash and always working to harvest mature products in declining industries to support new ones in growing industries.

Underlying the BCG growth-share matrix is the concept of the experience curve (discussed in Chapter 5). The key to success is market share. Those firms with the highest market share will tend to have a cost leadership position based on economies of scale, among other things. If a company is able to use the experience curve to its advantage, it should be able to manufacture and sell new products at a price low enough to garner early market share leadership. Once it becomes a star, it is destined to be very profitable, considering its inevitable future as a cash cow.

Research into the growth-share matrix generally supports its assumptions and recommendations except for the advice that dogs should be promptly harvested or liquidated.[11] A product with a low share in a declining industry can be very profitable if the product has a niche in which market demand remains stable and predictable.[12] If enough of the competition leaves the industry, a product's market share can increase by default until the dog becomes the market leader and thus a cash cow. All in all, the BCG growth-share matrix is a very popular technique. It is quantifiable and easy to use. The animal analogies of cash cows and dogs have become trendy buzz-words in management circles.

However, the growth-share matrix has been criticized for several reasons.

- The use of highs and lows to make just four categories is too simplistic.
- The link between market share and profitability is not necessarily strong. Low-share businesses can be profitable, too (and vice versa).
- The highest growth rate markets are not always the best.
- It considers the product or SBU only in relation to one competitor: the market leader. It misses small competitors with fast-growing market shares.
- Growth rate is only one aspect of industry attractiveness.
- Market share is only one aspect of overall competitive position.[13]

Nine-Cell GE Business Screen

A more complicated matrix is that developed by General Electric with the assistance of the McKinsey and Company consulting firm. As depicted in Fig. 6.5, it includes nine cells based on long-term industry attractiveness and business strength/ competitive position. Interestingly, this nine-cell matrix is almost identical to the *Directional Policy Matrix* developed by Shell Oil and used extensively by European firms. Both use the same factors and both use nine cells. The GE Business Screen, in contrast to the BCG growth-share matrix, includes much more data in its two key factors than just business growth rate and comparable market share. For example, at GE, industry attractiveness includes market growth rate, industry profitability, size, and pricing practices, among other possible opportunities and threats. Business strength or competitive position includes market share as well as technological position, profitability, and size, among other possible strengths and weaknesses.[14]

The individual products or SBUs are identified by a letter and plotted as circles on the GE Screen. The area of each circle is in proportion to the size of the industry

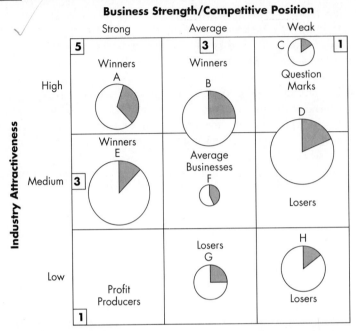

FIGURE 6.5 | General Electric's Business Screen

Source: Adapted from *Strategic Management in GE*, Corporate Planning and Development, General Electric Corporation. Used by permission of General Electric Company.

in terms of sales. The pie slices within the circles depict the market share of each product or SBU.

The following four steps are recommended for the plotting of products or SBUs on the GE Business Screen:[15]

1. **Assess industry attractiveness.**
   a) Select general criteria by which the industry will be rated. These criteria should be key aspects of the industry, such as its potential for sales growth and likely profitability. Table 6.1 lists 15 criteria for one specific industry.
   b) Weight each criterion according to management's perception of the criterion's importance to the achievement of corporate objectives. For example, because the key criterion of the corporation in Table 6.1 is profitability, it receives the highest weight, 0.20.
   c) Rate the industry on each of these criteria from 1 (*very unattractive*) to 5 (*very attractive*). For example, if an industry is facing a long-term decline in profitability, this criterion should be rated 2 or less.
   d) To get a weighted score, multiply the weight for each criterion by its rating. When these scores are added, the weighted attractiveness score for the industry as a whole is provided for a particular SBU. (The weighted industry attractiveness score is 3.38 for the SBU considered in Table 6.1.)

TABLE 6.1	An Example of an Industry Attractiveness Assessment Matrix		

Attractiveness Criteria	Weight[1]	Rating[2]	Weighted Score
Size	0.15	4	0.60
Growth	0.12	3	0.36
Pricing	0.05	3	0.15
Market diversity	0.05	2	0.10
Competitive structure	0.05	3	0.15
Industry profitability	0.20	3	0.60
Technical role	0.05	4	0.20
Inflation vulnerability	0.05	2	0.10
Cyclicality	0.05	2	0.10
Customer financials	0.10	5	0.50
Energy impact	0.08	4	0.32
Social	GO	4	—
Environmental	GO	4	—
Legal	GO	4	—
Human	0.05	4	0.20
	1.00		3.38

[1] Some criteria may be of a GO/NO GO type. For example, many Fortune 500 firms probably would decide not to invest in industries that are viewed negatively by our society, such as gambling, even if it were both legal and very profitable to do so.

[2] 1 (*very unattractive*) through 5 (*highly attractive*).

Source: Reprinted by permission from *Strategy Formulation: Analytical Concepts* by C. W. Hofer and D. Schendel. Copyright © 1978 by West Publishing Company. All rights reserved.

2. **Assess business strength/competitive position.**
   a) Identify the SBU's key factors for success in the industry. Table 6.2 lists 17 such factors for a specific industry.
   b) Weight each success factor (market share, for instance) in terms of its relative importance to profitability or some other measure of success within the industry. For example, because market share was believed to have a relatively small impact on most firms in the industry of Table 6.2, this success factor was given a weight of only 0.10.
   c) Rate the SBU on each of the factors from 1 (*very weak competitive position*) to 5 (*very strong competitive position*). For example, as the products of the SBU of Table 6.2 have a very high market share, market share received a rating of 5.
   d) To get a weighted score, multiply the weight of each factor by its rating. When these scores are added, the sum provides a weighted business strength/competitive position score for the SBU as a whole. (The weighted business strength/competitive position score for the SBU considered in Table 6.2 is 4.30.)

| TABLE 6.2 | An Example of a Business Strength/Competitive Position Assessment Matrix for an SBU |

Key Success Factors	Weight	Rating[2]	Weighted Score
Market share	0.10	5	.50
SBU growth rate	X[1]	3	—
Breadth of product line	.05	4	.20
Sales distribution effectiveness	.20	4	.80
Proprietary and key account advantages	X	3	—
Price competitiveness	X	4	—
Advertising and promotion effectiveness	.05	4	.20
Facilities' location and newness	.05	5	.25
Capacity and productivity	X	3	—
Experience curve effects	.15	4	.60
Raw materials cost	.05	4	.20
Value added	X	4	—
Relative product quality	.15	4	.60
R&D advantages/position	.05	4	.20
Cash throw-off	.10	5	.50
Caliber of personnel	X	4	—
General image	.05	5	.25
	1.00		4.30

[1] For any particular industry, there will be some factors that, while important in general, will have little or no effect on the relative competitive position of firms within that industry. It is usually better to drop such factors from the analysis than to assign them very low weights.

[2] 1 *(very weak competitive position)* through 5 *(very strong competitive position)*.

Source: Reprinted by permission from *Strategy Formulation: Analytical Concepts* by C. W. Hofer and D. Schendel. Copyright © 1978 by West Publishing Company. All rights reserved.

3. **Plot each SBU's current position.**
Once industry attractiveness and business strength/competitive position are calculated for each SBU, the actual position of all the corporation's SBUs should be plotted on a matrix like the one illustrated in Fig. 6.5. The areas of the circles should be proportional to the sizes of the various industries involved (in terms of sales); the company's current market share in each industry should be depicted as a pie-shaped wedge; and the circles should be centered on the coordinates of the SBU's industry attractiveness and business strength/competitive position scores.
   To develop a range of scores for the *industry attractiveness* axis of the matrix, look at Table 6.1. A highly attractive industry should have mostly 5s in the rating column. An industry of medium attractiveness should have mostly 3s in the rating column. An industry of low attractiveness should have

mostly 1s in the rating column. Because the weights of the criteria used for each industry must sum to 1.00 regardless of the number of criteria used, the attractiveness axis of the GE Business Screen matrix should range from 1.00 (*low attractiveness*) to 5.00 (*high attractiveness*), with 3.00 as the midpoint. The SBU evaluated in Table 6.1 with an industry attractiveness score of 3.38 is thus classified as "medium" on this factor.

Similarly, the range of scores for the *business strength/competitive position* axis of the GE Business Screen matrix should also range from 1.00 (*weak*) to 5.00 (*strong*), with 3.00 as the midpoint (*average*). This can be more clearly understood with another look at Table 6.2. Because the criteria weights must sum to 1.00 regardless of the number of criteria used for each SBU, an SBU with a very strong competitive position might have all 5s in the rating column and thus a total weighted score of 5.00. The SBU evaluated in Table 6.2 with a business strength/competitive position score of 4.30 is thus classified as "strong" on this factor.

The resulting matrix shows the corporation's current portfolio situation. The position on the GE matrix for the SBU just calculated would be similar to that of SBU E in Fig. 6.5. The actual situation of a company's SBUs is then contrasted with an ideal portfolio.

4. **Plot the firm's future portfolio.**

An assessment of the current situation is complete only when the present portfolio is projected into the future. Assuming that the present corporate and SBU strategies continue unchanged, top management should assess the probable impact that likely changes to the corporation's task and societal environments will have, on both future industry attractiveness and SBU competitive position. They should ask themselves whether future matrixes show an improving or deteriorating portfolio position. Is there a *performance gap* between projected and desired portfolios? If the answer is yes, this gap should serve as a stimulus for them to seriously review the corporation's current mission, objectives, strategies, and policies.

Overall, the nine-cell GE Business Screen is an improvement over the Boston Consulting Group growth-share matrix. The GE Screen considers many more variables and does not lead to such simplistic conclusions. It recognizes, for example, that there are many different ways to assess the attractiveness of an industry (other than simply using growth rate) and thus allows users to select whatever criteria they feel are most appropriate to their situation.[16] Nevertheless, it can get quite complicated and cumbersome. The calculations used in Tables 6.1 and 6.2 give the appearance of objectiviy but are in reality subjective judgments that may vary from one person to another. Another shortcoming of this portfolio matrix is that it cannot effectively depict the positions of new products or SBUs in developing industries.

Fifteen-Cell Product/Market Evolution Matrix

Developed by Hofer and based on the product life cycle, the 15-cell product/market evolution matrix (shown in Fig. 6.6) depicts the developing types of products or SBUs that cannot be easily shown on the GE Business Screen. Products or SBUs are

FIGURE 6.6 | **Product/Market Evolution Portfolio Matrix**

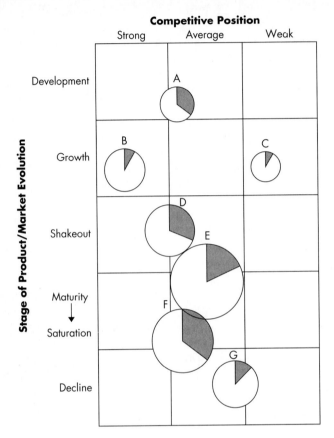

Source: C. W. Hofer and D. Schendel, *Strategy Formulation: Analytical Concepts* (St. Paul, Minn.: West Publishing Co., 1978), p. 34. From C. W. Hofer, "Conceptual Constructs for Formulating Corporate and Business Strategies" (Dover, Mass: Case Publishing), no. BP-0041, p. 3. Copyright © 1977 by Charles W. Hofer. Reprinted by permission.

plotted in terms of their competitive positions and their stages of product/market evolution.[17] As on the GE Business Screen, the circles represent the sizes of the industries involved, and the pie wedges represent the market shares of the firm's SBUs or products. Present and future matrixes can be developed to identify strategic issues. In response to Fig. 6.6, for example, one could ask why product or SBU B does not have a greater share of the market, given its strong competitive position. A limitation of this matrix is that the product life cycle does not always hold for every product. Many products, for example, do not inevitably fall into decline but (like Tide detergent and Colgate toothpaste) are revitalized and put back on a growth track.[18]

Advantages and Limitations of Portfolio Analysis

Portfolio analysis is commonly used in strategy formulation because it offers certain **advantages**:

- It encourages top management to evaluate each of the corporation's businesses individually and to set objectives and allocate resources for each.
- It stimulates the use of externally oriented data to supplement management's judgment.
- It raises the issue of cash flow availability for use in expansion and growth.
- Its graphic depiction facilitates communication.

Portfolio analysis does, however, have some very real **limitations** that have caused some companies to reduce their use of the matrixes:

- It is not easy to define product/market segments.
- It suggests the use of standard strategies that can miss opportunities or be impractical.
- It provides an illusion of scientific rigor when in reality positions are based on subjective judgments.
- Its value-laden terms like *cash cow* and *dog* can lead to self-fulfilling prophecies. General Mills' Chief Executive H. Brewster Atwater, for example, cites his company's Bisquick brand of flour as a product that would have been written off years ago based on portfolio analysis. "This product is 57 years old. By all rights it should have been overtaken by newer products. But with the proper research to improve the product and promotion to keep customers excited, it's doing very well."[19]
- It is not always clear what makes an industry attractive or what stage a product is in its life cycle.[20]

6.2 REVIEW OF MISSION AND OBJECTIVES

A reexamination of a corporation's current mission and objectives must be made before alternative strategies can be generated and evaluated. The seriousness of this step is emphasized by Tregoe and Zimmerman.

> When making a decision, there is an almost universal tendency to concentrate on the alternatives—the action possibilities—rather than on the objectives we want to achieve. This tendency is widespread because it is much easier to deal with alternative courses of action that exist right here and now than to really think about what we want to accomplish in the future. Projecting a set of values forward is hard work. The end result is that we make choices that set our objectives for us, rather than having our choices incorporate clear objectives.[21]

Problems in corporate performance can derive from an inappropriate statement of mission, which may be too narrow or too broad. If the mission does not provide a **common thread** (a unifying theme) for a corporation's businesses, managers may be unclear about where the corporation is heading. Objectives and strategies might be in conflict with each other. Divisions might be competing against one another, rather than against outside competition—to the detriment of the corporation as a whole. According to Lorange, "Rapid changes in the environment suggest that the definition of businesses should be reviewed frequently, so that the relevance of the business definitions can be maintained."[22]

An example of a revision of a corporation's mission statement is that by American Telephone and Telegraph (AT&T). The revised mission was published in AT&T's 1980 annual report to the stockholders and had important implications for future corporate strategy.

> No longer do we perceive that our business will be limited to telephony or, for that matter, telecommunications. Ours is the business of information handling, the knowledge business. And the market that we seek is global.

A corporation's objectives can also be inappropriately stated. They can either focus too much on short-term operational goals or be so general that they provide little real guidance. Consequently, objectives should be constantly reviewed so that their usefulness is ensured.

6.3 CORPORATE STRATEGY

A key part of strategy formulation is the development of alternative courses of action that specify the means by which the corporate mission and objectives are to be accomplished. As depicted in Fig. 6.1, the generation, evaluation, and selection of the best strategic alternative is the sixth step of the strategic decision-making process. The typical large, multidivisional business corporation operating in several different industries has three levels of strategy: *corporate, business,* and *functional.* The remainder of this chapter deals in particular with the generation of alternative corporate strategies. Business and functional strategies are discussed in the next chapter.

As described in Chapter 1, **corporate strategy** specifies the firm's overall direction in terms of its general orientation toward growth and the management of its various businesses and product lines to achieve a balanced portfolio of products and services. It is the pattern of decisions regarding the types of businesses and industries in which a firm should be involved, the flow of financial and other resources to and from its divisions, the relationship of the corporation to key groups in its environment, and the approach a corporation takes to achieve its mission and objectives. Even the smallest company operating in only one industry with one product line must, at one time or another, consider the questions embedded within corporate strategy:

- Should we expand, cut back, or continue our operations unchanged?
- If we want to grow and expand, should we do so through internal development or through external acquisitions, mergers, or joint ventures?
- Should we concentrate our activities within our current industry or should we diversify into other industries?

Corporate strategy is composed of three general orientations (sometimes called grand strategies); *growth, stability,* and *retrenchment.* This follows the common-sense notion that a corporation, like a person, can either move forward, stay where it is, or take a step back. Once the general orientation (such as growth) is chosen, a corporation's strategic managers can select from several more specific corporate strategies, such as concentration within one industry or diversification into other industries.

Assume for the purposes of this section that the corporation operates either in one industry *only,* like Caterpillar in heavy construction equipment, or in one industry *primarily,* like Anheuser-Busch, which derives approximately 80% of its sales and over 90% of its profits from beer and related products. This is a reasonable assumption given that the vast majority of U.S. business firms tends to be small companies—each concentrating in one industry.[23] In addition, a study of 145 diversified manufacturing firms by Wiersema and Ulrich from the Fortune 1000 revealed that the average U.S. corporation studied derived half of its total sales from its "core" business. The researchers concluded that "management of the organization's core business is central to any decision about strategic direction. . . . Today, despite the diversity of large firms, an organization's core business is still of prime importance. Without a strong core business, a firm cannot aggressively pursue new directions."[24]

Strategic managers must decide the overall direction of the firm through its corporate strategy. Management can do so by combining *industry attractiveness* with the company's *business strength/competitive position* within its primary industry (core business) into a nine-cell matrix similar to the GE Business Screen. The resulting matrix, depicted in Fig. 6.7, may be used as a model to plot some of the alternative corporate strategies that might fit the company's situation. This model suggests which corporate strategy from 12 possible strategies may be most appropriate. The placement of the strategies are in general agreement with research in the area regarding top management's reported motives for choosing one strategy over another.[25] The model does not state that these are the *only* strategies that should be used, just that these strategies seem the most likely.

Figure 6.7 identifies nine cells containing well-known corporate strategies that fit under the categories of growth, stability, and retrenchment. **Growth** strategies are either concentration, that is, expansion within the firm's current industry (*Cells 1, 2, and 5*), or diversification (*Cells 7 and 8*), where growth is generated outside of the firm's current industry. **Stability** strategies (*Cells 4 and 5*) represent a firm's choice to retain its current mission and objectives without any significant change in strategic direction. **Retrenchment** strategies (*Cells 3, 6, and 9*) are the reduction in scope and magnitude of the firm's efforts.

FIGURE 6.7	Proposed Model of Corporate Strategies

Business Strengths/Competitive Position

	Strong	Average	Weak
High	**1** **Growth** Concentration via Vertical Integration	**2** **Growth** Concentration via Horizontal Integration	**3** **Retrenchment** Turnaround
Medium	**4** **Stability** Pause or Proceed with Caution	**5** **Growth** Concentration via Horizontal Integration – – – – – – – – **Stability** No Change in Profit Strategy	**6** **Retrenchment** Captive Company or Divestment
Low	**7** **Growth** Concentric Diversification	**8** **Growth** Conglomerate Diversification	**9** **Retrenchment** Bankruptcy or Liquidation

Industry Attractiveness (vertical axis label)

Source: J. D. Hunger, E. J. Flynn, and T. L. Wheelen, "Contingency Corporate Strategy: A Proposed Typology with Research Propositions," Paper presented to the Midwest Division of the Academy of Management, Milwaukee, Wisconsin, April 1990. Copyright © 1990 by Wheelen and Hunger Associates. Reprinted by permission.

GROWTH STRATEGIES

By far the most widely pursued corporate strategies of business firms are those designed to achieve growth in either sales, assets, profits, or some combination.[26] This can be achieved by reducing price, developing new features, adding new products or services, or by gaining access to markets not currently served. Those corporations that do business in dynamic environments *must* grow in order to survive. Continuing growth means increasing sales and a chance to take advantage of the experience curve to reduce the per-unit cost of products sold, thereby increasing profits. This cost reduction becomes extremely important if a corporation's industry is growing quickly and competitors are engaging in price wars in attempts to increase their shares of the market. Those firms that have not reached "critical mass" (that is, gained the necessary economy of large-scale production) will face large losses unless they can find and fill a small, but profitable, niche where higher prices can be offset by special product or service features. That is why Motorola, Inc. continued to spend large sums on the product development of cellular phones, pagers, and two-way radios, despite a serious drop in profits in 1990. According to Motorola's Chairman George Fisher, "What's at stake here is leadership." Even though the industry was changing quickly, the company was working to avoid the erosion of its market share by jumping into new wireless markets as fast as possible.

Continuing as the market leader in this industry would almost guarantee Motorola enormous future returns.[27]

Growth is, however, a very seductive strategy for two key reasons:

- A growing firm can cover up mistakes and inefficiencies more easily than can a stable one. A growing flow of revenue into a highly leveraged corporation can create a large amount of "organization slack" (unused resources) that can be used to quickly resolve problems and conflicts between departments and divisions. There is also a big cushion for a turnaround in case a strategic error is made. Larger firms also have more clout and are more likely to receive support in case of impending bankruptcy, as was the situation with Chrysler Corporation in 1979.
- There are more opportunities for advancement, promotion, and interesting jobs in a growing firm. Growth itself is exciting and ego-enhancing for CEOs. A growing corporation tends to be seen as a "winner" or "on the move" by the marketplace and by potential investors. Large firms are also more difficult to acquire than are smaller ones; thus, an executive's job is more secure.[28]

Concentration and Diversification Growth Strategies

There are two basic growth strategies at the corporate level: *concentration* in one industry and *diversification* into other industries. If, as depicted in Fig. 6.7, the current industry is very attractive in terms of growth rate and other criteria, concentration of resources on that one industry makes sense as a strategy for growth. If, however, the current industry has little attractiveness, it makes sense for a corporation to diversify out of that industry if management wishes to pursue growth. Research does indicate that high-performing firms are less likely to diversify and that low-performing firms may seek diversification in order to improve firm performance.[29] If it chooses concentration, the company can grow through vertical or horizontal integration either internally, by using its own resources, or externally, by acquiring the resources of others. If it chooses diversification, the company can grow through concentric or conglomerate diversification either internally, through new product development, or externally, through acquisition. Figure 6.7 illustrates these growth strategies in *Cells 1, 2, 5, 7, and 8.*

Concentration Through Vertical Integration (*Cell 1*)   Growth through concentration in the firm's current industry can be achieved via vertical integration by taking over a function previously provided by a supplier (**backward integration**) or by a distributor (**forward integration**). This is a logical strategy for a corporation having a strong competitive position (high market share) in a highly attractive industry.[30] The attractiveness of the industry compels the firm to stay within the industry. That very attractiveness, however, will likely result in a higher level of competition as new competitors enter the industry and current competitors work to increase their sales. To keep and even improve its business strength/competitive position, the company may act to minimize resource acquisition costs and inefficient operations as well as

TABLE 6.3	Some Advantages and Disadvantages of Vertical Integration

Advantages	Disadvantages
Internal Benefits	*Internal Costs*
Integration economies reduce costs by eliminating steps, reducing duplicate overhead, and cutting costs (technology dependent).	Need for overhead to coordinate vertical integration increases costs.
Improved coordination of activities reduces inventorying and other costs.	Burden of excess capacity from unevenly balanced minimum efficient scale plants (technology dependent).
Avoid time-consuming tasks, such as price shopping, communicating design details, or negotiating contracts.	Poorly organized vertically integrated firms do not enjoy synergies that compensate for higher costs.
Competitive Benefits	*Competitive Dangers*
Avoid foreclosure to inputs, services, or markets.	Obsolete processes may be perpetuated.
Improved marketing or technological intelligence.	Creates mobility (or exit) barriers.
Opportunity to create product differentiation (increased value added).	Links firm to sick adjacent businesses.
Superior control of firm's economic environment (market power).	Lose access to information from suppliers or distributors.
Create credibility for new products.	Synergies created through vertical integration may be overrated.
Synergies could be created by coordinating vertical activities skillfully.	Managers integrated before thinking through the most appropriate way to do so.

Source: K. R. Harrigan, "Formulating Vertical Integration Strategies," *Academy of Management Review* (October 1984), p. 639. Copyright © 1984 by the Academy of Management. Reprinted by permission.

to gain more control over quality and product distribution. The firm, in effect, builds on its strengths to gain greater competitive advantage.

Vertical integration can be achieved either internally or externally by the firm. Henry Ford, for example, used internal company resources to build his River Rouge Plant outside Detroit. The manufacturing process was integrated to the point that iron ore entered one end of the long plant and finished automobiles rolled out the other end into a huge parking lot. In contrast, DuPont, the huge chemical company, chose the external route to backward vertical integration by acquiring Conoco for oil needed in the production of DuPont's synthetic fabrics.

Vertical integration is quite common in the oil, basic metals, automobile, and forest products industries. As pointed out in Table 6.3, some of its advantages are the lowering of costs and the improvement of coordination and control. It is a good way for a strong firm to increase its competitive advantage in an attractive industry. Although backward integration is usually more profitable than forward integration,[31] it can reduce a corporation's strategic flexibility: by creating an encumbrance of expensive assets that might be hard to sell, it can thus create an exit barrier to the corporation's leaving that particular industry.[32]

A study by Harrigan reveals at least four types of vertical integration ranging from **full integration** to **long-term contracts**.[33] For example, if a corporation does not want to have the disadvantages of full vertical integration, it may choose either taper or quasi-integration strategies. With **taper integration**, a firm produces part of its own requirements and buys the rest from outside suppliers. In the case of **quasi integration**, a company gets most of its requirements from an outside supplier that is under its partial control. For example, by purchasing 10% of the common stock of Interactive Images, Inc., IBM guaranteed its access to Interactive's graphics software.[34]

Concentration Through Horizontal Integration (*Cells 2 and 5*)   Growth through concentration in the firm's current industry can be achieved via horizontal integration by expanding the firm's business into other geographic locations and/or by increasing the range of products and services offered to current markets. Although in Cells 2 and 5 the corporation is in a highly or moderately attractive industry where it wishes to remain, its competitive strength is only average. The company's manufacturing or marketing functions may be operating satisfactorily, but in a mediocre manner providing no significant competitive advantage. A firm in this position may attempt to solidify and strengthen its presence in its current industry by working to shore up its weaknesses. When operating in a highly attractive industry (Cell 2), its objectives are generally to increase the sales and profits of the firm's current business through larger economies of scale in production and marketing, as well as to reduce current and/or potential competition for customers and supplies. When operating in a moderately attractive industry that is probably going through some consolidation (Cell 5), its objectives are more defensive in nature—avoiding current or expected future losses in sales and profits.

A company in these cells can acquire market share, production facilities, or specialized technology through internal development or externally through acquisitions or via joint ventures with another firm in the same industry.[35] For example, American Airlines in 1990 chose to expand horizontally through internal means into international service instead of externally as United Airlines did earlier when it purchased Pan American Airlines' Asian division.[36] Maytag Corporation also chose to grow through external means. See the *boxed example* of Maytag (p. 178) for a discussion of Maytag's choice of acquisitions.

Concentric Diversification (*Cell 7*)   Growth through diversification out of an industry into a *related* industry may be a very appropriate corporate strategy when a firm's competitive position is strong but industry attractiveness is low. By focusing on the characteristics that have given the company its competitive strength, the company uses those very strengths as its means of diversification. The firm attempts to secure strategic fit in a new industry where the firm's product knowledge, manufacturing capabilities, and marketing skills it used so effectively in the original industry can be put to good use. The search is for **synergy**—the concept that 2 + 2 = 5. It is hoped that two businesses will be able to generate more profits together than they could separately. The corporation's lines of business possess some common thread that serves to relate them in some manner. The point of commonality

Maytag Corporation: A Growth Strategy of Horizontal Integration Through External Means

Maytag management realized in 1978 that the company would be unable to continue competing effectively in the U.S. major home appliance industry if it remained only a high-quality niche manufacturer of automatic washers and dryers. The industry was rapidly consolidating around those appliance companies with a complete line of products at all price and quality levels in all three key lines of "white goods": laundry (washers and dryers), cooking (stoves and ovens), and cooling (refrigerators and freezers) appliances. Maytag's top management concluded that it would soon have to acquire other companies or risk being bought out itself. Given the long time frame needed to acquire the technology as well as the manufacturing and marketing expertise necessary to produce and sell these other lines of appliances, Maytag chose to grow externally by acquiring Jenn-Air and Magic Chef in the mid-1980s. Similarly, in 1989 Maytag's management concluded that the best way to ensure a global presence in major home appliances was to purchase Hoover, the well-known vacuum cleaner company with a solid position in white goods in Europe and Australia.

may be similar technology, customer usage, distribution, managerial skills, or product similarity. Those corporations most likely to diversify out of their current industry into related industries are those that are the leaders in their core business and have the capabilities needed for success in the new industry.[37]

The firm may choose to diversify concentrically, either through internal or external means. Anheuser-Busch, for example, took the internal path when it created its Busch Gardens theme parks (to better use the land around its breweries) and Eagle Snacks food line (to provide snacks to complement beer drinking). Only after the success of these relatively small diversification efforts and the continued drop in attractiveness of the brewing industry did the company take the external route in acquiring Campbell Taggart bakery and Sea World amusement parks during the 1980s. Philip Morris, in contrast, took the external route to concentric diversification by purchasing Miller Brewing in the early 1970s when the swell of the college-age population made the beer industry attractive. The company chose to apply the strong product development, marketing, and distribution skills it had developed earlier in its core tobacco business (which by then was becoming an unattractive industry) to the brewing and selling of beer. Miller soon became a dominant force in the brewing industry, second only to Anheuser-Busch. In both instances, the new products complemented the company's existing products. Combining the new with the old seemed likely to provide some product-market synergy that would then increase sales or reduce the costs of current products as well as new ones.

Conglomerate Diversification (*Cell 8*) Growth through diversification out of an industry into an *unrelated* industry may be a very appropriate corporate strategy when a firm's competitive position is only average and industry attractiveness is low.

These two factors force the firm to put its developmental efforts into other industries. The company is probably able to attain a reasonably good level of sales and profits in its current business so long as the industry is growing and has more opportunities than threats. Once its markets reach maturity, however, a company with only an average competitive position begins to realize lower levels of performance. When top management realizes that the company's current industry is unattractive and that the firm lacks outstanding abilities or skills it could easily transfer to related products or services in other industries, the most likely strategy will be diversifying into an industry unrelated to its current one. Such a move can be made via internal or external routes. In conglomerate diversification, timing is important—early entry seems to be a key to success when established companies move into a younger industry.[38]

Rather than maintaining a common thread throughout their corporation, top managers who adopt this strategy are primarily concerned with the criterion of return on investment: Will it increase the corporation's level of profitability? The addition may, however, be justified in terms of strategic fit. The emphasis in conglomerate diversification is on financial synergy rather than on the product-market synergy common to concentric diversification. A cash-rich corporation with few opportunities for growth in its industry might, for example, move into another industry where opportunities are great, but cash is hard to find. Another instance of conglomerate diversification might be the purchase by a corporation with a seasonal and, therefore, uneven cash flow of a firm in an unrelated industry with complementing seasonal sales that will level out the cash flow. The purchase of a natural gas transmission business (Texas Gas Resources) by the railroad, CSX Corporation, was considered by CSX management to be a good fit because most of the gas transmission revenue was realized in the winter months when railroads experience a seasonally lean period.

Other examples of conglomerate diversification are the many acquisitions and mergers that occur throughout the world as established corporations attempt to move into more attractive industries without carrying along the baggage they were forced to support in their core business. U.S. Steel (now called USX), for example, began its slow movement out of a very mature steel industry in which it saw little value in further investment into the still reasonably attractive petroleum industry with its purchase of Marathon Oil. Top management decided to change industries while the corporation still had the resources to support such a move. By 1989, Marathon Oil generated 55% of USX's operating profit![39]

Given the rationale behind conglomerate diversification, it is easy to understand why most examples are of the external variety—acquisitions and mergers. By the time a corporation's top management realizes that the company's industry is no longer attractive, it is very likely too late to change industries through internal means. Examples can be provided, however, of companies that developed a product or service in another industry strictly as a sideline to their current business. See Illustrative Example 6.3 for the reason behind Hoover Company's original decision to make vacuum cleaners.

There are other examples of companies that, through serendipity, planning, or research efforts, developed interests in secondary areas that evolved into industries

ILLUSTRATIVE EXAMPLE 6.3

Vacuum Cleaners Were Originally a Sideline at the Hoover Company

The Hoover Company, now a part of Maytag Corporation, began as a successful maker and seller of leather goods. The company got involved with vacuum cleaners only when Frank Hoover's wife, Susan, bought one of the new inventions of Murray Spangler. The Hoovers were so impressed with the product that they agreed to take over the manufacture and sale of Spangler's cleaners in 1908 as a sideline when the inventor ran out of money to keep his small enterprise operating. When the Hoover Company's leather business faded with the advent of mass-produced automobiles and the end of World War II (saddles, cable traces, and leggings were no longer in much demand!), management decided to switch industries and focus on their "little cleaner business."

unrelated to the company's original business. Maytag began as a farm implement manufacturer. Polaroid Corporation was founded to make polarized filters and sunglasses. Xerox Corporation's Palo Alto Research Center originated much of the technology later used by Apple Computer to develop the Apple Macintosh family of computers.[40]

Controversies in Growth Strategies

There are many controversial issues surrounding the growth strategies just mentioned. One issue deals with the impact on corporate performance of concentric versus conglomerate diversification. Another concerns the value of mergers versus acquisitions versus joint ventures. A third issue questions whether internal or external growth is the best strategy for a corporation.

Concentric versus Conglomerate Diversification   Beginning with the classic study by Rumelt, several researchers have argued that conglomerate (unrelated) diversification into other industries is less profitable than concentric (related) diversification.[41] Peters and Waterman support this proposition in their book, *In Search of Excellence.*

> Our principal finding is clear and simple. Organizations that do branch out (whether by acquisition or internal diversification) but stick very close to their knitting outperform the others. The most successful of all are those diversified around a single skill—the coating and bonding technology at 3M, for example.
>
> The second group, in descending order, comprises those companies that branch out into related fields—the leap from electric power generation turbines to jet engines (another turbine) from GE, for example.
>
> Least successful, as a general rule, are those companies that diversify into a wide variety of fields. Acquisitions, especially among this group, tend to wither on the vine.[42]

Supporting this argument are the recent spin-offs by conglomerate corporations of formerly acquired units. In the past few years, ITT, RCA, Gulf & Western, Beatrice Foods, Quaker Oats, General Electric, Exxon, and R. J. Reynolds have sold off major nonrelated holdings. Nevertheless, other studies have found that *both* concentric (related) and conglomerate (unrelated) acquisitions create value, and that one is *not* any better than the other in terms of financial performance.[43]

It is most probable that concentric and conglomerate diversification are equally valuable strategies for corporate growth, but are successful in different situations.[44] Figure 6.7 suggests that a corporation with a strong competitive position in a particular industry will do better if it diversifies concentrically into a related industry where it can most easily apply its distinctive competence. Corporations with only average competitive positions should thus do better by diversifying into unrelated industries. Leontiades, a well-known scholar in the area, argues that conglomerate acquisitions do not at first appear to be as successful as concentric because the conglomerate acquisition causes an initial reduction in efficiency. (This conclusion, of course, assumes diversification through external means.) He states:

> Until a company learns to manage and integrate its acquisitions, it is dependent on autonomous units operating profitably enough to overcome the lack of administrative coordination. This leaves the company vulnerable to unexpected downturns in the new businesses which it cannot directly control nor totally avoid. Over time, the level of administrative control tends to rise. If this aspect of diversification is mastered, and an optimum "family" of businesses emerges, then the fruits of the labor of diversification can be enjoyed.[45]

This argument thus suggests that the real issue may not be concentric versus conglomerate diversification, but concerns the level of difficulty of managing an acquisition. If the firms are managed with a similar *dominant logic*, they can be integrated quickly and profitably.[46] This concept is exemplified by the comments of F. Ross Johnson, Chief Executive of Nabisco Brands, upon the company's acquisition by R. J. Reynolds Industries:

> We studied each other's track records and hit a common road. How we manage our businesses is practically identical. What we believe in—divesting the bad businesses, tight control of the balance sheet, understanding cash flow—is pretty much the same.[47]

External versus Internal Growth   Corporations can follow the growth strategies of either concentration or diversification through the internal development of new products and services, or through external acquisitions, mergers, and joint ventures. There is some evidence that firms that engage in acquisitions reduce their commitment to innovation. Acquisitions may therefore serve as a substitute for investing in R&D.[48] There is also evidence that acquiring firms tend *not* to do as well in terms of profits as they did before the acquisition.[49] A study of 42 large U.S. business firms that had engaged in diversification over a five-year period revealed that 45% diversified through internal means, 19% diversified through external means, and 36% diversified through both internal and external methods. It is interesting that the economic performances of the companies in the three categories were very similar.

Overall, there appears to be no conclusive sales or profits advantages to either external or internal growth.[50]

Mergers, Acquisitions, and Joint Ventures   Some of the more common examples of external growth strategies are mergers, acquisitions, and joint ventures. A **merger** is a transaction involving two or more corporations in which stock is exchanged, but from which only one corporation survives. Mergers usually occur between firms of somewhat similar size and are usually "friendly." The resulting firm is likely to have a name derived from its composite firms. One example is the merging of Allied Corporation and Signal Companies to form Allied Signal.

An **acquisition** is the purchase of a corporation that is completely absorbed as an operating subsidiary or division of the acquiring corporation. Examples are Procter & Gamble's acquisition of Richardson-Vicks and the purchase of the Chicago Cubs baseball team by the Tribune Company (parent company of the *Chicago Tribune* newspaper and TV superstation WGN). Acquisitions usually occur between firms of different sizes and can be either *friendly* or *hostile*. A friendly acquisition usually begins with the acquiring corporation discussing its desires with the other firm's top management. The top management of the firm to be acquired agrees to work for the acquisition, in return for fair consideration after acquisition. Friendly acquisitions are thus similar to mergers. Hostile acquisitions, in contrast, are often called "takeovers." The acquiring firm ignores the other firm's top management or board of directors and simply begins buying up the other firm's stock until it owns a controlling interest. The takeover target, in response, begins defensive maneuvers, such as buying up its own stock, calling in the Justice Department to initiate an antitrust suit in order to stop the acquisition, or looking for a friendly merger partner (as Gulf Oil did with Standard Oil of California when Texas oilman T. Boone Pickens mounted a takeover effort to buy Gulf's stock).

Slang terms are very popular in mergers and acquisitions. For example, a "pigeon" (highly vulnerable target) or "sleeping beauty" (more desirable than a pigeon) might take a "cyanide pill" (taking on a huge long-term debt on the condition that the debt falls due immediately upon the firm's acquisition) so that it can avoid being "raped" (being subjected to a forcible hostile takeover, sometimes accompanied by looting the target's profitability) by a "shark" (extremely predatory takeover artist) using "hired guns" (lawyers, merger and acquisition specialists, and certain investment bankers).[51] To avoid takeover threats, many corporations have chosen to stagger the elections of board members, to prohibit two-tier tender offers (the offering of a higher price to stockholders who sell their shares first), to prohibit "green-mail" (the buying back of a company's stock from a "shark" at a premium price), and to require an 80% shareholder vote for approval of a takeover. The ultimate countermeasure appears to be the *poison pill*, a procedure granting present shareholders the right to acquire at a substantial discount a large equity stake in an acquiring company whose offer does not have the support of the acquired company's board of directors.

A **joint venture** is a "cooperative business activity, formed by two or more separate organizations for strategic purposes, that creates an independent business entity and allocates ownership, operational responsibilities, and financial risks and rewards to each member, while preserving their separate identity/autonomy."[52] Joint ventures occur because the corporations involved do not wish to or cannot legally merge permanently. Joint ventures provide a way to temporarily fit the different strengths of partners together so that an outcome of value to both is achieved.[53] For example, in 1990 the pharmaceutical firm Merck & Company agreed with the chemical giant DuPont Company to form a new company called DuPont Merck Pharmaceutical Company. Under the terms of the joint venture agreement, the two companies owned, in a 50-50 partnership, DuPont's entire pharmaceutical operations. Merck provided the new company its foreign marketing rights to some prescription medicines plus some cash. In return, Merck got access to all of DuPont's experimental drugs and its small but productive research operation. According to Roy Vagelos, Chairman and CEO of Merck, "We're convinced that we have to increase our access to R&D if we want to increase our world-wide market share [of the pharmaceutical business]." Given that outright acquisitions of other drug producers would be too expensive, Vagelos said that "we looked to a company with a top-notch research operation, but that needed the marketing and development skills we could offer."[54]

Joint ventures are one type of increasingly popular cooperative arrangements (also called **strategic alliances**) ranging from joint venture equity arrangements to nonownership cooperative agreements, R&D partnerships, and cross-licensing.[55] Extremely popular in international undertakings because of financial and political-legal constraints, joint ventures are a convenient way for a privately owned and a publicly owned (state-owned) corporation to work together. Joint ventures and other strategic alliances are discussed further in Chapter 11.[56]

STABILITY STRATEGIES

The stability family of corporate strategies is probably most appropriate for a reasonably successful corporation operating in an industry of medium attractiveness. The industry may be only medium in attractiveness because (1) it is facing a situation of modest or no growth or (2) key forces in the environment are in the process of great change and no one is able to predict if the threats will soon outnumber the opportunities, or vice versa. Stability strategies can be very useful in the short run, but can be dangerous if followed for too long a period. Some of the more popular of these are pause, proceed with caution, no change, and the profit strategy. Figure 6.7 illustrates these strategies in *Cells 4 and 5.*

Pause or Proceed with Caution (*Cell 4*)

A corporation with a strong competitive position in an industry of only moderate attractiveness may pursue no significant change in corporate strategy. A **pause** strategy may be very appropriate as a temporary strategy to enable a corporation to consolidate its resources after prolonged rapid growth in an industry now facing an uncertain future. For example, Cincinnati Millicron changed its emphasis in 1988 from growth to stability after a series of acquisitions and successful product developments positioned the firm at the forefront of robotics and computer-controlled parts manufacturing systems. Unfortunately for the company, the industry was no longer growing at its previous pace.

The situation within the industry may call for a **proceed with caution** strategy. "Steady as she goes" is the appropriate nautical phrase, but all eyes should be trained to spot shallow water or a quick change in weather. The competitive environment is perceived as highly changeable and unpredictable. Since the external environment could soon become highly attractive with many new opportunities or unattractive with many new threats, top management is not likely to be disposed to make sudden moves or take unjustified risks by either investing in or out of the industry. This was the situation faced by CSX Corporation in 1985 while top management waited for the federal government to decide what it was going to do with Conrail, the government-owned railroad operating in the northeastern U.S. CSX operated railroads in the eastern U.S. in competition with Conrail and Norfolk Southern railroads. From CSX management's point of view, if the government sold Conrail to Norfolk Southern, Norfolk Southern would dominate the eastern part of the country and the industry would become very unattractive for CSX. If, however, Conrail was split between CSX and Norfolk Southern, the industry would be very attractive for CSX. As a result, CSX followed a proceed with caution strategy while it lobbied vigorously at the state and federal levels and generated contingency plans for a variety of likely scenarios.

No Change or Profit Strategies (*Cell 5*)

Either no change or profit stability strategies may be pursued when a corporation is operating in an industry of medium attractiveness and has only an average competitive position. The relative stability created by the firm's modest competitive position in an industry facing little or no growth encourages the company to continue on its current course, making only small adjustments for inflation in its sales and profit objectives. There are no obvious opportunities and threats. The company in this cell has no significant strengths or weaknesses. Few aggressive new competitors are likely to enter such an industry. The leaders in the industry are probably holding off any significant investment until the industry becomes more attractive. Weaker competitors are likely to retrench by cutting costs in an attempt to stay profitable. Unless the industry is undergoing consolidation, the relative comfort possessed by a company in this situation is likely to result in its following a **no change** strategy in which the future is expected to continue as an extension of the present. Rarely articulated as a definite strategy, a no change strategy's success depends on a lack of significant change in a corporation's situation. This strategy might also evolve from a lack of interest in or need to engage in hard strategic analysis. For example, between 1955 and 1976 Air Canada operated in a relatively stable and protected environment. The very success of the company worked against any planning for change. The same mission and strategies went unchanged, for the most part, for 21 years![57]

In those cases when the industry is reaching maturity and has dropped from high attractiveness to medium attractiveness (and may even be on its way to becoming unattractive), a corporation with only an average competitive position may find its sales and profits leveling off, and perhaps even beginning to decrease. Rather than announcing this to its stockholders and the investment community at large, top management may be tempted to follow the **profit** strategy. Wishing to believe this drop in industry attractiveness is only temporary, management defers or cuts some short-term discretionary expenses, such as R&D, maintenance, and advertising, to keep profits at a stable level during this period. For example, many U.S. airlines were accused during the 1980s of reducing their maintenance budgets and of canceling contracts for the purchase of new planes so that they could remain profitable during a period of aggressive price competition. Obviously, the profit strategy is useful only to help a company get through a temporary difficulty when the industry is dropping in attractiveness. Unfortunately, the strategy is seductive and if continued long enough will lead to a drop in a corporation's business strength/competitive position—as several airlines discovered to their chagrin when the industry continued to be less attractive than expected and the airlines found themselves unable to compete in any way other than price. The profit strategy is thus a passive, short-term response to the situation described in *Cell 5*. As described earlier, a more active response to this situation is horizontal growth through the acquisition of some of the weaker firms in the industry.

RETRENCHMENT STRATEGIES

Retrenchment strategies may be pursued when a corporation has a weak competitive position regardless of the industry's attractiveness. The weak competitive position typically results in poor performance—sales are down and profits may become losses. With these strategies there is a great deal of pressure to improve performance. As is the coach of a losing football team, the CEO here is typically under pressure to do something quickly or be fired. In an attempt to eliminate the weaknesses that are dragging the company down, management may follow one of several retrenchment strategies. Depending on the attractiveness of the industry, managers could select from the strategies presented in Fig. 6.7 of turnaround (*Cell 3*), captive company or divestment (*Cell 6*), and bankruptcy or liquidation (*Cell 9*).

Turnaround (*Cell 3*)

The turnaround strategy is probably most appropriate when a corporation is in a highly attractive industry and when the corporation's problems are pervasive, but not yet critical. The strategy emphasizes the improvement of operational efficiency. Analogous to a diet, the two basic phases of turnaround strategy include contraction and consolidation. *Contraction* is the initial effort to quickly "stop the bleeding" with a general across-the-board cutback in size and costs. The second phase, *consolidation*, is the implementation of a program to stabilize the now-leaner corporation. To streamline the company, plans are developed to reduce unnecessary overhead and to make functional activities cost-justified. This is a crucial time for the corporation. If the consolidation phase is not conducted in a positive manner, many of the best people will leave the organization. If, however, all employees are encouraged to get involved in productivity improvements, the corporation is likely to emerge from this strategic retrenchment period a much stronger and better-

ILLUSTRATIVE EXAMPLE 6.4

Turnaround Strategy at Toro Company

After discovering in 1974 that the Toro brand name ranked second only to Hershey chocolate in consumer recognition, Toro's management decided to diversify by placing the Toro name on a wide range of products, from snow throwers to chain saws. Unfortunately, the pressure to increase sales led to a slide in quality across all product lines and conflict within the distribution channels. Even though the lawn products industry continued to be attractive, two snowless winters virtually stopped all sales of snow-related equipment—including Toro's huge inventory of snow throwers. In early 1981, after ten straight quarters of losses, a new president shifted the company to a turnaround strategy. Dividends were suspended; the work force was cut in half; sales and administrative costs were reduced by 23%; and three plants were closed. By 1985, the Minneapolis firm was a much slimmer, more carefully managed, and profitable company. The company had effectively improved its business strength/competitive position to the point that it was ready to expand again—only this time concentrating in the lawn-care industry. Consequently, it engaged in the growth strategy of horizontal integration by buying Lawn Boy, one of Toro's competitors in quality lawn-care products.

organized company. It has improved its business strength/competitive position and is able once again to expand the business.[58] A good example of the successful use of the turnaround strategy is Toro Company, the lawn mower manufacturer. See Illustrative Example 6.4.

Captive Company or Divestment (*Cell 6*)

A corporation with a weak competitive position in an industry of only medium (and probably declining) attractiveness may not be able to engage in a full-blown turnaround strategy. The industry is not sufficiently attractive to justify such an effort from either the current management or from investors. Nevertheless, a company in this situation faces poor sales and increasing losses unless it takes some action. Sometimes referred to using the chess term "endgame," this situation of slow growth, no growth, or negative growth in an industry forms the second half of a business's life.[59] Management desperately searches for an "angel" to guarantee the company's continued existence. If it is successful, the corporation is able to reduce the scope of some of its functional activities, such as marketing (thus reducing costs) by becoming a **captive company** to a key customer. The weaker company gains certainty of sales and production in return for becoming heavily dependent on another firm for at least 75% of its sales. This became a popular strategy during the 1980s in the moderately attractive auto parts and electronic parts industries for small firms with weak competitive positions. For example, in order to become the sole supplier of a part to General Motors, Simpson Industries of Birmingham, Michigan, agreed to have its engine parts facilities and books inspected and its employees interviewed by a special team from GM. In return, nearly 80% of the company's production was sold to GM through long-term contracts.[60]

In a moderately attractive industry, economies of scale in manufacturing, marketing/distribution, and purchasing may become critical to keeping costs down and profits up. If a corporation with a weak competitive position in this industry is unable either to pull itself up by its bootstraps or to find a customer to which it can become a captive company, it may have no choice but to **divest**, that is, sell out and leave the industry completely. This strategy makes sense if a company does not see any way to build some strengths or shore up its weaknesses and management feels that the industry is not soon likely to become more attractive. Horizontal integration through acquisition may be a popular strategy in this moderately attractive industry as firms with only average competitive positions (*Cell 5*) look to build their strengths by buying the weaker companies positioned in *Cell 6*. To the extent that a company with a weak competitive position in this industry can sell out at a good price for its stockholders (before the industry becomes even more unattractive), divestment makes a lot of sense as a strategy. This was certainly the rationale used by the Joseph Schlitz Brewing Company in agreeing to its sale to The Stroh Brewery in 1982. The turnaround strategy implemented earlier by Schlitz top management no longer appeared realistic given the deterioration in the industry's attractiveness in the early 1980s.

Divestment may also be appropriate for a multibusiness corporation when corporate problems can be traced to the poor performance of an SBU or product line, or when a division or SBU is a "misfit," unable to synchronize itself with the rest of the corporation. Divestment may be especially appropriate when a weak SBU operates in an industry of falling attractiveness. Because over 50% of acquisitions fail to achieve their objectives, it is not surprising that divestment is a popular strategy for corporations that had earlier chosen to grow through external means.[61]

Still another situation appropriate for divestment is when a division needs more resources to be competitive than a multibusiness corporation is willing to provide. Some corporations elect divestment instead of the more painful turnaround strategy. With divestment, top management is able to do one of two things: (1) select a scapegoat to be blamed for all of the corporation's problems, or (2) generate a lot of cash in the sale, which can be used to reduce debt and buy time. The second reason might explain why Pan American chose to sell the most profitable parts of its corporation, the Pan Am Building in New York and Intercontinental Hotels, while keeping its money-losing airline.[62]

Bankruptcy or Liquidation (*Cell 9*)

When a corporation finds itself in the worst possible situation with a weak competitive position in an industry of low attractiveness, management has only a limited number of alternatives—all of them distasteful. To the extent that top management identifies with the corporation, bankruptcy or liquidation may be perceived as an admission of failure. Pride and reputation are liquidated as well as jobs and financial assets. Options center on getting out of the industry before continued losses drain off all assets. To the extent that the corporation operates primarily in one industry, it may pursue a bankruptcy or liquidation strategy. **Bankruptcy** involves giving up management of the firm to the courts in return for some settlement of the corporation's obligations. The increasing use of bankruptcy as a strategy in the U.S. dates to 1978 when the Federal Bankruptcy Law was substantially revised to provide court protection from creditors while a debtor reorganized the company and established a plan to pay the creditors.[63] In such a strategy, management hopes that once the claims on the company are decided by the court, the company will be stronger and better able to compete in a more attractive industry. This was the strategy followed by Johns-Manville, the asbestos manufacturer, when it declared Chapter 11 bankruptcy because of the huge number of lawsuits it faced. After the court took over control of the corporation, the company changed its name to Manville Corporation, got completely out of the asbestos business, and focused its efforts in the reasonably attractive building products industry. Although the bankruptcy strategy appeared to save the corporation, everyone connected with the company experienced a great deal of pain and anguish in the process.

In contrast to bankruptcy, which seeks to perpetuate the corporation, **liquidation** is the termination of the firm. Since the industry is unattractive and the company too weak to be sold as a going concern, management may choose to convert as many saleable assets as possible to cash, which is then distributed to the stockholders once all obligations are paid. No matter how bad the condition of some seriously ill railroads or airlines, for example, rail rights-of-way and airport gates usually have some value. The benefit of liquidation over bankruptcy is that the board of directors, as representatives of the stockholders, together with top management make the decisions instead of turning them over to the court, which may choose to ignore stockholders completely. Even in bankruptcy, however, the court may still choose to liquidate the company instead of resuscitating it as the best way of satisfying the most claims.

EVALUATION OF CORPORATE STRATEGIES

Before it selects a particular corporate strategy, top management must critically analyze the pros and cons of each feasible alternative in light of the corporation's situation. The tendency to select the most obvious strategy can sometimes lead to serious trouble in the long run. The orientation of most top management toward growth strategies has resulted in a strong preference for acquisitions and mergers. In fact, a survey of 236 chief executive officers of the 1,000 largest U.S. industrial firms found that CEOs prefer diversification and acquisition over new product planning and development as a growth strategy.[64] A similar survey of chief financial officers found that the major motive for the acquisition of another firm was the generation of fast growth.[65] Given these attitudes of strategic managers, it is not surprising that the top executives of Fortune 1000 U.S. companies predicted that merger activity will continue to dominate the business community during the 1990s.[66]

There will be times when top management must be willing to select a retrenchment strategy. Unfortunately, some top managers do not like to admit that their company has serious weaknesses. From their research of companies in difficulty, Nystrom and Starbuck conclude that top management very often does not perceive that crises are developing. When top managers do eventually notice trouble, they are prone to attribute the problems to temporary environmental disturbances and tend to follow profit strategies of postponing investments, reducing maintenance, halting training, liquidating assets, denying credit to customers, and raising prices. They adopt a "weathering-the-storm" attitude. "A major activity becomes changing the accounting procedures in order to conceal the symptoms."[67] Even when things are going terribly wrong, there is a strong temptation for top management to avoid liquidation in the hope of a miracle.[68] It is for this reason that a corporation needs a strong board of directors that, to safeguard stockholders' interests, can tell top management when to quit.

SUMMARY AND CONCLUSION

Following the strategic decision-making model presented in Fig. 6.1, this chapter recommends that strategic managers engage in Step 5(a): analyzing strategic factors in light of the current situation. S.W.O.T. analysis and portfolio analysis are presented as two popular methods of conducting this situation analysis. *S.W.O.T.* is an acronym of a corporation's strategic factors: those key internal **S**trengths and **W**eaknesses and external **O**pportunities and **T**hreats. They should include not only those external factors that are most likely to occur and to have a serious impact on the company, but also those internal factors that are most likely to affect the implementation of present and future strategic decisions. *Portfolio analysis* recommends that each product, strategic business unit (SBU), or division be considered separately for purposes of strategy formulation. The most well known matrixes used in portfolio analysis are the four-cell Boston Consulting Group growth-share matrix, the nine-cell General Electric Business Screen, and the 15-cell product/market evolution matrix. Although each matrix looks at a different set of variables, each sums up key *internal* factors on one axis and key *external* factors on the other axis of a two-dimensional matrix. Positioning these two sets of strategic factors in a matrix thus results in an easy-to-grasp graphical representation of a firm's strategic situation.

This chapter further suggests that before generating feasible alternative strategies, strategic managers should review and revise as necessary the firm's current mission and objectives, as shown in Step 5(b) of Fig. 6.1. This leads to Step 6—the generation, evaluation, and selection of the best strategic alternatives.

This chapter then presents some of the many possible alternative corporate strategies and suggests when some of them might be most useful. Corporate strategy is composed of three general orientations (sometimes called grand strategies): growth, stability, and retrenchment. The very popular *growth strategies* are concentration, with its substrategies of vertical and horizontal integration, and diversification, both concentric and conglomerate. Any of these growth strategies can be achieved through internal development or through external acquisition. Epitomized by a philosophy of maintaining an even keel, *stability strategies* are pause, proceed with caution, no change, and profit. *Retrenchment strategies* include turnaround, captive company, divestment, and bankruptcy or liquidation. Before it selects a particular corporate strategy, top management must critically analyze the pros and cons of each feasible alternative in light of the corporation's situation.

Alternative business and functional strategies will be presented and discussed in the next chapter.

DISCUSSION QUESTIONS

1. Is it necessary that a corporation have a common thread running through its many activities in order to be successful? Why or why not?

2. What is likely to happen to an SBU that loses its propitious niche?

3. What value has portfolio analysis in the consideration of strategic factors?

4. Compare and contrast S.W.O.T. analysis with portfolio analysis.

5. What concepts underlie the BCG growth-share matrix? Are these concepts valid?

6. Is the GE Business Screen just a more complicated version of the BCG growth-share matrix? Why or why not?

7. Why is growth the most frequently used corporate-level strategy?

8. How does horizontal integration differ from concentric diversification?

9. What are the tradeoffs between an internal and an external growth strategy?

10. Is the profit strategy really a stability strategy? Why or why not?

NOTES

1. S. P. Sherman, "Inside the Mind of Jack Welch," *Fortune* (March 27, 1989), p. 50.

2. R. Reed and R. J. DeFillipi, "Causal Ambiguity, Barriers to Imitation, and Sustainable Competitive Advantage," *Academy of Management Review* (January 1990), pp. 89–90.

3. G. S. Hansen and B. Wernerfelt, "Determinants of Firm Performance: The Relative Importance of Economic and Organizational Factors," *Strategic Management Journal* (September-October 1989), pp. 399–411.

4. W. H. Newman, "Shaping the Master Strategy of Your Firm," *California Management Review*, Vol. 9, No. 3 (1967), pp. 77–88.

5. D. F. Abell, "Strategic Windows," *Journal of Marketing* (July 1978), pp. 21–26, as reported by K. R. Harrigan, "Entry Barriers in Mature Manufacturing Industries" in *Advances in Strategic Management*, Vol. 2, edited by R. Lamb (Greenwich, Conn.: JAI Press, 1983), pp. 67–97.

6. D. K. Clifford and R. E. Cavanagh, "The Winning Performance of Midsized Growth Companies," *Planning Review* (November 1984), pp. 18–23, 35.

7. L. Fahey and H. K. Christensen, "Evaluating the Research on Strategy Content," *Journal of Management* (Summer 1986), p. 180.

8. D. R. Gilbert, Jr., E. Hartman, J. J. Mauriel, and R. E. Freeman, *A Logic For Strategy* (Cambridge, Mass.: Ballinger, 1988), p. 55.

9. R. G. Hamermesh, "Making Planning Effective," *Harvard Business Review* (July-August 1986), p. 115.

10. B. Hedley, "Strategy and the Business Portfolio," *Long Range Planning* (February 1977), p. 9.

11. D. C. Hambrick, I. C. MacMillan, and D. L. Day, "Strategic Attributes and Performance in the BCG Matrix—A PIMS-Based Analysis of Industrial Product Businesses," *Academy of Management Journal* (September 1982), pp. 510–531.

12. C. Y. Woo and A. C. Cooper, "The Surprising Case for Low Market Share," *Harvard Business Review* (November-December 1982), pp. 106–113.

C. Carr, "Strategy Alternatives for Vehicle Component Manufacturers," *Long Range Planning* (August 1988), pp. 86–97.

13. P. McNamee, "Competitive Analysis Using Matrix Displays," *Long Range Planning* (June 1984), pp. 98–114.

R. E. Walker, "Portfolio Analysis in Practice," *Long Range Planning* (June 1984), pp. 63–71.

D. A. Aaker and G. S. Day, "The Perils of High-Growth Markets," *Strategic Management Journal* (September-October 1986), pp. 409–421.

14. R. G. Hamermesh, *Making Strategy Work* (New York: John Wiley and Sons, 1986), p. 14.

For a more complete list of characteristics, see McNamee, "Competitive Analysis," pp. 102–103.

15. C. W. Hofer and D. Schendel, *Strategy Formulation: Analytical Concepts* (St. Paul, Minn.: West Publishing Co., 1978), pp. 72–87.

16. B. Wernerfelt and C. A. Montgomery, "What Is an Attractive Industry?" *Management Science* (October 1986), pp. 1223–1230.

17. Similar to the Hofer model, but using 20 instead of 15 cells, is the Arthur D. Little (ADL) strategic planning matrix. For details see M. B. Coate, "Pitfalls in Portfolio Planning," *Long Range Planning* (June 1983), pp. 47–56.

18. A. Hiam, "Exposing Four Myths of Strategic Planning," *Journal of Business Strategy* (September-October 1990), pp. 27–28.

19. J. J. Curran, "Companies That Rob the Future," *Fortune* (July 4, 1988), p. 84.

20. F. W. Gluck, "A Fresh Look at Strategic Management," *Journal of Business Strategy* (Fall 1985), pp. 4–19.

    Gilbert et al., *A Logic for Strategy*, pp. 65–74.

21. B. B. Tregoe and J. W. Zimmerman, "The New Strategic Manager," *Business* (May-June 1981), p. 19.

22. P. Lorange, *Implementation of Strategic Planning* (Englewood Cliffs, N.J.: Prentice Hall, 1982), p. 211.

23. A. Conard, "The Corporate Census: A Preliminary Exploration," *California Law Review*, 65 (1975), pp. 440–462.

24. M. F. Wiersema and D. Ulrich, "Strategic Redirection and the Role of Top Management," in *Handbook of Business Strategy, 1989/90 Yearbook*, edited by H. E. Glass (Boston: Warren, Gorham and Lamont, 1989), pp. 14.13–14.14.

25. G. A. Walter and J. B. Barney, "Management Objectives in Mergers and Acquisitions," *Strategic Management Journal* (January 1990), pp. 79–86. This research study reported that the main objectives for engaging in the following strategies were: *Vertical Integration*—manage critical dependencies; *Horizontal Integration*—enter new businesses, economies of scale and scope, expand along product lines, and manage critical dependencies; *Concentric Diversification*—expand along product lines; *Conglomerate Diversification*—utilize financial capability and enter new businesses. This supports our rationale for the placement of the four growth strategies in the particular cells depicted in Figure 6.7.

26. W. F. Glueck, *Business Policy and Strategic Management*, 3rd ed. (New York: McGraw-Hill, 1980), pp. 197–231.

27. L. Therrien, P. Coy, and N. Gross, "Motorola: How Much Will It Cost to Stay No. 1?" *Business Week* (October 29, 1990), pp. 96–97.

28. D. R. Dalton and I. F. Kesner, "Organizational Growth: Big Is Beautiful," *Journal of Business Strategy* (Summer 1985), pp. 38–48.

29. R. E. Hoskisson and M. A. Hitt, "Antecedents and Performance Outcomes of Diversification: A Review and Critique of Theoretical Perspectives," *Journal of Management* (June 1990), 461–509.

30. R. D. Buzzell, "Is Vertical Integration Profitable?" *Harvard Business Review* (January-February 1983), pp. 92–102.

31. J. Vesey, "Vertical Integration: Its Effects on Business Performance," *Managerial Planning* (May-June 1978), pp. 11–15.

32. K. R. Harringan, "Exit Barriers and Vertical Integration," *Academy of Management Journal* (September, 1985), pp. 686–697.

33. K. R. Harrigan, *Strategies for Vertical Integration* (Lexington, Mass.: Lexington Books, D. C. Heath, 1983), pp. 16–21.

34. D. A. Depke, S. M. Gelfond, and J. W. Verity, "Suddenly, Software Houses Have a Big Blue Buddy," *Business Week* (August 7, 1989), pp. 68–69.

35. Horizontal integration is viewed as a useful means of managing competitive uncertainty. See J. Pfeffer and G. Salancik, *The External Control of Organizations* (New York: HarperCollins, 1978).

36. K. Labich, "American Takes On the World," *Fortune* (September 24, 1990), pp. 40–48.

37. R. Calori and CESMA, "How Successful Companies Manage Diverse Businesses," *Long Range Planning* (June 1988), p. 83.

38. C. G. Smith and A. C. Cooper, "Established Companies Diversifying into Young Industries: A Comparison of Firms with Different Levels of Performance," *Strategic Management Journal* (March-April, 1988), pp. 111–121.

39. C. Ansberry, "USX, Unlike Most Oil-Related Companies, Hasn't Benefited from Persian Gulf Conflict," *Wall Street Journal* (August 21, 1990), p. C2.

40. Xerox failed to take advantage of this technology probably because the reprographics industry was still very attractive at the time and demanded all of management's attention and resources. Only later did Xerox realize that with the expiration of its patents it had lost its strong position in the industry. Consequently, in a still highly controversial decision, Xerox management chose to diversify in 1982 into the unrelated industry of insurance with its purchase of Crum and Forster.

41. R. P. Rumelt, *Strategy, Structure, and Economic Performance* (Cambridge, Mass.: Harvard University Press, 1974).

    H. Singh and C. A. Montgomery, "Corporate Acquisition Strategies and Economic Performance," *Strategic Management Journal* (July-August 1987), pp. 377–386.

    R. Amit and J. Livnot, "A Concept of Conglomerate Diversification," *Journal of Management* (December 1988), pp. 593–604.

    M. Capon, J. M. Hulbert, J. U. Farley, and L. E. Martin, "Corporate Diversity and Economic Performance: The Impact of Market Specialization," *Strategic Management Journal* (January-February 1988), pp. 61–74.

    C. W. L. Hill and S. A. Snell, "Effects of Ownership

Structure and Control on Corporate Productivity," *Academy of Management Journal* (March 1989), pp. 25–46.

42. T. J. Peters and R. H. Waterman, Jr., *In Search of Excellence* (New York: HarperCollins, 1982), pp. 293–294.

43. A. Seth, "Value Creation in Acquisitions: A Re-Examination of Performance Issues," *Strategic Management Journal* (February 1990), pp. 99–115.

    B. W. Keats, "Diversification and Business Economic Performance Revisited: Issues of Measurement and Causality," *Journal of Management* (March 1990), pp. 61–72.

    J. B. Barney, "Returns to Bidding Firms in Mergers and Acquisitions: Reconsidering the Relatedness Hypothesis," *Strategic Management Journal* (Summer 1988), pp. 71–78.

44. G. Johnson and H. Thomas, "The Industry Context of Strategy, Structure, and Performance: The U.K. Brewing Industry," *Strategic Management Journal* (July-August 1987), pp. 343–361.

    S. Chatterjee and M. Lubatkin, "Corporate Mergers, Stockholder Diversification, and Changes in Systematic Risk," *Strategic Management Journal* (May-June 1990), pp. 255–268.

    V. Blackburn and J. R. Lang, "Toward a Market/Ownership Constrained Theory of Merger Behavior," *Journal of Management* (March 1989), pp. 77–88.

45. M. Leontiades, *Managing the Unmanageable* (Reading, Mass.: Addison-Wesley, 1986), pp. 62–63.

46. C. K. Prahalad and R. A. Bettis, "The Dominant Logic: A New Linkage Between Diversity and Performance," *Strategic Management Journal* (November-December 1986), pp. 485–501.

    R. M. Grant, "On 'Dominant Logic,' Relatedness and the Link Between Diversity and Performance," *Strategic Management Journal* (November-December 1988), pp. 639–642.

47. S. Scredon and A. Dunkin, "Why Nabisco and Reynolds Were Made for Each Other," *Business Week* (June 17, 1985), p. 34.

48. M. A. Hitt, R. E. Hoskisson, and R. D. Ireland, "Mergers and Acquisitions and Managerial Commitment to Innovation in M-Form Firms," *Strategic Management Journal* (Summer 1990), pp. 29–47.

49. K. L. Fowler and D. R. Schmidt, "Tender Offers, Acquisitions, and Subsequent Performance in Manufacturing Firms," *Academy of Management Journal* (December 1988), pp. 962–974.

50. B. T. Lamont and C. A. Anderson, "Mode of Corporate Diversification and Economic Performance," *Academy of Management Journal* (December 1985), pp. 926–936.

51. P. M. Hirsch, "Ambushes, Shootouts, and Knights of the Roundtable: The Language of Corporate Takeovers," Paper presented to the 40th Meeting of the Academy of Management, Detroit, Mich., August 1980.

52. R. P. Lynch, *The Practical Guide to Joint Ventures and Corporate Alliances* (New York: John Wiley and Sons, 1989), p. 7.

53. K. R. Harrigan, "Joint Ventures: Linking For a Leap Forward," *Planning Review* (July 1986), pp. 10–14.

54. M. Waldholz, "Merck-DuPont Venture Certain to Stir Drug Industry," *Wall Street Journal* (July 26, 1990), pp. B1, B4.

55. K. R. Harrigan, *Managing for Joint Venture Success* (Lexington, Mass.: Lexington Books, D. C. Heath, 1986), p. 4.

56. For more information on cooperative arrangements, see: P. Pekar, Jr., "How Battle-tested Managers Assess Strategic Alliances," *Planning Review* (July–August 1989), pp. 34–37; R. M. Kanter, "Becoming PALS: Pooling, Allying, and Linking Across Companies," *Academy of Management Executive* (August 1989), pp. 183–193.

57. H. Mintzberg, J. P. Brunet, and J. A. Waters, "Does Planning Impede Strategic Thinking? Tracking the Strategies of Air Canada from 1937 to 1976," in *Advances in Strategic Management*, Vol. 4, edited by R. Lamb and P. Shrivastava (Greenwich, Conn.: JAI Press, 1986), p. 29.

58. D. C. Hambrick, "Turnaround Strategies," in *Handbook of Business Strategy*, edited by W. D. Guth (Boston, Mass.: Warren, Gorham, and Lamont, 1985), pp. 10.1–10.32.

    F. M. Zimmerman, "Managing a Successful Turnaround," *Long Range Planning* (June 1989), pp. 105–124.

59. K. R. Harrigan, *Managing Maturing Businesses* (Lexington, Mass.: Lexington Books, D. C. Heath, 1988), p. 1.

60. J. B. Treece, "U.S. Parts Makers Just Won't Say 'Uncle,'" *Business Week* (August 10, 1987), pp. 76–77.

61. J. W. Hunt, "Changing Pattern of Acquisition Behavior in Takeovers and the Consequences for Acquisition Processes," *Strategic Management Journal* (January 1990), pp. 69–77.

62. For more information on reasons for divestment and the divestment process, see M. L. Taylor, *Divesting Business Units* (Lexington, Mass.: Lexington Books, D. C. Heath, 1988).

63. A. Stark and R. D. Frawley, "Bankrupt Firms Can Be

Attractive Acquisitions," *Journal of Business Strategy* (March/April 1989), pp. 34–37.

64. R. Hise and S. McDonald, "CEOs' Views on Strategy: A Survey," *Journal of Business Strategy* (Winter 1984), pp. 81, 86.

65. H. K. Baker, T. O. Miller, and B. J. Ramsperger, "An Inside Look at Corporate Mergers and Acquisitions," *MSU Business Topics* (Winter 1981), p. 51.

66. T. Doorley, "Merger Activity Expected to Remain High in the 1990s," *Journal of Business Strategy* (March/April 1990), pp. 63–64.

67. P. C. Nystrom and W. H. Starbuck, "To Avoid Organizational Crises, Unlearn," *Organizational Dynamics* (Spring 1984), p. 55.

68. For an interesting analysis of management's persistence in attempting to save a firm characterized by sustained low performance, see M. W. Meyer and L. G. Zucker, *Permanently Failing Organizations* (Newbury Park, California: Sage Publications, 1989).

CHAPTER SEVEN

Business and
Functional Strategies

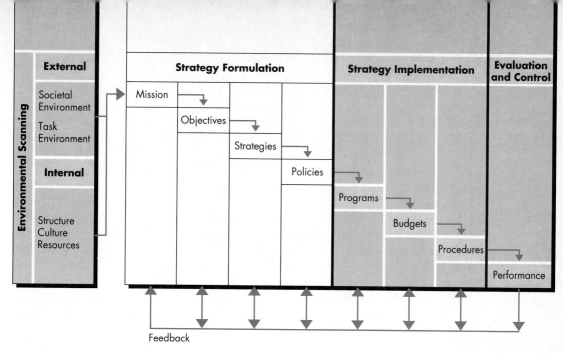

STRATEGIC MANAGEMENT MODEL

We are a Dunkin' Donuts, a Kentucky Fried Chicken, and a Pizza Hut, all rolled into one, for towns like Slater and Mitchellville.[1]

Donald F. Lamberti,
President,
Casey's General Stores

When Donald Lamberti incorporated Casey's General Stores in 1967, he formulated a strategy unknown at that time in the convenience store industry. Instead of targeting the large, growing metropolitan areas of the eastern, western, and southern U.S. where potential sales were high, he chose to focus on the small towns in the agricultural heartland of the Midwest. At first, Casey's appeared to be just another imitator of the successful Seven-Eleven convenience stores offering gasoline and basic groceries.

Operating out of Des Moines, Iowa, Lamberti noticed that many small towns in his part of the country were losing their retail businesses. Regional shopping malls were siphoning off customers attracted by their wider selections and merchandising attractiveness. Even the major gasoline retailers, such as Shell Oil, chose to leave the small towns of Illinois, Iowa, Nebraska, and the Dakotas. Into this developing retail vacuum stepped Casey's General Stores. Contrary to all the conventional wisdom arguing against beginning a business in a declining market, Lamberti avoided direct competition with Seven-Eleven and moved into these increasingly ignored small markets.

By the end of 1990, Casey's operated 777 convenience stores (up from 653 stores in 1988) in its eight-state marketing area of Illinois, Iowa, Kansas, Minnesota, Nebraska, South Dakota, and Wisconsin. Constantly thinking of ways to improve the offerings of his stores, Lamberti decided to expand from gasoline and basic groceries to include fast food. In 1988 Casey's began offering fried chicken and pizza in those stores located in small towns without direct fast-food competition. "We want to have an exclusive," explained Lamberti. Next were videotape rentals and in-store bakeries. In many small towns of the Midwest, Casey's was now the only retail business left. Like any convenience store, prices were somewhat higher than in larger, more specialized stores in the cities. But small-town people did not want to have to drive 10 to 20 miles for a loaf of bread or a pizza. At a time when other convenience stores were struggling to show a profit and avoid bankruptcy, Casey's recorded continuing growth and profitability.

Casey's General Stores is successful because its strategic managers formulated a new strategy designed to give it an advantage in a very competitive industry. A key part of this strategy formulation is the development of alternative courses of action that specify means by which the corporate mission and objectives are to be accomplished. As explained in Chapter 6 and depicted in Fig. 6.1, the generation, evaluation, and selection of the best strategic alternatives form the sixth step of the strategic decision-making process. Once the best strategy is selected, appropriate policies must be established to define the ground rules for implementation. One example is Casey's policy that a new service or product line may be added to its stores only when the product or service can be justified in terms of increasing store traffic. This chapter, therefore, will (1) explain the many business and functional alternative strategies available at the divisional and functional levels of the corporation; (2) suggest criteria for use in the evaluation of these strategies; (3) explain how an optimal strategy is selected; and (4) suggest how strategy is translated into policies.

As described in Chapter 1, the typical large, multidivisional business corporation operating in several different industries has three levels of strategy: corporate, business, and functional. Chapter Six discussed alternative corporate strategies—the strategies that specify the firm's overall direction and its portfolio of businesses, that is, the industries within which the firm operates. This chapter, in contrast, deals with the generation and selection of business and functional strategies—the strategies of most importance at the divisional and departmental levels that determine a company's competitive advantage.

7.1 BUSINESS (COMPETITIVE) STRATEGY

Sometimes referred to as division or competitive strategy, business strategy focuses on improving the competitive position of a corporation's products or services within the specific industry or market segment that the company or division serves. Business strategy raises the following questions:

- Should we compete on the basis of low cost, or should we differentiate our products/services on some basis other than cost, such as quality or service?

in icebreakers) in which they can gain competitive advantage in a narrower arena."[9] Another example of a company in danger of being stuck in the middle is Tandy Corporation. In 1990, Tandy's strategy of selling personal computers to the average person was not generating hoped-for sales. Its computers had neither the exciting new features found on Compaq's products nor the low price of the PC clones like those sold through the mail by Dell. Sales were stagnating. Attempting to increase its sales to business through its GRID Systems subsidiary while keeping up its Radio Shack sales, Tandy was confronted with the dilemma of trying to be all things to all people.[10]

Research generally supports Porter's contention that a firm that fails to achieve a generic strategy is going to be stuck in the middle with no competitive advantage.[11] There is some evidence, however, that businesses with *both* a low-cost and a high differentiation position can be very successful.[12] The Japanese auto companies of Toyota, Nissan, and Honda are often presented as examples of firms able to achieve both a low-cost and a high-quality position. Day refers to this as "playing the spread" and cites Kellogg as an example of a firm prospering by simultaneously lowering costs and selling at premium prices by offering superior customer value. Day contends that improving product quality can indirectly lower costs.[13] This is in agreement with W. Edwards Deming (the quality control expert who helped rebuild Japanese industry after World War II), who argues that quality and productivity (that is, lower-cost production) are compatible. One of Deming's famous 14 points for the transformation of industry states: "Improve constantly and forever the system of production and service, to improve quality and productivity, *and thus constantly decrease costs* [italics added]."[14] Instead of viewing cost leadership and differentiation as separate strategies, the two competitive strategies can be combined as shown in Fig. 7.3. Following this reasoning, Porter's stuck-in-the-middle situation is really the cell shown in Fig. 7.3 with the high cost and low differentiation position labeled as "no competitive advantage."

Although Porter agrees that it is possible for a company or an SBU to achieve low cost and differentiation simultaneously, he argues that this state is often temporary. "Achieving cost leadership and differentiation are also usually inconsistent, because differentiation is usually costly. . . . Eventually a competitor will choose a generic strategy and begin to implement it well, exposing the tradeoffs between cost and differentiation."[15] Porter does admit, however, that there are many different kinds of potentially profitable competitive strategies. Many variations are possible. Although there is generally room for only one company to successfully pursue the mass market cost leadership strategy (because it is so dependent on achieving dominant market share), there is room for an almost unlimited number of differentiation and focus strategies (depending on the range of possible desirable features and the number of identifiable market niches).

Research comparing Porter's generic competitive strategies with Miles and Snow's strategic types (discussed earlier in Chapter 4 under Industry Analysis) reveals that the two concepts are somewhat compatible. A *prospector* tends to follow a differentiation or differentiation focus strategy, whereas a *defender* tends to follow a cost leadership or cost focus strategy. A *reactor* follows no consistent strategy and is thus stuck in the middle. Since the *analyzer* refers to a corporation

| FIGURE 7.3 | **Combining Porter's Generic Competitive Strategies** |

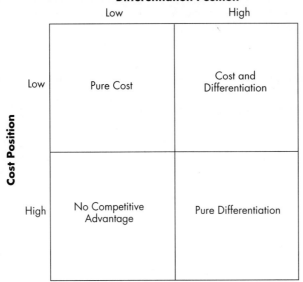

Differentiation Position

Source: R. E. White, "Generic Business Strategies, Organizational Context and Performance: An Empirical Investigation," *Strategic Management Journal* (May-June 1986), p. 226. Reprinted by permission of John Wiley & Sons, Ltd.

using different strategies in the different industries in which it competes, no one business-level competitive strategy quite fits this type of firm.[16]

INDUSTRY STRUCTURE AND COMPETITIVE STRATEGY

Although each of Porter's generic competitive strategies may be used in any industry, there are some instances when certain strategies are more likely to succeed than others. In a **fragmented industry**, for example, where many small and medium-sized local companies compete for relatively small shares of the total market, focus strategies will likely predominate. Fragmented industries are typical for products in the early stages of their life cycle. If there are few economies to be gained through size, no large firms will emerge and entry barriers will be low—allowing a stream of new entrants into the industry. If a company is able to overcome the limitations of a fragmented market, however, it can reap the benefits of a cost leadership or differentiation strategy. Until Pizza Hut was able to use advertising to differentiate itself from local competitors, the pizza fast-food business was composed primarily of locally owned pizza parlors, each with its own distinctive product and service offering. Subsequently, Domino's used the cost leader strategy to achieve U.S. national market share. The same was true of the computer software industry until a few companies, such as Microsoft, WordPerfect, Lotus, and Ashton-Tate, were able to achieve dominant positions in specific product offerings through the use of a differentiation strategy.

As an industry matures, fragmentation is overcome and the industry tends to become a **consolidated industry** dominated by a small number of large companies. Although most industries begin by being fragmented, battles for market share and creative attempts to overcome local or niche market boundaries will often result in a few companies' obtaining increasingly larger market shares. This happened in the fast-food, pizza, and computer software industries mentioned earlier. Once product standards become established for minimum quality and features, competition shifts to a greater emphasis on cost and service. Slower growth combined with over-capacity and knowledgeable buyers put a premium on a firm's ability to achieve cost leadership or differentiation along the dimensions most desired by the market. Research and development shifts from product to process improvements. Overall product quality improves and costs are reduced significantly. This is the type of industry in which cost leadership and differentiation tend to be combined to various degrees. A firm can no longer gain high market share simply through low price. The buyers are more sophisticated and demand a certain minimum level of quality for price paid. The same is true for firms emphasizing high quality. Either the quality must be high enough and valued by the customer enough to justify the higher price or the price must be dropped (through lowering costs) to compete effectively with the lower-priced products. This consolidation is taking place worldwide in the automobile, airline, and home appliance industries.

When an industry begins to consolidate, distinct strategic groups emerge as competitors combine various features in innovative ways to gain competitive advantage. New entrants into the industry are not as much of a threat as is the danger of a company or business unit moving from one strategic group to another (as the Japanese automakers did when they moved from low-priced dependable cars to high-priced performance cars in the late 1980s). Companies attempt to reduce the level of competitive rivalry through the use of market signals. A **market signal** is any action by a company or business unit that provides a direct or indirect indication of its intentions, motives, goals, or internal situation.[17] These signals become important in a consolidated industry that has developed some "rules of the game" and in which the potential for cutthroat competition is high. For example, Airline Tariff Publishing publishes daily U.S. airfare changes. Centralizing this information makes it easier for airlines to enter the data in their computer reservation systems for access by travel agents. It also provides an industry-only system that enables airlines to communicate pricing intentions to one another. According to people in the industry, a particular fare change could signal that an airline may be saying, in effect, "Let me determine the prices at my hub airport and I'll let you do the same at yours." According to Donald Garvett, a former Vice-President at Pan American World Airways: "It's almost like electronic negotiation. I wouldn't like to suggest that anyone is doing anything illegal. It's normal procedure to defend your turf."[18]

COMPETITIVE TACTICS

As defined in Chapter 1, a strategy is a comprehensive plan stating how the corporation will achieve its mission and objectives. A **tactic**, in comparison, is a specific operating plan specifying how a strategy is to be implemented in terms of *when* and *where* it is to be put into action. By their nature, tactics are narrower in their scope and shorter in their time horizon than are strategies. Tactics may therefore be viewed (like policies) as a link between the formulation and implementation of strategy. Some of the tactics available to implement competitive strategies are those dealing with timing (when) and location (where).

Timing Tactics

The first company to manufacture and sell a new product or service is called the **first mover**. Because it is a pioneer, it has certain advantages in the marketplace. According to Porter, "First mover advantages rest on the role of timing in improving a firm's position vis-à-vis sustainable sources of cost advantage or differentiation. In general terms, a first mover gets the opportunity to *define the competitive rules* in a variety of areas."[19] Research indicates that first movers not only tend to obtain higher market shares than do all later entrants, but that they also tend to enjoy a long-term profit advantage over their rivals. This high return is generally necessary to compensate the pioneer for its heavy investment in designing the product and developing the market.[20] Some of the advantages of being a first mover are that the company is able to establish a reputation as a leader in the industry, move down the learning curve to assume the cost leader position, and earn temporarily high profits from buyers who value the product or service very highly.[21]

Being a first mover does, however, have its disadvantages. These disadvantages are, conversely, advantages enjoyed by **late mover** firms. Late movers may be able to imitate others' technological advances (and thus keep R&D costs low), keep risks down by waiting until a new market is established, and take advantage of the natural inclination of the first mover to ignore market segments.[22]

Location Tactics

A company or business unit can implement a competitive strategy either offensively or defensively. Whereas an offensive tactic usually takes place in a location away from one's current position in the marketplace, a defensive tactic usually takes place in one's current market position.

Offensive Tactics   Some of the methods used to attack a competitor are:

- **Frontal Assault**: The attacking firm goes head-to-head with its competitor. It matches the competitor in every category from price to promotion to distribution channel. To be successful, the attacker must not only have superior resources, but also have the willingness to persevere. This is generally a very expensive tactic and may serve to awaken a sleeping giant (as MCI and Sprint did to AT&T in long distance telephone service), depressing profits for all in the industry.
- **Flanking Maneuver**: Rather than going straight for a competitor's position of strength with a frontal assault, a firm may attack a part of the market where the competitor is weak. Toyota and Nissan followed this tactic with their entry into the U.S. market during the 1960s when they emphasized the small, fuel-efficient cars then being ignored by General Motors, Ford, and Chrysler.

To be successful, the flanker must be patient and willing to slowly expand out of the relatively undefended market niche or else face retaliation by an established competitor.

■ **Encirclement**: Usually evolving out of a frontal assault or flanking maneuver, encirclement occurs as an attacking company or unit encircles the competitor's position in terms of products or markets or both. The encircler has greater product variety (a complete product line ranging from low to high price) and/or serves more markets (it dominates every secondary market). Honda successfully took this approach in motorcycles by taking every market segment except for the heavy-weight segment in the U.S. controlled by Harley-Davidson. To be successful, the encircler must have the wide variety of abilities and resources necessary to attack multiple market segments.

■ **Bypass Attack**: Rather than directly attacking the established competitor frontally or on its flanks, a company or business unit may choose to change the rules of the game. Made famous by Douglas MacArthur's island-hopping military campaign in the Pacific during World War II, this tactic attempts to cut the market out from under the established defender. The most common form of this tactic is the development of a new product that will satisfy customer needs that are currently unserved by any competitor. In 1990, Matsushita, Hitachi, Toshiba, and Mitsubishi were experimenting with the use of "fuzzy logic" software in their attempts to build major home appliances superior to those being made and sold throughout North America and Europe. Washing machines using this technology, for example, would be able automatically to adjust water level and cycle time depending on the size and dirtiness of the load and so do away with the need for selector switches. To be successful, the firm using the bypass strategy must be able to develop a product with the type of features desired by the marketplace or else its time and money are wasted.

■ **Guerrilla Warfare**: Instead of a continual and extensive resource-expensive attack on a competitor, a firm or business unit may choose to "hit and run." Guerrilla warfare is characterized by the use of small, intermittent assaults on different market segments held by the competitor. Using special promotions or advertising campaigns, a firm attempts to make a series of small market-share gains. In this way a new entrant or small firm can make some gains without seriously threatening a large, established competitor and evoking some form of retaliation. To be successful, the firm or unit conducting guerrilla warfare must be patient enough to accept small gains and to avoid pushing the established competitor to the point when it must make a response or else lose face.[23]

Defensive Tactics According to Porter, defensive tactics aim to lower the probability of attack, divert attacks to less-threatening avenues, or lessen the intensity of an attack. Instead of increasing competitive advantage per se, defensive tactics make a company's or business unit's competitive advantage more sustainable by causing a challenger to conclude that an attack is unattractive. Defensive tactics deliberately reduce short-term profitability to ensure long-term profitability.[24] Some of the methods used to defend against attacks by new entrants or established competitors are:

- **Raise Structural Barriers**: Structural barriers, like entry or mobility barriers, act to block a challenger's logical avenues of attack. Some of the most important according to Porter are to (1) offer a full line of products in every profitable market segment to close off any entry points, (2) block channel access by signing exclusive agreements with distributors, (3) raise buyer switching costs by offering low-cost training to users, (4) raise the cost of gaining trial users by keeping prices low on items most likely to be purchased by new users, (5) increase scale economies to reduce unit costs, (6) foreclose alternative technologies through patenting or licensing, (7) limit outside access to facilities and personnel, (8) tie up suppliers by obtaining exclusive contracts or purchasing key locations, (9) avoid suppliers that also serve competitors, and (10) encourage the government to raise barriers such as safety and pollution standards or favorable trade policies.

- **Increase Expected Retaliation**: A second type of defensive tactic is an action that increases the perceived threat of retaliation for an attack. Some of these actions may be market signals such as announced intentions by management to defend market share in certain product lines or plans to add to current capacity. Another action is to set an example by strongly defending any erosion of market share by drastically cutting prices or matching a challenger's promotion through a policy of accepting any price-reduction coupons for a competitor's product. For example, when Clorox Company challenged Procter & Gamble Company in the detergent market with Clorox Super Detergent, P&G retaliated by test marketing its liquid bleach Lemon Fresh Comet in an attempt to scare Clorox into retreating from the detergent market.[25] During an attack, a firm or business unit may disrupt a challenger's test or introductory markets by an exceptionally high or low level of advertising and promotion. These actions must be tempered, however, by keeping in mind that according to PIMS research the typical new entrant does not represent a serious threat, and aggressive retaliation can be very costly.[26]

- **Lower the Inducement for Attack**: A third type of defensive tactic is to reduce a challenger's expectations of future profits in the industry. Like Urshel Laboratories, a company can deliberately choose to forgo current profits by keeping its prices low and by investing in cost-reducing investments. With prices kept very low, there is little profit incentive for a new entrant. A firm can also use the media to let people know about problems facing the industry, which a challenger would have to consider in its strategic planning.

CHOOSING A BUSINESS STRATEGY

Before selecting one of these generic competitive strategies (and the appropriate competitive tactic) for a company or business unit, management should assess its feasibility in terms of company and divisional strengths and weaknesses. Porter lists

TABLE 7.1	**Requirements for Generic Competitive Strategies**	
Generic Strategy	Commonly Required Skills and Resources	Common Organizational Requirements
Overall Cost Leadership	Sustained capital investment and access to capital Process engineering skills Intense supervision of labor Products designed for ease of manufacture Low-cost distribution system	Tight cost control Frequent, detailed control reports Structured organization and responsibilities Incentives based on meeting strict quantitative targets
Differentiation	Strong marketing abilities Product engineering Creative flair Strong capability in basic research Corporate reputation for quality or technological leadership Long tradition in the industry or unique combination of skills drawn from other businesses Strong cooperation from channels	Strong coordination among functions in R&D, product development, and marketing Subjective measurement and incentives instead of quantitative measures Amenities to attract highly skilled labor, scientists, or creative people
Focus	Combination of the above policies directed at the particular strategic target	Combination of the above policies directed at the particular strategic target

Source: Adapted/reprinted with permission of The Free Press, a Division of Macmillan, Inc., from *Competitive Strategy: Techniques for Analyzing Industries and Competitors* by Michael E. Porter, pp. 40–41. Copyright © 1980 by The Free Press.

some of the commonly required skills and resources, as well as organizational requirements, in Table 7.1.

7.2 FUNCTIONAL STRATEGY

The principal goal of functional strategy is to maximize corporate and divisional resource productivity so that a distinctive competence will develop to provide a company or business unit a competitive advantage. Within the constraints of corporate and divisional strategies, functional strategies are developed to pull together the various activities and competencies of each function (typically housed within a department) so that performance improves. For example, a manufacturing department is very concerned with developing a strategy to reduce costs and to improve the quality of its output. Marketing, in comparison, is typically concerned with developing strategies to increase sales. Some of the many possible functional strategies are listed in the decision tree depicted in Fig. 7.4. These are some of the many functional strategic decisions that need to be made if corporate and divisional strategies are to be implemented properly by functional managers.

Functional strategies can be identified within the areas of marketing, finance, research and development, operations, and human resources, among other areas. The formulation and implementation of these strategies are important ways to build on an area's strengths or to reduce its weaknesses so that corporate and business strategies have a greater likelihood of success.

MARKETING STRATEGY

Two basic marketing strategies are market development and product development. Under **market development** a company or unit can (1) capture a larger share of an *existing* market for current products through market saturation and market penetration or (2) develop *new* markets for current products. Consumer product giants such as Procter & Gamble, Colgate-Palmolive, and Unilever are experts at using advertising and promotion to implement a market saturation/penetration strategy in order to gain the dominant market share in a product category. As seeming masters of the product life cycle, these companies are able to extend product life almost indefinitely through "new and improved" variations of product and packaging that appeal to most market niches. These companies also follow the second market development strategy by taking a successful product they market in one part of the world and marketing it elsewhere. Noting the success of their presoak detergents in Europe in the 1960s, both P&G and Colgate successfully introduced this type of laundry product to North America under the trade names of Biz and Axion.

Under **product development** a company or unit can (1) develop new products for *existing* markets or (2) develop new products for *new* markets. Church and Dwight has had great success following the first product development strategy (sometimes called "line extensions") by developing new products to sell to its current customers. Acknowledging the widespread appeal of its Arm & Hammer–brand baking soda, the company generated new uses for its sodium bicarbonate by reformulating it as toothpaste, deodorant, and detergent. In a brilliant bit of marketing, the company actually advertised that a good use of its baking soda was to throw it down the drain as a way to reduce sink odor! General Mills is an example of a company successfully following the second product development strategy. This company is not only a master of developing new kinds of breakfast cereals and baking products to appeal to changing tastes in its existing home-based market, it has developed new products for new markets through its restaurant segment. Avoiding the traditional fast-food industry, General Mills successfully established its Red Lobster and Olive Garden restaurants as moderately priced, national U.S. chains specializing in seafood and Italian cuisine.

Generally speaking, the market development strategy supports a corporate strategy of concentration, whereas the product development strategy supports a corporate strategy of diversification. There are many other marketing strategies.

| FIGURE 7.4 | **Functional Strategy Decision Tree** |

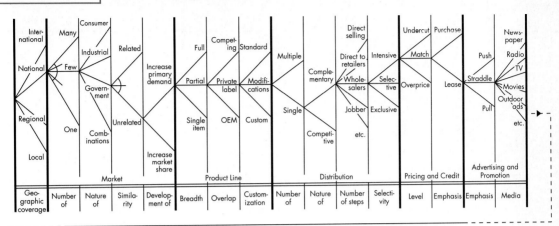

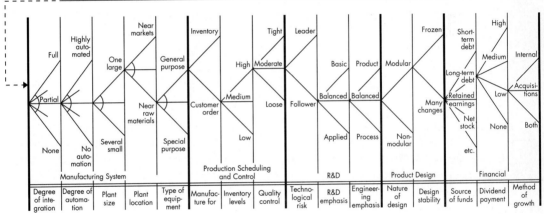

Source: Adapted from C. W. Hofer, "The Uses and Limitations of Statistical Decision Theory," (Boston: Intercollegiate Case Clearing House), No. 9-171-653, 1971, p. 34. Copyright © 1971 by C. W. Hofer. Reprinted by permission.

Some of them are depicted in the functional strategy decision tree presented in Fig. 7.4 in the categories of market, product line, distribution, pricing and credit, and advertising and promotion. Under advertising and promotion, for example, a company or business unit can choose between a "push" or a "pull" marketing strategy. Many large food and consumer products companies in the U.S. and Canada have followed a **push** strategy by spending a large amount of money on trade promotion in order to gain or hold shelf space in retail outlets. Trade promotion includes discounts and in-store special offers, as well as advertising allowances designed to "push" products through the distribution system. In 1990, however, Kellogg Company decided to change its emphasis from a push strategy by spending more money on consumer advertising designed to **pull** products off the shelf by building brand awareness before shoppers enter the store. According to Joseph Stewart, Kellogg's Senior Vice-President of Corporate Affairs, the company wanted to increase con-

MAYTAG CORPORATION: SUPPORTS DEALERS AS PART OF ITS MARKETING STRATEGY

Sales in the U.S. of major home appliances (white goods) such as washing machines, stoves, and refrigerators are made through three main retail outlets: (1) national chain store/mass merchandisers; (2) department, furniture, and discount stores; and (3) appliance dealers. An additional, but smaller outlet is the commercial market, composed of laundromats and institutions, such as hospitals and dormitories. Sales through national chain stores and mass merchandisers are usually composed of private brands promoted by the retailers. For example, Whirlpool Corporation has traditionally been a heavy supplier of Sears- and Kenmore-brand appliances to Sears, Roebuck. Magic Chef sells similar private-brand appliances to Montgomery Ward. Approximately 30%–40% of white goods are traditionally sold in the U.S. through this channel. Sears, Roebuck is so strong in major home appliance sales that it alone sells one out of every four major appliances in the U.S.

In the late 1980s, Sears instituted its new "Brand Central" format to sell white goods. In addition to offering its own private brands, the retail giant offered nationally known brands such as General Electric, Whirlpool, Amana, Speedqueen, and Jenn-Air. Except for its Jenn-Air products, Maytag Corporation chose not to join Sears' Brand Central concept. Leonard Hadley, Chief Operating Officer of Maytag Corporation, explained that the company did not want to antagonize its carefully nurtured appliance dealers who had always considered Sears their major retail competition. Maytag Company's emphasis on quality and higher price rather than market share as its business competitive strategy made the Maytag brand more dependent on appliance dealers than either General Electric or Whirlpool. In addition, some Maytag people feared that Sears might use the Maytag-brand image to attract customers into the stores, but then persuade them to buy a less-expensive Sears brand carrying a higher markup.

sumer brand loyalty through heavy television advertising. "We are driving our business to the consumer, to consumption," said Stewart.[27]

Other marketing strategies deal with distribution and pricing. A push strategy, for example, can be combined with the strategy of developing a close relationship with wholesalers and dealers. As shown in the *boxed example* of Maytag, the corporation chose not to sell its Maytag-brand home appliances through Sears' "Brand Central" because management did not want to alienate existing Maytag dealers. In another example, Chairman Robert Hanson of Deere and Company referred to Deere's 1,700 North American farm-equipment dealers as the company's "firing line." According to Hanson, "We can design and manufacture the best products in the world, but until the dealer is motivated to sell to the farmer, it's an exercise."[28]

When pricing a new product, a company or business unit can follow a marketing strategy of skim pricing or penetration pricing. For new-product pioneers, **skim pricing** offers the opportunity to "skim the cream" from the top of the demand curve while the product is novel and competitors are few. **Penetration pricing**, in contrast, attempts to hasten market development and offers the pioneer the opportunity to utilize the experience curve to gain market share and dominate the industry. Depending on corporate and business unit objectives and strategies, either of these choices may be desirable to a particular company or unit. Research does reveal, however, that penetration pricing is more likely than skim pricing to raise a unit's operating profit in the long term.[29]

FINANCIAL STRATEGY

Financial strategy's goal is providing the corporation with the appropriate financial structure and funds to achieve its overall objectives. In addition, it examines the financial implications of corporate and business-level strategic options and identifies the best financial course of action. It can also provide competitive advantage through a lower cost of funds and a flexible ability to raise capital to support a business strategy.[30] Financial strategy usually attempts to maximize the financial value of the firm. Some of the more popular methods for measuring firm value are listed in Table 7.2.

As shown in Fig. 7.4, the desired level of debt versus equity versus internal long-term financing via cash flow is a key issue in financial strategy. For example, until Maytag decided in 1978 to expand its product lines by acquiring other companies, it financed its growth primarily through internal cash flow and sales of stock. Other companies, such as Urschel Laboratories, try to avoid *all* external sources of funds in order to avoid outside entanglements and to keep control of the company within the family. During the 1980s, a large number of corporations used long-term debt to finance a corporate strategy of growth through acquisitions. The $24.5 billion debt-financed takeover of RJR Nabisco, Inc. by Kohlberg Kravis Roberts & Co. in 1988 is one such example. The use of high-risk "junk" bonds to finance many of these acquisitions was one reason Campeau Corporation was forced to declare bankruptcy in 1989. Campeau was unable to generate the internal cash flow necessary to make the required interest payments for its earlier purchases of Allied Stores and Federated Department Stores.[31]

A very popular financial strategy is the **leveraged buy out** (LBO). In a leveraged buy out, a company is acquired in a transaction financed largely by debt. Ultimately, the debt is paid with money generated by the acquired company's operations or by sales of its assets. This is what happened when Westray Transportation, Inc., an affiliate of Westray Corporation, purchased Atlas Van Lines. Under the leveraged buy out plan, Atlas stockholders received $18.35 for each share of stock outstanding and the company was taken private by Westray. The money was funded by Merrill Lynch Interfunding, Inc. and Acquisition Funding Corporation. Westray then paid the debt from the operations of its new subsidiary, Atlas Van Lines.[32] Research on the use of LBOs in the U.S. and the U.K. during the 1980s reveals that the financial results of these LBOs were generally positive, but not as high in the U.S. as was originally predicted.[33]

The management of dividends to stockholders is an important part of a corporation's financial strategy. Corporations in fast-growing industries, such as computers and computer software, often do not declare dividends. They use the money they might have spent on dividends to finance rapid growth. If the company is successful,

TABLE 7.2	Main Measures of the Financial Value of the Firm

Name	Definition	Limitations
Transaction Value	The value for which a company can be bought or sold.	Only known after a transaction.
Merger Market Value	Approximated by examining comparable transactions.	Comparability with other transactions is usually limited.
Market Capitalization	Number of shares × current share price.	Based on the few shares changing hands on a particular day. A bid would give a different value.
Price Earnings Ratio (P/E)	Share price ÷ Profit per share after tax gives P/E; × posttax earnings gives estimated value.	Normally based on historic performance and reflects daily transactions only.
Net Asset Value	Current assets − Current liabilities + Fixed assets − Long-term debt + Financial investments	Based on book values that may not reflect current asset values or earning potential.
Asset Value	Estimates of the current value of net assets.	Only relevant if the earnings stream is of lower value than assets.
Net Present Value of Future Cash Flows	Future net cash flow stream discounted to today's value.	Theoretically the best method of valuation but can vary wildly if strategic assumptions are changed.
		Requires detailed strategic information and analysis to be useful.

Source: C. J. Clarke, "Using Finance for Competitive Advantage," *Long Range Planning* (April 1988), p. 65. Copyright © 1988 by Pergamon Press. Reprinted with permission of Pergamon Press, Inc.

its growth in sales and profits is reflected in a higher stock price—eventually resulting in a hefty capital gain when shareholders sell their common stock. Other corporations, such as electric utilities, that do not face rapid growth must support the value of their stock by offering generous and consistent dividends.

RESEARCH AND DEVELOPMENT STRATEGY

Those corporations that are dependent on technology for their success are becoming increasingly concerned with the development of R&D strategies that complement business-level strategies.[34] As shown in Fig. 7.4, one of the R&D choices is to be either a **leader** or a **follower**. Porter suggests that making the decision to become a technological leader or follower can be a way of achieving either overall low cost or differentiation.[35] This choice is described in more detail in Table 7.3.

TABLE 7.3	Research and Development Strategy and Competitive Advantage	
	Technological Leadership	Technological Followership
Cost Advantage	Pioneer the lowest-cost product design	Lower the cost of the product or value activities by learning from the leader's experience
	Be the first firm down the learning curve	
	Create low-cost ways of performing value activities	Avoid R&D costs through imitation
Differentiation	Pioneer a unique product that increases buyer value	Adapt the product or delivery system more closely to buyer needs by learning from the leader's experience
	Innovate in other activities to increase buyer value	

Source: Reprinted with permission of The Free Press, a Division of Macmillan, Inc., from *Competitive Advantage: Creating and Sustaining Superior Performance* by Michael E. Porter, p. 181. Copyright © 1985 by Michael E. Porter.

One example of an effective use of the follower R&D functional strategy to achieve a low-cost competitive advantage is Dean Foods Company. Discussed earlier in this chapter, Dean Foods uses its R&D strictly to develop low-cost imitations of expensive brand name dairy products that it sells as private label brands to supermarket chains throughout the U.S. and Canada. "We're able to have the customer come to us and say, 'If you can produce X, Y, and Z product for the same quality and service, but at a lower price and without that expensive label on it, you can have the business,'" says Howard Dean, president of the company.[36] Nike, Inc., in contrast, uses the leader R&D strategy. As detailed in Illustrative Example 7.1, Nike spends more than most in the industry on R&D in order to differentiate its athletic shoes from its competitors on a performance dimension. As a result, its products have become the favorite of the serious athlete.

Research and development strategy also deals with a company's mix of basic versus applied and product versus process R&D. The particular mix should suit the level of industry development and the firm's particular corporate and business strategies. General Motors, for example, takes a very applied orientation. Eighty percent of its R&D is applied (47% directed toward long-range efforts, with the balance toward the short range). Basic research accounts for only 12% of the lab's efforts. Product development occupies the remaining 8% of the researchers' time. According to Robert Frosch, Vice-President in charge of GM Research Laboratories, "We do applied research with a basic research attitude."[37]

The make or buy decision can be an important one in a firm's R&D strategy. Although in-house R&D has traditionally been an important source of technical knowledge for companies, firms can also tap the R&D capabilities of competitors, suppliers, and other organizations through contractual agreements such as licensing, R&D agreements, and joint ventures. During a time of technological discontinuity in an industry, a company may have no choice but to purchase the new technology

---

ILLUSTRATIVE EXAMPLE 7.1

Nike Uses a Leader R&D Strategy to Achieve Differentiation

In an industry in which companies routinely spend tens of millions of dollars on advertising campaigns featuring superstar athletes like Michael Jordan and Bo Jackson, Nike, Inc. spends more on research and development for its athletic shoes than does any competitor except Japan's ASICS Corp. Industry analysts evaluate Nike's R&D lab as "far and away the best" in the industry. In 1979, the company introduced the air-cushioning system. In the mid-1980s, however, Nike emphasized fashion and lost market share to Reebok International Ltd. In 1987, Nike fought back with its Visible Air line of athletic shoes. Each shoe had a tiny window in the heel so consumers could see the air bag providing extra cushioning. In the two years following the Visible Air introduction, Nike surpassed Reebok in both market share (25% versus 23%) and sales. Needless to say, with Nike's return to an emphasis on performance, R&D people played a dominant role in the company's strategy making.

After the success of the Visible Air line, Bruce Kilgore, head of Nike's R&D department, wanted to develop a shoe whose entire heel was a visible air bag. Working behind a cagelike door guarded by a stuffed gorilla, ten advanced-products engineers, who called themselves APEs, labored to make Kilgore's idea a reality. Once the shoe was readied for mass production as the Nike Air 180, the company engaged 186 athletes from Alaska to the Virgin Islands to test the shoes for 90 days over all kinds of terrain. The runners' comments were then used when making the minor modifications needed to ensure that the shoe would last over 500 miles of use. The bottom of the shoe's heel held a large urethane window, bonded to the shoe by a new Nike-developed compound, that allowed a 180-degree view of a greatly expanded air bag. Nike's management reported that not only did the Nike 180 have the most cushioning of any of its running shoes, but that retailers were showing great interest. Even though the new shoe was not to be available in stores until January 1991, advance orders were beyond expectations by August 1990. According to Nike's founder Philip H. Knight, "We're already overbooked."

Source: D. Jones Yang and R. Buderi, "Step by Step with Nike," *Business Week* (August 13, 1990), pp. 116–117.

---

from others if it wishes to remain competitive. Firms that are unable to finance alone the huge costs of developing a new technology may coordinate their R&D with other firms. By 1990, more than 150 industry consortia involving 1,000 companies were operating in the U.S. and many more were operating throughout Europe and Asia.[38] Research suggests, however, that companies must have at least a minimal R&D capability if they are to correctly assess the value of technology developed by others. R&D creates a capacity in a firm to assimilate and exploit new knowledge. This is called a company's *absorptive capacity* and is a valuable by-product of routine in-house R&D activity.[39]

OPERATIONS STRATEGY

A corporation's operations strategy determines how and where a product or service is to be manufactured, the level of vertical integration, the deployment of physical resources, and relationships with suppliers.[40] To begin with, a firm's manufacturing strategy will be affected by the product/process life cycle conceptualized by Hayes and Wheelwright.[41] This concept describes the increase in production volume ranging from lot sizes as low as one in a **job shop** (one-of-a-kind production using skilled labor) through **connected line batch flow** (components are standardized; each machine functions like a job shop, but is positioned in the same order as the parts are processed) to lot sizes as high as 100,000 or more per year for **flexible manufacturing systems** (parts are grouped into manufacturing families to produce a wide variety of mass-produced items) and **dedicated transfer lines** (highly automated assembly lines making one mass-produced product using little human labor). According to this concept, the product becomes standardized into a commodity over time in conjunction with increasing demand, as flexibility gives way to efficiency. Nevertheless, a company's competitive business strategy can be the key determinant of the manufacturing process. For example, Pratt & Whitney selected the connected line batch flow approach in making disks and hubs for its jet engines, whereas General Electric selected the flexible manufacturing system. General Electric was geared to the global mass market. Pratt & Whitney, in contrast, was interested in satisfying lucrative market segments with particular needs.[42]

Kotha and Orne recommend that operations strategy should have certain characteristics based on the competitive strategy of the company or business unit of which operations is a part.[43] Some of these characteristics are presented in Table 7.4. The manufacturing strategy should also address the issue of how much a company or business unit should be vertically integrated. Until recently, once a product reached the stage of its life cycle in which it assumed characteristics of a

TABLE 7.4	**Impact of Business Competitive Strategy on Operations Strategy**
Business Competitive Strategy	Characteristics of Operations Strategy
Strong Cost Leadership Emphasis	Strong emphasis on cost reduction and control
	High level of process engineering skills
	Strong emphasis on elimination of inventories
	High level of production standards
	High level of machine pacing of material flow
Strong Differentiation Emphasis	Strong emphasis on premium-value products and services
	Relatively high end-product complexity
	Wide variety of final products
	High level of product engineering skills
	High level of production scheduling flexibility (flexible service and order lead times)

Source: Adapted from S. Kotha and D. Orne, "Generic Manufacturing Strategies: A Conceptual Synthesis," *Strategic Management Journal* (May-June 1989), p. 227. Reprinted by permission of John Wiley & Sons, Ltd.

commodity, the manufacturing strategy was one of full vertical integration to reduce costs and to standardize the manufacturing process for mass production. Thanks to new technologies in communications, logistics, and information systems, vertical integration of the manufacturing process does not always now make the most sense. Company-owned internal suppliers can be replaced by a network of independently owned external suppliers linked together with long-term contracts and close personal relationships. Quinn, Doorly, and Paquette propose that companies "strip" themselves down to the essential core skills necessary to make a product or service and "outsource" (purchase) as much of the rest as possible.

> Thanks to new technologies, executives can divide up their companies' value chains, handle the key strategic elements internally, outsource others advantageously anywhere in the world with minimal transaction costs, and yet coordinate all essential activities more effectively to meet customers' needs. Under these circumstances, moving to a less integrated but more focused organization is not just feasible but imperative for competitive success. . . . By limiting or shedding activities that provide no strategic advantage, a company can increase the value it delivers to both customers and shareholders and, in the process, lower its costs and investments.[44]

HUMAN RESOURCES AND OTHER FUNCTIONAL STRATEGIES

In addition to functional strategies in marketing, finance, R&D, and operations, there are those in human resource management (HRM), information systems (IS), and other areas of functional significance to corporations depending on the industry. As depicted in Fig. 7.4, production scheduling and product design might be considered as functions separate from manufacturing. Insofar as human resources is concerned, an HRM strategy needs to address the issue of whether a company or business unit should hire a large number of low-skilled employees who receive low pay, perform repetitive jobs, and most likely quit after a short time (the McDonald's restaurant strategy) or hire skilled employees who receive relatively high pay and are cross-trained in order to participate in self-managed work teams. As work increases in complexity, the more suited it is for teams. A recent survey of 476 Fortune 1000 U.S. companies revealed that although only 7% of their work force was organized into self-managed teams, half the companies reported that they would be relying significantly more on them in the years ahead.[45] Other HRM strategies deal with the question of promotion from within or recruitment of managers from outside the company. These and other options within functional strategies are summarized in Table 7.5.

STRATEGIES TO AVOID

Several strategies, used at various levels, are very dangerous. Managers who have made a poor analysis or lack creativity may be trapped into considering them.

- **Follow the Leader.** Imitating the strategy of a leading competitor might seem a good idea, but it ignores a firm's particular strengths and weaknesses as well as the possibility that the leader may be wrong. The decision by Stan-

| **TABLE 7.5** | **Some Functional Strategy Options** |

Marketing
- Expand sales into new classes of customers
  1. Geographic expansion
  2. Additional related products—line extension
  3. Develop completely new products
  4. New applications for same products
  5. Develop customized products
- Increase penetration in market segments of existing customers
  1. Develop competing products—product overlap
  2. Product customization
  3. Product system concept
  4. Find pricing and service mix to give competitive edge
  5. Seek promotional techniques to drown out competitive ads
  6. Pinpoint markets by reducing variety of products and models
- Hold market share
  1. Copy, do not innovate
  2. Emphasize larger product sizes or more durable products to keep current customers out of the marketplace
  3. Increase switching costs by offering special services to current customers

Finance
- Borrow short term
  1. Credit line
  2. Bank notes
  3. Factor accounts receivable
- Borrow long term
  1. Secured debt of three to five years
  2. Bonds or debentures
  3. Commercial paper
- Equity funding
  1. Private placement
  2. Public placement
  3. Voting or nonvoting

- Refinancing
  1. Refinance long term with short term
  2. Refinance short term with long term
  3. Purchase treasury stock
  4. Split shares
  5. Liquidate debt by selling shares
- Dividend policy
  1. Begin dividend payout
  2. Increase dividend payout
  3. Reduce dividend payout
  4. Maintain present dividend payout
  5. Discontinue dividend payout

R&D and Operations
- Research and development emphasis
  1. Increase funds
  2. No change in funding
  3. Decrease funding
  4. Mix of basic and applied efforts
  5. Mix of product and process technology emphasis
- Technology
  1. Upgrade
  2. Retain
  3. Subcontract
- Operations capacity
  1. Build new capacity
  2. Maintain current capacity
  3. Expand current capacity
  4. Increase size of workforce
  5. Add shifts
  6. Reduce workforce
  7. Reduce inventory
  8. Consolidate and centralize
  9. Decentralize to smaller facilities
  10. Decentralize to functional facilities

(continued)

TABLE 7.5	**Some Functional Strategy Options** *(continued)*

R&D and Operations (continued)
- Material and supply
  1. Obtain new domestic sources
  2. Obtain new import sources
  3. Substitute materials
  4. Negotiate lower costs
  5. Centralize procurement
  6. Decentralize procurement
- Quality/productivity
  1. Use team concept
  2. Switch to modular
  3. Superautomate with robots and computers
  4. Japanese management techniques

Human Resources
- Recruitment and training
  1. Use internal employee recruitment, selection, and placement
  2. Use external employee recruitment, selection, and placement
  3. Establish management development program
  4. Link career paths to corporate and business strategy
  5. Establish specific job skill training
  6. Establish assessment centers for selection and development

- Appraisal and benefits
  1. Link pay and benefits to corporate and business strategy
  2. Link appraisal system to corporate and business strategy
  3. Use cafeteria benefits package

Information Systems
- Hardware and software
  1. Upgrade mainframe central processor
  2. Purchase new central processor
  3. Upgrade existing distributed microprocessors
  4. Purchase new distributed microprocessors and networking system
  5. Switch from central processor to distributed system
  6. Use centralized software support system
  7. Use decentralized software support system
- Link information systems to corporate and business competitive strategy
  1. Establish and maintain environmental scanning system
  2. Automate routine clerical operations
  3. Assist managers in making decisions
  4. Use information systems (IS) to provide improved service to customers
  5. Develop new uses of current IS that can be sold to current or new customers

Source: Suggested by V. A. Quarstein, Old Dominion University.

dard Oil of Ohio to follow Exxon and Mobil Oil into conglomerate diversification resulted in poor corporate performance and the company's complete loss of autonomy to British Petroleum.

- **Hit Another Home Run.** If a corporation is successful because it pioneered an extremely successful product, it has a tendency to search for another super-product that will ensure growth and prosperity. Like betting on long shots at the horse races, the probability of finding a second winner is slight. Polaroid spent a lot of money developing an "instant" movie camera, but the public ignored it. In 1990, Xerox introduced a revolutionary new product called "Xenith," which combined computing, scanning, faxing, and copying in an attempt to duplicate the great success of its original copier. According to Chairman David Kearns: "This is a really, really big deal for us."[46]

- **Arms Race.** Entering into a spirited battle with another firm for an increase in market share might increase sales revenue, but that increase will probably be more than offset by increases in advertising, promotion, R&D, and manufacturing costs. Since the deregulation of airlines, price wars and rate "specials" have contributed to the low profit margins or bankruptcy of many major airlines, such as Eastern and Continental.
- **Do Everything.** When faced with several interesting opportunities, management might tend to leap at all of them. At first, a corporation might have enough resources to develop each idea into a project, but money, time, and energy are soon exhausted as each of the many projects demand large infusions of resources. Convinced that its brand name would serve as an effective umbrella for a whole series of new products, Toro Company quickly ran out of money and time (see Illustrative Example 6.4).
- **Losing Hand.** A corporation might have invested so much in a particular strategy that top management is unwilling to accept the fact that the strategy is not successful. Believing that it has too much invested to quit, the corporation continues to throw "good money after bad." Pan American, for example, chose to sell its Pan Am Building and Intercontinental Hotels, the most profitable parts of the corporation, to keep its money-losing airline flying. Subsequently—after four years of consecutive net losses from 1986 through 1989—management in 1990 continued to follow this strategy of shedding assets to remedy the company's cash problems by selling its East Coast Pan Am shuttle and its inter-German routes.[47]

7.3 SELECTION OF THE BEST STRATEGY

Once potential strategic alternatives have been identified and evaluated in terms of their pros and cons, one must be selected for implementation. By this point, it is likely that many alternatives will have emerged as feasible. How is the decision made that determines the best strategy?

Choosing among a set of acceptable alternative strategies is often not easy. Each alternative is likely to have its proponents as well as critics. Steiner and Miner suggest using the 20 questions listed in Table 7.6 before one strategy is selected over another. Perhaps the most important criterion is the ability of the proposed strategy to deal with the specific **strategic factors** developed earlier in the S.W.O.T. analysis. If the alternative doesn't take advantage of environmental opportunities and corporate strengths, and lead away from environmental threats and corporate weaknesses, it will probably fail.[48]

Another important consideration in the selection of a strategy is the ability of each alternative to satisfy agreed-on objectives with the least use of resources and with the fewest number of negative side effects. It is therefore important to develop a tentative implementation plan so that the difficulties that management is likely to face are addressed. Is the alternative worth the probable short-term as well as long-term costs?

TABLE 7.6	Twenty Questions for Use in Evaluating Strategies

1. Does the strategy conform to the basic mission and purpose of the corporation? If not, a new competitive arena with which management is not familiar might be entered.

2. Is the strategy consistent with the corporation's external environment?

3. Is the strategy consistent with the internal strengths, objectives, policies, resources, and personal values of managers and employees? A strategy might not be completely in tune with all of these, but major dissonance should be avoided.

4. Does the strategy reflect the acceptance of minimum potential risk, balancing it against the maximum potential profit consistent with the corporation's resources and prospects?

5. Does the strategy fit a niche in the corporation's market not now filled by others? Is this niche likely to remain open long enough for the corporation to return capital investment plus the required level of profit? (Niches have a habit of filling up fast.)

6. Does the strategy conflict with other corporate strategies?

7. Is the strategy divided into substrategies that interrelate properly?

8. Has the strategy been tested with appropriate criteria (such as consistency with past, present, and prospective trends) and by the appropriate analytical tools (such as risk analysis, discounted cash flows, and so on)?

9. Has the strategy been tested by developing feasible implementation plans?

10. Does the strategy really fit the life cycles of the corporation's products?

11. Is the timing of the strategy correct?

12. Does the strategy pit the product against a powerful competitor? If so, reevaluate carefully.

13. Does the strategy leave the corporation vulnerable to the power of one major customer? If so, reconsider carefully.

14. Does the strategy involve the production of a new product for a new market? If so, reconsider carefully.

15. Is the corporation rushing a revolutionary product to market? If so, reconsider carefully.

16. Does the strategy imitate that of a competitor? If so, reconsider carefully.

17. Is it likely that the corporation can get to the market first with the new product or service? If so, this is a great advantage. (The second firm to market has much less chance of high returns on investment than the first.)

18. Has a really honest and accurate appraisal been made of the competition? Is the competition under- or overestimated?

19. Is the corporation trying to sell abroad something it cannot sell at home? (This is not usually a successful strategy.)

20. Is the market share likely to be sufficient to assure a required return on investment? (Market share and return on investment are generally closely related but differ from product to product and market to market.) Has this relationship of market and product been calculated?

Source: Adapted with permission of Macmillan Publishing Company from *Management Policy and Strategy* by George A. Steiner and John B. Miner, pp. 219–221. Copyright © 1977 by Macmillan Publishing Company.

Several techniques to aid strategic planners in estimating the likely effects of strategic changes are available. One of these was derived from the research project on the Profit Impact of Market Strategies (PIMS), which was discussed in Chapter 5. As part of PIMS, reports for a participating corporation's business units show how its expected level of ROI is influenced by various factors. A second report shows how ROI can be expected to change, both in the short and long runs, if particular changes are made in its strategy.

One of the best ways to assess the likely economic impact of each alternative on the future of the corporation is through the construction of detailed scenarios. Once these scenarios are adjusted for management's attitude toward risk, pressures from the external and internal environments, and the personal needs and desires of key managers, they are invaluable aids to management's selecting the alternative with the best chance of achieving corporate objectives.

SCENARIO CONSTRUCTION

Using **pro forma** balance sheets and income statements, management can construct detailed **scenarios** to forecast the likely effect of each alternative strategy and its various programs on division and corporate return on investment.[49] These scenarios are simply extensions of the industry scenarios discussed in Chapter 4. If, for example, industry scenarios suggest the probable emergence of a strong market demand for certain products, a series of alternative strategy scenarios can be developed. The alternative of acquiring another company having these products can be compared with the alternative of developing the products internally. Using three sets of estimated sales figures (optimistic, pessimistic, and most likely) for the new products over the next five years, the two alternatives can be evaluated in terms of their effect on future company performance as reflected in its probable future financial statements. *Pro forma* **balance sheets** and **income statements** can be generated with spreadsheet software, such as Lotus 1-2-3, on a personal computer.

To construct a scenario, *first* use the industry scenarios discussed earlier in Chapter 4 and develop a set of assumptions about the task environment. At 3M, for example, the general manager of each business unit is required annually to describe what his or her industry will look like in 15 years.[50] Optimistic, pessimistic, and most likely assumptions should be listed for key economic factors such as the GNP, CPI (Consumer Price Index), and prime interest rate, as well as for other key external strategic factors, such as governmental regulation and industry trends. These same underlying assumptions should be listed for each of the alternative scenarios to be developed.

Second, for each strategic alternative, develop a set of optimistic, pessimistic, and most likely assumptions about the impact of key variables on the company's future financial statements. Forecast three sets of sales and cost of goods sold figures for at least five years into the future. Look at historical data from past financial statements (use common-size income statements and balance sheets—see Chapter 14) and make adjustments based on the environmental assumptions listed above. Do the same for other figures that can vary significantly. For the rest, assume that they will continue in their historical relationship to sales or some other key determining factor. Plug in expected inventory levels, accounts receivable, accounts payable, R&D expenses, advertising and promotion expenses, capital expenditures, and debt payments (assuming that debt is used to finance the strategy), among others. Consider not only historical trends, but also programs that might be needed for the implementation of each alternative strategy (such as building a new manufacturing facility or expanding the sales force).

Third, construct detailed *pro forma* financial statements for *each* of the strategic alternatives. Using a spreadsheet program, list the *actual* figures from this year's financial statements in the left column. To the right of this column, list the *optimistic* figures for year one, year two, year three, year four, and year five. Go through this same process with the same strategic alternative, but now list the *pessimistic* figures for the next five years. Do the same with the *most likely* figures. Once this is done, develop a similar set of optimistic (O), pessimistic (P), and most likely (ML) *pro forma* statements for the second strategic alternative. This process will generate six different *pro forma* scenarios reflecting three different situations (O, P, and ML) for two strategic alternatives. Next, calculate financial ratios and common-sized income statements, and balance sheets to accompany the *pro formas*. To determine the feasibility of the scenarios, compare assumptions underlying the scenarios with these financial statements and ratios. For example, if cost of goods sold drops from 70% to 50% of total sales revenue in the *pro forma* income statements, this drop should result from a change in the production process or a shift to cheaper raw materials or labor costs, rather than from a failure to keep the cost of goods sold in its usual percentage relationship to sales revenue when the predicted statement was developed.

The result of this detailed scenario construction should be anticipated net profits, cash flow, and net working capital for each of three versions of the two alternatives for five years into the future. Once this is done, the strategist might wish to go further into the future if the strategy is expected to have a major impact on the company's financial statements beyond five years. The result of this work should provide sufficient information on which forecasts of the likely feasibility and probable profitability of each of the strategic alternatives could be based.

Obviously, these scenarios can quickly become very complicated, especially if three sets of acquisition prices as well as development costs are calculated. Nevertheless, this sort of detailed "what if" analysis is needed for realistic comparisons of the projected outcome of each reasonable alternative strategy and its attendant programs, budgets, and procedures. Regardless of the quantifiable pros and cons of each alternative, the actual decision will probably be influenced by several subjective factors that are difficult to quantify. Some of these factors are management's attitude toward risk, pressures from the external environment, influences from the corporate culture, and the personal needs and desires of key managers.

✓ MANAGEMENT'S ATTITUDE TOWARD RISK

The attractiveness of a particular strategic alternative is partially a function of the amount of risk it entails. The risk is composed not only of the *probability* that the strategy will be effective, but also of the amount of *assets* the corporation must allocate to that strategy, and the length of *time* the assets will be unavailable for other uses. To quantify this risk, many people suggest the use of the **Capital Asset Pricing Model** (CAPM). CAPM is a financial method for linking the risk involved in a particular alternative with expected returns on a company's equity.[51] Research by Stahl, however, found little evidence that corporate planners actually use the CAPM as a tool for either acquisition or divestment decisions.[52] Another proposed technique is the **Arbitrage Pricing Model** (APM), which screens acquisition candidates.[53] In response to these and other complicated approaches to risk quantification, Everett proposes a simpler approach for the assessment of the probability of success or failure for a particular strategic alternative; his approach uses a Lotus 1-2-3 spreadsheet to consider risk-return tradeoffs.[54]

The greater the assets involved and the longer they are tied up, the more likely top management is to demand a high probability of success. This might be one reason innovations seem to occur more often in small firms than in large, established corporations.[55] The small firm managed by an entrepreneur is willing to accept greater risk than would a large firm of diversified ownership run by professional managers. It is one thing to take a chance if you are the primary stockholder and are not concerned with periodic changes in the value of the company's common stock. It is something else if the corporation's stock is widely held and acquisition-hungry competitors or takeover artists surround the company like sharks every time the company's stock price falls below some external assessment of the firm's value!

Hayes and Garvin make the point that too much emphasis is being placed on discounted rate of return as an aid to strategic decision making in professionally managed corporations. High hurdle rates based on unrealistic assumptions often discourage investment in a firm's existing businesses whose risks are known and direct it toward acquiring businesses whose risks are less known. Over time, this results in a "disinvestment spiral"—deferred investment in a firm's core businesses that leads to reduced profitability, which further reduces the incentive to invest. "Faced with these circumstances, top management often concludes that a division or product line is unsalvageable and purposely continues the process of disinvestment."[56] This reasoning helps to explain the emphasis on growth through unrelated acquisitions during the 1970s and 1980s and the corresponding poor performance and divestment decisions in the late 1980s of many of the corporations following this corporate strategy of conglomerate diversification.

PRESSURES FROM THE EXTERNAL ENVIRONMENT

The attractiveness of a strategic alternative will be affected by its perceived compatibility with the key stakeholders in a corporation's task environment. These stakeholders are typically concerned with certain aspects of a corporation's activities. Creditors want to be paid on time. Unions exert pressure for comparable wage and employment security. Governments and interest groups demand social responsibility. Stockholders want dividends. All of these pressures must be considered in the selection of the best alternative. Hicks B. Waldron, Chairman of Avon Products, argues that corporations have duties beyond the maximizing of value for shareholders:

We have a number of suppliers, institutions, customers, communities. None of them have the democratic freedom as shareholders do to buy or sell their shares. They have much deeper and much more important stakes in our company than our shareholders.[57]

Questions management should raise in their attempt to assess the importance to the corporation of stakeholder concerns are the following:

1. What stakeholders are most crucial for corporate success?
2. How much of what they want are they likely to get, under this alternative?
3. What are they likely to do if they don't get what they want?
4. What is the probability that they will do it?

By ranking the key stakeholders in a corporation's task environment and asking these questions, strategy-makers should be better able to choose strategic alternatives that minimize external pressures and maximize the probability of gaining stakeholder support.[58] In addition, top management can propose a political strategy to influence its key stakeholders. Some of the most commonly used political strategies are constituency building, political action committee contributions, advocacy advertising, lobbying, and coalition building.[59] For example, in response to public concerns about its disposable diapers contributing to the growing landfill problem in the U.S., Procter & Gamble not only promoted the use of a new process to dispose of solid waste, but also promised to spend $20 million on R&D to develop disposable diapers that break down completely in such systems.[60]

PRESSURES FROM THE CORPORATE CULTURE

As pointed out in Chapter 5, the norms and values shared by the members of a corporation do affect the attractiveness of certain alternatives. If a strategy is incompatible with the corporate culture, the likelihood of its success will be very low. Foot-dragging and even sabotage will result, as employees fight to resist a radical change in corporate philosophy. Precedents from the past tend to restrict the kinds of objectives and strategies that can be seriously considered. The "aura" of the founders of a corporation can linger long past their lifetimes because their values have been imprinted on a corporation's members. According to Cyert and March:

> Organizations have memories in the form of precedents, and individuals in the coalition are strongly motivated to accept the precedents as binding. Whether precedents are formalized in the shape of an official standard operating procedure or are less formally stored, they remove from conscious consideration many agreements, decisions, and commitments that might well be subject to renegotiation in an organization without a memory.[61]

In considering a strategic alternative, the strategy-makers must assess its compatibility with the corporate culture. If there is little fit, management must decide if it should (1) *take a chance on ignoring the culture*, (2) *manage around the culture and change the implementation plan*, (3) *try to change the culture to fit the strategy*, or (4) *change the strategy to fit the culture*.[62] If the culture will be strongly opposed to a strategy, it is foolhardy to ignore the culture. Further, a decision to proceed with a particular strategy without a commitment to change the culture or manage around the culture (both very tricky and time-consuming) is dangerous. Nevertheless, restricting a corporation to those strategies only that are completely compatible with its culture might eliminate from consideration the most profitable alternatives. Further information on managing corporate culture is presented in Chapter 8 as part of strategy implementation.

NEEDS AND DESIRES OF KEY MANAGERS

Even the most attractive alternative might not be selected if it is contrary to the needs and desires of important top managers. A person's ego may be tied to a particular proposal to the extent that all other alternatives are strongly lobbied against. Key executives in operating divisions, for example, might be able to influence other people in top management in favor of a particular alternative so that objections to it are ignored.

Evidence suggests there is a tendency to maintain the status quo, which means that decision makers continue with existing goals and plans beyond the point when an objective observer would recommend a change in course. Silver and Mitchell propose that negative information about a particular course of action to which a person is committed may be ignored because of a desire to appear competent (e.g., "A manager shouldn't be wishy-washy") and strongly held values regarding consistency (e.g., "Don't change horses in midstream").[63] It may take a crisis or an unlikely event to cause strategic decision makers to seriously consider an alternative they had previously ignored or discounted. For example, it wasn't until the CEO of ConAgra, a multinational food products company, had a heart attack that ConAgra and others started producing whole lines of low-fat, low-cholesterol, low-sodium frozen-food entrees. ConAgra led the industry with its introduction of Healthy Choice—frozen dinners and boil-in-bag entrees consumers could eat without worrying about nutrition.[64]

STRATEGIC CHOICE

There is an old story at General Motors about Alfred Sloan. At a meeting with his key executives, Sloan proposed a controversial strategic decision. When asked for comments, each executive responded with supportive comments and praise. After announcing that they were all in apparent agreement, Sloan stated that they were not going to proceed with the decision. Either his executives didn't know enough to point out potential downsides of the decision, or they were agreeing to avoid upsetting the boss and disrupting the cohesion of the group. The decision was delayed until a debate could occur over the pros and cons.[65]

Once scenarios have been constructed for each feasible alternative strategy and strategic managers have acknowledged their attitudes toward risk, the pressures from the external and internal environments, as well as their own personal needs and desires, one strategy among many must be chosen for implementation. Although some people urge consensus in decision making, there is mounting evidence that the best strategic decisions are not unanimous—they actually involve a certain amount of heated disagreement, and even conflict.[66] Since unmanaged conflict often carries a high emotional cost, authorities in decision making propose that strategic managers use "programmed conflict" to raise different opinions, regardless of the personal feelings of the people involved. Two techniques are suggested to help strategic managers avoid the consensus trap that Alfred Sloan found in the example mentioned earlier: the devil's advocate and dialectical inquiry.

Devil's Advocate

The devil's advocate originated in the medieval Roman Catholic Church as a way of ensuring that impostors were not canonized as saints. Once sufficient evidence was assembled to begin canonization proceedings, the Pope would select one of his most trusted and competent aides to serve as the advocate of Satan. The advocate's job was to question every bit of evidence in favor of a person's sainthood and to uncover any indications of the person's poor moral character or evidence of wrongdoing. This was to ensure that all sides of an issue were considered regardless of the popularity of any one point of view. It was made clear to all that criticism by the devil's advocate was to be taken neither personally nor as evidence of the advocate's true feelings on the issue.

When applied to strategic decision making, the devil's advocate (who may be an individual or a group) is assigned to identify potential pitfalls and problems with a proposed alternative strategy in a formal presentation. Cosier and Schwenk, authorities on the subject, suggest that people should be rotated through the devil's advocate position so that one person is not identified as the critic on all issues. Steve Huse, Chairman and CEO of Huse Food Group, states that the devil's advocate role is an opportunity for employees to demonstrate their presentation and debating skills as well as their ability to do in-depth research and to understand both sides of an issue.[67]

Dialectical Inquiry

The dialectic philosophy, which can be traced back to Plato and Aristotle and more recently to Hegel, involves combining two conflicting views—the *thesis* and the *antithesis*—into a *synthesis*. Most of the world's legal systems reflect the dialectic process through their belief that the eventual truth of a crime will emerge out of the conflict between prosecuting and defense attorneys.

When applied to strategic decision making, dialectical inquiry requires that two proposals using different assumptions be generated for each alternative strategy under consideration. After advocates of each position present and debate the merits of their arguments before key decision makers, either one of the alternatives or a new compromise alternative is selected as the strategy to be implemented. At Compaq Computer Corporation, for example, strategic managers follow a process of dialectical inquiry as a way to choose the best alternative, not just the one supported by the highest-ranking executive in the room. To ensure that issues are thoroughly discussed, President Rod Canion takes one side and Michael Swavely, President of Compaq's North American operation, or Gary Stimac, Compaq's Senior Vice-President of Systems Engineering, takes the other side. In theory, there are no winners or losers trying to make points with the boss. "We have to leave our egos at the door," says Swavely. "But we can put any question on the table without fear of being wrong." Once a project is approved or disapproved at Compaq, however, everyone is expected to support the decision. "Above all, we want team players, not individualists," comments Canion.[68]

Research generally supports the conclusion that both the devil's advocate and dialectical inquiry are equally superior to consensus in decision making. The debate itself, rather than its particular format, appears to improve the quality of decisions by formalizing and legitimizing constructive conflict and by encouraging critical evaluation. Both lead to better assumptions and recommendations and to a higher level of critical thinking among the people involved.[69]

7.4 DEVELOPMENT OF POLICIES

The selection of the best strategic alternative is not the end of strategy formulation. Policies to define the ground rules for implementation must now be established. Flowing from the selected strategy, they provide guidance for decision making throughout the organization. Corporate policies are broad guidelines for divisions to follow in compliance with corporate strategy. These policies are interpreted and implemented through each division's own objectives and strategies. Divisions may then develop their own policies that will be guidelines for their functional areas to follow. At General Electric, for example, Chairman Welch insists that GE be Number One or Number Two wherever it competes. This policy gives clear guidance to managers throughout the organization.

Another example of a corporate policy is that developed by Ford Motor Company. Concerned with the historic lack of cooperation between Ford U.S. and Ford of Europe, Ford's top management developed a companywide policy requiring any new car design to be easily adaptable to any market in the world. Before this policy was implemented, Ford of Europe developed cars strictly for its own market, while engineers in the U.S. separately designed their own products. The new policy was a natural result of Ford's emphasis on manufacturing efficiency and global integration as a corporation. One result of this new policy was the program to produce the European Sierra and its U.S. counterpart, the Merkur. The cost to convert the European Sierra to meet all U.S. safety and emission standards was about one-fourth of what the conversion of previous European models would have cost. The Taurus and Sable models were also engineered for easy conversion to overseas markets.[70]

Some policies will be expressions of a corporation's **critical success factors** (CSF). Critical success factors are those elements of a company that determine its strategic success or failure. Research indicates that organizations that possess strengths in their key success factors outperform the competition.[71] Critical success factors will likely vary from company to company. IBM, for example, sees customer service as its critical success factor. McDonald's CSFs are quality, cleanliness, and value. Hewlett-Packard is concerned with new-product development. Dick Mahoney, Chairman and CEO of Monsanto Company, acknowledges research and development of new chemical products as the critical success factor of his company when he says, "R&D isn't part of the strategy. R&D *is* the strategy."[72] As guidelines for decision making, policies can therefore be based on a corporation's critical success factors. At Lazarus Department Store in Columbus, Ohio, for example, customer service is a critical success factor. Store policies state that the customer is *always* right. Even if a department manager believes that a customer who is returning a shirt bought that shirt from a competitor, the manager is bound by policy to accept it and to give money to the customer in return. Lazarus's top management believes that even though a few people might take advantage of the store in the short run, the store will make up for it in the long run with goodwill and increased market share.

Policies tend to be rather long lived and can even outlast the particular strategy that created them. Interestingly, these general policies, such as "The customer is always right" or "Research and development should get first priority on all budget requests," can become, in time, part of a corporation's culture. Such policies can make the implementation of specific strategies easier. They can also restrict top management's·strategic options in the future. It is for this reason that a change in strategy should be followed quickly by a change in policies. Managing policy is one way to manage the corporate culture.

SUMMARY AND CONCLUSION

The typical large, multidivisional business corporation operating in several different industries has three levels of strategy: corporate, business, and functional. Chapter 6 discussed alternative corporate strategies—the strategies that specify the firm's overall direction and its portfolio of businesses, that is, the industries within which the firm operates. This chapter, in contrast, deals with the generation and evaluation of business and functional strategies—the strategies of most importance at the divisional and departmental levels that determine a company's competitive advantage.

Sometimes referred to as division or competitive strategy, business strategy focuses on improving the competitive position of a corporation's products or services within a particular industry or market segment. Porter proposes two "generic" competitive strategies for outperforming other corporations in a particular industry. Lower cost is the ability of the company or its business unit to design, produce, and market a comparable product more efficiently than its competitors. Differentiation is the ability to provide unique and superior value to the buyer in terms of product quality, special features, or after-sale service. Porter further proposes that a firm's competitive advantage in an industry will be determined by its competitive scope, that is, the breadth of the company's target market. When the lower cost and differentiation strategies have a broad mass-market target, they are called cost leadership and differentiation. When they are focused on a market niche, they are called cost focus and focused differentiation. Porter argues that, to be successful, a company or business unit must achieve one of these four strategies. Otherwise, the company or unit will be stuck in the middle of the competitive marketplace with no competitive advantage and be doomed to below-average performance. Various timing and location competitive tactics, such as being first mover or late mover, can be used to implement these competitive business strategies.

Functional strategy acts to maximize corporate and divisional resource productivity, so that a distinctive competence will develop to provide a company or business unit a competitive advantage. Functional strategies can be identified within marketing, finance, research and development, operations, and human resources, among other areas. The formulation and implementation of these strategies are important ways to build on an area's strengths or reduce its weaknesses so that corporate and business strategies have a greater likelihood of success. Within any corporation, these three levels of corporate, business, and functional strategy must fit together in a mutually supporting manner so that they form an integrated hierarchy of strategy.

One of the best ways to assess the likely impact of alternative strategies is through the construction of detailed scenarios. The selection of the best strategic alternative from these projected scenarios will probably be affected by several factors. Among them are management's attitude toward risk, pressures from the external environment, influences from the corporate culture, and the personal needs and desires of key managers. Two approaches to strategic choice that help avoid the dangers of early consensus are the use of the devil's advocate and dialectical inquiry.

Once a strategy has been selected, policies are established to define the ground rules for implementation. As broad guidelines for divisions to follow, corporate policies assure the divisions' compliance with corporate strategy. Divisions may then generate their own internal policies to be followed by their functional areas. These policies define the ground rules for strategy implementation and serve to align corporate activities in the new strategic direction.

DISCUSSION QUESTIONS

1. Is it possible for a company or business unit to follow a cost leadership strategy and a differentiation strategy simultaneously? Why or why not?

2. How can a company overcome the limitations of being in a fragmented industry?

3. What are the advantages and disadvantages of being the first mover in an industry? Give some examples of first mover and late mover firms. Were they successful?

4. Should functional strategies be categorized under strategy formulation or under strategy implementation?

5. Why is penetration pricing more likely than skim pricing to raise a company's or a business unit's operating profit in the long run?

6. What are the pros and cons of R&D leadership versus R&D followership as a functional strategy?

7. What are the pros and cons of the devil's advocate versus dialectical inquiry versus consensus in strategic choice?

8. What is the relationship of policies to strategies? Should policies be categorized under strategy formulation or under strategy implementation?

NOTES

1. L. Collins, "Casey's Wants Exclusive Markets for Its Fried Chicken, Pizza," *Des Moines Register* (June 23, 1988), p. 5S.

2. M. E. Porter, *Competitive Strategy* (New York: The Free Press, 1980), pp. 34–41 as revised in M. E. Porter, *The Competitive Advantage of Nations* (New York: The Free Press, 1990), pp. 37–40. In his 1980 book Porter originally proposed focus as a third generic competitive strategy. In his subsequent 1985 *Competitive Advantage* he introduced differentiation focus and cost focus as categories of the focus strategy. In the 1990 book cited above Porter finally dropped focus as a separate strategy and began viewing it instead as a category of competitive scope rather than a separate competitive strategy. This was in agreement with a developing stream of research on generic competitive strategies.

3. Porter, *The Competitive Advantage of Nations*, p. 37.

4. Porter, *Competitive Strategy*, p. 35.

5. L. Therrien, "Dean Goes Looking for a Diet Supplement," *Business Week* (March 14, 1988), p. 92.

6. S. S. Atchison, "A Perfectly Good Word for WordPerfect: Gutsy," *Business Week* (October 2, 1989), pp. 99–102.

7. M. E. Porter, *Competitive Advantage* (New York: The Free Press, 1985), p. 15.

8. T. Y. Wiltz, "Johnson Products Tries to Catch a New Wave," *Business Week* (August 27, 1990), p. 56.

9. Porter, *The Competitive Advantage of Nations*, p. 40.

10. A. Zipser, "Tandy Corp. Loses Luster in Glitzy Lines," *Wall Street Journal* (January 23, 1990), p. A12.

11. T. G. M. Van Asseldonk, "Porter Quantified," in *Handbook of Business Strategy, 1989/90 Yearbook,*

edited by H. E. Glass (Boston: Warren, Gorham and Lamont, 1989), pp. 12.1–12.14.

G. G. Dess and P. S. Davis, "Porter's (1980) Generic Strategies as Determinants of Strategic Group Membership and Organizational Performance," *Academy of Management Journal* (September 1984), pp. 467–488.

12. G. R. Jones and J. E. Butler, "Costs, Revenue, and Business-Level Strategy," *Academy of Management Review* (April 1988), pp. 202–213.

C. W. L. Hill, "Differentiation versus Low Cost or Differentiation and Low Cost: A Contingency Approach," *Academy of Management Review* (July 1988), pp. 401–412.

R. E. White, "Generic Business Strategies, Organizational Context and Performance: An Empirical Investigation," *Strategic Management Journal* (May-June 1986), pp. 217–231.

13. G. S. Day, "Deciding How to Compete," *Planning Review* (September-October 1989), pp. 18–23.

14. W. E. Deming, *Out of the Crisis* (Cambridge, Mass.: Massachusetts Institute of Technology, Center for Advanced Engineering Study, 1986), p. 23.

15. Porter, *Competitive Advantage*, pp. 18–19.

16. E. Segev, "A Systematic Comparative Analysis and Synthesis of Two Business-Level Strategic Typologies," *Strategic Management Journal* (September-October 1989), pp. 487–505.

17. Porter, *Competitive Strategy*, p. 75.

18. A. Q. Nomani, "Airlines May Be Using a Price-Data Network to Lessen Competition," *Wall Street Journal* (June 28, 1990), p. A1.

19. Porter, *Competitive Advantage*, p. 186.

20. M. Lambkin, "Order of Entry and Performance in New Markets," *Strategic Management Journal* (Summer 1988), pp. 127–140.

21. Porter, *Competitive Advantage*, pp. 186–187.

22. M. B. Lieberman and D. B. Montgomery, "First-Mover Advantages," *Strategic Management Journal* (Summer 1988), pp. 41–58. See also M. B. Lieberman and D. B. Montgomery, "Strategy of Market Entry: To Pioneer or Follow?" in *Handbook of Business Strategy*, 2nd ed., edited by H. E. Glass (Boston: Warren, Gorham and Lamont, 1991), pp. 21.0–21.29.

23. Summarized from various articles by L. Fahey in *The Strategic Management Reader*, edited by L. Fahey (Englewood Cliffs, N.J.: Prentice Hall, 1989), pp. 178–205.

24. This information on defensive tactics is summarized from Porter, *Competitive Advantage*, pp. 482–512.

25. "P&G Ends Test Marketing of Its Liquid Bleach Entry," *Wall Street Journal* (May 23, 1989), p. A8.

26. W. T. Robinson, "Marketing Mix Reactions to New Business Ventures," *The PIMSletter on Business Strategy*, No. 42 (Cambridge, Mass.: Strategic Planning Institute, 1988), p. 9.

27. R. Gibson, "Kellogg Shifts Strategy to Pull Consumers In," *Wall Street Journal* (January 22, 1990), p. B1.

28. R. L. Rose, "Deere Faces Challenge Just When Farmers Are Shopping Again," *Wall Street Journal* (February 8, 1990), p. A1.

29. W. Redmond, "Innovation, Price Strategy, and Long-Term Performance," in *Handbook of Business Strategy, 1988/1989 Yearbook*, edited by H. E. Glass (Boston: Warren, Gorham and Lamont, 1988), pp. 3.1–3.11.

30. C. J. Clarke, "Using Finance for Competitive Advantage," *Long Range Planning* (April 1988), pp. 63–64.

31. "Mergers Take Drastic Drop in 1990," *Des Moines Register*, December 27, 1990, p. 5S.

32. J. Zaslow, "Atlas Van Lines Agrees to Buyout for $71.6 Million," *Wall Street Journal* (June 25, 1984), p. A10.

33. J. Kitching, "Early Returns on LBOs," *Harvard Business Review* (November-December, 1989), pp. 74–81.

34. N. K. Sethi, B. Movsesian, and K. D. Hickey, "Can Technology Be Managed Strategically?" *Long Range Planning* (August 1985), pp. 89–99.

35. Porter, *Competitive Advantage*, p. 181.

36. T. Due, "Dean Foods Thrives on Regional Off-Brand Products," *Wall Street Journal* (September 17, 1987), p. A6.

37. E. Koerner, "Technology Planning at General Motors," *Long Range Planning* (April 1989), p. 18.

38. M. Silva and B. Sjogren, *Europe 1992 and the New World Power Game* (New York: John Wiley and Sons, 1990), pp. 239–241. See also P. Nueno and J. Oosterveld, "Managing Technology Alliances," *Long Range Planning* (June 1988), pp. 11–17.

39. W. M. Cohen and D. A. Levinthal, "Absorptive Capacity: A New Perspective on Learning and Innovation," *Administrative Science Quarterly* (March 1990), pp. 128–152.

40. R. J. Mayer, "Winning Strategies for Manufacturers in Mature Industries," *Journal of Business Strategy* (Fall 1987), p. 24.

41. R. H. Hayes and S. C. Wheelwright, *Restoring Our Competitive Edge: Competing Through Manufacturing* (New York: John Wiley and Sons, 1984).

42. J. R. Williams and R. S. Novak, "Aligning CIM Strategies to Different Markets," *Long Range Planning* (February 1990), pp. 126–135.

43. S. Kotha and D. Orne, "Generic Manufacturing Strat-

egies: A Conceptual Synthesis," *Strategic Management Journal* (May-June 1989), pp. 211–231.

44. J. B. Quinn, T. L. Doorley, and P. C. Paquette, "Beyond Products: Services-Based Strategy," *Harvard Business Review* (March-April 1990), pp. 58, 65.

45. B. Dumaine, "Who Needs a Boss?" *Fortune* (May 7, 1990), pp. 52–60.

46. L. Hooper, "Xerox Tries to Shed Its Has-Been Image with Big New Machine," *Wall Street Journal* (September 20, 1990), p. A1.

47. A. Q. Nomani, "Pan Am to Slash Payroll, Trim Service as Fuel Costs Surge and Demand Drops," *Wall Street Journal* (September 20, 1990), p. A3.

48. R. L. Kuhn, "How Strategic Management Builds Company Value," *Journal of Business Strategy* (November-December 1989), pp. 57–59.

49. W. Whipple III, "Evaluating Alternative Strategies Using Scenarios," *Long Range Planning* (June 1989), pp. 82–86.

50. J. F. Bandrowski, "Taking Creative Leaps," *Planning Review* (January/February 1990), p. 35.

51. M. Hergert, "Strategic Resources Allocation Using Divisional Hurdle Rates," *Planning Review* (January/February 1987), pp. 28–32.

52. M. J. Stahl, *Strategic Executive Decisions* (New York: Quorum Books, 1989), pp. 27–55.

53. M. Kroll and S. Caples, "Managing Acquisitions of Strategic Business Units with the Aid of the Arbitrage Pricing Model," *Academy of Management Review* (October 1987), pp. 676–685.

54. M. D. Everett, "A Simplified Guide to Capital Investment Risk Analysis," *Planning Review* (July 1986), pp. 32–36.

55. H. L. Mathews and T. W. Harvey, "The Sugar Daddy Gambit: Funding Strategic Alliances with Venture Capital," *Planning Review* (November/December 1988), pp. 36–41. See also T. J. Peters and R. H. Waterman, *In Search of Excellence* (New York: HarperCollins, 1982), pp. 115–116.

56. R. H. Hayes and D. A. Garvin, "Managing As If Tomorrow Mattered," *Harvard Business Review* (May-June 1982), p. 79.

57. B. Nussbaum and J. H. Dobrzynski, "The Battle for Corporate Control," *Business Week* (May 18, 1987), p. 103.

58. E. Weiner and A. Brown, "Stakeholder Analysis for Effective Issues Management," *Planning Review* (May 1986), pp. 27–31.

59. For further information on stakeholder management

and political strategy, see I. C. MacMillan and P. E. Jones, *Strategy Formulation: Power and Politics*, 2nd ed. (St. Paul, Minn.: West Publishing Co., 1986).

60. Z. Schiller, "Turning Pampers into Plant Food?" *Business Week* (October 22, 1990), pp. 38–40.

61. R. M. Cyert and J. G. March, "A Behavioral Theory of Organizational Objectives," in *Management Classics*, edited by M. T. Matteson and J. M. Ivancevich (Santa Monica, Calif.: Goodyear Publishing, 1977), p. 114.

62. H. Schwartz and S. M. Davis, "Matching Corporate Culture and Business Strategy," *Organizational Dynamics* (Summer 1981), p. 43.

63. W. S. Silver and T. R. Mitchell, "The Status Quo Tendency in Decision Making," *Organizational Dynamics* (Spring 1990), pp. 34–46.

64. B. Tandy Leblang and C. Wyman, "1990 Was the Year of the 'Lite' Products," *The Ames* [Iowa] *Daily Tribune* (January 2, 1991), p. A6.

65. R. A. Cosier and C. R. Schwenk, "Agreement and Thinking Alike: Ingredients for Poor Decisions," *Academy of Management Executive* (February 1990), p. 69.

66. D. M. Schweiger, W. R. Sandberg, and P. L. Rechner, "Experiential Effects of Dialectical Inquiry, Devil's Advocacy, and Consensus Approaches to Strategic Decision Making," *Academy of Management Journal* (December 1989), pp. 745–772.

   K. M. Eisenhardt, "Making Fast Strategic Decisions in High-Velocity Environments," *Academy of Management Journal* (September 1989), pp. 543–576.

   Cosier and Schwenk, "Agreement and Thinking Alike," pp. 69–74.

67. *Ibid.*, p. 72.

68. M. Ivey and G. Lewis, "How Compaq Gets There Firstest with the Mostest," *Business Week* (June 26, 1989), pp. 146–150.

69. Schweiger et al., "Experiential Effects," pp. 745–772.

70. M. Edid and W. J. Hampton, "Now That It's Cruising, Can Ford Keep Its Foot on the Gas?" *Business Week* (February 11, 1985), pp. 48–52.

71. J. A. S. de Vasconcellos e Sa and D. C. Hambrick, "Key Success Factors: Test of a General Theory in the Mature Industrial-Product Sector," *Strategic Management Journal* (July-August 1989), pp. 367–382.

   J. A. S. De Vasconcellos e Sa, "The Impact of Key Success Factors on Company Performance," *Long Range Planning* (December 1988), pp. 56–64.

72. J. E. Ellis, "Why Monsanto Is Plunking Down Its Chips on R&D," *Business Week* (August 21, 1989), p. 66.

STRATEGY IMPLEMENTATION AND CONTROL

PART FOUR

CHAPTER EIGHT

Strategy Implementation: Organizing for Action

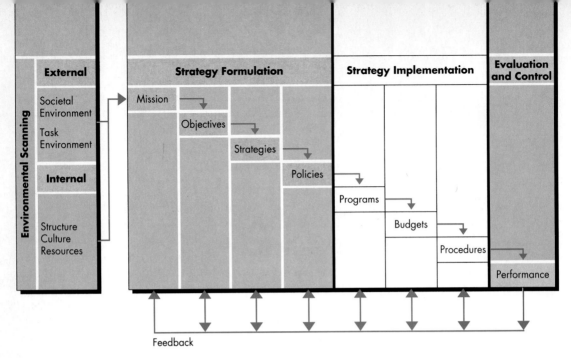

STRATEGIC MANAGEMENT MODEL

If you're going to take $100 a family, you had better make sure that everything is working. Even the vendors ran out of soda![1]

Sheryl Leibert, disgruntled customer at Universal Studios, Florida

Once a strategy and a set of policies have been formulated, the focus of strategic management shifts to implementation. **Strategy implementation** is the sum total of the activities and choices required for the execution of a strategic plan. It is the process by which strategies and policies are put into action through the development of programs, budgets, and procedures. Although implementation is usually considered after strategy has been formulated, implementation is a key part of strategic management. As Hambrick and Cannella point out, "Without successful implementation, a strategy is but a fantasy."[2] Strategy formulation and strategy implementation should thus be considered as two sides of the same coin.[3]

To begin the implementation process, strategy-makers must consider three questions.

Who are the people who will carry out the strategic plan?

What must be done?

How are they going to do what is needed?

These questions and similar ones should have been addressed initially when the pros and cons of strategic alternatives were analyzed. They must also be addressed again before appropriate implementation plans can be made. Unless top management can answer these basic questions in a satisfactory manner, even the best-planned strategy is unlikely to provide the desired outcome.

For example, based on the huge success of its Hollywood, California, Universal Studios tour, MCA, Inc. had planned since 1969 to establish a bigger version of the studio tour in Orlando, Florida. MCA bought land in central Florida, but management's reservations about the project delayed construction until the late 1980s—too late to beat Walt Disney World and its Disney-MGM Studios operation. Finally deciding to go ahead in 1989, the year the Disney-MGM studio tour opened, top management rushed to open the project well before it was ready. For instance, work on an amusement ride based on the movie *Back to the Future* was not yet finished when the studio opened in June 1990. Three months after opening its 444-acre combination studio tour and theme park, customers were still demanding refunds on poorly operating rides and attractions. The rides, which were based on Universal's movies *Jaws*, *Earthquake*, and *King Kong*, rarely operated as planned. One group of customers, having paid the full-price $29 admission, charged up to assembled television cameras, thrust down their thumbs, and shouted: "We're going to Disney World!" After expecting the Florida operation to add as much as $25 million a year to MCA's earnings, management revised its estimates and was hoping merely to break even. Theme park Chief Jay Stein commented in retrospect that he was misled by the rides' designers. Said Stein, "We bought a lemon."[4]

Alexander's survey of 93 company presidents and divisional managers revealed that over half of the group experienced the following ten problems when they attempted to implement a strategic change. These problems are listed in order of frequency of occurrence.

1. More time needed for implementation than originally planned.
2. Unanticipated major problems.
3. Ineffective coordination of activities.
4. Crises that distracted attention away from implementation.
5. Insufficient capabilities of the involved employees.
6. Inadequate training and instruction of lower-level employees.
7. Uncontrollable external environmental factors.
8. Inadequate leadership and direction by departmental managers.
9. Poor definition of key implementation tasks and activities.
10. Inadequate monitoring of activities by the information system.[5]

Poor implementation of an appropriate strategy can result in the failure of that strategy. An excellent implementation plan, however, will not only cause the success of an appropriate strategy, it can also rescue an inappropriate strategy. This is why an increasing number of chief executives are turning their attention to the problems of implementation. Now more than ever before they realize that a successful strategy depends on having in place the right organization structure, resource allocation, compensation program, information system, and corporate culture, among other resources.[6] Supporting their view is recent research on companies in 31 U.S. manufacturing industries revealing that firm performance is not so much a result of a company's strategy, but of the company's capabilities to effectively carry out that strategy.[7] For an example of a successful implementation, see Illustrative Example 8.1.

8.1 *WHO* IMPLEMENTS STRATEGY?

Depending on how the corporation is organized, those who implement corporate strategy might be a different set of people from those who formulate it. In most large, multi-industry corporations, the implementers will be everyone in the organization except top management and the board of directors. Vice-presidents of functional areas and directors of divisions of SBUs will work with their subordinates to put together large-scale implementation plans. From these plans, plant managers, project managers, and unit heads will put together plans for their specific plants, departments, and units. Therefore, every operational manager down to the first-line supervisor will be involved in some way in the implementing of corporate, divisional, and functional strategies.

It is important to note that most of the people in the corporation who are crucial to successful strategy implementation probably had little, if anything, to do with the development of the corporate strategy. Therefore, they might be entirely ignorant of the vast amount of data and work that went into the formulation process. Unless changes in mission, objectives, strategies, and policies and their importance to the corporation are communicated clearly to all operational managers, there can be a lot of resistance and foot-dragging. When top management formulates a strategy that challenges the corporation's culture, lower-level managers might even sabotage the implementation. These managers might hope to influence top management into abandoning its new plans and returning to its old ways. This is one reason why involving middle managers in the formulation as well as in the implementation of strategy tends to result in better organizational performance.[8]

8.2 *WHAT* MUST BE DONE?

The managers of divisions and functional areas work with their fellow managers to develop *programs*, *budgets*, and *procedures* for the implementation of strategy. They also work to achieve synergy among the divisions and functional areas in order to establish and maintain a company's distinctive competence.

DEVELOPING PROGRAMS, BUDGETS, AND PROCEDURES

A **program** is a statement of the activities or steps needed to accomplish a single-use plan, the purpose of which is to make the strategy action-oriented. For example, top management might have chosen forward vertical integration as its best strategy for growth. It purchased existing retail outlets from another firm instead of building its

ILLUSTRATIVE EXAMPLE 8.1

Successful Strategy Implementation at AAL

The Aid Association for Lutherans (AAL) is a nonprofit fraternal society whose mission is two-fold: (1) to provide charitable services to people in need, and (2) to sell life, health, and disability income policies to members of Lutheran congregations and their families. With current assets of $6 billion, the AAL ranks among the top 2% of U.S. life insurers. Despite (or because of) its past success in insurance, the association decided in 1986 to transform itself. From 1982 to 1986, its workforce expanded by 40% to keep pace with insurance volume. As a result, the once-small, family-style organization turned into "just another big company," remarked unhappy employees to an AAL survey team. Organized according to products and functions, all life insurance cases were handled by one section, health insurance by a second, and support services, such as billing, by a third section. When any of AAL's 1,900 field agents contacted the home office to make policy changes or to learn the status of a case, they were often shunted from one section to another and from clerk to clerk. Service to the policyholders deteriorated. "A case would get lost in the maze and sometimes take 30 days to find," said Jerome H. Laubenstein, Vice-President of the insurance department. In an industry characterized by low profit margins and increasing competition, top management concluded that AAL had to cut costs by $50 million over five years in order to be competitive. But how does a charitable organization cut costs without putting its own people out of work and adding to the very problem it is trying to solve?

At precisely noon on August 14, 1987, the entire insurance staff of 500 clerks, technicians, and managers piled all their belongings on office chairs and pushed them along the crowded corridors of the two-story headquarters to their newly assigned work areas. Within two hours, this "organized chaos" sorted itself into a new organizational structure based on work teams. Under the new system, the insurance department is divided into five groups, each serving agents in a different region. Each group consists of three or four teams of 20 to 30 employees who perform all 167 tasks that were formerly divided among the three separate sections. Team members are cross-trained in other functional skills so that they can help each other as needed.

Under the new structure, field agents now need to deal with only one team and can develop relationships with its members. The time required to process complicated cases is now down from an average of 20 days to five days. Although a manager heads each of the 17 teams, three other levels of management (a total of 55 positions) were eliminated as the span of control was widened and team members took on managerial responsibilities. Under a no-layoff policy, top management helped displaced employees to find new jobs elsewhere in the organization. The new structure resulted in 10% less personnel in the insurance department, a 20% increase in productivity, and a reduction in case-processing time by 75%. In addition, the smaller work force is able to handle 10% more transactions of all kinds.

AAL is one of the few organizations to successfully redesign the way it works in an already existing office. Richard L. Gunderson, President and Chief Executive Officer, remarked: "I've felt for years if you provide the right environment for people, they want to do a good job." Each employee has a roomy workstation. Team members schedule their own hours in a flextime program, assign themselves tasks, and exchange jobs with one another. They put up banners to proclaim their excellence and hold parties when they achieve production and quality objectives. "We celebrate a lot these days," remarked Jerome Laubenstein, who headed the reorganization. "That's something we never did before, celebrate."

Source: J. Hoerr, "Work Teams Can Rev Up Paper-Pushers, Too," *Business Week* (November 28, 1988), pp. 64–72.

own. To integrate the new stores into the corporation, various programs, such as the following, would now have to be developed:

1. A restructuring program to move the stores into the existing marketing chain of command, so that store managers report to regional managers, who report to the merchandising manager, who reports to the vice-president in charge of marketing.
2. An advertising program. ("Jones Surplus is now a part of Ajax Continental. Prices are lower. Selection is better.")
3. A training program for newly hired store managers as well as for those Jones Surplus managers the corporation has chosen to keep.
4. A program to develop reporting procedures that will integrate the stores into the corporation's accounting system.
5. A program to modernize the stores and to prepare them for a "grand opening."

Once these and other programs are developed, the budget process begins. A **budget** is a statement of a corporation's programs in terms of dollars. The detailed cost of each program is listed for planning and control purposes. Planning a budget is the last real check a corporation has on the feasibility of its selected strategy. An ideal strategy might be found to be completely impractical only after specific implementation programs are costed in detail.

Once program, divisional, and corporate budgets are approved, procedures to guide the employees in their day-to-day actions must be developed. Sometimes referred to as Standard Operating Procedures (SOP), **procedures** are a system of sequential steps or techniques that describe in detail how a particular task or job is to be done. They typically detail the various activities that must be carried out to complete a corporation's programs. In the case of the corporation that decided to acquire another firm's retail outlets, new operating procedures must be established for, among others, in-store promotions, inventory ordering, stock selection, customer relations, credits and collections, warehouse distribution, pricing, paycheck timing, grievance handling, and raises and promotions. These procedures ensure that the day-to-day store operations will be consistent over time (that is, next week's work activities will be the same as this week's) and consistent among stores (that is, each store will operate in the same manner as the others). For example, to ensure that its policies are carried out to the letter in every one of its fast-food retail outlets, McDonald's has done an excellent job of developing very detailed procedures (and policing them!).

ACHIEVING SYNERGY

One of the goals to be achieved in strategy implementation is synergy between and among functions and business units. This is the reason why corporations commonly reorganize after an acquisition.[9] **Synergy** is said to exist for a divisional corporation if the return on investment (ROI) of each division is greater than what the return would be if each division was an independent business.[10] The acquisition or development of additional product lines is often justified on the basis of achieving some

Copy

advantages of scale in one or more of a company's functional areas. For example, when Ralston Purina acquired Union Carbide's Eveready and Energizer lines of batteries, Ralston's CEO argued that his company would earn better profit margins on batteries than Union Carbide because of Ralston's expertise in developing and marketing branded consumer products. Ralston Purina felt it could lower the costs of the batteries by taking advantage of synergies in advertising, promotion, and distribution.

Ansoff, an authority in strategic management, proposes the existence of four types of synergy. These often affect the success of an implemented strategy.

1. **Marketing Synergy.** Common distribution channels, sales force, and/or warehousing create synergies. A complete line of related products increases the productivity of the sales force. Common advertising and promotions can have multiple returns for the same dollar spent.
2. **Operating Synergy.** The greater utilization of facilities and personnel, the spreading of overhead, and large-lot purchasing create operating synergies.
3. **Investment Synergy.** The joint use of plant, common raw materials inventories, transfer of R&D among products, common tooling and machinery, and increased access to sources of capital create investment synergies.
4. **Management Synergy.** Since competent management is often a scarce commodity, the addition of new products or businesses can enhance overall performance if management finds the new problems to be similar to the ones it has successfully overcome earlier with its current products or businesses.[11]

These synergies are not automatic. In order to achieve them, a corporation must develop an implementation program reorganizing and combining its operations. An example of such a program developed at Philip Morris to integrate its recently acquired General Foods and Kraft subsidiaries is provided in Illustrative Example 8.2.

8.3 *HOW* IS STRATEGY TO BE IMPLEMENTED? *ORGANIZING* FOR ACTION

Up to this point, both strategy formulation and implementation have been discussed in terms of planning. Programs, budgets, and procedures are simply more greatly detailed plans for the eventual implementation of strategy. The total strategic management process includes, however, several additional action-oriented activities crucial to implementation, such as organizing, staffing, directing, and controlling. Before *plans* can lead to actual performance, top management must ensure that the corporation is appropriately *organized*, programs are adequately *staffed*, and activities are being *directed* toward the achievement of desired objectives. Organizing activities are reviewed briefly in this chapter. Staffing and directing activities are discussed in Chapter 9. Top management must also ensure that there is progress toward the objectives, according to plan; this is a *control* function that is discussed in Chapter 10.

ILLUSTRATIVE EXAMPLE 8.2

Philip Morris Reorganizes to Achieve Synergies

Just three months after acquiring Kraft, Inc. for $12.9 billion, Philip Morris began implementing a reorganization plan to combine Kraft with its previously acquired General Foods subsidiary. Taking effect on March 1, 1989, the reorganization plan created the Kraft General Foods Group. Consisting of seven separate operating units, the new group became the largest U.S. food and beverage business in terms of overseas sales. The plan called for John M. Richman, Vice-Chairman of Philip Morris, to oversee the integration of the two companies in his new capacity as Chairman and Chief Executive Officer of Kraft General Foods. Michael A. Miles, President and CEO of Kraft and rumored to be a leading candidate for the CEO position at RJR Nabisco, became President and Chief Operating Officer of the new unit.

The reorganization plan also involved the transfer of other Kraft and General Foods executives. For example, the president of Kraft's operations and technology became president of General Foods USA. Similarly, the president of General Foods USA became president of Kraft USA. The new company was based in Glenview, Illinois, the site of Kraft's old headquarters. In general, analysts reacted favorably to Philip Morris' plan to quickly integrate the acquired companies. "Philip Morris dragged its feet with General Foods and doesn't want to make the same mistake twice," explained Emanuel Goldman of Paine Webber Group. Regarding the use of Kraft's old headquarters as the site of the new group's headquarters, Roy Burry of Kidder, Peabody & Company remarked: "They wanted distribution synergies and Kraft's proven management."

Source: A. M. Freedman, "Philip Morris, Moving Swiftly, Unveils Plan to Meld Kraft and General Foods," *Wall Street Journal* (February 21, 1989), p. A6.

FUNDAMENTALS OF ORGANIZING: MECHANISTIC AND ORGANIC STRUCTURE

Establishing some sort of structure is the primary means of organizing the many activities and people in a large organization in order to get work done. As defined earlier in Chapter 5, the **structure** of a corporation is its formal arrangement of people's roles and relationships, so that the work is directed toward meeting the goals and accomplishing the mission of the corporation. Sometimes it is referred to as the chain of command and is often graphically described in an organization chart.

It is very likely that a change in corporate strategy will require some sort of change in the way a corporation is structured and in the kind of skills needed in particular positions. There is a developing consensus among scholars that changes in the environment primarily affect organizational structure through changes in the organization's corporate and/or business-level strategies.[12] The conclusion seems to be that strategy, structure, and the environment need to be closely aligned; otherwise, organizational performance will likely suffer.[13] Strategic managers must therefore closely examine the way their company is structured in order to decide what, if any, changes should be made in the way work is accomplished. Should activities be grouped differently? Should the authority to make key decisions be centralized at headquarters or decentralized to managers in distant locations? Should the company be managed like a "tight ship" with many rules and controls, or "loosely" with few rules and controls? Should the corporation be organized into a "tall" structure with many layers of managers, each having a narrow span of control (that is, few employees to supervise) to better control his or her subordinates; *or* should it be organized into a "flat" structure with fewer layers of managers, each having a wide span of control (that is, more employees to supervise) to give more freedom to his or her subordinates? For example, Ford has a fairly tall structure with 15 layers of managers, whereas Toyota has a relatively flat structure (for an automaker) composed of seven layers.[14] Is Toyota's or Ford's structure "better"? Before these and other questions can be answered, the strategic manager must understand the differences between mechanistic and organic structures.

Research by Burns and Stalker concluded that a **mechanistic structure**, with its emphasis on a centralization of decision making and bureaucratic rules and procedures, appears to be well suited to organizations operating in a reasonably stable environment. In contrast, however, they found that successful firms operating in a constantly changing environment, such as those in the electronics and aerospace industries, use a more **organic structure**, with a decentralization of decision making and flexible procedures.[15] Studies by Lawrence and Lorsch support this conclusion. They found that successful firms in a reasonably stable environment, such as the container industry, coordinate activities primarily through fairly centralized corporate hierarchies, which place some reliance on direct contact by managers as well as on written directives. Successful firms in more dynamic environments, such as the plastics industry, coordinate activities through integrative departments and permanent cross-functional teams as well as through hierarchical contact and memos.[16] These differences in the use of structural integrating devices are detailed in Table 8.1. The container industry is the most stable; foods, intermediate; plastics, the least stable.

The general conclusion of these studies is that traditional mechanistic structure with few horizontal linkages and many layers of managers is most appropriate for

TABLE 8.1	**Integrating Mechanisms in Three Different Industries**		
	Plastics	Food	Container
Percentage of New Products in Last 20 Years	35%	15%	0%
Integrating Devices	Rules	Rules	Rules
	Hierarchy	Hierarchy	Hierarchy
	Goal setting	Goal setting	Goal setting
	Direct contact	Direct contact	Direct contact
	Teams at 3 levels	Task forces	
	Integrating departments	Integrators	
Percentage of Integrators/Managers	22%	17%	0%

Source: J. Galbraith, *Designing Complex Organizations.* Copyright © 1973 by Addison-Wesley Publishing Co., Inc. Table on Page 111. Reprinted by permission of the publisher.

organizations operating in a relatively certain, stable environment, but that a looser organic structure with more horizontal linkages and fewer layers of managers is most appropriate for those organizations operating in a relatively uncertain, changing environment. This conclusion has been generally supported by further research.[17]

One example of an organization becoming more organic to better adjust to a more uncertain environment is IBM. Realizing that research and development activities needed to be better connected with other parts of the organization, IBM created about 18 special groups throughout the company to link research people with product development people. These special teams work at the cutting edge of technology to produce workable prototypes. "We've gone to tremendous lengths to make that link," says Ralph Gomory, Vice-President of Research and Advanced Technology at IBM. "Instead of doing pieces of technology, we produce a coherent whole."[18]

Other large corporations are also trying to become more efficient and more adaptable to more competitive conditions by decentralizing decision making further down the hierarchy and by reducing the number of middle managers to result in a flatter and more flexible structure. Caterpillar, Inc., for example, unveiled a major reorganization in 1990 designed to "push decision making downward" in the organization. In order to flatten its structure, Caterpillar replaced its tall functional structure with a flatter divisional structure composed of highly autonomous profit centers and support divisions.[19]

ADVANCED STRUCTURES

The basic structures (simple, functional, divisional, and conglomerate) were discussed earlier in Chapter 5 and depicted in Fig. 5.2. A new strategy may, however, require more flexible and organic characteristics of a more advanced structure. Under conditions of (1) increasing environmental uncertainty, (2) greater use of sophisticated technological production methods, (3) the increasing size and scope of worldwide business corporations, (4) a greater emphasis on multi-industry competitive strategy, and (5) a more educated cadre of managers and employees, new advanced forms of organizational structure emerged during the latter half of the twentieth century. Although there are many variations and hybrid structures, three forms stand out as being real advances in organizational structure: strategic business units, matrix structure, and the network organization.

Strategic Business Units

A successful method for the structuring of a large and complex business corporation was developed in 1971 by General Electric (GE) as a variant of the divisional structure. Referred to as **strategic business units**, or SBUs, organizational groups composed of discrete, independent product-market segments served by the firm were identified and given primary responsibility and authority for management of their own functional areas. An SBU may be of any size or level, but it must have (1) *a unique mission*, (2) *identifiable competitors*, (3) *an external market focus*, and (4) *control of its business functions*.[20]

Recognizing that its structure of decentralized operating divisions was not working efficiently (massive sales growth was not being matched by profit growth), GE's top management decided to reorganize. They restructured nine groups and 48 divisions into 43 strategic business units, many of which crossed traditional group, divisional, and profit center lines. For example, food-preparation appliances in three separate divisions were merged into a single SBU serving the housewares market.[21] The concept thus is to decentralize on the basis of strategic elements rather than on the basis of size or span of control and to create horizontal linkages among units previously kept separate. Following GE's lead, other firms, such as Honeywell, Mead Corporation, Eastman Kodak, Campbell Soup, Union Carbide, and Armco Steel, have implemented the concept of the strategic business unit. In introducing the concept, General Foods organized certain products on the basis of menu segments: breakfast food, beverage, main meal, dessert, and pet foods.

Once a large corporation is organized on a divisional basis around strategic business units, there still may be too many SBUs for top management to manage effectively. In this case, an additional management layer, *group executives*, is added between top management and the division or SBU chiefs. The group executive is thus responsible for the management of several similar SBUs, such as housewares, building materials, and auto accessories. Approximately 70% of the Fortune 500 corporations are combining divisions or SBUs around group executives.[22]

This type of reorganization on the basis of markets is one way a **horizontal strategy**, based on competitive considerations that cut across divisional boundaries, is developed. The group or sector executive therefore is responsible for developing and implementing a horizontal strategy to coordinate the various goals and strategies of related business units. This strategy can help a firm compete with **multipoint competitors**, that is, firms that compete with each other not only in one business unit, but in several related business units.[23] For example, Procter & Gamble, Kimberly-Clark, Scott Paper, and Johnson and Johnson compete with one another in varying combinations of consumer paper products, from disposable diapers to facial tissue. If (purely hypothetically) Johnson and Johnson had just developed a toilet tissue with which it chose to challenge Procter & Gamble's high-share Charmin brand in a particular district, it might charge a low price for its new brand to build sales quickly. Procter & Gamble might not choose to respond to this attack on its share by cutting prices on Charmin. Because of Charmin's high market share, Procter & Gamble would lose significantly more sales dollars in a price war than Johnson and Johnson would with its initially low-share brand. To retaliate, Procter & Gamble might thus challenge Johnson and Johnson's high-share baby shampoo with Procter & Gamble's own low-share brand of baby shampoo in a different district. Once Johnson and Johnson had perceived Procter & Gamble's response, it might choose to stop challenging Charmin so that Procter & Gamble would stop challenging Johnson and Johnson's baby shampoo.

Matrix Structure

Most organizations find that organizing around either functions (in the functional structure) or around products (in the divisional structure) provides an appropriate organizational structure. The strategic business unit form is simply a more advanced version of the divisional structure developed originally at General Motors and DuPont. SBUs provide horizontal links for related product divisions so that the organization as a whole can better address changing product-market issues. The matrix structure, in contrast, may be very appropriate when organizations conclude that neither functional nor divisional forms, even when combined with horizontal linking mechanisms, are right for their situations. In **matrix structures,** functional and product forms are combined *simultaneously* at the same level of the organization. Employees have two superiors, a product or project manager and a functional manager. The "home" department—that is, engineering, manufacturing, or sales—is usually functional and is reasonably permanent. People from these functional units are often assigned on a temporary basis to one or more product units. The product units act like divisions in that they are differentiated on a product-market basis. Pioneered in the aerospace industry, the matrix structure was developed to combine the stability of the functional structure with the flexibility of the product form. The matrix structure is very useful when the external environment (especially its technological and market aspects) is very complex and changeable. It does, however, produce conflicts revolving around duties, authority, and resource allocation. To the extent that the goals to be achieved are vague and the technology used is poorly understood, there is likely to be a continuous battle for power between product and functional managers.[24] For a graphical depiction of the matrix structure, see Fig. 8.1. The matrix structure is likely to be used in an organization or within an SBU when the following three conditions exist:

- There is a need for cross-fertilization of ideas across projects or products.
- Resources are scarce.
- There is a need to improve the abilities to process information and to make decisions.[25]

Stanley Davis and Paul Lawrence, authorities on the matrix form of organization, propose that there are *three distinct phases* in the development of the matrix structure.[26] *At first,* **temporary cross-functional task forces** are used when a new product line is being introduced. A project manager is in charge as the key horizontal link.

If the cross-functional task forces become permanent, the project manager becomes a product or brand manager and a *second phase* begins. In this arrangement, function is still the primary organizational structure, but **product or brand managers act as the integrators of semipermanent products or brands.** Considered by many a key to the success of Procter & Gamble, brand management has been widely imitated by other consumer products firms around the world.[27]

The *third and final phase* of matrix development involves a **true dual-authority structure.** Both the functional and product structures are permanent. All employees are connected to both a vertical functional superior and a horizontal product manager. Functional and product managers have equal authority and must work well together to resolve disagreements over resources and priorities. TRW Systems, the aerospace company, is an example of a company that uses a mature matrix.

| FIGURE 8.1 | Matrix and Network Structures |

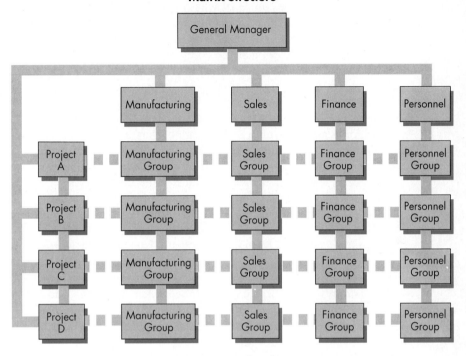

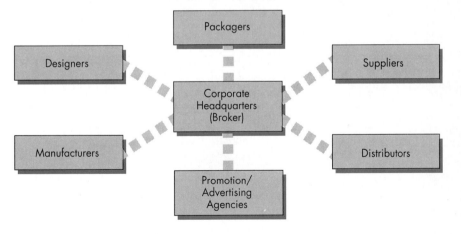

Network Structure

Perhaps the newest and most radical organizational design, the network structure (see Fig. 8.1), is an example of what could be termed a nonstructure by its virtual elimination of in-house business functions. Following the logic of *transaction costs economics*, long-term contracts with suppliers and other "strategic alliances" are used to replace services that the company could provide for itself through vertical integration.[28] The existence of electronic markets and sophisticated information systems reduces the transaction costs of the marketplace, thus justifying a "buy" over a "make" decision.[29] Rather than being located in a single building or area, an organization's business functions are scattered worldwide. The organization is, in effect, only a shell, with a small headquarters acting as a "broker," electronically connected to some completely owned divisions, partially owned subsidiaries, and other independent companies.[30] In its ultimate form, the network organization is a series of independent firms or business units linked together by computers in an information system that designs, produces, and markets a product or service.

Nike, the sports shoe company, has used the network form since the company's beginning in 1964. Nike views itself as a research, development, and marketing corporation, and uses contract manufacturers around the world to produce all of its products. Another example of a complete network organization is Lewis Galoob Toys, one of the most successful toy companies in the U.S. A mere 115 employees run Galoob's entire organization. Independent inventors and entertainment companies conceive of the products, and outside specialists handle the design and engineering work. Manufacturing and packaging are contracted out to a dozen or so firms in Hong Kong, which in turn pass on the most labor-intensive work to factories in China. The toys are distributed by independent manufacturers' representatives. Accounts receivables are sold to Commercial Credit Corporation—Galoob does not bother with collecting monies from its customers![31]

The network organization structure provides an organization with increased flexibility and adaptability to cope with rapid technological change and shifting patterns of international trade and competition. It allows a company to specialize in those activities that are essential to its competitive advantage. Raymond Miles and Charles Snow, authorities on the network organization, point out: "A properly constructed network can display the technical specialization of the functional structure, the market responsiveness of the divisional structure, and the balanced orientation of the matrix."[32] Increased efficiency and effectiveness are thus the basic reasons to use the network organization structure.[33]

STRUCTURE FOLLOWS STRATEGY

In a classic study of large U.S. corporations, such as DuPont, General Motors, Sears, and Standard Oil, Alfred Chandler concluded that changes in corporate strategy lead to changes in organizational structure. He also concluded that organizations follow a pattern of development from one kind of structural arrangement to another as they expand. According to him, these structural changes occur because inefficiencies caused by the old structure have, by being pushed too far, become too obviously detrimental to live with. "The thesis deduced from these several propositions is then that structure follows strategy and that the most complex type of structure is the result of the concatenation [linking together] of several basic strategies."[34] Chandler therefore proposed the following as the sequence of what occurs:

1. New strategy is created.
2. New administrative problems emerge.
3. Economic performance declines.
4. New appropriate structure is invented.
5. Profit returns to its previous level.

Chandler found that in their early years, corporations such as DuPont tend to have a centralized functional organizational structure that is well suited to their producing and selling a limited range of products. As they add new product lines, purchase their own sources of supply, and create their own distribution networks, they become too complex for highly centralized structures. In order to remain successful, this type of organization needs to shift to a decentralized structure with several semiautonomous divisions (referred to in Chapter 5 as the divisional structure). This type of structure is also called the *M-form* (for multidivisional structure) by the noted economist O. E. Williamson.[35]

In his book *My Years with General Motors*, Alfred P. Sloan detailed how General Motors conducted such structural changes in the 1920s.[36] He saw *decentralization of structure* as "centralized policy determination coupled with decentralized operating management." Once a strategy was developed for the total corporation by top management, the individual divisions, such as Chevrolet, Buick, and so on, were free to choose how to implement that strategy. Patterned after DuPont, GM found the decentralized multidivisional structure to be extremely effective in allowing the maximum amount of freedom for product development. Return on investment was used as a financial control.

Research generally supports Chandler's proposition that *structure follows strategy* (as well as the reverse proposition from Chapter 5 that structure influences strategy).[37] As mentioned earlier, changes in the environment tend to be reflected in changes in a corporation's strategy, thus leading to changes in a corporation's structure. Strategy, structure, and the environment need to be closely aligned; otherwise, organizational performance will likely suffer. For example, in one study of 110 business firms, those firms having very uncertain environments reacted by divesting (selling off) business units and developing a simpler structure. They tended to sell off units having the least in common with the rest of the organization. The higher degree of relatedness among the remaining units and a simpler divisional structure made the organizations easier to manage. The top managers were better able to understand markets of related products, so environmental uncertainty decreased for them. Less divisionalization created a relatively simpler, more predictable structure.[38]

When strategies are changed, the early adoption of an appropriate structure can give a company a competitive advantage.[39] In support of this argument, research indicates that when companies that diversify into unrelated products change from a functional structure to a divisional structure, the companies' rates of return increase. Teece, in particular, found reorganization to contribute approximately 1.2 percentage points to a company's return on assets.[40] Research also reveals that the fit between a business-level strategy and the amount of autonomy that corporate headquarters allows the business unit has an effect on business unit performance.[41]

There is some evidence, however, that a change in strategy might not necessarily result in a corresponding change in structure if the corporation has very little competition. If a firm occupies a monopolistic position, with tariffs in its favor or close ties to a government, it can raise prices to cover internal administrative inefficiencies. This is an easier path for these firms to take than going through the pain of corporate reorganization.[42]

Although it is agreed that organizational structure must vary with different environmental conditions, which, in turn, affect an organization's strategy, there is no agreement about an optimal organizational design.[43] What was appropriate for DuPont and General Motors in the 1920s might not be appropriate today. Firms in the same industry do, however, tend to organize themselves in a similar fashion. For example, automobile manufacturers tend to emulate General Motors' decentralized division concept, whereas consumer-goods producers tend to emulate the brand-management concept pioneered by Procter & Gamble Company. The general conclusion seems to be that firms following similar strategies tend to adopt similar structures.[44]

STAGES OF CORPORATE DEVELOPMENT

A key proposition of Chandler's was that successful corporations tend to follow a pattern of structural development as they grow and expand. Further work by Thain, Scott, and Tuason specifically delineates three distinct structural stages.[45]

Stage I: Simple Structure

Stage I is typified by the entrepreneur, who founds the corporation to promote an idea (product or service). The entrepreneur tends to make all the important decisions personally, and is involved in every detail and phase of the organization. The Stage I corporation has a structure allowing the entrepreneur directly to supervise the activities of every employee (see Fig. 5.2). The corporation in Stage I is thus characterized by little formal structure. Planning is usually short range or reactive. The typical managerial functions of planning, organizing, directing, staffing, and controlling are usually performed to a very limited degree, if at all. The greatest strengths of a Stage I corporation are its flexibility and dynamism. The drive of the entrepreneur energizes the corporation in its struggle for growth. Its greatest weakness is its extreme reliance on the entrepreneur to decide general strategies as well as detailed procedures. If the entrepreneur falters, the corporation usually flounders.

Stage I describes Polaroid Corporation, whose founder, Dr. Edwin Land, championed *Polarvision*, a financially disastrous instant home-movie system, while ignoring its potential industrial and commercial uses. Growing concern by stockholders over declines in sales and net income resulted in Dr. Land's resignation from his top management position in 1980 and from the board of directors in 1982. By 1983, analysts reported that Polaroid was in the throes of a "mid-life crisis," worrying about its mortality and the loss of Dr. Land's inspiring vision.[46] Polaroid Corporation was, in effect, a Stage II corporation being managed by Dr. Land as if it were still in Stage I.

This is an example of what Greiner calls the *crisis of leadership*, which an organization must solve before it can move into the second stage of growth.[47]

Stage II: Functional Structure

At Stage II, the entrepreneur is replaced by a team of managers who have functional specializations. The transition to this state requires a substantial managerial style change for the chief officer of the corporation, especially if the chief officer was the Stage I entrepreneur. Otherwise, having additional staff members yields no benefits to the corporation. At this juncture, the corporate strategy favors protectivism through dominance of the industry, often through vertical or horizontal integration. The great strength of a Stage II corporation lies in its concentration and specialization in one industry. Its great weakness is that all of its eggs are in one basket.

Specialized Bicycle Components, Inc. is an example of a company that recently moved from a Stage I, freewheeling, fast-growing company founded by bike enthusiast Mike Sinyard to a Stage II firm run by professional managers. The originator of "mountain bikes," Specialized controlled 65% of the market for these fat-tired bicycles in 1989, but was having difficulty managing its growth. Consequently, Sinyard hired some professional managers to bring about some order. One of these managers, Erik Eidsmo, left Citicorp to manage Specialized's marketing and sales. Since his arrival, Eidsmo introduced into the company Management By Objectives, detailed project planning, and forecasting (see Chapter 9). According to Eidsmo, "We're finally getting—and it's been very painful—some understanding of what the company's long-term horizon should begin to look like."[48]

By concentrating on one industry so long as that industry remains attractive, a Stage II company, like Specialized Bicycle Components, can be very successful. Once a functionally structured firm diversifies into other products in other industries, however, the advantages of the functional structure break down. A crisis of autonomy can develop, in which people managing diversified product lines need more decision-making freedom than top management is willing to delegate to them.

Stage III: Divisional, SBU, and Conglomerate Structures

The Stage III corporation focuses on managing diverse product lines in numerous industries; it decentralizes decision-making authority. These corporations grow by diversifying their product lines and expanding to cover wider geographical areas. These corporations move to a divisional or strategic business unit structure with a central headquarters and decentralized operating divisions—each division or business unit is a functionally organized Stage II company. They may also use a conglomerate structure if top management chooses to keep its collection of Stage II subsidiaries operating autonomously. Headquarters attempts to coordinate the activities of its operating divisions through performance- and results-oriented control and reporting systems, and by stressing corporate planning techniques. The divisions are not tightly controlled, but are held responsible for their own performance results. Therefore, to be effective, the corporation has to have a decentralized decision process. The greatest strength of a Stage III corporation is its almost unlimited

TABLE 8.2	Key Factors Differentiating Stage I, II, and III Companies		
Function	Stage I	Stage II	Stage III
1. Sizing up: Major problems	Survival and growth dealing with short-term operating problems.	Growth, rationalization, and expansion of resources, providing for adequate attention to product problems.	Trusteeship in management and investment and control of large, increasing, and diversified resource. Also, important to diagnose and take action on problems at division level.
2. Objectives	Personal and subjective.	Profits and meeting functionally oriented budgets and performance targets.	ROI, profits, earnings per share.
3. Strategy	Implicit and personal; exploitation of immediate opportunities seen by owner-manager.	Functionally oriented moves restricted to "one product" scope; exploitation of one basic product or service field.	Growth and product diversification; exploitation of general business opportunities.
4. Organization: Major characteristic of structure	One unit, "one-man show."	One-unit, functionally specialized group.	Multiunit general staff office and decentralized operating divisions.
5. (a) Measurement and control	Personal, subjective control based on simple accounting system and daily communication and observation.	Control grows beyond one person; assessment of functional operations necessary; structured control systems evolve.	Complex formal system geared to comparative assessment of performance measures, indicating problems and opportunities and assessing management ability of division managers.
5. (b) Key performance indicators	Personal criteria, relationships with owner, operating efficiency, ability to solve operating problems.	Functional and internal criteria such as sales, performance compared to budget, size of empire, status in group, personal relationships, etc.	More impersonal application of comparisons such as profits, ROI, P/E ratio, sales, market share, productivity, product leadership, personnel development, employee attitudes, public responsibility.

(continued)

TABLE 8.2	Key Factors Differentiating Stage I, II, and III Companies *(continued)*		
Function	Stage I	Stage II	Stage III
6. Reward-punishment system	Informal, personal, subjective; used to maintain control and divide small pool of resources to provide personal incentives for key performers.	More structured; usually based to a greater extent on agreed policies as opposed to personal opinion and relationships.	Allotment by "due process" of a wide variety of different rewards and punishments on a formal and systematic basis. Companywide policies usually apply to many different classes of managers and workers with few major exceptions for individual cases.

Source: D. H. Thain, "Stages of Corporate Development," *Business Quarterly* (Winter 1969), p. 37. Copyright © 1969 by *Business Quarterly*. Reprinted by permission.

resources. Its most significant weakness is that it is usually so large and complex that it tends to become relatively inflexible. General Electric, DuPont, and General Motors are Stage III corporations.

These descriptions of the three stages of corporate development are supported by research.[49] The differences among the stages are specified in more detail by Thain in Table 8.2.

Stage IV: Network or Matrix?

Galbraith and Kazanjian propose the existence of an additional *Stage IV* corporation based on the *matrix* structure. They argue that the matrix is the essential form for diversified multinational corporations.[50] Others disagree. (Refer to Chapter 11 for additional information on multinational corporations.) A growing number of people are suggesting that the further development of corporations will be based on *networks* instead of hierarchies.[51] The increasing use of joint ventures, strategic alliances, and quasi-vertical integration strategies, coupled with the popularity of just-in-time delivery using captive company suppliers, does support the proposal of the network organization as a possible fourth stage of corporate development. At this time, however, neither the matrix nor the network structure has received the degree of usage necessary for either to be considered the next stage of corporate development.

Blocks to Changing Stages

In his study, Chandler noted that the empire builder was rarely the person who created the new structure to fit the new strategy, and that, as a result, the transition from one stage to another is often a painful one.[52] (See Table 8.3 for a listing of some of the possible blocks.) This was true of General Motors Corporation under

TABLE 8.3	Blocks to Development

A) Internal Blocks

Stage I to II	Stage II to III
Lack of ambition and drive.	Unwillingness to take the risks involved.
Personal reasons of owner-manager for avoiding change in status quo.	Management resistance to change for a variety of reasons including old age, aversion to risk taking, desire to protect personal empires, etc.
Lack of operating efficiency.	
Lack of quantity and quality of operating personnel.	Personal reasons among managers for defending the status quo.
Lack of resources such as borrowing power, plant and equipment, salesmen, etc.	Lack of control system related to appraisal of investment of decentralized operations.
Product problems and weaknesses.	Lack of budgetary control ability.
Lack of planning and organizational ability.	Organizational inflexibility.
	Lack of management vision to see opportunities for expansion.
	Lack of management development, i.e., not enough managers to handle expansion.
	Management turnover and loss of promising young managers.
	Lack of ability to formulate and implement strategy that makes company relevant to changing conditions.
	Refusal to delegate power and authority for diversification.

B) External Blocks

Stage I to II	Stage II to III
Unfavorable economic conditions.	Unfavorable economic, political, technological, and social conditions and/or trends.
Lack of market growth.	
Tight money or lack of an underwriter who will assist the company "to go public."	Lack of access to financial or management resources.
Labor shortages in quality and quantity.	Overly conservative accountants, lawyers, investment bankers, etc.
Technological obsolescence of product.	Lack of domestic markets necessary to support large diversified corporation.
	"The conservative mentality," e.g., cultural contentment with the status quo and lack of desire to grow and develop.

Source: D. H. Thain, "Stages of Corporate Development," *Business Quarterly* (Winter 1969), pp. 43–44. Copyright © 1969 by *Business Quarterly.* Reprinted by permission.

the management of William Durant, Ford Motor Company under its founder, Henry Ford, Polaroid Corporation under Edwin Land, and Apple Computer under its founder, Steven Jobs. (See Illustrative Example 8.3.) This difficulty in moving to a new stage is compounded by the founder's tendency to maneuver around the need to delegate by carefully hiring, training, and grooming his or her own team of managers. These managers eventually hold the same beliefs and attitudes as the founder who hired them. In this way a corporation's culture is formed and perpetuated. The team tends to maintain the founder's influence throughout the organization long after the founder is gone.[53]

ORGANIZATIONAL LIFE CYCLE

Another approach to a better understanding of the development of corporations is that of the organizational life cycle.[54] Instead of considering stages in terms of structure, this approach places the primary emphasis on the dominant issue facing the corporation. The specific organizational structure, therefore, becomes a secondary concern. These stages are *Birth* (Stage I), *Growth* (Stage II), *Maturity* (Stage III), *Decline* (Stage IV), and *Death* (Stage V). The impact of these stages on corporate strategy and structure is summarized in Table 8.4. Note that the first three stages of the organizational life cycle are similar to the three commonly accepted stages of corporate development mentioned previously. The only significant difference is the addition of decline and death stages to complete the cycle.

Miller and Friesen place a *Revival* phase between Maturity and Decline; this reflects how the corporation's life cycle can be extended by innovations in a manner similar to the extension of a product's life cycle. Nevertheless, revival is not included here as a separate stage because it can occur anytime during a corporation's maturity stage, when a new growth strategy is implemented, or during its decline stage, when a turnaround strategy is being followed. At Maytag Corporation, for example, the revival phase was initiated in the 1970s under the leadership of Daniel Krumm while

TABLE 8.4	**Organizational Life Cycle**				
	Stage I	Stage II	Stage III	Stage IV	Stage V
Dominant Issue	Birth	Growth	Maturity	Decline	Death
Popular Strategies	Concentration in a niche	Horizontal and vertical integration	Concentric and conglomerate diversification	Profit strategy followed by retrenchment	Liquidation or bankruptcy
Likely Structure	Entrepreneur-dominated	Functional management emphasized	Decentralization into profit or investment centers	Structural surgery	Dismemberment of structure

ILLUSTRATIVE EXAMPLE 8.3

Corporations Recently Moving from STAGE I to STAGE II

What do Apple Computer, Wang Laboratories, Control Data Corporation, and Lotus Development Corporation have in common—other than computers and computer software? Answer: All are successful corporations that have recently made or are in the process of making a transition from an entrepreneur-managed Stage I small business to a professionally managed Stage II corporation.

In the case of Apple Computer, Chairman and co-founder Steven P. Jobs resigned from the company in 1985 after several years of management turmoil. After only eight years of existence, the original two-man company had become a $2 billion company with 5,000 employees. The company grew either because of or in spite of spur-of-the-moment decisions by founders Jobs and Stephen Wozniak and fights by staff over competing projects. John Sculley, Jobs's handpicked successor as Chairman at Apple, restructured the company and introduced rules, strict financial controls, and product-development deadlines in accordance with his strategy of selling Apple computers to businesses. In selecting Sculley one of its "business people of the year," *Fortune* stated:

What makes him one of the top business people of the year is his success in harnessing Apple's famous combination of blue-jeaned idealism and arrogance—and turning the company, once widely dismissed as a glorified toymaker, into a highly profitable producer of serious computers for the desktops of corporate America.

In the first two months after taking office as President of Wang Laboratories, Inc. in 1986, Frederick Wang, son of founder An Wang, reorganized the company's marketing operation and began implementing a retrenchment strategy. The company had been faltering for two years while the founder had been unable to delegate authority for its operation. Even though Wang Laboratories' products were excellent, its lack of marketing skills was crippling its growth. "Wang couldn't sell life jackets on the Titanic," said Vincent Flanders, Associate Editor of *Access 87*, an independent magazine for Wang customers, in comments on the company's marketing weakness under its founder. Unfortunately, even Fred Wang could not keep the company from posting losses and was forced to resign the president's position in 1989. Former employees commented that Fred

Maytag was still in its mature stage of development. As pointed out in the *boxed example* of Maytag (p. 258), the transition from aggressive growth to a rather passive and complacent maturity left the company vulnerable to competitive advances and the possibility of being acquired.

Why do companies go into decline? In *The Icarus Paradox*, Miller proposes that companies go into decline because the very characteristics that helped make them successful tend to be taken to extremes over time and eventually cause a decrease in performance. A successful firm develops a theme based on a mission and a mutually supportive **configuration** composed of strategies, policies, structure, and culture. Success creates **momentum**, causing organizations to keep extending their theme and configuration until they push too far and eventually start to decline. Based on studying over 100 companies, Miller found four very common "**trajectories**" of decline.[55]

was often overruled by his father, who continued to serve as CEO of the company.

___

By the time William C. Norris, the founder and Chief Executive Officer of Control Data Corporation, resigned from the company in 1986, there was a rising chorus of critics complaining that Norris had stayed too long. Through the late 1960s and most of the 1970s, Control Data had been the world's leading maker of computer peripherals. Increased competition during the 1980s cut into the company's sales and profits to the point that the company was forced in 1985 to sell some of its businesses to raise cash. Just before Norris resigned, a banker involved with the debt negotiations stated, "They really need outside people—especially in the financial area. There's a sense that this management isn't prepared for the situation."

___

On July 10, 1986, Mitchell "Mitch" Kapor, founder and Chairman of Lotus Development Corporation, resigned unexpectedly and handed the chairman's position to Jim Manzi, a marketing-oriented consultant whom Kapor had hired earlier from McKinsey and Company to help manage the growing corporation. Kapor, widely regarded as a software "guru," had developed Lotus 1-2-3, the highly successful spreadsheet program—a product that accounted for more than 70% of the company's operating profits. Kapor had been turning over management responsibilities to Manzi for the past year, a trend that was capped by Manzi's assumption of the chief executive office in April 1986. Commenting on his resignation, Kapor stated that he had been rethinking his role at Lotus for several months. He said that leaving a large company "is a natural evolution for founders and entrepreneurs." Five years ago, he added, "We were a small band setting out on a great adventure. Now we have 1,200 employees and two million customers. It's a radically different situation."

Sources: B. O'Reilly, "Growing Apple Anew for the Business Market," *Fortune* (January 4, 1988), pp. 36–37; A. Beam, "Strong Medicine from the Son of Doctor Wang," *Business Week* (January 19, 1987), p. 33; L. Jereski, "The Boss's Son Logs Off," *Business Week* (August 21, 1989), p. 31; R. Gibson, "Control Data Betting Smaller Is Better," *Wall Street Journal* (December 3, 1985), p. 6; W. M. Bulkeley, "Kapor, Founder of Lotus Development, Resigns as Chairman of Software Firm," *Wall Street Journal* (July 11, 1986), p. 2.

- **Focusing** trajectory turns quality-driven *"Craftsmen"* with masterful engineers and excellent operations into rigidly controlled, detail-obsessed *"Tinkerers"* making perfect products with little appeal to the marketplace. By focusing on perfection and not on the marketplace, they alienate customers. By the end of World War II and before Daniel Krumm revitalized the company, Maytag was probably well on its way to becoming a tinkerer.
- **Venturing** trajectory converts growth-driven, entrepreneurial *"Builders"* with imaginative leaders and brilliant financial staffs into impulsive, greedy *"Imperialists"* who squander their resources by expanding helter-skelter into businesses they know nothing about. ITT under Harold Geneen was first a brilliant success in conglomerate diversification, but eventually could not keep track of all its acquisitions and went into decline.
- **Inventing** trajectory turns *"Pioneers"* with unexcelled R&D and state-of-the-

MAYTAG CORPORATION: INITIATING A REVIVAL PHASE

Under the leadership of Lewis B. Maytag, a son of the founder, Maytag Company expanded from 1920 to 1926 into a national company. In terms of the organizational life cycle, this was Maytag Company's **growth stage**. The increasing demand for home laundry equipment caused the company to further reduce its production of farm implements and accessories and to concentrate all of its efforts on washing machines. The company went from a $280,000 loss in 1921 to profits exceeding $6.8 million in 1926. Throughout the 1920s and 1930s, Maytag Company had an average U.S. market share of 40%–45% in washing machines. During the Great Depression of the 1930s, Maytag never suffered a loss. During World War II, the company suspended the manufacture of washers and instead produced components for military aircraft.

At the end of World War II in 1945, the Maytag Company returned to the manufacture of washing machines. Unfortunately, the innovative genius and entrepreneurial drive of the company's early years were no longer present. By then, Maytag had become the most successful washing machine company in the U.S. and had reached its **maturity stage**. Bendix, a newcomer to the industry, introduced an automatic washing machine that used an automatic spin cycle instead of a hand-cranked wringer to squeeze excess rinse water out of clothes. Maytag, however, did not immediately convert to the manufacture of automatic washers. This reluctance cost the company its leadership of the industry. Even with automatics, Maytag's share of the U.S. washer market was only 8% in 1954.

Upon the death in 1962 of CEO Fred Maytag II, professional managers took charge of the company and Maytag family members were no longer involved in company management. Until 1972, George M. Umbreit served as Chairman and CEO, and E. G. Higdon served as President.

These two men were very conservative and were mainly concerned with continuing practices that had served the company well in its past. Product quality and cost control were strongly emphasized. The company had become complacent and somewhat self-satisfied, but it continued to build on its reputation for quality. It also added related products such as clothes dryers to its product line. By 1969, Maytag's market shares in washers and dryers were 10% and 9%, respectively.

Taking over as company President in 1972, Daniel Krumm was not satisfied with Maytag's situation. Although the company had added products to its original line of washers, Krumm saw Maytag as merely a successful niche manufacturer in a maturing U.S. market and vulnerable to aggressive actions by larger competitors. Consequently, Maytag's management adopted a strategy to become a full-line manufacturer and develop a stronger position in the U.S. appliance industry. The decision was made to grow by acquisition within the appliance industry. The **revival phase** of Maytag's organizational life had begun.

In 1981, Maytag purchased Hardwick Stove Company, followed by Jenn-Air a year later, and Magic Chef in 1986. Maytag Company and the Magic Chef family of companies were then merged under the parent Maytag Corporation on May 30, 1986, headed by Chairman and CEO Daniel Krumm. In 1988, the top management of the new Maytag Corporation decided to extend the corporation's growth strategy by buying the Chicago Pacific Corporation to acquire the Hoover Company. In this one step Maytag Corporation moved into the international home appliance marketplace with nine manufacturing operations in the U.K., France, Australia, Mexico, Colombia, and Portugal. Maytag Corporation was now positioned as one of the "Big Four" U.S. appliance manufacturers able to have a strong presence in the developing global home appliance industry.

art products into utopian *"Escapists,"* dominated by cults of free-spirited scientists in pursuit of interesting inventions with little market appeal. Polaroid under Dr. Land became an escapist firm when it continued to develop wonderfully innovative products, but forgot about the marketplace.

■ **Decoupling** trajectory converts *"Salesmen"* with superior market skills and prominent brand names into aimless, bureaucratic *"Drifters"* whose sales orientation ignores product development and produces a stale and disjointed line of "me-too" products. Procter & Gamble in the 1970s and early 1980s continued to emphasize its powerful marketing brilliance, but was no longer developing innovative products to sell.

Table 8.5 illustrates these four trajectories in terms of the company's preferred strategy, goals, culture, and structure.

TABLE 8.5	Four Trajectories of Decline	

	Craftsman ——————→ *Tinkerer*		*Focusing*
Strategy	Quality leadership	Technical tinkering	
Goals	Quality	Perfection	
Culture	Engineering	Technocratic	
Structure	Orderly	Rigid	
	Builder ——————→ *Imperialist*		*Venturing*
Strategy	Building	Overexpansion	
Goals	Growth	Grandeur	
Culture	Entrepreneurial	Gamesman	
Structure	Divisionalized	Fractured	
	Pioneer ——————→ *Escapist*		*Inventing*
Strategy	Innovation	High-tech escapism	
Goals	Science-for-society	Technical utopia	
Culture	R&D	Think-tank	
Structure	Organic	Chaotic	
	Salesman ——————→ *Drifter*		*Decoupling*
Strategy	Brilliant marketing	Bland proliferation	
Goals	Market share	Quarterly numbers	
Culture	Organization man	Insipid and political	
Structure	Decentralized-bureaucratic	Oppressively bureaucratic	

Source: D. Miller, *The Icarus Paradox* (New York: Harper Business, 1990), p. 5. Copyright © 1990 by Danny Miller. Reprinted by permission.

The declining (Stage IV) firm became a widespread phenomenon in the western world during the 1970s and 1980s as many corporations in basic industries such as steel and automobiles seemed to lose their vitality and competitiveness. In decline, the major objective becomes survival. Retrenchment, coupled with pleas for government assistance, is the only feasible strategy.

Unless a corporation is able to resolve the critical issues facing it in Stage IV (as Chrysler was able to do in the early 1980s), it is likely to move into Stage V, corporate death. This is what happened to AM International (previously known as the Addressograph-Multigraph Corporation), Baldwin-United, Eastern Airlines, and Osborne Computers, as well as to many other firms. The corporation is forced into bankruptcy. As in the cases of Johns Manville and International Harvester, both of which went bankrupt in the 1980s, a corporation might nevertheless rise like a phoenix from its own ashes and live again (as Manville Corporation and Navistar International Corporation, respectively). The company may be reorganized or liquidated, depending on individual circumstances. In some liquidations, the corporation's name is purchased, and the purchasing corporation places that name on some or all of its products. For example, Wordtronix, a maker of stand-alone word processors, acquired the Remington Rand trademark, even though Remington Rand no longer made typewriters. Top management planned to change the Wordtronix name to Remington Rand to give its machines some name recognition in the marketplace.

It is important to realize that few corporations will move through these five stages in order.[56] Some corporations, for example, might never move past Stage II. Others, like General Motors, might go directly from Stage I to Stage III. A large number will jump from Stage I into Stages IV and V. Ford, for example, was unable to move from Stage I into Stage II as long as Henry Ford I was in command. Its inability to realign itself no doubt contributed to its movement into Stage IV just before World War II. After the war, Henry Ford II's turnaround strategy successfully restructured the corporation as a Stage II firm.

ORGANIZING FOR INNOVATION—CORPORATE ENTREPRENEURSHIP

One reason proposed for the eventual slide of many established business corporations into Stage IV decline is their inability to innovate. In a special issue of *Strategic Management Journal* devoted to corporate entrepreneurship, Lant and Mezias assert: "Successfully choosing and implementing entrepreneurial strategies is especially difficult in established organizations because they have developed routines and structures which constrain activities."[57] After reviewing the difficulty of generating new technology and innovations within established companies, the Business Environment Study Group of the Strategic Planning Society concluded that much of the future innovation will occur in new small firms rather than in existing ones. They proposed the existence of three types of innovation.

1. Improving existing products.
2. Producing new products.
3. Developing a new technology.

After admitting that large firms are generally able to implement only the first type of innovation (in this way postponing their eventual demise), the Study Group concluded: "Thus, for the foreseeable future, firms will rise and fall along with the product cycle of the industries concerned."[58] Can anything be done by established corporations to avoid this pessimistic fate?

Both scholars and practicing managers are now calling for corporate entrepreneurship as the way to increase meaningful innovation within established corporations. **Corporate entrepreneurship** (also called *intrapreneurship*) is defined by Guth and Ginsburg as "the birth of new businesses within existing organizations, i.e., internal innovation or venturing; and the transformation of organizations through renewal of the key ideas on which they are built, i.e., strategic renewal."[59] A study by Kuratko, Montagno, and Hornsby reveals that for corporate entrepreneurship to be successful, there needs to be management support, appropriate organizational structure, and available resources.[60]

A large corporation that wishes to encourage innovation and creativity within its firm must choose a type of structure that will give the new business unit an appropriate amount of freedom while headquarters still has some degree of control. This is in agreement with the views of authorities in the area that the entrepreneurial project has to be organized separately from the existing, mainstream organization.[61] This separation is needed because the large, successful corporation tends to have a fairly bureaucratic corporate culture emphasizing efficiency, and thus tends to conflict with the type of loose, often freewheeling culture that is needed to nurture innovation.

Burgelman proposes (see Fig. 8.2) that the use of a particular organizational design should be determined by the **strategic importance** of the new business to the

FIGURE 8.2	**Organizational Designs for Corporate Entrepreneurship**

Organizational Designs for Corporate Entrepreneurship

		Very Important	Uncertain	Not Important
Operational Relatedness	Unrelated	3. Special Business Units	6. Independent Business Units	9. Complete Spin-Off
	Partly Related	2. New Product Business Department	5. New Venture Division	8. Contracting
	Strongly Related	1. Direct Integration	4. Micro New Ventures Department	7. Nurturing and Contracting
		Strategic Importance		

Source: Reprinted from R. A. Burgelman, "Designs for Corporate Entrepreneurship in Established Firms." Copyright © 1984 by the Regents of the University of California. Reprinted/condensed from *California Management Review*, Vol. 26, No. 3, p. 161. By permission of The Regents.

corporation and the **relatedness** of the unit's operations to those of the corporation.[62] The combination of these two factors results in nine organizational designs for corporate entrepreneurship.

1. **Direct Integration.** If the new business has a great deal of strategic importance and operational relatedness, it must be a part of the corporation's mainstream. Product "champions"—people who are respected by others in the corporation and who know how to work the system—are needed to manage these projects. When he was with Ford Motor Company, Lee Iacocca, for example, championed the Mustang.

2. **New Product Business Department.** If the new business has a great deal of strategic importance and partial operational relatedness, it should be a separate department, organized around an entrepreneurial project in the division where skills and capabilities can be shared.

3. **Special Business Units.** If the new business has a great deal of strategic importance and low operational relatedness, it should be a special new business unit with specific objectives and time horizons. General Motors' Saturn unit is one example of this approach.

4. **Micro New Ventures Department.** If the new business has uncertain strategic importance and high operational relatedness, it is a peripheral project, which is likely to emerge in the operating divisions on a continuous basis. Each division thus has its own new ventures department. Xerox Corporation, for example, uses its SBUs to generate and nurture new ideas. Small product-synthesis teams within each SBU test the feasibility of new ideas. Those concepts receiving a "go" are managed by an SBU product-delivery team, headed by a chief engineer, that takes the prototype from development through manufacturing.[63]

5. **New Venture Division.** When the new business has uncertain strategic importance and is only partly related to present corporate operations, it belongs in a new venture division. It brings together projects that either exist in various parts of the corporation or can be acquired externally; sizable new businesses are built. R. J. Reynolds Industries, for example, established a separate company, R. J. Reynolds Development, to evaluate new business concepts with growth potential. The development company nurtures and develops businesses that might have the potential to become one of RJR's core businesses.[64]

6. **Independent Business Units.** Uncertain strategic importance coupled with no relationship to present corporate activities can make external arrangements attractive. Procter & Gamble took this approach when it established a separate unit to manage the uncertain, but potentially major, business created by the synthetic fat substitute, olestra, invented by the company. The company claimed that olestra as a food additive was free of calories and cholesterol, and that it had no serious side effects. While awaiting the Food and Drug Administration's approval for marketing the product, the new unit had to decide which uses of olestra it should reserve for its own products and which it should license.[65]

7. **Nurturing and Contracting.** When an entrepreneurial proposal might not be important strategically to the corporation but is strongly related to present operations, top management might help the entrepreneurial unit to spin off from the corporation. This allows a friendly competitor, instead of one of the corporation's major rivals, to capture a small niche. For example, Tektronix, a maker of oscilloscopes, formed a unit to act as an in-house venture capitalist to its own employees; this relationship allowed the corporation to swap the parent company's operational knowledge for equity in the new company. The arrangement is intended to provide Tektronix with a better return on its R&D expenditures and to help it maintain ties with innovative employees who want to run their own companies.[66] Because of research revealing that related spin-offs tend to be poorer performers than nonrelated spin-offs (presumably owing to the loss of benefits enjoyed with a larger company), it is especially important that the parent company continue to support the development of the spun-off unit in this cell.[67]

8. **Contracting.** As the required capabilities and skills of the new business are less related to those of the corporation, the parent corporation may spin off the strategically unimportant unit yet keep some relationship through a contractual arrangement with the new firm. The connection is useful in case the new firm eventually develops something of value to the corporation.

9. **Complete Spin-off.** If both the strategic importance and the operational relatedness of the new business are negligible, the corporation is likely to completely sell off the business to another firm or to the present employees in some form of ESOP (Employee Stock Ownership Plan). Or the corporation can sell off the unit through a leveraged buy out (executives of the unit buy the unit from the parent company with money from a third source, to be repaid out of the unit's anticipated earnings). This is what happened to Lifeline Technology, originally a part of Allied Corporation. Lifeline, an inventory management system, had been developed in Allied's new ventures unit (Cell 5 in Fig. 8.2). After Allied's merger with Signal Companies in 1985, new ventures that didn't fit into the company's existing businesses were refused further funding. Noting that Lifeline lacked any strategic fit with Allied, Stephen Fields, Lifeline's manager, quit Allied and, together with six partners from Allied, formed Lifeline Technology to market the product.[68]

Organizing for innovation has become especially important for those corporations in high-tech industries that wish to recapture the entrepreneurial spirit but are really too large to do so. These new structural designs cannot work by themselves, however. As pointed out earlier by Kuratko, Montagno, and Hornsby, in order to promote successful innovation, new structural designs must also have the support of management and sufficient resources. They must also have employees who are risk takers willing to purchase an ownership interest in the new venture, and a corporate culture supportive of new ventures. Eastman Kodak, for example, established a program in 1984 to encourage employees to manage new ventures within the company. By 1990, of the 14 ventures created by Kodak, six had been closed, four had been merged into the company, and only one still operated independently. Most of the venture managers had been Kodak employees with no experience running an entrepreneurial venture and who had no equity stake in the start-up. According to Stephen Sayles, a former Kodak venture manager: "If you're running a small business, you have to be willing to give up your home, your wife, your kids—you have to be dedicated. People who take jobs with big companies usually aren't those types of people." Kodak management contends that it didn't monitor the ventures closely enough. "Technologists believe that a good idea will make a good business, but it's tougher than that," commented Dennis Deleo, Manager in charge of Kodak's venture program.[69] In response, former venture managers accused Kodak of not giving them the autonomy they said they needed. Because of similar problems, Control Data Corporation and U S West have also ended their corporate entrepreneurship programs.

Rather than attempting such in-house innovation, many corporations are investing venture capital in existing small firms. Wang, for example, purchased a minority interest in InteCom, Inc., a maker of telephone switching equipment. General Motors, Procter & Gamble, and six other companies did the same by buying $20 million of equity in a small artificial-intelligence company called Teknowledge. GM hoped that Teknowledge's expert systems software would help it to design cars and to prepare factory schedules. Increasingly referred to as *strategic partnerships*, these joint ventures are similar to Burgelman's nurturing and contracting design (Cell 7 in Fig. 8.2) and can be viewed as a form of quasi-vertical integration as well.[70] In such arrangements, it often becomes difficult to tell where one firm begins and the other leaves off!

DESIGNING JOBS

Organizing a company's activities and people to implement strategy involves more than simply redesigning a corporation's overall structure; it also involves redesigning the way jobs are done.[71] Looking at Japanese manufacturing methods, many companies are beginning the process of rethinking their work processes with an eye toward phasing unnecessary people and activities out of the process. Harley-Davidson, for example, has managed to reduce total plant employment by 25% while reducing by 50% the time needed to build a motorcycle. Whereas this job-oriented form of restructuring does involve some changes in an organization's structure, such as reducing the number of levels in the hierarchy, its focus is on challenging the basic assumptions and old habits concerning how to get work done. Restructuring through fewer people requires broadening the scope of jobs and encouraging teamwork. This involves moving away from job specialization, a cornerstone of the industrial revolution. It also involves reducing the time it takes a company to complete any major task. The design of jobs and subsequent job performance are increasingly being considered as sources of competitive advantage.

Job design refers to the study of individual tasks in an attempt to make them more relevant to the company and to the employee(s). From the organization's point of view, jobs that are performed efficiently and effectively are optimal. From the individual's perspective, it is important that the jobs be enjoyable and motivating.

The main problem with the traditional cornerstone of job design—specialization—is that people tend to find simplified and highly specialized jobs boring. Boredom results in workers not acting in the best interest of the company; they form unions, are absent, quit, and reduce the quality if not the quantity of their productivity.[72] This has been a serious problem in particular for the U.S. automobile industry ever since Henry Ford invented the moving assembly line. Before purchasing a new car during the 1970s, prospective customers learned to ask *when* the car was built. People knowledgeable in the industry advised purchasers never to buy a car built on a Friday or a Monday: Fridays were bad because many workers called in sick or, if present, spent more time thinking about the weekend than the job. Mondays were also bad because workers tended to arrive late. On both days, management had to use inexperienced part-timers to fill in for the absentees so that production quotas could be met. Quality was a minor concern compared with the pressure to meet production quotas. Manufacturers faced similar problems around the world.

In an effort to minimize some of the adverse consequences of task specialization, theorists and practitioners turned to new job design techniques: **job enlargement** (combine tasks to give a worker more of the same type of duties to perform), **job rotation** (move workers through several jobs to increase variety), and **job enrichment** (altering the jobs by giving the worker more autonomy and control over activities). Although each of these methods had their adherents, none of them seemed to work in all situations. A newer approach to job design is the job characteristics model.

The **job characteristics model** is based on the belief that tasks can be described in terms of certain objective characteristics and that these characteristics affect employee motivation. In order for the job to be motivating, (1) the worker needs to feel a sense of responsibility, feel the task to be meaningful, and receive useful feedback on his/her performance, and (2) the job has to satisfy needs that are important to the worker.[73] The model proposes that managers follow five principles for redesigning work:

- **Combine tasks** to increase task variety and to enable workers to identify with what they are doing.
- **Form natural work units** to make a worker more responsible and accountable for the performance of the job.
- **Establish client relationships** so the worker will know what performance is required and why.
- **Vertically load** the job by giving workers increased authority and responsibility over their activities.
- **Open feedback channels** by providing workers information on how they are performing.[74]

Although there are several other approaches to job design besides the job characteristics model, practicing managers seem increasingly to follow the prescriptions of the model as a way of improving productivity and product quality. For example, Corning, Inc., the glass manufacturer, introduced team-based production in its Blacksburg, Virginia, plant in 1989. With union approval, Corning reduced job classifications from 47 to 4 to enable production workers to rotate jobs after learning new skills. The workers were divided into 14-member teams that, in effect, managed themselves. The plant had only two levels of management: Plant Manager Robert Hoover and two line leaders who only advised the teams. Employees worked a demanding 12½ hour shift, alternating three-day and four-day weeks. The teams made managerial decisions, imposed discipline on fellow workers, and were given the task of learning three "skill modules" within two years or else lose their jobs. As a result of this new job design, a Blacksburg team, made up of workers with interchangeable skills, can retool a line to produce a different type of filter in only ten minutes—six times faster than workers in a traditionally designed filter plant. The Blacksburg plant earned a $2 million profit in its first eight months of production, instead of losing the $2.3 million projected for the start-up period. The plant performed so well that Corning's top management acted to convert the company's 27 other factories to team-based production.[75]

Similar experiences are being reported at other corporations, such as Caterpillar, the earth-moving machine manufacturer, which is trying to reduce costs and improve quality as part of its competitive strategy. Using "cellular manufacturing," Caterpillar's workers are trained to handle multiple tasks, work in teams, and take responsibility for the quality of the parts they produce. "Five years ago the foreman wouldn't even listen to you, never mind the general foreman or the plant supervisor," said Gary Hatmaker, an assembly-line worker. "Now everyone will listen." When Hatmaker installs hydraulic hoses, he, not a quality control inspector, does the spot check. Says Hatmaker: "I know how these things are supposed to fit."[76]

SUMMARY AND CONCLUSION

This chapter explains the implementation of strategy in terms of (1) *who* the operational managers are who must carry out strategic plans, (2) *what* they must do in order to implement strategy, and (3) *how* they should go about their activities. Vice-presidents of functional areas and directors of divisions or SBUs work with their subordinates to put together large-scale implementation plans. These plans include programs, budgets, and procedures and become more detailed as they move down the corporate "chain of command."

Strategy is implemented by management through planning, organizing, staffing, and directing activities. This chapter deals with planning and organizing. Planning results in fairly detailed programs, budgets, and procedures. Organizing deals with the design of an appropriate structure for the corporation. Research generally supports Chandler's proposal that changes in corporate strategy in response to changes in the environment tend to lead to changes in organizational structure. The growing use of strategic business unit, matrix, and network structures reflects a need for more flexible organizational designs to manage increasingly diversified corporations.

Not only should a firm work to make its structure congruent with its strategy, it should also be aware that there is an organizational life cycle composed of stages of corporate development through which a corporation is likely to move. As a way to avoid a corporation's eventual slide into decline, both scholars and practicing managers are proposing corporate entrepreneurship as the way to increase meaningful innovation within established corporations. Burgelman proposes that the use of a particular organizational design for new ventures should be determined by the *strategic importance* of the new business to the corporation and the *relatedness* of the unit's operations to those of the corporation.

Organizing a company's activities and people to implement strategy involves more than just redesigning a corporation's overall structure; it also involves redesigning the way jobs are done. The job characteristics model is one approach to use to introduce team-based production as a way of implementing strategies to reduce cost and improve quality.

Other aspects of strategy implementation, such as staffing and directing, will be discussed in the following chapter. Evaluation and control will be discussed in Chapter 10.

DISCUSSION QUESTIONS

1. Japanese corporations typically involve many more organizational levels and people in the development of implementation plans than do U.S. corporations. Is this appropriate? Why or why not?

2. To what extent should top management be involved in strategy implementation?

3. Does structure follow strategy or does strategy follow structure? Why?

4. What can be done to encourage innovation in large corporations?

5. To what extent should a corporation attempt to achieve synergy between and among functions and business units?

6. What are the pros and cons of the network structure?

7. How should an owner-manager prepare the company for its movement from Stage I to Stage II?

8. How can a corporation keep from sliding into decline as part of the organizational life cycle?

9. According to the job characteristics model, how should task activities be organized in order to improve product quality and productivity?

NOTES

1. R. Grover and A. N. Fins, "MCA May Have Created a Monster," *Business Week* (September 10, 1990), p. 37.

2. D. C. Hambrick and A. A. Cannella, "Strategy Implementation as Substance and Selling," *Academy of Management Executive* (November 1989), p. 278.

3. R. M. Prasad and S. B. Prasad, "Strategic Planning in Banks: Senior Executives' Views," *International Journal of Management* (December 1989), p. 436.

4. R. Turner, "Missed Opportunities, Old-Fashioned Style Push MCA to Merge," *Wall Street Journal* (September 26, 1990), pp. A1, A12.

   Grover and Fins, "MCA," pp. 37–38.

5. L. D. Alexander, "Successfully Implementing Strategic Decisions," *Long Range Planning* (June 1985), p. 92.

6. J. R. Galbraith and R. K. Kazanjian, *Strategy Implementation: Structure, Systems, and Process*, 2nd ed. (St. Paul, Minn.: West Publishing Co., 1986), p. 108.

   P. Miesing, "Integrating Planning with Management," *Long Range Planning* (October 1984), pp. 118–124.

7. M. W. Lawless, D. D. Bergh, and W. D. Wilsted, "Performance Variations Among Strategic Group Members: An Examination of Individual Firm Capability," *Journal of Management* (December 1989),

pp. 649–661. See also C. K. Prahalad and G. Hamel, "The Core Competence of the Corporation," *Harvard Business Review* (May-June 1990), pp. 79–91; and D. A. Aaker, "Managing Assets and Skills: The Key to a Sustainable Competitive Advantage," *California Management Review* (Winter 1989), pp. 91–106.

8. B. Wooldridge and S. W. Floyd, "The Strategy Process, Middle Management Involvement, and Organizational Performance," *Strategic Management Journal* (March-April 1990), pp. 231–241.

9. A. F. de Noble, L. T. Gustafson, and M. Herger, "Planning for Post-merger Integration—Eight Lessons for Merger Success," *Long Range Planning* (August 1988), pp. 82–85.

10. J. A. S. de Vasconcellos e Sa, "A Practical Way to Evaluate Synergy," in *Handbook of Business Strategy, 1989/90 Yearbook*, edited by H. E. Glass (Boston: Warren, Gorham and Lamont, 1989), pp. 11.1–11.19.

11. H. I. Ansoff, *The New Corporate Strategy* (New York: John Wiley and Sons, 1988), pp. 55–58.

12. D. Miller, "Relating Porter's Business Strategies to Environment and Structure: Analysis and Performance Implications," *Academy of Management Journal* (June 1988), pp. 280–308.

C. Oliver, "The Collective Strategy Framework: An Application to Competing Predictors of Isomorphism," *Administrative Science Quarterly* (December 1988), pp. 543–561.

13. Miller, "Porter's Business Strategies," p. 304.

    R. E. Miles and C. C. Snow, "Fit, Failure and the Hall of Fame," in *Strategy and Organization: A West Coast Perspective*, edited by G. Carroll and D. Vogel (Boston: Pittman Publishing, 1984), pp. 1–19.

14. T. F. O'Boyle, "From Pyramid to Pancake," *Wall Street Journal* (June 4, 1990), p. R37.

15. T. Burns and G. M. Stalker, *The Management of Innovation* (London: Tavistock Publications, 1961).

16. P. R. Lawrence and J. W. Lorsch, *Organization and Environment* (Homewood, Ill.: Irwin, 1969), p. 138.

17. J. G. Covin and D. P. Slevin, "Strategic Management of Small Firms in Hostile and Benign Environments," *Strategic Management Journal* (January-February 1989), pp. 75–87.

    P. F. Buller, "Successful Partnerships: HR and Strategic Planning at Eight Top Firms," *Organizational Dynamics* (Autumn 1988), pp. 27–43.

18. M. Schrage, "R&D Just Ain't What It Used to Be," *Wall Street Journal* (October 10, 1988), p. A8.

19. "Caterpillar Says Fites to Be Its Chairman; Wogsland in New Job," *Wall Street Journal* (January 30, 1990), p. B7.

20. M. Leontiades, "A Diagnostic Framework for Planning," *Strategic Management Journal* (January-March 1983), p. 14.

21. W. K. Hall, "SBUs: Hot New Topic in the Management of Diversification," *Business Horizons* (February 1978), p. 19.

22. J. M. Stengrevics, "Managing the Group Executive's Job," *Organization Dynamics* (Winter 1984), p. 21.

23. M. E. Porter, *Competitive Advantage* (New York: The Free Press, 1985), pp. 322, 395–398.

24. E. W. Larson and D. H. Gobeli, "Matrix Management: Contradictions and Insights," *California Management Review* (Summer 1987), pp. 131–132.

25. L. G. Hrebiniak and W. F. Joyce, *Implementing Strategy* (New York: Macmillan, 1984), pp. 85–86.

26. S. M. Davis and P. R. Lawrence, *Matrix* (Reading, Mass.: Addison-Wesley, 1977), pp. 11–24.

27. J. Solomon and C. Hymowitz, "P&G Makes Changes in the Way It Develops and Sells Its Products," *Wall Street Journal* (August 11, 1987), pp. 1, 10.

28. O. E. Williamson, *Markets and Hierarchies* (New York: The Free Press, 1975).

    O. E. Williamson, *The Economic Institutions of Capitalism* (New York: The Free Press, 1985).

C. W. L. Hill, "The Emergence of Cooperation Without Hierarchical Governance: Implications for Transaction Cost Theory and the Theory of the Firm," in *Proceedings, Conference on Corporate Governance and Competitive Strategy* (Minneapolis: Carlson School of Management, University of Minnesota, October 25–26, 1990), pp. 1–45.

29. T. W. Malone, J. Yates, and R. I. Benjamin, "The Logic of Electronic Markets," *Harvard Business Review* (May-June 1989), pp. 166–172.

30. R. E. Miles and C. C. Snow, "Organizations: New Concepts for New Forms," *California Management Review* (Spring 1986), pp. 62–73.

31. E. J. Ottensmeyer and C. C. Snow, "Managing Strategies and Technologies," in *Proceedings, Managing the High Technology Firm Conference*, edited by L. R. Gomez-Mejia and M. W. Lawless (Boulder, Colo.: University of Colorado, January 13–15, 1988), p. 428.

32. Miles and Snow, "Organizations," p. 65.

33. J. C. Jarillo, "On Strategic Networks," *Strategic Management Journal* (January-February 1988), p. 36.

34. A. D. Chandler, *Strategy and Structure* (Cambridge, Mass.: MIT Press, 1962), p. 14.

35. O. E. Williamson, "The Multidivisional Structure," in *Markets and Hierarchies* (New York: The Free Press, 1975), as reprinted in *Organizational Economics*, edited by J. B. Barney and W. G. Ouchi (San Francisco: Jossey-Bass, 1986), pp. 163–187.

36. A. P. Sloan, Jr., *My Years with General Motors* (Garden City, N.Y.: Doubleday, 1964).

37. H. L. Boschken, "Strategy and Structure: Reconceiving the Relationship," *Journal of Management* (March 1990), pp. 135–150.

    L. Donaldson, "Strategy and Structural Adjustment to Regain Fit and Performance: In Defense of Contingency Theory," *Journal of Management Studies* (January 1987), pp. 1–24.

    D. Miller, "Strategy Making and Structure: Analysis and Implications for Performance," *Academy of Management Journal* (March 1987), pp. 7–32.

    Galbraith and Kazanjian, *Strategy Implementation*, pp. 13–27.

38. B. W. Keats and M. A. Hitt, "A Causal Model of Linkages Among Environmental Dimensions, Macro Organizational Characteristics, and Performance," *Academy of Management Journal* (September 1988), pp. 570–598.

    See also J. R. Williams, B. L. Paez, and L. Sanders, "Conglomerates Revisited," *Strategic Management Journal* (September-October 1988), pp. 403–414.

39. Galbraith and Kazanjian, *Strategy Implementation*, p. 45.

40. R. E. Hoskisson, "Multidivisional Structure and Performance: The Contingency of Diversification Strategy," *Academy of Management Journal* (December 1987), pp. 625–644.

R. E. Hoskisson and C. S. Galbraith, "The Effect of Quantum versus Incremental M-form Reorganization on Performance: A Time-Series Exploration of Intervention Dynamics," *Journal of Management* (Fall-Winter 1985), pp. 55–70.

D. J. Teece, "Internal Organization and Economic Performance: An Empirical Analysis of the Profitability of Principal Firms," *The Journal of Industrial Economics* (Vol. 30, 1981), pp. 173–199.

41. R. E. White, "Generic Business Strategies, Organizational Context and Performance: An Empirical Investigation," *Strategic Management Journal* (May-June 1986), pp. 217–231.

A. K. Gupta, "SBU Strategies, Corporate-SBU Relations, and SBU Effectiveness in Strategy Implementation," *Academy of Management Journal* (September 1987), pp. 477–500.

42. Galbraith and Kazanjian, *Strategy Implementation,* p. 24.

43. D. R. Dalton, W. D. Todor, M. J. Spendolini, G. J. Fielding, and L. W. Porter, "Organization Structure and Performance: A Critical Review," *Academy of Management Review* (January 1980), pp. 49–64.

44. Hrebiniak and Joyce, *Implementing Strategy,* p. 70.

45. D. H. Thain, "Stages of Corporate Development," *The Business Quarterly* (Winter 1969), pp. 32–45.

B. R. Scott, "Stages of Corporate Development" (Boston: Intercollegiate Case Clearing House, No. 9-371-294, 1971); and "The Industrial State: Old Myths and New Realities," *Harvard Business Review* (March-April 1973).

R. V. Tuason, "Corporate Life Cycle and the Evaluation of Corporate Strategy," *Proceedings, The Academy of Management* (August 1973), pp. 35–40.

46. W. M. Bulkeley, "As Polaroid Matures, Some Lament a Decline in Creative Excitement," *Wall Street Journal* (May 10, 1983), p. 1.

47. L. E. Greiner, "Evolution and Revolution as Organizations Grow," *Harvard Business Review* (July-August 1972), pp. 37–46.

48. M. Selz, "Mountain-Bike Firm Performs Tough Balancing Act," *Wall Street Journal* (October 31, 1989), p. B2.

49. N. R. Smith and J. B. Miner, "Type of Entrepreneur, Type of Firm, and Managerial Motivation: Implications for Organizational Life Cycle Theory," *Strategic Management Journal* (October-December 1983), pp. 325–340.

F. Hoy, B. C. Vaught, and W. W. Buchanan, "Managing Managers of Firms in Transition from Stage I to Stage II," *Proceedings, Southern Management Association* (November 1982), pp. 152–153.

K. Smith and T. Mitchell, "An Investigation into the Effect of Changes in Stages of Organizational Maturation on a Decision Maker's Decision Priorities," *Proceedings, Southern Management Association* (November 1983), pp. 7–9.

50. Galbraith and Kazanjian, *Strategy Implementation,* pp. 153–154.

51. J. Child, "Information Technology, Organization, and the Response to Strategic Challenges," *California Management Review* (Fall 1987), pp. 33–50.

R. L. Drake, "Innovative Structures for Managing Change," *Planning Review* (November 1986), pp. 18–22.

B. Borys and D. B. Jemison, "Hybrid Arrangements as Strategic Alliances: Theoretical Issues in Organizational Combinations," *Academy of Management Review* (April 1989), pp. 234–249.

52. G. D. Meyer, R. M. Lenoir, and T. J. Dean, "The Executive Limit Scenario in High Technology Firms," in *Proceedings, Managing the High Technology Firm Conference,* edited by L. R. Gomez-Mejia and M. W. Lawless (Boulder: University of Colorado, January 13–15, 1988), pp. 342–349.

53. K. G. Smith and J. K. Harrison, "In Search of Excellent Leaders," in *Handbook of Business Strategy, 1986/87 Yearbook,* edited by W. D. Guth (Boston: Warren, Gorham and Lamont, 1986), p. 27.8.

54. D. Miller and P. H. Friesen, "A Longitudinal Study of the Corporate Life Cycle," *Management Science* (October 1984), pp. 1161–1183.

J. R. Kimberly, R. H. Miles, and Associates, *The Organizational Life Cycle* (San Francisco: Jossey-Bass, 1980).

55. D. Miller, *The Icarus Paradox: How Exceptional Companies Bring About Their Own Downfall* (New York: Harper Business, 1990).

56. R. Drazin and R. K. Kazanjian, "A Reanalysis of Miller and Friesen's Life Cycle Data," *Strategic Management Journal* (May-June 1990), pp. 319–325.

57. T. K. Lant and S. J. Mezias, "Managing Discontinuous Change: A Simulation Study of Organizational Learning and Entrepreneurship," *Strategic Management Journal* (Summer 1990), p. 147.

58. R. Whaley and B. Burrows, "How Will Technology Impact Your Business?" *Long Range Planning* (October 1987), p. 113.

59. W. D. Guth and A. Ginsberg, "Corporate Entrepreneurship," *Strategic Management Journal* (Summer 1990), p. 5.

60. D. F. Kuratko, R. V. Montagno, and J. S. Hornsby, "Developing an Intrapreneurial Assessment Instrument for an Effective Corporate Entrepreneurial Environment," *Strategic Management Journal* (Summer 1990), pp. 49–58.

61. P. F. Drucker, *Innovation and Entrepreneurship* (New York: HarperCollins, 1985), pp. 161–170.

    J. R. Galbraith, "Human Resource Policies for the Innovating Organization," in *Strategic Human Resources Management*, edited by C. J. Fombrun, N. M. Tichy, and M. A. Devanna (New York: John Wiley and Sons, 1984), pp. 319–341.

    P. Strebel, "Organizing for Innovation over an Industry Cycle," *Strategic Management Journal* (March-April 1987), pp. 117–124.

62. R. A. Burgelman, "Designs for Corporate Entrepreneurship," *California Management Review* (Spring 1984), pp. 154–166.

    R. A. Burgelman and L. R. Sayles, *Inside Corporate Innovation* (New York: The Free Press, 1986).

63. "How Xerox Speeds Up the Birth of New Products," *Business Week* (March 19, 1984), pp. 58–59.

64. J. T. Wilson, "Strategic Planning at R. J. Reynolds Industries," *Journal of Business Strategy* (Fall 1985), p. 26.

65. R. Koenig, "P&G Establishes Division to Manage Fat Substitute Line," *Wall Street Journal* (September 9, 1987), p. 20.

66. C. Dolan, "Tektronix New-Venture Subsidiary Brings Benefits to Parent, Spinoffs," *Wall Street Journal* (September 18, 1984), p. 31.

67. C. Y. Woo, G. E. Willard, and S. M. Beckstead, "Spin-Offs: What Are the Gains?" *Journal of Business Strategy* (March-April 1989), pp. 29–32.

68. U. Gupta, "The Perils of a Corporate Entrepreneur," *Wall Street Journal* (September 10, 1987), p. 35.

69. J. S. Hirsch, "At Giant Kodak, 'Intrapreneurs' Lose Foothold," *Wall Street Journal* (August 17, 1990), p. B1, B8.

70. N. W. Miller, "Art of 'Strategic Partnerships' Is Refined by California Firm," *Wall Street Journal* (December 6, 1985), p. 25.

71. Much of this section was suggested by J. McElroy of Iowa State University.

72. R. B. Dunham, "Job Design and Redesign," in *Organizational Behavior*, edited by S. Kerr (Columbus, Ohio: Grid, 1979), pp. 337–354.

73. J. R. Hackman and E. E. Lawler, "Employee Reactions to Job Characteristics," *Journal of Applied Psychology* (1971), pp. 259–286.

74. J. R. Hackman and G. R. Oldham, *Work Redesign* (Reading, Mass.: Addison-Wesley, 1980), pp. 135–141.

75. J. Hoerr, "Sharpening Minds for a Competitive Edge," *Business Week* (December 17, 1990), pp. 72–78.

76. R. Henkoff, "This Cat Is Acting Like a Tiger," *Fortune* (December 19, 1988), pp. 69–76.

CHAPTER NINE

Strategy Implementation: Staffing and Directing

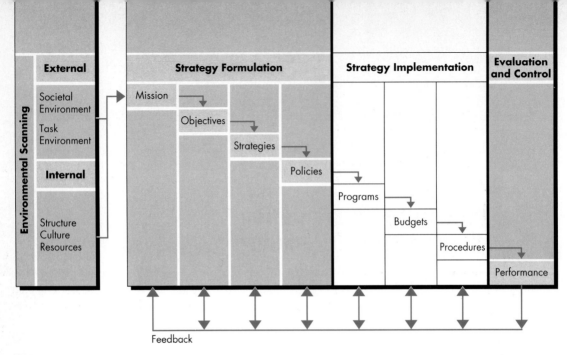

STRATEGIC MANAGEMENT MODEL

Without the dedication of all its employees, no company can have long-term success.[1]

Richard Teerlink, CEO
Harley-Davidson, Inc.

As mentioned in Chapter 8, strategy implementation is the sum total of the activities and choices required for the execution of a strategic plan. It is the process by which strategies and policies are put into action, through the development of programs, budgets, and procedures. Although it certainly involves some planning activities, the major emphasis in strategy implementation is on *organizing* into units people and activities for maximum effectiveness and efficiency, *staffing* these units with people having the appropriate mix of abilities and skills, and on *directing* people to use their abilities and skills most effectively and efficiently to achieve organizational objectives. Organizing was discussed in Chapter 8 in terms of organizational structure and job design. This chapter discusses staffing and directing. Staffing focuses on the selection and utilization of employees. Directing emphasizes the management of corporate culture, the development of action plans, Management By Objectives (MBO), and incentive management.

9.1 STAFFING

The implementation of new strategies and policies often calls for new human resource management priorities and a different utilization of personnel.[2] This may mean hiring new people with new skills, firing people with inappropriate or substandard skills, and/or training existing employees to learn new skills.

If growth strategies are to be implemented, new people may need to be hired and trained. Experienced people with the necessary skills need to be found for promotion to newly created managerial positions. For example, if a manufacturing firm has decided to integrate forward by opening its own retail outlets, one key concern is the ability of the corporation to find, hire, and train store managers. When a corporation follows a growth through acquisition strategy, it may find that it will need to replace several managers in the acquired company. Research by Walsh of 102 companies following an acquisition revealed that the percentage of the acquired company's top management team that either quit or was asked to leave was 26% after the first year and 61% after five years.[3]

If a corporation adopts a retrenchment strategy, however, a large number of people may need to be laid off or fired; and top management, as well as the divisional managers, needs to specify criteria used in making these personnel decisions. Should employees be fired on the basis of low seniority or on the basis of poor performance? Sometimes corporations find it easier to close an entire division than to choose which individuals to fire.

PROBLEMS IN RETRENCHMENT

In a study of **downsizing** (laying off employees and reducing the corporate hierarchy) at 30 automobile-related industrial companies in the U.S., Cameron concluded that most of these cutbacks in personnel were handled poorly. In about two-thirds of the cases either the wrong jobs were eliminated or blanket offers of early retirement prompted managers, even those considered invaluable, to leave. After the layoffs, the employees who were left had to do not only their work, but also the work of the people who had gone. Says Cameron, "There's a general approach of throwing a hand grenade at a bunch of employees, and whoever survives has to do all the work there was before." Since the survivors often didn't know how to do the departeds' work, morale and productivity plummeted.[4] When this occurs, reducing the number of layers in an organization's structure may result in less rather than more productivity.

In a survey of 1,468 downsized companies, more than half reported that employee productivity either stayed the same or deteriorated after the layoffs. Part of the reason was that cost-conscious executives tended to defer maintenance, skimp on training, delay new product introductions, and avoid risky new businesses. According to Robert Gunn, management consultant, "You get a bottom-line benefit from the payroll cut, but then all these other things have gone wrong. The net change is zero."[5]

A good retrenchment strategy can thus be implemented well in terms of organizing, but poorly in terms of staffing. A situation can develop in which retrenchment feeds on itself and acts to further weaken instead of strengthen the company. Eric Greenberg, editor of the American Management Association's research reports, comments: "The best indication of whether a company will downsize next year is whether it has downsized in the past." During 1990, for example, Eastman Kodak was shrinking for the third time in six years; Honeywell was also shrinking, for the second time in four years.[6]

Following are proposed guidelines for successful downsizing:[7]

- **Eliminate Unnecessary Work Instead of Making Across-the-Board Cuts.** Spend the time to research where money is going and eliminate the task if it doesn't add value to what the firm is producing. For example, the productivity of Colgate-Palmolive's R&D scientists increased significantly once they were freed from an excessive amount of supervising and reporting.

- **Contract Out Work That Others Can Do Cheaper.** For example, Bankers Trust of New York contracts out to a division of Xerox its mail room and printing services, as well as some of its payroll and accounts payable activities. About 70 Bankers Trust employees were transferred to Xerox, but never left the building! According to Peter Hawes of Xerox Reproduction Centers, "Sometimes we can find efficiencies in these businesses because they are our specialty."[8]

- **Plan for Long-Run Efficiencies.** Don't simply eliminate all postponable expenses, such as maintenance, R&D, and advertising, in the unjustifiable hope that the environment will become more supportive. (Remember when U.S. automakers predicted that Americans would soon tire of driving those small Japanese cars?) Some companies like Ford, General Electric, and Citicorp are following long-term strategies for the redeployment of their human and physical resources.

- **Communicate the Reasons for Actions.** Tell employees not only why the company is downsizing, but also what the company is trying to achieve. Sharpen and emphasize the mission statement. For example, Square D, a leading manufacturer of electrical equipment, had all its 19,200 employees attend a two-day program stressing the importance of quality and customer service.

- **Invest in the Remaining Employees.** Since most "survivors" in a corporate downsizing will probably be doing different tasks from what they were doing before the change, firms need to draft new job specifications, performance standards, appraisal techniques, and compensation packages. Additional training will be needed to ensure that everyone has the proper skills to deal with expanded jobs and responsibilities. After eliminating many of its supervisors, for example, DuPont created work teams and rotated the management of each team to train its members to take responsibility for performing critical tasks.

- **Develop Value-Added Jobs to Balance Out Job Elimination.** IBM, among other companies, has for years been able to avoid firing people by transferring them from one job to another. Sometimes, however, there are no other jobs currently available and management must consider some other staffing alternatives. After a series of production-improvement programs eliminated many jobs, management at Harley-Davidson, the motorcycle manufacturer, worked with the company's unions to find other work for their surplus employees. Through an active "in-sourcing" program, in which work previously done by suppliers was moved into Harley-Davidson plants, the unions helped the company transfer people to new jobs. According to Peter Reid, author of *Well Made in America*: "This joint union-management effort has brought in 60 jobs, improved quality, and reduced costs by over $2 million. Employment security has been increased, and Harley-Davidson has been able to utilize the plant space it freed up through successful inventory reduction."[9]

STAFFING FOLLOWS STRATEGY

As in the case of structure, staffing requirements are also likely to follow a change in strategy. Once a new strategy is formulated, either different kinds of people may be needed or the current employees may need to be retrained to implement the new strategy.

Staffing Requirements Change

A change in strategy is likely to have a significant impact on staffing needs. For example, when J. C. Penney's management decided to make its stores more competitive by appealing directly to local market segments, it realized that it was no longer appropriate for a set of buyers centrally located at headquarters to dictate the merchandise mix for all stores. Consequently, it decentralized purchasing authority down to store level so that individual store managers would have greater opportunity to buy only the merchandise they deemed most suited to their regional needs. Although it seemed that this strategy would help Penney to better compete with local stores, top management was concerned with implementation. Instead of a corporate buyer purchasing entire lines of merchandise and requiring all stores to carry them, the buyer now presented the items on Penney's satellite television network, and gave local buyers the opportunity to choose all the lines, some of the lines, or none of the lines. Penney's top management and suppliers feared that some local buyers weren't experienced enough to spot potentially popular fashion trends. The job of the corporate buyer had also become riskier. "Their job is going to be selling merchandise on television," said a Penney official. "You may buy good products but might not be able to sell. If the person showing the merchandise turns you off, you as a buyer in Omaha may not go for the lines." Although Penney officials denied that a lack of TV skills would cost corporate buyers their jobs, the company considered using video screen tests to help select future buyers.[10]

Another example of a change in strategy causing a change in staffing requirements is the example, given earlier in Chapter 8, of the introduction of team-based production at Corning's Blacksburg, Virginia, filter plant. Employee selection and training were crucial to the success of the new manufacturing strategy. Plant Manager Robert Hoover sorted through 8,000 job applications before hiring 150 people with the best problem-solving ability and a willingness to work in a team setting.

The majority had finished at least one year of college. Those selected received extensive training in technical and interpersonal skills. During the first year of production, 25% of all hours worked were devoted to training at a cost of $750,000. The company's decision to introduce team-based production at all of its plants meant that Corning's strategic managers had chosen to compete in world markets on the basis of a highly skilled, well-paid work force, rather than by cutting wages or moving manufacturing to low-wage nations. Since two-thirds of Corning's 20,000 employees in 1990 were either weak or seriously deficient in reading and math comprehension, they needed to receive remedial education along with job training. One of Corning's human resource objectives for 1991 was therefore to devote 5% of all hours worked to classroom training—up from 4% in 1989 and far more than the 1%–2% spent on training at most companies.[11]

Matching the Manager to the Strategy

As mentioned earlier in Chapter 2, research has found that chief executive officers and other top managers have a significant impact on corporate performance, particularly in companies in industries where there is a high degree of discretion in terms of strategic actions.[12] According to Day and Lord, ". . . executive leadership can explain as much as 45% of an organization's performance."[13] Building on these and other findings, several authorities suggest that the "best" or most appropriate type of general manager needed to effectively implement a new divisional, corporate, or Strategic Business Unit (SBU) strategy depends on the desired strategic direction of that firm or business unit.[14] This was certainly the thinking of Porsche AG, the German automaker, when it selected the financially oriented Heinz Branitzky to be

FIGURE 9.1	Matching Proposed Chief Executive "Types" with Corporate Strategy

Business Strength/Competitive Position

		Strong	Average	Weak
Industry Attractiveness	High	**Growth — Concentration** *Dynamic Industry Expert*		**Retrenchment — Save Company** *Turnaround Specialist*
	Medium		**Stability** *Cautious Profit Planner*	
	Low	**Growth — Diversification** *Analytical Portfolio Manager*		**Retrenchment — Close Company** *Professional Liquidator*

Source: Thomas L. Wheelen and J. David Hunger, "Matching Proposed Chief Executive 'Types' with Corporate Strategy." Copyright © 1991 by Wheelen and Hunger Associates. Reprinted by permission.

ILLUSTRATIVE EXAMPLE 9.1

Porsche Selects a New Chairman to Match Its New Strategy

During most of the 1980s, Porsche AG had successfully followed a growth strategy. Led by Peter W. Schutz as Chairman, the German company designed and manufactured sleek, high-performance automobiles. Schutz had a strong marketing orientation and constantly pressed for new ideas and expansion. Under his guidance, Porsche's production doubled between 1981 and 1986 to 53,600 units. With a strong emphasis on expanding its sales in the U.S., the company ran into trouble in 1987 when the U.S. dollar weakened against the German mark. Losing the support of Porsche's family owners, Schutz resigned from the company at the end of 1987. The board turned to Heinz Branitzky, the company's Chief Financial Officer, to bring order to the firm. Dealers were reporting large inventories of unsold cars—15,000 worldwide including 8,000 languishing in U.S. showrooms alone. Profit in fiscal 1987 decreased 31% from a year earlier to 51.9 million marks. This was quite a change from the profit of 120.4 million marks in fiscal 1985.

Branitzky's first task was to initiate and implement a strategy designed to stabilize the company. Consequently, he reduced dividends, slashed production to 31,000 autos from the 50,700 cars made in 1987, stopped all new hiring, and put workers on shorter shifts. According to one longtime Porsche executive, "A lot is going to change. Branitzky and Schutz are completely different types. Schutz loved publicity and cars and was always pressing new ideas and action. Branitzky is all precision. He is more reticent and thoughtful, looking for potential problems that could arise."

Heinz Branitzky's first job was as a tax analyst for an accounting firm. After eight years, he joined the finance department of the Carl Zeiss optics company, where he worked for five more years. He came to Porsche's finance office in 1965 and worked his way up to Chief Financial Officer and membership on the company's management board. An avid chess player who liked to spend time reading history or hiking in the mountains, Branitzky's personality reflected his no-frills management style. Compared with his predecessors, he showed little interest in Porsche's successful racing program—considered by many to be a key to the company's marketing. When making a presentation to the press detailing his plans to restructure the company, he went so deep into analyzing the financial reports that the reporters got confused. In response to their questions, Branitzky said: "Please be patient. I don't want to sound like a preacher, but it must be this way. I don't think much of loose finances. Finances are an absolutely important point; it's what I grew up with."

Source: T. Roth, "Porsche Puts a Numbers Man in Charge to Get Its Sales Back in High Gear," *Wall Street Journal* (February 10, 1988), p. A14.

---

the first Chairman in the company's 57-year history not to have an engineering background. See Illustrative Example 9.1 for details.

Executives with a particular mix of skills and experiences may be classified as an executive "type" and paired with a specific corporate strategy. Some of these proposed chief executive "types" are given in Fig. 9.1 in a modified form of the matrix of corporate strategies presented earlier in Fig. 6.7. For example, a corporation following a concentration strategy emphasizing vertical or horizontal integration would probably want an aggressive new chief executive with a great deal of experience in that particular industry—a **dynamic industry expert**. A diversification strategy, in contrast, might call for someone with an analytical mind who is highly knowledgeable in other industries and can manage diverse product lines—an **analytical portfolio manager**. A corporation choosing to follow a stability strategy would probably want as its CEO a **cautious profit planner**, a person with a conservative style, a production or engineering background, and experience with controlling budgets, capital expenditures, inventories, and standardization procedures.[15] Weak companies in a relatively attractive industry tend to turn to a type of challenge-oriented executive known as the **turnaround specialist** to save the company.[16] Illustrative Example 9.2 provides a description of one of these turnaround specialists: Stephen Pistner of Ames Department Stores. If a company cannot be saved, a **professional liquidator** might be called on by a bankruptcy court to close the firm and liquidate its assets.

Successful business unit managers with a particular mix of experiences, skills, and personality factors tend to be linked with one type of strategy; those with a different mix, to a different type of strategy.[17] For example, one research study of SBU executives has found that strategic business units with a "build" strategy, as compared with SBUs with a "harvest" strategy, tend to be headed by managers with a greater willingness to take risks, a higher tolerance for ambiguity, and greater sales/marketing experience.[18] In addition, those executives who successfully implement a differentiation business strategy tend to have a high internal locus of control, that is, they tend to view personal hard work and ability rather than some external cause as the reason for an outcome. They also tend to have more experience in R&D. Units following a low-cost business strategy tend to be run by a manager with greater experience in production.[19]

One interesting study of 173 firms over a 25-year period revealed that CEOs in these corporations tended to have the same functional specialization as the former CEO, especially when the past CEO's strategy continued to be successful. The researchers concluded that there is a tendency to continue with the CEO specializations that fit a successful corporate strategy and that this may be a pattern for successful corporations.[20] This may explain why so many prosperous companies tend to recruit their top executives from one particular area. At Procter & Gamble, for example, the route to the CEO's position has always been through brand management. In other firms, the route may be through manufacturing, marketing, accounting, or finance—depending on what the corporation has always considered its key area.

Studies have also found that since priorities change over an organization's life cycle, successful corporations tend to select managers who have skills and characteristics appropriate to the organization's particular stage of development.[21] In general agreement with previously cited work in Chapter 8, Miller, in his book *Barbarians to Bureaucrats*, proposes a different chief executive leadership style for each stage of corporate development. The styles range from the "Prophet" who creates the company to the "Administrator" who imposes controls, and finally to the "Synergist" who unifies and continues the growth of the large, complex corporation.[22]

In summary, there is growing support for matching executive "types" with the dominant strategic direction of a corporation or a business unit. Unfortunately,

ILLUSTRATIVE EXAMPLE 9.2

Stephen Pistner Implements Turnaround Strategy at Ames Department Stores

Stephen Pistner (pronounced *Pies*-ner) is an executive who works to save ailing companies. Often thought of as a turnaround specialist, Pistner was hired in April 1990 as CEO of Ames Department Stores. In the process of filing for Chapter 11 bankruptcy protection, Ames needed Pistner for his proven ability to save retail chains. Previously Pistner had directed turnarounds at McCrory Corporation, Montgomery Ward, and Dayton-Hudson's Target Stores.

Pistner described Ames Department Stores as "the worst pressurized mess you can conceive of." The $5 billion-a-year discount retailer had expanded too quickly at a time when the economy was weakening. Its $800 million acquisition of the Zayre Corporation discount chain was the last straw. After losing $228 million in 1989, Ames lost $583 million during the first half of 1990. By April, the company was about to default on its debt and suppliers had stopped shipping merchandise. Indicating that gentle diplomacy was not his style, Pistner met with Ames' suppliers in his second week on the job to tell them in effect: "Get off your tails and get in line to ship merchandise." He assured them that he could pay for the goods by winning court approval for a $250 million loan from Chemical Bank. Next, he quickly shut 221 stores, laid off 18,000 employees, and hired a new management team who had worked with him on earlier turnarounds. Through these store closings and liquidation sales, he generated $210 million in cash. He also worked to renegoti-

ate the corporation's debt. Meanwhile, although suspicious, vendors continued to ship merchandise to Ames, based on Pistner's promises and "surgical" skills. Although others still had their doubts about the chains' ability to survive, the Ames CEO continued to be optimistic. Said Pistner, "The patient is off the operating table and in the recovery room."

Like many other successful turnaround managers, Pistner never likes to stay long at any one company. According to Leo Shapiro, a Chicago consultant who worked with Pistner at McCrory: "He's like Moses—a good leader taking people through the desert and adversity. But he doesn't quite make it to the land of milk and honey." Part of the reason could be his need for novelty and excitement. Pistner hunts, sails, flies small planes, and goes white-water canoeing. At the last minute he once canceled his plans to buy a yacht that he would have used to spend a year sailing around the world. Focusing on one pursuit that long, according to Pistner, would probably drive him "screwy." His philosophy in both work and play is the same: "Move fast." Another reason for his mobility could be his sometimes outrageous actions. At staff meetings, he is extremely animated and is known to jump out of his seat, shouting or bursting into raucous laughter when something amuses him. On weekends, he puts on dungarees and wanders Ames' aisles incognito. How long will he stay with Ames? That remains to be seen.

Source: L. Driscoll, "The Fix-It Doctor with a Rough Bedside Manner," *Business Week* (October 29, 1990), pp. 106–108.

there is little available to help top management or the board select the most appropriate manager when a corporation or SBU does not have a specific strategy formulated for that manager to implement. In this instance, top management or the board has no choice; it must search for a person with a proven capability to exercise initiative and leadership in the industry, and hope that the person selected can lead other strategic managers in formulating and implementing a strategy.[23]

SELECTION AND DEVELOPMENT

Selection and development are important not only to ensure that people with the right mix of skills and experiences are initially hired, but also to help them grow on the job so that they might be prepared for future promotions. This is relevant to all levels of employees.

Executive Succession: Insiders versus Outsiders

Given that the typical large U.S. corporation changes its chief executive every eight years, it is important that the firm plan for this eventual executive succession.[24] It is especially important for a company that usually promotes from within to prepare its current managers for promotion. Research indicates that firms with succession planning programs in place for top management have an advantage (about 15% above expected return on investment [ROI] for firms in similar strategic positions) over firms that do not have formal programs.[25]

Research into the value of selecting a CEO from outside the company instead of promoting someone already with the company has mixed conclusions. Some studies report that the top performing companies hire their CEOs from within and that insider succession leads to increased firm performance;[26] however, other studies report that the percentage of CEOs hired from outside the corporation is higher for prosperous firms than for firms in decline.[27] Another study reports that the incidence of outsiders becoming CEOs of failing (bankrupt) firms is higher than that of solvent firms.[28] A further study reveals that internal candidates are more likely to be selected following the death of the CEO than under any other circumstances.[29] Obviously, more research is needed before any clear conclusion can be reached regarding the superiority of either inside or outside candidates for a top management position.

Identifying Abilities and Potential

There are several ways that a company can promote continuous cultivation of inside people for important positions. One approach is to establish a sound **performance appraisal system** to identify good performers with promotion potential. A survey of 34 corporate planners and human resource executives from 24 large U.S. corporations revealed that approximately 80% made some attempt to identify managers' talents and behavioral tendencies, so that they could place a manager with a likely fit to a given competitive strategy.[30]

Many large organizations are using **assessment centers** to evaluate a person's suitability for an advanced position. Popularized by AT&T in the mid-1950s, assessment centers have been used by corporations such as Standard Oil, IBM, Sears, and GE. Because each is specifically tailored to its corporation, these assessment centers are unique. They use special interviews, management games, in-basket exercises, leaderless group discussions, case analyses, decision-making exercises, and oral presentations to assess the potential of employees for specific positions. Promotions into these positions are based on performance levels in the assessment center. According to Joiner's evaluation of assessment center performance,

. . . assessment centers are appropriate and likely to result in better predictions, when the target job requires a variety of complex skills, the requirements of the target job vary substantially from those at the next lowest level in the organization or when applicants come from a variety of different backgrounds or locations making it difficult to obtain objective data upon which to make accurate predictions.[31]

Many assessment centers have proved to be highly predictive of subsequent job performance.[32]

The implementation of strategy should be concerned with the selection and training of the appropriate mix of professional, skilled, and unskilled labor. For example, in their expectation that market growth would soon begin to slow for mainframe computers, IBM's top management decided to emphasize software development in its reach for corporate growth objectives. Key divisions were then directed to expand their programming staffs by 20% per year for the next ten years, even though at that time there was nothing for the new programmers to do![33] To ensure that managers with potential for promotion have a grasp of many areas within the company other than the functional area in which they started work, many companies rotate people through different divisions and locations. Research reveals that corporations that pursue related diversification strategies through internal development make greater use of interdivisional transfers of people than do companies that grow through unrelated acquisitions. Apparently, the companies that grow internally attempt to transfer important knowledge and skills throughout the corporation, so that some sort of managerial synergy is achieved.[34]

9.2 DIRECTING

Organizing activities into meaningful units and then staffing them with the appropriate people are important aspects of strategy implementation. This is not enough, however, to complete the task. Implementation also involves directing people to use their abilities and skills most effectively and efficiently to achieve organizational objectives. Without direction, people tend to do their work according to their personal view of what tasks should be done, how, and in what order. They may approach their work as they have in the past or emphasize those tasks that they most enjoy—regardless of what needs prioritizing.

To effectively direct a new strategy, top management must delegate appropriate authority and responsibility to the operational managers. People should be motivated to act in ways desired by the organization. Further, the actions must be coordinated so that they result in effective performance. Managers should be stimulated to find creative solutions to implementation problems without getting bogged down in conflict. Sometimes this is informally accomplished through a strong corporate culture, with accepted norms and values regarding teamwork and commitment to the company's objectives and strategies. It may also be accomplished more formally through action planning, Managing By Objectives, and linking an incentive program to the new strategy.

MANAGING CORPORATE CULTURE

Described earlier in Chapter 5, a corporation's culture is the collection of beliefs, expectations, and values *learned* and *shared* by the corporation's members and *transmitted* from one generation of employees to another. These create norms (rules of conduct) that define acceptable behavior, from top management to the operative employee. Corporate culture generally reflects the mission of the firm. It includes the dominant orientation of the company and gives a corporation a sense of identity.

Corporate culture appears to have two distinct attributes: intensity and integration.[35] **Intensity** is "the extent to which members of a unit agree on the norms, values, or other culture content associated with the unit." Organizations with strong norms promoting a particular value, such as quality at Maytag, have intensive cultures, whereas new firms (or those in transition) have weaker, less intensive cultures. Employees of a company with an intensive culture tend to exhibit consistency in behavior, that is, they tend to act similarly over time. **Integration** is "the extent to which units within an organization share a common culture." Organizations with a pervasive dominant culture may be hierarchically controlled and power-oriented, such as a military unit, and have highly integrated cultures. All employees tend to hold the same cultural values and norms. In contrast, a company that is structured into diverse units by functions or divisions usually exhibits some strong subcultures (e.g., R&D versus manufacturing) and an overall weaker corporate culture.

Because an organization's culture can exert a powerful influence on the behavior of all employees, it can strongly affect a corporation's ability to shift its strategic direction. As mentioned in Chapter 5, a strongly held corporate culture can produce "strategic myopia" and restrict top management's ability to perceive developing problems at a time when the corporation most needs to change its strategic direction. An additional problem for a strong culture is that a change in mission, objectives, strategies, or policies is not likely to be successful if it is in opposition to the accepted culture of the corporation. For an example of corporate culture acting as a barrier to strategic change, see Illustrative Example 9.3.

Research indicates that there is no one best corporate culture.[36] An optimal culture is one that best supports the mission and strategy of the company of which it is a part. This means that for all practical purposes **corporate culture** (like structure and staffing) **should follow strategy**. A significant change in strategy should thus be followed by a change in the organization's culture.

Assessing Strategy-Culture Compatibility

When implementing a new strategy, consider the following questions regarding the corporation's culture:

1. **Is the planned strategy compatible with the company's current culture?**
   If yes, full steam ahead. Tie organizational changes into the company's culture by identifying how the new strategy will better achieve the mission than the current strategy does.

ILLUSTRATIVE EXAMPLE 9.3

Corporate Culture Acts as a Barrier to Strategic Change

Originally developed in the U.S. in the 1940s, Statistical Process Control (SPC) was largely ignored until W. Edward Deming, an M.I.T. professor, introduced it to the Japanese in 1950. *Statistical process control* is a method that attempts to facilitate understanding of the critical variables in each sequence of a manufacturing process and their intercorrelation. Following Deming's guidelines, workers in Japanese factories sampled parts as they moved through manufacturing processes and, through the use of control charts, ensured that any deviations from specifications were quickly corrected. Thus, SPC ensures that virtually all finished products meet or exceed specification. In this way quality is built into the product instead of having workers correct for it after the fact by tossing out rejects—the more traditional (and more expensive) route to quality control.

An automotive company that had heard about SPC attempted to introduce it in the U.S. at one of its manufacturing plants. After two and a half years, the attempt had ground to a halt. There was deep pessimism about SPC's future at the plant. Members of the SPC coordination team in charge of implementing the change were considering a mass resignation. The change had clearly failed. Why?

The culture at the manufacturing plant contained three key values that ran counter to those values that underlie statistical process control.

- *First*, the plant had a norm valuing performance over learning. **Workers were paid to work, not to think.** Unfortunately, SPC goes against this value. The introduction of SPC involves not only a period of learning about SPC itself, but also a period of learning about every manufacturing process in which it is to be implemented. Managers in the plant interpreted acts through a filter of questions like "What did you do for me?" instead of "What did you learn?"

- *Second*, public information was used in terms of one of three things: expectations of future performance, reports of bad performance, and assignment of responsibility. **Information was not valued for its use in actually fixing problems, only in placing blame or assigning responsibility elsewhere.** In contrast, SPC uses public information to highlight problems and to help fix them. Data collection involves workers and managers together maintaining charts and graphs throughout the work area for anyone to see. Unfortunately, as time went by, management returned primarily to looking at results and assigning responsibility. People were told to fix their own problems. The feelings of the employees became, "Why make my problems visible with SPC?"

- *Third*, following the traditional structural concept of division of work, the plant's work was split into tiny segments parcelled out to individual operators and units in assembly-line fashion. Strong lines of demarcation existed between workers and managers, manufacturing and service, plant and division. **There was a tendency to compartmentalize problems and information.** Statistical process control, however, takes a holistic approach rather than the traditional segmentalist approach. It requires thinking about the interactions of many variables in a process and managing their interdependencies. As a result, attempts to improve productivity through joint efforts among groups and departments were sabotaged by the tendency for highly paid and educated staff at division headquarters to ignore suggestions for improvement from "lowly" production employees.

Source: Summarized from G. R. Bushe, "Cultural Contradictions of Statistical Process Control in American Manufacturing Organizations," *Journal of Management* (March 1988), pp. 19–31.

2. **If the strategy is not compatible with the current culture, can the culture be easily modified to make it more compatible with the new strategy?**

   If yes, move forward carefully by introducing a set of culture-changing activities, such as minor structural modifications, training and development activities, and/or hiring new managers who are more compatible with the new strategy. Procter & Gamble's top management decided in the mid-1980s, for example, that in order to implement the new companywide emphasis on a low-cost strategy, they had to make some changes in the firm's almost-sacred brand management system and alter the way salespeople dealt with customers. The culture needed only slight modifications to make it compatible with the new strategy. Brand managers were instructed to report to a "category" manager, who coordinated advertising and sales to minimize the products' "cannibalizing" each other. Salespeople, long noted by retailers for their arrogance, were directed to pay more attention to retailers' needs and to woo them with special promotions. Even with these and other changes, none of the company's basic values was directly attacked. After a few years, the new system was generating a significant increase in performance.[37]

3. **If the culture cannot be easily changed to make it more compatible with the new strategy, is management willing and able to make major organizational changes and accept probable delays and a likely increase in costs?**

   If yes, manage around the culture by establishing a new structural unit to implement the new strategy. At General Motors, for example, top management realized that in order to compete with the Japanese automakers, the company had to make some radical changes in the way it produced cars. Since the current structure and culture were very inflexible, management decided to establish a completely new division (GM's first new division since 1918) called Saturn to build its new auto. In cooperation with the United Auto Workers, an entirely new labor agreement was developed based on decisions reached by consensus. Carefully selected employees received five days of "awareness training" to teach them how to work together in teams. They then received from 100 to 750 hours of training, including how to read financial statements, so they would understand how much their operations affected the cost of the car. A whole new culture was built piece by piece. According to James Lewandowski, Vice-President of Human Resources, "There's a real cause here. It's been described as almost like a cult." Originally conceived in 1983, the first Saturn took until 1990 to roll off the modular assembly line in the Spring Hill, Tennessee, plant.[38]

4. **If management is not willing to make the major organizational changes required to manage around the culture, are they still committed to implementing the strategy?**

   If yes, find a joint-venture partner or contract with another company to carry out the strategy.

   If no, formulate a different strategy.

Managing Change Through Communication

Communication is key to the effective management of change in culture. After observing the corporate culture of over 100 different companies, Gordon reports that the companies in which major cultural changes had successfully taken place had the following characteristics in common:

1. The CEO had a strategic vision of what the company could become.
2. The vision was translated into the key elements necessary to accomplish that vision. For example, if the vision called for the company to become a leader in quality or service, aspects of quality and service were pinpointed for improvement and appropriate measurement systems were developed to monitor them. These measures were communicated widely through contests, formal and informal recognition, and monetary rewards, among other devices.
3. The CEO and other top managers were obsessive about communicating as widely as possible to employees at all levels three key bits of information:
   a) The current state of the company in comparison with its competition plus the outlook for the future.
   b) The vision of *what* the company was to become and *how* it would achieve that vision.
   c) The progress of the company in those elements identified as important to achieve the vision.[39]

One way of communicating the new vision of the corporation is through training and development programs. At General Electric, for example, top management wanted to change the corporate culture. The pre-1981 culture was built around a core set of principles based on growth in sales greater than GNP, with many SBUs, relying on financial savvy, meticulous staff work, and a domestically focused company. Jack Welch, the new CEO, wanted the company to think in terms of building shareholder value in a slow-growth environment through operating competitive advantage with dynamic leadership at all levels of the organization. Since top management viewed GE's management development institute (at Crotonville, New York) as an instrument for cultural change, training was drastically changed to reflect the new emphasis on aggressive global competitiveness. In 1989, for example, Crotonville spearheaded an effort to change the way GE's middle managers operated. The emphasis in its workshops was on radically altering the old hierarchical bureaucracy to create a new nonhierarchical, fast-paced, flexible organization. Management development was thus viewed as a catalyst for mobilizing the energies of the 30,000 to 40,000 middle managers to enable them to lead the change from the middle of the company.[40]

Managing Cultures in Mergers and Acquisitions

When merging with or acquiring another company, top management must give some consideration to a potential clash of cultures. It's dangerous to assume that the firms can simply be integrated into the same reporting structure and all will be well. A classic example of the mismanagement of corporate cultures occurred when Exxon Corporation decided to purchase some high-tech companies. Exxon's top management decided in the early 1970s to diversify away from the company's dependence on the declining petroleum business into the "office of the future." By buying firms from creative entrepreneurs, Exxon acquired three new word processing and printing technologies (named QWIP, QYX, and Vydec) to form Exxon Office Systems. As part of the bargain, the entrepreneurs who had developed these new products were also hired. Unfortunately, the entrepreneurs, who thrived in a helter-skelter world of exciting ideas and quick, risky decisions, were placed under the authority of Exxon's senior executives, people who lived by corporate policy and procedures manuals and made decisions only after many group meetings. One by one, the creative but undisciplined "kids" left the company, with its meetings and paperwork, and started something new somewhere else. Exxon replaced them with professional managers hired from other office-equipment companies like IBM, Xerox, and Burroughs. Accustomed to large staffs and generous support, the new managers staffed these small business units as if they were the large firms they had just left. Instead of emphasizing research and innovation, they focused on advertising and promotion. The result was an estimated loss of approximately $2 billion and the eventual sale of Exxon Office Systems to Olivetti and Lanier in 1985. One analyst summarized the basic problem:

> Obviously, Exxon never thought to analyze the subtle nuances of what it takes to run a collection of small technology-driven businesses because it simply wasn't a part of their culture. . . . [Management] never seemed to learn that the lethargic machinery and process technique that works so well in the oil business, simply wouldn't work in the fast-paced office equipment industry.[41]

After reviewing the impact of corporate cultures on the effectiveness of mergers and acquisitions, Malekzadeh and Nahavandi propose four general methods of managing disparate cultures: *integration, assimilation, separation,* and *deculturation.*[42] As shown in Fig. 9.2, the most appropriate method hinges on (1) *how much members of the acquired firm value preservation of their own culture* and (2) *their perception of the attractiveness of the acquirer.*

Integration involves a relatively balanced give-and-take of cultural and managerial practices between the merger partners, and no strong imposition of cultural change on either company. It merges the two cultures in such a way that the separate cultures of both firms are preserved in the resulting culture. This is what occurred when the Seaboard and Chesapeake & Ohio railroads merged in 1980 to form CSX Corporation. The top executives were so concerned that both cultures be equally respected that they kept referred to the company as a "partnership of equals."

Under **assimilation**, one organization dominates the other. The domination is not forced, but is welcomed by members of the acquired firm, who may feel for many reasons that their culture and managerial practices have not produced success. The acquired firm surrenders its culture and adopts the culture of the acquiring company. The *boxed example* of Maytag (p. 288) describes this method of acculturation when Admiral, a subsidiary of Magic Chef, joined Maytag Corporation.

The **separation** method is characterized by a separation of the two companies'

| FIGURE 9.2 | Methods of Managing the Culture of an Acquired Firm |

**How Much Members of the Acquired Firm Value
Preservation of Their Own Culture**

Source: A. Nahavandi and A. R. Malekzadeh, "Acculturation in Mergers and Acquisitions," *Academy of Management Review* (January 1988), p. 83. Copyright © 1988 by the Academy of Management. Reprinted by permission.

cultures. They are structurally separated, without cultural exchange. In the case of the Shearson–American Express merger, both parties agreed to keep the fast-paced Shearson completely separate from the planning-oriented American Express.

Deculturation is the most common and most destructive method of dealing with two different cultures. It involves the disintegration of one company's culture resulting from unwanted and extreme pressure from the other to impose its culture and practices. As discussed earlier in the example of Exxon Corporation, this method is often accompanied by a great deal of confusion, conflict, resentment, and stress. Such a merger typically results in poor performance by the acquired company and its eventual divestment.

ACTION PLANNING

Activities can be directed toward accomplishing strategic goals through action planning. At a minimum, an **action plan** states what actions are going to be taken, by whom, during what time frame, and with what expected results. Once a program has been selected to implement a particular strategy, an action plan should be developed to put the program in place.

Take the example, mentioned earlier in Chapter 8, of a company choosing forward vertical integration through the acquisition of a retailing chain as its growth strategy. Now that it owns its own retail outlets, it must integrate the stores into the company. One of the many programs it would have to develop is a new advertising program for the stores. The resulting action plan to develop a new advertising program should include much of the following:[43]

MAYTAG CORPORATION: ASSIMILATING ADMIRAL'S CULTURE

Headquartered in Galesburg, Illinois, Admiral was the refrigeration division of Maytag Corporation. It manufactured refrigerators for the corporation's Maytag, Jenn-Air, and Magic Chef companies. Prior to Maytag's purchase of Magic Chef (and thus Admiral) in 1986, Admiral had been owned by three different corporations. In order to better fit the company into the corporation, all functional departments, except marketing, reported directly to Richard Haines, Maytag Company President. One result of Admiral's relationship with Maytag was a heavier emphasis on quality. Maytag's management had always wanted to have its own Maytag-brand refrigerator, but it was worried that Admiral might not be able to produce a quality product to Maytag's specifications.

Maytag's corporate culture had been dominated almost from the beginning of the company by the concept of quality. Maytag employees took great pride in being known as the "dependability people." Over the years, Maytag Company consistently advertised that their repairmen were "lonely" because Maytag-brand products rarely, if ever, needed repair. The importance of quality to Maytag Corporation was highlighted in Chairman and CEO Daniel Krumm's comments regarding the specific resources that gave the corporation a competitive edge:

[Quality], of course, has been Maytag's hallmark for as long as any of us can remember. We believe quality and reliability are, ultimately, what the consumer wants. That has been a challenge to us as we have acquired companies that may have had a different emphasis, but we have made significant recent strides in improving the quality of all our products.

Under the direction of Leonard Hadley, while he was serving as Maytag Company President, a project was initiated to design and manufacture a Maytag-brand refrigerator at the Admiral plant in Galesburg. It combined Admiral's engineering expertise in refrigeration with Maytag Company's manufacturing and quality skills. When Hadley first visited Admiral's facilities to discuss the design of a Maytag line of refrigerators, Admiral personnel asked Hadley when the name on their plant's water tower would be changed from Admiral to Maytag. Hadley (acknowledging Maytag's cultural concerns regarding quality) responded: "When you earn it."

The refrigerator resulting from the Maytag-Admiral collaboration was a huge success. The project crystallized corporate management's philosophy for forging synergies among the Maytag companies, while simultaneously allowing the individual expertise of those units to flourish. Admiral's employees were willing to accept the dominance of Maytag's strong quality-oriented culture because they respected it. In turn, they expected to be treated with some respect for their tradition of skill in refrigeration technology. Daniel Krumm acknowledged the importance of respecting Admiral's culture in an interview with *Appliance* magazine.

The engineers at Admiral developed the Maytag brand refrigerator in close collaboration with R&D here in Newton. The people in Newton did not design that refrigerator, but they did make specifications. . . . We have no intention of designing refrigerators in Newton. Admiral is the expert in that area. . . . Creating these synergies is a very important element in our long-term strategy—sharing the expertise of each of our companies. As we bring all these companies together, our hope is that one-plus-one will ultimately add up to more than two.

1. **Specific actions to be taken to make the program operational.** One action might be to contact three reputable ad agencies and ask them to prepare a proposal for a new radio and newspaper ad campaign based on the theme "Jones Surplus is now a part of Ajax Continental. Prices are lower. Selection is better."

2. **Dates to begin and end each action.** Time would have to be allotted not only to select three agencies to contact, but also to contact them and to allow them sufficient time to prepare a detailed proposal. For example, allow one week to select and contact the agencies plus three months for them to prepare detailed proposals for presentation to the company's marketing director. Also allow some time to make a decision on which proposal to accept.

3. **Person (identified by name and title) responsible for carrying out each action.** List someone—such as Jan Lewis, advertising manager—who can be put in charge of the program.

4. **Person responsible for monitoring the timeliness and effectiveness of each action.** Indicate that Jan Lewis is responsible for ensuring that the proposals are of good quality and are priced within the planned program budget. She will be the primary contact for the ad agencies and will report on the progress of the program once a week to the company's marketing director.

5. **Expected financial and physical consequences of each action.** Estimate when a completed ad campaign will be ready to show top management and how long it will take after approval to begin to air the ads. Estimate also the expected increase in store sales over the six-month period after the ads are first aired. Indicate if "recall" measures will be used to help assess the ad campaign's effectiveness plus how, when, and by whom the recall data will be collected and analyzed.

6. **Contingency plans.** Indicate how long it will take to get an acceptable ad campaign to show top management if none of the initial proposals is acceptable.

According to Camillus, an authority on strategy implementation and control, action plans are important for several reasons. First, they serve as a link between strategy formulation and evaluation and control. Second, the action plan specifies what needs to be done differently from the way operations are currently carried out. Third, during the evaluation and control process that comes later, an action plan helps in both the appraisal of performance and in the identification of any remedial actions, as needed. In addition, the explicit assignment of responsibilities for implementing and monitoring the programs may contribute to better motivation.[44]

MANAGEMENT BY OBJECTIVES (MBO)

Activities can also be directed toward accomplishing strategic goals through programs such as Management By Objectives (MBO). MBO is an organizationwide approach to help assure purposeful action toward desired objectives. MBO links organizational objectives and the behavior of individuals. Because it is a system that links plans with performance, it is a powerful implementation technique.

Value of MBO

Although there is some disagreement about the purpose of MBO, most authorities agree that this approach involves (1) establishing and communicating organizational objectives, (2) setting individual objectives (through superior-subordinate interaction) that help implement organizational ones, (3) developing an action plan of activities needed to achieve the objectives, and (4) periodically (at least quarterly) reviewing performance as it relates to the objectives and including the results in the annual performance appraisal.[45] MBO provides an opportunity for the corporation to connect the objectives of people at each level to those at the next higher level: "If carried out logically and ideally, the goals at each level would be contributing most directly toward overall organizational objectives. . . . MBO provides a potential method of integrating the physical, financial, and human resource plans of the organization to the goals that an individual is expected to achieve."[46] MBO, therefore, acts to tie together corporate, business, and functional objectives, as well as the strategies developed to achieve them. This tying together forms a hierarchy of objectives similar to the hierarchy of strategy discussed in Chapter 1. The MBO process is depicted in Fig. 9.3.

| **FIGURE 9.3** | **The Process of Management By Objectives** |

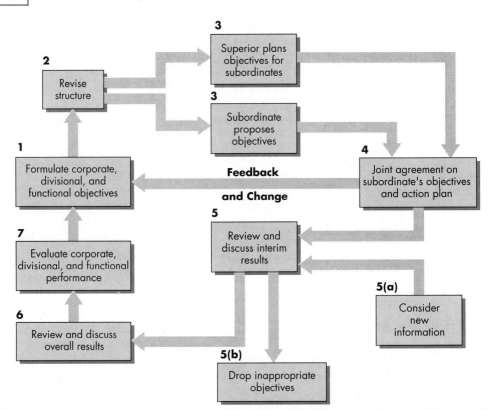

Research conclusions on the effectiveness of corporate MBO programs are mixed, but tend to support the belief that MBO should result in higher levels of performance than would be achieved by other approaches that do not include performance goals, relevant feedback, and joint supervisor/subordinate goal setting.[47] In addition, there is some evidence that MBO can be successfully used not only in a company managed in a democratic and participative manner, but also in a company managed in an autocratic and directive manner.[48] According to Carroll, an expert on MBO,

> In general, managers react favorably to MBO systems provided they are being carefully implemented, managed in a flexible manner, and receive the full backing of top organizational management.[49]

Impact of MBO on Internal Politics and Interpersonal Conflict

One of the real benefits of MBO is that it can reduce the amount of internal politics operating within a large corporation. **Internal politics** is defined as influence attempts outside formal channels that are intended to promote the self-interests of individuals or groups and that threaten the self-interests of others in the organization.[50] Such political actions can cause conflict and create divisions between the very people and groups who should be working together to implement strategy. People are less likely to jockey for position if the company's mission and objectives are clear and they know that the reward system is based not on game playing, but on achieving clearly communicated, measurable objectives.

Research by Jones of 39 aerospace firms reveals that the presence of clear, measurable objectives reduces the amount of internal politics. The study also indicates that the transmission of strategic objectives to lower-level units in a corporation decreases internal politics.[51] In addition, Galbraith and Kazanjian point out that the existence of an MBO program at Dow-Corning permits its matrix structure to function effectively: "Because people work against goals and problems, rather than against each other, they have less need for hierarchy and tie-breaking."[52] At Dow-Corning, the agreed-upon objectives are used to help reach consensus and thus reduce the potential for the conflict inherent in a matrix-style organization.

INCENTIVE MANAGEMENT

To ensure that there is a congruence between the needs of the corporation as a whole and the needs of the employees as individuals, management should develop an incentive program that rewards desired performance. Research confirms the conventional wisdom that when pay is tied to performance, it motivates higher productivity, and strongly affects both absenteeism and work quality.[53] Corporations have, therefore, developed various types of incentives for executives that range from stock options to cash bonuses. A study of compensation plans in all types of companies— manufacturing and service, large and small, growing and declining, businesses in stable as well as turbulent markets—found that the higher the percentage of management's compensation that is linked to performance, the greater the company's profitability.[54]

Incentive plans should be linked in some way to corporate and divisional strategy. For example, a survey of 600 business units indicates that the pay mix associated with a growth strategy emphasizes bonuses and other incentives over salary and benefits, whereas the pay mix associated with a maintenance strategy has the reverse emphasis.[55] Ansoff, an authority on strategic management, proposes that one of the key means of changing corporate culture is by changing formal and informal rewards and incentives.[56] Performance appraisal and incentive systems are discussed in more detail in Section 10.6, Strategic Incentive Management, in the next chapter.

SUMMARY AND CONCLUSION

This chapter continues the discussion of strategy implementation that began in Chapter 8. Strategy implementation is the process by which strategies and policies are put into action, through the development of programs, budgets, and procedures. Although it certainly involves some planning activities, the major emphasis in strategy implementation is on *organizing* into units people and activities for maximum effectiveness and efficiency, *staffing* these units with people having the appropriate mix of abilities and skills, and on *directing* people to use their abilities and skills most effectively and efficiently to achieve organizational objectives. Organizing was discussed in Chapter 8 in terms of organizational structure and job design. This chapter discusses staffing and directing.

Staffing focuses on finding and developing appropriate people for key positions. Without capable and committed employees, strategy can never be implemented satisfactorily. As in the case of structure, staffing requirements are also likely to follow a change in strategy. Once a new strategy is formulated, either different kinds of people may be needed or the current employees may need to be retrained to implement the new strategy. Research does indicate that managers with a particular mix of skills and experiences should be selected to implement a particular strategy. To survey and develop candidates, performance appraisal systems and assessment centers are used by many large corporations.

Directing deals with programs that direct operational managers and employees to implement corporate, business, and functional strategies. It em-

phasizes the management of corporate culture, the development of action plans, Management By Objectives (MBO), and incentive management. Described earlier in Chapter 5, *corporate culture* is the collection of beliefs, expectations, and values learned and shared by the corporation's members and transmitted from one generation of employees to the next. These create norms (rules of conduct) that define acceptable behavior, from top management to the operative employee. There is no one best corporate culture. An optimal culture is one that best supports the mission and strategy of the company of which it is a part. A significant change in strategy should therefore be followed by a change in the organization's culture.

Activities can also be directed toward accomplishing strategic goals through action planning and MBO. An *action plan* states what actions are going to be taken, by whom, during what time frame, and with what expected results. Once a program has been selected to implement a particular strategy, an action plan should be developed to put the program in place. *MBO* is an organizationwide program to link organizational objectives with the behavior of individuals. Because it is a system that links plans with performance, it is a powerful implementation technique. One of the real benefits of MBO is that it can reduce the amount of internal politics operating within a large corporation.

The proper use of incentives, when integrated with a change in corporate culture or with a goal-centered approach such as MBO, is another method by which effort is directed toward the desired results.

DISCUSSION QUESTIONS

1. What are some of the ways a retrenchment strategy can be implemented without creating a lot of resentment and conflict with labor unions?

2. Assuming that the best person to implement a particular strategy is the one with a special mix of skills and experiences, what kinds of skills should a person have who is selected to manage a business unit using a differentiation strategy? Why? What if this type of person is not available internally and the company has a policy of promotion only from within?

3. What type of person should be selected to manage a company or business unit when no clear strategy has been formulated?

4. When should someone from outside the company be hired to manage the company or one of its business units?

5. Does culture follow strategy or does strategy follow culture?

6. How can corporate culture be changed?

7. Compare and contrast action planning with Management By Objectives.

8. How can MBO help improve the implementation of strategy?

9. Why is internal politics a problem in strategy implementation? What, if anything, can be done about it?

NOTES

1. P. C. Reid, *Well Made In America* (New York: McGraw-Hill, 1990), p. 6.

2. R. S. Schuler and S. E. Jackson, "Determinants of Human Resource Management Priorities and Implications for Industrial Relations," *Journal of Management* (March 1989), pp. 89–99.

3. J. P. Walsh, "Doing a Deal: Merger and Acquisition Negotiations and Their Impact Upon Target Company Top Management Turnover," *Strategic Management Journal* (July-August 1989), pp. 307–322.

4. B. O'Reilly, "Is Your Company Asking Too Much?" *Fortune* (March 12, 1990), p. 41.

5. R. Henkoff, "Cost Cutting: How to Do It Right," *Fortune* (April 9, 1990), pp. 40–49.

6. *Ibid.*, p. 40.

7. Suggested by D. A. Heenan, "The Downside of Downsizing," *Journal of Business Strategy* (November-December 1989), pp. 18–23; and by R. Henkoff.

8. P. Truell, "Bankers Trust Transfers Departments to Xerox in Bid to Cut Costs and Staff," *Wall Street Journal* (June 17, 1988), p. A2.

9. Reid, *Well Made*, p. 171.

10. H. Gilman, "J. C. Penney Decentralizes Its Purchasing," *Wall Street Journal* (May 8, 1986), p. 6.

11. J. Hoerr, "Sharpening Minds for a Competitive Edge," *Business Week* (December 17, 1990), pp. 72–78.

12. E. J. Zajac, "CEO Selection, Succession, Compensation and Firm Performance: A Theoretical Integration and Empirical Analysis," *Strategic Management Journal* (March-April 1990), pp. 217–230.

S. Finkelstein and D. C. Hambrick, "Top-Management-Team Tenure and Organizational Outcomes: The Moderating Role of Managerial Discretion," *Administrative Science Quarterly* (September 1990), pp. 484–503.

K. M. Eisenhardt and C. B. Shoonhoven, "Organizational Growth: Linking Founding Team, Strategy, Environment, and Growth Among U.S. Semiconductor Ventures, 1978–1988," *Administrative Science Quarterly* (September 1990), pp. 504–529.

13. D. V. Day and R. G. Lord, "Executive Leadership and Organizational Performance: Suggestions for a New Theory and Methodology" *Journal of Management* (September 1988), pp. 453–464.

14. S. F. Slater, "The Influence of Managerial Style on Business Unit Performance," *Journal of Management* (September 1989), pp. 441–455.

T. T. Herbert and H. Deresky, "Should General Managers Match Their Business Strategies?" *Organizational Dynamics* (Winter 1987), pp. 40–51.

R. Chaganti and R. Sambharya, "Strategic Orientation and Characteristics of Upper Management," *Strategic Management Journal* (July-August 1987), pp. 393–401.

A. D. Szilagyi, Jr., and D. M. Schweiger, "Matching

Managers to Strategies: A Review and Suggested Framework," *Academy of Management Review* (October 1984), pp. 626–637.

15. Herbert and Deresky, "Should General Managers Match Their Business Strategies?" pp. 43–44.

16. G. L. Miles et al., "The Green Berets of Corporate Management," *Business Week* (September 21, 1987), pp. 110–114.

17. R. M. Grant, "Competing Against Low Cost Cutlery Imports," *Long Range Planning* (October 1989), pp. 59–68.

18. A. K. Gupta and V. Govindarajan, "Business Unit Strategy, Managerial Characteristics, and Business Unit Effectiveness at Strategy Implementation," *Academy of Management Journal* (March 1984), pp. 25–41.

19. V. Govindarajan, "A Contingence Approach to Strategy Implementation at the Business-Unit Level: Integrating Administrative Mechanisms with Strategy," *Academy of Management Journal* (December 1988), pp. 828–853.

V. Govindarajan, "Implementing Competitive Strategies at the Business Unit Level: Implications of Matching Managers to Strategies," *Strategic Management Journal* (May-June 1989), pp. 251–269.

20. M. Smith and M. C. White, "Strategy, CEO Specialization, and Succession," *Administrative Science Quarterly* (June 1987), pp. 263–280.

21. K. G. Smith, T. R. Mitchell, and C. E. Summer, "Top Level Management Priorities in Different Stages of the Organizational Life Cycle," *Academy of Management Journal* (December 1985), pp. 799–820.

B. Virany and M. L. Tushman, "Executive Succession: The Changing Characteristics of Top Management Teams," *Proceedings, Academy of Management* (1986), pp. 155–159.

J. Muczyk and B. C. Reimann, "The Case for Directive Leadership," *Academy of Management Executive* (November 1987), pp. 301–311.

G. D. Hughes, "Managing High-Tech Product Cycles," *Academy of Management Executive* (May 1990), pp. 44–55.

22. L. M. Miller, *Barbarians to Bureaucrats* (New York: Clarkson N. Potter, 1989).

23. W. F. McCanna and T. E. Comte, "The CEO Succession Dilemma: How Boards Function in Turnover at the Top," *Business Horizons* (May-June 1986), pp. 17–22.

24. R. F. Vancil, *Passing the Baton* (Boston: Harvard Business School Press, 1987).

25. D. A. Hofrichter and G. J. Myszkowski, "Developing Managers Who Can Implement the Strategy: Competency-Based Succession Planning," in *Handbook of Business Strategy, 1989/90 Yearbook*, edited by H. E. Glass (Boston: Warren, Gorham and Lamont, 1989), pp. 18.1–18.12.

26. W. N. Davidson III, D. L. Worrell, and L. Cheng, "Key Executive Succession and Stockholder Wealth: The Influence of Successor's Origin, Position, and Age," *Journal of Management* (September 1990), pp. 647–664.

D. R. Dalton and I. F. Kesner, "Organizational Performance As an Antecedent of Inside/Outside Chief Executive Succession: An Empirical Assessment," *Academy of Management Journal* (December 1985), pp. 749–762.

27. K. H. Chung, R. C. Rogers, M. Lubatkin, and J. E. Owers, "Do Insiders Make Better CEOs Than Outsiders?" *Academy of Management Executive* (November 1987), pp. 323–329.

R. S. Schuler and S. E. Jackson, "Linking Competitive Strategies with Human Resource Management Practices," *Academy of Management Executive* (August 1987), pp. 207–219.

28. K. B. Schwartz and K. Menon, "Executive Succession in Failing Firms," *Academy of Management Journal* (September 1985), pp. 680–686.

29. D. L. Worrell and W. N. Davidson, "Inside Versus Outside Succession Following Key Executive Death," *International Journal of Management* (December 1987), pp. 546–552.

30. P. Lorange and D. Murphy, "Bringing Human Resources Into Strategic Planning: System Design Characteristics," in *Strategic Human Resource Management*, edited by C. J. Fombrun, N. M. Tichy, and M. A. Devanna (New York: John Wiley and Sons, 1984), pp. 281–283.

31. D. A. Joiner, "Assessment Centers in the Public Sector: A Practical Approach," in *Perspectives on Personnel/Human Resources Management*, edited by H. G. Heneman and D. P. Schwab (Homewood, Ill.: Irwin, 1986), pp. 192–204.

32. H. G. Heneman III, D. P. Schwab, J. A. Fossum, and L. D. Dyer, *Personnel/Human Resources Management*, 3rd ed. (Homewood, Ill.: Irwin, 1986), pp. 351–353.

33. M. A. Harris, "IBM: More Worlds to Conquer," *Business Week* (February 18, 1985), p. 85.

34. R. A. Pitts, "Strategies and Structures for Diversification," *Academy of Management Journal* (June 1977), pp. 197–208.

35. D. M. Rousseau, "Assessing Organizational Culture: The Case for Multiple Methods," in *Organizational Climate and Culture*, edited by B. Schneider (San Francisco: Jossey-Bass, 1990), pp. 153–192. Quotes are taken from pp. 181–182.

36. G. Hofstede, B. Neuijen, D. D. Ohayv, and G. Sanders,

"Measuring Organizational Cultures: A Qualitative and Quantitative Study Across Twenty Cases," *Administrative Science Quarterly* (June 1990), pp. 286–316.

M. C. Cooper, "Managing Cultural Change to Achieve Competitive Advantage," in *Handbook of Business Strategy, 1987/1988 Yearbook*, edited by H. Babian and H. E. Glass (Boston: Warren, Gorham and Lamont, 1987), pp. 11.1–11.21.

37. A. Swasy, "In a Fast-Paced World, Procter & Gamble Sets Its Store in Old Values," *Wall Street Journal* (September 21, 1989), pp. A1, A14.

38. J. B. Treece, "Here Comes GM's Saturn," *Business Week* (April 9, 1990), pp. 56–62.

39. G. G. Gordon, "The Relationship of Corporate Culture to Industry Sector and Corporate Performance," in *Gaining Control of the Corporate Culture*, edited by R. H. Kilmann, M. J. Saxton, R. Serpa, and Associates (San Francisco: Jossey-Bass, 1985), p. 123.

40. N. M. Tichy, "GE's Crotonville: A Staging Ground for Corporate Revolution," *Academy of Management Executive* (May 1989), pp. 99–106.

41. R. M. Donnelly, "Exxon's 'Office of the Future' Fiasco," *Planning Review* (July/August, 1987), pp. 13, 14.

42. A. R. Malekzadeh and A. Nahavandi, "Making Mergers Work by Managing Cultures," *Journal of Business Strategy* (May/June 1990), pp. 53–57.

A. Nahavandi and A. R. Malekzadeh, "Acculturation in Mergers and Acquisitions," *Academy of Management Review* (January 1988), pp. 79–90.

43. Suggested by J. C. Camillus, *Strategic Planning and Management Control* (Lexington, Mass.: Lexington Books, 1986), pp. 170–172.

44. Camillus, *Strategic Planning*, pp. 171–172.

45. S. J. Carroll, Jr., and H. L. Tosi, Jr., *Management by Objectives* (New York: Macmillan, 1973), p. 3.

S. J. Carroll, Jr., "Management By Objectives: Three Decades of Research and Experience," in *Current Is-*

sues in Human Resource Management, edited by S. L. Rynes and G. T. Milkovich (Plano, Texas: Business Publications, Inc., 1986), pp. 295–312.

J. P. Muczyk and B. C. Reimann, "MBO as a Complement to Effective Leadership," *Academy of Management Executive* (May 1989), pp. 131–138.

46. M. D. Richards, *Setting Strategic Goals and Objectives*, 2nd ed. (St. Paul, Minn.: West Publishing Co., 1986), pp. 122–123.

47. E. J. Seyna, "MBO: The Fad That Changed Management," *Long Range Planning* (December 1986), pp. 116–123.

Carroll, "Management by Objectives."

48. Muczyk and Reimann, "MBO."

49. Carroll, "Management by Objectives," p. 309.

50. L. Porter, R. Allen, and R. Angle, "The Politics of Upward Influences in Organizations," in *Organizational Influence Processes*, edited by R. W. Allen and L. W. Porter (Glenview, Ill.: Scott, Foresman, 1983), p. 409.

51. R. E Jones, "Managing the Political Context in PMS Organizations," *European Journal of Operations Research*, in press.

52. J. R. Galbraith and R. K. Kazanjian, *Strategy Implementation: Structure, Systems, and Process*, 2nd ed. (St. Paul, Minn.: West Publishing Co., 1986), p. 120.

53. E. E. Lawler III, *Strategic Pay* (San Francisco: Jossey-Bass, 1990), p. 13.

54. H. D. Friedeck, "Changing Working Arrangements and Variable Pay: Does Pay-for-Performance Really Work?" in *Handbook of Business Strategy, 1989/1990 Yearbook* (Boston: Warren, Gorham and Lamont, 1989), pp. 20.1–20.13.

55. D. B. Balkin and L. R. Gomez-Mejia, "Matching Compensation and Organizational Strategies," *Strategic Management Journal* (February 1990), pp. 153–169.

56. H. I. Ansoff, "Strategic Management of Technology," *Journal of Business Strategy* (Winter 1987), p. 37.

CHAPTER TEN

Evaluation and Control

CHAPTER OUTLINE

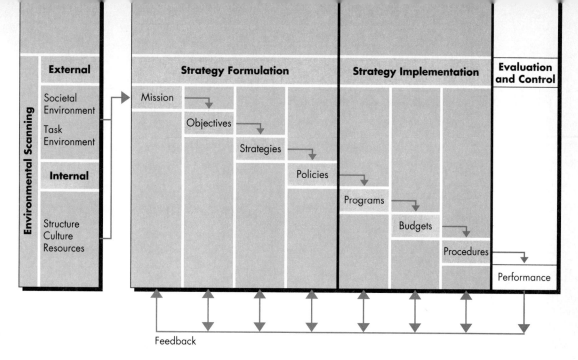

| Environmental Scanning | | Strategy Formulation | Strategy Implementation | Evaluation and Control |

External

Societal Environment

Task Environment

Internal

Structure
Culture
Resources

Strategy Formulation

Mission

Objectives

Strategies

Policies

Strategy Implementation

Programs

Budgets

Procedures

Evaluation and Control

Performance

Feedback

STRATEGIC MANAGEMENT MODEL

Things for which we can devise indicators can be managed; things for which we have no indicators can be out of control before we realize it.[1]

George S. Odiorne

The last part of the strategic management model is the evaluation of performance and the control of work activities. Control follows planning. It ensures that the corporation is achieving what it set out to accomplish. Just as planning involves the setting of objectives along with the strategies and programs necessary to accomplish them, the control process compares performance with desired results and provides the feedback necessary for management to evaluate results and take corrective action, as needed.[2] This process can be viewed as a five-step feedback model, as depicted in Fig. 10.1.

1. **Determine what to measure.** Top managers as well as operational managers need to specify what implementation processes and results will be monitored and evaluated. The processes and results must be capable of being measured in a reasonably objective and consistent manner. The focus should be on the most significant elements in a process—the ones that account for the highest proportion of expense or the greatest number of problems.

2. **Establish standards of performance.** Standards used to measure performance are detailed expressions of strategic objectives. They are *measures* of acceptable performance results. Each standard usually includes a *tolerance*

FIGURE 10.1 | **Evaluation and Control Process**

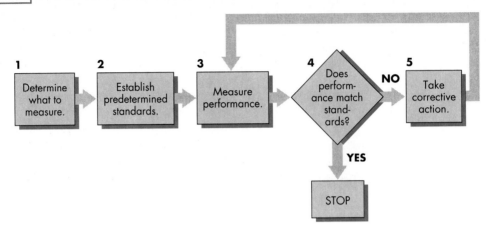

range within which deviations accepted as satisfactory are defined. Standards can be set not only for final output, but also for intermediate stages of production output.

3. **Measure actual performance.** Measurements must be made at predetermined times.

4. **Compare actual performance with the standard.** If actual performance results are within the desired tolerance range, the measurement process stops here.

5. **Take corrective action.** If actual results fall outside the desired tolerance range, action must be taken to correct the deviation. The following must be determined:
   a. Is the deviation only a chance fluctuation?
   b. Are the processes being carried out incorrectly?
   c. Are the processes appropriate to the achievement of the desired standard? Action must be taken that will not only correct the deviation, but will also prevent its happening again.

10.1 EVALUATION AND CONTROL IN STRATEGIC MANAGEMENT

The representation of the strategic management model that prefaces each chapter shows that evaluation and control information is fed back and assimilated into the entire management process. This information consists of performance data and activity reports (gathered in Step 3 of Fig. 10.1). If undesired performance is the result of an inappropriate *use* of the strategic management processes, operational managers must know about it so that they can correct the employee activity. Top management need not be involved. If, however, undesired performance results from the processes themselves, top managers, as well as operational managers, must know about it so that they can develop new implementation programs or procedures.

An application of the control process to strategic management is depicted in Fig. 10.2. Beginning with the central question "Did the existing strategies produce the desired results?" it provides strategic managers with a series of questions to use in the evaluation of strategies formulated and implemented. Such a strategy review is usually initiated when a "*planning gap*" appears between a company's financial objectives and the expected results of current activities.[3] Short-term measurements are beginning to suggest that the firm is likely to perform below expectations. After answering the proposed set of questions, a manager should have a good idea of where the problem originated and what must be done to correct the situation.

Lorange, Morton, and Ghoshal, in their book on strategic control, propose three types of control: strategic, tactical, and operational.[4] **Strategic control** deals with the basic strategic direction of the corporation in terms of its relationship with its environment. It focuses on the corporation as a whole and might emphasize long-term measures (considering one year or more), such as return on investment and changes in shareholder value. **Tactical control**, in contrast, deals primarily with the implementation of the strategic plan. It emphasizes the implementation of programs and might use medium-range measures (considering six months to a year), such as market share in particular product categories. **Operational control** deals with near-term (considering today to six months) corporate activities and focuses on what might be going on now to achieve near- and long-term success. An example of an operational control is the use of "statistical process control" as proposed by Deming (and discussed in Illustrative Example 9.3) to provide immediate feedback to the workers to enable them to better limit defects in the production process.[5]

Lorange, Morton, and Ghoshal further suggest that just as there is a hierarchy of strategy, there is also a **hierarchy of control,** as depicted in Fig. 10.3. At the corporate level, control focuses on maintaining a balance among the various activities of the corporation as a whole. Strategic and tactical controls are most important. Overall annual profitability is key. At the divisional level, control is primarily concerned with the maintenance and improvement of competitive position. Tactical control dominates. Market share and unit costs are watched carefully on a monthly and quarterly basis. At the functional level, the role of control becomes one of developing and enhancing function-based distinctive competencies. Such things as number of sales calls completed, number of customer complaints, and number of defects are watched daily and weekly. Because of the short-term time horizon, operational and tactical controls are most important at this level, where there is only a modest concern for strategic control.[6]

To help achieve organizational objectives, strategic managers have an obligation to ensure that the entire hierarchy of control is integrated and working properly. According to W. Edwards Deming, the quality-control expert who helped the Japanese build their successful business economy (see Illustrative Example 9.3), 85% of the causes of product defects are caused by the system within which the worker must perform and only 15% can be directly traced to the worker.[7] Unfortunately, in the last few decades top management has almost forgotten the importance of strategic control, and when control was called for, it has reverted to more direct tactical and operational control—often becoming crisis management.[8]

FIGURE 10.2   **Evaluating an Implemented Strategy**

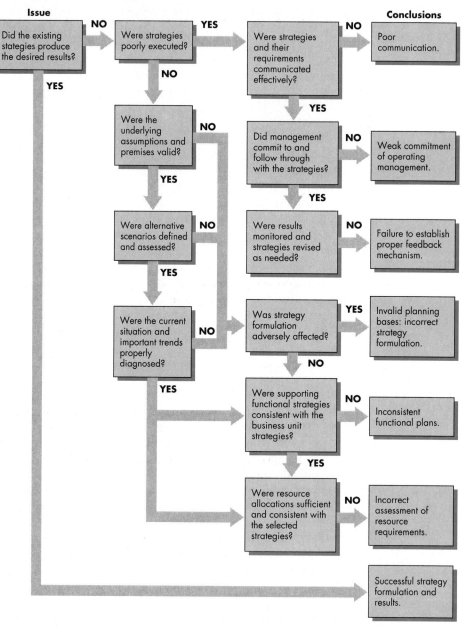

Source: Jeffrey A. Schmidt, "The Strategic Review," *Planning Review* (July/August 1988), p. 15. Copyright © 1988 by The Planning Forum, Oxford, Ohio.

| FIGURE 10.3 | **Hierarchy of Control** |

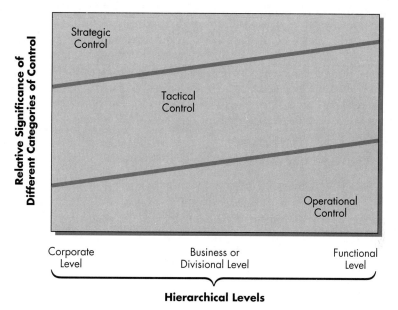

Source: Reprinted by permission from *Strategic Control* by P. Lorange, M. F. S. Morton, and S. Ghoshal. Copyright © 1986 by West Publishing Company. All rights reserved.

10.2 MEASURING PERFORMANCE

Which measures will be used to assess performance depends on the organizational unit to be appraised, as well as on the objectives to be achieved. Different measures are required for different objectives. Some measures, such as return on investment (ROI), are appropriate for evaluating the corporation's or division's ability to achieve a profitability objective. These measures, however, are inadequate for evaluating other objectives that a corporation might want to achieve: social responsibility or employee development, for instance. Even though profitability is the major objective for a corporation, ROI alone might be insufficient as a control device. ROI, for example, can be computed only *after* profits are totaled for a period. It tells what happened after the fact—not what *is* happening or what *will* happen. A firm, therefore, needs to develop measures that predict likely profitability. These are referred to as "steering" or "feed-forward" controls because they measure variables that influence future profitability.

Controls can be established to focus either on actual performance results (output) or on the activities that generate the performance (behavior). **Behavior controls** specify *how* something is to be done through policies, rules, standard operating procedures, and orders from a superior. **Output controls** specify *what* is to be accomplished by focusing on the end result of the behaviors through the use of objectives and performance targets or milestones. Behavior and output controls are not interchangeable. Behavior controls are most appropriate for those situations in which performance results are hard to measure and there is a clear cause-effect connection between activities and results. Output controls are most appropriate for those situations in which there are specific agreed-upon output measures and there is no clear cause-effect connection between activities and results. Generally, output measures serve the control needs of the corporation as a whole, whereas behavior measures serve the control needs of the individual manager.[9]

MEASURES OF CORPORATE PERFORMANCE

The most commonly used measure of corporate performance (in terms of profits) is ROI. It is simply the result of dividing net income after taxes by total assets. Although there are several advantages to the use of ROI, there are also several distinct limitations. (See Table 10.1 for list of some advantages and limitations of ROI.)

Other popular measures are earnings per share (EPS) and return on equity (ROE). Earnings per share also has several deficiencies as an evaluation of past and future performance. For one thing, because alternative accounting principles are available, EPS can have several different but equally acceptable values, depending on the principle selected for its computation. Second, because EPS is based on accrual income, the conversion of income to cash can be near term or delayed. Therefore, EPS does not consider the time value of money. Return on equity also has its share of limitations because it is also derived from accounting-based data. In addition, there is some evidence that EPS and ROE are often unrelated to a company's stock price.[10] Because of these and other limitations, EPS and ROE *by themselves* are not adequate measures of corporate performance.[11]

Stakeholder Measures

As mentioned in Chapter 4, stakeholders in the corporation's task environment are often very concerned about corporate activities and performance. Each has its own set of criteria to determine how well the corporation is performing. These criteria typically deal with the direct and indirect impact of corporate activities on stakeholder interests. Freeman proposes that top management needs to "keep score" with these stakeholders; it should establish one or more simple measures for each stakeholder category.[12] A few of these measures are listed in Table 10.2.

Value-Added Measures

Assuming that any one measure is bound to have some shortcomings, Hofer recommends the use of three new measures in an evaluation of a corporation's performance results (see Table 10.3). These are based on *value-added* measures and are attempts to assess directly the contribution a corporation makes to society. **Value added** is the difference between dollar sales and the cost of raw materials and

TABLE 10.1	Advantages and Limitations of ROI as a Measure of Corporate Performance

Advantages

1. ROI is a single comprehensive figure influenced by everything that happens.
2. It measures how well the division manager uses the property of the company to generate profits. It is also a good way to check on the accuracy of capital investment proposals.
3. It is a common denominator that can be compared with many entities.
4. It provides an incentive to use existing assets efficiently.
5. It provides an incentive to acquire new assets only when doing so would increase the return.

Limitations

1. ROI is very sensitive to depreciation policy. Depreciation write-off variances between divisions affect ROI performance. Accelerated depreciation techniques reduce ROI, conflicting with capital budgeting discounted cash-flow analysis.
2. ROI is sensitive to book value. Older plants with more depreciated assets have relatively lower investment bases than newer plants (note also the effect of inflation), thus increasing ROI. Note that asset investment may be held down or assets disposed of in order to increase ROI performance.
3. In many firms that use ROI, one division sells to another. As a result, transfer pricing must occur. Expenses incurred affect profit. Since, in theory, the transfer price should be based on the total impact on firm profit, some investment center managers are bound to suffer. Equitable transfer prices are difficult to determine.
4. If one division operates in an industry that has favorable conditions and another division operates in an industry that has unfavorable conditions, the former division will automatically "look" better than the other.
5. The time span of concern here is short range. The performance of division managers should be measured in the long run. This is top management's timespan capacity.
6. The business cycle strongly affects ROI performance, often despite managerial performance.

Source: Table, "Advantages and Limitations of ROI as a Measure of Corporate Performance" from *Organizational Policy and Strategic Management,* 2nd ed. Copyright © 1983 by The Dryden Press, a division of Holt, Rinehart and Winston, Inc. Reprinted by permission of the publisher.

purchased parts. Return on value added (ROVA) is a measure that divides net profits before tax by value added and converts the quotient to a percentage. Preliminary studies by Hofer suggest that ROVA tends to stabilize in the range of 12%–18% for most industries in the maturity or saturation phases of market evolution. Hofer argues that ROVA might be a better measure of corporate performance across various industries than other measures currently in use.[13]

Unfortunately, the major disadvantage of using value added is that the figures are not readily available. There is no way to calculate value added from traditional financial reports in the U.S., for example, because of the allocation and application of direct labor, indirect costs, and overhead that become part of the cost of goods manufactured. Nevertheless, authorities on the subject argue that combining value-added measures with traditional performance measures creates a more complete and realistic picture of a corporation's performance.[14]

TABLE 10.2	A Sample Scorecard for "Keeping Score" with Stakeholders

Stakeholder Category	Possible Near-Term Measures	Possible Long-Term Measures
Customers	Sales ($ and volume) New customers Number of new customer needs met ("tries")	Growth in sales Turnover of customer base Ability to control price

Suppliers	Cost of raw material
	Delivery time
	Inventory
	Availability of raw material
		Growth rates of:
		  Raw material costs
		  Delivery time
		  Inventory
		New ideas from suppliers

Financial community	EPS Stock price Number of "buy" lists ROE	Ability to convince Wall Street of strategy Growth in ROE
Employees	Number of suggestions Productivity Number of grievances	Number of internal promotions Turnover
Congress	Number of new pieces of legislation that affect the firm Access to key members and staff	Number of new regulations that affect industry Ratio of "cooperative" vs. "competitive" encounters
Consumer advocate	Number of meetings Number of "hostile" encounters Number of times coalitions formed Number of legal actions	Number of changes in policy due to C.A. Number of C.A.-initiated "calls for help"
Environmentalists	Number of meetings Number of hostile encounters Number of times coalitions formed Number of EPA complaints Number of legal actions	Number of changes in policy due to environmentalists Number of environmentalist "calls for help"

Source: R. E. Freeman, *Strategic Management: A Stakeholder Approach* (Boston: Ballinger Publishing Company, 1984), p. 179. Copyright © 1984 by R. E. Freeman. Reprinted by permission.

TABLE 10.3	Value-Added Measures of Corporate Performance	

Performance Characteristic	Some Traditional Measures	Proposed New Measures
Growth	Dollar sales, unit sales, dollar assets	Value added[1]
Efficiency	Gross margin, net profits, net profits/dollar sales	ROVA[2]
Asset utilization	ROI, return on equity, earnings per share	ROVA/ROI

[1] Value added = Dollar sales − Cost of raw materials and purchased parts.

[2] ROVA: Return on Value Added $= \dfrac{\text{Net profits before tax}}{\text{Value added}} \times 100\%$.

Source: C. W. Hofer, "ROVA: A New Measure for Assessing Organizational Performance," in *Advances in Strategic Management,* vol. 2, edited by R. Lamb (Greenwich, Conn.: JAI Press, 1983), p. 50. Copyright © 1983 by C. W. Hofer. Reprinted by permission.

Shareholder Value

Because of the belief that accounting-based numbers such as return on investment, return on equity, and earnings per share are not reliable indicators of a corporation's economic value, many corporations are using shareholder value as a better measure of corporate performance and strategic management effectiveness.[15] Among them are PepsiCo, Westinghouse, Heinz, Disney, and Dexter Corporation. Arguing that the purpose of a company is to increase shareholder wealth, shareholder value analysis concentrates on cash flow as the key measure of performance. The value of a corporation is thus the value of its cash flows discounted back to their present value, using the business's cost of capital as the discount rate. As long as the returns from a business exceed its cost of capital, the business will create value and be worth more than the capital invested in it.[16] Rappaport, one of the principal advocates of this measure, explains its use in evaluating strategy:

> What I have termed the "shareholder value approach" estimates the economic value of any strategy as the expected cash flows discounted by the market discount rate. These cash flows in turn serve as the basis for expected shareholder returns from dividends and stock-price appreciation.[17]

A survey of the senior managers of Fortune 500 companies revealed that 30% of their selections of investment proposals are based on their expected contributions to shareholder wealth. The survey also noted that many corporations not now using this approach are starting to experiment with value-based techniques.[18]

Performance Objectives

The objectives that were established earlier in the strategy formulation stage of the strategic management process should certainly be used to measure corporate performance once the strategies have been implemented. Drucker, one of the originators of Management By Objectives, proposed eight key areas in which overall corporate objectives should be established and monitored.

1. Market standing.
2. Innovation.
3. Productivity.
4. Use of physical and financial resources.
5. Profitability.
6. Manager performance and development.
7. Worker performance and attitude.
8. Public responsibility.[19]

Westinghouse Electric Corporation, for example, established an objective of productivity improvement for the entire corporation. Concerned that the company had slipped from the position of Number Two in the world in its industry, top management decided in 1979 that the firm had to do a better job with the resources it controlled. Consequently, it developed a series of productivity-improvement programs, such as the introduction of quality circles, improved inventory control, and the global location of its manufacturing facilities. To measure the overall impact of these programs on the corporation, Westinghouse's top management developed a productivity improvement (PI) formula:

$$\frac{\text{Constant dollar value-added change}}{\text{Total employee costs}} = \% \text{ PI}$$

Top management established an overall corporate objective for productivity improvement at $6 + \%$ per year. This was quite a challenging objective given that the overall U.S. manufacturing PI had been less than 1% when Westinghouse began its use of the measure. The productivity improvement measure thus became one of the key indicators of corporate performance.[20]

Evaluation of Top Management

Through its strategy, audit, and compensation committees, a board of directors closely evaluates the job performance of the CEO and the top management team. Of course, it is concerned primarily with overall profitability as measured by return on investment, return on equity, earnings per share, and shareholder value. The absence of short-run profitability is certainly a factor contributing to the firing of any CEO. The board will also, however, be concerned with other factors.

Members of the compensation committees of today's boards of directors generally agree that measuring a CEO's ability to establish strategic direction, build a management team, and provide leadership is more critical in the long run than are a few quantitative measures.[21] The board should evaluate top management not only on the typical output-oriented quantitative measures (see Fig. 10.4), but also on behavioral measures—factors relating to its strategic management practices. Has the top management team set reasonable long-run as well as short-run objectives? Has it formulated innovative strategies? Has it worked closely with operational managers in the development of realistic implementation plans, schedules, and budgets? Has it developed and used appropriate measures of corporate and divisional performance for feedback and control? Has it provided the board with appropriate feedback on corporate performance in advance of key decision points? These and other questions

FIGURE 10.4 | **Assessing Top Management's Performance**

Measure	Excellent	Above Average	Average	Below Average	Poor
Qualitative Establishing strategic direction					
Building management team					
Leadership qualities					
Providing for succession					
Implementing strategy					
Employee/labor relations					
Technology leadership					
Board relations					
Investor relations					
Community/gov't relations					
Quantitative EPS over 2–5 years					
Total return to shareholders					
Return on invested capital					
Return measure trends					
Return on stockholder equity					
Cash flow					
Yearly/quarterly EPS					
Stock price performance					
Book value performance					
Dividend payout ratio					

Source: Suggested by R. Brossy, "What Directors Say About Their Role in Managing Executive Pay," *Directors & Boards* (Summer 1986), pp. 38–40.

should be raised by a board of directors as it evaluates the performance of top management.

The specific items that are used by a board to evaluate its top management should be derived from the objectives agreed on earlier by both the board and top management. If better relations with the local community and improved safety practices in work areas were selected as objecties for the year (or for five years), these items should be included in the evaluation. In addition, other factors that tend to lead to profitability might be included, such as market share, product quality, or investment intensity (from the PIMS research discussed in Chapter 5).

Strategic Audits

Used by various consulting firms as a way to measure performance, audits of corporate activities are frequently suggested for use by boards of directors as well as by others in managerial positions. Management audits have been developed to evaluate activities such as corporate social responsibility, functional areas such as the marketing department, and divisions such as the international division, as well as to evaluate the corporation itself in a strategic audit (see Chapter 2). The strategic audit is likely to be used increasingly by corporations that have begun to monitor closely those activities that affect overall corporate effectiveness and efficiency, because it incorporates both output and behavioral control measures. To be effective, the strategic audit should parallel the corporation's strategic management process and/or model.

MEASURES OF DIVISIONAL AND FUNCTIONAL UNIT PERFORMANCE

Corporations use a variety of techniques to evaluate and control performance in divisions, SBUs, and functional units. If a corporation is composed of SBUs or divisions, it will use many of the same performance measures (ROI, for instance) that it uses to assess overall corporation performance. To the extent that it can isolate specific functional units, such as R&D, the corporation may develop responsibility centers.

Budgets are certainly an important control device. During strategy formulation and implementation, top management approves a series of programs and supporting operating budgets from its business units.[22] During evaluation and control, actual expenses are contrasted with planned expenditures and the degree of variance is assessed. This is typically done on a monthly basis. In addition, top management will probably require *periodic statistical reports* summarizing data on key factors, such as the number of new customer contracts, volume of received orders, and productivity figures, among others.[23]

Control and Business Unit Strategy

The strategy chosen by an SBU should influence the type of controls chosen.[24] Research by Govindarajan and Fisher indicates that high-performing SBUs following a cost leadership competitive strategy tend to use output controls, such as piece rate or straight commission. This is appropriate since costs can usually be easily determined. High-performing SBUs following a differentiation competitive strategy, in contrast, tend to use behavior controls, such as salaried compensation. Factors such as creative flair, strong R&D, and innovative product development are extremely important to this strategy, but are difficult to quantify.[25]

Two successful computer companies can be given as examples. Digital Equipment Corporation (DEC) follows a differentiation strategy and Data General follows a low-cost strategy. The control systems differ accordingly. DEC's salespeople are on straight salary, but Data General's salespeople receive 50% of their pay on a commission basis. DEC's product managers are evaluated primarily on the basis of the quality of their customer relationships, whereas Data General's product managers are evaluated strictly on the basis of results, that is, profits. Research concludes that "for increased effectiveness, cost leadership and differentiation strategies need to be matched with output and behavior controls, respectively."[26]

Responsibility Centers

Control systems can be established to monitor specific functions, projects, or divisions. Budgets are one type of control system that are typically used to control the financial indicators of performance. **Responsibility centers** are used to isolate a unit so that it can be evaluated separately from the rest of the corporation. Each responsibility center therefore has its own budget and is evaluated on its use of budgeted resources. A responsibility center is headed by the manager responsible for the center's performance. The center uses resources (measured in terms of costs or expenses) to produce a service or a product (measured in terms of volume or revenues). There are five major types of responsibility centers. The type is determined by the way these resources and services or products are measured by the corporation's control system.[27]

1. **Standard cost centers.** Primarily used in manufacturing facilities, standard (or expected) costs are computed for each operation on the basis of historical data. In evaluation of the center's performance, its total standard costs are multiplied by the units produced; the result is the expected cost of production, which is then compared to the actual cost of production.
2. **Revenue centers.** Production, usually in terms of unit or dollar sales, is measured without consideration of resource costs (e.g., salaries). The center is thus judged in terms of effectiveness rather than efficiency. The effectiveness of a sales region, for example, is determined by the comparison of its actual sales to its projected or previous year's sales. Profits are not considered because sales departments have very limited influence over the cost of the products they sell.
3. **Expense centers.** Resources are measured in dollars without consideration of service or product costs. Thus, budgets will have been prepared for "engineered" expenses (those costs that can be calculated) and for "discretionary" expenses (those costs that can be only estimated). Typical expense centers are administrative, service, and research departments. They cost an organization money, but they only indirectly contribute to revenues.
4. **Profit centers.** Performance is measured in terms of the difference between revenues (which measure production) and expenditures (which measure

resources). A profit center is typically established whenever an organizational unit has control over both its resources and its products or services. By having such centers, a corporation can be organized into divisions of separate product lines. The manager of each division is given autonomy to the extent that she or he is able to keep profits at a satisfactory (or better) level.

Some organizational units that are not usually considered potentially autonomous can, for the purpose of profit-center evaluations, be made so. A manufacturing department, for example, can be converted from a standard cost center (or expense center) into a profit center: it is allowed to charge a **transfer price** for each product it "sells" to the sales department. The difference between the manufacturing cost per unit and the agreed-upon transfer price is the unit's "profit." Transfer pricing is commonly used in vertically integrated corporations and can work well when a price can be easily determined for a designated amount of product. When a price cannot be set easily, however, the relative bargaining power of the centers, rather than strategic considerations, tends to influence the agreed-upon price.[28] Top management has an obligation to make sure that these political considerations do not overwhelm the strategic ones. Otherwise, profit figures for each center will be biased and provide poor information for strategic decisions at the corporate level.

5. **Investment centers.** As with profit centers, an investment center's performance is measured in terms of the difference between its revenues and its costs and expenses. Most divisions in large manufacturing corporations use huge assets, such as plants and equipment, to make their products, and evaluating their performance on the basis of profits alone can be misleading because it ignores the size of their assets. For example, two divisions in a corporation made identical profits, but one division owns a $3 million plant, whereas the other owns a $1 million plant. Both make the same profits, but one is obviously more efficient: the smaller plant provides the stockholders with a better return on their investment.

The most widely used measure of investment center performance is return on investment (ROI). Another measure, called *"residual income"* or *"after-capital charge,"* is found by subtracting an interest charge from the net income. This interest charge could be based on the interest the corporation is actually paying to lenders for the assets being used. It could also be based on the amount of income that could have been earned if the assets had been invested somewhere else. According to Camillus, an authority on measures of control: "The return after capital charge is superior to the ROI measure in that it takes into account the corporate cost of capital rather than the particular division's rate of return on investment."[29]

Sloan reports that the concept of rate of return on investments was crucial to General Motors' exercise of its permanent control of the whole corporation in a way consistent with its decentralized organization.[30] Donaldson Brown, who came to GM from DuPont in 1921, defined return on investment as a function of the profit margin and the rate of turnover of invested capital. Multiplying the profit margin by the investment turnover equals the percentage of return on investment. To increase the return on investment, management can, therefore, increase the rate of capital turnover in relation to sales (that is, increase volume) or increase profit margins (increase revenue and/or cut costs and expenses).[31]

Investment center performance can also be measured in terms of its contribution to shareholder value. One example is given by the CEO of a large corporation.

> We value our businesses by computing the net present value of each unit's equity cash flow, using the appropriate cost of capital. Then we subtract out the market value of assigned debt and arrive at an estimate of the warranted market value of the unit. These techniques allow us to evaluate and rank our units based on their relative contribution to the creation of overall corporate equity value, which is our overall objective.[32]

Most single-business corporations tend to use a combination of cost, expense, and revenue centers. In these corporations, most managers are functional specialists and manage against a budget. Total profitability is integrated at the corporate level. Dominant-product companies, which have diversified into a few small businesses but which still depend on a single product line for most of their revenue and income, generally use a combination of cost, expense, revenue, plus profit centers. Multidivisional corporations, however, will tend to emphasize investment centers—although in various units throughout the corporation other types of responsibility centers will also be used.[33] One problem with using responsibility centers, however, is that they sometimes make it difficult to do the calculations necessary for the kind of value chain analysis that looks for synergistic linkages among units.[34]

10.3 STRATEGIC INFORMATION SYSTEMS

Before performance measures can have any impact on strategic management, they must first be communicated to those people responsible for formulating and implementing strategic plans. Strategic information systems can perform this function. They can be computer-based or manual, formal or informal. They serve the information needs of top management.[35] As discussed in Chapter 5, an information system is meant to provide a basis for early warning signals that can originate either externally or internally. These warning signals grow out of the corporation's need to ensure that programs and procedures are being implemented in ways that will achieve corporate and divisional objectives. One of the key reasons given for the bankruptcy of International Harvester was the inability of the corporation's top management to precisely determine its income by major class of similar products. Because of this inability, management kept trying to fix ailing businesses and was unable to respond flexibly to major changes and unexpected events.[36] In contrast, one of the key reasons for the success of Toys "R" Us has been management's use of the company's sophisticated information system to control purchasing decisions. (See Illustrative Example 10.1 for details.)

ILLUSTRATIVE EXAMPLE 10.1

Toys "R" Us Uses Information Systems to Control Purchasing

Since 1978, sales at Toys "R" Us have been growing at a compounded rate of 28% annually. Sales topped $3 billion by 1988. At the root of the success of the company is a sophisticated information system. Cash registers in the company's 300 + U.S. stores transmit information daily to computers at the company's headquarters in Rochelle Park, New Jersey. Consequently, managers know every morning exactly how many of each item have been sold the day before, how many have been sold so far in the year, and how this year's sales compare to last year's.

The information system allows all reordering to be done automatically by computers without any managerial input. It also allows the company to experiment with new toys without committing to big orders in advance. In effect, the system allows the customers to decide through their purchases what gets reordered. Chairman Charles Lazarus respects the information system so much that when the computer's decision conflicts with his judgment, he defers to the computer. For example, he personally thought Cabbage Patch dolls were ugly and didn't think children would want to hold them. The information system, on the other hand, recognized consumer buying patterns and reordered accordingly. The system is also able to recognize drops in demand, such as when a fad like Trivial Pursuit begins to fade.

Source: S. N. Chakravarty, "Will Toys 'B' Great?" *Forbes* (February 22, 1988), pp. 37–39.

As mentioned in Chapter 5, the information system should focus managers' attention on the critical success factors in their jobs. **Critical success factors** (CSFs) are those few things that must go well if a corporation's success is to be ensured.[37] They are typically the 20% of the total factors that determine 80% of the corporation's or business unit's performance.[38] They therefore represent those areas that must be given the special and continuous attention needed for high performance. Each CSF is therefore very likely to be a strategic factor for the corporation. Critical success factors should be

- Important to achieving overall corporate goals and objectives.
- Measurable and controllable by the organization to which they apply.
- Relatively few in number—not everything can be critical.
- Expressed as things that must be done.
- Applicable to all companies in the industry with similar objectives and strategies.
- Hierarchical in nature—some CSFs will pertain to the overall corporation, whereas others will be more narrowly focused in one functional area.[39]

These critical success factors provide a focal point from which a computer-based information system can be developed. Such an information system will thus pinpoint key areas that require a manager's attention.

The Diversified Products and Service Group of GTE, for example, established a formal system, based on critical success factors, to track the implementation of the group's strategic plans. Management referred to this system as their Strategic Tracking System (STS). Charles M. Jones, Vice-President of Administration for GTE Diversified Products, relates how it was done.

> We called the things that had to be done well Critical Success Factors (CSFs). The first criterion in defining CSFs was that they had to be very specific and action oriented. In addition, we developed performance measures for each CSF. Then we set up a monthly STS reporting system, reviewed by the president of Diversified Products. . . .
>
> Each organization developed its own STS reporting process, determining from the various line managers what factors were critical to their particular operation. At the next higher level, these success factors and performance measures were reviewed and the most important were selected as monitors for the monthly report. In theory, and in practice, there's nothing in the STS that general managers don't use to run their businesses, but not everything they use was included.[40]

At the divisional or SBU level of a corporation, the information system should be used to support, reinforce, or enlarge its business-level strategy through its decision support system.[41] An SBU pursuing a strategy of overall cost leadership could use its information system to reduce costs either by the improvement of labor productivity or the utilization of other resources such as inventory or machinery. Merrill Lynch took this approach when it developed PRISM software to provide its 500 U.S. retail offices quick access to financial information in order to boost the efficiency of its brokers.[42] Another SBU, in contrast, might wish to pursue a differentiation strategy. It could use its information system to add uniqueness to the product or service and contribute to quality, service, or image through the functional areas.[43] American Hospital Supply and both United and American Airlines took this approach to increase their market shares: they offered unique information-systems services to their customers.

The choice of the business-level strategy will thus dictate the type of information system that the SBU needs both to implement and to control strategic activities. Table 10.4 lists the differences between an information system needed to evaluate and control a low-cost strategy and an information system needed for product differentiation. The information systems will be constructed differently to monitor different activities because the two types of business-level strategies have different critical-success factors.[44]

10.4 PROBLEMS IN MEASURING PERFORMANCE

The measurement of performance is a crucial part of evaluation and control. The lack of quantifiable objectives or performance standards and the inability of the information system to provide timely, valid information are two obvious control problems.[45] Without objective and timely measurements, it would be extremely difficult to make operational, let alone strategic, decisions. Nevertheless, the use of timely, quantifiable standards does not guarantee good performance. The very act of monitoring and measuring performance can cause side effects that interfere with overall corporate performance. Among the most frequent negative side effects are a short-term orientation and goal displacement.

TABLE 10.4	Use of Information Systems to Monitor Implementation of Business Strategies	

	Generic Strategies	
	Low Cost	Product Differentiation
Product Design and Development	Product engineering systems Project control systems	R&D data bases Professional workstations Electronic mail CAD Custom engineering systems Integrated systems for manufacturing
Operations	Process engineering systems Process control systems Labor control systems Inventory management systems Procurement systems Quality monitoring systems	CAM Quality assurance systems Systems for suppliers Quality monitoring systems
Marketing	Streamlined distribution systems Centralized control systems Econometric modeling systems	Sophisticated marketing systems Market data bases Graphic display systems Telemarketing systems Competition analysis systems Modeling systems Service-oriented distribution systems
Sales	Sales control systems Advertising monitoring systems Systems to consolidate sales function Strict incentive/monitoring systems	Differential pricing systems Office/field communications Customer/sales support systems Dealer support systems Customer order-entry systems
Administration	Cost control systems Quantitative planning and budgeting systems Office automation for staff reduction	Office automation to integrate functions Environment scanning and nonquantitative planning systems Teleconferencing systems

Source: G. L. Parsons, "Information Technology: A New Competitive Weapon," *Sloan Management Review* (Fall 1983), p. 12. Reprinted by permission of the publisher. Copyright © 1983 by the Sloan Management Review Association. All rights reserved.

SHORT-TERM ORIENTATION

Hodgetts and Wortman state that in many situations top executives do not analyze *either* the long-term implications of present operations on the strategy they have adopted *or* the operational impact of a strategy on the corporate mission. They report that long-run evaluations are *not* conducted because executives (1) may not realize their importance, (2) may believe that short-run considerations are more important than long-run considerations, (3) may not be personally evaluated on a long-term basis, or (4) may not have the time to make a long-run analysis.[46] There is no real justification for the first and last "reasons." If executives realize the importance of long-run evaluations, they make the time needed to conduct them. Even though many chief executives point to immediate pressures from the investment community and to short-term incentive and promotion plans to support the second and third reasons, evidence does not always support their claims.

A survey of 400 U.S. chief executives revealed that 98% of them agreed that their industry could be justifiably criticized for focusing on next quarter's earnings or tomorrow's stock price. Over half of them felt that institutional investors were placing heavy pressure on them for short-term performance and that this pressure was increasing.[47] Recent research suggests, however, that this view of short-term pressure may be based more on personal interest and conventional wisdom than on actual pressures. Studies reveal that the stock market does value long-term investment and that investors (even institutional investors) place considerable value on profits that won't be earned for another five or more years.[48] Nevertheless, there are times when the stock market does *not* value a particular strategic investment. See the *boxed example* of Maytag (p. 316) for the response of the investment community to Maytag Corporation's acquisition of Hoover (in terms of Maytag's stock market price).

Regarding long-term evaluations, there does appear to be a trend in U.S. executive compensation toward evaluating and rewarding long-run performance.[49] A study by the Hay Group indicated that long-term incentives made up 27% of the total annual income of CEOs of major U.S. corporations in 1990—an increase from just 15% in 1975. The rest of the typical chief executive's annual compensation in 1990 came from salary (38%), benefits (13%), and an annual bonus (22%).[50]

Many accounting-based measures do, however, encourage a short-term emphasis. Table 10.1 indicates that one of the limitations of ROI as a performance measure is its short-term nature. In theory, ROI is not limited to the short run, but in practice it is often difficult to use this measure to realize long-term benefits for the corporation. If the performance of corporate and divisional managers is evaluated primarily on the basis of an annual ROI, the managers tend to focus their effort on those factors that have positive short-term effects. Therefore, divisional managers often undertake capital investments with early paybacks that will establish a favorable track record for the division. These results are often inconsistent with corporate long-run objectives. Because managers can often manipulate both the numerator (earnings) as well as the denominator (investment), the resulting ROI figure can be meaningless. Advertising, maintenance, and research efforts can be reduced. Mergers can be undertaken that will do more for this year's earnings (and next year's paycheck) than for the division's or corporation's future profits. (Research of 55

MAYTAG CORPORATION: STOCK PRICE DROPS AFTER HOOVER ACQUISITION

When Maytag Corporation purchased Chicago Pacific Corporation (CP) in order to acquire one of its companies, Hoover, for its international appliance business, its debt soared to $923 million from $134 million just nine months earlier. Maytag's total outstanding shares swelled to 105 million from 75 million during the same time period. Although Maytag's debt was soon reduced by $200 million with the sale of CP's furniture companies, interest payments leaped to $70 million in 1989 from $20 million in 1988 and its stock price dropped from $26.50 in October 1988 to $20.00 in January 1989. This was a significant change for a company that, until eight years earlier, had had no long-term debt!

By the April 1990 annual meeting most of the corporation's stockholders knew how much the company had changed since the days when Maytag sold washing machines only as a sideline. Most appreciated management's attempts to build the company. Many were concerned, however, that the corporation no longer maintained the best profit margin in the industry. After describing some of the recent trends in the industry to those present at the annual meeting, Chairman and CEO Daniel Krumm summarized the corporation's financial performance in 1989:

> Maytag Corporation's sales of major appliances and floor care products in North America were strong in 1989 and we out-performed our competitors in

these respective industries. Pricing was very competitive and we experienced margin pressures most of the year. . . . A major problem area last year was Hoover's business in the U.K. This impacted net income negatively, as did our interest payments on our higher long-term debt.

Krumm also summarized first quarter results for 1990. Compared to the first quarter of 1989, net sales had increased from $678,573,000 to $762,074,000. Although unit sales were down, price increases kept dollar sales up. Operating income also improved from $67,673,000 to $71,233,000 but was insufficient to offset the interest payments associated with the corporation's higher level of debt. Consequently, net income dropped from $34,113,000 to $32,649,000. Commenting on the decline in the corporation's per share stock price to $16 by April 24, 1990, and the lack of interest in Maytag's stock by Wall Street, Krumm commented:

> There is nothing particularly unusual about any of these situations—in fact they are all either logical or inevitable. But as such they do not generate the interest or attention of many people in the financial community who tend to be shorter term in their investment perspective.

firms that engaged in major acquisitions revealed that even though the firms performed poorly after the acquisition, top management still received significant increases in compensation!)[51] Expensive retooling and plant modernization can be delayed as long as a manager can manipulate figures on production defects and absenteeism.

Efforts to compensate for these distortions tend to create a burdensome accounting-control system, which stifles creativity and flexibility, and leads to even more questionable "creative accounting" practices.[52] For example, the top management of Regina Corporation, a manufacturer of vacuum cleaners, admitted to the SEC in 1988 that it had inflated sales, profits, and revenues by omitting from the financial statements one annoying detail—products returned by the customers. Although buyers normally return around 5% of all vacuum cleaners sold in the U.S., Regina's customers were returning 20%–25%—totaling over $13 million worth of vacuums! Other "cute tricks" to massage the "bottom line" include shipping products on the last day of the year to reduce inventory (thus flooding distributors) and extending (or contracting) years of inventory depreciation either to boost this year's profits to impress the stock market or to decrease profits in order to reduce taxes.[53]

GOAL DISPLACEMENT

The very monitoring and measuring of performance (if not carefully done) can actually result in a decline in overall corporate performance. A dysfunctional side effect known as *goal displacement* can occur. This is the confusion of means with ends. Goal displacement occurs when activities originally intended to help managers attain corporate objectives become ends in themselves—or are adapted to meet ends other than those for which they were intended.[54] Two types of goal displacement are behavior substitution and suboptimization.

Behavior Substitution

Not all activities or aspects of performance can be easily quantified and measured. It can be very difficult to set standards for such desired activities as cooperation or initiative. Therefore, managers tend to focus more of their attention on those behaviors that are clearly measurable than on those that are not.[55] They thus reward those people who do well on these types of measures. Because managers tend to ignore behaviors that are either unmeasurable or difficult to measure, people receive little to no reward for engaging in these activities. The problem with this phenomenon is that the easy-to-measure activities might have little to no relationship to the desired good performance. Rational people, nevertheless, will tend to work for those rewards that the system has to offer. Therefore, employees will tend to substitute behaviors that are recognized and rewarded for those behaviors that are ignored, without regard to their contribution to goal accomplishment.[56] A U.S. Navy quip sums up this situation: "What you inspect is what you get." If the evaluation and control system of an auto plant rewards the meeting of quantitative goals and pays only lip service to qualitative goals, consumers can expect to get a very large number of very poorly built cars!

The most frequently mentioned problem with Management By Objectives (MBO) is that the measurement process partially distorts the realities of the job. Objectives are made for areas in which the measurement of accomplishments is relatively easy, such as ROI, increased sales, or reduced cost. But these might not always be the most important areas. This problem becomes crucial in professional, service, or staff activities in which the making of quantitative measurements is difficult. If, for example, a divisional manager is achieving all of the quantifiable objectives but, in so doing, alienates the work force, the result could be a long-term drop in the division's performance. If promotions are strictly based on measurable short-term performance results, this manager is very likely to be promoted or transferred before the employees' negative attitudes result in complaints to the personnel office, strikes, or sabotage. The law governing the effect of measurement on behavior seems to be that *quantifiable measures drive out nonquantifiable measures.*

Suboptimization

The emphasis in large corporations on developing separate responsibility centers can create some problems for the corporation as a whole. To the extent that a division or functional unit views itself as a separate entity, it might refuse to cooperate with other units or divisions in the same corporation if cooperation could in some way negatively affect its performance evaluation. The competition between divisions to achieve a high ROI can result in one division's refusal to share its new technology or work-process improvements. One division's attempt to optimize the accomplishment of its goals can cause other divisions to fall behind and thus negatively affect overall corporate performance. One common example of this type of suboptimization occurs when a marketing department approves an early shipment date to a customer as a means of getting an order and forces the manufacturing department into overtime production for this one order. Production costs are raised, which reduces the manufacturing department's overall efficiency. The end result might be that, although marketing achieves its sales goal, the corporation as a whole fails to achieve its expected profitability.

10.5 GUIDELINES FOR PROPER CONTROL

In designing a control system, top management should remember that *controls should follow strategy.* Unless controls ensure the use of the proper strategy to achieve objectives, there is a strong likelihood that dysfunctional side effects will completely undermine the implementation of the objectives. The following guidelines are recommended:

1. **Control should involve only the minimum amount of information** needed to give a reliable picture of events. Too many controls create confusion. Focus on that 20% of the factors that determine 80% of the results.
2. **Controls should monitor only meaningful activities and results,** regardless of measurement difficulty. If cooperation between divisions is important to corporate performance, some form of qualitative or quantitative measure should be established to monitor cooperation.
3. **Controls should be timely** so that corrective action can be taken before it is too late. *Steering controls,* controls that monitor or measure the factors influencing performance, should be stressed so that advance notice of problems is given.
4. **Long-term as well as short-term controls should be used.** If only short-term measures are emphasized, a short-term managerial orientation is likely.
5. **Controls should aim at pinpointing exceptions.** Only those activities or

results that fall outside a predetermined tolerance range should call for action.

6. **Emphasize the reward of meeting or exceeding standards rather than punishment for failing to meet standards.** Heavy punishment of failure will typically result in goal displacement. Managers will "fudge" reports and lobby for lower standards.

It is surprising that the best-managed companies often have only a few formal objective controls. They focus on measuring the critical success factors—those few things whose individual success ensures overall success. Other factors are controlled by the social system in the form of the corporate culture.[57] To the extent that the culture complements and reinforces the strategic orientation of the firm, there is less need for an extensive formal control system. In their book *In Search of Excellence*, Peters and Waterman state that "the stronger the culture and the more it was directed toward the marketplace, the less need was there for policy manuals, organization charts, or detailed procedures and rules. In these companies, people way down the line know what they are supposed to do in most situations because the handful of guiding values is crystal clear."[58]

10.6 STRATEGIC INCENTIVE MANAGEMENT

Traditionally, the level of compensation for chief executive officers has been a function of compensation received in comparable firms.[59] Therefore, CEO compensation is related more to the size of the corporation than to the size of its profits.[60] The gap between CEO compensation and corporate performance is most noticeable in those corporations with widely dispersed stock ownership and no dominant stockholder group to demand performance-based pay.[61] This association between firm size and executive compensation, according to Rappaport, can only serve to fuel top management's natural inclination to grow businesses as quickly as possible.[62]

Boards of directors need to take the initiative in the development of long-term controls and corresponding incentive plans. According to Andrews, "The best criterion for appraising the quality of management performance, in the absence of personal failures or unexpected breakdowns, is management's success over time in executing a demanding and approved strategy that is continually tested against opportunity and need."[63]

Executive compensation must be clearly linked to strategic performance—to the management of the corporate portfolio, to the business unit's mission, to short-term financial as well as long-term strategic performance, and to the degree of risk involved in the effective and efficient management of a portfolio. Recent research has found that although there is usually no relationship between the salary portion of a CEO's compensation and the company's subsequent performance, there is a strong relationship between the incentive portion of a CEO's compensation and the company's subsequent ROA and ROE.[64] A study of 58 business units in 15 different corporations concluded that "the payment of incentive compensation to managers is associated with more profitable businesses of all types."[65] There is some evidence, however, that successful SBUs following a growth strategy tend to have a pay mix with a strong incentive component, whereas SBUs following a maintenance or stability strategy tend to have a pay mix emphasizing salary and benefits.[66]

The following three approaches are tailored to help match measurements and rewards with explicit strategic objectives and time frames: (1) the weighted-factor method, (2) the long-term evaluation method, and (3) the strategic-funds method. These approaches can also be combined to best suit a corporation's circumstances.[67]

1. **Weighted-factor method.** The weighted-factor method is particularly appropriate for measuring and rewarding the performance of top SBU managers and group-level executives when performance factors and their importance vary from one SBU to another. The measurements used by one corporation might contain the following variations: the performance of high-growth SBUs measured in terms of market share, sales growth, designated future payoff, and progress on several future-oriented strategic projects; the performance of low-growth SBUs, in contrast, measured in terms of ROI and cash generation; and the performance of medium-growth SBUs measured for a combination of these factors. Refer to Table 10.5 for an example of the weighted-factor method applied to three different SBUs.

TABLE 10.5	Weighted-Factor Approach to Strategic Incentive Management

Strategic Business Unit Category	Factor	Weight
High Growth	Return on assets	10%
	Cash flow	0%
	Strategic-funds programs	45%
	Market-share increase	45%
		100%
Medium Growth	Return on assets	25%
	Cash flow	25%
	Strategic-funds programs	25%
	Market-share increase	25%
		100%
Low Growth	Return on assets	50%
	Cash flow	50%
	Strategic-funds programs	0%
	Market-share increase	0%
		100%

Source: Reprinted, by permission of the publisher, from "The Performance Measurement and Reward System: Critical to Strategic Management," by Paul J. Stonich, from *Organization Dynamics* (Winter 1984), p. 51. Copyright © 1984 by American Management Association, New York. All rights reserved.

2. **Long-term evaluation method.** The long-term evaluation method compensates managers for achieving objectives set over a multiyear period. An executive is promised some company stock or "performance units" (convertible into money) in amounts to be based on long-term performance. An executive committee, for example, might set a particular objective in terms of growth in earnings per share during a five-year period. The giving of awards would be contingent on the corporation's meeting that objective within the designated time limit. Any executive who leaves the corporation before the objective is met receives nothing. The typical emphasis on stock price makes this approach more applicable to top management than to business unit managers.

3. **Strategic-funds method.** The strategic-funds method encourages executives to look at developmental expenses as being different from those expenses required for current operations. The accounting statement for a corporate unit enters strategic funds as a separate entry below the current ROI. It is therefore possible to distinguish between those expense dollars consumed in the generation of current revenues and those invested in the future of the business. Therefore, the manager can be evaluated on both a short- and a long-term basis and has an incentive to invest strategic funds in the future. Refer to Table 10.6 for an example of the strategic-funds method applied to a business unit.

According to Stonich, "An effective way to achieve the desired strategic results through a reward system is to combine the weighted-factor, long-term evaluation, and strategic-funds approaches."[68] To do this, *first* segregate strategic funds from short-term funds, as is done in the strategic-funds method. *Second*, develop a weighted-factor chart for each SBU. *Third*, measure performance on three bases: the pretax profit indicted by the strategic-funds approach; the weighted factors; and the long-term evaluation of the SBUs' and the corporation's performance. These incentive plans will probably gain increasing acceptance by business corporations in the near future. General Electric and Westinghouse are two firms using a version of these measures.

TABLE 10.6	**Strategic-Funds Approach Applied to an SBU's Profit-and-Loss Statement**
Sales	$ 12,300,000
Cost of sales	− 6,900,000
Gross margin	$ 5,400,000
General and administrative expenses	− 3,700,000
Operating profit (return on sales)	$ 1,700,000
Strategic funds	− 1,000,000
Pretax profit	$ 700,000

Source: Reprinted, by permission of the publisher, from "The Performance Measurement and Reward System: Critical to Strategic Management" by Paul J. Stonich, *Organizational Dynamics* (Winter 1984). Copyright © 1984 by American Management Association, New York. All rights reserved.

SUMMARY AND CONCLUSION

The evaluation and control of performance is a five-step process: (1) determine what to measure, (2) establish standards for performance, (3) measure actual performance, (4) compare actual performance with the standard, and (5) take corrective action. Information coming from this process is fed back into the strategic control system so that managers at all levels in the hierarchy of control can monitor and correct for performance deviations.

Although the most commonly used measures of corporate performance are the various return ratios, measures based on a value-added or shareholder value approach can be of some use. Most corporations also monitor key performance objectives. If a corporation sets goals other than simple profitability or return on investment, it might wish to follow the example of Westinghouse and establish specific performance objectives, such as productivity improvement, for special attention. A stakeholder scorecard can also be of some value in the assessment of the corporation's impact on its environment. The strategic audit is recommended as a method by which activities throughout the corporation can be evaluated.

Divisions, SBUs, and functional units are often broken down into responsibility centers to aid control. Such areas are often categorized as standard cost centers, revenue centers, expense centers, profit centers, and investment centers. Budgets and periodic statistical reports are important control devices used in the monitoring of the implementation of major programs in business units.

A strategic information system is an important part of the evaluation and control process. By focusing on critical success factors, it can provide early warning signals to strategic managers. The system can be tailored to the business-level strategy being implemented in the SBU, so that the success of the strategy is ensured.

The monitoring and measurement of performance can result in dysfunctional side effects that negatively affect overall corporate performance. Among the likely side effects are a short-term orientation and goal displacement. These problems can be reduced if top management remembers that controls must focus on strategic goals. There should be as few controls as possible, and only meaningful activities and results should be monitored. Controls should be timely to both long-term and short-term orientations They should pinpoint exceptions, but should be used more to reward than to punish individuals.

Incentive plans should be based on long-term as well as short-term considerations. Three suggested approaches are the weighted-factor method, the long-term evaluation method, and the strategic-funds method.

A proper evaluation and control system should act to complete the loop shown in the strategic management model. It should feed back information important not only to the implementation of strategy, but also to the initial formulation of strategy. In terms of the strategic decision-making process depicted in Fig. 2.4, the data coming from evaluation and control are the basis for Step 1—evaluating current performance results. Because of this feedback effect, evaluation and control are the beginning as well as the end of the strategic management process.

DISCUSSION QUESTIONS

1. Is Fig. 10.1 a realistic model of the evaluation and control process? Why or why not?

2. Why bother with value-added measures, shareholder value, or a stakeholder's scorecard? Isn't it simpler to evaluate a corporation and its SBUs just by using standard measures like ROI or earnings per share?

3. What are the differences between strategic, tactical, and operational controls?

4. What are the pros and cons of using performance objectives to evaluate performance?

5. What is the difference between performance objectives and critical success factors?

6. What are the major types of responsibility centers? Briefly describe each type of center.

7. How much faith can a division or SBU manager place in a transfer price as a surrogate for a market price, in measurement of a profit center's performance?

8. Why are goal displacement and short-run orientation likely side effects of the monitoring of performance? What can a corporation do to avoid them?

9. Is the evaluation and control process appropriate for a corporation that emphasizes creativity? Are control and creativity compatible? Explain.

10. What are the guidelines for proper control?

NOTES

1. G. S Odiorne, "Measuring the Unmeasurable: Setting Standards for Management Performance," *Business Horizons* (July/August 1987), p. 73. Copyright © 1987 by the Foundation for the School of Business at Indiana University. Used with permission.

2. J. C. Camillus, *Strategic Planning and Management Control* (Lexington, Mass.: D. C. Heath, Lexington Books, 1986), p. 11.

3. J. A. Schmidt, "The Strategic Review," *Planning Review* (July/August 1988), pp. 14–19.

4. P. Lorange, M. F. S. Morton, and S. Ghoshal, *Strategic Control* (St. Paul, Minn.: West Publishing Co., 1986), pp. 11–14.

5. W. E. Deming, *Out of the Crisis* (Cambridge, Mass.: M.I.T. Center for Advanced Engineering Study, 1986).

6. Lorange, et al., *Strategic Control*, p. 124.

7. J. R. Meredith, "Strategic Control of Factory Automation," *Long Range Planning* (December 1987), p. 109.

8. *Ibid.*, p. 112.

9. W. G. Ouchi and M. A. Maguire, "Organizational Control: Two Functions," *Administrative Science Quarterly* (December 1975), pp. 559–569.

10. B. C. Reimann reporting on a presentation by W. H. Quick to The Conference Board, "A Session For Students of Shareholder Value Creation," *Planning Review* (May/June 1990), pp. 43–44.

11. B. C. Reimann and R. Thomas, "Value-Based Portfolio Planning: Improving Shareholder Return," in *Handbook of Business Strategy, 1986/87 Yearbook*, edited by W. D. Guth (Boston: Warren, Gorham and Lamont, 1986), pp. 21.2–21.3.

    J. Stern, "Think Cash and Risk—Forget Earnings Per Share," *Planning Review* (January/February 1988), pp. 6–9, 48.

12. R. E. Freeman, *Strategic Management: A Stakeholder Approach* (Boston: Pitman Publishing Co., 1984), pp. 177–181.

13. C. W. Hofer, "ROVA: A New Measure for Assessing Organizational Performance," in *Advances in Strategic Management*, Vol. 2, edited by R. Lamb (Greenwich, Conn.: JAI Press, 1983), pp. 43–55.

    C. W. Hofer and D. Schendel, *Strategy Formulation: Analytical Concepts* (St. Paul, Minn.: West Publishing Co., 1978), p. 130.

14. N. E. Swanson and L. A. Digman, "Organizational Performance Measures for Strategic Decisions: A PIMS-Based Investigation," in *Handbook of Business Strategy, 1986/1987 Yearbook*, edited by W. D. Guth (Boston: Warren, Gorham and Lamont, 1986), pp. 17.2–17.4.

    J. Bryant, "Assessing Company Strength Using Added Value," *Long Range Planning* (June 1989), pp. 34–44.

15. D. L. Wenner and R. W. LeBer, "Managing for Shareholder Value—From Top to Bottom," *Harvard Business Review* (November-December 1989), pp. 52–66.

16. B. Reimann, *Managing for Value: A Guide to Value-Based Strategic Management* (Oxford, Ohio: The Planning Forum, 1990).

    W. Kiechel III, "Corporate Strategy for the 1990s," *Fortune* (February 28, 1988), pp. 34–42.

17. A. Rappaport, "Have We Been Measuring Success with the Wrong Ruler?" *Wall Street Journal* (June 25, 1984), p. 22.

18. V. E. Millar, "The Evolution Toward Value-Based Financial Planning," *Information Strategy: The Executive's Journal* (Winter 1985), pp. 29–30.

    For more information on shareholder value analysis and its application, see the January/February and March/April 1988 issues of *Planning Review*.

19. P. Drucker, *The Practice of Management* (New York: Harper and Brothers, 1954, as reported by M. D. Richards, *Setting Strategic Goals and Objectives* (St. Paul, Minn.: West Publishing Co., 1986), pp. 16–17.

20. C. C. Barucki and G. D. Childs, "Productivity and

Quality Improvement: The Westinghouse Story," in *Strategic Human Resources Management*, edited by C. Fombrun, N. Tichy, and M. A. Devanna (New York: John Wiley and Sons, 1984), pp. 381–401.

21. S. J. Burchman and C. E. Schneier, "Assessing CEO Performance: It Goes Beyond the Numbers," *Directors and Boards* (Winter 1989), pp. 26–30.

22. P. Lorange, "Monitoring Strategic Progress and Ad Hoc Strategy Modification," in *Strategic Management Frontiers*, edited by J. H. Grant (Greenwich, Conn.: JAI Press, 1988), pp. 261–285.

23. R. L. Daft and N. B. Macintosh, "The Nature and Use of Formal Control Systems for Management Control and Strategy Implementation," *Journal of Management* (Spring 1984), pp. 43–66.

24. V. Govindarajan, "A Contingency Approach to Strategy Implementation at the Business-Unit Level: Integrating Administrative Mechanisms with Strategy," *Academy of Management Journal* (December 1988), pp. 828–853.

25. V. Govindarajan and J. Fisher, "Strategy, Control, Systems, and Resource Sharing: Effects on Business-Unit Performance," *Academy of Management Journal* (June 1990), pp. 259–285.

26. *Ibid.*, p. 280.

27. This discussion is based on R. N. Anthony, J. Dearden, and R. F. Vancil, *Management Control Systems* (Homewood, Ill.: Irwin, 1972), pp. 200–203.

28. Lorange, et al., *Strategic Control*, p. 69. Camillus, *Strategic Planning*, pp. 193–195.

29. Camillus, *Strategic Planning*, p. 196.

30. A. P. Sloan, Jr., *My Years with General Motors* (Garden City, N.Y.: Doubleday, Anchor Books, 1972), p. 159.

31. *Ibid.*, p. 161.

32. Millar, "Value-Based Financial Planning," p. 30.

33. J. R. Galbraith and R. K. Kazanjian, *Strategy Implementation: Structure, Systems and Process* (St. Paul, Minn.: West Publishing Co., 1986), pp. 85–86.

34. M. Hergert and D. Morris, "Accounting Data for Value Chain Analysis," *Strategic Management Journal* (March-April 1989), pp. 175–188.

35. J. A. Turner and H. C. Lucas, Jr., "Developing Strategic Information Systems," in *Handbook of Business Strategy*, edited by W. D. Guth (Boston: Warren, Gorham and Lamont, 1985), p. 21.2.

36. N. Gross, "Inquest for International Harvester," *Planning Review* (July-August 1987), p. 9.

37. J. Rockart, "Chief Executives Define Their Own Data Needs," *Harvard Business Review* (March-April 1979).

P. V. Jenster, "Using Critical Success Factors in Planning," *Long Range Planning* (August 1987), pp. 102–109.

38. Vilfredo Pareto, a nineteenth-century Italian economist, originated what is sometimes called the 80-20 rule—meaning that 20% of the known variables will produce 80% of the results. Business executives have found the rule to apply to many areas of their companies. For example, Illinois Tool Works found that 80% of the business at any one plant tends to come from 20% of the customers—people who order only a handful of products but in huge quantities. Bank executives report a similar phenomenon regarding customer deposits. See R. Henkoff, "The Ultimate Nuts & Bolts Co.," *Fortune* (July 16, 1990), pp. 70–73.

39. Y. P. Freund, "Critical Success Factors," *Planning Review* (July/August 1988), p. 20.

40. C. M. Jones, "GTE's Strategic Tracking System," *Planning Review* (September 1986), p. 28.

41. W. R. King, "Strategic Management Decision Support Systems," in *Strategic Management Frontiers*, edited by J. H. Grant (Greenwich, Conn.: JAI Press, 1988) pp. 237–259.

42. E. M. Koerner, "Integrating Information Systems for Competitive Advantage at Merrill Lynch," *Long Range Planning* (April 1990), pp. 27–34.

43. G. L. Parsons, "Information Technology: A New Competitive Weapon," *Sloan Management Review* (Fall 1983), p. 11.

44. For other examples of the use of computerized strategic information systems to gain competitive advantage, see R. I. Benjamin, D. W. de Long, and M. F. S. Morton, "Electronic Data Interchange: How Much Competitive Advantage?" *Long Range Planning* (February 1990), pp. 29–40; and B. C. Reimann, "Strategic Management in an Electronic Age: Exploiting the Power of Information Technology," *International Journal of Management* (September 1987), pp. 438–451.

45. L. G. Hrebiniak and W. F. Joyce, *Implementing Strategy* (New York: Macmillan, 1984), pp. 198–199.

46. R. M. Hodgetts and M. S. Wortman, *Administrative Policy*, 2nd ed. (New York: John Wiley and Sons, 1980), p. 128.

47. S. B. Graves and S. A. Waddock, "Institutional Ownership and Control: Implications for Long-term Corporate Strategy," *Academy of Management Executive* (February 1990), pp. 75–83.

48. J. R. Wooldridge and C. C. Snow, "Stock Market Reaction to Strategic Investment Decisions," *Strategic Management Journal* (September 1990), pp. 353–363. G. Hector, "Yes, You *Can* Manage Long Term," *Fortune* (November 21, 1988), pp. 64–76.

49. R. Ferracone, "More Executive Pay Linked to Company Performance," *Journal of Business Strategy* (May/June 1990), pp. 63–64.

50. "Executive Compensation: Even Those Awarding Pay Aren't Sure They're Doing It Right," *Wall Street Journal* (July 3, 1990), p. A1.

51. D. R. Schmidt and K. L. Fowler, "Post-Acquisition Financial Performance and Executive Compensation," *Strategic Management Journal* (November-December 1990), pp. 559–569.

52. T. A Stewart, "Why Budgets Are Bad for Business," *Fortune* (June 4, 1990), pp. 179–190.

53. G. Hector, "Cute Tricks on the Bottom Line," *Fortune* (April 24, 1990), pp. 193–200.

    C. K. Bart, "Budgeting Gamesmanship," *Academy of Management Executive* (November 1988), pp. 285–294.

54. H. R. Bobbitt, Jr., R. H. Breinholt, R. H. Doktor, and J. P. McNaul, *Organizational Behavior*, 2nd ed. (Englewood Cliffs, N.J.: Prentice Hall, 1978), p. 99.

55. J. C. Worthy and R. P. Neuschel, *Emerging Issues in Corporate Governance* (Evanston, Ill.: Northwestern University Press, 1984), p. 84.

56. S. Kerr, "On the Folly of Rewarding A, While Hoping for B," *Academy of Management Journal* (December 1975), pp. 769–783.

57. Ouchi calls this "clan control." See W. Ouchi, *Theory Z* (Reading, Mass.: Addison-Wesley, 1981).

58. T. J. Peters and R. H. Waterman, *In Search of Excellence* (New York: HarperCollins, 1982), pp. 75–76.

59. C. A. O'Reilly III, B. G. Main, and G. S. Crystal, "CEO Compensation as Tournament and Social Comparison: A Tale of Two Theories," *Administrative Science Quarterly* (June 1988), pp. 257–274.

60. Schmidt and Fowler, "Post-Acquisition Financial Performance."

M. C. Jensen and K. J. Murphy, "CEO Incentives—It's Not How Much You Pay, But How," *Harvard Business Review* (May-June 1990), pp. 138–153.

61. L. R. Gomez-Mejia, H. Tosi, and T. Hinkin, "Managerial Control, Performance, and Executive Compensation," *Academy of Management Journal* (March 1987), pp. 51–70.

62. A. Rappaport, "How To Design Value-Contributing Executive Incentives," *Journal of Business Strategy* (Fall 1983), p. 50.

63. K. R. Andrews, "Directors' Responsibility for Corporate Strategy," *Harvard Business Review* (November-December 1980), p. 32.

64. B. Gerhart and G. T. Milkovich, "Organizational Differences in Managerial Compensation and Financial Performance," *Academy of Management Journal* (December 1990), pp. 663–691.

    S. Finkelstein and D. C. Hambrick, "Chief Executive Compensation: A Study of the Intersection of Markets and Political Processes," *Strategic Management Journal* (March-April 1989), pp. 121–134.

65. A. Giller, "Organizational Characteristics of Successful Business Units," in *Handbook of Business Strategy, 1987/1988 Yearbook*, edited by H. Babian and H. E. Glass (Boston: Warren, Gorham and Lamont, 1987), p. 8.7.

66. D. B. Balkin and L. R. Gomez-Mejia, "Matching Compensation and Organizational Strategies," *Strategic Management Journal* (February 1990), pp. 153–169.

67. P. J. Stonich, "The Performance Measurement and Reward System: Critical to Strategic Management," *Organizational Dynamics* (Winter 1984), pp. 45–57.

68. *Ibid.*, p. 53.

OTHER STRATEGIC ISSUES

CHAPTER ELEVEN

Strategic Issues in Multinational Corporations

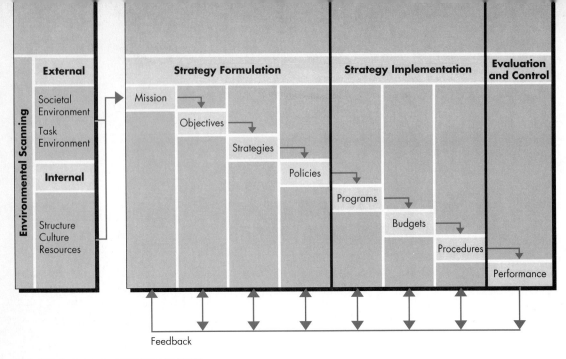

STRATEGIC MANAGEMENT MODEL

The revolutionary thing that is occurring is that national economies can no longer be understood—or operated within—unless you understand them in connection with all other economies. There are no islands anymore.
. . . Countries will not make and export products in the way they have in the past. Instead you will have value added: You will make a transistor in Korea and a plastic case in Taiwan, you will assemble it in Ireland, and sell it in all the countries that will buy it.[1]

Walter Wriston, Past CEO of Citicorp

In 1965, Marshall McLuhan suggested that advances in communications and transportation technologies were drawing the peoples of the world closer together. As intercontinental travel times decreased, the world started to shrink to become a "*global village*" of interdependent people.[2] Indeed, the modern world is rapidly reaching into the most remote locations (and vice versa). Television is a global phenomenon—linking nations together as they watch the Olympics as well as the bombing of Baghdad. Ted Turner's Cable Network News (CNN) was the first truly global television channel, reaching 50.8 million U.S. homes and beaming news to viewers in 83 nations via satellite. CNN is even sold as an over-the-air subscription service in Moscow.[3]

Since 1950, world trade has grown twice as fast as world economic production. This expansion in trade has been supported by a 50% increase in foreign direct investment and even more growth in international stock, bond, and foreign exchange markets.[4] The global economy is now close to 50% integrated versus 25% in 1980 and 10% in 1950.[5] Countries throughout the world are courting multinational corporations as never before in hopes of capturing jobs, technology, capital, and greater economic prosperity.[6]

In the U.S. alone, there are more than 3,500 multinational corporations (MNCs), 30,000 exporting manufacturers, 25,000 companies with overseas branches and affiliates, and 40,000 firms operating in other countries on an *ad hoc* basis. Not only are U.S. based multinationals increasing their investments in production facilities and companies in other countries, but foreign-based MNCs are also doing the same in the U.S., Canada, and Mexico. IBM's sales from its overseas operations account for over 50% of its total revenues. The same is true for Coca Cola and General Motors.[7] As shown in Illustrative Example 11.1, which describes recent developments in the tire and rubber industry, international considerations have become crucial to the strategic decisions of any large business corporation.

11.1 THE MULTINATIONAL CORPORATION (MNC)

The multinational corporation is a very special type of international firm. Any U.S. company can call itself "international" if it has a small branch office in, say, Juárez or Toronto. An **international company** is one that engages in any combination of activities, from exporting/importing to full-scale manufacturing, in foreign countries. The **multinational corporation** (MNC), in contrast, is a highly developed international company with a deep worldwide involvement, plus a global perspective in its management and decision making. A more specific definition of an MNC is suggested by Dymsza.[8]

1. Although a multinational corporation may not do business in every region of the world, its *decision makers consider opportunities globally.*
2. A *considerable portion of an MNC's assets are invested internationally.* One authority suggests that a firm becomes global when 20% of its assets are in other countries. Another suggests that the point is reached when operations in other nations account for at least 35% of the corporation's total sales and profits.
3. The corporation *engages in international production and operates plants in several countries.* These plants may range from assembly to fully integrated facilities.
4. *Managerial decision making is based on a worldwide perspective.* The international business is no longer a sideline or segregated activity. International operations are integrated into the corporation's overall business.

Porter proposes that multinationals operate in world industries that vary on a continuum from multidomestic to global (see Fig. 11.1).[9] **Multidomestic industries** are specific to each country or group of countries. This type of international industry

ILLUSTRATIVE EXAMPLE 11.1

Global Competition in the Tire and Rubber Industry

The tire and rubber industry has recently experienced one of the most difficult times in its existence. Intense global competition beginning in the 1960s led industry experts to predict that only four or five tire companies would be strong enough to survive as independent profitable entities through the end of the century. It was agreed during the 1970s that Goodyear Tire and Rubber would be one of those strong enough to survive the coming shakeout to continue dominating the stagnant worldwide tire market. But what would be the future of well-known U.S. companies such as Firestone, B. F. Goodrich, General Tire, Cooper, Mohawk, Armstrong, and Uniroyal, as well as the venerable European firms of Dunlop of Britain, Michelin of France, Continental of Germany, and Pirelli of Italy?

By the early 1980s, Firestone, in particular, was in desperate trouble. The third-largest tire company in the world and second-largest in the U.S., Firestone was burdened with obsolete plants, a bloated payroll, and a mountain of debt. In 1988, after an unsuccessful attempt by Pirelli to acquire Firestone, Japan's Bridgestone Corporation purchased Firestone's tire manufacturing business for $2.6 million. It was a case of acquire or be acquired as the now-global tire and rubber industry consolidated into a few survivors.

By 1991, the worldwide tire industry was dominated by three multinational corporations, each with approximately 20% of the world market share: Goodyear, Michelin, and Bridgestone. Michelin, with its acquisition in 1989 of the previously merged Uniroyal Goodrich Tire Company, was arguably the world's largest tire maker. Pirelli and Continental each had about 8% of the world market. Pirelli had reacted to its failure to acquire Firestone by purchasing Armstrong Tire—a key supplier of tires to Sears, Roebuck and Company. Continental of Germany bought General Tire in 1987 and initiated a joint venture with Yokohama Rubber Company and Toyo Tire and Rubber Company of Japan. Through its 1990 joint ventures with East German and Czechoslovakian tire companies, Continental appeared to pass Pirelli as the world's fourth-largest tire company. Dunlop, the U.K. company founded by the inventor of the pneumatic tire, was mostly owned by Sumitomo, a Japanese trading company. In addition to Goodyear, only medium-sized Cooper Tire and Rubber of Findlay, Ohio, survived as the last publicly owned U.S. tire company.

The future of the tire and rubber industry appears to be one of continuing acquisitions and joint ventures as the remaining companies jostle to see which will survive intact at the end of the twentieth century. Pirelli is already making overtures to Continental to merge their tire businesses in order to challenge the dominance of the three giants in the world market. Dennis Rich, Goodyear's Director of Business Planning, stated his company's view: "We no longer have U.S. competition. They're all foreign names now. They're rapidly growing and they're very capable."

Sources: J. Peterson, "Why Firestone Gave Up on Tiremaking," *Des Moines Register* (March 27, 1988), p. 1; G. Collins and T. Roth, "Pirelli Proposes Tire Merger to Continental," *Wall Street Journal* (September 18, 1990), p. A4; T. Roth, "Continental AG and Czech Firm Sign Tire Accord," *Wall Street Journal* (June 20, 1990), p. A15; E. S. Browning, "Long-Term Thinking and Paternalistic Ways Carry Michelin to Top," *Wall Street Journal* (January 5, 1990), p. A1, A8.

FIGURE 11.1	Continuum of International Industries

Multidomestic ←———————————————————————→ Global

Industry in which companies tailor their products to the specific needs of consumers in a particular country.

- Retailing
- Insurance
- Banking

Industry in which companies manufacture and sell the same products, with only minor adjustents made for individual countries around the world.

- Automobiles
- Tires
- Television sets

---

is a collection of essentially domestic industries, like retailing and insurance. The activities in an MNC's subsidiary in this type of industry are essentially independent of the activities of the MNC's subsidiaries in other countries. In each country the MNC tailors its products or services to the very specific needs of consumers in that particular country. **Global industries,** in contrast, operate worldwide, with only small adjustments made by MNCs for country-specific circumstances. A global industry is one in which an MNC's activities in one country are significantly affected by its activities in other countries. MNCs produce products or services in various locations throughout the world and sell them, making only minor adjustments for specific country requirements, all over the world. Examples of global industries are commercial aircraft, television sets, semiconductors, copiers, automobiles, watches, and, of course, tires. The largest industrial corporations in the world in terms of dollar sales are, for the most part, multinational corporations operating in global industries.

≈ 230

11.2 BASIC CONCEPTS OF INTERNATIONAL TRADE

The economic theories underlying the concept of free international trade among nations are those of absolute advantage and comparative advantage. Recently, these concepts have been challenged by the notion that it is competitive advantage, not comparative advantage, that determines a nation's wealth.

ABSOLUTE ADVANTAGE

In his book *Wealth of Nations*, Adam Smith proposed the theory of **absolute advantage,** which states that certain countries are able to produce certain goods more efficiently than others. Their advantage may stem from a natural situation, such as natural resources and climate, or it may evolve from a learned skill or technology, such as the Danish skill in designing distinctive silver tableware. Smith reasoned that if international trade was completely unrestricted (in effect, an international laissez-faire), each country would specialize in those products in which it had an absolute advantage. Through specialization, the companies in each country would become larger and more efficient. A country could then use the excess of its specialized production to buy more imports than it could otherwise have produced.

COMPARATIVE ADVANTAGE

In 1817, David Ricardo expanded on Smith's theory by proposing the theory of **comparative advantage.** This theory states that even if one country has an absolute advantage in producing *all* the products it wants, it will still gain from international trade if it specializes in those products that it can produce more efficiently than other products. Because the country's companies focus their energies on those products from which they can derive the greatest advantage, they will produce more goods at lower costs than could companies anywhere else in the world. Ricardo's conclusion reinforced Smith's. Everyone receives the maximum benefit of international trade when nations allow their business organizations to exchange the products resulting from their comparative advantage, unencumbered by tariffs and other trade barriers. For a simplified example of absolute and comparative advantage, see Illustrative Example 11.2.[10]

PORTER'S COMPETITIVE ADVANTAGE VERSUS COMPARATIVE ADVANTAGE

The value of these economic theories in explaining international trade fell considerably in the latter half of the twentieth century. Both Smith and Ricardo assumed the factors of production to be immobile between nations and thus not an influence in the flow of international trade. Today, of course, people, capital, and technology travel the globe freely—and comparative advantage moves with them.[11] In addition, the increasing globalization of industries means that many multinational corporations are "decoupled" from a particular country. As Walter Wriston pointed out in the quotation beginning this chapter, MNCs operating in global industries produce various parts of a product in many locations throughout the world, assemble them somewhere else, and sell them to markets worldwide. With technology circumventing the use of many scarce elements in production (for example, ceramics substituting for aluminum) and many less-developed countries reaching a basic "threshold level" of development, competitive advantage replaces comparative advantage as the most useful concept in today's international trade.[12]

National Competitive Advantage

In his book *The Competitive Advantage of Nations*, Porter proposes that four factors determine the creation of **competitive advantage** of nations (see Fig. 11.2).

1. **Factor Conditions.** The nation's position in the basic factors of production, such as labor or infrastructure, necessary to compete in a given industry.
2. **Demand Conditions.** The nature of home demand (demand within the specific nation under consideration) for the industry's product or service.
3. **Related and Supporting Industries.** The presence or absence in the nation of supplier industries and related industries that are internationally competitive.
4. **Firm Strategy, Structure, and Rivalry.** The conditions in the nation governing

copy

ILLUSTRATIVE EXAMPLE 11.2

Examples of Absolute and Comparative Advantage

Suppose a country produces 1 million bushels of corn and 5 million bushels of beans each year, but its people want more corn. Should it simply plant more corn and less beans? This seems like a reasonable solution until one notes that the soil and water are much better for growing beans than for corn. Each acre planted can produce twice as much bean crop as corn. It takes the same amount of work, and the seeds, fertilizer, and other costs are the same for the farmers regardless of the crop planted. Suppose that the neighboring country has different soil and on every acre planted is able to produce twice as much corn as beans.

The concept of *absolute advantage* in international trade suggests that when both countries are considered, the first country has an advantage over the second country in producing beans, but the second has an advantage over the first in producing corn. The logical conclusion is that the first country should specialize in producing beans (where it has absolute advantage) and the second should plant only corn (where it also has absolute advantage). The result would be that the first country would produce 7 million bushels of beans each year and *no* corn (with the 2 to 1 advantage of beans to corn, the 1 million bushels of corn would be replaced by 2 million bushels of beans). The reverse would be true in the second country. If the countries are able to trade freely with each other, both countries will be able to have more corn and beans if they each specialize in the crop with which there is advantage, than if both countries try to produce both crops.

Therefore, in answer to the question posed earlier, if a country wants more corn but has an absolute advantage in the production of beans, it should plant more beans. The bean excess can be exported to another country in exchange for more corn than the first country could ever produce with the same resources.

What happens, however, when the first country can produce more corn *and* beans per acre planted than can its neighboring country? Is there any benefit to trade? According to the concept of *comparative advantage*, it still makes sense to specialize as long as the first country is able to grow more of one crop than another crop per acre planted. As an analogy, suppose the best architect in town also happens to be the best carpenter. Would it make sense for him to build his own house? Certainly not, because he can earn more money per hour by devoting all his time to his job as an architect even though he has to employ a carpenter less skillful than himself to build the house. In the same manner, the first country will gain if it concentrates its resources on the production of that commodity it can produce most efficiently. It will earn enough money from the export of that commodity to still import what it needs from its less-efficient neighbor country.

how companies are created, organized, and managed, plus the nature of domestic rivalry.[13]

According to Porter: "Gaining advantage in the first place requires a new approach to competing, whether it is perceiving and then exploiting a factor advantage, discovering an underserved segment, creating new product features, or changing the process by which a product is made. . . . The determinants of the 'diamond' [depicted in Fig. 11.2] and the interactions among them create the forces that shape the likelihood, direction, and speed of improvement and innovation by a nation's firms in an industry."[14] Porter thus extends the Ricardian concept of comparative

FIGURE 11.2 | **Determinants of National Competitive Advantage**

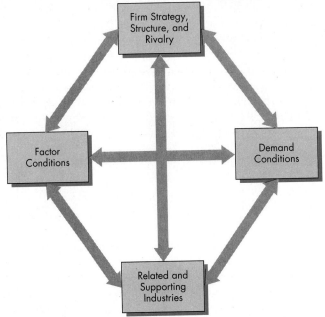

Source: M. E. Porter, *The Competitive Advantage of Nations* (New York: The Free Press, 1990), p. 72. Copyright © 1990 by Michael Porter. Reprinted by permission of The Free Press.

advantage to include not only the basic (and somewhat constant) factors of production, but also shifting differences in technology, factor quality, and methods of competing.

Stages of National Competitive Development

Porter further proposes that nations evolve through four stages of competitive development, reflecting the sources of advantage of a nation's firms in international competition and the nature and extent of internationally successful industries:

■ **Stage 1: Factor Driven.** In Stage 1 of development, industries within the nation draw their advantage almost solely from the basic factors of production. For example, the huge supply of cheap oil drives the success of oil companies in the Middle East. This stage fits Smith's and Ricardo's concepts of absolute and comparative advantage. In this stage, nations that wish to advance to the next stage are concerned with the process of technology transfer. *International technology transfer* refers not to the process of taking new technology from the lab to the marketplace (as defined in Chapter 5), but to the movement of sophisticated technology from an economically advanced country to a less-developed country.[15]

■ **Stage 2: Investment Driven.** In Stage 2, foreign technology and methods are not just applied (as in Stage 1) but improved on. Competitive advantages result from improving basic factor conditions as well as firm strategy, structure, and rivalry. Korea, for example, has invested heavily in shipbuilding to stretch well beyond its factor advantages in ocean harbors (a factor shared with many other nations) and to gain worldwide competitive advantage.

- **Stage 3: Innovation Driven.** At Stage 3 the full "diamond" (Fig. 11.2) is in place in a wide range of industries that support and reinforce each other. (For example, steel, electronics, and plastics industries, among others, are needed to support the development of a successful automobile industry.) Firms in this stage not only borrow and improve technology from other nations, they actually create new innovations. The U.K. achieved this stage in the first half of the nineteenth century. The U.S., Germany, and Sweden did so about the beginning of the twentieth century. Japan achieved this stage during the 1970s.

- **Stage 4: Wealth Driven.** According to Porter, nations pass through the first three stages of competitive development if they are willing and able to sustain the process of upgrading national competitive advantage. In Stage 4 the driving force is the wealth that has been achieved in the earlier stages. This stage thus leads ultimately to economic decline as individual firms and then industries lose their competitive advantage—costs go up, quality drops, and innovation slows. There is a narrowing of the range of industries in which firms can sustain competitive advantage. During the 1970s, for example, firms within the steel, auto, and electronics industries in the U.S. lost many of their advantages to Japanese companies. In the 1990s, the still-strong U.S. computer and aerospace industries were facing stronger competition worldwide. Even the strong financial institutions (characteristic of wealth-driven nations) of the U.K. and the U.S. were being strongly challenged. Stage 4 decline is not inevitable. According to Porter, "The decline of a wealth-driven economy can be arrested through policy changes, major discontinuities, or shifts in social values."[16]

11.3 INTERNATIONAL ISSUES IN ENVIRONMENTAL SCANNING

As described in Chapter 1, the strategic management process includes environmental scanning, strategy formulation, strategy implementation, and evaluation and control. To begin the process, the strategic managers of a multinational corporation must scan both the external international environment for opportunities and threats, and its own internal environment for strengths and weaknesses.

SCANNING FOR INTERNATIONAL OPPORTUNITIES AND THREATS

The dominant issue in the management of an organization operating internationally is the external environment. For each country or group of countries in which a company operates, there is a whole new societal environment with a different set of economic, technological, political-legal, and sociocultural variables for it to face. The type of relationship a multinational corporation can have with each factor in its task environment varies from one country to another and from one region to another. International societal environments vary so widely that a corporation's internal environment and strategic management process must be very flexible. Cultural trends in Germany, for example, have resulted in the inclusion of worker representatives in corporate strategic planning. Differences in societal environments strongly affect the ways in which an MNC conducts its marketing, financial, manufacturing, and other functional activities. Some of the variables to be monitored in the various international societal environments are listed in Table 11.1.

Before a company plans its strategy for a particular international location, it must scan the particular societal and task environment(s) in question for opportunities and threats, and compare these with its own organizational strengths and weaknesses. For example, if a company wishes to operate successfully in a global industry such as automobiles, tires, electronics, or watches, it must be prepared to establish a significant presence in the three developed areas of the world known collectively as **the triad**. Coined by Kenichi Ohmae, Managing Director of the Tokyo office of McKinsey & Company, this term stands for the three markets of Japan, North America, and Western Europe, which now form a single market with common needs.[17] Arguing that consumers' behavior is influenced more by their educational background and disposable income than by ethnic characteristics, Ohmae proposes that strategic managers of MNCs must treat the inhabitants of the triad as a single race of consumers with shared needs and aspirations. The decision by the 12 partners of the European Community to abolish national frontiers in 1992 to allow the free movement of goods and people certainly supports Ohmae's argument.

Focusing on the triad is essential for an MNC pursuing success in a global industry, according to Ohmae, because close to 90% of all high-value-added, high-technology manufactured goods are produced and consumed in North America, Western Europe, and Japan. Ideally, a company should have a significant presence in each of these regions so that it can produce and market its products simultaneously in all three areas. Otherwise, it will lose competitive advantage to triad-oriented MNCs. No longer can an MNC develop and market a new product in one part of the world before it exports it to other developed countries.

In searching for an advantageous market or manufacturing location, a multinational corporation must gather and evaluate data on strategic factors in many countries and regions. Because of its global perspective, an MNC might use comparative advantage to its benefit by making machine parts in Brazil, assembling them as engines in Germany, installing the engines in auto bodies in Italy, and shipping completed cars to the U.S. for sale. This strategy serves to reduce the risk to the MNC of operating in only one country, but exposes it to a series of smaller risks in more countries. Therefore, multinational corporations must be able to deal with political and economic risk in many diverse countries and regions.

Some firms, such as American Can Company, develop an elaborate computerized system to rank investment risks. Small companies can hire outside consultants such as Chicago's Associated Consultants International or Boston's Arthur D. Little, Inc. to provide political-risk assessments. Among the many systems that exist to assess political and economic risks are the Political System Stability Index, the Business Environment Risk Index, Business International's Country Assessment Service, and Frost and Sullivan's World Political Risk Forecasts.[18] (For a summary

TABLE 11.1	Some Important Variables in International Societal Environments		
Economic	**Technological**	**Political-Legal**	**Sociocultural**
Economic development	Regulations on technology transfer	Form of government	Customs, norms, values
Per capita income	Energy availability/cost	Political ideology	Language
Climate	Natural resource availability	Tax laws	Demographics
GNP trends	Transportation network	Stability of government	Life expectancies
Monetary and fiscal policies	Skill level of work force	Government attitude toward foreign companies	Social institutions
Unemployment level	Patent-trademark protection	Regulations on foreign ownership of assets	Status symbols
Currency convertibility	Information-flow infrastructure	Strength of opposition groups	Life-style
Wage levels		Trade regulations	Religious beliefs
Nature of competition		Protectionist sentiment	Attitudes toward foreigners
Membership in regional economic associations		Foreign policies	Literacy level
		Terrorist activity	
		Legal system	

of Frost and Sullivan's risk index, see the March/April 1990 issue of *Planning Review*.)[19] Regardless of the source of data, a firm must develop its own method of assessing risk.[20] It must decide on its most important risk factors and then assign weights to each.

SCANNING FOR INTERNATIONAL STRENGTHS AND WEAKNESSES

Any company desiring to move into the international arena will need to assess its own strengths and weaknesses. An organization's chances for success are enhanced if it has or can develop the following capabilities:

1. **Technological Lead.** An innovative approach or a new product or a new process gives one a short-term monopolistic position.
2. **A Strong Trade Name.** If a well-known product has snob appeal, a higher profit margin can cover initial entry costs.
3. **Advantage of Scale.** A large corporation has the advantage of low unit costs and a financial base strong enough that it can weather setbacks.
4. **A Scanning Capability.** An ability to search successfully and efficiently for opportunities will take on greater importance in international dealings.
5. **An Outstanding Product or Service.** A solid product or service is more likely to have staying power in international competition.
6. **An Outstanding International Executive.** The presence of an executive who understands international situations and can develop a core of local execu-

tives who can work well with the home office is likely to result in the building of a strong and long-lasting international organization.[21]

11.4 INTERNATIONAL ISSUES IN STRATEGY FORMULATION

Strategy formulation becomes much more complex as a company moves into the international arena. Top management must review its current mission and objectives to decide if they are still relevant for international activities.[22] International strategic alternatives must be considered in light of a company's strengths and weaknesses and the opportunities and threats present in the country under consideration. International portfolio analysis may be used to help evaluate these strategic factors.

INTERNATIONAL PORTFOLIO ANALYSIS

To aid international strategic planning, Harrell and Kiefer show how portfolio analysis can be applied to international markets.[23] As depicted in Fig. 11.3, each axis summarizes a host of data concerning the attractiveness of a particular country and the competitive strength of a particular product.

A country's **attractiveness** is composed of its market size, the market rate of growth, the extent and type of government regulation, and economic and political factors. A product's **competitive strength** is composed of its market share, product fit, contribution margin, and market support. The two scales form the axes of the matrix in Fig. 11.3. Those products falling in the upper left generally should receive funding for growth, whereas products in the lower right are prime for "harvesting," or divesting. Those products falling in the lower left to upper right diagonal require selective funding strategies. Those falling in the upper right block require additional funding if the product is to contribute in the future to the firm's profits. Joint ventures or divestitures would be most appropriate if cash is limited. Those falling in the center and lower left blocks are probably good candidates for "milking." They can produce strong cash flows in the short run.[24]

Portfolio analysis might not be useful, however, to those MNCs operating in a global industry rather than a multidomestic one. In discussing the importance of global industries, Porter argues against the use of Harrell and Kiefer's recommended portfolio analysis on a country-by-country basis:

> In a global industry, however, managing international activities like a portfolio will undermine the possibility of achieving competitive advantage. In a global industry, a firm must in some way integrate its activities on a worldwide basis to capture the linkage among countries.[25]

POPULAR INTERNATIONAL STRATEGIES

Depending on its situation and its mission and objectives, a multinational corporation can select from several strategic options the most appropriate methods for it to use in entering a foreign market or establishing manufacturing facilities in another country. Some of the more popular international strategies are exporting, licensing,

| FIGURE 11.3 | **Portfolio Matrix for Plotting Products by Country** |

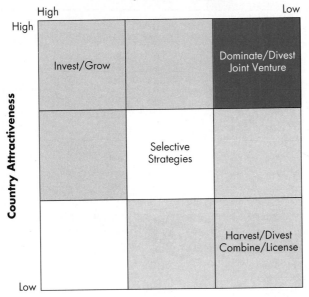

Source: G. D. Harrell and R. O. Kiefer, "Multinational Strategic Market Portfolios," *MSU Business Topics* (Winter 1981), p. 7. Reprinted by permission.

joint ventures, acquisitions, green-field development, production sharing, turnkey operations, and management contracts.

- **Exporting.** Simply shipping goods produced in the company's home country to other countries for marketing is a good way to minimize risk and to experiment with a specific product. It can be conducted in several ways. For instance, the company could choose to handle all critical functions itself, or it could contract these functions to an export management company.
- **Licensing.** Under a licensing agreement, the licensing firm grants rights to another firm in the host country to produce and/or sell a product. The licensee pays compensation to the licensing firm in return for technical expertise. This is an especially useful strategy if the trademark or brand name is well known, but the MNC does not have sufficient funds to finance its entering the country directly. Anheuser-Busch is using this strategy to produce and market Budweiser beer in the U.K., Japan, Israel, Australia, Korea, and the Philippines. This strategy also becomes important if the country makes entry via investment either difficult or impossible. There is always the danger, however, that the licensee might develop its competence to the point that it becomes a competitor to the licensing firm.
- **Joint Ventures.** Joint ventures are very popular with MNCs. Companies often form joint ventures to combine the resources and expertise needed for the development of new products or technologies.[26] The corporation engages in

Maytag Corporation: The Emerging Global Appliance Market

The focus of attention in the major home appliance industry in the early 1990s was on Europe—specifically, on the economic integration of the European Community (EC) and the rapidly opening markets of Eastern Europe. The 12-nation European Community was unifying into a true common market. Barriers to free trade were being eliminated or standardized, including borders and customs controls, technical product and safety standards, and excise and value-added taxes. The goal was to enable European companies to operate as easily throughout the 12 nations as companies operated in the United States. The largest U.S. appliance manufacturers wanted to be a part of this European phenomenon while the doors were still open to outsiders. The EC requirement of at least 60% local content (amount of the product actually produced in an EC country) to avoid tariffs made a European presence imperative. The Japanese companies Hitachi, Mitsubishi, Panasonic, Sanyo, Sharp, and Toshiba wanted to use their strengths in the production of microwave ovens and compact appliances to become a strong force in Europe as well.

The European appliance manufacturers did not want to be left out of future developments. The Swedish firm of A.B. Electrolux was in good position to dominate the coming global market. The Dutch firm of Philips (traditionally the second largest European producer of white goods after A.B. Electrolux) had decided to pool its appliance resources with Whirlpool in a joint venture to generate a single brand that they would sell globally. Other strong European competitors were Thomson-Brandt, which traditionally dominated France, Siemens-Bosch and AEG Telefunken, which used their domination of the German market to export aggressively, and Merloni and Candy of Italy. The British General Electric Company (GEC) and Hoover dominated the United Kingdom's appliance market. Concerned about its future, GEC joined General Electric (GE) of the U.S. in a joint venture and planned to grow with GE through acquisitions.

Home appliances were becoming more alike throughout the world as the European visual style of appliance design was being copied in Asia and the Americas. Technology and materials used in

international ownership at a much lower risk. A joint venture may be an association between an MNC and a firm in the host country or a government agency in that country. A quick method of obtaining local management, it also reduces the risks of expropriation and harassment by host country officials. Disadvantages of joint ventures include loss of control, lower profits, probability of conflicts with partners, and the likely transfer of technological advantage to the local partner. Joint ventures are typically meant to be temporary, especially by the Japanese, who view them as a way to rectify a competitive weakness until they can achieve long-term dominance in the partnership.[27]

- **Acquisitions.** A relatively quick way to move into an international area is to purchase another company already operating in that area. Synergistic benefits can result if the MNC acquires a firm with strong complementary product lines and a good distribution network. Maytag Corporation's acquisition of

~ 150

CONTINUED

the manufacturing process were easily obtainable. Consequently, developments in one part of the world were being quickly copied elsewhere. During the 1990s, the major home appliance industry was expected to continue evolving from a multi-domestic to a global industry.

Through its acquisition of the Hoover Company in 1988, Maytag Corporation moved into the international home appliance marketplace. Hoover was known worldwide for its floor care products and throughout Europe and Australia for its washers, dryers, dishwashers, microwave ovens, and refrigerators. Previous to the acquisition, Maytag's international revenues were too small to even report. Maytag's CEO Daniel Krumm pointed out the importance to Maytag Corporation of this international acquisition strategy:

> American appliances are virtually un-salable in Europe, or most places in the world, and vice versa. Our homes are different, the sizes of our kitchens, even the standard dimensions of things are so different. . . . . The addition of Hoover

makes Maytag about a $3 billion-a-year corporation consisting of 12 companies. We now have 28 manufacturing operations in eight countries, and approximately 28,000 employees.

Unfortunately, the now-multinational Maytag Corporation was not in the best position to compete globally as the twentieth century was coming to an end. Its acquisition of Hoover was completed just as the major home appliance market in the U.K. slumped. Elsewhere in Europe, Hoover was important in vacuum cleaners, but only a minor player in major appliances. The combination of heavy debt and low stock price in 1991 prevented Maytag from using acquisitions to push deeper into Europe. Meanwhile, the excitement of a newly integrating Europe prevented many from noticing the rapidly growing markets of Asia. The aggressive growth of A.B. Electrolux and Whirlpool in the Western world and of various Japanese appliance makers in the Eastern world might squeeze out not only the purely domestic appliance companies like Raytheon, but also emerging global companies like Maytag.

Hoover gave it entry into Europe through Hoover's strength in home appliances in the U.K. and in its vacuum cleaner distribution centers on the European continent (see the *boxed example* of Maytag). In some countries, however, acquisitions can be difficult to arrange because of a lack of available information about potential candidates. Government restrictions on ownership, such as the U.K.'s requirement that limits foreign ownership of British corporations handling defense work to only 15% of total common stock, can also discourage acquisitions.[28]

- **Green-Field Development**. If a corporation does not want to attain another firm's existing facilities through acquisition, it may choose a green-field development, or the building of a manufacturing facility from scratch. This is usually a far more complicated and expensive operation than acquisition, but it allows the MNC more freedom in designing the plant, choosing suppliers, and hiring a work force. An Italian semiconductor manufacturer, SGS-Ates Componenti Elettronici S.p.A., selected this strategy. According to its Vice-President of Marketing, Richard Pieranunzi: "To find a company that exactly matched our needs would be difficult. And we didn't want to buy other people's problems."[29]

- **Production Sharing.** Coined by Peter Drucker, the term *production sharing* means the process of combining the higher labor skills and technology available in the developed countries with the lower-cost labor available in developing countries. Since 1970, U.S. imports under production-sharing arrangements have been increasing at a rate of more than 20% a year.[30] By locating an assembly plant, called a **maquiladora**, in Ciudad Juarez, Mexico, and a packaging plant across the border in El Paso, Texas, companies like Hoover are able to take advantage of Mexico's low labor costs. This opportunity is a result of the Mexican government's relaxation of its laws against foreign ownership of factories and its reduction of import taxes on raw materials.[31]

- **Turnkey Operations.** Turnkey operations are typically contracts for the construction of operating facilities in exchange for a fee. The facilities are transferred to the host country or firm when they are complete. The customer is usually a government agency of, say, China or a Middle Eastern country that has decreed that a particular product must be produced locally and under its control. MNCs that perform turnkey operations are frequently industrial equipment manufacturers that supply some of their own equipment for the project and that commonly sell to the host country replacement parts and maintenance services. They thereby create customers as well as future competitors.

- **Management Contracts.** A large multinational corporation is likely to have a large amount of management talent at its disposal. Management contracts offer a means through which an MNC may use part of its personnel to assist a firm in a host country for a specified fee and period of time. Such arrangements are useful when a multinational corporation builds a turnkey operation in a less-developed country where people do not have the knowledge and skills needed to operate a manufacturing facility. Management contracts are also common when a host government expropriates part or all of an MNC's holdings in its country. The contracts allow the MNC to continue to earn some income from its investment and keep the operations going until local management is trained.[32]

11.5 INTERNATIONAL ISSUES IN STRATEGY IMPLEMENTATION

To be effective, international strategies must be implemented in concurrence with national and cultural differences. Among the many considerations of an MNC, three of the most important are (1) selecting the local partner for a joint venture or licensing arrangement, (2) designing an appropriate organizational structure, and (3) encouraging global rather than national management practices.

INTERNATIONAL PARTNER SELECTION

Joint ventures and licensing agreements between a multinational company and a local partner in a host country are becoming increasingly popular as a means by which an MNC can gain entry into other countries, especially less-developed countries. National policies as well as the complexity of the host country's market often make these the preferred strategies for the balancing of a country's attractiveness against financial risk. The key to the successful implementation of these strategies is the selection of the local partner.[33] In Fig. 11.4, Lasserre proposes a model describing the many variables to be considered by both sides when they are assessing a partnership. Each party needs to assess not only the strategic fit of each company's project strategy, but also the fit of each company's respective resources. Lasserre contends that this process requires a minimum of one to two years of prior contacts

---

FIGURE 11.4 | **Assessing Potential International Partners**

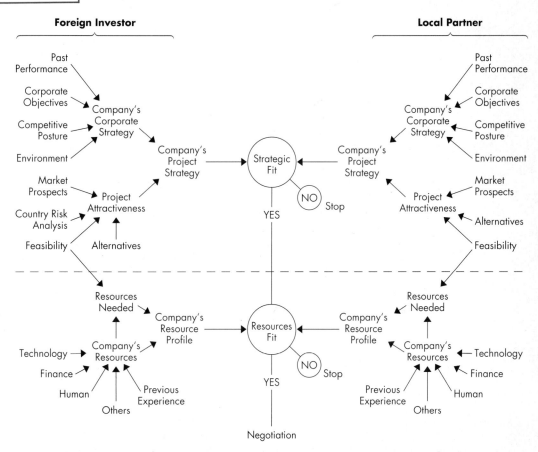

Source: P. Lasserre, "Selecting a Foreign Partner for Technology Transfer," *Long Range Planning* (December 1984), p. 45, Copyright © 1984 by Pergamon Press, Ltd. Reprinted by permission.

between both parties. The fact that joint ventures tend to have a high rate of costly failures suggests that few multinationals use such a careful selection process.[34]

INTERNATIONAL ORGANIZATIONAL DESIGN

The design of an organization's structure is strongly affected by the company's stage of development in international activities and the types of industries in which the company is involved. The issue of centralization versus decentralization becomes especially important for a multinational corporation operating in both multi-domestic and global industries.

Stages of International Development

Rarely, if ever, do multinational corporations suddenly appear as full-blown worldwide organizations. They tend to evolve through five common stages, both in their relationships with widely dispersed geographic markets and in the manner in which they structure their operations and programs.[35] These stages of development are listed in Table 11.2.

- **Stage 1.** The primarily domestic company exports some of its products through local dealers and distributors in the foreign countries. The impact on the organization's structure is minimal since everything is handled through an export department at corporate headquarters.
- **Stage 2.** Success in Stage 1 leads the company to establish its own sales company with offices in other countries to eliminate the middlemen and to take more control over its marketing. Since exports have now become more important, the company establishes an export division to oversee foreign sales offices.
- **Stage 3.** Success in earlier stages leads the company to establish manufacturing facilities in addition to sales and service offices in key countries. By now, the company adds an international division with responsibilities for most of the business functions conducted in other countries.
- **Stage 4.** Now a full-fledged multinational corporation, the company increases its investments in other countries. The company establishes a local operating division or company in the host country, such as Ford of Britain, to better serve the market. The product line is expanded. Local manufacturing capacity is established. Managerial functions (product development, finance, marketing, and so on) are organized locally. As time goes by, other related businesses are acquired by the parent company so that the base of the local operating division is broadened. As the subsidiary in the host country successfully develops a strong regional presence, it achieves greater autonomy and self-sufficiency. An international headquarters division may be established as a wholly owned subsidiary of the original domestic company. The international headquarters oversees all foreign operations and can work very well to administer international operations in a multidomestic industry where different countries and regions manufacture and buy an array of differentiated products.

TABLE 11.2	**Stages of Development of a Multinational Corporation**

Stage	**Activities of Company**	**Organization Responsible for International Activities**	**Executive in Charge**
1	Exports directly and indirectly, but trade is minor.	Export department.	Export manager, reporting to domestic marketing executive.
2	Exports become more important.	Export division.	Division manager.
3	Company undertakes licensing and invests in production overseas.	International division.	Director of international operations, usually vice-president.
4	International investments increase.	Sometimes international headquarters company as wholly owned subsidiary [of domestic parent company].	President, who is vice-president in parent company.
5	International investments substantial and widespread; diversified international business activities.	Global organizational structure by geographic areas, product lines, functions, or some combination. Also worldwide staff support.	No single executive in charge of international business.

Source: Adapted from W. A. Dymsza, *Multinational Business Strategy* (New York: McGraw-Hill, 1972), p. 22. Copyright © 1972 by McGraw-Hill, Inc. Reprinted by permission.

■ **Stage 5.** A few of the most successful multinational corporations move into a fifth stage in which they have worldwide personnel, R&D, and financing strategies. Typically operating in a global industry, the MNC denationalizes its operations and plans product design, manufacturing, and marketing around worldwide considerations. The company is now a global MNC, not a multidomestic MNC. Global considerations now dominate organizational design. The global MNC structures itself around some combination of geographic areas, product lines, and functions. All managers are now responsible for dealing with international as well as domestic issues.

Even though most international and multinational corporations move through these stages in their involvement with host countries, any one corporation can be at different stages simultaneously, with different products in different markets at different levels. An example of corporate diversity in international operations is Hewlett-Packard. In the beginning of its international activity, the company exported its products. It used its own staff to oversee exports to Canada, and export management companies (export intermediaries operating on a buy-and-sell basis and providing financing for export shipments) to oversee exports to other countries. These exports were then sold in both cases to middlemen abroad. As sales expanded,

Hewlett-Packard took over the exporting functions, opened its own sales office in Mexico, purchased a warehousing facility in Switzerland, organized a wholly owned manufacturing subsidiary in Germany, and entered into a partly owned venture in Japan.[36]

Centralization versus Decentralization

A basic dilemma facing the multinational corporation is how to organize authority centrally so that it operates as a vast interlocking system that achieves synergy, and at the same time decentralize authority, so that local managers can make the decisions necessary to meet the demands of the local market or host government.[37] To deal with this problem, MNCs tend to structure themselves either along product groups or geographic areas. They may even combine both in a matrix structure.

Typically, multinational corporations do not organize themselves around business functions, such as marketing or manufacturing, unless they are in an extractive raw-materials industry. Basic functions are thus subsumed under either product or geographic units.[38] Two examples of the usual international structures are Nestlé and American Cyanamid. Nestlé's structure is one in which significant power and authority have been decentralized to geographic entities. This structure is similar to that depicted in Fig. 11.5, in which each geographic set of operating companies has a different group of products. In contrast, American Cyanamid has a series of product groups with worldwide responsibilities. To depict Cyanamid's structure, the geographical entities in Fig. 11.5 would have to be replaced by product groups or strategic business units.

The **product-group structure** enables the company to introduce and manage a similar line of products around the world. The **geographic-area structure**, in contrast, allows a company to tailor products to regional differences and to achieve regional coordination. NV Philips, the Dutch electronics firm, recently switched from a geographical structure, oriented to local needs, to a product structure, oriented to global needs. Philips is known for its light bulbs, for Magnavox, Sylvania, and Philco electronic products, and for Norelco shavers. The company's production facilities were small and high-cost because they were designed only for regional markets. The switch to a product struture was believed by top management to be crucial if Philips was to compete effectively with the Japanese MNCs. "We are still weak," stated Dick Snijders, a Director of Corporate Finance at Philips, "because our emphasis is still too much on the national, and we need to achieve much greater economies of scale."[39]

A survey of 37 large, U.S.-based multinational corporations in various industries reveals that 43% use an international division; 35% are organized according to product group; 14% are structured according to geographic areas; 5% use a functional structure; and 3% utilize the matrix structure. The international division is much more commonly used by U.S.-based MNCs than European-based MNCs. This is probably a result of the size difference between the domestic markets of the typical U.S.-based and the typical Swiss or British MNC.[40] Further research also noted the popularity of the international division and product-group structure in U.S.-based MNCs.[41]

FIGURE 11.5 | **Geographic Area Structure for a Multinational Corporation**

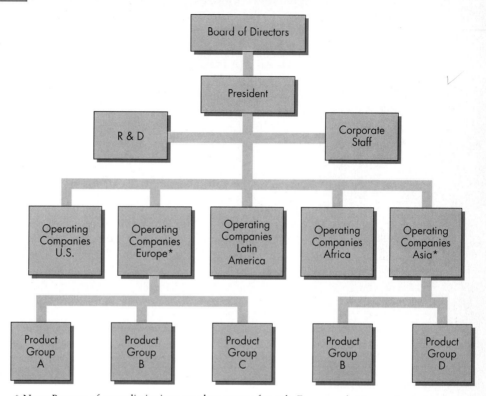

* Note: Because of space limitations, product groups for only Europe and Asia are shown here.

INTERNATIONAL MANAGEMENT PRACTICES AND HUMAN RESOURCE MANAGEMENT

Important international issues for a multinational corporation are the universality of accepted management practices and the proper management of human resources. Are people from different countries basically the same once differences in language and race are resolved, or are they so different that each country needs a whole new style of management?

Cultural Values and Management Practices

There is no simple answer to the question raised above. People around the world are alike, but also different. For example, a study of 14,644 people in eight western countries revealed that work is a central interest for most people in all countries and that interesting work and good pay are the most important elements to jobs.[42] Another study of managers from the U.K., Hungary, Japan, and the U.S. found no significant differences among the attributes preferred in jobs. Type of work was ranked most important, followed by pay and opportunity for advancement for all groups surveyed. Working conditions, benefits, and hours worked tended to be ranked last out of ten for all four groups.[43] Nevertheless, there is some evidence that what the U.S. emphasizes in occupations is fundamentally different from that of other countries. For example, Americans tend to emphasize their career over their employer. In Japan, however, a first loyalty to the organization rather than to one's occupation or profession is listed as one of the fundamental characteristics of the Japanese style of management.[44]

As most people from any industrial society tend to think, managers usually believe that what works well in their own society will work well anywhere. Thus, someone well schooled in the virtues of MBO, participative decision making, theory Y practices, job enrichment, quality circles, and management science will tend to transplant these practices without alteration to foreign nations. Unfortunately, just as products often need to be altered to appeal to a new market, so too do most management practices.

In a study of 53 different national cultures, Hofstede found that he could explain the success or failure of certain management practices on the basis of four cultural dimensions: (1) power distance, (2) uncertainty avoidance, (3) individualism-collectivism, and (4) masculinity-femininity.[45] The following dimensions list the countries with the lowest and highest scores on each dimension, plus the scores of Canada, France, Germany, Japan, Mexico, and the U.S. for comparison purposes.*

1. **Power Distance.** Power distance (PD) is the extent to which a society accepts an unequal distribution of power in organizations. People in those countries scoring high on this dimension tend to prefer autocratic to more participative managers. Power distance scores range from 11 to 104.

   Highest PD score   Lowest PD score

Malaysia	Mexico	France	Japan	U.S.	Canada	Germany	Austria
(104)	(81)	(68)	(54)	(46)	(39)	(35)	(11)

2. **Uncertainty Avoidance.** Uncertainty avoidance (UA) is the extent to which a society feels threatened by uncertain and ambiguous situations. People in those nations scoring high on this dimension tend to want career stability, formal rules, and clear-cut measures of performance. Uncertainty avoidance scores range from 8 to 112.

   Highest UA score   Lowest UA score

Greece	Japan	France	Mexico	Germany	Canada	U.S.	Singapore
(112)	(92)	(86)	(82)	(65)	(48)	(46)	(8)

* Hofstede and Bond do not tell the numerical significance of the scores for each dimension. They merely indicate that the scores are *relative*: the scales were chosen to allow around 100 points between the lowest- and highest-scoring country (p. 14).

3. **Individualism-Collectivism.** Individualism-collectivism (IC) is the extent to which a society values individual freedom and independence of action compared with a tight social framework and loyalty to the group. People in those nations scoring high on individualism tend to value individual success through competition, whereas people scoring low on individualism would tend to value group success through collective cooperation. Individualism scores range from 6 to 91.

Highest IC score						Lowest IC score
U.S. (91)	Canada (80)	France (71)	Germany (67)	Japan (46)	Mexico (30)	Guatemala (6)

4. **Masculinity-Femininity.** Masculinity-Femininity is the extent to which society is oriented toward money and things (which Hofstede labels masculine) or toward people (which Hofstede labels feminine). People in those nations scoring high on masculinity tend to value clearly defined sex roles where men dominate, and to emphasize performance and independence, whereas people scoring low on masculinity (and thus high on femininity) would tend to value equality of the sexes where power is shared, and to emphasize the quality of life and interdependence. Masculinity (M) scores range from 5 to 95.

Highest M score						Lowest M score
Japan (95)	Mexico (69)	Germany (66)	U.S. (62)	Canada (52)	France (43)	Sweden (5)

The many differences in these four dimensions on national culture explain why some management practices work well in some countries, but not in others. Management By Objectives (MBO), originated in the U.S., has succeeded in Germany, according to Hofstede, because the idea of replacing the arbitrary authority of the boss with the impersonal authority of mutually agreed-upon objectives fits the small power distance and strong uncertainty avoidance that are dimensions of the German culture. It has failed in France, however, because the French are used to large power distances—to accepting orders from a highly personalized authority. This French cultural dimension runs counter to key aspects of MBO: the small power distance between superior and subordinate, and impersonal, objective goal setting. This same cultural dimension explains why the French, for whom vertical authority lines are very important, are significantly more reluctant than Americans to accept the multiple authority structures of project management or matrix structure.[46] Some of the difficulties experienced by U.S. companies in using Japanese-style quality circles may stem from the extremely high value U.S. culture places on individualism.

Further research using Hofstede's dimensions points to some interesting conclusions. For example, the chief executive officer of a multinational corporation tends to demonstrate behavior in line with the dominant cultural values of the country in which the MNC is located. Thus, the management style of Pehr Gyllenhammar of Volvo reflects the individual initiative (high individualism score), high risk taking (low UA score), combined with a people-oriented approach (low masculinity score) of Sweden. In contrast, the emphasis by Y. C. Wang, founder of Formosa Plastics Group, on tradition, family, and company is consistent with the jen philosophy of the Taiwanese people.[47] Other researchers conclude that technology transfer is most successful in countries with individualistic orientations and/or high masculinity scores. Collectivism tends to dampen innovation in organizations. Masculinity values economic growth over social welfare. Exceptions can, of course, be found to these rather sweeping, but still tentative, research conclusions. Sweden, for example, scores very low on the masculinity (and thus high on the femininity) dimension, but is highly developed economically. Technology transfer has successfully occurred in Venezuela even though, as a culture, it scores low on individualism (and thus high on collectivism).[48]

Additional work by Hofstede and Bond on national cultures reveals the existence of a *fifth dimension* labeled **Confucian Dynamism** (CD), the extent to which society follows the principles commonly ascribed to Confucius. These principles, according to Hofstede and Bond, are, briefly, (1) the arrangement of relationships by status and a sensitivity to social contracts; (2) the importance placed on hard work, education, and persistence; (3) the importance of thrift; and (4) the treatment of others as one would like to be treated. A study of this dimension in 22 countries shows that Confucian Dynamism is strongly associated with economic growth. The countries scoring highest on this dimension are Hong Kong, Taiwan, Japan, and South Korea, four of the most economically prosperous countries in Asia. The cultures scoring lowest are Pakistan and West Africa. Confucian Dynamism scores range from 0 to 96.

Highest CD score					Lowest CD score
Hong Kong (96)	Japan (80)	Germany (31)	U.S. (29)	Canada (23)	Pakistan (0)

Hofstede and Bond propose that multinational corporations must pay attention to the many differences in cultural dimensions around the world and make appropriate adjustments in their management practices. Cultural differences can easily go unrecognized by a headquarters staff that may interpret these differences as personality defects, whether the people in the subsidiaries are locals or expatriates. Ethnocentric people at headquarters will likely explain that a person who was previously very competent while at headquarters suddenly became incompetent in a foreign setting because he or she "went native." Hofstede and Bond conclude: "Whether they like it or not, the headquarters of multinationals are in the business of multicultural management."[49]

Management practices
and

International Human Resource Management

IKEA

Because of cultural differences, managerial style and practices must be tailored to fit the particular situations in other countries. Most multinational corporations therefore attempt to fill managerial positions in their subsidiaries with well-qualified citizens of the host countries. More than 95% of all managers employed by Unilever are nationals of the country in which they work.[50] IBM follows a similar policy. This policy serves to placate nationalistic governments and to better attune management practices to the host country's culture. The danger in using primarily foreign nationals to staff managerial positions in subsidiaries is the increased likelihood of suboptimization. This makes it difficult for a multinational corporation to meet its long-term, worldwide objectives. To a local national in an MNC subsidiary, the corporation as a whole is an abstraction. Communication and coordination across subsidiaries become more difficult.[51] As it becomes harder to coordinate the activities of several international subsidiaries, an MNC will have serious problems operating in a global industry. The North American subsidiary of NV Philips, for example, had earned a reputation as being an independent "maverick" within the NV Philips MNC. This independence may have been acceptable and even useful to the Netherlands–based MNC while it was operating in multidomestic industries. Once the industries became global, however, NV Philips had to take control of the North American subsidiary. It began to staff the top positions with non-Americans who could view the global situation and the MNC as a whole.

drawbacks of using local mgrs. ↓ Quote IKEA Foreign Expansion plan.

Another approach to staffing the managerial positions of multinational corporations is to use people with an "international" orientation, regardless of their country of origin or host country assignment. This approach to using "third-country nationals" allows for more opportunities for promotion than does Unilever's policy but it can result in a greater number of misunderstandings and conflicts with the local employees and with the host country's government.

Staffing foreign subsidiaries with either home-country or third-country nationals can be very expensive for an MNC. It is estimated that approximately 35% of **expatriate managers** (people from a country other than the host country) of U.S.-based MNCs fail to adjust to a particular host country's social and business environment.[52] This failure is very costly in terms of management performance, operations efficiency, and customer relations. The average cost to a company of repatriating an executive and family exceeds $100,000.[53]

To improve their chances of success using expatriates, multinational corporations are now putting more emphasis on intercultural training for those managers being sent on an assignment to a foreign country.[54] This training is one of the commonly cited reasons for the lower expatriate failure rates—6% or less—for European and Japanese MNCs, compared with U.S.-based MNCs.[55] Given that multinational corporations want their people to have greater international experience, it is important to minimize the career risks for people accepting foreign assignments. Otherwise, the company may find itself at a competitive disadvantage in an increasingly global business world.

≈ 360

11.6 INTERNATIONAL ISSUES IN EVALUATION AND CONTROL

As MNCs increase the scope of their activities around the world, timely information becomes even more important for effective evaluation and control. In evaluating the activities of its international operations, the MNC should consider not only financial measures, but also the effects of its activities on the host country.

TRANSBORDER DATA FLOW

Multinational corporations are relying increasingly on transborder data flow (TDF) and international data networks to coordinate their international operations and control their subsidiaries. TDF, the electronic movement of data across national boundaries, has been made possible by the rapid growth and convergence of new technologies, such as telecommunications and computer networks. A survey of 89 MNCs concludes that these companies are already dependent on international data flow for their foreign operations and will become even more so in the future. Transborder data flow appears to be a major information-systems issue for multinational corporations. More and more countries are taking steps to control the flow of data across their borders and thus handicap an MNC in its evaluation and control function.[56]

FINANCIAL MEASURES

The three most widely used techniques for international performance evaluation are return on investment, budget analysis, and historical comparisons. In one study, 95% of the corporate officers interviewed stated that they use the same evaluation techniques for foreign and domestic operations. Rate of return was mentioned as the single most important measure.[57] The use of ROI, however, can cause problems when it is applied to international operations: "Because of foreign currencies, different rates of inflation, different tax laws, and the use of transfer pricing, both the net income figure and the investment base may be seriously distorted."[58]

Authorities in international business recommend that the controls and reward systems used by a global MNC be different from those used by a multidomestic MNC.[59] The *multidomestic* MNC should use loose controls on its foreign units. The management of each geographic unit should be given considerable operational latitude, but be expected to meet some performance targets. Because profit and ROI measures are often unreliable in international operations, it is recommended that the MNC's top management in this instance emphasize budgets and nonfinancial measures of performance, such as market share, productivity, public image, employee morale, and relations with the host country government, to name a few.[60] Multiple measures should be used to differentiate between the worth of the subsidiary and the performance of its management.

An MNC with a *global perspective*, however, needs tight controls over its many units. In order to reduce costs and gain competitive advantage, it is trying to spread the manufacturing and marketing operations of a few fairly uniform products around the world; therefore, its key strategic operational decisions must be centralized. Its environmental scanning must include research not only into each of the national markets in which the MNC competes, but also into the "global arena" of the interaction between markets. Foreign units are thus evaluated more as cost centers, revenue centers, or expense centers than as investment or profit centers because MNCs operating in a global industry do not often make the entire product in the country in which it is sold.

As mentioned earlier, NV Philips decided to change from being primarily a multidomestic to a more global MNC. Therefore, in 1987 it purchased the 42% of the stock it did not already own of the MNC's subsidiary, the North American Philips Corporation. NV Philips also replaced the Chairman of the North American subsidiary with Gerrit Jeelof, a top executive of the MNC. Jeelof had spent much of his career in Latin America and the U.K. Cornelis van der Klugt, the President of North American Philips who reported to Jeelof, stated that he wants more production, ideas, and managers to originate in the U.S. and to be spread throughout NV Philips' worldwide operations. In referring to the actions by NV Philips to increase its ownership of the North American subsidiary, a spokesperson of the Netherlands–based MNC stated: "This should be seen as part of our global strategy to bring U.S. activities under the full control of Philips."[61]

MNC/HOST COUNTRY RELATIONSHIPS

As multinational corporations grow and spread across the world, nations find themselves in a dilemma. Most countries, especially the less-developed ones, want to have the many benefits an MNC can bring: technology transfer, employment opportunities, tax revenues, and the opportunity for domestic business corporations to be built in partnership with powerful and well-connected foreign-based companies. These countries also fear the problems an MNC can bring. Having welcomed an MNC with tax benefits and subsidies of various types, the host country can find itself in a double bind regarding the repatriation of profits. Either it can allow the MNC to export its profits to corporate headquarters in its home country—thereby draining the nation of potential investment capital—or it can allow the MNC to send home only a small portion of its profits—thereby making the host country unattractive to other MNCs. For example, research reveals that between 1960 and 1968, profits sent to the U.S. from Latin America by MNCs exceeded new investment there by $6.7 billion.[62] Research on joint ventures in the Middle East indicates that "benefits and profits accruing to the foreign partner far exceeded those gained by the host government despite its holding between 70 and 84 percent of the equity."[63] Host countries also note that MNCs' technology transfer to less-developed countries seldom increases their exports. MNCs also have a tradition of placing business values above the cultural values of the host country.[64] For example, an MNC's need to continue manufacturing operations in order to meet a deadline dictated by the home office may conflict with a country's desire to honor a special event by declaring a national holiday that would force plant closures for a specified period.

Research does suggest, however, that developing countries are beginning to revise their attitudes and policies toward multinational corporations as MNCs become more willing to contribute to rather than to exploit host countries. The number of times a host country's government has expropriated or nationalized an MNC's operations substantially decreased during the 1980s from the 1960s. Researchers concluded from their study of Latin America that "the relationship between multinational companies and the host governments seems to be shifting from confrontation to mutual understanding and cooperation."[65]

SUMMARY AND CONCLUSION

A knowledge of international considerations is becoming extremely important to the proper understanding of the strategic management processes in large corporations. Just as North American firms are becoming more involved every year with operations and markets in other countries, imports and subsidiaries from other countries are becoming more a part of the U.S. landscape. International corporations have been transforming themselves slowly into multinational corporations (MNCs) with a global orientation and flexible management styles. The venerable economic concepts of absolute and comparative advantage in international trade are giving way to the more modern concept of competitive advantage.

The dominant issue in the strategic management process of a multinational corporation is the effect of widely different external environments on the firm's internal activities. A firm's strategic managers must therefore be well schooled in the national differences in sociocultural, economic, political-legal, and technological environmental variables. They must also be aware of any shifts in industries away from the multidomestic to the global. Data-search procedures and analytical techniques must be used in assessments of the many possible investment opportunities and their risks in world business. Once top management believes that the corporation has the requisite internal qualifications to become multinational, it must then determine the appropriate set of strategies for entering and investing in potential host countries. These may vary from simple exportation to the formation with other companies of very complex consortiums. The corporation's product portfolio must be constantly monitored for strengths and weaknesses.

Attention must also be paid to the selection of the most appropriate local partner, organizational structure, and management system for a worldwide enterprise. An overall system of control and coordination must be balanced against a host country's need for local flexibility and autonomy. Consideration must be given to industry emphasis, either multidomestic or global. An MNC should use a series of performance indicators so that return on investment, budget analysis, and historical comparisons can be viewed in the context of a strategic audit of operations in the host country. Above all, the top management of a multinational corporation has the responsibility to ensure that the MNC contributes to and reinforces the functioning of the host nation, rather than frustrating or undermining its government and culture.

DISCUSSION QUESTIONS

1. What differentiates a multidomestic from a global industry? Cite some industries that are now in the process of converting from multidomestic to global. What underlying factors are causing this change in these industries?

2. If the basic concepts of absolute and comparative advantage suggest free trade as the best route to prosperity for all nations, why do so many countries use protectionist measures to discourage imports?

3. What can be done to reverse the economic decline of a country that has reached the wealth-

driven fourth stage of economic development? Is this a country to be avoided by a multinational corporation?

4. Discuss the pros and cons of using portfolio analysis in international strategic analysis.

5. What popular strategies are available to a company entering a foreign market or establishing manufacturing facilities in another country? List and describe each strategy.

6. Should MNCs be allowed to own more than half the stock of a subsidiary based in a host country? Why or why not?

7. There are many disadvantages to the joint venture—loss of control, lower profits, probability of conflicts with partners, the likely transfer of technological advantage to a partner, plus its typical temporary nature. So why is it such a popular strategy?

8. What are the stages of development of a multinational corporation? List and briefly describe each stage.

9. What are the advantages and disadvantages of using a product-group structure compared with a geographic-area structure in a multinational corporation? Which MNC structure do you think will be increasingly used in the future?

10. Given the differences in national cultural values pointed out by Hofstede, how can a multinational corporation ensure the consistency and reliability of its worldwide activities (e.g., make sure a McDonald's hamburger served in Moscow is the same as one served in Akron) without ignoring local customs and traditions?

11. What is the overall impact of multinational corporations on world peace? How do they help? How do they hinder?

NOTES

1. "Stars of the 1980s Cast Their Light," *Fortune* (July 3, 1989), p. 66. © 1989 The Time Inc. Magazine Company. All rights reserved.

2. M. McLuhan, *Understanding Media: The Extensions of Man* (New York: McGraw-Hill Paperbacks, 1965).

3. S. Ticer, W. C. Symonds, P. Finch, and D. Lieberman, "Captain Comeback," *Business Week* (July 17, 1989), pp. 98–106.

4. P. Nulty, "How the World Will Change," *Fortune* (January 15, 1990), p. 45.

5. D. A. Heenan, "The Case for Convergent Capitalism," *Journal of Business Strategy* (November/December 1988), pp. 54–57.

6. D. A. Heenan, "The Courtship of the Multinational Corporation," *Journal of Business Strategy* (March/April 1988), pp. 49–52.

7. "The Stateless Corporation," *Business Week* (May 14, 1990), p. 99.

8. W. A. Dymsza, *Multinational Business Strategy* (New York: McGraw-Hill, 1972), pp. 5–6.

9. M. E. Porter, "Changing Patterns of International Competition," *California Management Review* (Winter 1986), pp. 9–40. Also in *The Competitive Challenge*, edited by D. J. Teece (Cambridge, Mass.: Ballinger, 1987), pp. 27–57.

10. For more information on the theories of absolute and comparative advantage, see J. D. Daniels and L. H. Radebaugh, *International Business*, 5th ed. (Reading, Mass.: Addison-Wesley, 1989), pp. 126–135.

11. Heenan, "Convergent Capitalism," p. 55.

12. M. E. Porter in a presentation to the 1988 *Strategic Management Society* as summarized by B. C. Reimann in "Selected Highlights of the 1988 Strategic Management Society Conference," *Planning Review* (January/February 1989), pp. 26–27.

13. M. E. Porter, *The Competitive Advantage of Nations* (New York: The Free Press, 1990), p 71.

14. *Ibid.*, 1990, p. 173.

15. R. Stobaugh and L. T. Wells, Jr., eds., *Technology Crossing Borders* (Boston: Harvard Business School Press, 1984).

16. Porter, *The Competitive Advantage of Nations*, p. 565.

17. K. Ohmae, "The Triad World View," *Journal of Business Strategy* (Spring 1987), pp. 8–19.

18. T. N. Gladwin, "Assessing the Multinational Environment for Corporate Opportunity," in *Handbook of Business Strategy*, edited by W. D. Guth (Boston: Warren, Gorham and Lamont, 1985), pp. 7.28–7.41.

19. W. D. Coplin and M. K. O'Leary, "1990 World Political Risk Forecast," *Planning Review* (March/April 1990), pp. 41–47.

20. For further information about international environ-

mental scanning, see I. Walter, "Country-Risk Assessment" and S. J. Kobrin, "Political Risk Evaluation" in *Handbook of International Management*, edited by I. Walter and T. Murray (New York: John Wiley and Sons, 1988), pp. 7.1–8.24; J. F. Preble, P. A. Rau, and A. Reichel, "The Environmental Scanning Practices of Multinational Firms—An Assessment," *International Journal of Management* (March 1989), pp. 18–28; and W. Teng, *Multinational Risk Assessment and Management* (New York: Quorum Books, 1988).

21. Y. N. Chang and F. Campo-Flores, *Business Policy and Strategy* (Santa Monica, Calif.: Goodyear Publishing, 1980), pp. 602–604.

22. J. A. Pearce II and K. Roth, "Multinationalization of the Mission Statement," *SAM Advanced Management Journal* (Summer 1988), pp. 39–44.

23. G. D. Harrell and R. O. Kiefer, "Multinational Strategic Market Portfolios," *MSU Business Topics* (Winter 1981), p. 5.

24. *Ibid.*, p. 8.

25. M. E. Porter, "Changing Patterns of International Competition," *California Management Review* (Winter 1986), p. 12.

26. F. J. Contractor and P. Lorange, "Why Should Firms Cooperate? The Strategy and Economics Basis for Cooperative Ventures," in *Cooperative Strategies in International Business*, edited by F. J. Contractor and P. Lorange (Lexington, Mass.: Lexington Books, 1988), pp. 3–30.

   J. S. Harrison, "Alternatives to Merger—Joint Ventures and Other Strategies," *Long Range Planning* (December 1987), p. 80.

27. V. Pucik and N. Hatvany, "Management Practices in Japan and Their Impact on Business Strategy," in *Advances in Strategic Management*, Vol. I, edited by R. Lamb (Greenwich, Conn.: JAI Press, 1983), p. 124.

28. "EC, Rolls-Royce Reach Compromise on Limiting Holdings by Foreigners," *Wall Street Journal* (July 20, 1989), p. A9.

29. S. P. Galante, "Foreign Semiconductor Firms Try New Strategy in U.S.," *Wall Street Journal* (August 23, 1984), p. 20.

30. K. P. Power, "Now We Can Move Office Work Offshore to Enhance Output," *Wall Street Journal* (June 9, 1983), p. 30.

31. For an excellent summary of U.S.–Mexican maquiladora operations, see J. P. McCray and J. J. Gonzalez, "Increasing Global Competitiveness with U.S.–Mexican Maquiladora Operations," *SAM Advanced Management Journal* (Summer 1989), pp. 4–7, 23, 28.

32. For further information on various international entry

strategies, see S. H. Akhter and R. Friedman, "International Market Entry Strategies and Level of Involvement in Marketing Activities," in *International Strategic Management*, edited by A. R. Negandhi and A. Savara (Lexington, Mass.: Lexington Books, 1989), pp. 157–172.

33. P. Lasserre, "Selecting a Foreign Partner for Technology Transfer," *Long Range Planning* (December 1984), pp. 43–49.

   J. M. Geringer, *Joint Venture Partner Selection* (New York: Quorum Books, 1988), pp. 176–187.

34. W. H. Davidson, "Creating and Managing Joint Ventures in China," *California Management Review* (Summer 1987), p. 77.

35. K. Ohmae, "Planting for a Global Harvest," *Harvard Business Review* (July-August 1989), pp. 136–145.

   K. Ohmae, "No Manufacturing Exodus, No Great Comeback," *Wall Street Journal* (April 25, 1988), p. 18.

   N. Kobayashi, "Strategic Alliances with Japanese Firms," *Long Range Planning* (April 1988), pp. 29–34.

36. J. D. Daniels, E. W. Ogram, Jr., and L. H. Radebaugh, *International Business: Environments and Operations*, 2nd ed. (Reading, Mass.: Addison-Wesley, 1979), p. 359.

37. C. K. Prahalad and Y. L. Doz, *The Multinational Mission* (New York: The Free Press, 1987).

38. J. Garland and R. N. Farmer, *International Dimensions of Business Policy and Strategy* (Boston: Kent Publishing, 1986), pp. 98–102.

39. G. Turner, "Inside Europe's Giant Companies: Cultural Revolution at Philips," *Long Range Planning* (August 1986), p. 14.

40. J. D. Daniels, R. A. Pitts, and M. J. Tretter, "Organizing for Dual Strategies of Product Diversity and International Expansion," *Strategic Management Journal* (July-September 1985), pp. 223–237.

41. P. S. Lewis and P. M. Fandt, "The Strategy-Structure Fit in Multinational Corporations: A Revised Model," *International Journal of Management* (June 1990), pp. 137–147.

42. MOW International Research Team, *The Meaning of Work* (London: Academic Press, 1987), as reviewed by G. Akin and L. D. Loehr in *Administrative Science Quarterly* (December 1988), pp. 648–651.

43. W. S. Blumenfeld, D. C. Brenenstuhl, and L. F. Jordan, "A Comparison of the Job Attribute Preferences of British, Hungarian, Japanese, and United States Managers," *International Journal of Management* (September 1988), pp. 323–332.

44. W. A. Jones, Jr., and V. E. Johnson, "The Large Organization as a Community of Games: Another View of

the 'Culture' Phenomenon," *International Journal of Management* (March 1988), pp. 74–76.

45. G. Hofstede and M. H. Bond, "The Confucius Connection: From Cultural Roots to Economic Growth," *Organizational Dynamics* (Spring 1988), pp. 5–21.

    G. Hofstede, "The Cultural Relativity of the Quality of Life Concept," *Academy of Management Review* (July 1984), pp. 389–398.

    G. Hofstede, "National Cultures in Four Dimensions: A Research-Based Theory of Cultural Differences among Nations," *International Journal of Management and Organization* (Spring-Summer 1983), pp. 46–74.

    G. Hofstede, "Motivation, Leadership, and Organization: Do American Theories Apply Abroad?" *Organizational Dynamics* (Summer 1980), pp. 42–63.

    The scores for each of the dimensions were taken from Hofstede and Bond, "The Confucius Connection," pp. 12–13.

46. G. Inzerilli and A. Laurent, "Managerial Views of Organization Structure in France and the USA," *International Studies of Management and Organization* (Spring-Summer 1983), p. 113.

47. E. F. Jackofsky, J. W. Slocum, Jr., and S. J. McQuaid, "Cultural Values and the CEO: Alluring Companions?" *Academy of Management Executive* (February 1988), pp. 39–49.

48. B. L. Kedia and R. S. Bhagat, "Cultural Constraints on Transfer of Technology Across Nations: Implications for Research in International and Comparative Management," *Academy of Management Review* (October 1988), pp. 559–571.

49. Hofstede and Bond, "The Confucius Connection," p. 20.

50. W. C. Kim and R. A. Mauborgne, "Cross-Cultural Strategies," *Journal of Business Strategy* (Spring 1987), p. 30.

51. S. J. Kobrin, "Are Multinationals Better After the Yankees Go Home?" *Wall Street Journal* (May 8, 1989), p. A14.

52. R. L. Tung, *The New Expatriates* (Cambridge, Mass.: Ballinger, 1988), as reviewed by D. J. Cohen in *Academy of Management Executive* (May 1988), pp. 171–172.

53. N. J. Adler, *International Dimensions of Organizational Behavior*, 2nd ed. (Boston: PWS/Kent, 1991), p. 257.

54. P. C. Earley, "Intercultural Training for Managers: A Comparison of Documentary and Interpersonal Methods," *Academy of Management Journal* (December 1987), pp. 685–698.

55. Tung, *The New Expatriates*.

56. W. B. Carper, "Transborder Data Flows in the Information Age: Implications for International Management," *International Journal of Management* (December 1989), pp. 418–425.

    R. Chandran, A. Phatak, and R. Sambharya, "Transborder Data Flows: Implication for Multinational Corporations," *Business Horizons* (November-December 1987), pp. 74–82.

57. S. M. Robbins and R. B. Stobaugh, "The Bent Measuring Stick for Foreign Subsidiaries," *Harvard Business Review* (September-October 1973), p. 82.

58. Daniels and Radebaugh, *International Business*, pp. 673–674.

59. C. W. L. Hill, P. Hwang, and W. C. Kim, "An Eclectic Theory of the Choice of International Entry Mode," *Strategic Management Journal* (February 1990), pp. 117–128.

    D. Lei, J. W. Slocum, Jr., and R. W. Slater, "Global Strategy and Reward Systems: The Key Roles of Management Development and Corporate Culture," *Organizational Dynamics* (Autumn 1990), pp. 27–41.

    W. R. Fannin and A. F. Rodriques, "National or Global?—Control vs. Flexibility," *Long Range Planning* (October 1986), pp. 84–188.

60. A. V. Phatak, *International Dimensions of Management*, 2nd ed. (Boston: Kent, 1989), pp. 155–157.

61. M. M. Nelson, "NV Philips Plans to Tighten Control of U.S. Operations," *Wall Street Journal* (August 2, 1988), p. 18.

62. K. Paul and R. Barbato, "The Multinational Corporation in the Less Developed Country: The Economic Development Model versus the North-South Model," *Academy of Management Review* (January 1985), p. 9.

63. S. M. Afifi, "The Management Component in Strategies for the Export of Technology to the Gulf States: A Key to Competitiveness," *SAM Advanced Management Journal* (Summer 1989), p. 26.

64. P. Wright, "MNC-Third World Business Unit Performance: Application of Strategic Elements," *Strategic Management Journal* (July-September 1984), pp. 231–240.

65. K. Fatehi-Sedeh and M. H. Safizadeh, "Sociopolitical Events and Foreign Direct Investment: American Investments in South and Central American Countries, 1950–1982," *Journal of Management* (March 1988), p. 105.

CHAPTER TWELVE

Strategic Issues in Entrepreneurial Ventures and Small Businesses

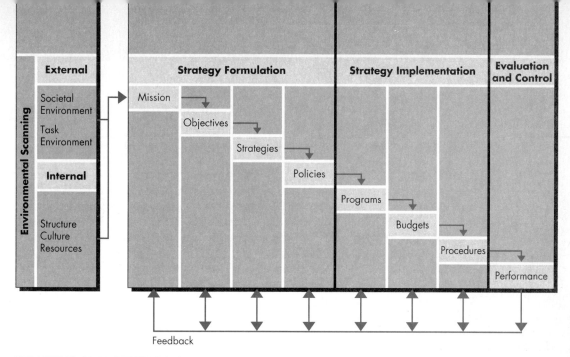

STRATEGIC MANAGEMENT MODEL

If you asked a hundred business owners what they think is most important in successfully starting a company, you may get a hundred different answers. But to me, there is only one: persistence.[1]

Ed Wilkes, Founder of
Sunsign Manufacturing Co.

Strategic management as a field of study typically deals with large, established business corporations and, until lately, has virtually ignored small-business firms. Muldowney and D'Amboise, in their recent review of small-business research, conclude that "knowledge about small business management is fragmented."[2] In a separate review of research on entrepreneurship, Wortman states that "there are no theories in the entrepreneurship field."[3] There is a tendency to treat small companies as if they were just a smaller version of larger companies and to apply standard management concepts and techniques to their situation. This "little big-business" orientation can be a serious mistake. For example, single-product companies cannot readily apply the strategic planning technique of portfolio analysis to their situation. Because many small businesses and entrepreneurial ventures make only one product or product line, portfolio analysis has little, if any, relevance to their planning.

Small business cannot be ignored, however, when strategic management is discussed. Approximately 99% of the 17 million businesses in the U.S. employ fewer than 100 people. Small business accounts for approximately half of all U.S. employment. Over 80% of all new jobs created in the U.S. between 1960 and 1985 were created by small businesses. Well over 60% of this total were created by new ventures. Between 1980 and 1988, 3 million jobs were lost in the Fortune 500 companies, whereas 17 million jobs were created by small businesses.[4] Research reveals that not only do small firms spend almost twice as much of their R&D dollars on fundamental research as do large firms, but also that small companies are responsible for a high proportion of innovations in products and services.[5] For example, new small firms produce 24 times more innovation per research dollar than do the much larger Fortune 500 firms.[6] The National Science Foundation estimates that 98% of "radical" product developments result from the research done in labs of small companies.[7]

Despite the overall success of small business, however, every year tens of thousands of small companies fail. A study by Dun and Bradstreet revealed that 53% of all failures and bankruptcies posted in 1980 occurred in less than five years from a firm's founding, and that 83% of businesses failed in less than ten years from inception.[8] Another study found that 34% of the small businesses in existence during 1982 had discontinued operations by late 1986. For those firms with sales in 1982 of less than $5,000, 50% went out of existence.[9] Although some studies are more positive regarding the survival rate of new entrepreneurial ventures,[10] new businesses are definitely considered risky. The causes of small-business failure (depending on the study cited) range from inadequate accounting systems to inability to cope with growth. The underlying problem appears to be an overall lack of strategic management—beginning with an inability to plan a strategy to reach the customer, and ending with a failure to develop a system of controls to keep track of performance.[11]

12.1 THE ENTREPRENEUR AS STRATEGIC MANAGER

Often defined as a person who organizes and manages a business undertaking and who assumes risk for the sake of a profit, the **entrepreneur** is the ultimate strategic manager. He or she makes all the strategic as well as operational decisions. All three levels of strategy—corporate, business, and functional—are the concerns of this founder and owner-manager of a company. As one entrepreneur puts it: "Entrepreneurs are strategic planners without realizing it."[12]

Illustrative Example 12.1 describing the founding of Sunshine Manufacturing Company captures the key elements of the entrepreneurial venture: a basic business idea that has not yet been successfully tried and a gutsy entrepreneur who, while working on a shoestring budget, creates a new business through a lot of trial and error and persistent hard work. Similar stories can be told of other people, such as Will Parish, who founded National Energy Associates, and Debbi Fields, who created Mrs. Fields Cookies. Both were ridiculed at one time or another for their desire to start a business. Friends and family told Debbi Fields that starting a business to sell chocolate chip cookies "was a stupid idea." Will Parish, who built a power plant in California's Imperial Valley that burns "pasture patties," is called an

ILLUSTRATIVE EXAMPLE 12.1

The Founding of a New Business: Sunsign Manufacturing

Ed Wilkes has just begun a new venture called Sunsign Manufacturing Company. He describes the product it makes this way: "I have a new enterprise with a new product—signs lighted with solar power. My signs can be seen after dark in places where you wouldn't expect to see them, such as building sites and vacant lots, giving them special advertising value for many types of businesses." Wilkes also owns and manages a successful dealership in Norman, Oklahoma, selling solar-powered home-heating and water-heating systems. This business was the springboard for his idea of making and selling solar-powered signs. Wilkes describes the process of developing the signs.

> Originally, I had planned a sign with a light that would shine down on the surface. I started from zero; I had no engineering background, and I did the work myself. I found, however, that an internal light made a sign look brighter and more attractive. So I changed the design. . . . It took months to develop a satisfactory sign. I would try something, and try again if it didn't work. Persistence.

The sign I developed operates with what is, in a sense, a little transmitter, powered by a portable generating plant.

The transmitter can function in a yard, a vacant lot, even the middle of a lake. The sign has a photovoltaic panel, better known as a solar panel, which captures sunlight that charges a battery inside the sign. The battery powers the fluorescent tube that illuminates the sign's message from behind.

The sign's message can be changed easily because it is on a sheet of plastic that slides in and out of a frame like a removable storm window. If the message needs no change, however, the sign needs no service for years.

Because his capital is limited, Wilkes distributes his signs through dealers. A small Arizona company agreed to produce photovoltaic panels in the tiny quantities the new venture initially needed. The billing is prepared by another company at a cost of $.50 a month per account. Wilkes sums up his entrepreneurial venture this way:

> My business has a long way to go. The first dealerships are just getting under way. But with little money or experience, I have come a long way, too. Thanks to persistence.

Source: E. Wilkes, "Something New Under the Sun," *Nation's Business* (August 1989), p. 9. Copyright © 1989, U.S. Chamber of Commerce.

"entre-manure." Every day the plant burns 900 tons of manure collected from nearby feedlots to generate 15 megawatts of electricity—enough to light 20,000 homes. The power is sold to Southern California Edison. Parish got the idea from a trip to India where the fuel used to heat a meal was cow dung. Now that the plant is earning a profit, Parish is building a larger plant nearby that will burn wheat straw and other crop wastes. The plants provide an environmentally sound as well as profitable way to dispose of waste. Says Parish, who is very interested in conservation, "I wanted to combine doing well with doing good."[13]

12.2 DEFINITION OF SMALL-BUSINESS FIRMS AND ENTREPRENEURIAL VENTURES

The most commonly accepted definition of a small-business firm is one employing fewer than 500 people and that generates sales of less than $20 million annually. According to the United States Small Business Administration: "A small business is one which is independently owned and operated, and which is not dominant in its field of operation."[14]

Although there is considerable overlap between what is meant by the terms "small business" and "entrepreneurship," the concepts are different. The **small-business firm** is independently owned and operated, not dominant in its field, and does not engage in innovative practices. The **entrepreneurial venture**, in contrast, is any business whose primary goals are profitability and growth and that can be characterized by innovative strategic practices.[15] The basic difference between the small-business firm and the entrepreneurial venture, therefore, lies not in the type of goods or services provided, but in their fundamental views on growth and innovation.

12.3 USE OF STRATEGIC MANAGEMENT

Sexton, an authority on entrepreneurship, proposes that strategic planning is more likely to be present in an entrepreneurial venture than in the typical small-business firm:

> Most firms start with just a single product. Those oriented toward growth immediately start looking for another one. It's that planning approach that separates the entrepreneur from the small-business owner.[16]

The reasons often cited for the apparent lack of strategic planning practices in many small-business firms are fourfold:

- **Not Enough Time.** Day-to-day operating problems take up the time necessary for long-term planning. It's relatively easy to justify avoiding strategic planning on the basis of day-to-day crisis management. Some will ask: "How can I be expected to do strategic planning when I don't know if I'm going to be in business next week?"
- **Unfamiliar with Strategic Planning.** The small-business CEO may be unaware of strategic planning, or view it as irrelevant to the small-business situation. Planning may be viewed as a straitjacket that limits flexibility.
- **Lack of Skills.** Small-business managers often lack the skills necessary to begin strategic planning and do not have or wish to spend the money necessary to import trained consultants. Future uncertainty may be used to justify a lack of planning. One entrepreneur admits, "Deep down, I know I should plan. But I don't know what to do. I'm the leader but I don't know how to lead the planning process."

■ **Lack of Trust and Openness.** Many small-business owner managers are very sensitive regarding key information about the business and are thus unwilling to share strategic planning with employees or outsiders. For this reason, boards of directors are often composed only of close friends and relatives of the owner-manager: people unlikely to provide an objective viewpoint or professional advice.[17]

VALUE OF STRATEGIC PLANNING

Although many small companies still do not use it, strategic planning is being practiced by a growing number of small businesses and entrepreneurial companies. Research shows that strategic planning is strongly related to small-business financial performance.[18] For example, a study of 265 dry cleaners revealed that firms that had engaged in strategic planning for more than five years significantly outperformed, in terms of revenue growth and net profits, those firms with less than five years of experience in strategic planning.[19] Another study of 135 small businesses in six different industries concluded that firms that engaged in strategic planning had greater increases in both sales and profits over a three-year period than did nonplanners.[20]

There is some evidence that an increasing number of entrepreneurial ventures are introducing strategic management very early in their existence. A 1990 survey by the national accounting and consulting firm of BDO Seidman found that 81% of firms one to ten years old had strategic plans, whereas only 67% of companies 11 to 20 years old had such plans. Herb Goldstein, a partner with BDO Seidman, commented that older entrepreneurs were more likely to "manage by the seat of their pants." Of those firms with a strategic plan, 89% indicated that the plan had been effective. Reasons given for its effectiveness were that it had specific goals (64%), gave staff a unified vision (25%), and set up a time frame for achievements (11%). Reasons given for an ineffective strategic plan were that it was too vague (43%), lacked a time frame for goals (29%), did not identify goals (17%), and lacked staff input (11%).[21]

DEGREE OF FORMALITY IN STRATEGIC PLANNING

Research generally concludes that the strategic planning process should be far more informal in small companies than it is in large corporations.[22] A study of 220 of the fastest-growing, privately held companies in the U.S. found that the strategic planning activity was more short-run–oriented than that conducted by large corporations.[23] Some studies have even found that too much formalization of the strategic planning process may actually result in reduced performance.[24] It is possible that a heavy emphasis on structured, written plans can be dysfunctional to the small entrepreneurial firms because it detracts from the very flexibility that is a benefit of small size.

Nevertheless, there is some evidence that a certain degree of formality and structure in the strategic management process can be beneficial to the small and developing company. In the dry cleaner study mentioned earlier, companies with formal, written plans (resulting from an analysis of internal strengths and weaknesses and external opportunities and threats) had higher sales and profits than did those firms with strictly intuitive plans developed by the entrepreneurs, or without any planning process at all. The study concluded that *the process of strategic planning, not the plan itself, was a key component of business performance.*[25]

These observations suggest that new entrepreneurial ventures begin life in Mintzberg's *entrepreneurial mode* of strategic planning (explained in Chapter 2), and move toward the *planning mode* as the company becomes established and wants to continue its strong growth. If, after becoming successfully established, the entrepreneur instead chooses stability over growth, the venture moves more toward the *adaptive mode* so common to many small businesses.

USEFULNESS OF STRATEGIC MANAGEMENT MODEL

The descriptive model of strategic management, which was presented in Chapter 1 as Fig. 1.2 and which prefaces each chapter in the book, is also relevant to entrepreneurial ventures and small businesses. As does the large corporation, the small company must go through (1) *environmental scanning*, (2) *strategy formulation*, (3) *strategy implementation*, and (4) *evaluation and control*. Using an assessment of the company's external and internal environments, top management (often just the CEO-entrepreneur) must first decide the company's mission, objectives, strategies, and policies, and then implement them with the appropriate programs, budgets, and procedures, so that the company's performance meets or exceeds expectations.

This basic model holds for both an established small company and a new entrepreneurial venture. As the research mentioned earlier concluded, small and developing companies increase their chances of success if they make a serious attempt to work through the strategic issues embedded in the strategic management model. The terms used in the process are relatively unimportant. The key is to focus on what's important—that set of managerial decisions and actions that determines the long-run performance of the company. The list of informal questions presented in Table 12.1 may be more useful to a small company than their more formal counterparts used by large corporations.

USEFULNESS OF STRATEGIC DECISION-MAKING PROCESS

As mentioned in Chapters 2 and 6, one way in which the strategic management model can be made action-oriented is to follow the strategic decision-making model presented in Figs. 2.4 and 6.1. The eight steps presented in that model are just as appropriate for small companies as they are for large corporations. Unfortunately, the process does not fit new entrepreneurial ventures. It makes no sense to begin the process with an evaluation of current performance results if the company has not yet begun operations. In the same manner, an entrepreneurial venture has no current mission, objectives, strategies, and policies to be evaluated. It must develop new ones out of a comparison of its external opportunities and threats to its potential strengths and weaknesses.

TABLE 12.1	Informal Questions to Begin the Strategic Management Process in a Small Company or Entrepreneurial Venture

Formal	Informal
Define mission	What do we stand for?
Set objectives	What are we trying to achieve?
Formulate strategy	How are we going to get there? How can we beat the competition?
Determine policies	What sort of ground rules should we all be following to get the job done right?
Establish programs	How should we organize this operation to get what we want done as cheaply as possible with the highest quality possible?
Prepare pro forma *budgets*	How much is it going to cost us and where can we get the cash?
Specify procedures	In how much detail do we have to lay things out, so that everybody knows what to do?
Determine performance measures	What are those few key things that will determine whether we make it? How can we keep track of them?

Consequently, we propose in Fig. 12.1 a modified version of the strategic decision-making process; this version more closely suits the new entrepreneurial business.

The *strategic decision-making process for new ventures* is composed of the following eight interrelated steps:

1. **Development of the basic business idea**—a product and/or service having target customers and/or markets. The idea can be developed from a person's experience or it can be generated in a moment of creative insight. As shown in Illustrative Example 12.1, Ed Wilkes conceived of the solar-powered sign long before such a product was feasible.

2. **A scanning of the external environment, to locate strategic factors** in the societal and task environments that pose opportunities and threats. The scanning should focus particularly on market potential and resource accessibility.

3. **A scanning of the internal strategic factors** relevant to the new business. The entrepreneur should objectively consider personal assets, areas of expertise, abilities, and experience, all in terms of the organizational needs of the new venture.

4. **Analysis of the strategic factors,** in light of the current situation. The venture's potential strengths and weaknesses must be evaluated in light of opportunities and threats.

5. **Decision point**. If the basic business ideas appears to be a feasible business opportunity, the process should be continued. Otherwise, further development of the idea should be canceled unless the strategic factors change.

6. **Generation of a business plan** specifying how the idea will be transformed into reality. See Table 12.2 for the suggested contents of a strategic business

FIGURE 12.1 | **Strategic Decision-Making Process for New Ventures**

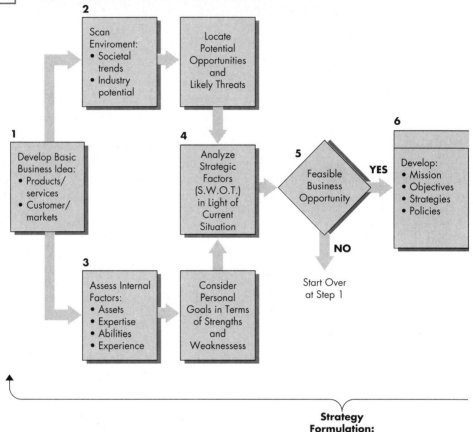

Source: T. L. Wheelen and C. E. Michaels, Jr., "Model for Strategic Decision-Making Process for New Ventures." Copyright © 1987 by T. L. Wheelen. Reprinted by permission.

plan. The proposed venture's mission, objectives, strategies, and policies, as well as its likely board of directors (if a corporation) and key managers should be developed. Key internal factors should be specified and performance projections generated. The business plan serves as a vehicle through which financial support is obtained from potential investors and creditors. Starting a business without a business plan is the quickest way to kill a new venture.[26]

7. **Implementation of the business plan,** via the use of action plans and procedures.

8. **Evaluation of the implemented business plan,** through comparison of actual performance against projected performance results. This step leads to Step 1(b) of the strategic decision-making process shown in Figs. 2.4 and 6.1. To

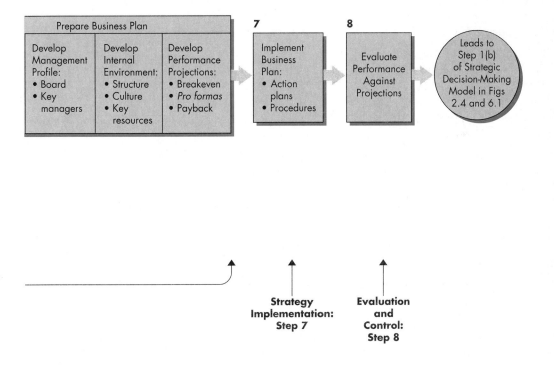

the extent that actual results are less than or much greater than the anticipated results, the entrepreneur needs to reconsider the company's current mission, objectives, strategies, policies, and programs, and possibly make changes to the original business plan.

12.4 ISSUES IN ENVIRONMENTAL SCANNING AND STRATEGY FORMULATION

Environmental scanning in small businesses is much less sophisticated than in large corporations. The business is usually too small to justify hiring someone to do only environmental scanning or strategic planning. Top managers, especially if they are the founders, tend to believe that they know the business and can follow it better

TABLE 12.2	Contents of a Strategic Business Plan for an Entrepreneurial Venture

I. Table of Contents	X. Human Resources Plan
II. Executive Summary	XI. Ownership
III. Nature of the Business	XII. Risk Analysis
IV. Strategy Formulation	XIII. Timetables and Milestones
V. Market Analysis	XIV. Strategy Implementation—
VI. Marketing Plan	Action Plans
VII. Operational Plans—Service/	XV. Evaluation and Control
Product	XVI. Summary
VIII. Financial Plans	XVII. Appendixes
IX. Organization and Management	

Source: Thomas L. Wheelen, "Contents of a Strategic Business Plan for an Entrepreneurial Venture." Copyright © 1988 by Thomas L. Wheelen. Reprinted by permission.

than anyone else. A study of 220 small rapid-growth companies revealed that the majority of the CEOs were actively and personally involved in all phases of the planning process, but especially in the setting of objectives. Only 15% of the companies used a planning officer or formed a planning group to assist in the planning process. In the rest of the firms, operating managers who participated in strategic planning provided input only to the CEO, who then formulated the plan.[27]

A fundamental reason for differences in strategy formulation between large and small companies lies in the relationship between owners and managers.[28] The CEO of a large corporation has to consider and balance the varied needs of the corporation's many stakeholders. The CEO of a small business, however, is very likely also to be the owner—the company's primary stakeholder. Personal and family needs can thus strongly affect the company's mission and objectives and can overrule other considerations. For example, large corporations often choose growth strategies for their many side benefits for management as well as for stockholders. A small company may, however, choose a stability strategy because the entrepreneur is interested mostly in generating employment for family members, providing the family a "decent living," and in being the "boss" of a firm small enough that he/she can manage it comfortably. "Thus in order to understand the goals of a small organization, it is first necessary to understand the motivation of the owner since the two are indistinguishable, certainly in the early days of the firm's start-up."[29]

The basic S.W.O.T. analysis is just as relevant to small businesses as it is to large ones. Both the greatest strength and the greatest weakness of the small firm, at least in the beginning, rest with the entrepreneur—the owner-manager of the business. The entrepreneur is *the* manager, the source of product/market strategy, and the dynamo who energizes the company. That is why the internal assessment of a new venture's strengths and weaknesses focuses in Fig. 12.1 on the personal characteristics of the founder—his or her assets, expertise, abilities, and experience. Just as an entrepreneur's strengths can be the key to company success, personal weaknesses can be a primary cause of failure. For example, the reason for the failure of many small retail businesses is the founders' lack of knowledge of retailing skills.[30]

SOURCES OF INNOVATION

Drucker, in his book *Innovation and Entrepreneurship*, proposes the existence of seven sources for innovative opportunity that should be monitored by those interested in starting an entrepreneurial venture, either within an established company or as an independent small business.[31] The first four sources of innovation lie within the industry itself. The last three arise in the societal environment. These seven sources are:

1. **The Unexpected.** An unexpected success, an unexpected failure, or an unexpected outside event can be a symptom of a unique opportunity. When Don Cullen of Transmet Corporation spilled a box of very fine aluminum flakes onto his company's parking lot, he discovered that their presence in the asphalt prevented it from turning sticky in high temperatures. His company now produces aluminum chips for use in roofing. Sales have doubled every year since introduction and will soon dominate the business.[32]

2. **The Incongruity.** A discrepancy between reality and what everyone assumes it to be, or between what is and what ought to be, can create an opportunity for innovation. Realizing that the real costs of ocean freighter haulage were not crew wages but the time spent loading and unloading at port, Sea-Land changed the entire industry by introducing efficient containerized shipping to reduce handling time and costs.

3. **Innovation Based on Process Need.** When a weak link is evident in a particular process, but people work around it instead of doing something about it, an opportunity is present for the person or company willing to forge a stronger one. For example, Alcon Laboratories was developed based on the discovery that a specific enzyme could enable doctors to avoid cutting a particular ligament when performing eye surgery.

4. **Changes in Industry or Market Structure.** A business is ready for an innovative product, service, or approach to the business when the underlying foundation of the industry or market shifts. Johnson Products was born when George Johnson noted that none of the established cosmetics firms was paying any attention to the needs of blacks and other ethnic groups who wanted to use hair straighteners.

5. **Demographics.** Changes in the population's size, age structure, composition, employment, level of education, and income can create opportunities for innovation. For example, as the large bulge of "baby boomers" in the U.S. population aged, overall interest in beer drinking and X-rated movies declined and interest shifted to those products and services dealing with family and career, such as day care and physical fitness centers. As this group enters its 50s, expect increasing general interest in health care, cultural activities, travel, and financial planning.

6. **Changes in Perception, Mood, and Meaning.** Opportunities for innovation can develop when a society's general assumptions, attitudes, and beliefs change. For example, the trend to two-career families, increasing divorce, and fewer children in the developed countries has not adversely affected the toy market. People simply spend more money on fewer children! The growth of Toys "R" Us is a result of this phenomenon.

7. **New Knowledge.** Advances in scientific and nonscientific knowledge can create new products and new markets. Advances in two different areas can sometimes be integrated to form the basis of a new product. For example, new software firms emerge weekly as new programs are needed to take advantage of technological advances in computers and telecommunications.

FACTORS AFFECTING A NEW VENTURE'S SUCCESS

According to Hofer and Sandberg, there are three factors that have a substantial impact on a new venture's performance. In order of importance, they are (1) the structure of the industry entered, (2) the new venture's business strategy, and (3) behavioral characteristics of the entrepreneur.[33]

Industry Structure

Research shows that the chances for success are greater for those entrepreneurial ventures that enter rapidly changing industries than for those that enter stable industries. In addition, prospects are better in industries that are in the early, high-growth stages of development. There is often less intense competition. Fast market growth also allows new ventures to make some mistakes without serious penalty. New ventures also increase their chances of success when they enter markets in which they can erect entry barriers to keep out competitors.

PIMS data reveal that a new venture is more likely to be successful entering an industry in which one dominant competitor has a 50% or more market share than entering an industry in which the largest competitor has less than a 25% market share. To explain this phenomenon, Hofer and Sandberg point out that when an industry has one dominant firm, the remaining competitors are relatively weak and are easy prey for an aggressive entrepreneur. To avoid direct competition with a major rival, the new venture can focus on a market segment that is being ignored.

Industry product characteristics also have a significant impact on a new venture's success. First, a new venture is more likely to be successful when it enters an industry with heterogeneous (different) products than when it enters one with homogeneous (similar) products. In a heterogeneous industry, a new venture can differentiate itself from competitors with a unique product; or, by focusing on the unique needs of a market segment, it can find a market niche. Second, a new venture is, according to research data, more likely to be successful if the product is relatively unimportant to the customer's total purchasing needs than if it is important. Customers are more likely to experiment with a new product if the costs are low and product failure will not create a problem.

Business Strategy

According to Hofer and Sandberg, the key to success in new-venture strategy is (1) *to differentiate the product from other competitors in the areas of quality and service* and (2) *to focus the product on customer needs in a segment of the market so that a dominant share of that part of the market is achieved.* Adopting guerrilla-warfare tactics, these companies go after opportunities in market niches too small to justify retaliation from the market leaders.[34]

To continue its growth once it has found a niche, the entrepreneurial firm can emphasize continued innovation and pursue natural growth in its current markets. It can expand into related markets in which the company's core skills, resources, and facilities offer the keys to further success.

Entrepreneurial Characteristics

Hofer and Sandberg propose four behavioral factors as key to a new venture's success.[35]

1. Successful entrepreneurs are able to *identify potential venture opportunities* better than are most people. They focus on opportunities—not on problems—and try to learn from failure. Entrepreneurs are goal-oriented and have a strong impact on the emerging culture of an organization. They are able to envision where the company is going and are thus able to provide an overall strong sense of strategic direction.[36]
2. Successful entrepreneurs have a *sense of urgency* that makes them action-oriented. They have a high need for achievement, which motivates them to put their ideas into action. They tend to have an internal locus of control that leads them to believe that they can determine their own fate through their own behavior. They also have a significantly greater capacity to tolerate ambiguity than do many in established organizations.[37] They also have a high need for control and may even be viewed as "misfits who need to create their own environment." They tend to distrust others and often have a need "to show others that they amount to something, that they cannot be ignored."[38]
3. Successful entrepreneurs have a *detailed knowledge of the key factors* needed for success in the industry and have the physical stamina needed to make their work their lives. More than half of all entrepreneurs work at least 60 hours a week in the start-up year, according to a study by the National Federation of Independent Business.[39]
4. Successful entrepreneurs *seek outside help* to supplement their skills, knowledge, and abilities. Through their enthusiasm, they are able to attract key investors, partners, creditors, and employees. As mentioned previously in Illustrative Example 8.3, Mitch Kapor, founder of Lotus Development Corporation, did not hesitate to bring in Jim Manzi as President, because Manzi had the managerial skills that Kapor lacked.

TABLE 12.3	**Some Guidelines for New-Venture Success**

- Focus on industries facing substantial technological or regulatory changes, especially those with recent exits by established competitors.
- Seek industries whose smaller firms have relatively weak competitive positions.
- Seek industries that are in early, high-growth stages of evolution.
- Seek industries in which it is possible to create high barriers to subsequent entry.
- Seek industries with heterogeneous products that are relatively unimportant to the customer's overall success.
- Seek to differentiate your products from those of your competitors in ways that are meaningful to your customers.
- Focus such differentiation efforts on product quality, marketing approaches, and customer service—and charge enough to cover the costs of doing so.
- Seek to dominate the market segments in which you compete. If necessary, either segment the market differently or change the nature and focus of your differentiation efforts to increase your domination of the segments you serve.
- Stress innovation, especially new product innovation, that is built on existing organizational capabilities.
- Seek natural, organic growth through flexibility and opportunism that builds on existing organizational strengths.

Source: C. W. Hofer and W. R. Sandberg, "Improving New Venture Performance: Some Guidelines for Success," *American Journal of Small Business* (Summer 1987), pp. 17, 19. Copyright © 1987 by C. W. Hofer and W. R. Sandberg. Reprinted by permission.

In summarizing their conclusions regarding factors affecting the success of entrepreneurial ventures, Hofer and Sandberg propose guidelines presented in Table 12.3.

12.5 ISSUES IN STRATEGY IMPLEMENTATION

The implementation of strategy in a small business involves many of the same issues, mentioned in Chapters 8 and 9, that concern a large corporation. Programs, budgets, and procedures to make the strategy action-oriented must be developed and used. Resources must be organized so that the work can be done efficiently and effectively; the proper people must be selected for key jobs; and employees' efforts need to be directed toward task accomplishment and coordinated so that the company achieves its objectives and fulfills its mission. The major difference between the large and small company is *who* must implement the strategy. In a large corporation, the implementors are often a very different group of people from those who formulated the strategy. In a small business, the formulators of the strategy are usually the ones to implement it. It is for this reason that the imaginary line between strategy formulation and implementation often becomes blurred in most small businesses. Two key implementation issues in small companies are organizing and staffing the growing company and transferring ownership of the company to the next generation.

STAGES OF SMALL BUSINESS DEVELOPMENT

The implementation problems of a small business change as the company grows and develops over time. Just as the decision-making process for entrepreneurial ventures is different from that of established businesses, so do the managerial systems in small companies often vary from those of large corporations. Those variations are based on their stage of development. The stages of corporate growth and development discussed in Chapter 8 suggest that all small businesses are either in Stage I or trying to move into Stage II. These models imply that all successful new ventures eventually become Stage II, functionally organized companies. This is not always true, however. In attempting to show clearly how small businesses develop, Churchill and Lewis propose five *substages* of small business development: (A) Existence, (B) Survival, (C) Success, (D) Take-off, and (E) Resource Maturity.[40] (See Table 12.4.) A review of these small-business sub-stages shows in more detail how a company can move through the entrepreneurial Stage I (as described in Chapter 8) into a functionally oriented, professionally managed Stage II.

Stage A: Existence

At this point, the entrepreneurial venture faces the problems of obtaining customers and delivering the promised product or service. The organizational structure is a simple one. The entrepreneur does everything and directly supervises subordinates. Systems are minimal. The owner *is* the business.

TABLE 12.4 | **Substages of Small-Business Development[1]**

A. Existence
B. Survival
C. Success
   1. Disengagement
   2. Growth
D. Take-off
E. Resource Maturity

---

[1] These are actually substages within the stages of development discussed in Chapter 8. Thus, small business Stages A through D are really substages of Stage I, entrepreneurial management, whereas Stage E is the first substage of Stage II, functional management. Refer to Table 8.2.

Source: N. C. Churchill and V. L. Lewis, "The Five Stages of Small Business Growth," *Harvard Business Review* (May–June 1983), pp. 30–50.

Stage B: Survival

Those ventures able to satisfy a sufficient number of customers enter this stage. The rest of the ventures close when the owners run out of start-up capital. Those reaching the survival stage are concerned about generating the cash flow needed to repair and replace capital assets as they wear out, and to finance the growth to continue satisfying the market segment it has found.

At this stage, the organizational structure is still simple, but it probably has a sales manager or general supervisor to carry out the well-defined orders of the owner. A major problem of many small businesses at this stage is finding a person who is qualified to supervise the business when the owner can't be present but who is still willing to work for a very modest salary.[41] Entrepreneurs usually try to use family members rather than to hire an outsider, who lacks the entrepreneur's dedication to the business and (in the words of one owner-manager) "steals them blind." A company that remains in this stage for a long time will earn marginal returns on invested time and capital (with lots of psychic income!) and eventually go out of business when "mom and pop" give up or retire.

Stage C: Success

By this point the company's sales have reached a level where the firm is not only profitable, but has sufficient cash flow to reinvest in itself. The key issue at this stage is whether the company should be used as a platform for growth or as a means of support for the owners as they completely or partially disengage from the company. The company is transforming into a functionally structured organization, but still relies on the entrepreneur for all key decisions. The two options are:

C(1) Disengagement   The company can now successfully follow a stability strategy and remain at this stage almost indefinitely—provided that environmental change does not destroy its niche or poor management reduce its competitive abilities. By now functional managers have taken over some duties of the entrepreneur. The company at this stage may be incorporated, but it is still primarily owned by the founder or founder's family. Consequently, the board of directors is either a rubber stamp for the entrepreneur or a forum for family squabbles. Growth strategies are not pursued, either because the market niche will not allow growth or because the owner is content with the company at a size he or she can still manage comfortably.

C(2) Growth   The entrepreneur risks all available cash and the established borrowing power of the company in financing further growth. Strategic as well as operational planning is extensive and deeply involves the owner. Managers with an eye to the company's future rather than for its current situation are hired. The emphasis now is on teamwork rather than on the entrepreneur's personal actions and energy. As noted in the *boxed example* of Maytag, a corporate culture based on the personal values and philosophy of the founder begins to form as the founder hires and trains a dedicated team of successors.[42]

MAYTAG CORPORATION: THE IMPACT OF F. L. MAYTAG

Much of Maytag Corporation's corporate culture derives from founder F. L. Maytag's personal philosophy and from lessons he learned when starting the business at the turn of the twentieth century. F. L. Maytag made a direct impact on the Maytag Company's development and indirectly on the Maytag Corporation's philosophy of management in the following areas:

- **Commitment to Quality.** In the company's first year of operation (selling attachments to threshing machines), almost half the products sold were defective in some way. F. L.'s insistence on fixing or buying back the faulty products resulted in losses for the new company, but set a strong example in emphasizing the importance of quality. F. L. commented that *"nothing was actually 'sold' until it was in the hands of a satisfied user."*
- **Concern for Employees.** Wages at Maytag have traditionally been some of the highest in the industry. Fred Maytag's philosophy was that an *"uncommonly good company wants to pay its employees uncommonly well."*
- **Concern for the Community.** F. L. Maytag played a significant role in the development of the Newton (Iowa) YMCA. He also built a water plant and sold it to the city at cost. Continuing his example, Maytag management has been active in community affairs and concerned about pollution.
- **View of Innovation.** In the company's early years when the factory itself sent service people out to far-flung dealers to repair de-

fective products, F. L. Maytag noted that few calls ever came from a Minnesota dealer that employed a mechanic named Howard Snyder. Consequently, he hired Snyder to improve the company's products. Snyder was not interested in cosmetic changes for the sake of sales, but in internal improvements related to quality, durability, and safety. This emphasis became the company's dominant view of product development.

- **Promotion from Within.** F. L. Maytag was very concerned about building company loyalty and trust. He was committed to hiring and training people to do the best work possible. He constantly told people: *"I'd rather make men than money . . . and I would because I can give money away. I can't give men away; I need them."*
- **Dedication to Hard Work.** Imbued with the strong work ethic of the Midwest, F. L. Maytag spent huge amounts of time to establish and maintain the company. His trip West while Chairman of the Board to personally sell a traincar load of washers set an example to his sales force and became a permanent part of company lore.
- **Emphasis on Performance.** F. L. Maytag did not like to boast about himself or his company. Preferring to be judged by his work rather than by his words, he was quoted in a company newsletter as saying: *"It's a good idea for a fellow to have a fair opinion of himself. . . . But it doesn't sound well to hear him broadcast it. It's a better idea to let his associates discover it by his deeds."*

Stage D: Take-Off

The key problems in this stage are how to grow rapidly and how to finance that growth. The entrepreneur must learn to delegate to the specialized professional managers who now form the top management of the company.[43] A functional structure for the organization should now be solidly in place. Operational and strategic planning greatly involves the hired managers, but the company is still dominated by the entrepreneur's presence and stock control. Vertical and horizontal growth strategies are being seriously considered as the firm's management debates when and how to grow. This is the point at which the entrepreneur either is able to manage the transition from a small to a large company, or recognizes personal limitations, sells his or her stock for a profit, and leaves the firm. The composition of the board of directors changes, from dominance by friends and relatives of the owner to a large percentage of outsiders with managerial experience, who can help the owner during the transition to a professionally managed company. The biggest danger facing the firm in this stage is the owner's desire to remain in total control as if it were still a small entrepreneurial venture, even though he or she lacks the managerial skills necessary to run an established corporation.[44]

Stage E: Resource Maturity

It is at this point, Stage E, that the small company has adopted most of the characteristics of an established, large company. It may still be a small-to-medium-sized company, but it is recognized as an important force in the industry and a possible candidate for the Fortune 500 someday. The greatest concerns of a company at this stage are (1) controlling the financial gains brought on by rapid growth, and (2) retaining its flexibility and entrepreneurial spirit. In the terms of the stages of organizational growth and development discussed in Chapter 8, the company has become a full-fledged Stage II functional corporation.

TRANSFER OF POWER AND WEALTH IN FAMILY BUSINESSES

Small businesses are often family businesses. Even though the founders of the companies are the primary forces in starting the entrepreneurial ventures, their needs for business support and financial assistance will cause them to turn to family members, who can be trusted, over unknown outsiders of questionable integrity, who may demand more salary than the enterprise can afford. Sooner or later the founder's spouse and children are drafted into business operations, either because (1) the family standard of living is directly tied to the business, or (2) the entrepreneur is in desperate need of help just to staff the operation. The children are guaranteed summer jobs and the business changes from dad's or mom's company to "our" company. The family members are extremely valuable assets to the entrepreneur because they are often also willing, to help the business succeed, to put in long hours at low pay. Even though the spouse and children might have no official stock in the company, they know that they will somehow share in its future and perhaps even inherit the business. The problem is that only 30% of family firms in

TABLE 12.5	**Transfer of Power in a Family Business**

Phase 1. **Owner-managed business.** Phase 1 begins at start-up and continues until the entrance of another family member into the business on a full-time basis. Family considerations influence but are not yet a directing part of the firm. At this point, the founder (entrepreneur) and the business are one.

Phase 2. **Training and development of new generation.** The children begin to learn the business at the dining room table during early childhood and then through part-time and vacation employment. The family and the business become one. Just as the entrepreneur identified with the business earlier, the family now begins to identify itself with the business.

Phase 3. **Partnership between generations.** At this point, a son or daughter of the founder has acquired sufficient business and managerial competence so that he or she can be involved in key decisions for at least a part of the company. The entrepreneur's offspring, however, has to first gain respect from the firm's employees and other managers and show that he or she can do the job right. Another issue is the lack of willingness of the founder to share authority with the son or daughter. Consequently, a common tactic taken by sons and daughters in family businesses is to take a job in a large, established corporation where they can gain valuable experience and respect for their skills.

Phase 4. **Transfer of power.** Instead of being forced to sell the company when he or she can no longer manage the business, the founder has the option in a family business of turning it over to the next generation as part of their inheritance. Often the founder moves to the position of Chairman of the Board and promotes one of the children to the position of CEO. Unfortunately, some founders cannot resist meddling in operating affairs and unintentionally undermine the leadership position of the son or daughter. To avoid this problem, the founder should sell his or her stock (probably through a leveraged buy out to the children) and physically leave the company to allow the next generation the freedom it needs to adapt to changing conditions.

Source: N. C. Churchill and K. J. Hatten, "Non-Market-Based Transfers of Wealth and Power: A Research Framework for Family Businesses," *American Journal of Small Business* (Winter 1987), pp. 51–64.

the U.S. make it to the second generation, and just 13% survive to the third generation.[45]

Churchill and Hatten propose that family businesses go through four sequential phases, from the time in which the venture is strictly managed by the founder to the time in which the next generation takes charge.[46] Each of these phases must be well managed if the company is to survive past the average family-firm life expectancy of 24 years—the average tenure of the founder.[47] These phases are detailed in Table 12.5.

12.6 ISSUES IN EVALUATION AND CONTROL

As a means by which the corporation's implementation of strategy can be evaluated, the control systems of large corporations have evolved over a long period of time in response to pressures from the environment (particularly the government). Conversely, the entrepreneur creates what is needed as the business grows. Because of a personal involvement in decision making, the entrepreneur managing a small business has little need for a formal, detailed reporting system.[48] Thus, the founder who has little understanding of accounting and a shortness of cash might employ a bookkeeper instead of an accountant. A formal personnel function might never appear because the entrepreneur lumps it in with simple bookkeeping and uses a secretary to handle personnel files. As an entrepreneurial venture becomes more established, it will develop more complex evaluation and control systems, but they are often not the kind used in large corporations and are probably used for different purposes.

Financial statements, in particular, tell only half the story in small, privately owned companies. The formality of the financial reporting system in such a company is usually a result of pressures from government tax agencies, not from management's desire for an objective evaluation and control system. Because balance sheets and income statements do not always give an accurate picture, standard ratios such as return on assets and debt-equity are unreliable. Levin and Travis provide five reasons why owners, operators, and outside observers should be wary of using standard financial methods to indicate the health of a small, privately owned company.[49]

- **The line between debt and equity is blurred**. In some instances, what appears as a loan is really an easy-to-retrieve equity investment. The entrepreneur in this instance doesn't want to lose his or her investment if the company fails. Another condition is that retained earnings seldom reflect the amount of internal financing needed for the company's growth. This account may merely be a place in which cash is left so that the owner can avoid double taxation. To avoid other taxes, owner-managers may own fixed assets that they lease to the corporation. The equity that was used to buy those assets is really the company's equity, but it doesn't appear on the books.
- **Life-style is a part of financial statements**. The life-style of the owner and the owner's family is often reflected in the balance sheet. The assets of some firms include beach cottages, mountain chalets, and automobiles. In others, plants and warehouses that are used for company operations are not shown because they are held separately by the family. Income statements may not reflect how well the company is operating. Profitability is not so important in decision making in small, private companies as it is in large, publicly held corporations. For example, spending for recreation or transportation and paying rents or salaries above market rates to relatives put artificially high costs on the books of small firms. The business might appear to be poorly managed to an outsider, but the owner is acting rationally. The owner-manager wants dependable income or its equivalent with the least-painful tax consequences. Because the standard profitability measures such as ROI are not useful in the evaluation of such a firm, Levin and Travis recommend return on current assets as a better measure of corporate productivity.[50]
- **Standard financial formulas don't always apply**. Following practices that are in contrast to standard financial recomendations, small companies will often use short-term debt to finance fixed assets. The absence of well-organized

capital markets for small businesses, along with the typical banker's resistance to making loans without personal guarantees, leaves the private owner little choice.

- **Personal preference determines financial policies.** Because the owner is often the manager of the small firm, dividend policy is largely irrelevant. Dividend decisions are based not on stock price (which is usually unknown because the stock is not traded), but on the owner's life-style and the tradeoff between taking wealth from the corporation and double taxation.

- **Banks combine personal and business wealth.** Because of the large percentage of small businesses that go bankrupt every year, bank loan officers are reluctant to lend money to a small business unless the owner also provides some personal guarantees for the loan. In some instances, part of the loan may be composed of a second mortgage on the owner's house. If the owner does not want to succumb to this pressure by lenders to include the owner's personal assets as part of the collateral, the owner-manager must be willing to pay high interest rates for a loan that does not put the family's assets at risk.

SUMMARY AND CONCLUSION

Entrepreneurial ventures and small businesses are managed far more informally than are the large, established business corporations discussed elsewhere in this book. Some of the more popular strategic management concepts and techniques, such as portfolio analysis, are not very useful to the typical small-business manager or entrepreneur. As Mintzberg pointed out in Chapter 2, small, rapidly growing companies tend to follow the entrepreneurial mode of strategy formulation—characterized by bold moves and intuitive decisions.

Small firms that engage in strategic management usually outperform those that do not. This does not mean, however, that formal procedures are necessary. The process of strategic planning, not the plan itself, appears to be a key component of business performance. The strategic management model that was introduced in Chapter 1 and is used to introduce every chapter in this book is just as useful to small and entrepreneurial companies as it is to large business corporations and not-for-profit organizations. Even the strategic decision-making process discussed in Chapters 2 and 6 is valuable to existing small businesses with a few adjustments made for entrepreneurial ventures.

This chapter presents some issues in environmental scanning and strategy formulation that apply to new ventures and small businesses. S.W.O.T. anal-

ysis is very useful, but environmental scanning can be much more informal than that performed in large corporations. Seven sources of innovation should be carefully monitored by any prospective entrepreneur. A new venture's success is largely determined by (1) the industry's structure, (2) the venture's business strategy, and (3) the behavioral characteristics of the entrepreneur.

Although the implementation process for small and entrepreneurial businesses is similar to that used by large corporations, there are some important differences. Small-business managers tend to make little distinction between formulation and implementation. The stages of growth and development for a small business are also very different from those presented in Chapter 8. Between Stages I and II are five distinct substages that characterize many small companies. The implementation of strategy is also different for those many small companies (and for a few large ones as well) that are privately held family businesses. The next generation must always be considered in decisions concerning the staffing of key positions and the company's organization for future growth.

Evaluation and control in small businesses and entrepreneurial ventures is different from that practiced by most large, publicly held corporations. For the small operator, the procedures are far less formal and are usually the result of the owner-manager's preferences and government taxation policies rather than of any strategic considerations. Businesses are often run on a cash basis and have minimum reporting procedures. For these and other reasons, owners, operators, and outside observers should be wary of using standard evaluation methods to measure the health of a small, privately owned company.

In conclusion, this chapter provides the reader with a basic understanding of the differences between large corporations and small businesses in terms of their use of strategic management. Entrepreneurs and top managers of other small businesses inhabit a very different kind of world from that occupied by their counterparts in large corporations. These managers have few resources to draw on, and operate with the knowledge that the difference between success and bankruptcy can be their willingness to risk all their personal possessions on a dream.

DISCUSSION QUESTIONS

1. What are some arguments for and against the use of strategic management concepts and techniques in a small or entrepreneurial business?

2. If the owner-manager of a small company asked you for some advice concerning the introduction of strategic planning, what would you tell her?

3. In terms of strategic management, how does a new venture's situation differ from that of an ongoing small company?

4. The strategic decision-making process for new ventures comprises interrelated steps. List and describe each step in sequential order.

5. How should a small company engage in environmental scanning? To what aspects of the environment should management pay most attention?

6. What are the characteristics of an attractive industry from an entrepreneur's point of view?

7. What considerations should small-business entrepreneurs keep in mind when they are deciding if a company should follow a growth or a stability strategy?

8. What are the substages of small business development? List and explain each stage.

9. How does being family-owned as compared to publicly owned affect a firm's strategic management?

10. What are the pros and cons of using a standard financial reporting system in a small business?

NOTES

1. E. Wilkes, "Something New Under the Sun," *Nation's Business* (August 1989), p. 9.

2. G. d'Amboise and M. Muldowney, "Management Theory for Small Business: Attempts and Requirements," *Academy of Management Review* (April 1988), p. 226.

3. M. S. Wortman, Jr., "Entrepreneurship: An Integrating Typology and Evaluation of the Empirical Research in the Field," *Journal of Management* (Summer 1987), p. 264.

4. *The State of Small Business: A Report to the President* (Washington, D.C.: U.S. Government Printing Office, 1987), pp. 12–20; and "ABC World News Tonight" (May 6, 1988).

   C. W. Hofer and W. R. Sandberg, "Improving New Venture Performance: Some Guidelines for Success,"

American Journal of Small Business (Summer 1987), pp. 11–12.

5. *The State of Small Business: A Report to the President*, p. 117.

6. B. Keats and J. Bracker, "Toward a Theory of Small Firm Performance: A Conceptual Model," *American Journal of Small Business* (Spring 1988), pp. 41–58.

7. J. Castro, J. McDowell, and W. McWhirter, "Big vs. Small," *Time* (September 5, 1988), p. 49.

8. E. Romanelli, "Environments and Strategies of Organization Start-up: Effects on Early Survival," *Administrative Science Quarterly* (September 1989), p. 369.

9. T. Bates and A. Nucci, "Analysis of Small Business Size and Rate of Discontinuance," *Journal of Small Business Management* (October 1989), pp. 1–7.

10. Research commissioned by American Express Company and the National Federation of Independent Businesses conducted by A. C. Cooper, W. C. Dunkelberg, and C. Y. Woo of 2,994 new U.S. businesses found 77% survived past three years of existence. Favorable economic conditions may have contributed to the surprisingly high rate of new-venture success. For a summary of the controversial study, see R. Ricklefs, "Road to Success Becomes Less Littered with Failures," *Wall Street Journal* (October 10, 1989), p. B2.

11. M. J. Sanford, *New Enterprise Management* (Reston, Va.: Reston Publishing Co., 1982), p. 4.

12. S. Shirley, "Corporate Strategy and Entrepreneurial Vision," *Long Range Planning* (December 1989), p. 107.

13. D. Fields, "Mrs. Fields' Weekends," *USA Weekend* (February 3–5, 1989), p. 16.

    M. Alpert, "In the Chips," *Fortune* (July 17, 1989), pp. 115–116.

14. D'Amboise and Muldowney, "Management Theory for Small Business."

15. J. W. Carland, F. Hoy, W. R. Boulton, and J. A. C. Carland, "Differentiating Entrepreneurs from Small Business Owners: A Conceptualization," *Academy of Management Review* (April 1984), p. 358.

    J. W. Carland, J. C. Carland, F. Hoy, and W. R. Boulton, "Distinctions Between Entrepreneurial and Small Business Ventures," *International Journal of Management* (March 1988), pp. 98–103.

16. S. P. Galante, "Counting on a Narrow Market Can Cloud Company's Future," *Wall Street Journal* (January 20, 1986), p. 17.

17. C. B. Shrader, C. L. Mulford, and V. L. Blackburn, "Strategic and Operational Planning, Uncertainty, and Performance in Small Firms," *Journal of Small Business Management* (October 1989), pp. 45–60.

    R. B. Robinson, Jr., and J. A. Pearce II, "Research Thrusts in Small Firm Strategic Planning," *Academy of Management Review* (January 1984), p. 129.

    C. E. Aronoff and J. L. Ward, "Why Owners Don't Plan," *Nation's Business* (June 1990), pp. 59–60.

18. J. S. Bracker, B. W. Keats, and J. N. Pearson, "Planning and Financial Performance Among Small Firms in a Growth Industry," *Strategic Management Journal* (November-December 1988), pp. 591–603.

19. J. S. Bracker and J. N. Pearson, "Planning and Financial Performance of Small, Mature Firms," *Strategic Management Journal* (November-December 1986), pp. 503–522.

20. R. Ackelsberg and P. Arlow, "Small Businesses Do Plan and It Pays Off," *Long Range Planning* (October 1985), pp. 61–67.

21. J. Walsh, *1990 Pulse of the Middle Market,* as reported in "A Solid Strategy Helps Companies' Growth," *Nation's Business* (October 1990), p. 10.

22. Robinson and Pearce, "Research Thrusts," p. 130.

    A. Thomas, "Less Is More: How Less Formal Planning Can Be Best," in *The Strategic Planning Management Reader,* edited by L. Fahey (Englewood Cliffs, N.J.: Prentice Hall, 1989), pp. 331–336.

    Shrader, et al., "Strategic and Operational Planning," pp. 45–60.

23. J. C. Shuman and J. A. Seeger, "The Theory and Practice of Strategic Management in Smaller Rapid Growth Firms," *American Journal of Small Business* (Summer 1986), pp. 7–18; and J. C. Shuman, J. D. Shaw, and G. Sussman, "Strategic Planning in Smaller Rapid Growth Companies," *Long Range Planning* (December 1985), pp. 48–53.

24. R. B. Robinson, Jr., and J. A. Pearce II, "The Impact of Formalized Strategic Planning on Financial Performance in Small Organizations," *Strategic Management Journal* (July-September 1983), pp. 197–207.

    Ackelsberg and Arlow, "Small Businesses Do Plan," pp. 61–67.

25. Bracker and Pearson, "Planning and Financial Performance," p. 512.

26. R. R. Roha and B. Kainen, "7 Mistakes That Can Kill Your Business," *Changing Times* (August 1988), pp. 47–50.

    For information on preparing a business plan, see S. R. Rich and D. E. Gumpert, "How to Write a Winning Business Plan," *Harvard Business Review* (May-June 1985), pp. 156–163; and L. Hosmer and R. Guiles, *Creating the Successful Business Plan for New Ventures* (New York: McGraw-Hill, 1985).

27. Shuman and Seeger, "Strategic Management in Smaller Rapid Growth Firms," p. 14.

28. S. Birley and D. Norburn, "Small vs. Large Companies: The Entrepreneurial Conundrum," *Journal of Business Strategy* (Summer 1985), pp. 81–87.

29. *Ibid.*, p. 82.

30. *Ibid.*, p. 83.

31. P. F. Drucker, *Innovation and Entrepreneurship* (New York: HarperCollins, 1985), pp. 30–129.

32. C. A. Jaffe, "Success by Surprise," *Nation's Business* (September 1989), pp. 30–33.

33. Hofer and Sandberg, "Improving New Venture Performance," pp. 12–23.

34. J. L. Ward and S. F. Stasch, "How Small-Share Firms Can Uncover Winning Strategies," *Journal of Business Strategy* (September/October 1988), pp. 26–31.

    K. R. Harrigan, "Guerrilla Strategies for Underdog

Competitors," *Planning Review* (November 1986), pp. 4–11, 44–45.

35. Hofer and Sandberg, "Improving New Venture Performance," p. 22.

36. B. Bird, "Implementing Entrepreneurial Ideas: The Case for Intention," *Academy of Management Review* (July 1988), pp. 442–453.

    S. L. Hart and D. R. Denison, "Strategy-Making in New Technology-Based Firms: Comparing Process and Performance," in *Proceedings, Managing the High Technology Firm Conference,* edited by L. R. Gomez-Mejia and M. W. Lawless (Boulder: University of Colorado, January 13–15, 1988), pp. 188–194.

37. M. B. Low and I. C. MacMillan, "Entrepreneurship: Past Research and Future Challenges" *Journal of Management* (June 1988), p. 147.

38. M. Kets de Vries, "The Dark Side of Entrepreneurship," *Harvard Business Review* (November-December 1985), pp. 160–167.

39. R. Ricklefs and U. Gupta, "Traumas of a New Entrepreneur," *Wall Street Journal* (May 10, 1989), p. B1.

40. N. C. Churchill and V. L. Lewis, "The Five Stages of Small Business Growth," *Harvard Business Review* (May-June 1983), pp. 30–50.

    R. K. Kazanjian, in "Relation of Dominant Problems to Stages of Growth in Technology-Based New Ventures," *Academy of Management Journal* (June 1988), pp. 257–279, proposes the four stages of (1) conception and development, (2) commercialization, (3) growth, and (4) stability. Kazanjian's first two stages are similar to Churchill and Lewis's Stage A. Growth and stability are similar to Churchill and Lewis's Survival (Stage B) and Success (Stage C). The Churchill and Lewis model is used in this text because it is more comprehensive and generalizable to more types of entrepreneurial ventures than is the Kazanjian model.

41. R. Johnson, "Trying Harder to Find a No. 2 Executive," *Wall Street Journal* (June 19, 1989), p. B1.

42. K. G. Smith and J. K. Harrison, "In Search of Excellent Leaders," in *Handbook of Business Strategy, 1986/87 Yearbook,* edited by W. D. Guth (Boston: Warren, Gorham and Lamont, 1986), p. 27.8.

43. E. G. Flamholtz, *How to Make the Transition from an Entrepreneurship to a Professionally Managed Firm* (San Francisco: Jossey-Bass, 1986).

44. G. D. Meyer, R. M. Lenoir, and T. J. Dean, "The Executive Limit Scenario in High Technology Firms," in *Proceedings, Managing the High Technology Firm Conference,* edited by L. R. Gomez-Mejia and M. W. Lawless (Boulder: University of Colorado, January 13–15, 1988), pp. 342–349.

45. J. Ward, *Keeping the Family Business Healthy* (San Francisco: Jossey-Bass, 1987), as reported by U. Gupta and M. Robichaux, "Reins Tangle Easily at Family Firms," *Wall Street Journal* (August 9, 1989), p. B1.

46. N. C. Churchill and K. J. Hatten, "Non-Market-Based Transfers of Wealth and Power: A Research Framework for Family Businesses," *American Journal of Small Business* (Winter 1987), pp. 51–64.

47. R. Beckhard and W. G. Dyer, Jr., "Managing Continuity in the Family-Owned Business," *Organizational Dynamics* (Summer 1983), pp. 5–12.

48. Birley and Norburn, "Small vs. Large Companies," p. 85.

    S. S. Cowen and J. K. Middaugh II, "Designing an Effective Financial Planning and Control System," *Long Range Planning* (December 1988), pp. 83–92.

49. R. I. Levin and V. R. Travis, "Small Company Finance: What the Books Don't Say," *Harvard Business Review* (November-December 1987), pp. 30–32.

50. *Ibid.,* p. 31.

CHAPTER THIRTEEN

Strategic Issues in Not-for-Profit Organizations

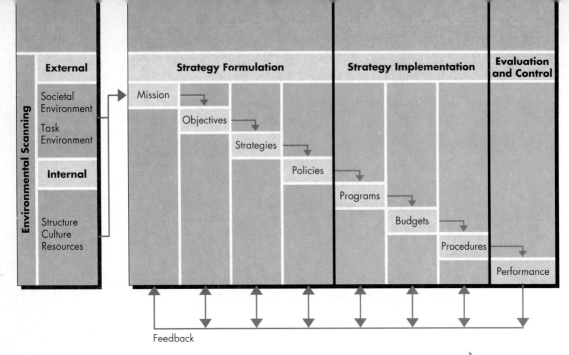

STRATEGIC MANAGEMENT MODEL

Twenty years ago, management was a dirty word for those involved in nonprofit organizations. It meant business, and nonprofits prided themselves on being free of the taint of commercialism and above such sordid considerations as the bottom line. Now most of them have learned that non-profits need management even more than business does, precisely because they lack the discipline of the bottom line.[1]

Peter Drucker

Traditionally, studies in strategic management have dealt with profit-making firms to the exclusion of nonprofit or governmental organizations. The little, but growing, empirical research suggests that not-for-profit organizations are in the initial stages of using strategic management.[2] An increasing number of not-for-profits, especially hospitals, colleges, and even charities, are concerned with strategic issues and strategic planning, even though their use of it might be only an informal process.

A knowledge of not-for-profit organizations would be important even if there were no other reason than the fact that they employ over 25% of the U.S. work force and own approximately 15% of the nation's private wealth.[3] Private nonprofit organizations, in particular, represent 5.2% of all corporations, partnerships, and proprietorships in the U.S., receive 3.5% of all revenue, and hold about 4.3% of the total assets of business firms.[4] In the U.S. alone, in addition to various federal, state, and local government agencies, there are about 10,000 not-for-profit hospitals and nursing homes (84% of all hospitals), 4,600 colleges and universities, over 100,000 private and public elementary and secondary schools, and almost 350,000 churches and synagogues, plus many thousands of charities and service organizations.[5]

The first 12 chapters of this book dealt primarily with the strategic management of profit-making corporations. Scholars and practitioners are concluding, however, that many strategic management concepts and techniques can be successfully adapted for not-for-profit organizations.[6] Although the evidence is not yet conclusive, there appears to be an association between strategic planning efforts and performance measures such as growth.[7] The purpose of this chapter is, therefore, to highlight briefly the major differences between the profit-making and the not-for-profit organization, so that the effects of their differences on the strategic management process can be understood.

13.1 CATEGORIES OF ORGANIZATIONS

All profit-making and not-for-profit organizations can be grouped into four basic categories.

1. **Private for-profit** businesses that depend on the market economy to generate the means of their survival. (These range from small businesses to major corporations.)
2. **Private quasi-public organizations** created by legislative authority and given a limited monopoly to provide particular goods or services to a population subgroup. (These are primarily public utilities.)
3. **Private nonprofit organizations** that operate on public goodwill (donations, contributions, and endowments or government stipends), but are constituted outside the authority of governmental agencies or legislative bodies.
4. **Public** agencies of the government (federal, state, and local) that are constituted by law and authorized to collect taxes and provide services.[8]

Typically, the term **not-for-profit** includes *private nonprofit corporations* (such as hospitals, institutes, private colleges, and organized charities) as well as *public governmental units or agencies* (such as welfare departments, prisons, and state universities). Regulated public utilities are in a gray area somewhere between profit and not-for-profit. They are profit making and have stockholders, but take on many of the characteristics of the not-for-profit organization, such as a greater dependence on rate-setting government commissions than on customers.

13.2 WHY NOT-FOR-PROFIT?

The not-for-profit sector of an economy is important for several reasons. *First,* society desires certain goods and services that profit-making firms cannot or will not provide. These are referred to as "public" or "collective" goods because people who might not have paid for the goods also receive benefits from them. Paved roads, police protection, museums, and schools are examples of public goods. A person cannot use a private good unless she or he pays for it. Generally once a public good is provided, however, anyone can use or enjoy it.

Second, a private nonprofit firm tends to receive benefits from society that a private profit-making firm cannot obtain. Preferred tax status to nonstock corporations is given in section 501(c)(3) of the U.S. Internal Revenue code in the form of exemptions from corporate income taxes. Private nonprofit firms also enjoy exemptions from various other state, local, and federal taxes. Under certain conditions these firms also benefit from the tax deductibility of donors' contributions and membership dues. In addition, they qualify for special third-class mailing privileges.[9] These benefits are allowed because private nonprofit organizations are typically service organizations, which are expected to use any excess of revenue over costs and expenses either to improve service or to reduce the price of their service. This service orientation is reflected in the fact that not-for-profit organizations do not use the term *customer* to refer to the recipient of the service. The recipient is typically referred to as a patient, student, client, case, or simply "the public."

13.3 IMPORTANCE OF REVENUE SOURCE

The feature that best differentiates not-for-profit organizations from each other as well as from profit-making corporations is their source of income.[10] The **profit-making firm** depends on revenues obtained from the sale of its goods and services to customers. Its source of income is the customer who buys and uses the product, and who typically pays for the product when it is received. Profits result when revenues are greater than the costs of making and distributing the product, and are thus a measure of the corporation's **effectiveness** (a product is valued because customers purchase it for use) and **efficiency** (costs are kept below selling price).

SOURCES OF NOT-FOR-PROFIT REVENUE

The **not-for-profit organization**, in contrast to the business firm, depends heavily on dues, assessments, or donations from its membership, or on funding from a sponsoring agency such as the United Way or the federal government. Revenue, therefore, is generated from a variety of sources—*not* just from sales to customers and clients. It can come from people who do not even receive the services they are subsidizing. Such charitable organizations as the American Cancer Society and CARE are examples. In another type of not-for-profit organization—such as unions and voluntary medical plans—revenue comes mostly from the members, the people who receive the service. Nevertheless, the members typically pay dues *in advance* and must accept later whatever service is provided whether they want it or not, whether it is what they expected or not. The service is often received long after the dues are paid. Therefore, some members who have paid into a fund for many years leave the organization or die without having received services, whereas newcomers may receive many services, even though they have paid only a small amount into the fund.

Therefore, in profit-making corporations, there is typically a simple and direct connection between the customer or client and the organization. The organization tends to be totally dependent on sales of its products or services to the customer for revenue, and is therefore extremely interested in pleasing the customer. As shown in Fig. 13.1, the profit-making organization (organization A) tries to influence the customer to continue to buy and use its services. Either by buying or not buying the

---

FIGURE 13.1 | **The Effects of Sources of Revenue on Patterns of Client-Organization Influence**

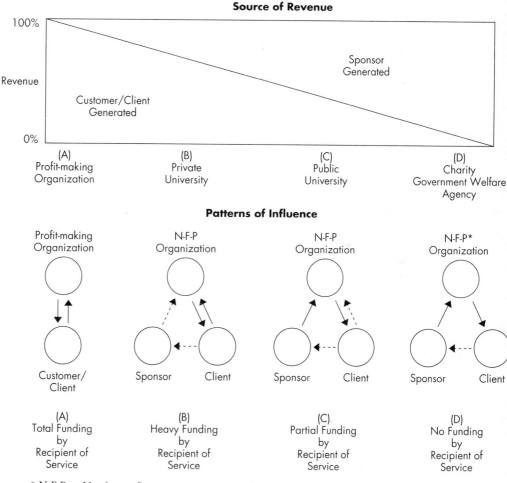

* N-F-P = Not-for-profit.

Source: Thomas L. Wheelen and J. David Hunger, "The Effect of Revenue Upon Patterns of Client-Organization Influence." Copyright © 1982 by Wheelen and Hunger Associates. Revised 1991. Reprinted by permission.

item offered, the customer, in turn, directly influences the organization's decision-making process.

In the case of the typical not-for-profit organization, however, there is likely to be a very different sort of relationship between the organization providing and the person receiving the service. Because the recipient of the service typically does not pay the entire cost of the service, outside sponsors are required. In most instances, the sponsors receive none of the service but provide partial to total funding of the needed revenues. As indicated earlier, these sponsors can be the government (using taxpayers' money) or charitable organizations, such as the United Way (using voluntary donations). As shown in Fig. 13.1, the not-for-profit (N-F-P) organization can be partially dependent on sponsors for funding (organizations B and C) or totally dependent on the sponsors (organization D).

PATTERNS OF INFLUENCE ON STRATEGIC DECISION MAKING

The pattern of influence on the organization's strategic decision making derives from its sources of revenue. As shown in Fig. 13.1, a private university (organization B) is heavily dependent on student tuition and other client-generated funds for about 71% of its revenue.[11] Therefore, the students' desires are likely to have a stronger influence (as shown by an unbroken line) on the university's decision making than are the desires of the various sponsors, such as alumni and private foundations. The sponsors' relatively marginal influence on the organization is reflected by a broken line. In contrast, a public university (depicted in Fig. 13.1 as organization C) is more heavily dependent on outside sponsors, such as a state legislature, for revenue funding. Student tuition and other client-generated funds form a small percentage (typically only 37%) of total revenue. Therefore, the university's decision making is heavily influenced by the sponsors (unbroken line) and only marginally influenced directly by the students (broken line). In the case of organization D in Fig. 13.1, however, the client has no direct influence on the organization because the client pays nothing for the services received. In this type of situation, the organization tends to measure its effectiveness in terms of sponsor satisfaction. It has no real measure of its efficiency other than its ability to carry out its mission and achieve its objectives within the dollar contributions it has received from its sponsors. In contrast to other organizations in which the client contributes a significant proportion of the needed revenue, this type of not-for-profit organization (D) actually might be able to increase the amount of its revenue by heavily lobbying its sponsors while reducing the level of its service to its clients!

Regardless of the percentage of total funding generated by the client, the client may attempt to indirectly influence the not-for-profit organization through the sponsors. This is depicted by the broken lines connecting the client and the sponsor in organizations B, C, and D in the figure. Welfare clients or prison inmates, for example, may be able to indirectly improve the services they receive if they pressure government officials with letters to legislators, or even by rioting. And students at public universities can lobby state officials for student representation on governing boards.

The key to understanding the management of a not-for-profit organization is thus learning who pays for the delivered services. If the recipients of the service pay only a small proportion of the total cost of the service, it is likely that strategic managers will be more concerned with satisfying the needs and desires of the funding sponsors or agency than those of the people receiving the service. As previous studies indicate, acquisition of resources can become an end in itself.[12]

USEFULNESS OF STRATEGIC MANAGEMENT CONCEPTS AND TECHNIQUES

To the extent that a not-for-profit organization depends more on its sponsors than on its clients for revenue, the less useful will be the standard concepts, techniques, and prescriptions of strategic management. The marketplace orientation underlying portfolio analysis and PIMS research does not translate into situations in which there are only indirect links between client satisfaction and revenue.[13] It is even more obscure when the organization's output is difficult to measure objectively, as is the case with most not-for-profit organizations. Thus, it is very likely that not-for-profit organizations are not for the most part using strategic management because its concepts, techniques, and prescriptions do not lend themselves to situations where sponsors, rather than the marketplace, determine revenue. Even when strategic management concepts and techniques can be applied to not-for-profit organizations, various constraints mean that strategy formulation, implementation, and evaluation and control must be modified.[14]

13.4 IMPACT OF CONSTRAINTS ON STRATEGIC MANAGEMENT

Because not-for-profit organizations are truly different from profit-making organizations, there are several characteristics peculiar to the former that constrain its behavior and affect its strategic management. Newman and Wallender list the following five **constraining characteristics**:

1. **Service is often intangible and hard to measure.** This difficulty is typically compounded by the existence of multiple service objectives developed in order to satisfy multiple sponsors.
2. **Client influence may be weak.** Often the organization has a local monopoly, and payments by customers may be a very small source of funds.
3. **Strong employee commitment to professions or to a cause** may undermine their allegiance to the organization employing them.
4. **Resource contributors**—notably fund contributors and government—**may intrude** on the organization's internal management.
5. **Restraints on the use of rewards and punishments** may result from characteristics 1, 3, and 4 above.[15]

It is true that several of these characteristics can be found in profit-making as well as in not-for-profit organizations. Nevertheless, as Newman and Wallender state, the ". . . frequency of strong impact is much higher in not-for-profit enterprises. . . .''[16] As a result, the strategic management process for any given situation will be different in a not-for-profit organization from that in the typical profit-making corporations discussed in earlier chapters.

IMPACT ON STRATEGY FORMULATION

The five constraining characteristics serve to add at least four **complications** to strategy formulation.

1. **Goal conflicts interfere with rational planning.** Because the not-for-profit organization typically lacks a single clear-cut performance criterion (such as profits), divergent goals and objectives are likely.[17] This divergence is especially likely if there are multiple sponsors. Differences in the concerns of various important sponsors can prevent top management from stating the organization's mission in anything but very broad terms, if they fear that a sponsor who disagrees with a particular, narrow definition of mission might cancel its funding. According to Heffron, an authority in public administration: "The greater openness within which they are compelled to operate—the fishbowl atmosphere—impedes thorough discussion of issues and discourages long-range plans that might alienate stakeholders."[18] In such organizations it is the reduced influence of the clients that permits this diversity of values and goals to occur without a clear market check.

2. **An integrated planning focus tends to shift from results to resources.** Because not-for-profit organizations tend to provide services that are hard to measure, they rarely have a net bottom line. Planning, therefore, becomes more concerned with resource inputs, which can easily be measured, than with service, which cannot. Goal displacement, therefore, becomes even more likely than it is in business organizations.[19]

3. **Ambiguous operating objectives create opportunities for internal politics and goal displacement.** The combination of vague objectives and a heavy concern with resources allows managers considerable leeway in their activities. Such leeway makes possible political maneuvering for personal ends. In addition, because the effectiveness of the not-for-profit organization hinges on the satisfaction of the sponsoring group, there is a tendency for management to ignore the needs of the client while focusing on the desires of the powerful sponsor. This problem is compounded by the fact that boards of trustees are often selected not on the basis of their managerial experience, but on the basis of their ability to contribute money, raise funds, and work with politicians. Their lack of interest in overseeing management is reflected in an overall board-meeting attendance rate of only 50%, compared with 90% for boards of directors of business corporations. Board members of not-for-profit organizations, therefore, tend to ignore the task of determining strategies and policies—leaving this to the paid (or sometimes unpaid) executive director.[20]

4. **Professionalization simplifies detailed planning but adds rigidity.** In those not-for-profit organizations in which professionals play important roles (as in

hospitals or colleges), professional values and traditions can prevent the organization from changing its conventional behavior patterns to fit new service missions tuned to changing social needs. This rigidity, of course, can occur in any organization that hires professionals. The strong service orientation of most not-for-profit organizations, however, tends to encourage the development of static professional norms and attitudes.

IMPACT ON STRATEGY IMPLEMENTATION

The five constraining characteristics affect how a not-for-profit organization is organized in both its structure and job design. Three *complications*, in particular, can be highlighted.

1. **Decentralization is complicated.** The difficulty of setting objectives for an intangible, hard-to-measure service mission complicates the delegation of decision-making authority. Important matters are therefore often centralized, and low-level managers are forced to wait until top management makes a decision. Because of the heavy dependence on sponsors for revenue support, the top management of a not-for-profit organization must be always alert to the sponsors' view of an organizational activity. This necessary caution leads to "defensive centralization," in which top management retains all decision-making authority so that low-level managers cannot take any actions to which the sponsors may object.

2. **Linking pins for external-internal integration become important.** Because of the heavy dependence on outside sponsors, a special need arises for people in "buffer" roles to relate to both inside and outside groups. This role is especially necessary when the sponsors are diverse (revenue comes from donations, membership fees, and federal funds), and the service is intangible (for instance, a "good" education) with a broad mission and multiple shifting objectives. The job of a "Dean for External Affairs," for example, consists primarily of working with the school's alumnae and raising funds.

3. **Job enlargement and executive development can be restrained by professionalism.** In organizations that employ a large number of professionals, managers must design jobs that appeal to prevailing professional norms. Professionals have rather clear ideas about which activities are, and which are not, within their province. Enriching a nurse's job by expanding his or her decision-making authority for drug dosage, for example, can cause conflict with medical doctors who believe that such authority is theirs alone. In addition, a professional's promotion into a managerial job might be viewed as a punishment rather than as a reward.

IMPACT ON EVALUATION AND CONTROL

Special *complications* arising from the constraining characteristics also affect how behavior is motivated and performance is controlled. Two problems, in particular, are often noticed.

1. **Rewards and penalties have little or no relation to performance.** When desired results are vague and the judgment of success is subjective, predictable and impersonal feedback cannot be established. Performance is judged either intuitively ("You don't seem to be taking your job seriously") or on the basis of those small aspects of a job that can be measured ("You were late to work twice last month").

2. **Inputs rather than outputs are heavily controlled.** Because its inputs can be measured much more easily than outputs, the not-for-profit organization tends to focus more on the resources going into performance than on the performance itself.[21] The emphasis is thus on setting maximum limits for costs and expenses. Because there is little to no reward for meeting these standards, people usually respond negatively to controls.

13.5 POPULAR NOT-FOR-PROFIT STRATEGIES

Because the typical mission of the not-for-profit organization is to satisfy an unmet need of a segment of the general public, its objective becomes one of satisfying that need as much as possible. If revenues exceed costs and expenses, the not-for-profit therefore is likely to use the surplus (otherwise known as "profit") to expand or improve its services. If, however, revenues are less than costs and expenses, strong pressures from both within and outside the organization often prevent it from reducing its services. To the extent that management is able to find new sponsors, all may be well. For many not-for-profits, however, there is an eventual limit to contributions with no strings attached. The organization is thus painfully forced to reject contributions from sponsors who wish to alter a portion of the organization's basic mission as a requirement of the contribution. Because of various pressures on them to provide more services than the sponsors and clients can pay for, not-for-profit organizations are developing strategies to help them meet their desired service objectives. Two popular strategies are strategic piggybacking and interorganizational linking.

STRATEGIC PIGGYBACKING

Coined by Nielsen, the term **strategic piggybacking** refers to the development of a new activity for the not-for-profit organization that would generate the funds needed to make up the difference between revenues and expenses.[22] The new activity is related typically in some manner to the not-for-profit's mission, but its purpose is to help subsidize the primary service programs. In an inverted use of portfolio analysis, top management invests in new, safe cash cows to fund its current cash-hungry stars, question marks, and dogs.

Although this strategy is not a new one, it has become very popular recently. As early as 1874, for example, the Metropolitan Museum of Art retained a professional to photograph its collections and to sell copies of the prints. Profits were used to defray the museum's operating costs. More recently, various income-generation ventures have appeared under various auspices, from the Girl Scouts to UNICEF, and in numerous forms, from small gift shops to vast real estate developments. A study by the U.S. General Accounting Office revealed that the amount of funds resulting from income-producing activities has increased from 39% in 1975 to 81% in 1982 of all funds raised by charitable organizations.[23] The Small Business Administration, however, views this activity as "unfair competition." The Internal Revenue Service advises that a not-for-profit that engages in a business "not substantially related" to the organization's exempt purposes may jeopardize its tax-exempt status, particularly if the income from the business exceeds approximately 20% of total organizational revenues.[24]

Although strategic piggybacks can help not-for-profit organizations self-subsidize their primary missions and better utilize their resources, according to Nielsen, there are several *potential negative effects*.[25] First, the revenue-generating venture could actually lose money—especially in the short run. Second, the venture could subvert, interfere with, or even take over the primary mission. Third, the public, as well as the sponsors, could reduce their contributions because of negative responses to such "money-grubbing activities" or because of a mistaken belief that the organization is becoming self-supporting. Fourth, the venture could interfere with the internal operations of the not-for-profit organization.

Edward Skloot, President of the New York consulting firm New Ventures, suggests that a not-for-profit organization have five resources before it begins a revenue-earning activity.[26]

1. **Something to sell**. The organization should assess its resources to see if people might be willing to pay for goods or services closely related to the organization's primary activity.
2. **Critical mass of management talent**. There must be enough available people to nurture and sustain an income venture over the long haul.
3. **Trustee support**. If the trustees have strong feelings against earned-income ventures, they could actively or passively resist commercial involvement.
4. **Entrepreneurial attitude**. Management must be able to combine an interest in innovative ideas with businesslike practicality.
5. **Venture capital**. Because it often takes money to make money, engaging in a joint venture with a business corporation can provide the necessary start-up funds as well as the marketing and management support. For example, Massachusetts General Hospital receives $50 million from Hoechst, the German chemical company, for biological research in exchange for exclusive licenses to develop commercial products from particular research discoveries. The Children's Television Workshop, in partnership with Anheuser-Busch, developed a theme park for young children in Langhorne, Pennsylvania.

INTERORGANIZATIONAL LINKING

A major strategy, called interorganizational linking, often used by not-for-profit organizations to enhance their capacity to serve clients or to acquire resources is developing cooperative ties with other organizations.[27] Not-for-profit hospitals are increasing their use of this strategy as a way to cope with increasing costs and declining revenues. Services can be purchased and provided more efficiently through cooperation with other hospitals than if they were done for one hospital alone. Currently, close to one-third of all nongovernmental not-for-profit hospitals in the U.S. are part of a *multihospital system*, defined as "two or more acute care hospitals owned, leased, or contract-managed by a corporate office."[28] By belonging to a cooperative system, a formerly independent hospital can hope to benefit in terms of staff utilization and management efficiency.

These cooperatives (e.g., American Healthcare Systems, Voluntary Hospitals of America, and Consolidated Catholic Health Care, Inc.) represent over 1,500 hospitals. They not only pool their members' purchasing orders to reduce costs, they also develop for-profit ventures and access capital markets through investor-owned subsidiaries. Don Arnwine, Chairman of Voluntary Hospitals of America, commented on this trend: "It is time we in the not-for-profit sector got off our duffs and competed."[29]

SUMMARY AND CONCLUSION

Strategic management in not-for-profit organizations is still in its initial stages of development. Approaches and techniques such as strategic planning and MBO, which work reasonably well in profit-making corporations, are increasingly being tried in many not-for-profit organizations. Nevertheless, private nonprofit and public organizations differ in terms of their sources of revenue and thus must be treated differently.

The relationship between the organization and the client is more complicated in not-for-profit organizations than in business corporations. Moreover, not-for-profit organizations have certain constraining characteristics that affect the strategic management process. These characteristics cause variations in the ways that managers in not-for-profit organizations formulate and implement strategic decisions. As increasing numbers of not-for-profit organizations find it difficult to generate from sponsors the funds they need to achieve key service objectives, they are turning to strategic piggybacking and interorganizational linking strategies.

Not-for-profit organizations form an important part of society. It is therefore important to understand their reason for existence and their differences from profit-making corporations. The lack of a profit motive often results in vague statements of mission and unmeasurable objectives. This, coupled with a concern for funding from sponsors, can cause a lack of consideration for the very clients the organization was designed to serve. Programs that have little or no connection with the organization's mission can develop. Nevertheless, it is important to remember that not-for-profit organizations usually are established to provide goods and services judged valuable by society that profit-making firms cannot or will not provide. It is dangerous to judge their performance on the basis of simple economic considerations, because they are designed to deal with conditions under which profit-making corporations could not easily survive.

DISCUSSION QUESTIONS

1. Are not-for-profit organizations less efficient than profit-making organizations? Why or why not?

2. Do you agree that the source of revenue is the best way to differentiate between not-for-profit and profit-making organizations as well as among the many kinds of not-for-profit organizations? Why or why not?

3. Is client influence always weak in the not-for-profit organization? Why or why not?

4. Why does the employment of a large number of people who consider themselves to be professionals complicate the strategic management process? How can this also occur in profit-making firms?

5. How does the lack of a clear-cut performance measure, such as profits, affect the strategic management of a not-for-profit organization?

6. What are the pros and cons of strategic piggybacking?

7. In the past, many profit-making businesses such as city bus lines and railroad passenger services have changed their status to not-for-profit as governmental agencies took them over. Recently, however, many not-for-profit organizations in the U.S. have been converting to profit making. For example, more than 20 of the 115 nonprofit Health Maintenance Organizations (HMOs) formed with federal money have converted to for-profit status.[30] Why would a not-for-profit organization want to change its status to profit making?

NOTES

1. P. F. Drucker, "What Business Can Learn from Nonprofits," *Harvard Business Review* (July-August 1989), p. 89.

2. M. S. Wortman, Jr., "Strategic Management in Nonprofit Organizations: A Research Typology and Research Prospectus," in *Strategic Management Frontiers*, edited by J. H. Grant (Greenwich, Conn.: JAI Press, 1988), pp. 415–442.

   J. M. Bryson, *Strategic Planning for Public and Nonprofit Organizations* (San Francisco: Jossey-Bass, 1988), p. xii.

   N. Karagozoglu and R. Seglund, "Strategic Planning for a Public Sector Enterprise," *Long Range Planning* (April 1989), pp. 121–125.

   J. W. Harvey and K. F. McCrohan, "Strategic Issues for Charities and Philanthropies," *Long Range Planning* (December 1988), pp. 44–55.

3. G. Rudney, "The Scope and Dimensions of Nonprofit Activity," in *The Nonprofit Sector: A Research Handbook*, edited by W. W. Powell (New Haven: Yale University Press, 1987), p. 56.

   C. P. McLaughlin, *The Management of Nonprofit Organizations* (New York: John Wiley and Sons, 1986), p. 4.

4. D. R. Young, *If Not For Profit, For What?* (Lexington, Mass.: D. C. Heath, Lexington Books, 1983), p. 9.

5. M. O'Neill, *The Third America* (San Francisco: Jossey-Bass, 1989).

6. I. Unterman and R. H. Davis, *Strategic Management of Not-For-Profit Organizations* (New York: Praeger Press, 1984), p. 2.

7. P. V. Jenster and G. A. Overstreet, "Planning for a Non-Profit Service: A Study of U.S. Credit Unions," *Long Range Planning* (April 1990), pp. 103–111.

   G. J. Medley, "Strategic Planning for the World Wildlife Fund," *Long Range Planning* (February 1988), pp. 46–54.

8. M. D. Fottler, "Is Management Really Generic?" *Academy of Management Review* (January 1981), p. 2.

9. J. G. Simon, "The Tax Treatment of Nonprofit Organizations: A Review of Federal and State Policies," in *The Nonprofit Sector: A Research Handbook*, edited by W. W. Powell (New Haven: Yale University Press, 1987), pp. 67–98.

10. B. P. Keating and M. O. Keating, *Not-For-Profit* (Glen Ridge, N.J.: Thomas Horton & Daughters, 1980), p. 21.

11. "Revenues and Expenditures of Colleges and Universities, 1981–82," *The Chronicle of Higher Education* (April 4, 1984), p. 14.

12. D. Mott, *Characteristics of Effective Organizations* (San Francisco: HarperCollins, 1972), as reported by H. L. Tosi, Jr., and J. W. Slocum, Jr., "Contingency Theory: Some Suggested Directions," *Journal of Management* (Spring 1984), p. 11.

13. R. McGill, "Planning for Strategic Performance in Local Government," *Long Range Planning* (October 1988), pp. 77–84.

14. J. D. Hunger and T. L. Wheelen, "Is Strategic Management Appropriate for Not-for-Profit Organizations?" in *Handbook of Business Strategy, 1989/90 Yearbook*, edited by H. E. Glass (Boston: Warren, Gorham and Lamont, 1989), pp. 3.1–3.8.

   The contention that the pattern of environmental influence on the organization's strategic decision making derives from the organization's source(s) of income agrees with the work of Emerson, Thompson, and Pfeffer and Salancik. See R. E. Emerson, "Power-Dependence Relations," *American Sociological Review* (February 1962), pp. 31–41; J. D. Thompson, *Organizations In Action* (New York: McGraw-Hill, 1967), pp. 30–31; and J. Pfeffer and G. R. Salancik, *The External Control of Organizations: A Resource Dependence Perspective* (New York: HarperCollins, 1978), p. 44.

15. W. H. Newman and H. W. Wallender III, "Managing Not-For-Profit Enterprises," *Academy of Management Review* (January 1978), p. 26.

16. *Ibid.*, p. 27. The following discussion of the effects of these constraining characteristics is taken from pp. 27–31.

17. P. C. Nutt, "A Strategic Planning Network for Non-Profit Organizations," *Strategic Management Journal* (January-March 1984), p. 57.

    F. Heffron, *Organization Theory and Public Administration* (Englewood Cliffs, N.J.: Prentice Hall, 1989), pp. 100–103.

18. *Ibid.*, p. 132.

19. *Ibid.*, pp. 103–115.

20. Unterman and Davis, *Strategic Management of Not-for-Profit Organizations*, p. 174.

21. R. M. Kanter and D. V. Summers, "Doing Well While Doing Good: Dilemmas of Performance Measurement in Nonprofit Organizations and the Need for a Multiple-Constituency Approach," in *The Nonprofit Sector: A Research Handbook*, edited by W. W. Powell (New Haven: Yale University Press, 1987), p. 163.

22. R. P. Nielsen, "SMR Forum: Strategic Piggybacking— A Self-Subsidizing Strategy for Nonprofit Institutions,"

Sloan Management Review (Summer 1982), pp. 65–69.

R. P. Nielsen, "Piggybacking for Business and Nonprofits: A Strategy for Hard Times," *Long Range Planning* (April 1984), pp. 96–102.

23. D. C. Bacon, "Nonprofit Groups: An Unfair Edge?" *Nation's Business* (April 1989), pp. 33–34.

24. E. Skloot, "Should Not-For-Profits Go Into Business?" *Harvard Business Review* (January-February 1983), p. 21.

25. R. P. Nielsen, "Piggybacking Strategies for Nonprofits: A Shared Costs Approach," *Strategic Management Journal* (May-June 1986), pp. 209–211.

26. Skloot, "Should Not-for-Profits Go Into Business?" pp. 20–24.

27. K. G. Provan, "Interorganizational Cooperation and Decision Making Autonomy in a Consortium Multihospital System," *Academy of Management Review* (July 1984), pp. 494–504.

    R. D. Luke, J. W. Begun, and D. D. Pointer, "Quasi-Firms: Strategic Interorganizational Forms in the Health Care Industry," *Academy of Management Review* (January 1989), pp. 9–19.

28. *Directory of Multihospital Systems* (Chicago: American Hospital Association, 1980).

29. T. Mason, "Lifesaving Partnerships for Nonprofit Hospitals," *Business Week* (August 26, 1985), p. 84.

30. D. Wellel, "As HMOs Increasingly Become Big Businesses, Many of Them Convert to Profit-Making Status," *Wall Street Journal* (March 26, 1985), p. 4.

INTRODUCTION TO CASE ANALYSIS

Chapter Fourteen

Suggestions for Case Analysis

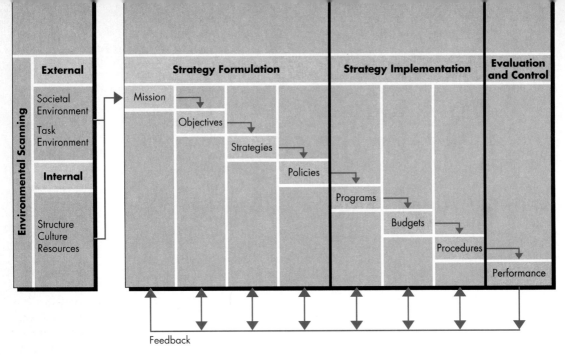

STRATEGIC MANAGEMENT MODEL

During the last 25 years the Case Method has enjoyed a steady and continuing increase in popularity and use. Once almost exclusively associated with Harvard University, the Case Method is now in use in many different parts of the world.[1]

Hans E. Klein

An analysis of a corporation's strategic management calls for a *comprehensive view* of the organization. The case method of analysis gives you the opportunity to move from a narrow, specialized view emphasizing technical skills to a broader, less precise analysis of the overall corporation emphasizing conceptual skills. Concentrating on strategic management processes forces you to develop a better understanding of the political, social, and economic environment of business, and to appreciate the interactions of the functional specialties required for corporate success.

14.1 THE CASE METHOD

The analysis and discussion of case problems has been the most popular method of teaching strategy and policy for many years.[2] Surveys indicate that approximately 70%–90% of business schools use cases in the strategic management course.[3]

Studies find that the case method emphasizes the manager's world, improves communication skills, offers the rewards of solving a mystery, possesses the quality of illustration, and establishes concrete reference points for connecting theory with practice.[4]

Cases present actual business situations and enable you to examine both successful and unsuccessful corporations. For example, you might be asked to critically analyze a situation in which a manager had to make a decision of long-run corporate importance. This approach gives you a feel for what it is like to work in a large corporation and to be faced with making a business decision.

14.2 FRAMEWORKS FOR CASE ANALYSIS

There is no one best way to analyze or present a case report. Each instructor has personal preferences for format and approach. Nevertheless, we present one suggested approach for both written and oral reports in Appendix 14.A, at the end of this chapter. This approach provides a systematic method for successfully attacking a case.

The presentation of case analysis can be organized on the basis of several frameworks. One obvious framework to follow is the *strategic audit* as detailed earlier in Chapter 2. Another is the McKinsey *7-S Framework,* composed of the seven organizational variables of **structure, strategy, staff, management style, systems and procedures, skills, and shared values.**[5] Regardless of the framework chosen, be especially careful to include a complete analysis of key environmental variables—especially of trends in the industry and of the competition.

The focus in case discussion is on critical analysis and logical development of thought. A solution is satisfactory if it resolves important problems and is likely to be implemented successfully. How the corporation actually dealt with the case problems has no real bearing on the analysis, because its management might have analyzed its problems incorrectly and implemented a series of flawed solutions.

14.3 LIBRARY RESEARCH

You should undertake outside research into the environmental setting of the case. Check each case to find out when the case situation occurred and then screen the business periodicals for that time. Use the computerized company and industry information services available at the library. This background will give you an appreciation for the situation as it was experienced by the people in the case. A company's annual report and 10K form from that year can be very helpful.[6] An understanding of the economy during that period will help you avoid making a serious error in your analysis—for example, suggesting a sale of stock when the stock market is at an all-time low or taking on more debt when the prime interest rate is over 15%. Information on the industry will provide insights on its competitive activities. Some resources available for research into the economy and a corporation's industry are suggested in Appendix 14.B at the end of the chapter.

If you are unfamiliar with these business resources, we urge you to read *How to Use the Business Library: With Sources of Business Information* by H. W. Johnson, A. J. Faria, and E. L. Maier, published by South-Western Publishing.

14.4 FINANCIAL ANALYSIS: A PLACE TO BEGIN

A review of key financial ratios can help you assess the company's overall situation and pinpoint some problem areas. Table 14.1 lists some of the most important financial ratios. Included are (1) **liquidity ratios**, which measure the corporation's ability to meet its financial obligations, (2) **profitability ratios**, which measure the degree of the corporation's success in achieving desired profit levels, (3) **activity ratios**, which measure the effectiveness of the corporation's use of resources, and (4) **leverage ratios**, which measure the contributions of owners' financing compared with creditors' financing.

ANALYZING FINANCIAL STATEMENTS

In your analysis do *not* simply make an exhibit including all the ratios, but select and discuss only those ratios that have an impact on the company's problems. For instance, accounts receivable and inventory may provide a source of funds. If receivables and inventories are double the industry average, reducing them may provide needed cash. In this situation, the case report should include not only sources of funds, but also the number of dollars freed for use.

A typical financial analysis of a firm would include a study of the operating statements for five or so years, including a trend analysis of sales, profits, earnings per share, debt to equity ratio, return on investment, and so on, plus a ratio study comparing the firm under study with industry standards. To begin, scrutinize *historical income statements and balance sheets*. These two basic statements provide most of the data needed for analysis. Compare the statements over time if a series of statements is available. Calculate changes that occur in individual categories from year to year, as well as the cumulative total change. Determine the change as a percentage as well as an absolute amount, and determine the amount *adjusted for inflation (constant dollars)*. Examination of this information may reveal developing trends. Compare trends in one category with trends in related categories. For example, an increase in sales of 15% over three years may appear to be satisfactory until you note an increase of 20% in the cost of goods sold during the same period. The outcome of this comparison might suggest that further investigation into the manufacturing process is necessary.

Some of the *red flags* to watch for in analyzing the financial statements in an annual report or prospectus are the following:

- **Special risks.** These are frequently grouped together in a section called "special considerations," "investment considerations," or "special risks." For example, the 1986 preliminary prospectus of the ZZZZ Best Company dis-

TABLE 14.1   Financial Ratio Analysis

	Formula	How Expressed	Meaning
1. Liquidity Ratios			
Current ratio	$\dfrac{\text{Current assets}}{\text{Current liabilities}}$	Decimal	A short-term indicator of the company's ability to pay its short-term liabilities from short-term assets; how much of current assets are available to cover each dollar of current liabilities.
Quick (acid test) ratio	$\dfrac{\text{Current assets} - \text{Inventory}}{\text{Current liabilities}}$	Decimal	Measures the company's ability to pay off its short-term obligations from current assets, excluding inventories.
Inventory to net working capital	$\dfrac{\text{Inventory}}{\text{Current assets} - \text{Current liabilities}}$	Decimal	A measure of inventory balance; measures the extent to which the cushion of excess current assets over current liabilities may be threatened by unfavorable changes in inventory.
Cash ratio	$\dfrac{\text{Cash} + \text{Cash equivalents}}{\text{Current liabilities}}$	Decimal	Measures the extent to which the company's capital is in cash or cash equivalents; shows how much of the current obligations can be paid from cash or near-cash assets.
2. Profitability Ratios			
Net profit margin	$\dfrac{\text{Net profit after taxes}}{\text{Net sales}}$	Percentage	Shows how much after-tax profits are generated by each dollar of sales.
Gross profit margin	$\dfrac{\text{Sales} - \text{Cost of goods sold}}{\text{Net sales}}$	Percentage	Indicates the total margin available to cover other expenses beyond cost of goods sold, and still yield a profit.
Return on investment (ROI)	$\dfrac{\text{Net profit after taxes}}{\text{Total assets}}$	Percentage	Measures the rate of return on the total assets utilized in the company; a measure of management's efficiency, it shows the return on all the assets under its control regardless of source of financing.
Return on equity (ROE)	$\dfrac{\text{Net profit after taxes}}{\text{Stockholders' equity}}$	Percentage	Measures the rate of return on the book value of stockholders' total investment in the company.

(continued)

TABLE 14.1 | **Financial Ratio Analysis** *(continued)*

	Formula	How Expressed	Meaning
Earnings per share (EPS)	$\dfrac{\text{Net profit after taxes} - \text{Preferred stock dividends}}{\text{Average number of common shares}}$	Dollar per share	Shows the after-tax earnings generated for each share of common stock.

3. Activity Ratios

	Formula	How Expressed	Meaning
Inventory turnover	$\dfrac{\text{Net sales}}{\text{Inventory}}$	Decimal	Measures the number of times that average inventory of finished goods was turned over or sold during a period of time, usually a year.
Days of inventory	$\dfrac{\text{Inventory}}{\text{Cost of goods sold} \div 365}$	Days	Measures the number of one day's worth of inventory that a company has on hand at any given time.
Net working capital turnover	$\dfrac{\text{Net sales}}{\text{Net working capital}}$	Decimal	Measures how effectively the net working capital is used to generate sales.
Asset turnover	$\dfrac{\text{Sales}}{\text{Total assets}}$	Decimal	Measures the utilization of all the company's assets; measures how many sales are generated by each dollar of assets.
Fixed asset turnover	$\dfrac{\text{Sales}}{\text{Fixed assets}}$	Decimal	Measures the utilization of the company's fixed assets (i.e., plant and equipment); measures how many sales are generated by each dollar of fixed assets.
Average collection period	$\dfrac{\text{Accounts receivable}}{\text{Sales for year} \div 365}$	Days	Indicates the average length of time in days that a company must wait to collect a sale after making it; may be compared to the credit terms offered by the company to its customers.
Accounts receivable turnover	$\dfrac{\text{Annual credit sales}}{\text{Accounts receivable}}$	Decimal	Indicates the number of times that accounts receivable are cycled during the period (usually a year).
Accounts payable period	$\dfrac{\text{Accounts payable}}{\text{Purchases for year} \div 365}$	Days	Indicates the average length of time in days that the company takes to pay its credit purchases.
Days of cash	$\dfrac{\text{Cash}}{\text{Net sales for year} \div 365}$	Days	Indicates the number of days of cash on hand, at present sales levels.

TABLE 14.1 | **Financial Ratio Analysis** *(continued)*

	Formula	How Expressed	Meaning
4. *Leverage Ratios*			
Debt to asset ratio	$\dfrac{\text{Total debt}}{\text{Total assets}}$	Percentage	Measures the extent to which borrowed funds have been used to finance the company's assets.
Debt to equity ratio	$\dfrac{\text{Total debt}}{\text{Stockholders' equity}}$	Percentage	Measures the funds provided by creditors versus the funds provided by owners.
Long-term debt to capital structure	$\dfrac{\text{Long-term debt}}{\text{Stockholders' equity}}$	Percentage	Measures the long-term component of capital structure.
Times interest earned	$\dfrac{\text{Profit before taxes} + \text{Interest charges}}{\text{Interest charges}}$	Decimal	Indicates the ability of the company to meet its annual interest costs.
Coverage of fixed charges	$\dfrac{\text{Profit before taxes} + \text{Interest charges} + \text{Lease charges}}{\text{Interest charges} + \text{Lease obligations}}$	Decimal	A measure of the company's ability to meet all of its fixed-charge obligations.
Current liabilities to equity	$\dfrac{\text{Current liabilities}}{\text{Stockholders' equity}}$	Percentage	Measures the short-term financing portion versus that provided by owners.
5. *Other Ratios*			
Price/earning ratio	$\dfrac{\text{Market price per share}}{\text{Earnings per share}}$	Decimal	Shows the current market's evaluation of a stock, based on its earnings; shows how much the investor is willing to pay for each dollar of earnings.
Dividend payout ratio	$\dfrac{\text{Annual dividends per share}}{\text{Annual earnings per share}}$	Percentage	Indicates the percentage of profit that is paid out as dividends.
Dividend yield on common stock	$\dfrac{\text{Annual dividends per share}}{\text{Current market price per share}}$	Percentage	Indicates the dividend rate of return to common stockholders at the current market price.

Note: In using ratios for analysis, calculate ratios for the corporation and compare them to the average ratios for the particular industry. Refer to Standard and Poor's and Robert Morris Associates for average industry data. For an in-depth discussion of ratios and their use, refer to a financial management text such as E. F. Brigham, *Fundamentals of Financial Management,* 5th ed. (Chicago, Ill.: Dryden Press, 1987), pp. 265–286. Special thanks to Dr. Moustafa H. Abdelsamad, Dean, Business School, Corpus Christi State University, Corpus Christi, Texas, for his writing of the meanings of these ratios.

closed that a single customer was responsible for 86% of the company's recent revenue. The company went bankrupt a year later.

- **Earnings problems.** Earnings trending downward should certainly raise a red flag. It also helps to know where the money comes from. Is the company dependent on a single product for its profits or are there special, one-time items that artificially boost earnings? Look closely at operating income to learn if the company is earning any profit in its primary business activity. The corporation may be showing a net profit only because management is selling the company's assets.

- **Too much debt.** Although the optimal ratio varies from industry to industry, most financial professionals believe that the amount of equity (common stock) should significantly exceed the amount of long-term debt.

- **Top management.** Some experts feel that officers and directors should own a significant amount of stock in the corporation—otherwise their interests may not be aligned with those of the stockholders.

- **Questionable transactions.** Watch out for strange items buried in the notes to the financial statements. A stock prospectus for Crazy Eddie, Inc. disclosed that before the company went public, it funded a medical school in the Caribbean, invested in oil and gas limited partnerships, and made interest-free loans to the chairman and other members of his family "to meet family needs." It's no surprise that this company, too, soon went bankrupt.

- **Lawsuits.** Legal actions against a company can be significant in themselves if they suggest that something may be seriously wrong with either the company's products or the way it conducts business.[7]

COMMON-SIZE STATEMENTS

Another approach to the analysis of financial statements is to convert both the income statement and balance sheet into **common-size statements.** Convert every category from dollar terms to percentages. For the income statement, net sales represent 100%: calculate the percentage of each category so that the categories sum to the net sales percentage (100%). For the balance sheet, give the total assets and liabilities a value of 100%, and calculate all other categories as percentages of the total assets or liabilities. (Individual asset and liability items, such as accounts receivable and accounts payable, can also be calculated as a percentage of net sales.)

When you convert statements to this form, it is relatively easy to note the percentage that each category represents of the total. Comparisons of these percentages over the years can point out areas for additional analysis. To get a proper picture, however, make comparisons with industry data, if available, to see if fluctuations are merely reflecting industrywide trends. If a firm's trends are generally in line with those of the rest of the industry, there is a lower likelihood of problems than if the firm's trends are worse than industry averages. These statements are especially helpful in developing *scenarios* (see Chapters 4 and 7) and *pro forma* statements, since they provide a series of historical relationships (for example, cost of goods sold to sales, interest to sales, and inventories as a percentage of assets).

OTHER USEFUL CALCULATIONS

If the corporation being studied appears to be in poor financial condition, use **Altman's bankruptcy formula** to calculate its *Z-value*. This formula combines five ratios by weighting them according to their importance to a corporation's financial strength (see Illustrative Example 14.1). The formula predicts the likelihood of the company going bankrupt. Firms in serious trouble have Z-values below 1.81.

Takeover artists and LBO (leveraged buy out) specialists look at a corporation's financial statements for **operating cash flow**: the amount of money generated by a company before the cost of financing and taxes. LBO specialists will take on as much debt as the company's operating cash flow can support. Although operating cash flow is a broad measure of a company's funds, some takeover artists look at a much narrower **free cash flow**: the amount of money a new owner can take out of the firm without harming the business. The various measures of cash flow are as follows:[8]

$$Cash\ Flow = \text{Net income} + \text{Depreciation} + \text{Depletion} + \text{Amortization}$$

$$Operating\ Cash\ Flow = \text{Cash Flow} + \text{Interest Expense} + \text{Income Tax Expense}$$

$$Free\ Cash\ Flow = \text{Cash Flow} - \text{Capital Expenditures} - \text{Dividends}$$

ILLUSTRATIVE EXAMPLE 14.1

The Altman Bankruptcy Formula

Edward I. Altman developed a formula to predict a company's likelihood of going bankrupt. His system of multiple discriminate analysis is used by stockholders to determine if the corporation is a good investment. The formula was developed from a study of 33 manufacturing companies with assets averaging $6.4 million that had filed Chapter X bankruptcies. These were paired with 33 similar but profitable firms with assets between $1 million and $25 million. The formula is:

$$Z = 1.2x_1 + 1.4x_2 + 3.3x_3 + 0.6x_4 + 1.0x_5$$

where

x_1 = Working capital divided by total assets.

x_2 = Retained earnings divided by total assets.

x_3 = Earnings before interest and taxes divided by total assets.

x_4 = Market value of equity divided by book value of total debt.

x_5 = Sales divided by total assets.

Z = Overall index of corporate fiscal health.

The range of the Z-value for most corporations is −4 to +8. According to Altman:

- *Financially strong* corporations have Z-values above 2.99.

- Corporations in *serious trouble* have Z-values below 1.81.

- Corporations between 1.81 and 2.99 are *question marks* that could go either way.

The closer a firm gets to bankruptcy, the more accurate is the Z-value as a predictor.

Source: M. Ball, "Z Factor: Rescue by the Numbers," *INC.* (December 1980), p. 48. Reprinted with permission, *INC.* magazine (December 1980). Copyright © 1980 by Goldhirsh Group, 38 Commercial Wharf, Boston, Mass. 02110.

ADJUSTING FOR INFLATION—CONVERTING TO CONSTANT DOLLARS

Several cases in business policy/strategy textbooks take place during a period of inflation. When analyzing these cases, you should calculate sales and profits in **constant dollars** (dollars adjusted for inflation) in order to perceive the "true" performance of the corporation in comparison with that of the industry, or of the economy in general. Remember that chief executive officers wish to keep their jobs and that some will tend to bias the figures in their favor. Sales stated in current dollars may seem to show substantial growth, but when they're converted to constant dollars, they may show a steady decline.

The return on investment (ROI) ratio is doubly susceptible to distortion. Because net income is generally measured in current dollars, it rises with inflation. Meanwhile, investment (generally valued in historical dollars) effectively falls. Thus ROI may appear to be rising when it is actually stable, or appear to be stable when it is actually falling.[9]

To adjust for general inflation, most firms use the Consumer Price Index (CPI), as given in Table 14.2. The simplest way to adjust financial statements for inflation is to divide each item by the CPI for that year. This changes each figure to 1967 constant dollars. The CPI uses 1967 as the base year (with a CPI of 100.0) against which all other years' prices are compared. Remember that the CPI for each year is a percentage. For example, to convert 1990 reported sales of $950,000 to constant (1967) dollars, divide 950,000 by the CPI for 1990 (3.914); 1990 sales are thus converted to constant (1967) dollars of $242,718. This conversion displays the fact that, in terms of general purchasing power, a U.S. dollar in 1990 was worth only $0.25 in 1967 dollars.

For a comparison of recent financial statements, it might help to use a more recent base year than 1967 in the adjustment for inflation. For example, in Table 14.3 selected figures are taken from Maytag Corporation's annual reports for 1988 through 1990. (The acquisition of Hoover is reflected in the 1989 and 1990 statements.) Instead of using 1967 as the base year for these comparisons, one may use 1988. To do so, divide the CPIs for 1989 and 1990 (as provided in Table 14.2) by the CPI for 1988; the appropriate adjustment factors are found to be 1.048 for 1989 and 1.105 for 1990. Table 14.3 shows net sales and net income figures first as reported (in 1989 and 1990 dollars) and second divided by each year's adjustment factor, to result in 1988 constant dollars. Once this conversion is done, the impact of inflation on a firm's revenues and earnings can be clearly seen. Note, for example, that reported net sales increased by 62% from 1988 to 1990 (primarily due to the Hoover acquisition). In constant 1988 dollars, however, they increased only 47%. Although net earnings as reported in 1990 decreased 38% from 1988, they decreased 44% when they are considered in constant dollar terms. The use of constant dollars serves to magnify the depressing effect on Maytag's earnings of the Hoover acquisition.

CONSIDERING INTEREST RATES

Another helpful aid in the analysis of cases in business policy is the chart on prime interest rates given in Table 14.4. For better assessments of strategic decisions, it can

TABLE 14.2	U.S. Consumer Price Index for All Items (1967 = 100.0)			
Year	CPI	Year	CPI	
1977	181.5	1984	311.1	
1978	195.4	1985	322.2	
1979	217.4	1986	328.4	
1980	246.8	1987	340.4	
1981	272.4	1988	354.3	
1982	289.1	1989	371.3	
1983	298.4	1990	391.4	

Source: U.S. Department of Commerce, *1988 Statistical Abstract of the United States,* 108th edition, Chart no. 740, p. 451. *Monthly Labor Review* (March 1991), p. 76.

TABLE 14.3	General Price-Level Adjustment for Inflation Using Consumer Price Index (Dollar amounts in millions)		
	1990	1989	1988
Net Sales, as reported	$3,057	$3,089	$1,886
% increase (decrease) over 1988	62%	64%	—
Net Sales			
Constant (1988) dollars	$2766.5	$2947.5	$1,886
% increase over 1988	47%	56%	—
Net Income, as reported	$99	$131	$159
% increase (decrease) over 1988	(38%)	(18%)	—
Net Income			
Constant (1988) dollars	$89	$125	$159
% increase (decrease) over 1988	(44%)	(21%)	—
CPI Adjustment Factor (1988 = 100%)	1.105	1.048	1.000
$\frac{\text{19xx CPI}}{\text{1988 CPI}}$	$\left(\frac{391.4}{354.3}\right)$	$\left(\frac{371.3}{354.3}\right)$	$\left(\frac{354.3}{354.3}\right)$

Source: Selected reported figures taken from Maytag Corporation, *1990 Annual Report,* p. 25.

be useful to note the level of the prime interest rate at the time of the case. A decision to borrow money to build a new plant would have been a good one in 1986, but somewhat foolhardy in 1981.

14.5 USING THE STRATEGIC AUDIT IN CASE ANALYSIS

The Appendix at the end of Chapter 2 is an example of a *strategic audit* proposed for use not only in strategic decision making, but also as a framework for the analysis of complex business policy cases.[10] The questions in the audit parallel the eight steps

TABLE 14.4	Changes in Prime Interest Rates[1]				
Year	Low	High	Year	Low	High
1977	6½	7¾	1984	10¾	12¾
1978	6	11¾	1985	9½	10¾
1979	11½	15¾	1986	7½	9
1980	11	21½	1987	7¾	9¾
1981	15¾	20½	1988	8½	10
1982	11½	17	1989	10½	11½
1983	10½	11½	1990	10	10

[1] The rate of interest that banks charge on the lowest-risk loans they make..

Source: D. S. Benton, "Banking and Financial Information," Table 1.1, p. 2 in *Thorndike Encyclopedia of Banking and Financial Tables,* 3rd ed., *1991 Yearbook* (Boston: Warren, Gorham and Lamont, 1991).

depicted in Fig. 2.4, the strategic decision-making process. The audit provides a checklist of questions, by area or issue, that enables a systematic analysis of various corporate activities to be made. It is extremely useful as a diagnostic tool to pinpoint problem areas and to highlight strengths and weaknesses. It is *not* an all-inclusive list, but it presents many of the critical questions needed for the strategic analysis of any business corporation. Some questions or even some areas might be inappropriate for a particular case; in other cases, the questions may be insufficient for a complete analysis. However, each question in a particular area of the strategic audit can be broken down into an additional series of subquestions. It is up to you to develop these subquestions when they are needed.

A strategic audit fulfills three major functions in a case-oriented strategy and policy course:

1. It serves to highlight and review important concepts from previously studied subject areas.
2. It provides a systematic framework for the analysis of complex cases. (It is especially useful if you are unfamiliar with the case method.)
3. It generally improves the quality of case analysis and reduces the amount of time you might spend in learning how to analyze a case.

Students also find the audit helpful in organizing a case for written or oral presentation and in seeing that all areas have been considered. The strategic audit thus enables both students and teachers to maximize their efficiency, both in analyzing why a certain area is creating problems for a corporation and in considering solutions to the problems.

14.6 STRATEGIC AUDIT WORKSHEET

The *Strategic Audit Worksheet* (as shown in Fig. 14.1) is provided as a systematic method to organize a student's strategic audit. The strategic audit worksheet is part

FIGURE 14.1 **Strategic Audit Worksheet**

Audit Heading	Text Pages	Strategic Audit Heading	Analysis		Comments
			(+) Factors	(−) Factors	
I	52	**Current Situation**			
IA	52	A. Past Corporate Performance Indexes			
IB	52	B. Strategic Posture: Mission, Objectives, Strategies, and Policies			
		S.W.O.T. Analysis Begins			
II	52	**Strategic Managers**			
IIA	52	A. Board of Directors			
IIB	52	B. Top Management			
III	53	**External Environment: Opportunities and Threats (S.W.O.T.)**			
IIIA	53	A. Societal Environment			
IIIB	53	B. Task Environment (Industry Analysis)			
IV	53	**Internal Environment: Strength and Weaknesses (S.W.O.T.)**			
IVA	53	A. Corporate Structure			
IVB	53	B. Corporate Culture			
IVC	53	C. Corporate Resources			
IVC1	53	1. Marketing			
IVC2	54	2. Finance			
IVC3	54	3. Research and Development			
IVC4	54	4. Operations (Manufacturing/Service)			
IVC5	55	5. Human Resources			
IVC6	55	6. Information Systems			
V	56	**Analysis of Strategic Factors**			
VA	56	A. Key Internal and External Strategic Factors (S.W.O.T.)			
VB	56	B. Review of Mission and Objectives			
		S.W.O.T. Analysis Ends			
VI	56	**Strategic Alternatives**	(Pros)	(Cons)	(Comments)
VII	56	**Recommendation**			
VIII	56	**Implementation**			
IX	57	**Evaluation and Control**			

Source: T. L. Wheelen and J. D. Hunger, "Strategic Audit Worksheet." Copyright © 1989 by Wheelen and Hunger Associates. Revised 1991. Reprinted by permission.

of the software, STrategic Financial ANalyzer (ST. FAN)™, which is available with this book. This computerized worksheet enables the student to organize information from the case by topic headings of the strategic audit.

SUMMARY AND CONCLUSION

The strategic management/business policy course is concerned with developing the conceptual skills that successful strategic managers need. The emphasis is therefore on improving your analytical and problem-solving abilities. The case method develops those skills and gives you an appreciation of environmental issues and the interdependencies among the functional units of a large corporation. This chapter reviews basic techniques of financial analysis to use with strategic management cases. It also recommends the strategic audit as a systematic way to analyze the fairly long and complex policy cases. Nevertheless, the strategic audit is only one of many techniques with which you can analyze and diagnose case problems. Use the framework of analysis with which you feel most comfortable.

DISCUSSION QUESTIONS

1. What value does the case method hold for the study of strategic management/business policy?

2. Why should one begin a case analysis with a financial analysis? When are other approaches appropriate?

3. What role does constant dollars play in analyzing financial statements over a long period of time?

4. What are the pros and cons of using the strategic audit as a framework for case analysis?

NOTES

1. H. E. Klein, "Introduction," in *Case Method Research and Application: New Vistas*, edited by H. E. Klein (Needham, Mass.: World Association for Case Method Research and Application, 1989), p. xv.

2. C. Boyd, D. Kopp, and L. Shufelt, "Evaluative Criteria in Business Policy Case Analysis: An Exploratory Study," *Proceedings, Midwest Academy of Management* (April 1984), pp. 287–292.

3. C. R. Decker and J. F. Bibb, "The Business Policy Course: Case and Other Course Components," (Millikin University Working Paper, 1990).

   C. H. Davis and G. T. Mills, "Offering Variety in Policy Case Courses," *Proceedings, Midwest Society for Case Research* (1990), pp. 89–95.

4. B. Keys and J. Wolfe, "Management Education and Development: Current Issues and Emerging Trends," *Journal of Management* (June 1988), p. 214.

5. T. J. Peters and R. W. Waterman, Jr., *In Search of Excellence* (New York: HarperCollins, 1982), pp. 9–12.

6. A survey of 6,000 investors and analysts in the U.S., U.K., and New Zealand revealed a strong belief in the importance of annual reports, especially the financial statement sections, for investment decisions. See L. S. Chang and K. S. Most, "An International Study of the Importance of Financial Statements," *International Journal of Management* (December 1985), p. 76–85.

7. G. Jasen, "Red Flags: Putting a Company in Its Proper Prospectus," *Wall Street Journal* (September 7, 1989), p. C1.

8. J. M. Laderman, "Earnings, Schmernings—Look at the Cash," *Business Week* (July 24, 1989), pp. 56–57.

9. M. J. Chussil, "Inflation and ROI," *The PIMSletter on Business Strategy*, Number 22 (Cambridge, Mass.: The Strategic Planning Institute, 1980), p. 1.

10. J. D. Hunger and T. L. Wheelen, "The Strategic Audit: An Integrative Approach To Teaching Business Policy" (Paper presented at the Forty-third Annual Meeting of the Academy of Management, Dallas, Tex., August 1983).

APPENDIX 14.A

Suggested Techniques
for Case Analysis
and Presentation

A. CASE ANALYSIS

1. Read the case rapidly, to get an overview of the nature of the corporation and its environment. Note the date on which the case was written so that you can put it into proper context.

2. Read the case a second time, and give it a detailed examination according to the strategic audit (see the Appendix to Chapter 2) or some other framework of analysis. The audit, for example, will provide a conceptual framework for the examination of the corporation's objectives, mission, policies, strategies, problems, symptoms, and issues. Regardless of the framework used, you should end up with a list of the salient issues and problems in the case. Perform a financial analysis.

3. Undertake outside research, when appropriate, to uncover economic and industrial information. Appendix 14.B suggests possible sources for outside research. These data should provide the environmental setting for the corporation. Conduct an in-depth analysis of the industry. Analyze the important *competitors*. Consider the bargaining power of *suppliers*, as well as *buyers* that might affect the firm's situation. Consider also the possible threats of *future competitors* in the industry, as well as the likelihood of new or different products or services that might *substitute* for the company's present ones. Consider *other stakeholders* who might affect strategic decision making in the industry.

4. Marshal facts and evidence to support selected issues and problems. Develop a framework or outline to organize the analysis. Your method of organization could be one of the following:
   a) The case as organized around the strategic audit.
   b) The case as organized around the key individual(s) in the case.
   c) The case as organized around the corporation's functional areas: production, management, finance, marketing, and R&D.

d) The case as organized around the decision-making process.

e) The case as organized around the seven variables (McKinsey 7-S Framework) of structure, strategy, staff, management style, systems and procedures, skills, and shared values.

5. Clearly identify and state the central problem(s) as supported by the information in the case. Use the *S.W.O.T.* format to sum up the key *strategic factors* facing the corporation: Strengths and Weaknesses of the company; Opportunities and Threats in the environment. Consider using the external (EFAS) and internal (IFAS) strategic factor analysis summary tables from Chapters 4, 5, and 6 (Tables 4.4, 5.3, and 6.2).

6. Develop a logical series of mutually exclusive alternatives that evolve from the analysis to resolve the problem(s) or issue(s) in the case. One of the alternatives should be to continue the company's current strategy. Develop at least two other strategy alternatives. Above all, don't present three alternatives and then recommend that all three be adopted. That's not three alternatives. That's one alternative presented in three parts!

7. Evaluate each of the alternatives in light of the company's environment (both external and internal), mission, objectives, strategies, and policies. Discuss *pros* and *cons*. For each alternative, consider both the possible obstacles to its implementation and its financial implications.

8. Make recommendations on the basis of the fact that action must be taken. (Don't say, "I don't have enough information." The individuals in the case may have had the same or even less information than is given by the case.)

a) Base your recommendations on a total analysis of the case.

b) Provide the evidence gathered in **Step A4** to justify suggested changes.

c) List the recommendations in order of priority.

d) Show clearly how your recommendations deal with each of the *strategic factors* that were mentioned earlier in **Step A5.** How do they build on corporate *Strengths* to take advantage of environmental *Opportunities*? How do they deal with environmental *Threats* and corporate *Weaknesses*?

e) Explain how each recommendation will be implemented. How will the plan(s) deal with anticipated resistance?

f) Suggest feedback and control systems to ensure that the recommendations are carried out as planned and to give advance warning of needed adjustments.

B. WRITTEN PRESENTATION

1. Use the outline from **Step A4** above to write the first draft of the case analysis. Follow **Steps A5** through **A8.**

a) Don't rehash the case material; rather, supply the salient evidence and data to support your recommendations.

b) Develop exhibits on financial ratios and other data, such as strategic factors summary, for inclusion in your report. The exhibits should provide meaningful information. Mention key elements of an exhibit in the text of the written analysis. If you include a ratio analysis as an exhibit, explain the meaning of the ratios in the text and cite only the critical ones in your analysis.

2. After it is written, review your case analysis for content and grammar. Remember to compare the outline (**Step A4**) with the final product. Make sure you've presented sufficient data or evidence to support your problem analysis and recommendations. If the final product requires rewriting, do so. Keep in mind that the written report is going to be judged not only on what is said but also on the manner in which it is said. *Style, grammar, and spelling are just as important as the content in a written case analysis!*

3. If your written or oral presentation requires *pro forma* statements, you may wish to develop a scenario for each quarter and/or year in your forecast. A *well-constructed scenario* will help improve the accuracy of your forecast. Chapters 4 and 7 suggest methods for the development of scenarios.

C. ORAL PRESENTATION BY TEAMS

1. The team should first decide on a framework or outline for analysis, as mentioned above in **Step A4**. Although teams often divide the analysis work among team members, it is helpful if each team member also follows **Steps A5** through **A8** in developing a preliminary analysis of the entire case to share and compare with team members.

2. The team should combine member input into one consolidated team analysis, including S.W.O.T. analysis, alternatives, and recomendation(s). Gain agreement on the strategic factors and the best alternative(s) to support.

3. Divide among the team's members the further development and presentation of the case analysis and recommendation(s). Agree on responsibilities for the preparation of visual aids and handouts. As in written reports, scenarios and *pro forma* financial statements should support any recommendation.

4. Modify the team outline, if necessary, and have one or two rehearsals of the presentation. If there is a time constraint for the final presentation, apply it to the practice presentation. If exhibits are used, make sure to allow sufficient time for their explanation. Check to ensure that any visual aids can be easily seen from the back of the room. Critique one another's presentations and make the necessary modifications to the analysis. Again, *style, grammar, and delivery are just as important in an oral presentation as is content*!

5. Begin your presentation by handing out a copy of the agenda specifying not only the topics to be covered, but also who will deal with each topic area. Introduce yourselves. Dress appropriately. During the class presentation, if a presenter misses a key fact, either slip a note to him or her, or deal with it in the summary speech.

6. Answer the specific questions raised by the instructor or classmates. If the team has done a good job of presenting, it should welcome questions. Start off the questioning period with a question from one of your friends that will enable you to impress the audience with your well-thought-out answer. You may wish to have one person act as a moderator who refers questions to the appropriate team member.

Resources for Case
Library Research

A. COMPANY INFORMATION

1. Annual Reports
2. *Moody's Manuals on Investment* (a listing of companies within certain industries that contains a brief history and a five-year financial statement of each company)
3. Securities and Exchange Commission Annual Report Form 10-K
4. *Standard and Poor's Register of Corporations, Directors, and Executives*
5. *Value Line Investment Survey*
6. *Findex: The Directory of Market Research Reports, Studies and Surveys* (a listing by Find/SVP of over 11,000 studies conducted by leading research firms)
7. *COMPUSTAT, Compact Disclosure,* and *CD/International* (computerized operating and financial information on thousands of publicly held corporations)

B. ECONOMIC INFORMATION

1. Regional statistics and local forecasts from large banks
2. *Business Cycle Development* (Department of Commerce)
3. Chase Econometric Associates' publications
4. Census Bureau publications on population, transportation, and housing
5. *Current Business Reports* (Department of Commerce)
6. *Economic Indicators* (Joint Economic Committee)

7. *Economic Report of the President to Congress*
8. *Long-Term Economic Growth* (Department of Commerce)
9. *Monthly Labor Review* (Department of Labor)
10. *Monthly Bulletin of Statistics* (United Nations)
11. "Survey of Buying Power," *Sales Management*
12. Standard and Poor's Statistical Service
13. *Statistical Abstract of the United States* (Department of Commerce)
14. *Statistical Yearbook* (United Nations)
15. *Survey of Current Business* (Department of Commerce)
16. *U.S. Industrial Outlook* (Department of Defense)
17. *World Trade Annual* (United Nations)
18. *Overseas Business Reports* (by country, published by U.S. Department of Commerce)

C. INDUSTRY INFORMATION

1. Analyses of companies and industries by investment brokerage firms
2. *Annual Report of American Industry* (a compilation of statistics by industry and company, published by *Fortune*)
3. *Business Week* (provides weekly economic and business information, and quarterly profit and sales rankings of corporations)
4. *Fortune* (each April publishes listings of financial information on corporations within certain industries)
5. *Industry Survey* (published quarterly by Standard and Poor's Corporation)
6. *Industry Week* (late March–early April issue provides information on 14 industry groups)
7. *Forbes* (mid-January issue provides performance data on firms in various industries)
8. *Inc.* (May and December issues give information on small companies)

D. DIRECTORY AND INDEX INFORMATION ON COMPANIES AND INDUSTRIES

1. *Business Information: How to Find and Use It*
2. *Business Periodical Index* (on computer in many libraries)
3. *Directory of National Trade Associations*
4. *Encyclopedia of Associations*
5. *Funk and Scott Index of Corporations and Industries*
6. *Thomas's Register of American Manufacturers*
7. *Wall Street Journal Index*
8. *Where to Find Business Information*

E. Ratio analysis information

1. *Almanac of Business and Industrial Financial Ratios* (Prentice Hall)
2. *Annual Statement Studies* (Robert Morris Associates)
3. *Dun's Review* (Dun and Bradstreet; published annually in September–December issues)
4. *Industry Norms and Key Business Ratios* (Dun and Bradstreet)
5. *How to Read a Financial Report* (Merrill Lynch, Pierce, Fenner and Smith, Inc.)
6. *Quality of Earnings: The Investor's Guide to How Much Money a Company Is Really Making* (T. L. O'Glove, Free Press, 1987)

F. General sources

1. *Commodity Yearbook*
2. *U. S. Census of Business*
3. *U. S. Census of Manufacturers*
4. *World Almanac and Book of Facts*

G. Business periodicals

1. *Business Week*
2. *Forbes*
3. *Wall Street Journal*
4. *Fortune*
5. Industry-specific periodicals (e.g., *Oil and Gas Journal, Appliance*)

H. Academic/Practitioner journals

1. *Harvard Business Review*
2. *Journal of Business Strategy*
3. *Long-Range Planning*
4. *Strategic Management Journal*
5. *Planning Review*
6. *Academy of Management Review*
7. *SAM Advanced Management Journal*

Note: For further information, see M. A. Young, "Sources of Competitive Data for the Management Strategist," *Strategic Management Journal* (May-June 1989), pp. 285–293.

NAME INDEX

SUBJECT INDEX